Schriften des
Zentrum für Europäische Integrationsforschung
Center for European Integration Studies
der Rheinischen Friedrich-Wilhelms-Universität Bonn

Herausgegeben von
Prof. Dr. Ludger Kühnhardt

Band 67

Ludger Kühnhardt

European Union – The Second Founding

The Changing Rationale of European Integration

2. revised edition

Nomos

Die Deutsche Nationalbibliothek lists this publication in the Deutsche Nationalbibliografie; detailed bibliographic data is available in the Internet at http://dnb.d-nb.de.

ISBN 978-3-8329-5505-2

2. Edition 2010

For Stephan Maximilian

whose century this is

Table of Contents

Introduction

I.

"The term Europeanization," one can read in a 1937 article of the "Encyclopedia of the Social Sciences," "is intended to express the effects on Asiatic, American and African cultures and civilizations of permeation by the peculiar social system set up in modern Europe as a consequence of the classical renaissance, the Protestant Reformation and the industrial revolution. Europeanization may be expressed politically by imposing the idea of democracy, in the sense of parliamentary and party government, or of sovereignty, in the sense of suppression or subordination of all governmental organs to the semireligious solidarity in support of that sovereignty. It may be expressed economically by imposing ideas of individualistic capitalism, competition and control on communities enjoying more elaborate and equitable, but less productive and progressive, collectivist or communal civilizations; or industrially by substituting the factory and the foundry for the hand look and home craft. It may be expressed in terms of education by convincing other continents of the advisability of acquiring attainments in European science to their material or even moral advantage, or by exposing the discipline of tribal tradition and training to the dissipation by the gospel of the missionary, the goods of the trader and the good intentions of the administrator."[1] If it were not for the rather rusty and politically incorrect language, eight decades later such an article – by and large – could have appeared in an Encyclopedia discussing the term "Americanization."

Even in its critique, America and Europe remain tied together to this day as each other's mirror. While in 1937, the US was critical about Europe's global colonialism, in the first decade of the twenty-first century Europe tended to criticize the global projection of American power and values. Will a 2037 Encyclopedia publish a balanced article on the link between "Europeanization" and "Americanization" in the age of globalization? Will it recognize that the American and European societies are complimentary expressions of an Atlantic civilization, each of them having dominated the other one at times? Will it finally recognize that in the end, both partners of the Atlantic civilization found a new balance, synchronizing values and interests and bringing their joint resources to the best possible use of managing global matters while yet living with inevitable differences and, at times, even conflicts?

Both partners of the Atlantic civilization have lately been forgetful of the bonds that hold. Instead they have engaged each other during the last decade of the twentieth century and the first years of the twenty-first century in endless rows over their

1 Young, George, "Europeanization," *Encyclopedia of the Social Sciences*, Vol. 5, New York: Macmillan, 1937: 623.

differences and the inevitable divorce that ought to follow – first strategic, then cultural. None of this has happened and will unlikely happen in the years ahead. Yet it remains an open question as to how transatlantic relations will relate to other coordinates that constitute world order-building in the twenty-first century.

The 1937 article mentioned that China "as a whole could not be Europeanized from outside. It could only Europeanize itself if and when it chose, and the early attitude of China toward Europeanization was as antagonistic and anti-European as anywhere."[2] In the first decade of the twenty-first century, a self-assured and strong China had become an indispensable partner for balancing and managing the world order of this century, no matter whether or not China will be called "Europeanized," "Americanized" or simply "globalized." The 1937 article spoke about the voluntary "sudden and sensational Europeanization of the Japanese" as an expression of its authentic nationalism during the second half of the nineteenth century.[3] The important role of Japan as a provider of global stability prevails, added by the economic contributions of South Korea that has gone through its own remarkable, sudden and sensational modernization during the last decades of the twentieth century. The 1937 article analyzed the "intellectual Europeanization" of the Indian elite. In the early twenty-first century, for the first time an Indian middle-class had emerged in this extremely diverse and fascinating country that has atomic bombs and the biggest number of impoverished people side by side. For the 1937 author, the Eurasian Empire Russia had been "Europeanized forcibly" by Peter the Great. During the first decade of the twenty-first century, Russia is still struggling with its identity amid aggravating poverty downgrading the former super-power to Third World levels of development while its political neo-authoritarianism is disconnecting Russia from becoming fully "European."[4] In 1937, an emerging Latin America was seen as a promising continent in which Europeanization "is producing new life from seed."[5] During the first decade of the twenty-first century, in spite of its cultural cohesion Latin America is still not recognizable as a global force although its biggest country, Brazil, is rallying support to play this role. The 1937 social science analysis concluded that the Arab region was "wholly recalcitrant to Europeanization whether imperialist, nationalist or socialist" and it mentioned the "artificial Europeanization of Iraq."[6] During the first decade of the twenty-first century and in spite of the military defeat of the terrible regime of Saddam Hussein, Iraq did not turn into an uncontested model for democracy in the Broader Middle East. The hope for modernization and more pluralism in Arab countries remained torn between reasonable

2 Ibid: 633.

3 Ibid: 625.

4 The GDP of Russia's 144 million people amounts to 347 billion US dollars (2005), much less than Mexico's GDP of 699 billion US dollars with 100 million people, less than the 399 billion US dollars GDP of Australia with 19 million people and less than Korea's GDP of 476 billion US dollars with its 47 million people.

5 Young, George, "Europeanization," op.cit.: 629.

6 Ibid: 631-632.

progress and the drawbacks of Islamic fundamentalism. Building sustainable peace between the Palestinians and Israel has remained the most pressing geopolitical issue for more than half a century. As in 1937, also in the early twenty-first century, Africa tends to be forgotten. This should not prevail for too long, for reasons of enlightened self-interest of both its Western and Arab neighbors and for reasons of historical justice to the whole continent.

Between 1937 and the first decade of the twenty-first century, imperialist Europeanization had been replaced by American-dominated globalization.[7] Whether or not Europe has been "provincializing" with the end of its colonialism, as an Indian author was suggesting,[8] both the US and Europe tended to forget that their own internal history has been one of colonization, empire-building and the language of power ever since their beginnings – since the Roman Empire in Europe and since the first colonial settlements on both sides of the North American coasts.[9] The issue in the twenty-first century is not any more one of colonization and hegemonic dominance; it is one of world order-building. Thus it is inherently a multidimensional and multipolar challenge. In shaping the world order, the US and Europe are indispensable partners.

The Europe engaged in this partnership is of an altogether different nature than the Europe characterized in 1937 as imperial initiator of "Europeanization" elsewhere.[10] It is an anti-colonial and anti-imperial, largely multilateral Europe that has enormously increased the level of its integration under the roof of the European Union. It is a Europe that has finally transformed its cultural diversity into its advantage. It is a Europe in which different nations and diverse, also non-overlapping interests prevail and yet democratic stability and peaceful affluence have reached levels unheard of in earlier periods of European history. Nevertheless, Europe is not free from conflicts. Populist nationalism and the challenge of integrating migrants, particularly of Muslim faith, are distant echoes of the colonial and imposed Europeanization of past centuries: Today, non-Europeans claim citizen rights in a continent which, in the past, has dominated many of their home countries. Although they could be "normal" citizens

7 On the imperial legacy of Europe see Raudzens, George, *Empires: Europe and Globalization, 1492-1788*, Stroud: Sutton, 1999; Chamberlain, Muriel Evelyn, *The Longman Companion to European Decolonization in the Twentieth Century*, London/New York: Longman, 1998; Waites, Bernard, *Europe and the Third World: From Colonization to Decolonization, 1500-1998*, New York: St.Martin's Press, 1999; Springhall, John, *Decolonization since 1945: the Collapse of European Overseas Empires*, New York: Palgrave, 2001.

8 Chakrabarty, Dipesh, *Provincializing Europe: Postcolonial Thought and Historical Difference*, Princeton: Princeton University Press, 2000.

9 See for some instructive reading Armitage, David (ed.), *Theories of Empire, 1450-1800*, Aldershot: Ashgate, 1998: passim.

10 For some traditional characteristics and contemporary dilemmas of Europe see Scales, Len, and Oliver Zimmer (eds.), *Power and the Nation in European History,* New York: Cambridge University Press, 2005; Gerrits, André W. M., and Dirk Jan Wolffram (eds.), *Political Democracy and Ethnic Diversity in Modern European History*, Stanford: Stanford University Press, 2005; Majone, Giandomenico, *Dilemmas of European Integrations: The Ambiguities and Pitfalls of Integration by Stealth,* Oxford: Oxford University Press, 2005.

there, surprisingly many people from distant lands voluntarily prefer to live in Europe, despite problems of integration, legal status and fear (if not xenophobia) among the indigenous European population they are confronted with.

America, on the other hand, is experiencing the curse and paradox of an Empire, which Europeans know only too well from their own nineteenth or early twentieth century dominance. Global leadership is coupled with a global fascination for the American way of life and yet it breeds mistrust, rejection, and even hatred toward America in many places around the globe.[11] Internally, America is as much confronted with issues of national identity as the European Union and its constituent parts are.[12] For the remainder of the twenty-first century, the defining question posed to the US and to the EU will not be what they are, but who they are, not how they operate, but what they intend to achieve, not how democratic they are, but what the purpose of their democracy and their power will be.

The European Union's homepage introduces its overview of EU relations with the United States under the headline: "The World's two greatest powers."[13] Whatever that means and implies, the European Union is today's Europe. Over the past five decades, Americans have used the term "Europeans" much more liberally than many Europeans do. Europeans still have mixed feelings about it as they divide their identity between their "European-ness" and their adherence to one of Europe's many nations, old or new, big or small. Yet, today the European Union signifies "political Europe" across the continent and around the world. The European Union comprises 0.86 percent of the globe (4.324.782 square kilometers) and roughly seven percent of the global population (491 million). Even with Turkey as an EU member, these figures would increase only insignificantly to 1.01 percent of global space and nine percent of global population. All in all, the European Union is, and will remain, the smallest of all continents. But, at last, it has achieved a level of unity unprecedented in its long and colorful history.

This has been easy so long as the EU was in its embryonic stage, still labeled the EEC (European Economic Community) and later the EC (European Community). The US had served as Europe's pacifier and federator after World War II. European integration was in the US's interest as it was largely dependent upon America's strategic goodwill and protection. As much as America has been the product of emancipation from Europe, after the end of the Cold War many in Europe claimed some sort of emancipation from the US. No matter how these phenomena are assessed, they are inevitable by-products of the reversion of the global role between Europe and America during the past four centuries. They do not imply divorce and the drifting apart

11 On the inevitability for the US to operate as an empire, on its merits and price see Ferguson, Niall, *Colossus: The Price of America's Empire*, New York: Penguin Press, 2004.

12 See Schlesinger jr., Arthur M., *The Disuniting of America: Reflections on a Multicultural Society*, New York: W.W. Norton & Co., 1998; Huntington, Samuel R., *Who are We?: The Challenges to America's National Identity*, New York: Simon & Schuster, 2004.

13 See European Union, European Commission, *The EU's Relation With the United States – Overview*, http://ec.europa.eu/external_relations/us/intro/index.htm.

of the Atlantic partners. Their self-interest is too strong to allow for this under any rational circumstances. These disputes echo rather temporary collisions among close partners, having to find a new balance among them and a new organizing principle to define their partnership and the purpose of their underlying civilization.

Unfortunately, there is no such thing as a "European dream." Europe has been created, but Europeans are still missing. A genuine European interest is only growing slowly, but steadily. And no matter how hard proponents try, it is difficult to decipher what "the European model" truly will mean as opposed to "American conditions," which is a favorite stereotype in Europe to blame America for its deficits without giving justice to all the positive dimensions of that great country. More realism and rational analysis would often be helpful to understand each other, including each other's differences and complementary strengths. Part of this necessary reevaluation of transatlantic realities on the side of Europeans is the need to stop caricaturing the US. And part of this necessary reevaluation of transatlantic realities on the side of the US is the need to take the European Union more seriously.

Since the founding of the European Economic Community in 1957, European states have transformed dramatically. No European state of the early twenty-first century was defined only ethnically. Compared with the long and often ideologically-obsessed period between the eighteenth and the twentieth century, other functions of the modern state prevail in contemporary Europe. The states in Europe are still the most important source for providing the social framework for Europe's economic development. But European citizens, by and large, have become market citizens, primarily interested in their economic well-being, in social security, safe jobs, and the delivery of social provisions by the state. Function and effect of the European state have turned primarily into that of an economic agency, sharing authority and power with the European Union. Yet, cultural integration prevails as aspiration and problem both on the national and on the European level. Unlike in the eighteenth to the twentieth century, the status of European citizens as cultural citizens is not defined against any of their neighbors in Europe. At times, it is however defined against close-by immigrants or far-away Americans. European patriotism might and, I believe, should grow step by step. But it should be based on values and constitutional principles, never on anti-American or any other anti-type of Euro-Gaullism. The emergence of some sort of a dangerous European nationalism is not an artificial worry for a continent in which "myth and nationhood" often went hand in hand.[14] Timothy Garton Ash has put this concern into clear words: "The whole of the new, enlarged Europe is engaged in a great argument between the forces of Euro-Gaullism and Euroatlanticism. This is the argument of the decade. On its outcome will depend the future of the West."[15] It is exactly because of this concern that

14 See Hosking, Geoffrey, and George Schöpflin (eds.), *Myths and Nationhood*, London: Hurst, 1997.

15 Garton Ash, Timothy, *Free World: Why a Crisis of the West Reveals the Opportunity of Our Time*, London: Allen Lane, 2004: 58; for an early study on the Atlantic civilization see Deutsch, Karl W.,

I suggest to reconcile a strong Atlantic partnership of the European Union with the internal evolution of a European constitutional patriotism.

Wherever states cannot deliver sufficient economic benefits for their citizens – or wherever political systems do not have to do this anymore in the very basic sense of the word – the state will inevitably change its character and meaning. The idea of cultural identification was never sufficient to integrate a state over a critically long period of time. Nation-building and state-building outside the Western world give ample proof to this experience. Yet economic impulses for integrating a large population are also insufficient if not embedded in a political purpose and perspective. This is what the European Union continuously looks for: Political purpose and popular approval for a successful economic integration amid cultural diversity in unity. This can only work as a permanent learning process and it requires the recognition of local and regional identities as enshrined in the concept of "subsidiarity," one of the linguistic monsters of Euro-speak (and one of the original structural principles of Catholic social doctrine since its development in the nineteenth century). Subsidiarity is not just an intelligent concept to protect political autonomy in an ever globalizing and homogenizing world, it is also the recognition of the cultural seed in which Europe grew and will continue to be fertile.

Despite the constitutional roller coaster ride of the first decade of the twenty-first century, the EU lives its symbols, among them the European flag, the European anthem (Beethoven's "Ode to Joy") and "Europe Day" on May 9. "United in diversity" is not simply a fine and appropriate motto for Europe. It is the very summary of the evolution of the European population since time immemorial. Demographically, Europe has always been a continent of emigration and immigration, of voluntary and enforced migrants.[16] Among European high-nobility, cross-national marriages have always been the norm and are well studied even as an instrument of power-formation. It would also be worth studying the degree of cross-national marriages among ordinary European citizens over all recorded periods: United in diversity is the demographic bond that has held Europe together ever since. Today, it constitutes the most successful post-national integration project in human history.

The formula "an ever closer union among the peoples of Europe," used already in the Treaties of Rome in March 1957, is a distant echo, of course, of the "more perfect union" invoked in the US Constitution of 1787. This is another indication of the mutually reinforcing character of the political processes on both sides of the Atlantic Ocean. The US Constitution was an early realization of European constitutional

et al., *Political Community and the North Atlantic Area: International Organization in the Light of Historical Experience*, Princeton, N.J.: Princeton University Press, 1957. For the current situation see Rien, Serges T., *Cultural Constructions of Europe: European Identity in the twenty-first Century*, Frankfurt/New York: Peter Lang, 2004.

16 See van de Kaa, Dirk, et al. (eds.), *European Populations: Unity in Diversity*, Dordrecht/Boston: Kluwer Academic Publishers, 1999.

evolution at that time, albeit on the national level only. In the early twenty-first century, the European Union, with its flag and anthem, currency and parliament, Europe Day and treaty-based rule of law, is a genuine contribution to the global development of political form and theory. Most of all, the European Union is a form in action, a vision turned practice. It is a process and not a static construction. The enlargement of the European Union by twelve new member states during the first decade of the twenty-first century – ten of them post-communist countries and the other two making the EU a neighbor of Tunisia, Libya and Egypt, Lebanon and Israel – was significant not only for the degree of complexity and regional asymmetries it created inside the EU; it was also very emotional, because in reality it meant the reunification of Europe under conditions of cooperative peace and parliamentary democracy. The enlargement marathon of the early years of the twenty-first century went hand in hand with a deep crisis of confidence, orientation and leadership. Nowhere was this crisis more evident than in the failure to ratify the Constitutional Treaty and in the difficulties to ratify its subsequent repair work, the Treaty of Lisbon. This double fiasco, in the end, was a crisis of adaptation: adaptation to a new set of member states, to a new rationale of integration in the globalized world, and to a new form of legitimacy, no longer rooting the EU solely in elite discourses but requiring a fresh and substantial connection with the feelings, aspirations and concerns of Union citizens. For the political leaders of the European Union, the result of the constitution-building crisis came with their signature under the Treaty of Lisbon on December 13, 2007. They called it metaphorically "Reform Treaty." For the citizens of the European Union, the EU's constitution-building process between 2001 and 2009 (when the Treaty of Lisbon finally entred into force) was a sequence of rifts between their growing recognition of the importance of European solutions to common challenges and their increasing skepticism about political leadership and backdoor politics in the European Union. The constitution-building process was the most intensive reform process of the EU so far, and yet it rather enhanced people's distance from the EU and its institutions. To complete the paradox of this decade, the majority of EU citizens were ahead of their leaders, still favoring a genuine European Constitution while their leaders were helplessly absorbed in implementing, at least, the repair work of what they initially had claimed to achieve. The confusing first decade of the twenty-first century was a turning point in European integration history. This decade of confusion, euphoria, backlash, a new, cautious beginning and, again, backlash and relieve over a moderate new beginning was the painful birth of a new European consensus between Europe's institutions and Europe's people. It was a decade equivalent to the Second Founding of the European Union.

European integration is the single most important event in European history in modern times, no matter the still pending cases of integration in South Eastern Europe and a long list of unfinished business as far as the implementation of EU policies is concerned.

The political, legal and economic development of Europe has always been accompanied by "the cultural gradient."[17] Ideas were transferred from their original place of construction into a new context and into social norms. Gradually they amalgamated into political form – or vanished into the big archives of Europe. The idea of European unity finally has been transformed into Europe's reality – with all the idiosyncrasies and disputes that will continue amid the diversity in united Europe. Limits of European-ness prevail, to be sure.[18] The term "Europeanization" is no longer used to delineate colonial empires and their cultural development. The term "Europeanization" has come home and refers to the often daunting process of applying EU legal norms in the member states of the European Union. European integration, to paraphrase the 1937 "Encyclopedia of Social Sciences" article, is permeating the nation states in Europe and the complex web of world order-building. At the end of a long journey, Europe is Europeanizing itself.

The guiding principle of the quest for European unity has been and remains the maintenance of peace. The search for peaceful solutions, for conflict-prevention and conflict resolution, if necessary also with the use of military might, has turned into the EU's central creed. Promoting the strategy of reconciliation is no longer necessary among Europeans, but it remains in short supply amid the many regional conflicts of the world. The European Union will stay committed to supporting peaceful order-building in the world, if necessary also with military means. The European Union would not want to become a superpower. But it would want to be respected as a power for peace and stability, freedom and prosperity in partnership with the world. Although its link with the US might remain contested, or at least uncertain for some time ahead, this is the new political identity of most Europeans, as Timothy Garton Ash has eloquently defined it: "We hope to become a superpower, fellow Europeans, in vain. Let us make ourselves, rather, comrades in a community of free people, working to build a free world."[19]

II.

This book introduces the first five decades of European unity and analyzes the European Union at a crossroads. It describes the changes and transformations during the first decade of the twenty-first century as the Second Founding of the EU. Following five decades of turbulent, often daunting, yet highly successful integration, the

17 See Evtuhov, Catherine, and Stephen Kotkin (eds.), *The Cultural Gradient: the Transmission of Ideas in Europe, 1789-1991*, Lanham: Rowman & Littlefield, 2003 (this book however is mainly dealing with Eastern European intellectual history).

18 See Ferguson, Niall, *Colossus: The Price of America's Empire*, op.cit.: 251–257.

19 Garton Ash, Timothy, *Free World: Why a Crisis of the West Reveals the Opportunity of Our Time*, op.cit.: 223.

European Union unintentionally yet with lasting effect began a process of refounding, symbolized in the enormous eastward enlargement, contested in the search for the constitutional parameters of European integration and visible in the all-pervasive effects of European integration on public life and politics across EU member states. European integration has become a matter of domestic politics everywhere in the EU while at the same time the EU is exponentially broadening its global role. This study puts the European Union and its evolution in the global context as defined by transatlantic relations, the impact of globalization on the rationale of European integration, and the global proliferation of regional integration schemes. It discusses the theoretical and normative issues related to the rise of the European Union and its challenges ahead. The book ends with an outlook on the prospects of a genuine European constitutional patriotism and the increased global role of the European Union.

This book offers a history-based political analysis with sensitivity for the cultural dimensions in which European integration is embedded. The first five decades of the quest for European unity have seen remarkable developments, and also failures, new beginnings and lasting success. The idea of reconciliation among former European foes has been the driving motivation at the beginning stages of European integration. After losing its global power as defined in the age of colonialism, Europe got a second chance with US support for its integration. Throughout this path, the ongoing division of Europe and the absence of freedom under totalitarian communism saddened the image of post-war Europe. Following its first successful peaceful and democratic revolution, symbolized in the fall of the Berlin Wall, and bringing the Cold War to its end, Europe's unity strengthened the European Union as the ever increasing embodiment of the political identity of a continent, whose cultural diversity will surely prevail as one of its charming advantages and sources of identity. It also confronted the European Union with its biggest ever adaptation crisis and the need to restore legitimacy to European integration as a project rooted in its citizens' identity and loyalty. A common political identity under the roof of the European Union is only gradually emerging. Yet it adds already a new dimension to the various cultural identities in Europe. One might even say that this new and gradually uniting political identity – as incomplete as it still is – protects the diverse cultural identities of Europe, not the least among its many small nations and for all of their languages.

European political identity has been shaped, challenged and advanced in the course of the first decade of the twenty-first century. Parallel with an unprecedented enlargement of the European Union, the need for deeper integration was confronted with the usual disputes between advocates and skeptics of integration. The search for constitution-building led the EU to its, so far, finest hour in institutional reform, but also into the deepest crisis ever. EU leaders signed a European Constitution all but in name. However, they were unable to manage the ratification process in a convincing way for many of their citizens. After the Constitutional Treaty came to a halt, the first ever constitutional debate in EU history followed. Its result was a repair treaty, relying on the traditional means of an inter-state bargain, and a citizenry in favor of a genuine European Constitution. Ironically, at first the reform treaty was rejected in the only public referendum at hand. The Irish went through a second referendum in order to prove to be good Europeans by not only wanting a better EU but accepting the compromises of their leaders. This paradoxical result of incremental and deliberative constitution-building will be discussed in Chapter I: Emerging European constitutionalism without a European Constitution is the result of almost a decade of adaptation crises. Since it also opened new dimensions to a renewed contract between citizens and political elites, it is no exaggeration to frame this period as the Second Founding of European integration. In Chapter II, I will analyze the European Constitutional Treaty of 2004, compare it with the so-called Reform Treaty of 2007 and assess the experiences of a unique reform period in European integration in which both treaties were rejected by European citizens in the name of a better EU. In three subsequent chapters (Chapter III, Chapter IV, Chapter V) that combine historical narrative and political science-based structural analysis, I will discuss the key turning points of this development as an interplay of "challenge and response," thereby recalling the famous argument of the great historian Arnold Toynbee about the dialectical sources of progress. In my understanding, the main turning points of European integration were a permanent interplay of "challenge and response," often requiring an external, and even more often an internal, crisis to advance to the next level of deepened integration. The debate about a possible alternative between the deepening of European integration and permanent widening of the process through four distinct series of enlargement turns out to be artificial. In the end, all enlargements served the purpose to strengthen European unity and hence the European Union as it is today. Deepening its structures and policies was, at the end, in the interest of all partners.

The internal evolution of the European Union never followed a blueprint. The goals of integration evolved step by step, and with them the very name for the project. From European Economic Community to European Community to European Union – that also marks the development of an often idiosyncratic yet stabilizing process of integration policies. From customs union to political solidarity, from the direct election of a European Parliament to a common currency, from qualified majority voting as contested principle of decision-making in very limited policy areas to an almost generalized joint EU legislation of the Council of the European Union (in the following: "Council") and the European Parliament, from heavily contested first steps in political cooperation to the doorsteps of introducing a European Foreign Minister in all but the name – at no point in European integration did it meet its finality. In fact, one might wonder about the very meaning of this term if one believes in political freedom and non-deterministic paths of life. Indeed, the debates about political finality in European integration have always been more of a wake-up call for prioritizing new stages of

European integration than a serious effort to delineate the ultimate boundaries of integration.

The imminent results of European integration were mostly supported, and at times were even made possible, by the European policies of the United States. Without Marshall Plan aid and protection under the Truman Doctrine, Western Europe would have found it extremely difficult after 1945 to reestablish viable democracies, to generate unprecedented affluence and to overcome centuries of mistrust, hatred and nationalism. Moreover, Western Europe would have had difficulties in organizing "the West" alone as a magnetic attraction for countries and people in Central and Eastern Europe forced to live under communist totalitarian rule. The integration process followed an idiosyncratic mechanism of "challenge and response," as I argue in the three historical chapters. Often, a crisis was followed by unintended consequences ultimately strengthening the integration process. Sometimes it seemed as if Europe needed a crisis – internal or external – in order to get its act together and reach the next goal of integration. Without a permanent US commitment to this process, it might have been impossible. At least it would have been extremely difficult, given the Soviet threat that was military and ideological at the same time. This argument is developed in Chapter VI. The US was Europe's federator and this immediate post war-experience prevailed in South East Europe amid the Wars of Yugoslavian Succession and their aftermath. This does not mean that relations in the Atlantic Alliance were always smooth. Far from it, their history could be written as one of permanent crisis and controversy. Yet, in the end, the Atlantic Alliance prevailed as an embodiment of Atlantic civilization and as the most successful military alliance ever. With the end of the Cold War, it has turned into transatlantic relations covering a much larger ground than before, being economically more interdependent than ever, but also encountering fundamental disputes, clashing moralities and interests on key issues relevant for the management of global affairs. The dispute over the usefulness of the war against Iraq in 2002/2003 escalated into an internal Cold War of the West. Yet, I argue, it was the culmination of a transformation of transatlantic relations and their link to a rapidly growing European integration. One experience prevailed from the ashes of this bitter dispute: Whenever transatlantic relations are not in good shape, European integration tends to suffer, too.

Over the course of the twenty-first century, the United States and the European Union will remain each other's most indispensable partner for economic, but likewise for political and cultural reasons. In the age of economic globalization, the US and the EU are destined to cooperate in the evolution of a common global agenda as part of an increasingly multipolar world order. In doing so, the European Union will continue its politically driven integration. Unlike market-driven globalization, I argue in Chapter VII, European integration remains a process led by the primacy of politics, defined by a community of law and a supranational parliamentary democracy. Globalization has changed the rationale for European integration. It has moved the process beyond internal European reconciliation toward an external projection of European interests and ambitions. European integration has also generated genuine and unique contributions to our understanding of key terminologies of political theory and philosophy: The notion of sovereignty has been expanded, and it now includes the notion of a supranationally pooled and shared sovereignty. The concept of governance has been broadened, and it now includes the category of multilevel governance as exercised among the various levels of rule in Europe, both horizontally and vertically. And the notion of democracy has been expanded, encompassing also multinational democracy without the ambition of becoming a state in the nineteenth century meaning of the word.

European integration has also found global resonance and raised the question of its applicability in other regions of the world. The EU has made it its explicit strategy to promote regional cooperation and integration elsewhere. An overview of regional integration schemes indicates an impressive array of related efforts in other parts of the world. The global proliferation of regional integration schemes is a new element in world order-building. Its success depends on criteria of regime cohesion and shared interests, to name just the two most evident. In Chapter VIII, I present an overview of non-European regional integration schemes, assess their flaws and potentials and express my concern about the fact that the geopolitically most troublesome regions, Northeast Asia and the Broader Middle East, are the least affected by integration ideas or realities so far. In fact, only in these parts of the world are both virtually absent to this day.

The global proliferation of regional integration raises a lot of questions for further research. One of them refers to the deficit of integration: Why does it not work and did not achieve the results the initiators had hoped for? This very question is also pertinent with regard to Europe's past. For two thousand years the European continent has been a cradle of continuous cultural developments, and yet it has never achieved peaceful and voluntary, law-based political integration. The failures of the past are related to the inability of Europeans to turn cultural experiences of commonality into the political will to work together and thus transform the political culture of their continent. This is all the more sad as European statesmen and intellectuals have contributed a good number of concepts favoring European unity. Instead of becoming reality, these concepts moved into archives and libraries, where they constitute the archaeology of European integration. For all too long, I argue in Chapter IX, hegemonic aspirations and nationalistic rivalries have prevented European unity from taking place in freedom and peace. All reasonable integration concepts of past centuries were lacking political sense and will as far as the necessary drive for their implementation was concerned. This remains the genius of the Founding Fathers of European unity to this day: They have turned European unity from a fine idea into a workable political process.

On the basis of this exceptional change in the political culture of Europe many problems were resolved. However numerous pragmatic conflicts and unresolved debates on principles prevail. Some of them, I argue in Chapter X, will advance European constitutionalism (and eventually, I am convinced, European patriotism in the best original meaning of this old Roman term), while others constantly activate the ever-present potential for slowing down European integration for a considerable period of time. Re-nationalization of European politics remains an unfortunate option, although in the end only to please parochial populists across the EU and to reduce the perspectives for the vast majority of EU citizens. The real issue is no longer the survival of the European Union; the real issue in this debate is the degree of relevance Europe can play in the world of the twenty-first century. The strongest argument against any parochialism in the European Union must grow from within Europe. It must be nurtured by the experience of EU citizens that European integration adds value to their lives and that of their societies. The most convincing argument against the often-invoked fear of failure lies in the experience of successful integration. Rightly so, politicians have lately formulated the concept of a Europe that works. A growing degree of shared memories reinforces the importance of defining common goals. The biggest challenge ahead of Europe might not be the organizing of the continent's unity, but the purposeful use of its rule of law-based democracy. European leaders need to continuously define Europe from its potential and not only from its limits.

Academic reflection has accompanied the European integration process ever since the beginning. Different schools of thought have contributed to a vast theoretical body of literature, some of which is more an exercise in logic than a reflection on European realities. Other theoretical contributions wavered between their descriptive and prescriptive character, while the best ones in the field have been able to inspire both colleagues and policy-makers as they were capable of feeling the true pulse of integration as it evolved. The fact that the academic penetration of European integration has attracted so many bright minds in the social sciences adds to its liveliness and underlines the all-permeable relevance of European integration. I discuss the evolution of academic theories in Chapter XI and argue – which might not please some of its proponents – that ultimately they can all be considered variations of a federal theory of European integration.

A critical assessment of academic exercises on European integration brings the circle of my study to a close. In the final chapters I discuss the preconditions and limits of European patriotism and the emerging global strategic role of Europe. It is my firm conviction that European patriotism – in the Ciceronian sense of the word – is not directed against anyone, any other country or region, culture or religion. Instead, European patriotism is rooted in the treaty-based constitution of European governance, in a community of recollections and driven by the desire to jointly approach the future as a matter of common destiny. At best, I dare to dream, European patriotism will one day have a (slim and trim) European Constitution as its point of political reference. In Chapter XII, I discuss the potential and the limits of a genuine European constitutional patriotism. I conclude my argument with several concrete practical proposals for how to advance the European sense of ownership even in the absence of a European Constitution that would truly deserve its name. Finally, in Chapter XIII, I outline the trajectory of the European Union into the role of a global political and strategic actor. The stronger the sense of European political identity will become, the more coherent one might expect Europe's foreign and security policy to be. Together with the US, the EU is the main player in the management of global affairs, both economical and political. It must therefore be in the continuing interest of the US to see the European Union flourish. There is no need to fear this and little reason to look at it with lack of understanding or even to look down on it with cynicism as the process of European unity enters the second half of its first century.

Although one cannot compare the two processes of federation-building, it is worth recalling the long and winding road the US has followed from independence through constitution-building – its Second Founding – to a common currency, a solidified and saturated territory, and to a global role. History does not repeat itself. Sometimes, it never reaches its goals and ends. Sometimes, it takes astonishing detours and unexpected jumps. And sometimes, it is faster, steadier and happier than most professional skeptics allow themselves to recognize. All in all, it will be exciting for the living to observe the next decades of European integration. I hope that it will remain a good story to be told one day to those who were just born (or not even born yet) as European unity turned fifty in 2007. All in all, it is a story whose characteristics shifted from fragile integration to multilevel governance, from market-building to security strategies, from internal reconciliation to global positioning, from institution-building to constitutional patriotism. It is the unique story of the European Union as the embodiment of the political identity of Europe.

III.

This book reflects the EU's journey through its fascinating success since 1957 and its deep crises of adaptation in the first decade of the twenty-first century. The preparation of this book suffered with the detours and impasses of European integration, and it echoes its joy, self-doubt and potential. It has accompanied much of my work as Director at Bonn University's Center for European Integration Studies, and it has benefited enormously from the many dimensions of this gratifying work. This book owes a lot to my experiences across Europe as they have helped me to look at Europe through the specific perspective of many of its peoples with their own hopes, fears and worries, as well as with their diverse interpretations of European history and their own ideas for Europe's future. This book also owes a lot to my experiences outside Europe as these experiences helped me to understand the worldwide perception of Europe. In the most diverse of places, policy makers, religious and other community leaders, as well as academic colleagues, have shaped my knowledge of the world and of Europe's place in its midst. Reading about European integration over the past decade, its internal dynamics and its external impact, has been a constant source of fresh knowledge that helped to clarify my own judgment. Working in different environments outside Germany during the years of incubation of this book has helped me to broaden my perspectives and test my hypotheses. The Woodrow Wilson Center for International Scholars in Washington D.C. was my host during extremely stimulating initial research months in 2002, which led to the publication of a book that can be considered a small prelude to this present study.[20] Walking around the Wilson Center, one can reach not only the White House within a few moments, but also a plaque at one of the corner's of the Willard Hotel, recalling the sojourn of Jean Monnet in Washington during the dark years of World War II. Looking at this sign reinforced my firm conviction that the Atlantic civilization exists and that Europeans and Americans can be proud of it while they also remain responsible to maintain it for the sake of others. The format and outline of this book grew from an idea basically conceived at Stanford University in 2004, where I had the pleasure to teach an exceptionally diverse and bright group of students from all over the world. Advising Seoul National University in 2004/2005 about the establishment of a Korean Center for European Studies reinforced my impression that European integration often finds more enthusiasm outside Europe than within the EU. At Oxford University's St. Antony's College I was privileged to organize a lecture series on the effects of crises in European integration during Hilary Term 2006. The Oxford debates have further sharpened my understanding of European integration, its opportunities and its limits. The prepration of the second edition of this book in early 2010 drew again heavily on the insights of students and colleagues from across the world.

At Bonn University's Center for European Integration Studies, Ingrid Maldonado, Simone Schmidt and Nora Iven went through the development of this book with patience and commitment, for which I am grateful indeed. As grateful as I am for the insights of many of my academic colleagues – from the ones I personally know to personally unknown authors of fine works on the topic quoted in this book – I especially appreciate the intellectual input of my students on several occasions during the past decade at different universities. Students in America, Asia, Africa and across Europe have helped me to better understand my own questions through the lenses of their good answers and even more so with their own succinct new questions. This unending

20 Kühnhardt, Ludger, *Constituting Europe: Identity, Institution-building and the Search for a Global Role*, Baden-Baden: Nomos, 2003.

interplay of question and answer is the spirit in which European unity may well flow, in diversity and for many generations to come.

Inspired by this hope, *European Union – The Second Founding* is dedicated to my son Stephan Maximilian, born in 2000, whose century this is.

Bonn, August 2008
Ludger Kühnhardt

The revised second edition of this book takes into account the ratification of the Treaty of Lisbon that has come into effect on December 1, 2009. In 2010, the debate over European economic governance in light of the Greek state deficit marked not only the latest EU crisis. Most likely, the debate would develop into the next stage of European integration through crisis and re-adjustment. Such has been the European experience for most of the past decades. There was no reason to believe that the constellation would fundamentally alter: Multi-level governance and competing legal norms, diverse political interests and incomplete integration structures would prevail, while the EU was increasingly growing into a global role. Such was the reality of the European Union amidst its second founding.

Bonn, May 2010
Ludger Kühnhardt

The Second Founding

I. From National Identities to European Constitutionalism

1. European Constitution-Building as a Dialectical Process

On October 29, 2004, the Treaty Establishing a Constitution for Europe was signed in Rome.[21] Immediately, "European Constitution" became the commonly used label for this long und unreadable text. Almost fifty years after the conclusion of the Treaties of Rome on March 25, 1957, the European Union opened a new chapter in its history. It began with shock and frustration. The Treaty Establishing a Constitution for Europe was never to become reality. After its ratification was rejected by majorities in referenda in France and in the Netherlands, a new effort was needed to achieve the realization of its objectives. At the occasion of the fiftieth anniversary of the Treaties of Rome, the Heads of State and Government of the European Union, the President of the European Parliament, and the President of the European Commission promised in a Berlin Declaration to reignite the institutional reform-process.[22] Within a few months, an Intergovernmental Conference (IGC) under the Portuguese EU Presidency negotiated the details of what was to become the Treaty of Lisbon. This treaty was signed on December 13, 2007, by the Heads of State and Government of twenty-seven EU member states in the Portuguese capital.[23] The media reaction was friendly but cautious in light of the pending ratification marathon. The political leaders of the EU preferred to talk about it as the Reform Treaty. In fact, it was never more than a repair treaty after the ratification of the European Constitution had failed: The EU's political leaders tried to repair the failure they had made by underestimating the ratification problems of the European Constitution. Returning to the intransparent mechanism of an Intergovernmental Conference they aimed at improving democracy and efficiency in the EU institutions by undermining the third objective of the constitution-building process, transparency. As the political leaders were afraid of the unpredictable reaction of their fellow citizens, they wanted to avoid another round of referenda. They brought the constitution-building process back to backdoor diplomacy. But a referendum was unavoidable in Ireland, and it failed their hopes: On June 12, 2008, the majority of Irish voters said "no" to the proposition of their leaders. The adaptation crisis aimed at achieving a new social and political contract between EU institutions and EU citizens

21 European Union, *Treaty Establishing a Constitution for Europe*, Luxembourg: Office for Official Publications of the European Communities, 2005.

22 European Union, *Declaration on the Occasion of the Fiftieth Anniversary of the Signature of the Treaties of Rome*, Berlin, March 25, 2007, http://eu2007.de/de/News/download_docs/ Maerz/0324-RAA/English.pdf.

23 European Union, "Treaty of Lisbon Amending the Treaty on European Union and the Treaty Establishing the European Community," *Official Journal of the European Union*, C 306/Vol.50, Luxembourg: Office for Official Publications of the European Communities, 2007, https://eur-lex.europa.eu/JOHtml.do?uri=OJ:C: 2007:306:SOM:EN:HTML.

continued. The Irish were granted some opting-out clauses and they were asked to vote again: On October 2, 2009, 67 percent of Irish voters said "yes", the excentric Czech President Vaclav Klaus also ratified and on December 1, 2009, at long last, the Treaty of Lisbon entered into force. At the end of a long decade of treaty revision, the main question was no longer: How about an outright constitution for Europe? The main question was: How can the condition of Europe be improved, even if only gradually? The constitution-building process of the first decade of the twenty-first century had returned to square one: defining the objectives of European integration and gaining legitimacy through successful and concrete work. Europe's political constitution is to remain a cumulative one, based on several treaties and treaty-revisions. Europe's inner constitution, its political condition, remains in need of permanent improvement, it can only achieve new acceptance through steady experiences with a Europe that works.

The daunting experience with European constitution-building has been part of a changing rationale of European integration. The changing rationale of European experience, in turn, has been part of the Second Founding of European integration. The American historian Joseph J. Ellis has characterized the completion of the American Constitution in 1787 as the Second Founding of the US. About half a generation after the United States had gained its independence in 1776, the work of the Founding Fathers was followed by the success of the Founding Brothers.[24] More appropriately, Ellis may have coined the American constitution-makers Founding Brethren. In the European context, the members of the European Convention that worked out the Treaty Establishing a Constitution for Europe in 2002/2003 could be considered the Founding Brethren, following the Founding Fathers of 1957. Both were followed by the repair workers who redesigned the 2007 Reform Treaty. Until the end end, the repair workers struggled with those EU citizens that had a chance to express their opinion in a referendum. In America, individual freedom had led to political sovereignty and constitutional order solidifying this individual freedom. In Europe, elite-driven integration has led to individual skepticism about content and perspective of a new covenant between the European Union citizens and the European Union institutions that remain essential to translate the European idea into reality. The difference is startling and yet, the European experience is extraordinary in its own right.

The painfully emerging Second Founding of the European Union brings together several trends and threads that are forming a new strong rationale for European integration before dispersing again into several directions:

- The changing rationale of European integration is related to the age of globalization and will continue for some time before being fully absorbed by the EU. The rapid development of a common foreign, security and defense policy is part of this process, but the redefinition of the rationale for European integration goes beyond specific policy areas. For the first five decades, European

24 Ellis, Joseph J., *Founding Brothers: The Revolutionary Generation*, New York: Knopf, 2000: 9.

integration was driven by the idea of internal reconciliation among the societies and the state of Europe. This path has been successful and has not yet come to full completion. Yet, it has been surpassed by the quest for a new global role for Europe. In past centuries, European countries had shaped the destiny of the world, for better or worse. In the age of globalization, the European Union needs to contribute to the management of global affairs if it wants to remain the subject of its own destiny. This fundamental shift in priorities impacts the rationale for European integration. This process is part of the Second Founding of the European Union.

- The changing basis for the legitimacy of integration is related to the process of re-calibrating the rationale for European integration. In the past, European integration was an elite-driven project for the benefit of a peaceful development in Europe. With deeper integration and with the growing global exposure of Europe, the citizens of the European Union are increasingly affected by the consequences of integration and the management of global affairs through EU institutions. The Second Founding of the European Union can only develop strong legitimacy if EU citizens recognize the work of EU institutions as helpful in improving public goods and realizing genuine political choices. The constitution-building process of European integration beyond the completion of a Single Market is not about institutional fine-tuning. It is about a necessary new contract between EU citizens and EU institutions. This remains an important part of the Second Founding of the EU.
- The long-term implications of enlarging the European Union with almost a dozen post-communist countries could not alone be accommodated by the formal acceptance of EU membership of Central and Southeast Europe and the formal acceptance of the EU's *acquis communautaire* by the candidate countries. The long-term accommodation of the enlargement effect requires a substantial and sustainable deepening of European integration. The constitution-building process that was accelerated during the first decade of the twenty-first century is part of the necessary balancing of the EU's widening with the necessary deepening of the European Union. Obviously, this process was too big too be achieved by one big stroke called the European Constitution. Yet, the gradual continuation of the treaty-based constitutionalization of European integration remains a fundamental requirement if the European Union is to maintain sustainable success. Therefore, the failed constitution-building experience of the first decade of the twenty-first century will remain an important part of the Second Founding of the EU.

The constitution-building experience during the first decade of the twenty-first century was a classical European reaction to a genuine European question: Integration through institutional designs remains abstract, cold and irrelevant for most of the EU citizens which these institutions are serving. The quest for a European Constitution has been the latest climax of an integration process that runs fundamentally counter to Europe's experience. European integration is the most successful utopia Europe has ever experienced in its political history. It is the antithesis to Europe's history of conflict, mistrust and balance of power. It should not come as a surprise that it was and remains a daunting struggle to frame the political and legal order of the European Union. In America, independence and constitution-making were expressions of hope, vision and optimism. In Europe, integration and its quest for constitutionalization are antitheses to the general European experience with politics. European integration was never utopian in its optimism but always utopian in its skepticism. All the more astonishing is its unbending success amidst uncertainty and crises. The crisis over the ratification of the Treaty Establishing a Constitution for Europe and the subsequent Reform Treaty had a paradoxical effect. Political leaders became cautious and timid. They began to question their own legitimacy and some of them questioned even that of the whole project of European integration. European citizens, in turn, became more outspoken than ever and began to claim ownership of the European integration project.

European integration remains inspired by the failure of centuries. The sustainable success of the European Union depends upon the continuous deepening of the integrative efforts that were already planted with the original inception of the European Economic Community. The tensions of this process will survive and also define the next decade in European integration beyond the double failure of implementing institutional reforms that remain abstract and insufficient for many citizens. What many understood as a crisis of integration was in fact a crisis in integration. The double rejection of leadership propositions by majorities of citizens in different European countries will eventually initiate and sharpen the need to reconnect the European idea between politicians and ordinary citizens. The constitution-building crisis of the first decade of the twenty-first century may turn out as a preparatory stage for an ever more strengthened and deepened quality integration. What was defined as period of reflection by the European Commission in 2005 became the first ever constitutional debate in the history of European integration.[25] What was meant to protect European politicians from criticism and further failure opened the door to a unique involvement of many Union citizens.

In the end, European Union citizens seem to be more courageous than their political leaders. While in the summer 2007 a majority of 66 percent of Union citizens were in favor of a full-fledged European Constitution and ready for sacrifices necessary to find

25 See Eschke, Nina, and Thomas Malick (eds.), *The European Constitution and its Ratification Crisis: Constitutional Debates in the EU Member States*, ZEI Discussion Paper C156, Bonn: Center for European Integration Studies, 2006; Kühnhardt, Ludger, *Europa neu begründen*, ZEI Discussion Paper C167, Bonn: Center for European Integration Studies, 2007.

a common ground, their leaders were hiding behind changes in nomenclature.[26] While in no country could a majority be identified that opposed a European Constitution, their leaders scrapped the symbolic components of the European Constitution with the argument that the invocation of the EU symbols could prevent the ratification of the eventual Reform Treaty out of fear it might look too much like state-building. This timid move may have rescued the Reform Treaty. But it remains true that European symbols remain essential for European Union citizens to identify with the EU. While European political leaders were hoping that a revision from the title Constitutional Treaty to the title Reform Treaty would help them to safeguard their credibility as European leaders, they watered down the original Treaty Establishing a Constitution for Europe without any public debate on the relevant issues (e.g., symbols, title of a European Foreign Minister, simplification of legislative procedures). The political leaders were convinced to have had no other political choice, but it was not a day of revolutionary refounding when they signed the Treaty of Lisbon on December 13, 2007. It was rather an act of helplessness, demonstrated by the fact that British Prime Minister Gordon Brown did not even participate in the signing ceremony. He appeared late and signed the Treaty in an adjacent room, wanting to show the lack of importance of the situation. Was it really a surprise that it took two Irish referenda to ratify the Reform Treaty? The bickering and self-applauding of the EU's political actors in late 2007 turned out to be nothing more than a helpless answer to a continuing "Europe's mid-life crisis."[27] In a way, their signing of the Treaty of Lisbon was the recognition of the limits of political leadership in a European Union that has not increased the sense of ownership for the EU among its citizens. This understanding will have long-term consequences for policy formulation and the organization of the European body politic: While democracy has entered the arena of European integration, its political leadership has become part of the transformation process. The dire need to form genuine European political parties and to extend the European policy agenda on the whole sphere of welfare-related social and societal matters must eventually be some of of the immediate and obvious consequences.

26 Eurobarometer findings in February 2004 showed that for the total of 25 EU member states, 62 percent of all respondents agreed that their country had to get ready to make concessions in order to enable the constitution of the EU come into life: European Union. European Commission, *Flash Eurobarometer, The Future "European Constitution"*, February 2004, http://ec.europa.eu/public_opinion/flash/fl159_fut_const.pdf. Eurobarometer findings in December 2006 found a majority of 53 percent of EU citizens in favour of a "European Constitution," with the highest level of support (63 percent) in Poland. The smallest gap between those in favour and those against a "European Constitution" was smallest in the United Kingdom (40 percent in favour, 35 percent against): European Union, European Commission, *Standard Eurobarometer, Eurobarometer 66: Public Opinion in the European Union*, December 2006, http://ec.europa.eu/public_opinion/archives/eb/eb66/eb66_highlights_en.pdf.

27 Thus the title of *The Economist*, "Europe's Mid-Life Crisis: A Special Report," March 17-23, (2007).

The bumpy dialectics of forward-backward-forward-backward was not new to past European experiences with constitution-building on the national level. In fact, constitution-building on the national level has always echoed a certain contemporary social transformation of the respective country. With any new upheavals and transformations, constitutions were also about to change. In fairness, it is in this context that the Treaty of Lisbon must be judged. For most of the past two decades, European national governments have been rather fragile coalition governments that needed to deliver to a broad array of clientele. Many of those majorities that were in power when the Treaty Establishing a Constitution for Europe was signed on October 29, 2004, had been replaced by another set of political leaders when the Treaty of Lisbon was signed on December 13, 2007.[28] The changes in government were echoed in different

28 In June 2004, when the Treaty Establishing a Constitution for Europe was agreed upon by the European Council, most governments in the European Union were coalitions, often rather weak because of divergent political orientations: Austria: coalition under the Christian Democratic Austrian People's Party (ÖVP) and the Nationalist Freedom Party of Austria (FPÖ) under Chancellor Wolfgang Schüssel, Federal Minister for Foreign Affairs Benita Ferrero-Waldner; Belgium: coalition under Liberals (VLD) with Socialists from Walloon and from Flanders under Prime Minister Guy Verhofstadt, Foreign Minister Louis Michel; Cyprus (Greek Republic): coalition under Social Democrats (AKEL) with Liberals (DIKO) and Conservatives (KISOS) (Turkish part: coalition under Social Democrats (CTP) and Conservatives (DP) under President Tassos Papadopoulos, Foreign Minister George Iacovou; Czech Republic: coalition under Social Democrats (SSD) with Christian Democrats (KDU-SL) and Liberals (US-DEL) under Prime Minister Vladimir Spidla, Foreign Minister Cyril Svoboda; Denmark: Liberal minority government (Venstre) with Conservatives under Prime Minister Anders Fogh Rasmussen, Foreign Minister Per Stig Møller; Estonia: right of center coalition under Conservatives (Res Publica) with Liberals (Estonian People's Union and Reform Party) under Prime Minister Juhan Parts, Foreign Minister Kristina Ojuland; Finland: left of center coalition of various Social Democrats and Socialists under Prime Minister Matti Vanhanen, Foreign Minister Erki Tuomioja; France: right of center coalition of Union for a Popular Movement (UMP) with Union for French Democracy (UDF) and the Liberal Democracy (DL) under Prime Minister Jean-Pierre Raffarin, Foreign Minister Michel Barnier; Germany: coalition government of Social Democrats (SPD) with Greens under Chancellor Gerhard Schröder, Foreign Minister Joseph Fischer; Greece: right of center absolute majority of Nea Democratia under Prime Minister Kostas Karamanlis, Foreign Minister Petros Molyviatis; Hungary: coalition under Socialists (MSZP) with left of center Liberals (SZDZS) under Prime Minister Peter Medgyessy, Foreign Minister László Kovács; Ireland: right of center majority under Fianna Fáil – The Republican Party with Progressive Democrats (PD) under Prime Minister Bertie Ahern, Foreign Minister Brian Cowen; Italy: populist conservative coalition under Forza Italia with Alleanza Nazionale, Lega Nord, Christian Democrats (CCD-CDU) and conservative Social Democrats (PSI) under Prime Minister Silvia Berlusconi, Foreign Minister Franco Frattini; Latvia: right of center coalition (with the first Green Prime Minister in Europe) under First Party with New Era Party under Prime Minister Indulis Emsis, Foreign Minister Rihard Pics; Lithuania: Socialist coalition under Social Democrats, Labour Party and Social Liberals under Prime Minister Algirdas Brazauskas, Foreign Minister Antanas Valionis; Luxembourg: right of center coalition under Christian Democrats (CSV) and Liberals (DP) under Prime Minister Jean Claude Juncker, Foreign Minister Lydie Polver; Malta: Christian Democratic majority (Nationalist Party) under Prime Minister Lawrence Gonzi, Foreign Minister John Dalli; the Netherlands: right of center coalition under Christian Democrats (CDA) with Conservative Liberals (VVD) and left of center Liberals (D66) under Prime Minister Jan Peter Balkenende, Foreign Minister Bernard R. Bot; Poland: Socialist minority government under Prime Minister Marek Belka, Foreign Minister Vlodzimierz Cimoszewicz; Portugal: right of center coalition under Social Democrats (in fact: Christian Social Conservatives) with Conservatives (Partido Popular) under Prime Minister José Manuel Durão Barroso, Foreign Minister Teresa Gouveia; Slovenia: coalition under Social Democrats with

Conservative People's Party and Party of Pensioners under Prime Minister Anton Rop, Foreign Minister Dimitrij Rupel; Slovakia: right of center coalition under Christian Democrats (SDKV and KDH) with Hungarian Party (MK), and Liberals (ANO) under Prime Minister Mikulas Dzurinda, Foreign Minister Eduard Kukan; Spain: Socialist coalition under PSOE under Prime Minister José Luis Rodriguez Zapatero, Foreign Minister Miguel Angel Moratinos; Sweden: Social-Democratic minority government (SDP) under Prime Minister Göran Persson, Foreign Minister Laila Freivalds; United Kingdom: majority of the Labor Party under Prime Minister Tony Blair, Secretary of State for Foreign and Commonwealth Affairs Jack Straw.

In June 2007, when the Treaty of Lisbon was agreed upon by the European Council, the following majorities were in charge of the governments of EU member states, still coalition governments for the most part and rather limited in their space for domestic maneuver: Austria: Grand Coalition under the Social Democratic Party of Austria (SPÖ) and the Christian Democratic Austrian People's Party (ÖVP) under Federal Chancellor Alfred Gusenbauer, Federal Minister for European and International Affairs Ursula Plassnik; Belgium: coalition of Liberals (VLD) with Socialists from Walloon and from Flanders under Prime Minister Guy Verhofstadt, Minister for Foreign Affairs Karel de Gucht; Bulgaria: coalition under the Bulgarian Socialist Party (BSP), the National Movement Simeon II and the Movements for Rights and Freedoms under Prime Minister Sergei Stanishev, Deputy Prime Minister and Minister for Foreign Affairs Ivaylo Kalfin; Cyprus (Greek Republic): coalition under the Democratic Party (DIKO), the Progressive Party of Working People (AKEL) and the Movement for Social Democracy (EDEK) under President Tassos Papadopoulos, Minister for Foreign Affairs Erato Kozakou-Marcoullis; Czech Republic: coalition under the Civic Democratic Party (ODS) the Christian and Democratic Union – Czechoslovak People's Party (KDU-ČSL) and the Green Party under Prime Minister Mirek Topolánek, Minister for Foreign Affairs Karel Schwarzenberg; Denmark: Liberal minority coalition under Liberal Party (VENSTRE) and Conservative People's Party (DKF) under Prime Minister Anders Fogh Rasmussen, Minister for Foreign Affairs Per Stig Møller; Estonia: coalition under the Estonian Reform Party, the Union of Pro Patria and Res Publica (IRL) and the Social Democratic Party under Prime Minister Andrus Ansip, Minister for Foreign Affairs Urmas Paet; Finland: coalition under the Centre Party (KESK), the National Coalition Party (KOK), the Green League and the Swedish People's Party under Prime Minister Matti Vanhanen, Minister for Foreign Affairs Ilkka Kanerva; France: right of center coalition under the Union for a Popular Movement (UMP), the Union for French Democracy (UDF), the New Centre (NC) and the Liberal Democracy (DL) under Prime Minister François Fillon, Minister for Foreign Affairs Bernard Kouchner; Germany: Grand Coalition under the Christian Democratic Union (CDU/CSU) and the Social Democratic Party of Germany (SPD) under Federal Chancellor Angela Merkel, Minister for Foreign Affairs Frank-Walter Steinmeier; Greece: right of center majority of the New Democracy (ND) under Prime Minister Kostas Karamanlis, Minister for Foreign Affairs Theodora Bakoyannis; Hungary: coalition under the Hungarian Socialist party (MSZP) and the Alliance of Free Democrats (SZDSZ) under Prime Minister Ferenc Gyurcsány, Minister for Foreign Affairs Kinga Göncz; Ireland: coalition under Fianna Fáil, the Green Party and the Progressive Democrats under Prime Minister Bertie Ahern, Minister for Foreign Affairs Dermot Ahern; Italy: coalition under the Democrats of the Left, the Communist Refoundation Party, Party of Italian Communists, Rose in the Fist, the Greens and others under Prime Minister Romano Prodi, Deputy Prime Minister and Minister for Foreign Affairs Massimo D'Alema; Latvia: coalition under the People's Party (TP), the Union of Greens and Farmers (ZZS), Latvia's First Party (LPP) and For Fatherland and Freedom/LNNK under Prime Minister Aigars Kalvītis, Minister for Foreign Affairs Maris Riekstinš; Lithuania: minority coalition under the Social Democratic Party of Lithuania (LSDP), the Lithuanian Peasant Popular Union (VNDS) and the Liberal and Centre Union under Prime Minister Gediminas Kirkilas, Minister for Foreign Affairs Petras Vaitiekūnas; Luxembourg: coalition under the Christian Social People's Party (CSV) and the Luxembourg Socialist Workers' Party (LSAP) under Prime Minister Jean-Claude Juncker, Minister for Foreign Affairs Jean Asselborn; Malta: majority of the Nationalist Party (PN) under Prime Minister Lawrence Gonzi, Minister for Foreign Affairs Michael Frendo; Netherlands: coalition of the Christian Democratic Appeal (CDA), the Labour Party (PvdA) and the Christian Union (CU) under Prime Minister Jan-Peter Balkenende, Minister for Foreign Affairs Maxime Verhagen; Poland: coalition under the Civic Platform (PO) and the Polish People's Party (PSL) under Prime Minister Donald Tusk, Minister for Foreign Affairs Radosław Sikorski; Portugal: majority of the Socialist Party (PS) under Prime Minister José Sócrates, Minister for Foreign Affairs Luís Amado; Romania: coalition of the negotiating positions and "red lines" in the European arena. This observation does not resolve the dilemma of democratic theory and legal philosophy posed by the fact that the European Constitution had after all been ratified by eighteen EU member states when it was officially buried in 2007. That much of its political substance was resurrected through the self-acclaimed Reform Treaty cannot be denied. However, the awkward decrease in public credibility if an international signature by an incumbent government does not have binding consequences for itself or its successor government is a serious diminution of the constellation of collective solidarity expressed in the signing of a treaty by twenty-seven partners. Initially, the repair workers of the European Constitution ran into the same trouble when the Treaty of Lisbon was rejected in the first Irish referendum on June 12, 2008. Only after they accepted repair of their repair work could the Treaty of Lisbon come into force.

For European states, constitutions have always been contracts rather than covenants, alterable when need be and when new insights had evolved into new contractual consensus. The American constitution was designed and is still respected as a covenant. In spite of its amendments, it has prevailed as the longest lasting constitution in the world. Following the model of French constitution building since 1789, all European countries have amended, altered and abandoned constitutions whenever a new political consent had emerged or a revolutionary breach had forced this upon a body politic.[29] Unlike the American Constitution, constitutions in Europe were never written for eternity. The path from the Treaty of Nice via the Treaty Establishing a Constitution for Europe to the Treaty of Lisbon thus reflects the continuously changing political consensus in Europe, often within an enormously short span of time. The revision of the treaties, procedures and policy competencies in the EU will continue to accompany future changes in the political consensus across Europe.

National Liberal Party (PNL) and the Democratic Union of Hungarians in Romania (UDMR) under Prime Minister Călin Popescu-Tăriceanu, Minister for Foreign Affairs Adrian-Mihai Cioroianu; Slovenia: coalition under the Slovenian Democratic Party (SDS), New Slovenia – Christian People's Party (NSi), the Slovenian People's Party (SLS) and the Democratic Party of Pensioners of Slovenia (DeSUS) under Prime Minister Janez Janša, Minister for Foreign Affairs Dimitrij Rupel; Slovakia: coalition under Direction – Social Democracy (Smer-SD), the People's Party – Movement for a Democratic Slovakia (LS-HZDS) and the Slovak National Party (SNS) under Prime Minister Robert Fico, Minister for Foreign Affairs Ján Kubiš; Spain: majority of the Spanish Socialist Workers' Party (PSOE) under Prime Minister José Luis Zapatero, Minister for Foreign Affairs Miguel Angel Moratinos; Sweden: coalition under the Moderate Party, the Centre Party, the Liberal People's Party and the Christian Democrats under Prime Minister Fredrik Reinfeldt, Minister for Foreign Affairs Carl Bildt; United Kingdom: majority of the Labour Party under Prime Minister Gordon Brown, Labour Party, Secretary of State for Foreign and Commonwealth Affairs David Miliband.

29 See van Caenegem, R.C., *An Historical Introduction to Western Constitutional Law*, New York/Cambridge: Cambridge University Press, 1999; Reinhardt, Wolfgang, *Geschichte der Staatsgewalt: Eine vergleichende Verfassungsgeschichte Europas von den Anfängen bis zur Gegenwart*, Munich: C.H. Beck, 1999; Schulze, Reiner (ed.), *Europäische Rechts- und Verfassungsgeschichte: Ergebnisse und Perspektiven der Forschung*, Berlin: Duncker&Humblot, 1991.

This inescapable insight was already evident when the Heads of State and Government of twenty-five EU member states agreed upon the original text of the Treaty Establishing a Constitution for Europe during a European Council meeting on June 18, 2004. Yet, they did not properly address the possible consequences of this insight. The text with its 448 articles was heavy-handed in style, contradictory in key aspects of its content, and insufficient in the eyes of many observers. It remained a serious political mistake not to have managed the subsequent ratification process in a more subtle way from its very beginning. Less understandable was the underestimation of the same process during the second try of treaty-based institutional reforms through the Treaty of Lisbon which was even less readable for ordinary citizens.

As the first treaty of the EU carrying the name Constitution, the Constitutional Treaty was and will remain a historical document. Immediately after it was signed, however, it became controversial. Some were afraid – and others were hoping – that the Treaty Establishing a Constitution for Europe would be the last document of its type before the EU might collapse.[30] In the end, the Constitutional Treaty did not become reality but it triggered the first ever constitutional debate on European identity and the rationale for European integration. The initial Irish rejection of the Treaty of Lisbon was a strong indication for the dire need to reconnect the citizens of the European Union with its institutions and political actors.

The Second Founding of European integration did not begin with the idea to write a European Constitution in 2002. It did not come to an end with the ratification of the Treaty of Lisbon and its implementation in the course of the subsequent cycle of European governance. Finding a new contract between the Union citizens and the idea of Europe, re-calibrating the global role for Europe, and reconciling democracy, transparency and efficiency on the European level of politics will remain major challenges for many years ahead. Yet, this process has begun. European integration has been contract-based from the very beginning.[31] A sequence of treaty revisions followed the original Treaties of Rome.[32] This sequence of treaties and treaty revisions has produced a cumulative "pre-constitution" of Europe.

30 See Booker, Christopher, and Richard North, *The Great Deception: Can the European Union Survive?*, London: Continuum, 2003; Jervis, Paul (ed.), *Resolving the European Crisis: Perspectives on the Future of the European Union*, Middlesex: Middlesex University Press, 2005.

31 See Frankenberg, Günter, "The Return of the Contract: Problems and Pitfalls of "European Constitutionalism"," *European Law Journal*, 6.3 (2000): 257-276.

32 The signatories of the Treaties of Rome were: for Belgium Foreign Minister Paul-Henri Spaak and the Secretary General of the Belgian Economic Ministry, Count Jean-Charles Snoy et d'Oppuers; for France Foreign Minister Christian Pineau and his State Secretary Maurice Faure; for the Federal Republic of Germany Chancellor Konrad Adenauer and the State Secretary in the Foreign Office Walter Hallstein; for Italy Prime Minister Antonio Segni and Foreign Minister Gaetano Martino; for Luxembourg State and Foreign Minister Joseph Bech and the Ambassador of Luxembourg in Brussels Lambertus Schaus; for the Netherlands Foreign Minister Joseph Luns and the Director for Montan Integration in the Dutch Economic Ministry Johannes Linthorst Homan.

Map 1: European Union (2010)

Based on these achievements and the fact that the European Union does not want to constitute a state in the classical sense of the word, it has been argued that the EU does not need a genuine Constitution. Some analysts have maintained the view that it would, in fact, be impossible for the enormously diverse European Union to agree upon any constitutional framework. The agreement on the Treaty Establishing a Constitution for Europe - after all signed by twenty-five responsible and democratically elected governments - has proven these skeptics wrong. The subsequent double ratification crisis only sharpened the awareness of the challenges inevitably linked with the ongoing constitution-building process of European integration.[33]

The relationship between democracy and constitutionalism has not been clarified once and for all with the double rejection of leadership propositions by informed citizens in selected EU member states. The continuing EU's constitutionalization will bring about further empirical and theoretical clarification and new contestations at each future level of agreement. The ongoing constitutional interpretation and review will continue to transform politics in the European Union from a sphere of negotiated compromises in elite-institutions to a sphere of publicly debated goals. It will continue to politicize the integration process and strengthen the claim that the EU is a community of destiny. The idea of Europe being a community of values has become a legal framework with a political face. In the meantime, the European Union has consolidated its role as the expression of political Europe. The Council of Europe, founded in 1949 as the first pan-European institution, has been relegated to a role in the process of protecting of human rights and contributioning to the European identity. The Council of Europe, to recall Walter Bagehot's classical distinction of the two parts of the British constitution, represents the symbolic parts of the European constitution; only the European Union represents the efficient part of the European constitution.[34] The European Union is the political center of Europe and it is increasingly at the heart of its multilevel governance system. This political fact of undeniable weight carries the EU beyond the formal textual basis of its *acquis communautaire*. While European law gives order to European integration, European governance gives authority to it.

33 On the issue of constitutionalization of European integration see Craig, Paul, "Constitutions, Constitutionalism and the European Union," *European Law Journal*, 7.2 (2001): 125-150; Gerstenberg, Oliver, "Expanding the Constitution Beyond the Court: The Case of Euro-Constitutionalism," *European Law Journal*, 8.1 (2002): 172-194; Mancini, Giuseppe Federico, *Democracy and Constitutionalism in the European Union*, Oxford: Hart Publishing, 2000; Pernice, Ingolf, "Multi-Level Constitutionalism in the European Union," *European Law Review*, 27.1/6(2002): 511-529; Lorente, Francisco Rubio, *Constitutionalism in the "Integrated" States of Europe*, Cambridge/Mass.: Harvard Law School, 1998; Ward, Ian, "Beyond Constitutionalism: The Search for a European Political Imagination," *European Law Journal*, 7.4 (2001): 24-40; Weiler, Joseph H. H., and Marlene Wind (eds.), *"European Constitutionalism:" Beyond the State*, Cambridge: Cambridge University Press, 2003; Wiener, Antje, "Evolving Norms of Constitutionalism," *European Law Journal*, 9.1 (2003): 1-13.

34 Bagehot, Walter, *The English Constitution*, Boston: Little Brown, 1873.

Democracy, the rule of law, respect for minorities, a corruption-free market economy – these became the official criteria for EU membership in 1993 (the Copenhagen Criteria) and thus have become the guidelines for membership negotiations since the mid-1990's. In fact, the EU stated that all European countries that comply with or accept the *acquis communautaire* are eligible for membership. The EU insists that its approved substance of common law and policy procedures should be the benchmark for future membership. This pre-constitutional criterion has become the guideline for the process of membership negotiation. The enlargement marathon was not completed with Bulgaria and Romania joining in 2007. It might well last until the end of the second decade of the twenty-first century in the course of which all of Southeast Europe (including Turkey) and possibly further Western European countries (Norway, Iceland, Switzerland) could potentially join the EU. Considering that the Ukraine, Moldova and Belarus are also sometimes mentioned as potential EU members, that in the long run full democratization and market economy in Georgia might lead to that country's EU-application, and that even the chance of independence for Greenland might lead to EU application, all cannot be fully excluded over the next decades and demonstrate that the EU enlargement process could last until the third decade of the twenty-first century. For the time being, only Russian EU membership seems unimaginable, given Russia's domestic situation and the fact that Russia is and wants to remain a global power in its own right.

Notwithstanding future discourses about the geographical borders of Europe, the political finality of European integration will not be answered by any geographical limit to EU membership. Whether or not the European Union will or can at some point overlap with the geographical scope of the Council of Europe is doubtful – even irrelevant – for outlining the political finality of the political borders of the EU. While the Council of Europe defines Europe geographically in the most inclusive way, the European Union has always defined and will continue to primarily define Europe in a political sense. During four decades of creating a common market and after more than a decade of preparing for enlargement into post-communist Europe, the political aspirations of the integration rationale have often been blurred or overshadowed. Moreover, they remain contested. Many inside and outside the EU still favor a lose integration of markets over political integration. This ongoing normative debate cannot hide the fact that from the very beginning, the intention of the Founding Fathers of 1957 was as political as the intention of the Founding Brethren that drafted the failed European Constitution of 2003.[35] The European Union is a political project with a

35 See Loth, Wilfried, *Der Weg nach Europa: Geschichte der europäischen Integration 1939–1957*, Göttingen: Vandenhoeck&Ruprecht, 1990; Dedman, Martin, "European Integration, Origins and Motives," *Modern History Review*, 2:.9 (1997): 30-33; Alting von Gesau, Frans A. M., (ed.), *European Unification in the Twentieth Century: A Treasury of Readings*, Nijmegen: Vidya Publishers, 1998; Burgess, Michael, *Federalism and European Union: The Building of Europe 1950-2000*, London: Routledge, 2000; Bonnefous, Edouard, *La construction de l'Europe par l'un de ses*

political ambition. The deepening of European integration has, therefore, always been the essential precondition to make any enlargement process successful.

The latest crisis in integration escalated during the dual process of accommodating twelve new EU member states while at the same time trying to deepen the constitutionalization of the European Union. This crisis was part of a larger process of adaptation and recalibration. The first cracks in the traditional wall of integration solidarity had already begun during the 1980's. When Great Britain's Prime Minister Margaret Thatcher demanded "her money back", it became evident that the consent for defining European interests was frail. Increasingly, the original question of European integration – "what can we do together?" – was steadily replaced by the search for the very limits of European integration. The fear of too strong integration effects became as vocal as the ambition to move ahead in deepening integration. Instead of defining European integration by its potential, the quest for limiting its effects was spreading across the member states of the EU. The more European integration advanced, the more its prerequisites came under pressure, i.e., reciprocal solidarity and recognition of a common law-based political aspiration. By the early twenty-first century, Europeans desired to become a world power. But they did not want to pay the price for it.[36] In many ways, their political leaders had acted in a similarly paradoxical way. European Union matters absorbed more and more of their time in office, yet they tried to relegate its effects and limit the implications of their own deeds. The uncertain question "What kind of Europe" was already in the air before the crisis over the European Constitution broke out[37] Its aftermath will last longer than the technical solution of this crisis in deepening integration. The European Union will not be allowed to stop in solidifying its legitimacy of being a law-based genuine body politic.

2. Constitutionalizing the Acquis Communautaire

The legal and political core of European Union is enshrined in the *acquis communautaire.* Not too many EU citizens will be able to properly define what this term means. In the context of the eastern EU-enlargement in the early years of the

initiateurs, Paris: Presse Universitaire Française, 2002; von der Groeben, Hans, *Europäische Integration aus historischer Erfahrung: Ein Zeitzeugengespräch mit Michael Gehler*, ZEI Discussion Paper C108, Bonn: Center for European Integration Studies, 2002; Dinan, Desmond, *Europe Recast: A History of European Union*, Boulder: Lynn Rieffer, 2004.

36 See *Frankfurter Allgemeine Zeitung*, "Europäer wollen Weltmacht sein," September 7, (2005): According to an opinion poll taken by the German Marshall Fund of the United States, seventy percent of European citizens expressed their desire that the EU should become a world power similar to the United States. But only 44 percent of EU citizens were ready to accept higher military spending for achieving that objective.

37 See Tsoukalis, Loukas, *What Kind of Europe?*, Oxford: Oxford University Press, 2005 (2nd rev. ed.); see also Mendrano, Juan Diez, *Framing Europe: Attitudes to European Integration in Germany, Spain and the United Kingdom*, Princeton: Princeton University Press, 2003.

twenty-first century, the *acquis communautaire* seemed to be better known in post-communist members of the EU than in the older member states. Their societies, legal systems and political regimes had to undergo a fundamental transformation prior to being allowed to join the EU. The term *acquis communautaire* became synonymous with the EU.[38] In Western Europe, among the fifteen "old" EU member states, the term *acquis communautaire* had never gained that much "fame" – neither positive nor negative. This was astonishing, because in reality also Western Europe was increasingly influenced by the *acquis communautaire* – that is to say by EU law – and had, in fact, brought it about.[39] The term *acquis communautaire* was and remains part of the technocratic jargon known to EU experts. In order to give Europe a soul and in order to reach the hearts of EU citizens, it would be necessary to define Europe in other terms. It would be necessary to demonstrate European integration as a success story for its citizens. It would be necessary to demonstrate that the EU could work effectively and efficiently. It would simply be necessary to define Europe again from its opportunities instead of burdening Europe by focusing only on its limits. This will remain the central leadership test for many years and well beyond the technical solution to the constitutional issue.

Whether taken seriously in public or not, the existence of the *acquis communautaire* has always demonstrated that the European Union is not only about rhetoric and diplomacy. The European Union is about the evolution of a common European law, a common European market, and a common European body politic. It is important to reiterate that European integration is not heading toward a superstate, but it is clearly more than an effort to create a common market.[40] Eventually, the European Union is about the formation of a community of law and common political destiny as the basis for a new global presence of Europe. In the early twenty-first century, only few observers and actors seem to be more optimistic than Europeans themselves about this prospect.[41]

For the enlarged European Union to succeed, it requires to connect its growing global role with the steady deepening of the integration process. This, of course, has implications not only for EU institutions, but also for the societies of all its member states. The broader European public – including the political elites – has only recently begun to take note of the fact that the EU is also streamlining national priorities in order

38 See Krenzler, Horst Günter (ed.), *Preparing for the Acquis Communautaire: Report on the Working Group on the Eastern Enlargement of the EU*, Florence: European University Institute, 1998.

39 See Craig, Paul, and Grainne de Burca (eds.), *The Evolution of EU Law*, Oxford: Oxford University Press, 1999.

40 See Gillingham, John, *European Integration, 1950-2003: Superstate or New Market Economy?*, Cambridge: Cambridge University Press, 2003.

41 See Rifkin, Jeremy *The European Dream: How Europe's Vision of the Future is Quietly Eclipsing the American Dream*, Cambridge: Polity Press, 2004; Leonhard, Mark *Why Europe will Run the twenty-first Century*, London, Fourth Estate, 2005; Verhofstadt, Guy, *The United States of Europe*, London: Federal Trust, 2006.

to forge a law-based economic and political union. The people of the EU are increasingly learning that this has consequences for their respective national political and socio-economic systems.[42] It should not come as a surprise that this realization provokes skepticism and resentment. Yet, it will continue to be a European reality.

From its very beginning, the European integration process has included a constitutional dimension. As part of an ongoing process, the 2007 Reform Treaty was nothing but the most recent expression of this trend that has grown over more than fifty years of European integration. Treaty revisions have added substantial weight to the primacy of the European Union in European governance and its *acquis communautaire* as the central legal body in Europe. The EU is not just about shared interests. It is increasingly also about shared destiny. This is why it can legitimately be considered a community of values.

Democracy is not unique about Europe. What is unique about Europe is the way Europeans have made use of democratic rule in their individual countries in order to set up a new political, legal, and economic order for their common continent.[43] What is unique about European integration is the consistent amalgamation of democratic nations into a Union based on law, consensus oriented policy processes, parliamentary governance with a strong executive, and a treaty-based constitutionalization. This transformation is generating pooled sovereignty and pooled democracy of EU member states and Union citizens, yet it preserves the individual nations and states as they have developed in the course of Europe's long history.

This politicized and constitutionalized Europe is unique compared with past modes of organizing and orchestrating interests and principles in Europe's order. A strong economy, growing into a common market, generated respect for European integration during the five decades of its existence. At the turn of the century, Europe had to go through an adaptation crisis. Yet, it has maintained its path and regained a certain sense of direction. In the decades ahead, it is this political dimension that will define the role and recognition of the European Union as a strong international player. There is an increasing realization – inside as well as outside of Europe – that Europe's affluence and social cohesion are rooted in the political and constitutional order of the continent. The order is not only the consequence of coordinated or pooled economic policies, but also the result of and the engine for further political and constitutional developments.

42 See Green Cowles, Maria, et al. (eds.), *Transforming Europe: Europeanization and Domestic Change*, Ithaca/London: Cornell University Press, 2001; Goldmann, Kjell, *Transforming the European Nation-State*, London: SAGE, 2001.

43 This thought is echoed in the philosophical discussion about European identity in Brague, Remi, and Peter Koslowski, *Vaterland Europa: Europäische und nationale Identität im Konflikt*, Vienna: Passagen Verlag, 1997. Brague talks about Europe as not being a tradition, but a horizon and a goal (page 38), while Koslowski compares European integration with the "translatio imperii" from the Roman Empire to the world of the Franks under Charlemagne, based on a limited mandate which is also the case with European Union competencies; on the origins of Europe see Davies, Norman, *Europe: A History*, Oxford: Oxford University Press, 1996: 213-290 ("Origo. The Birth of Europe AD c. 330-800").

The emerging European constitutionalism is both an answer to Europe's struggle with identity and the foundation for preserving freedom and affluence in the age of globalization through political means.

Democratic theory recognizes people for what they are and who they are. It promotes political and personal freedom in the name of the recognition of the individual. Checks and balances serve the pursuit of individual freedom and the protection of human rights. Democracy tends to mistrust institutions while institutions tend to tame democratic aspirations as absolutes. Constitutional procedures emphasize authority over freedom, while democracy tends to do the opposite. Yet, the lasting authority of a constitution depends largely upon the degree to which it can generate and guarantee freedom and democracy. This is why non-democratic constitutions lack legitimacy. Constitutions that reconcile democratic aspirations with the ability to generate authority and result-oriented decision-making through political processes tend to have a higher degree of legitimacy in the eyes of the citizens living under them. It can create and reproduce sustainable constitutionalism.[44]

All constitutions in the contemporary world provide for representational institutions, normally in the form of parliaments. That is why parliamentary democracy has become the most respected form of constitutional government. This theoretical understanding is at the root of reasoning about parliamentarian democracy, as it has become the guiding principle for governance in a constitutionalized European Union. Still, it is an emerging parliamentary democracy, which is multilayered and encompasses the national as well as the European parliaments, and it certainly remains incomplete as a constitution-based body politic.

Europe's evolving political order is a continent-wide continuation of the individual national European experiences in the age of early constitutionalism in the nineteenth century. The trend toward parliamentary and constitutional rule at the national level, which was repeating itself in stages, can be observed with detours and under different historical circumstances at the level of the European Union. All European nation states have grown from pre-constitutionalism to constitutionalism. As an emerging parliamentary and constitutionally-based democracy, the European Union follows the journey of parliamentary democracy in most European states over the past two hundred

44 See Bellamy, Richard (ed.), *Constitutionalism, Democracy and Sovereignty: American and European Perspectives*, Aldershot: Ashgate, 1996; Alexander, Larry, *Constitutionalism: Philosophical Foundations*, Cambridge: Cambridge University Press, 1999; Sajo, Andras, and Stephen Holmes, *Limiting Government: An Introduction to Constitutionalism*, Budapest: Central European University Press, 1999; Sampford, Charles, *Beyond the Republic: Meeting the Global Challenges to Constitutionalism*, Sydney: Federation Press, 2001; Gordon, Scott, *Controlling the State: Constitutionalism from Ancient Athens to Today*, Cambridge/Mass.: Harvard University Press, 2002; Berggren, Niclas, and Nils Karlson, "Constitutionalism, Division of Power and Transaction Costs," *Public Choice*, 117.1/2 (2003): 99-124.

years.[45] For the time being, the rule of law is stronger in the European Union than democracy while democracy is stronger than transparency.

The revival of parliamentary democracy in Western Europe after World War II stood in contrast to the prevailing totalitarian systems in the communist-ruled part of Europe. Nevertheless, the revival of Europe after a century of bloody national and ideological warfare was based on the principle of constitutional democracy. This revival began after 1945 on the national level – most remarkably in Italy, Germany and France, later followed by Greece, Spain and Portugal – and it has grown gradually to the European level. It is not surprising that most post-communist countries in Europe were heading in the very direction of redefining their political system as one based on parliamentary and constitutional rule of law after the peaceful revolutions of 1989. Theirs were revolutions in the name of freedom and democracy, intended to catch up with the established parliamentary democracies of Western Europe. Hence, it was logical and consistent that the quest in Central Europe to join the European integration structures was coupled with the effort to streamline their national political systems with the parliamentary-based democracies, constitution-based rule of law, and market-based economies in Western Europe. Since the late 1980's, the European integration process has increasingly been influenced by the promotion of the idea of a European Constitution. In hindsight this is not a mysterious surprise, but rather a logical consequence of the systemic reconciliation among European states and the national reconciliation among European people. The national experience of parliamentary democracy as the expression of political identity under conditions of freedom and rule of law found its echo at the level of the European Union. This was further proof of the over-lap of multilayered, multiple identities within the multilevel system of European governance.[46]

45 On the early national constitutionalism in Europe see Dippel, Horst (ed.), *Die Anfänge des Konstitutionalismus in Deutschland: Texte deutscher Verfassungsentwürfe am Ende des 18. Jahrhunderts*, Frankfurt/Main: Keip, 1991; Hye, Hans Peter, *Das politische System in der Habsburgermonarchie: Konstitutionalismus, Parlamentarismus und politische Partizipation*, Prague: Karolinum, 1998; Dippel, Horst (ed.), *Executive and Legislative Powers in the Constitutions of 1848-49*, Berlin: Duncker&Humblot, 1999; Kirsch, Martin, *Monarch und Parlament im 19. Jahrhundert - Der monarchische Konstitutionalismus als europäischer Verfassungstyp: Frankreich im Vergleich*, Göttingen: Vandenhoeck&Ruprecht, 1999; Kirsch, Martin, and Pierangelo Schiera, *Denken und Umsetzung des Konstitutionalismus in Deutschland und anderen europäischen Ländern in der ersten Hälfte des 19. Jahrhunderts*, Berlin: Duncker&Humblot, 1999; Kirsch, Martin, et al. (eds.), *Der Verfassungsstaat vor der Herausforderung der Massengesellschaft: Konstitutionalismus um 1900 im europäischen Vergleich*, Berlin: Duncker&Humblot, 2002.

46 Earlier efforts to draft a European Constitution remained academic exercises or precursory visions of politicians, such as Altiero Spinelli's work in the European parliament. The hope of matching the path toward monetary union with a path toward political union failed during the process that led to the Treaty of Maastricht in 1991. Nevertheless, the discourse about a European Constitution gained momentum during the 1990s – as a reaction to the institutional crisis which stemmed from the insufficient work of Intergovernmental Conferences during the 1990s and their incremental yet increasingly contradictory strife for institutional reforms.

After World War II, Western Europe had experienced a period of constitutional reconstruction as the answer to totalitarian politics. After 1989, a second wave of constitutional reconstruction took place in post-communist Europe. It was the second answer to totalitarian politics. In the early twenty-first century, both processes came together in the quest for a genuine European Constitution giving a political frame to united Europe. Even in its rejection by majorities of two European people, the failed European Constitution of 2004 remains part of a gradually emerging constitutionalization of the European Union, an experience that has begun with the Treaties of Rome. This process was shaped by further treaty revisions, most notably the Treaty of Maastricht (Treaty on European Union). The cumulative European constitution-building has already had and will continue to have ramifications for the individual democratic nations of Europe. They continue to gradually, yet cautiously, pool their constitutional sovereignty on the European level. Constitution-building on the European level affects the identity of the citizens of Europe, while it is inspired by a European broadening of the various national and regional identities in Europe. Unavoidable, European constitution-building impacts the political system of each member state of the EU. Resistance to a speedy continuation of this trend is rather natural. With all the accompanying skepticism, Europe is experiencing the increasing political dimension of a shared identity and destiny.

The constitutionalization of Europe raises the question about the degree of authority that can be expected from the European Union – what it represents to constitute the means to give form and direction to a political entity. A constitution is considered to be supreme law and should frame, or at least guide, a political system. It is useful to distinguish "between the authority a text asserts and the authority it exerts."[47] It remains open to historical judgment whether or not the European Union can claim a sustained degree of authority national constitutions have been able to accrue in the history of Europe. The question of whether or not the current European pre-constitutionalism can grow into full-fledged European constitutionalism will be answered by an open future.

Based on historical experience, constitutions can fulfill different functions:[48]

- They can be purely cosmetic in which case either a nation or a political system can hide its true intentions or failures behind the curtain of constitutional rhetoric.
- They can serve as a Charter for government, which is to say the constitution sketches out the rules of operation of a legitimate government, irrespective of the social fabric of the society which the government will shape.
- They can explicitly serve as guardian of fundamental human rights and values

47 Murphy, Walter F., "Constitutions, Constitutionalism, and Democracy," in: Greenberg, Douglas, et al. (eds.), *Constitutionalism and Democracy - Transitions in the Contemporary World*, New York/Oxford: Oxford University Press, 1993: 8.

48 Ibid.: 8-17.

and thus delineate the scope of political authority in order to protect basic human rights and fundamental values of a body politic.

- They can serve as the founding document of a body politic and as a symbol of its aspiration; by doing so, constitutions can be the foundation stone of a new political entity and serve the function of a covenant.

The existing cumulative European Constitution – the set of Treaties from Rome to Maastricht, to Nice and, as of 2009, to Lisbon – entails elements of all these functions as experienced in the history of constitution-building linked to nation states. The cumulative European Constitution challenges those who assume that a European Constitution can only be of a cosmetic nature. The European Union has become a genuine governance system although it does not represent a state in the traditional sense of the word.

More than five decades after the beginning of the European integration process, the difficult yet continuing constitutionalization of the European Union coincides with fundamental trends in European integration and anticipates some trends which will unfold as the twenty-first century develops:

- Internally, the European Union is challenged by the need to absorb its biggest and most complex enlargement and it will have to complete the enlargement process toward South Eastern Europe. Regional economic asymmetries and a strong gap between experiences and expectations accompany the consequences of enlargement toward post-communist countries in 2004 and 2007. At the same time, the European Union is confronted with the consequences of an aging population, thus putting even more pressure on the future struggle over social policies and the reallocation of limited resources.
- The European Union faces globalization and the challenge of the economic and social dynamics outside Europe while it has severe difficulties to convince the world that it ought to be considered the most innovative and dynamic economy. The biggest challenge for the EU in managing globalization relates to its ability to pursue internal structural economic reforms and generate coherent and efficient decision-making structures and mechanisms of implementing joint policies, which can support sustainable innovation and social dynamics. Simultaneously, the EU needs to grow into a force that is capable and willing to contribute to the global projection of stability and the management of the global political and economic system.
- In order to cope with internal frustration and external expectation, the European Union faces the need to gradually, but consistently politicize its identity and become a global political actor. The EU needs to better define policy preferences and priorities. It is not enough to accept economic path dependencies. Supporting diversity in unity cannot be accomplished by traditional means of promoting cultural identity. It requires the European Union to grow from a

community of institutions and organs into a community of practical will and political destiny. It requires the EU to generate leadership, which is apt to the task and courageous enough to take the necessary risks. And it requires the EU to truly generate European citizens with a sense of ownership in and commitment to the process.

Thus, the order of testing the meaning and consequences of the constitutionalized European Union is tall. The practical policy processes will generate debate, controversy and compromise. The gap between expectation and reality will probably always exist. But most important for the credibility and viability of the European Union are two questions that were relevant in the history of constitution-building and constitutionalism elsewhere: who will eventually judge the legitimacy of the implications of a constitutionalized European Union for the European body politic?[49] And: In which condition and on the basis of which constitution does the European Union present itself to the world?

3. Challenge and Response: Patterns of European Identity Formation

The relationship between integration and identity has changed over the first fifty years of European integration. In the course of five decades, a study of the "deepening" and "widening" European integration can lead to some comprehensive conclusions. One of them is the fact that both of these processes were never mutually exclusive. Of course, they did not necessarily go hand in hand smoothly. At times they blocked each other. However, they never prevented each other from developing further in their own right. Sometimes new dynamics stemmed surprisingly from dialectical processes, sometimes progress was the result of trial and error or of challenge and response. In fact, this classical concept of challenge and response, introduced by historian Arnold J. Toynbee in his seminal work on world history, is the best available key to understanding and rationalizing the course of European integration. The natural oscillation of European integration represents what Toynbee called the "alternating rhythm of static and dynamic, of movement and pause and movement fundamental to the nature of the universe"[50].

Toynbee explained with great erudition that challenges instigate responses, which, of course, can be either appropriate or inappropriate. Depending on the nature of the response, challenges can lead to negative, if not catastrophic, consequences for the form they are relating to. If the response is appropriate and well focused, it will strengthen and reinvigorate the form it touches upon. As Toynbee remarks: "In the language of

49 See Kumm, Matthias, *Who is the Final Arbiter of the Constitutionality in Europe?*, Cambridge/Mass.: Harvard Law School, 1998.

50 Toynbee, Arnold Joseph, *Studies of History: Abridgement of Volumes I-VI*, New York/London: Oxford University Press, 1947: 51.

science we may say that the function of the intruding factor is to supply that on which it intrudes with a stimulus of the kind best calculated to evoke the most potently creative variations."[51] None of the trendy social science theories is better equipped to explain the paths, detours, rough roads and happy endings of European integration over the first fifty years. It has been and it remains a path of challenges and responses.

This is, of course, not indicating that the rationale of this process (or rather, these processes) can simply be reduced to one specific explanation. If this were the case, we would approach deterministic notions of history that run counter to social theory and anthropological evidence. Nevertheless, it is not too far-fetched to outline the history of European integration as a permanent set of responses to contingently changing challenges. They were, of course, always executed by a series of political processes with their genuine strategic and tactical logics. But these were instrumental actions in reaction to structural challenges. The logic of "challenge and response" is the most comprehensive frame one can put around the many existing theoretical efforts to conceptualize European integration, why it began and how it developed.[52]

The most serious challenge for the creation of a new Europe stood at the very beginning. The destruction of Europe in two wars and the democratic revitalization of its Western regions (West Germany included), with the help of America's enlightened, but not selfless Marshall Plan, the founding of NATO, and the continuous strategic presence of the US as a European power, marked the beginning of Europe's second renaissance. The first renaissance can best be understood by Leonardo da Vinci's ambition to build a bridge wherever he saw a river and by Blaise Pascal's fear in face of the dark open sky at night. Europe's second renaissance is likewise driven by hope and fear.

51 Ibid.: 63.

52 In his small and concise book *The Origins and Development of the European Union 1945-1995* Martin Dedman (London: Routledge, 1996: 7-33) describes the three most influential approaches to the theory of European integration, although it remains questionable whether they can really be called "theories" or should rather be referred to as comprehensive assessments of analysis: 1.Functional theory that dominates contemporary Political Science. It assumes that an increase in international cooperation and consequently in integration is the logical precondition for states to enhance their scope of action in the modern state system. The scholarly works of David Mitrany (*A Working Peace System: An Argument for the Functional Development of International Organization*, New York: Russel&Russel Inc., 1943) and Ernst Haas (*The Uniting of Europe: Political, Social, and Economic Forces 1950-1957*, Stanford: Stanford University Press, 1958) laid the ground for this most influential integration theory. 2. Ideological approaches refer to the growth and influence of European federalist movements in the interwar period and during World War II. The erudite work of Walter Lipgen's (*Documents on the History of European Integration*, 2 Volumes, Berlin/New York: de Gruyter, 1985 and 1986) has contributed the best possible insights into their quest for a new normative beginning in building a European order. 3. Historical-systematizing research has focused primarily on the period from the Treaties of Rome until the Treaty of Maastricht. Alan Milward (*The European Rescue of the Nation State*, London: Routledge, 1992) in one of the most influential works of this nature has argued that integration occurs only when it is needed by the states that come together. Andrew Moravscik (*The Choice for Europe: Social Purpose and State Power from Messina to Maastricht*, Ithaca: Cornell University Press, 1998) has elaborated on the theme that European integration strengthened the European nation-states.

After 1945, the return of a Hitler-like dictator – anywhere, but mainly in Germany – or Stalin taking over all of Europe was as deep a fear as the hope of reinvigorating Europe's economic, social and cultural resources. The rise of an integrated Europe coincided with the end of Europe's colonial ambitions. This helped to convince the French to support the project of European integration although it did not prevent them from keeping their British rivals out as long as possible. Furthermore, integration was Germany's best choice in regaining recognition after the horrendous legacy of Hitler's totalitarian terror, with the Holocaust as its culmination, his war and Stalin's victory with the division of Europe as the most bitter and lasting price. West Germany's rehabilitation through integration coincided with the interests of the other Founding members of the European Economic Community. Italy was in a somewhat similar although less dramatic situation than the Germans were, because Mussolini's Fascism, as bad as it had been, paled by comparison to Hitler's totalitarian regime, a system whose communist variant prevailed behind the Iron Curtain after 1945. Meanwhile, Belgium, the Netherlands and Luxembourg were traditionally favorably disposed toward international and intra-European cooperation. Thus it is not surprising that many initiatives (and leaders) in support of European integration originated in these three countries.

The history of European integration has produced its own culture of memory. Some even go so far as saying that Europe's integration is the new great, triumphal story of our time.[53] It is certainly true that common experience, continuous testing through crises, and symbolic and substantial achievements have generated joint memories and shared feelings all across the European Union. They contribute to an evolving European political identity. It is a constructionist evolution. It is the ongoing work on a political construction site.

The relationship between "challenge and response" can be studied in many specific cases that are part of the integration experience. Most importantly, however, it can be detected in the context of the two most defining phases of integration development: The defining periods from 1945 to 1957 and from 1989 to 2009.

- The Treaties of Rome and the creation of the European Economic Community in 1957 were the ultimate European responses to the end of World War II and the renaissance of parliamentary democracy in the countries of Western Europe in 1945.
- The political proposal to deepen European integration through the advanced and formalized constitutionalization of European politics until 2009 was the ultimate response to the re-unification of Europe that began in 1989. It was also the beginning of a new era in European integration in which democracy and the

53 Peter Koslowski cites Japanese philosopher Naoshi Yamawaki as one of those points to the process of European integration as the greatest master story of our time, Brague, Remi, and Peter Koslowski, *Vaterland Europa*, op.cit.: 70.

participatory claims of Union citizens were entering the multilevel governance system of the EU, clashing with the elite-driven character of the past.

Both defining periods encompass complex historical developments that must be analyzed in their own right. Both ended with successful institutional and constitutional results in combining two factors whose relationship has been debated as mutually exclusive, the "deepening" and "widening". In 1957, integration started with six European countries and it became successful only because they brought about treaty-based common supranational institutions. At the signing of the Reform Treaty in 2007, European integration had advanced to 27 European countries. It could only remain successful over time through deepened integration in a constitutionally based supranational community of law, common interests, values, institutions and policies. Obviously, the EU needed more than new legal and constitutional provisions. It was in continuous need of a much stronger and focused "European spirit," which politicians like to invoke in order to appeal to European solidarity. The more successful the original integration process had become, the more Europe needed to widen and to include additional European countries that wanted to join the EU. The larger Europe has grown, the deeper the integration process inevitably needs to become. Understanding this dialectic as part of the mechanism of "challenge and response" is not always shared in the scholarly literature on European integration. Yet, the mechanism of "challenge and response" – coupled with the importance of leadership during critical periods for EU politics – is closer to the empirical evidence than many theory-driven assessments of the process of integration in Europe.

The founding of the European Economic Community in 1957 was the deepest structural response to the end of World War II in 1945, but it could not prevent the European Economic Community from encountering its own crises. Over time, while it developed from the European Economic Community into the European Community and ultimately into the European Union, the "original crises" of war and peace had been resolved through the aspiration of a common market. To stand against Soviet expansion, and to do so under the security umbrella provided by the United States with the creation of NATO, was the external constellation and condition under which Western Europe succeeded. Other crises followed over the next decades, in the end understood as crises in integration and not crises of integration:

- The crisis that broke out after the French National Assembly refused to ratify the European Defense Community in 1954 that France itself had launched two years earlier.
- The failure to proceed with concepts of political integration after the governments of the six member states refused the proposals for political integration expressed in two Fouchet Plans in 1961 and 1962 that they had commissioned themselves.
- The Luxembourg Compromise, which brought France back into the EEC

institutions in 1965 after France had left over disputes on agricultural policies.

- The failure of the EEC to implement the Werner Plan of 1970 that outlined the path toward monetary union and a common currency over the decade of the 1970's, which then had to wait until 2002 to become a reality.
- The frustrating refusal of the Treaty of Maastricht by the majority of Danes in a referendum in 1992, finally neutralized by the "invention" of dubious "opting out-clauses" for Denmark that helped to bring the majority back on the path of integration.
- The crisis over constitution-making that was brought about by the EU Heads of State and Government in December 2003 when they were initially unable to agree on the draft Treaty Establishing a Constitution for Europe which the Constitutional Convention had presented to them in unanimity in June 2003. Last minute compromises were found by the EU heads of state and government in the summer of 2004, which were face-saving although not uplifting.
- The double crisis of ratification which derailed the Treaty Establishing a Constitution of Europe and almost killed the subsequent Reform Treaty. More than ever, the political establishment in the EU is now forced to focus on a new contract between EU institutions and EU citizens by delivering a "Europe that works."

In summary, European integration has been nurtured, pushed forward and shaped by crises: It is as if crises were often the best engines for European integration.[54] But it can be said that all crises were crises in integration that never escalated into crises of integration. In this sense, also the constitutional crisis of the first decade of the twenty-first century must be considered a crisis of adaptation. The Treaty Establishing a Constitution for Europe in 2004 was intended to be the ultimate response to the challenge that the end of communist totalitarianism and the fall of the Iron Curtain had posed to the concept of European integration.[55] It was the last effort to pursue European integration as a top-down process. Although the Constitutional Convention had been the best possible indication for a change in the method of advancing institutional reforms in the EU, this effort was obviously neither enough or convincing. To put it blunt: It was not successful. With the crisis that broke out when majorities of French and Dutch voters said "no" in referenda, Europe's political elites were shocked. They drew, however, the wrong conclusion by retrenching to backdoor politics instead of fully democratizing the future process of constitutionalizing Europe. When Irish voters initially said "no" to the repair treaty, political leaders paid the bill for this unconvincing behaviour that undermined their credibility but did not destroy European integration.

54 See Kirt, Romain (ed.), *Die Europäische Union und ihre Krisen*, Baden-Baden: Nomos, 2001; Kühnhardt, Ludger (ed.), *Crises in European Integration: Challenge and Response 1945-2005*, Oxford and New York: Berghahn Books, 2008.

55 See Kühnhardt, Ludger, *Revolutionszeiten: Das Umbruchjahr 1989 im geschichtlichen Zusammenhang*, Munich: Olzog, 1994 (Turkish edition 2003).

"Challenge and response" accompanied the defining periods of European integration as much as many smaller events and developments during the first fifty years of its existence. No blueprints were available, no theory could be followed, but in the two most critical defining periods of European integration until this day, the actors involved had to cope with a web of challenges and bring about a web of answers. During both periods the process of framing a European answer to a European challenge was linked to the formulation of a European answer to the issue of transatlantic relations. In other words, whenever European integration went through defining critical years, transatlantic relations were undergoing parallel developments of uncertainty, crises and adaptation.

- The period from 1949 (the founding of NATO) until 1957 (the signing of the Treaties of Rome) was crucial for the making of the West. It was an integral part of the evolution of the European integration process.
- The period from 1991 (Yugoslavian Wars, Iraq Wars) until 2009 (reconstruction of Iraq and Afghanistan, EU and NATO enlargements, a new US presidency, new elections to the European Parliament) was crucial for redefining transatlantic relations. The search for a post-Cold War frame of mind was also essential inside Europe.

During both of these defining periods of European integration and of the concept of "the Western World," the Atlantic civilization several times went through divergent experiences: In 1945, Europe's self-destruction had ended with America's continuous presence as a European power. Immediately, a common frame of mind was organized around the notion of defending Western freedom against Soviet hegemony. After 1989, and especially after 2001, Europe and America had to gradually reconcile contrasting implications of "11/9" – the fall of the Berlin Wall on November 9, 1989 as Europe's "11/9" – and "9/11" – the terrorist attacks on New York and Washington on September 11, 2001. At the end, the transatlantic partners had no alternative but to come together again as the main agents of managing world affairs.

Between 1949 and 1957 three complex issues intertwined in the parallel and overlapping processes of shaping the European and the transatlantic architecture:

- The outbreak of the Cold War and Soviet expansionism, followed by the wars in Korea and Indochina as well as the Suez Crises, made France and Great Britain realize the limits of their global role. The ensuing US-Soviet hegemonic struggle facilitated the American guarantee for Europe's security.
- The start of functional European integration through the European Coal and Steel Community turned out to be a highly successful way of matching various ideas about integration and conflicting interests. Eventually, European integration turned into the most successful structure for rebuilding Western Europe as a society of affluence and freedom and a loyal partner of the United States.
- The establishment of an institutional network with NATO as the strategic and

military insurance policy for rebuilding Western Europe, the Council of Europe as a loose community of European values, and the European Economic Community as the first step to political integration in Europe were mutually supporting elements of a new and sustainable European peace order with the United States as one of its corner stones.

Between 1989 and 2009, again, three decisive and interconnected issues shaped the path of European integration and the transformation of the Atlantic community:

- The introduction of the euro opened the way to the further transfer of sovereignties from the national level to the supranational level of the European Union. A common European currency had a long-term impact on the American perception of European integration. United Europe eventually had to be taken seriously, eventually also as an emerging Home Affairs Union and a Foreign, Security and Defense Union.
- The enlargement of the European Union with post-communist countries went hand in hand with the gradual enlargement of NATO (by 2008 twenty-six NATO members and twenty-seven EU members were anticipating further enlargements) and proved that the Euro-Atlantic institutions remained valid as the core for the projection of stability beyond their own territory in a world facing enormous opportunities as a result of globalization, but also serious new threats emanating from the modernization crisis in the Broader Middle East, the terrorist threat of Islamic totalitarianism, and the proliferation of weapons of mass destruction.
- Ultimately, the most serious adaptation crisis in the history of transatlantic relations in the aftermath of the terrorist attacks of September 11, 2001 had to bring the US and Europe back as each others closest partners in managing world affairs. Neither the global economy nor any geopolitical challenge was handled successfully without joint transatlantic action.

European integration has never followed a theoretical blueprint. It is therefore hard to characterize and assess through the categories of theoretical models and concepts. European integration is constructionist and actor based, largely elite driven, often a response to external challenges and internal crises; its results have rarely been the consequence of simple and easy decisions. Often they were accompanied by frustrating detours. Almost always they were of an incremental and difficult nature. The governance system of the European Union still is contradictory and clumsy, its decision-making processes often non-transparent and inefficient. However, the alternative warrants consideration: The price of non-integration would be too high. Fragmented and limited national markets and weakness in the international arena can only be overcome by participating in a common European effort. Maintaining national exceptionalism because of a diverse national cultural identity is no longer a positive option for the vast majority of European states.

The existing nation states of Europe reflect the cultural diversity of the continent. They are a cultural product with strong political bonds holding them together. Yet, alone they are incapable of delivering most of those goods to their citizens for whom they were created in the first place for security, stability, and affluence. This is why European integration has become a political "must" for practically all-European countries. In order to preserve their cultural diversity and identity, European states and societies need to participate in the shaping of a joint political identity. Only a European frame of mind allows the growth of common interests and forms of solidarity. This transformation of culture and politics in Europe is neither easy nor can it be completed rapidly. Yet, it has been occurring for more than five decades, and it is shaping the political culture of Europe. It would not be overly speculative to assume that it will take another five decades before a comprehensive form will finally solidify. It will need to combine function and legitimacy of European integration with the interests, values, and multiple identities of the majority of EU citizens.

At the core of the transformation of the European order of states and people is the changing character of identity. In the past, matters of identity were limited to their role in shaping national public life. In the European Union, matters of identity become increasingly related to a common political will and destiny in Europe. As the European integration process is beginning to cut deeply into the domestic structures of all member states and nations, political identity is becoming the logical consequence of the European Union as a community of values.[56] The European Union represents the multiple identities in a diverse European culture.

The origins of the European integration process are an answer to the exploitation of European differences in the name of nationalism and even racism. After the antagonistic clashes and collective destructions of Europe's internal order and external relevance, the Founding Fathers of European integration were convinced that they had to define common interests and shared perspectives in order to overcome a culture of hatred and mistrust. They began with the economy. All too often, the subsequent path of European integration was accompanied by skepticism among intellectuals. Often, Jean Monnet[57] is quoted as having said that if he would have to restart the integration process, he would begin with culture. Extensive research could not find proof for the quotation. Moreover, being quoted time and again and with emphasis has not substantiated the argument that Europe missed a golden opportunity by not building its integration around the notion of culture.

Following World War II, cultural mistrust was so prevalent in Europe that it would hardly have been a good mirror for choreographing the idea of European integration:

56 See Banchoff, Thomas, and Mitchell P. Smith (eds.), *Legitimacy and the European Union: The Contested Polity*, London/New York: Routledge, 1999.

57 On his legacy for European integration see Roussel, Eric, *Jean Monnet 1888-1979*, Paris: Fayard, 1996; Fransen, Frederic J., *Supranational Politics of Jean Monnet: Ideas and Origins of the European Community*, Westport: Greenwood, 2001.

Who would have trusted the Germans immediately after 1945 on the sheer basis of a good cultural tradition that had proved incapable of preventing Hitler from rising to power? Who would have accepted a French concept of cultural superiority ("mission civilisatrice") as still practiced in French colonies? And whom would the French have recognized as equal to their concept of culture? Who would have been able to link Belgian culture with British culture or Italian culture in order to create an integrated Europe? Under the given conditions, the Council of Europe did its best to give credit to and generate respect for the diversity of European culture as the basis for revitalizing a deeply humiliated and destroyed continent.[58] But culture could have hardly served as the sufficient instrument to initiate and orchestrate sustainable political integration for a divided continent in ashes. It required the rational choice to pool common yet divisive economic interests in order to construct a new Europe.

Certainly, cultural considerations and underpinnings were present during the creation of the European integration process. It has been said that the European Economic Community was a "catholic project" as many leaders of the 1950's were Roman-Catholic. Robert Schuman was Catholic, so were Alcide de Gasperi, Konrad Adenauer and Joseph Bech – it is hard to deny the religious background of some of the most important Founding Fathers of the integration process. Yet, they did not insist on mentioning culture, values or even religion in the Treaties of Rome.[59] The Founding Fathers of the European Economic Community were united in the desire to prevent the outbreak of yet another war in Europe. No matter whether Catholic, Socialist (which was mutually exclusive at the time), Liberal or Agnostic, all had experienced the disastrous escalation of nationalism and terror and were deeply convinced that only supranational cooperation and subsequent integration could revitalize Europe, its culture and self-esteem. Non-overt normative consent accompanied the preparation for the Treaties of Rome. For Roman-Catholic leaders among the six founding states of the European Economic Community supranational thinking was an indirect reflection of

58 For the most recent efforts of the Council of Europe see Council of Europe (ed.), *The European Identity: Colloquy in Three Parts Organized by the Secretary General of the Council of Europe*, Strasbourg: Council of Europe, 2001-2003.

59 The governments of the six founding states of the European Economic Community in 1957 were composed as following: Belgium: coalition of Socialists (PSB) with Liberals under Prime Minister van Acker (1898-1975), Foreign Minister Paul Henri Spaak (Socialist); Germany: coalition of Christian Democrats (CDU and CSU) with Liberals (FDP) and some smaller parties (DP and GP-GHE) under Chancellor Konrad Adenauer (1876-1967), Foreign Minister Heinrich von Brentano; France: Government of the Republican Front under the leadership of the Socialist SFIO under Prime Minister Guy Mollet (1905-1975), Foreign Minister Christian Pineau; Italy: coalition of Christian Democrats (DC) with Social Democrats (PSDI) and Liberals (PLI) under Prime Minister Antonio Segni (1891-1972), Foreign Minister Gaetano Martino; Luxembourg: Christian Democratic government (CSV) under Prime Minister and Foreign Minister Joseph Bech (1887-1975); Netherlands: coalition of Socialists (PvdA) with Christian Democrats and Liberals (KVP , ARP and CHU) under Prime Minister Willem Drees (1886-1988), Foreign Minister Joseph Luns; explicitly Catholic were Adenauer, Bech, von Brentano, Luns, Segni. Jean Monnet, by the way, was agnostic, but came from a catholic family; in the early 1960s, his sister was the only woman attending the Vatican II Council.

their religious creed – with the Pope as Bishop of Rome as their natural spiritual center – and thus rather "normal". They did not need public reassurance from the church as they were united with many of their fellow liberals and socialists in post-War Europe. All of them looked to Europe's fine past and to its set of venerable values that could reinvigorate them with a sense of pride in light of a collective failure of politics and leadership across Europe over more than a generation. It was no coincidence that the founding Treaties of the European Economic Community were signed at the Capitol in Rome, following a service in San Lorenzo Fuori le Mure, where former Italian Foreign Minister Alcide de Gasperi had been buried less than three years earlier.[60] Yet, the European Economic Community was not simply "a catholic project" and the Treaties of Rome did not need to make any reference to religious belief or even to secular cultural norms and values in order to be understood as a new cultural and political beginning for Europe.

In the 1950's, the Founding Fathers knew what Europe needed and they were in consent with the silent majority of their citizens. Interestingly enough, five decades later and after Europe had experienced a substantial process of secularization, the debate leading to the Treaty Establishing a Constitution for Europe included a highly public and emotionally controversial debate about the relevance of religion and the meaning of God for the Constitution which Europe was about to give itself. What was unnecessary during times of much greater religious consent became divisive during times of excessive pluralistic and normative pluralism. In the course of the constitutional debate, the name of God was mentioned in the public media across the European Union more often than in decades. In light of this mixture of positions, the public debate about the inclusion of God in the Treaty Establishing a Constitution for Europe was serious, valuable and reasonably honest. The late Pope John Paul II, other church leaders and committed politicians had continuously claimed that Europe's identity could not be described without clear reference to God and Christian values. Their position gained respect beyond any political text and compromise. But in the end, God was not invoked in the Treaty Establishing a Constitution for Europe. The Reform Treaty came about without any new political debate on the matter of a public role for religion. Secularists, and even more so, rigid laicists continued to dominate the arena of European politics.

At the same time while Europe was doubtful about the public relevance of its Christian heritage and the Christian faith of many of its citizens, an increasingly secularized environment had become overly sensitive to the effects of Muslim migration to Europe that had taken place since the 1950's. Rising to the tide of Islam in Europe, many proponents of a post-Christian Europe were also willing to also give up the Christian roots of the continent. In the meantime, Islam has become the second largest religion in Europe and requires a new calibration of religious relations on the continent.

60 For a good essayistic description of the scenery, see Knipping, Franz, *Rom 25. März 1957, Die Einigung Europas*, Munich: Deutscher Taschenbuch Verlag, 2004: 9-18.

However, the main problem for the European Union in defining its roots and moral ressources has been the overly defensive and sometimes rapidly vanishing religiosity across Christian Europe. This phenomenon is exceptional indeed, especially when compared to the religiosity across all other continents in the early twenty-first century.[61]

Not only overly pious observers were astonished about the "precipitously declining religiosity" in Europe.[62] A Gallup millennium survey of religious attitudes in 1999 and related surveys had brought awareness to the fact that for 49 percent of Danes, 55 percent of Swedes and even 65 percent of Czechs God did not matter, while 82 percent of Americans stressed that God is "very important" in their lives. 48 percent of West Europeans hardly ever go to church, for Eastern Europe the figure was a little lower than 44 percent.[63] Eurobarometer surveys emphasize the continuous importance of religiosity in the life of all European people. In reality, however, the gap between theory and practice could hardly be bigger. Their own uncertainty about the public sphere of religion makes many Europeans react almost helplessly in the face of the firm belief of others with a distinct creed, Muslims in particular.

Sometimes, relativism has gone so far that Christian believers face outright resentment, pressure or cynicism in contemporary Europe, as an Italian candidate for the office of an EU Commissioner had to experience: In the autumn of 2004, Rocco Buttiglione's traditional (and thus not spectacular) Catholic convictions on morality, family and sexuality were held against him as if he represented the darkest ages of Europe. Buttiglione had to withdraw his candidacy and was forced to conform to the strange exceptionalism of Europe as far as the public role of religion is concerned. Buttiglione's faith prevented him from being acceptable for public office – a unique case of religious persecution in post-totalitarian Europe and astonishing for a continent being so proud of its protection of human rights, the right to religion included.

The role of religion in European public life has substantially changed in the half century since 1957. In the 1950's, Western Europe experienced a revival of Christian values in the aftermath of totalitarianism and the destructions of a Thirty Years War. At the same time, in Eastern Europe under communist rule, coupled with state-induced atheism, the public discourse became increasingly cynical toward religious and civic values in public institutions. In the 1990's and during the first decade of the twenty-first century, the picture seemed to change: While Western Europe has become widely secular and somewhat relativistic about religious and ethical norms, post-communist countries are struggling to again be "living in truth."[64] But they remain skeptical about the relationship between public institutions and value preferences. The transformation

61 See Weiler, Joseph H. H., *Ein christliches Europa*, Salzburg: Pustet, 2004.
62 Ferguson, Niall, *Colossus: The Price of America's Empire*, New York: Penguin Press, 2004: 236.
63 Ibid.: 237.
64 Havel, Václav, *Living in truth*, London: Faber, 1989.

of the political culture in the EU candidate states has not been an easy process. It has not come to an end with the formal accession to the European Union.[65]

As delicate as the public role of religion is the issue of cultural diversity for the shaping of Europe's identity and the implications it has on European political integration. In Western Europe, by and large, cultural diversity is no longer considered an obstacle to political cooperation and integration, although the notion of political solidarity – reflecting the idea of a common destiny –only gradually takes shape. Differences in identity are no longer a matter of mutually exclusive principles but have rather become a matter of different mentalities.[66] The Basque country is an exception to the rule: There, the discourse on cultural identity remains closer to the perception of identity in most of post-communist Europe. In most of Central and South Eastern Europe cultural differences remain essential for the definition of identity, dignity and pride. After the experiences with the Austro-Hungarian, the Turkish or the Russian and the Soviet Empire, most of post-communist Europe still links cultural identity and cultural recognition predominantly with genuine nationhood. National identities tend to be considered mutually exclusive.[67] Given these differences in attitude and perception, it cannot be an easy task to shape a common European identity and common European political interests.

In light of this situation, the result of the constitution-building decade can be perceived like a glass of water: for some, it may be half full, for others it may be half empty. For Europhiles, the work of the Constitutional Convention was historic, and they were failed by the national governments, which did not succeed in ensuring the ratification of the European Constitution. For Euroskeptics (and probably also for most Euro-realists) the rejection of the European Constitution and the difficulties in implementing the Treaty of Lisbon were the logical consequence of a wrong and naive turn in European integration. In any case, the debate about constitution-building in the European Union has been substantially advanced during the first decade of the twenty-first century. European constitutionalism has never been more substantiated.[68] As for the political outcome, it was remarkable enough that 27 European states recognized one common text as basis for their future deliberations and decision-making in the EU. They

65 See Brzezinski, Mark, *The Struggle for Constitutionalism in Poland*, Basingstoke: Macmillan, 2000; Goenenc, Levent, *Prospects for Constitutionalism in Post-Communist Countries*, The Hague: Nijhoff, 2002; Erdödy, Gabor (ed.), *Transformationserfahrungen: Zur Entwicklung der politischen Kultur in den EU-Kandidatenländern*, Baden-Baden, Nomos: 2003.

66 For an assessment of mentality conditions in North Western Europe see Delwaide, Jacobus, et al. (eds.), *Die Rheingesellschaft: Mentalitäten, Kulturen und Traditionen im Herzen Europas*, Baden-Baden: Nomos, 2003.

67 See Baier-Allen, Susanne, and Ljubomir Cucic (eds.), *The Challenges of Pluriculturality*, Baden-Baden: Nomos, 2000; Erdödy, Gabor (ed.), *Mitteleuropa: Politische Kultur und europäische Einigung*, Baden-Baden: Nomos, 2003.

68 See Brand, Michiel, *Affirming and Refining "European Constitutionalism": Towards the Establishment of the First Constitution for the European Union*, Florence: European University Institute, 2004.

succeeded in the formulation of a text but failed (in its interpretation) to convey it to the citizens. However, the double ratification crisis has helped to broaden the constitutional debate more than the political leaders of all EU member states could have dreamt of in 2001.

In 1991, the Treaty of Maastricht had established Union citizenship, without gaining strong public recognition among the European citizenry. Would the original Treaty Establishing a Constitution for Europe have been ratified without the controversy that included its formal failure, Europe would have probably missed the change of a deepened reflection and debate about its constitution, identity and future path. Paradoxical as it may seem, through the ratification crisis the Second Founding of European integration gained meaning and direction.

During five decades of European integration, European institutions have been established. They are strong and reasonably effective. The European Union has been established as a political system managed by multilevel governance.[69] But Europeans are still a rare species in the European Union. To facilitate the development of genuine Europeans must be the guiding principle of the new era of European integration. The formal introduction of a Union citizenship has provided for legal framework. To fill it with life and to make Union citizenship work will require many practical efforts. The Second Founding of European integration will remain a long-term project.

Claiming to define Europe's identity as political and yet recognizing the national or even regional cultural diversity as another level of identity requires philosophical clarity. Inter alia, it raises the issue of reciprocity, based on the recognition of mutually agreed differences, yet anchored in the explicit will and consent to share common interests, goals and destiny. Political solidarity can only grow in the new era of its development if the European Union initiates deeper integration through the resolution of pending issues instead of getting trapped again in idiosyncratic institutional designs that eventually may be more harmful to its legitimacy than even Euro-skeptics want it to be.

4. Cutting Through History: Periodizing European Integration

Since its beginnings in 1957, the European integration process has been enormously successful. However, by looking at the evolution of European integration in more detail, one can distinguish periods that advanced the process better than others. American historian Arthur M. Schlesinger Jr. has discussed cycles of history and rhythms of social and political development related to changing generations. It is certainly wrong to believe in cyclical political developments as if going from A to B would ultimately lead

69 See Scharpf, Fritz W., *Community and Autonomy Multilevel Policy-Making in the European Union*, Florence: European University Institute, 1994; Höreth, Marcus, *The Trilemma of Legitimacy: Multilevel Governance in the European Union and the Problem of Democracy*, ZEI Discussion Paper C11, Bonn: Center for European Integration Studies, 1998.

back to A. But it is worth considering the impact of generational changes on political developments. Referring to the sociological work of Karl Mannheim and José Ortega y Gasset, Schlesinger conceived the "model of a thirty-year alternation between public purpose and private interest"[70] as the key to understanding the impact of generational effects on political majorities. As he proposed, "each generation spends its first fifteen years after coming of political age in challenging the generation already entrenched in power. Then the new generation comes to power itself for another fifteen years, after which its policies pale and the generation coming up behind them claims the succession."[71] Schlesinger does not help us to understand why the changes occur and in which direction they may lead. Yet, it is sensible to identify distinct periods in the history of European integration and to consider defining experiences of each leadership generation and the marks that each has left on European integration.

1957 to 1979: The first period of European integration brought about the European Commission, the Court of Justice and the directly elected European Parliament as the first supranational institutions of European integration, while it focused on the completion of the customs union and ended with the first round of enlargement (to include Ireland, Denmark and the United Kingdom). This period also saw the failure of speedy political and military integration in Western Europe.

1979 to 1993: The second period of European integration led to the completion of the Single Market, two more rounds of enlargement (to include Greece and to Spain and Portugal) and the beginning of political cooperation on matters of foreign policy, based on the refounding of the European Community as European Union with the Treaty of Maastricht.

1993 to 2009: The third period of European integration was defined by the steady constitutionalization and politicization of European integration through treaty revisions, the introduction of the common currency and of Union citizenship, the fourth and fifth EU enlargement (first to include Austria, Finland and Sweden, and then to include Poland, Hungary, the Czech Republic, Slovakia, Slovenia, Estonia, Latvia, Lithuania, Malta, Cyprus, Romania and Bulgaria), the first military operations under the umbrella of a common foreign and security policy and the rise of people's power over elite-driven institutional arrangements.

It would be speculative to anticipate the outcome of the fourth period of European integration that will most likely last from 2009 until around 2025/2030. However, fifty years after the path to integration began, the most daunting challenges ahead of the EU seem obvious: Efforts to raise the degree of common European interests and to deepen integration amidst skepticism and fear; introduction of the principle of solidarity to the sphere of the welfare state; a stronger international political and military profile of the European Union; the issue of "the other" if not "the enemy," including the management

70 Schlesinger jr., Arthur M., *The Cycles of American History*, Boston: Houghton Mifflin, 1986: 31.
71 Ibid.: 30.

of migration to Europe; the need to increase economic dynamics in an aging European society; the relationship between cultural pluralism and universal moral claims; and further rounds of enlargement amidst the difficult process to strenghten and to improve the institutional arrangements on which the EU is based. Without doubt, a convincing application of coherent internal governance and of stronger contributions to global order building will challenge the EU in the years and decades ahead.

These challenges will have to be handled by a generation of leaders yet unknown. Most evident is the following: The youngest voters in the election to the European Parliament in 2009 were born in 1991. They cannot personally remember the fall of the Berlin Wall. The youngest voters in the elections to the European Parliament in 2024 were born in 2006. They will not even remember the ratification crisis of the Treaty Establishing a Constitution for Europe once they may go voting for the first time. The crisis over a European Constitution, the introduction of the euro, the terror attacks of 9/11 and 3/11 and the unification of Europe will be known to them only through the prism of their parents' and teachers' experiences. The cycle of experience of older generations, including their attitudes toward European integration, is not less revealing: Children born in 1945 were about to turn 65 shortly after the provisions of the Reform Treaty were to come to fruition. The Founding Fathers of the European Economic Community had been born before the beginning of the twentieth century. They did not live to see 1989 and the end of the Cold War. Children born in 1989, in turn, can expect to live until about 2070. In 2057, most of these children will celebrate the 100th anniversary of the European Union. The implication of generational aspects for the rhythm of ideas on Europe deserves further academic studies.

It is the generation born around 1957 that will now have to advance the idea of constitutional patriotism in Europe and the quest for a stronger global role of the EU, while the generation born around 1989 will take over power and responsibility before the work of the children of 1957 will be completed. Their formative experiences with European integration will matter as much as any economic model about path dependencies of European integration. The generation born in the late twentieth century will provide the leaders of tomorrow and the day after tomorrow. The leaders of the two generations of "1957" and of "1989" will direct and shape the European Union during the first half of the twenty-first century. Their work will have effects even beyond 2057. Political controversies and generational rifts are inevitable as they have ever been.

Ahead of the European Union and emerging generations of European leaders is a new set of priorities. Most of all, they have to develop a sense of orientation for guiding the European Union into a new and increasingly uncertain world. They have to define the opportunities of globalization for Europe and the benefits of European integration for the individual Union citizen. During the five past decades, Europe has tried to escape its past. In the decades ahead Europe will have to discover its common future.

Increasingly, culture and identity will be debated in a political and constitutional context.

The Second Founding of the European Union will be shaped and interpreted by the pragmatic results of integration in the decades ahead. With the change of generations and priorities, circumstances develop and challenges evolve. The main criteria for the continuous success of the European Union will be the degree of its ability to transform the notion of solidarity from a rhetorical principle into a viable and sustainable political reality – both inside the European Union and in Europe's encounters with partners all over the world.

The process of politicizing the identity of Europe is related to the meaning of memory for the citizens of the European Union. For over two millennia, European culture has evolved and different structures of society and statehood have emerged. Europeans discovered the world and Europeans conquered others – up to the point of generating a culture of guilt over the history of European expansionism. Europeans used to quarrel with each other, up until the complete self-destruction during the Thirty Years War that encompassed the first half of the twentieth century (1914-1945). They fought proxy wars in and over their colonies, up until the point that they began to return to seemingly remote places as peacekeepers and democracy-builders. They erected the magnificent structures, both material and immaterial, that are the visualizations of a common European heritage, from church spires to market squares, from the arts to music, from linguistic diversity to habits of lifestyle. They have defined time (through clocks and the calendar that is more or less universally approved today) and space (by delineating the borders of continents and of countries beyond Europe's borders). Europeans have exported more ideas and goods than any other region or culture, but they are still in the process of learning that others were and are as cultured as Europeans see themselves to be.

Europeans reconciled among themselves, beginning in the second half of the twentieth century and stretching into the first decades of the twenty-first century. Yet often, they did not understand the critique that they are erecting "fortress Europe" at the expense of others in matters of trade protection, agricultural subsidies and migration. In spite of this critique, most Europeans consider themselves generous, supportive of sustainable development and the eradication of poverty, and sympathetic to multilateralism and global cooperation.[72] Yet their image in the world has been, and remains so in some places, tainted with the history of colonialism, genocide and ethnic cleansing. None of this was exceptionally European, but all of it was exceptional for the development of a profoundly ambivalent, torn and contradictory set of European

72 See Tempini, Nadia, *Fortress Europe?: EC External Trade Relations and New Protectionism*, London: PNL Press, 1989; Baneth, Jean, *"Fortress Europe" and other Myths about Trade*, Washington D.C.: World Bank, 1993; Geddes, Andrew, *Immigration and European Integration: Towards Fortress Europe?*, Manchester: Manchester University Press, 2000; King, Russell, et al. (eds.), *Eldorado or Fortress?: Migration in Southern Europe*, Houndmills: Macmillan, 2000.

memories. It would not be historical to disregard these memories when reflecting on the identity of Europe.

The first set of formative memories for the evolution of a political identity of European integration is negative. It includes the memories of European wars, of nationalism and racism, of the Holocaust and the Gulag, of totalitarian politics under Nazi and communist rule. Over time, these darkest experiences in European history have blended into a new forward-looking denominator, at least within the European Union: "Never again." It was not easy to reach this stage and to root it into an atmosphere of mutual trust. It was not simple to generate sufficient readiness in Europe to share interests and even destiny with those who were enemies only a short while ago. As far as the memory of suffering is concerned, a short while can become a long haul. Yet, the European Union has achieved reconciliation, although the scars of the past still exist with varying degrees of intensity.

The second shared experience of Europeans in the second half of the twentieth century was a positive one. European integration has worked: as an order of peace and of freedom, as the fountain of unprecedented affluence, and as the source of respect all over the world. Before 1989, this experience could only be felt among the privileged Western Europeans.[73] With the peaceful revolutions of 1989, this experience began to spread to Central and Eastern Europe with the process of democratic transformation and gradual economic rehabilitation. The shared experience of freedom and market economy, of the benefits of cooperation and integration, and of pooled resources and sovereignties did not grow without ambiguities and skepticism. Rather, these grew and can be identified as the second cornerstone for a culture of memory preceding the growth of a political identity of European integration.[74]

The third shared experience is related to Europe's role in the world and the international perception of Europe. It often comes as a surprise to Europeans to realize how much they have in common with each other when they reflect on this issue outside Europe or in the presence of non-Europeans. In the early twenty-first century, in the presence of non-European circumstances or people, most Europeans, regardless of their national or social, regional or political background, see their "European-ness" as something non-antagonistic, non-imposing and non-partisan. And it is interesting to note that the European experience with transition to democracy, with conflict resolution and peace building has attracted enormous attention all over the globe.

73 See Bracher, Karl Dietrich, *The Age of Ideologies: A History of Political Thought in the Twentieth Century*, London: Palgrave Macmillan, 1984: 189-202 ("Post-War Experience: Re-Evaluation and Reconstruction").

74 See Garton Ash, Timothy, *History of the Present: Sketches and Dispatches from Europe in the 1990s*, London: Allen Lane, 1999: ix-xxi; Vinen, Richard, *A History in Fragments: Europe in the Twentieth Century*, London: Abacus, 2000: 265-474 ("Part III: Post-War Europe").

It remains central for the success and legitimacy of European integration to increase the common purpose about its objectives among EU citizens. In the course of the twentieth century, Europe had turned from being a subject, if not the leading subject of world events into the object of resentment, into a continent destroyed, divided and dependent upon external powers beyond Europe's shores. Since the end of the Cold War, its internal division and as a consequence of the success of European integration, Europe has once again become a leader in world order-building. The European Union is respected for its experiences of conflict resolution and modes of consensual politics, its affluence and its experiences with democratic transition and the primacy of law. This worldwide respect does not necessarily translate into domestic recognition and pride. The European Union needs to constantly reinvigorate its purpose in order to gain recognition and respect among its own citizens. A constant renewal of the contract between the political leaders and the citizens of the European Union is necessary to maintain a sufficient degree of loyalty to European integration and legitimacy of integration practices.

After the original founding of European integration, the freedom of travel and the emergence of a common market have been the most fascinating and inspiring experiences for many citizens. Any perusal of travel guides published before the outbreak of World War I shows how open Europe once was. Borders and minds were closed as a consequence of escalating nationalism. World War II was the climax of this self-destruction of the openness of Europe. The gradual return to open borders after 1957 was the most lauded improvement for the generations that had suffered the impact of nationalism and warfare. The shared experience of open EU borders is no longer an emotional driving force for younger Europeans. Neither is the visibility of the European flag in public buildings or the operation of European institutions. The strongest equivalent to the opening of borders for post-1957 Europeans was the physical introduction of the euro in 2002. This was not only the symbolic and logical outcome of the Single Market. The introduction of the euro for more than 300 million European citizens in twelve EU member states showed that European integration was impacting everybody's daily life. Critical assessments of the European Union's failure to couple the euro with a common political structure were expressed less loudly than complaints about price increases.[75] Yet, all in all, the euro was introduced smoothly, even in countries where the exchange rate to the old national currency was not at all easy. The Greeks had to give up the drachma, notably the oldest currency in Europe. The Germans had to relinquish the Deutschmark, the symbol of a successful and widely appreciated

75 Dyson, Kenneth (ed.), *European States and the EURO: Europeanization, Variation, and Convergence*, New York: Oxford University Press, 2002; Martinot, Bertrand, *L'Euro: une monnaie sans politique?*, Paris: Hamattan, 2003.

recovery after the dark years of Nazi rule. For others, pride in the national currency was weaker. In 2007, Slovenia was the first post-communist country to introduce the euro, followed in 2008 by Malta and Cyprus, and in 2009 by fellow post-communist Slovakia.

In the early twenty-first century, the introduction of the euro was the single most important demonstration that European integration is not only about "building Europe" at its top. Increasingly, European integration affects national traditions and structures: European integration is "striking back." While adding a new dimension to the structures of public life in Europe, European integration affects the daily life not only of politicians and bureaucrats, business leaders and academicians, but also each and every Union citizen. More than legal provisions of Union citizenship and probably more than political awareness about the relevance of decision-making in EU institutions, the euro has made Union citizens feel that European integration is a "real thing." But under these conditions, European integration has also encountered new skepticism and outright rejection among those of its citizens who believe that these processes happen too fast and reach too far.

The euro has become a successful currency. Yet, the experience with European integration shows that great visions tend to become meaningless once they are realized and consummated. This was the case with the vision of open borders. It was the case with the vision of a united Europe. And it is the case with the vision of a common European currency. The European Union needs to constantly define new visions, purposes and ideas in order to remain attractive for its citizens and regain the support and loyalty of new generations. At the core of this task lies the need to give the idea of Union citizenship a constant and emotional meaning. If EU citizens cannot identify with the European Union as being "owned" by them, they will at best remain passive consumers of EU gratifications. For a body politic to be actively supported by its citizens, it requires to constantly reinvigorate purpose and meaning. Only success nurtures loyalty and only loyalty nurtures political legitimacy. Ernest Renan's classical definition of politics as a "plébiscite de tous les jours"[76] is also relevant for the European Union.

Sovereignty has been defined as the supreme command of one's fiscal and economic destiny, of one's social safety and of one's external security.[77] Money, police and the military have always been considered the core expressions of a state's sovereignty. The process of European integration has transferred this experience to the European level without aiming to create a genuine "European state". Europeans have learned to live with the fact that the transfer of monetary sovereignty to the EU-level did not

76 Renan, Ernest, *Qu'est ce-qu' une nation?*, (in English: *What is a Nation?*), Toronto: Tapir Press, 1996.

77 See Guehenno, Jean-Marie, *The Typology of Sovereignty*, Washington D.C.: US Institute for Peace, 2000; Sim, Stuart, *The Discourse of Sovereignty - Hobbes to Fielding: The State of Nature and the Nature of the State*, Aldershot: Ashgate, 2003.

undermine their sense of national or even regional cultural identity. They pay with euros yet remain Greeks, Germans or Irish. They have begun to distinguish political sovereignty from cultural identity. In fact, they realized the value added by preserving cultural identity while transferring political sovereignty at the same time.

At the same time, they have begun to discover the link between pooled sovereignty and shared political identity. Since identity is relative and contingent, they can realize that multilayered and multiple identities are logically not exclusive. The effect of the introduction of the euro proved the opposite: As much as European integration is about pooling of sovereignties, its effects generate multilayered or multiple identities.[78]

While politically and legally integration is about the pooling of sovereignties, culturally it is about the broadening and sharing of identities. These arguments suggest that integration is "good" in itself and that it adds value through positive experiences and rationale arguments. Fact of the matter, however, is that the permanent inclination of any political or social system is to define itself against others. Since the days of ancient Greece, Europe has been struggling with the inclination to define itself against "the other." Defining "the good" in itself has always been the more difficult and often less successful task.

Also in the contemporary European Union, the issue of "the other" remains unresolved for many Europeans. European culture and intellectual history has always been torn between the understanding of Herodotus, that Greek identity was contrasted with the Persians as "the other," (representing barbarism) and the claim of Aristotle, the philosopher of same Greek roots, who stated that nothing is more difficult than defining "the good" out of itself without the need for "the other" or even for an enemy.[79] In the early twenty-first century, the European Union officially gave an indisputable answer: It wanted to be partners with a world of equals, promoting dialogue, understanding and cooperation. For many EU citizens, the case is less simple: Some of them are vocal in expressing their opposition to "American conditions" in Europe, whatever that might mean. School crime has entered Europe. Drugs, broken families and problems with migrants in the socially neglected parts of inner cities are no American prerogative. The extremely good quality of universities, including research universities, in the US encourages a majority of European Ph.D. students to stay in the US upon finishing their studies there. The Anglo-Saxon economic model is often quoted but seldom properly defined. Social and economic models in Europe are too manifold to reduce them to one European model that ought to be protected in the age of globalization. The emotional debates among Americans and Europeans in 2002/2003 over the war in Iraq and the role

78 See Dunkerley, David, et al. (eds.), *Changing Europe: Identities, Nations and Citizens*, London/New York: Routledge, 2002.

79 See Khan, H. A. (ed.), *The Birth of the European Identity: The Euro-Asia Contrast in Greek Thought 490-322 B.C.*, Nottingham: University of Nottingham, 1994.

of multilateralism in world politics came close to an internal Cold War of the West.[80] Anti-European sentiments in the US were echoed by strong anti-Americanism in Europe. This was often coupled with a changing attitude of many Europeans toward Israel. To the horrified surprise of many in Israel and elsewhere, more than 59 percent of Europeans consider Israel as the biggest threat to world peace in the twenty-first century.[81] America's strong support for Israel strengthened the dangerous trend of a transatlantic cultural divide.

This did not mean that the Arab world or Islam are the new attractions for Europe. On the contrary, many Europeans tend to be afraid of the weakness of Arab countries and the radicalism or even extremism associated with a certain version of political Islam. Often, the answers given in Europe remain ambiguous and unfocused. They also reflect uncertainty in dealing with the undeniable fact that Islam has become Europe's second largest religion next to Christianity. It is indicative that different EU countries give different answers to the question of Islamic veils in public schools.[82]

Others in Europe are afraid of the success of China and its rise to a new world power. Russia entails a certain attraction for some in Europe, but worries many because of its creeping return to authoritarianism and the threat of using Europe's dependency on energy supply as a political weapon.[83] It was indicative for the uncertain attitudes of Europe vis-à-vis "the other" that the relationship toward the geographical neighbors of the EU became an explicit issue in the deliberation of the Treaty Establishing a Constitution for Europe. Never before in the world did a Constitution explicitly include a chapter on neighborhood. This was a clear sign of how uncertain Europe is about the role of its "others."

Europe's relationship with the outside world, its perception of Europe and Europe's perception of the relevance of the world for Europe in the age of globalization are less clear than the official diplomatic rhetoric of the European Union suggests. It is beyond doubt that Europe, with its strongly export-oriented economy and dependency on the import of energy from the Middle East and from Russia, its links through migrant workers and emigrant communities to the Arab world, and its strategic investments with the United States could not afford to become myopic and exclusionary. Yet, Europe has often done so, or at least has been perceived as doing so. Struggling with the meaning of

80 See Gordon, Phillip H., and Jeremy Shapiro, *Allies at War: America, Europe and the Crisis over Iraq*, New York: MacGraw-Hill, 2004; Kühnhardt, Ludger, "German-American Relations: What Else Can Go Wrong?," in: American Institute for Contemporary German Studies (AICGS) (ed.), *Power and Principle - Prospects for Transatlantic Cooperation*, German-American Issues 02, Washington D.C.: 2004: 23-36.

81 See European Union, European Commission, *Flash Eurobarometer: Iraq and Peace in the World*, November 2003, http://ec.europa.eu/public_opinion/flash/fl151_iraq_full_report.pdf.

82 On the larger issue see Al Sayyad, Nezar, and Manuel Castells (eds.), *Muslim Europe or Euro-Islam: Politics, Culture and Citizenship in the Age of Globalization*, Lanham: Lexington Books, 2002.

83 See Neumann, Iver B., *Uses of the Other: "The East" in European Identity Formation*, Manchester: Manchester University Press, 1999.

"the others" is an echo of the ongoing quest for finding a renewed purpose for European integration.

The biggest challenge for the development of a culture of communication in a Europeanized public sphere is linked to Europe's demographic make-up and its long-term consequences. This complex issue is connected to the future of the (national) welfare state and to the search for European answers to globalization. The European welfare state is the twin sibling of the European nation state. While the latter has been undergoing substantial, albeit incomplete transformations since its nationalist overstretch, the welfare state has been only gradually forced to adjust to new realities. Whether Reaganomics in Margaret Thatcher's Great Britain, shock therapies in post-communist countries or resistance to reform in France, Germany or Belgium: Throughout the last quarter of the twentieth century, the transformation of the European welfare state remained bound to the decision-making prerogatives of the European nation state. While the European Union called upon its member states to embark on a path that will guarantee Europe's economic primacy in the year 2010, its constituent member states struggle with aging populations, fiscal problems, overly expensive health and pension systems and the fear both from Islamic migration and more children of their own. As a consequence, national political systems of the European Union were absorbed with the "old" agenda of readjusting social systems and reactions fearful to globalization while EU institutions were trying (often in vain) to define the "new" agenda of Europe's joint response to globalization and its opportunities. It remained unclear what the long-term implications of this ambivalence would be.

The conflict between old answers in aging welfare state societies and the need for innovation, creativity and a new sense of future to position Europe properly in the age of globalization will occupy institutions and policy-makers of the European Union for many years to come. Enormously increased regional asymmetries as the consequence of Eastern enlargement add to the social pressure. Coping with issues of equality and social solidarity and expressing skepticism against presumably Anglo-Saxon models of global capitalism will remain a strong topic in Europe. Moreover, the future role of the nation state and its government necessitate redefinition – a task easier said than done. The future of European governance has to be streamlined in order to foster the ambitious plans for the economic and technological future of the EU, which is as difficult to do. In terms of the quest for a European political identity, it means no less than confronting the most difficult task possible: In order to secure the identity and diversity that Europe is so proud of the European Union has to constantly reinvent itself by overcoming some of its dearest social traditions. This includes adjustments of the European Social Model, which is more often cited than properly defined.

For the time being, Europe is more populous than the US. This might not last for long. Between 1980 and 2003, the population of integrated Europe (EU 15) has grown by 6.1 percent, while the US population has grown by 27.8 percent.[84] By 2050, the EU population is supposed to shrink from 487 to 456 million (a decrease by 6 percent), while the US will grow from 282 million people in 2000 to 420 million in 2050. Estimates assume a median age for 2050 of 52.7 years in the EU, but only of 36.2 in the US. This will have enormous consequences for the welfare state, for pension and health systems in particular. Due to this aging population and its economic and welfare implications, the underlying economic growth in the EU could be reduced from 2 to 1.25 percent.[85] At the same time, developing countries are becoming an increasing demographic, social and migratory challenge for Europe: Their populations are young, growing, and often socially marginalized with all the known problems, including human trafficking and even terrorism. In 2050, the average Yemenite will be 32 years younger than the average European and 34 years younger than the average Japanese. At the same time, life expectancy will have grown enormously. The population of Yemen grew from 4.3 million in 1950 to 18.3 million in 2000. It could grow to 158.6 million by 2050. The German population, in contrast, might decrease from 82 million in 2000 to 51 million by 2050.[86] Whether or not this will eventually happen, more important is the growing age gap. While Europeans will be inclined to protect their welfare systems, people from other parts of the world will claim their share in Europe's affluence that is diminishing due to decreasing population and decreasing productivity. By 2020 the labor pool in the Arab world will have increased by 146 million, in sub-Saharan Africa by 402 million. On the other hand, the German age cohort born between 1995 and 1999 is 47 percent smaller than the group born between 1970 and 1974. By 2020, the European Union will experience a 20 percent decrease in its age group between 20 and 25. An American expert on demography, Paul S. Hewitt, foresees "age recessions" in Europe as a consequence of the unbalancing of Europe's demography.[87] It is no consolation for Europe that his view might express vested American interests?

By supporting development in other parts of the world and by limiting its own population, which often was considered wise in light of the limits of growth and the limits of global resources, Europe is creating the very problems it will be challenged with in the course of the twenty-first century. Europe's response to Europe's past is generating challenges that can endanger and undermine the success of those original responses. This paradoxical conclusion confirms yet another insight of Arnold Toynbee regarding the nexus between challenge and response.

84 See Wirtschaftskammern Österreich, *Bevölkerungsentwicklung*, http://wko.at/statistik/eu/europa-bevoelkerungsentwicklung.pdf.

85 Grant, Charles, *Transatlantic Rifts: How to Bring the Two Sides Together*, London: Centre for European Reform, 2003: 27.

86 See Hewitt, Paul S., "Die Geopolitik der globalen Alterungsprozesse," *Frankfurter Allgemeine Zeitung*, March 23, (2004): 39.

87 Hewitt, Paul S., "Depopulation and the Aging in Europe and Japan: The Hazardous Transition to a Labor Shortage Economy," *International Politics and Society*, 1 (2002), http://fes.de/ipg/ipg1_2002/ARTHEWITT.htm.

Related to this phenomenon is Europe's handling of the migration issue. Europeans tend to favor migration if it helps them to enhance their economic productivity in the absence of domestic fertility. Yet, they are worried, if not scared, about its consequences. This is related to the fundamental difference in migration effects in Europe and in the US. While in the US, the absorption capacity of its political culture has proven wrong all the fears that say that the US could lose its binding glue because of non-Caucasian migration, Europe was not properly equipped to integrate either more Muslim migration from its southern borders or more Russian or other post-Soviet migration from its eastern borders. Neither of the two groups connects with "a European dream" or a civil religion of Europe that could generate pride and a sense of belonging among immigrants. Quite the opposite, many immigrant communities in Europe remain marginalized and are considered a burden rather than a contribution, no matter what politicians suggest in tolerance speeches and beyond the certainly worrisome threat of Islamic totalitarianism. In 2003, for the first time Spain became the largest recipient country for migrants into the EU with 594,000 out of 1.6 million per year. Twice as many migrants went to Spain as France and Germany combined. This trend has continued ever since. Europe is a continent of migration, but the European Union still has to produce a breakthrough in terms of a consistent, forward-looking migration policy coupled with a future-oriented, child-friendly atmosphere. To generate such results would contribute more to the evolution of the European public sphere than many abstract academic discourses on the matter, most of which are stereotypically skeptical or simply focus on the issue of creating a more Europeanized media landscape in the EU.

In the early twenty-first century, while the EU embarks on the course toward constitutional patriotism and a more profiled global role, Europe's most serious challenge remains the reconciliation of diverse national cultural identities, and mentalities, including political habits, with a common political identity and the reconciliation of shared universal values with its distinct and often parochial habits of localism.[88] The perspective has to be living in reconciled difference. The most important legitimacy test for the European Union during the next decades will be whether or not it contributes to this reconciliation of differences while at the same time generating strength through shared interests and a future-oriented common perspective.

What should bother the EU is not the provocative question whether or not an artificial "point of no return" has been achieved in the integration process. What should

88 See Tiersky, Ronald (ed.), *Europe Today: National Politics, European Integration and European Security*, Lanham: Rowman&Littlefield, 1999; Cederman, Lars-Erik, *Nationalism and Bounded integration: What it Would Take to Construct a European Demos*, Fiesole: European University Institute, 2000; Malmborg, Mikael af, and Bo Strath (eds.), *The Meaning of Europe: Variety and Contention Within and Among Nations*, Oxford/New York: Berg, 2002; Gubbins, Paul, and Mike Holt (eds.), *Beyond Boundaries: Language and Identity in Contemporary Europe*, Clevedon: Multilingual Matters, 2002; Harmsen, Robert, and Menno Spiering (eds.), *Euroscepticism: Party Politics, National Identity and European Integration*, Amsterdam: Rodopi, 2004.

worry the European Union more is the perspective of a creeping deterioration of the base of its affluence and its capacity for influencing the path of global developments in the twenty-first century. The world might well live with a weak Europe, but Europe might not be happy to live with the consequences of a weakened role in the world.

As a result, Europe must pro-actively pursue the path toward a reconciled identity and shared destiny. It will have to challenge the myth of the missing demos as the root cause for its inability to generate a sufficiently solid public sphere. Europe will have to resort continuously to a pragmatism that argues in favor of issues and challenges of a future-oriented nature as first priority instead of becoming trapped by ghosts of past divisions. In the early twenty-first century, these ghosts still exist and could easily be more forcefully revived. It is thus all the more a question of responsible political leadership to guide the European body politic during the next periods of its development. Such guidance could help propel further transformations of European identity and the relationship between culture and politics. These transformations would not be the result of theories of integration but rather of responses to concrete challenges. This thought at least illustrates a reassuring realism.

The factors that bind united Europe are not different from whatever Europeans used to know about the glue of their nation states: shared memories, common suffering, and mutual success. Nothing less and nothing more is expected from the European Union during the period of its Second Founding. An initial sense of common purpose has clearly developed over the first fifty years of European integration, combined with a commonly shared memory and a growing evolution of a community of communication.[89] But now, first and foremost, Europe needs to redefine its purpose and live up to its new rationale. Through concrete and sustainable actions the EU must demonstrate that it represents "a Europe that works." It has been argued that Europe is building a new form of Commonwealth.[90] Whether Europe will live up to its global responsibilities and to the challenge of globalization is one, if not the most important, test case for its future path. To continuously generate a sufficient amount of internal legitimacy is the other testing ground for the future of Europe's Commonwealth.

Europe has embarked on the journey of its Second Founding on the basis of its genuine and often idiosyncratic political and legal contractualism. The concept of the contract as a basis for social and political consent has been known in political philosophy since the evolution of statehood in Europe. It once provided an authoritarian answer to European civil wars. With a cumulative European Constitution, consisting of a series of European treaties, democratic contract theory has entered the world of European integration. It will be tested time and again by political events to which the EU citizens expect the European Union institutions to give adequate answers.

89 For a critical assessment of this interpretation see Kielmannsegg, Peter Graf, "Integration und Demokratie," in: Jachtenfuchs, Markus, and Beate Kohler-Koch (eds.), *Europäische Integration*, Opladen: Westdeutscher Verlag, 1996: 47-71.

90 See Brague, Remi, and Peter Koslowski, *Vaterland Europa*, op.cit.: 64-70.

II. Europe's Constitution

1. The Initial Leadership Proposition: A Constitution for Europe

Between 2005 and 2007, the first ever European Constitution (formally called Treaty Establishing a Constitution for Europe or, less formal, Constitutional Treaty) was buried in order to be resurrected through the traditional channel of ordinary treaty-revision. The democratic aspiration of the European Constitution was curtailed when the repair work was handed back to the experience and camaraderie of intergovernmental backdoor bargaining. Two steps forward with the signing of the Constitutional Treaty in 2004, three steps backward with its rejection in referenda in France and in the Netherlands 2005, two steps forward again with the help of the Reform Treaty signed in Lisbon in 2007, again three steps backward with its rejection in a referendum in Ireland in 2008 and, finally, a step forward with the positive result of the second Irish referendum and the eventual ratification of the Reform Treaty in 2009 – European constitution-building during the first decade of the twenty-first century was truly a roller-coaster.

It had begun with a promising vision. October 29, 2004, European Constitutional history was rewritten. For the first time in the history of the European continent, a "European Constitution" was signed by the representatives of 28 countries.[1] The

1 The Treaty Establishing a Constitution for Europe was signed by Austria: Chancellor Dr. Wolfgang Schüssel, Christian Democratic Austrian People's Party (ÖVP), Federal Minister for International and European Affairs Dr.Ursula Plassnik, Christian Democratic Austrian People's Party (ÖVP); Belgium: Prime Minister Guy Verhofstadt, Flemish Liberals and Democrats (VLM), Foreign Minister Karel de Gucht, Reformist Movement (MR); Cyprus: (Greek Republic): President Tassos Papadopoulos, Democratic Party (DIKO), Foreign Minister George Iacovou, Independent; Czech Republic: Prime Minister Stanislav Gross, Social Democrats (CSSD), Foreign Minister Cyril Svoboda, Christian-Democratic Union – Czech People's Party (KDU-CSL); Denmark: Prime Minister Anders Fogh Rasmussen, Liberal Party (VENSTRE), Foreign Minister Per Stig Møller, Conservative Peoples Party (DKF); Estonia: Prime Minister Juhan Parts, Res Publica – Union for the Republic, Foreign Minister Kristiina Ojuland, Estonian Reform Party; Finland: Prime Minister Matti Vanhanen, Centre Party (KESK), Foreign Minister Erkki Tuomioja, Social Democratic Party of Finland (SDP); France: President Jacques Chirac, Union for a Popular Movement (UMP), Prime Minister Jean-Pierre Raffarin, Union for a Popular Movement (UMP), Foreign Minister Michel Barnier, Union for a Popular Movement (UMP); Germany: Chancellor Gerhard Schröder, Social Democrats (SPD), Foreign Minister: Joseph Fischer, Green Party; Greece: Prime Minister Kostas Karamanlis, New Democracy (ND), Foreign Minister Petros G. Molyviatis, New Democracy (ND); Hungary: Prime Minister Ferenc Gyurcsány, Socialist Party (MSZP), Foreign Minister László Kovács, Socialist Party (MSZP); Ireland: Prime Minister Bertie Ahern, Fianna Fáil – The Republican Party, Foreign Minister Dermot Ahern, Fianna Fáil – The Republican Party; Italy: Prime Minister Silvio Berlusconi, Forza Italia (FI), Foreign Minister Franco Frattini, Forza Italia (FI); Latvia: President Vaira Vike-Freiberga, Independent, Prime Minister Indulis Emsis, Green Party, Foreign Minister Artis Pabriks, Conservative People's Party; Lithuania: President Valdas Adamkus, Independent, Prime Minister Algirdas Mykolas Brazauskas, Social Democrats, Foreign Minister Antanas Valionis, Labour, Social Liberals – New Union; Luxembourg: Prime Minister Jean-Claude Juncker, Christian Social People's Party (CSV), Foreign Minister Jean Asselborn, Social Democrats

ceremony took place in the same room – the "Sala Degli Orazi e Curiazi" at the Rome City Hall Campidoglio on Capitoline Hill – as the signing of the Treaties of Rome (formally the Treaty Establishing the European Economic Community and the Treaty Establishing the European Atomic Energy Community) on March 25, 1957. The ceremony was much more crowded than the founding act of the European Economic Communities almost five decades earlier. But the signing ceremony of the Treaty Establishing a Constitution for Europe was not any less important. In fact, it was meant to symbolize the Second Founding of an integrated Europe. This, at least, was the initial ambition of the political leaders that came together on the solemn occasion. Three years later, the next generation of political leaders (or the same ones, after having gone through a reflection period that is ironically described as a period of abstention from thinking) in the European Union has had to realize that the political elite had failed in its initial ambition. They tried to rescue the substance by giving up on the symbolism.[2] This was less than what was planned in 2004. In the meantime, this was also below the expectation of many citizens of the EU. European integration was to continue as a process of incremental progress. This was not the only insight into the outcome of the constitution-building process of the first decade of the twenty-first century. Already the experience with the formulation of the Treaty Establishing a Constitution for Europe, and the subsequent decision-making process in the European Council, should have eliminated any hope of overcoming this realist approach any time soon.

Only after a bitter power struggle and psychological waves of mistrust, coupled with a lacking "esprit européenne" over much of 2002 and 2003, have the leaders of all EU member states and current candidate countries been ready to sign the Treaty

(LSAP); Malta: Prime Minister Lawrence Gonzi Nationalist Party (PN), Foreign Minister Michael Frendo, Nationalist Party (PN); The Netherlands: Prime Minister Jan Peter Balkenende, Christian Democratic Appeal (CDA), Foreign Minister Bernard R. Bot, Christian Democratic Appeal (CDA); Poland: Prime Minister Marek Belka, Independent, Foreign Minister Wlodzimierz Cimoszewicz, Socialist Party (SLD); Portugal: Prime Minister Pedro Miguel de Santana Lopes, Social Democratic Party, Foreign Minister António Victor Martins Monteiro, Independent; Slovakia: Prime Minister Mikulås Dzurinda, Slovakian Christian Democratic Union (SDKÚ), Foreign Minister Eduard Kukan, Slovakian Christian Democratic Union (SDKÚ); Slovenia: Prime Minister Anton Rop, Liberal Democrats (LDS), Foreign Minister Ivo Vajgl, Liberal Democrats (LDS); Spain: Prime Minister José Luis Rodriguez Zapatero, Socialist Party (PSOE), Foreign Minister Miguel Angel Moratinos Cuyaubé, Socialist Party (PSOE); Sweden: Prime Minister Göran Persson,Social Democrats, Foreign Minister Laila Freivalds, Social Democrats; United Kingdom Prime Minister Tony Blair, Labour Party, Secretary of State for Foreign and Commonwealth Affairs Jack Straw, Labour Party. The Final Act of the Treaty Establishing a Constitution for Europe was also signed in their capacity as candidate states for accession to the European Union by Bulgaria: Prime Minister Simeon Saxe-Coburg, National Movement Simeon II. (NDSV), Foreign Minister Solomon Passy, National Movement Simeon II. (NDSV); Romania: President Ion Iliescu, Social Democrats (PSD), Foreign Minister Mircea Geoana, Social Democrats (PSD);Turkey: Prime Minister Tayyip Erdogan, Justice and Development Party (AKP), Foreign Minister Abdullah Gül, Justice and Development Party (AKP). Present at the signatory ceremony were also representatives of Croatia. For the text see European Union, Treaty Establishing a Constitution for Europe, Luxembourg: Office for Official Publications of the European Communities, 2005.

2 On the meaning of political symbolism for European integration see Theiler, Tobias, *Political Symbolism and European Integration*, Manchester: Manchester University Press, 2005.

Establishing a Constitution for Europe. The optimists among them were convinced to move the European Union from early constitutionalism to a full European Constitution. Although the formal name Treaty Establishing a Constitution for Europe did not leave any doubt that this was another inter-state treaty arrangement, the colloquial use of the term European Constitution made it clear to skeptics and supporters of the project alike: This event did not have any precedent in European history. A European Constitution was truly news in the long history of old Europe. Even those who signed the Treaty Establishing a Constitution for Europe with reluctance had to admit this. Some of them, however, immediately began to back down. They began to reinterpret the European Constitution and tried to undermine this exceptional European project over the course of their respective national ratification processes.[3]

Constitutions are the product of a rearranged equilibrium of political power and social orientations in a society. They do not require the existence of firm identity of the body politic they are supposed to frame. The history of decolonization during the twentieth century gives ample proof of this experience. Constitutions time and again were meant to help in the formation of nation states. They did not have to be preceded by a solid nation state identity in order to make constitutional statehood possible. Often, constitutional orders were aspirations of a new beginning after the most daunting process of destruction of a nation (e.g., Afghanistan and Lebanon). Under other circumstances, a new constitutional order could prove the readiness of a population to mark a new beginning after deep societal cleavages and scars (e.g., South Africa and Russia).

The skeptics of constitution-building in Europe have perceived the potential of a European Constitution merely through the lenses of the historical experiences of Europe's long-standing nation states. They had developed constitutional orders – and had often changed them over time – in response to the historical evolution of national identities, significant developments in the national power equation and the redefinition of political or social goals. In the case of national histories, constitutions were evolving testimonies to the tenacity of the nation state they were meant to guide. In light of this pattern in Europe's national histories, it was easy to draw the wrong conclusion for the future of Europe as a whole. The "ingredients" needed for constitution-building and the tenacity of constitutional authority in many EU member states – skeptics argued – do not sufficiently exist on the European level. The experiences with failed constitutions in states with multiple identities (e.g., Yugoslavia and Soviet Union) were invoked as an alarm signal for the European Union. The example of Switzerland as a nation state with multiple identities and languages did not seem to be transferable because of different geographic dimensions and the enormous regional socio-economic asymmetries inside the European Union as a whole. And yet, the European Union has eventually reached the status of a constitutional entity. The EU is not a nation, and it is not a state. It

3 See Duff, Andrew, *The Struggle for Europe's Constitution*, London: Federal Trust, 2005.

contains multiple identities, multilevel structures of governance and enormous regional socio-economic asymmetries. It has become a political entity with a cumulative constitution. This is unknown to the history of national constitution-making.

The most promising sign of political leadership during the first decade of the twenty-first century stood at the very beginning of this most recent series of constitution-building efforts: The highly forward-looking work of the Convention on the Future of Europe, soon labeled the Constitutional Convention of Europe, was an extraordinary construction. This unique forum was installed by a decision of the European Council meeting on December 15, 2001. Meeting in Laeken one year after the highly unsuccessful European Council in Nice that had left bitter memories across the EU, the Heads of State and Government were under enormous public pressure not to lose further authority as leaders of Europe. The Declaration they presented to the public at the end of their meeting echoed this sense of cautious self-criticism.

Five decades after the beginning of European integration, the Laeken Declaration admitted, the EU "stands at a crossroads, a defining moment in its existence". While the European Union was preparing for the biggest ever enlargement through the admittance of former communist countries in Central and Eastern Europe, the EU itself was facing the challenge of a democratic deficit – a term often to be heard across the EU during the following years. While the institutions and actions of the European Union "must be brought closer to the citizens", the EU must respond to the challenges and opportunities of globalization, playing a "stabilizing role worldwide and to point the way ahead for many countries and peoples".[4]

The Laeken Declaration made explicit reference to new global threats manifested in the terrorist attacks in New York and Washington on September 11, 2001 ("9/11"). Invoking the Magna Carta, the Bill of Rights, the French Revolution, and the fall of the Berlin Wall, the Laeken Declaration defined Europe as "the continent of liberty, solidarity and above all diversity, meaning respect for other's languages, cultures and traditions". The Declaration used to proud language: "The European Union's one boundary is democracy and human rights." At the same time, it recognized that the actions and goals of the European Union were not always properly understood or appreciated by the EU's own citizens: "Citizens are calling for a clear, open, effective, democratically controlled Community approach, developing a Europe which points the way ahead for the world." What was expected from their leaders was left unspecified. The Laeken Declaration defined four fundamental mandates for the institutional reform process ahead:

- A better division and definition of competencies in the European Union, an issue especially dear to representatives of federal EU member states and those trying to prevent further transfer of competencies to the EU level.

4 European Union, European Council, *The Laeken Declaration on the Future of the European Union,* http://ec.europa.eu/justice_home/unit/charte/en/declarations-laeken.html.

- The need to simplify the Union's legislative instruments, an issue usually more contentious among political players than of interest to the broader public.
- A stronger involvement of national parliaments in the EU policy-making processes, an issue meant to enhance national legitimacy for the European process. The future structure of the EU's rotating presidency and the various Council formations as well as the mechanisms for the EU's foreign policy were included in the mandate.
- A simplification of the Treaty structure of the European Union in order to enhance transparency.

At the European Council meeting in Laeken on December 15, 2001, the possibility of the creation of a European Constitution was only a vague option ahead at the Convention that was to begin its work. The establishment of the Convention on the Future of Europe was an innovative rupture with the past method of treaty revisions through secretive intergovernmental conferences. Under the Presidency of former liberal French President Valéry Giscard d'Estaing, the Convention on the Future of Europe began its deliberations on March 1, 2002, in Brussels. The former Heads of Government of Italy, Giuliano Amato, a Social Democrat, and Belgium, Jean-Luc Dehaene, a Christian Democrat, had been appointed Giscard's deputies.

The Convention on the Future of Europe was composed of 15 representatives of the Heads of State and Government of EU member states (one from each state), 30 members of national parliaments (two from each state), 16 members of the European Parliament and two representatives of the European Commission. 13 accession countries were fully involved in the deliberations of the Convention on the Future of Europe, represented in the same way as the 15 current EU member states (one government representative and two representatives of each national parliament). The Praesidium of the Convention was composed of the Chairman and his two deputies and nine members drawn from the Convention: the representatives of all governments holding the Council Presidency during the work of the Convention – Spain, Denmark and Greece – two representatives of national parliaments, two representatives of the European Parliament and two representatives of the European Commission.[5] Three representatives from the Economic and Social Committee of the European Union and six representatives from the Committee of the Regions and the European Ombudsman were invited to attend as observers. The Presidents of the European Court of Justice and of the European Court of Auditors were invited to address the Convention. The work of

5 The other members of the Praesidium of the Convention were: Alfonso Dastis, Henning Christophersen, Georges Papandreou representing the governments holding the Council Presidency during the Convention, John Bruton and Gisela Stuart representing the national parliaments, Klaus Hänsch and Inigo Mendez de Vigo representing the European Parliament, Michel Barnier and Antonio Vitorino representing the European Commission; Alojz Peterle, representing the candidate countries, attended the meetings of the Praesidium as an invitee; the Council's Secretariat was headed by Sir John Kerr, a distinguished British career diplomat.

the Convention's Presidium was supported by a Secretariat with experts from the Commission, the European Parliament and the Council General Secretariat.

During its initial meeting, the Convention on the Future of Europe elected the remaining members of its Presidium and organized its work for the next fifteen months. The Convention came together on 28 occasions, discussing publicly in Brussels a politically loaded agenda.[6] The Convention's President structured the debate, allowing for an open exchange of general ideas at the beginning, while structuring the debate more carefully the closer the Praesidium and its secretariat came to preparing the final text on the Convention's work. The most courageous and far-sighted decision was taken by the Convention early on, namely the decision that the Convention would present a comprehensive text to the EU governments. This was the breakthrough for the concept of a European Constitution. What had been a taboo across Europe until then became thereafter a common reference across the EU's media, policy circles, and academia. The efforts of the Convention to frame a coherent text acceptable to all its members were supported by eleven Working Groups with members of the Convention dealing with the most crucial issues on the Convention's agenda:

- Subsidiarity.
- The Role of the European Charter of Basic Rights.
- The Legal personality of the European Union.
- The Role of national parliaments.
- Complementary competencies.
- Economic governance.
- External actions.
- Defense.
- The Simplification of European Treaties.
- European Space of Freedom, Security and Justice.
- Social Europe.[7]

Three specialized Discussion Circles dealt with the future status of the European Court of Justice, the possible future budgetary procedures, and the issue of possible own resources for the European Union.[8]

6 For all deliberations of the "Convention on the Future of Europe", see: European Union, The European Convention, http://european-convention.eu.int/sessplen.asp?lang=EN; on the Convention also Shaw, Jo, *The "Convention on the Future of Europe": Working Towards an EU Constitution*, London: Federal Trust for Education&Research, 2003; Michalski, Anna, and Matthias Heise (eds.), *European Convention on the Future of Europe: An Analysis of the Official Positions of EU Member States, Future Member States, Applicant and Candidate Countries*, The Hague: Netherlands Institute of International Relations, 2003.

7 For all deliberations in these Working Groups see: European Union, The European Convention, http://european-convention.eu.int/doc_wg.asp?lang=EN.

8 See: European Union, The European Convention, http://european-convention.eu.int/doc_CIRCLE.asp?lang=EN.

The Convention on the Future of Europe was a highly political body and was meant to be one. Unknown in former institutional reform processes, its deliberations took place in a very consensual atmosphere, intended to make full use of the possible impact of its work. It was soon labeled the Constitutional Convention of Europe. In light of the final result of the reform process, this was a premature assessment. But the members of the Convention deserve to be recognized as the Founding Brethren (and Sisters) of a new era in European integration. On July 10, 2003, the Constitutional Convention concluded its work. Without a formal vote, the Convention unanimously agreed to the final text prepared by its secretariat and presented by its President. This was a unique act in the history of European integration. Though politicians and government officials could split over issues the size of a hair without ever coming to any reasonable agreement, the Convention for the Future of Europe unanimously adopted a text with enormous implications for generations of Europeans to come. It was not only proof of their ability to generate a common denominator; it was a sign of leadership and authority, so often a rare commodity in European politics over past decade(s).

On July 18, 2003, Valéry Giscard d'Estaing presented the Draft Constitutional Treaty to the European Council and the European public.[9] It was now in their hands to decide about the fate of the first ever European Constitution. The Draft Constitutional Treaty was an extraordinary piece of work. It went far beyond the original expectations of the work of the Convention on the Future of Europe. The Convention had made full use of its mandate without overstretching it to a point at which its members would engage in so much controversy that splitting votes was inevitable. Of course, the Draft Constitutional Treaty did not satisfy everyone in the EU. In fact, practically everybody would have been able to identify with one or the other point of disagreement and contention. This was probably the best possible criterion for measuring the success of the Convention's work; while nobody could euphorically claim complete victory, everybody was able to point to one or the other endearing aspects of achievement.

The future of Europe was not be changed dramatically only because of the very text of a constitution. But the framework for future deliberations, policy decisions and – most importantly – expectations and standards of accountability was to be dramatically changed, enlarged and deepened with this text. The press coverage of the presentation of the Draft Constitutional Treaty already indicated that the text would soon only be known and referred to as the European Constitution. Two bottlenecks remained: The text would have to gain the blessing of the European Council and it would have to be ratified by each nation across the European Union.

The European Council handed the Draft Constitutional Treaty over to an Intergovernmental Conference. This procedural decision was an enormous success for a

9 European Union, *Draft Treaty Establishing a Constitution for Europe: adopted by consensus by the European Convention on 13 June and 10 July 2003: submitted to the President of the European Council in Rome, July 8, 2003*, Luxembourg: Office for Official Publications of European Communities, 2003.

Constitutional Convention that hardly anyone had believed to be possible two years before. Hope was aired that this might be the last Intergovernmental Conference dealing with EU institution-making. In the future, more public and political Conventions were to be the only instrument to amend EU treaties. Bureaucratic and non-transparent Intergovernmental Conferences would be declared outlived. This hope was premature. Yet, a constitutional debate in Europe had begun. The Draft Constitutional Treaty was recognized as the basis for further deliberations in European constitution-building. During the 1980's and 1990's, Intergovernmental Conferences had become notorious for being unable to achieve more than bureaucratic fine-tuning in EU institution-making. The failure of the Intergovernmental Conference preceding the Treaty of Nice was on everybody's mind when yet another IGC with representatives from member state governments was summoned in autumn 2003. The eventual failure of this IGC to come to terms with the most daunting controversies still in the European air was therefore no real surprise. It was, however, an unpleasant surprise that subsequently the Heads of State and Government also failed to achieve the necessary compromise when they convened for their regular European Council meeting in Brussels on December 11 and 12, 2003. They could not yet agree on the Constitutional Treaty.

Spain and Poland were tainted as the "bad boys;" such, at least was the superficial and highly prejudicial impression conveyed by many in the EU media. Spain and Poland were unwilling to accept demands by France and Germany concerning the future decision-making mechanisms in the Council. As the Italian EU Presidency was unable to overcome the deadlock, the European Council meeting ended early and without result. When the Treaty of Nice was negotiated in 2000, France had insisted on parity with Germany in the institutions of an enlarged EU. While both countries finally had agreed upon this principle, they also accepted an equal proportion of voting rights in the Council for Spain and Poland. Spain and Poland, together representing 80 million people, were granted 54 votes while Germany with 82 million citizens received 29 votes. It was so confusing and contradictory that only three years later, the Nice decision was considered invalid by its very inventors; suddenly, France and Germany insisted on a new share of voting rights in the Council, hoping to reduce the bargaining position of Spain and Poland while maintaining and even strengthening their own. It was no surprise that Spain and Poland said "no" to this "Big Power diplomacy." The idea to install a double majority for decision-making in the European Council – meaning that decisions could only be taken if a majority of both EU member states and EU citizens would agree – was not convincing to the representatives of Spain and Poland.

The controversy was not simply a matter of the arithmetic of the weighing of votes. The constitutional deadlock of December 2003 was rather the honest expression of antagonisms that had escalated since 2000. Instead of advancing the European Union, France and Germany had increasingly antagonized some of their EU partners – old and new – with a behavior that others were describing as counter-productive to the spirit of the European Union. Since the notorious Nice Summit, France and Germany had developed from pro-active engines of EU integration into veto powers, at least so it appeared to many of their EU partners. France and Germany were perceived as veto powers against the future new EU member states (i.e., on matters of EU budgeting), against provisions of EU law launched by themselves (i.e,. on the issue of the EU Stability and Growth Pact), against the United States (i.e., on the war in Iraq), and ultimately leading to suspicious among themselves (i.e., on voting rights in EU institutions). At the same time, France and Germany were confronted with enormous and growing difficulties to launch necessary structural reforms in their labor markets and welfare state mechanisms, health and pension policies in particular. They were not able to reinvigorate productivity and growth at home. Germany and France had turned from the central economic engines of Europe into the economically "sick men" of Europe.

By the end of 2003, many of their EU partners saw the Franco-German position on voting rights in the Council as yet another expression of their ambition to lead the EU and impose their will if necessary against the interests of other member states. This had become visible for them during the Iraq crisis of 2002/2003 when Spain, under conservative Prime Minister José Maria Aznar, and Poland, under Socialist Prime Minister Leszek Miller, were siding with the US administration of President George W. Bush, while France, under Gaullist President Jacques Chirac, and Germany, under Social Democratic Chancellor Gerhard Schröder, were opposing the American position. Their "bilateral unilateralism" was no more helpful than the one for which they criticized the US administration. The escalation of this internal Cold War in the West left deep wounds and scars all across the EU. One of its collateral victims – at least for a time being – was the European Constitution. An old law of European politics was confirmed: Whenever transatlantic relations are in bad shape, European integration will not work well.

By June 2004, transatlantic relations were not yet really repaired. More than ever, the growing frustration about the unaccomplished mission in Iraq overshadowed all efforts of damage control in order to rebuild the Atlantic alliance around the logic of a new transatlantic partnership.[10] In fact, the most severe wounds seemed to have healed in Europe. The terrorist attacks in Madrid on March 11, 2004 ("3/11") had shocked Europe and strengthened the sense of European solidarity with the US in an unprecedented way. The EU invoked the solidarity clause that was only to be used in reference to the Constitution itself. In the midst of the horror of the terrorist attack, the ruling conservative People's Party under Prime Minister Aznar lost the Spanish parliamentary elections. They were blamed for not being honest about the origin of the

10 On this matter see Asmus, Ronald D., and Kenneth M. Pollack, "The New Transatlantic Project," *Policy Review*, 115 (2002): 3-18.

terrorist act and trying to cover up what was seen as a consequence of their pro-American policy on Iraq. The new Socialist majority under Prime Minister José Luis Rodríguez Zapatero immediately announced an attitude of compromise on the European Constitution. Poland followed suit while its Premier Leszek Miller stepped down the morning after Poland formally acceded to the European Union on May 1, 2004, being replaced by a caretaker government under Marek Belka. Germany and France had also indicated their readiness to compromise. A result was imminent when the European Council convened again on June 17 and 18, 2004, in Brussels. It was called upon to repair the damage to Europe's future that had been inflicted six months earlier, and it did.

In the meantime, the principle of "double majority" as the basis for strengthening EU legitimacy had been widely discussed in the EU. Twofold legitimacy meant to recognize both the role of the states and the role of citizens in a Union of States and Citizens alike. According to international law, a Union of States would have to recognize equality among them. This would leave aside the sharp difference in the distribution of people among EU countries while all of them would be subject to binding EU law. According to democratic theory, a Union of Citizens would have to recognize equality among them. In the context of the European Union, this would marginalize the citizens of Malta, Luxembourg or Estonia in light of the much bigger populations in other EU countries.

A balance between the concept of a Union of States and the concept of a Union of Citizens was necessary, should the European Union maintain and broaden its popular, as well as its political and academic, legitimacy. Both principles – those referring to the Union of States and those referring to the Union of Citizens – had to be balanced in all EU institutions. As far as the European Parliament is concerned, degressive proportionality in the distribution of parliamentary mandates provides for this balance. In the case of the European Commission, the number of commissioners is decoupled from the number of member states. And as far as voting rights in the Council are concerned, a qualified majority in Council decisions is defined by a combined majority of member states and a majority of EU citizens.

After months of uncertainty, the European Council agreed on compromises on all pending issues during its session on June 17 and 18, 2004, in Brussels. The principle of "double majority" found agreement, with 55 percent of states representing 65 percent of the union citizens necessary to pass legislation under the principle of qualified majority voting. For an interim period (until 2009), the EU would keep 25 commissioners, but the overall number would be reduced to 18 once the EU consisted of more than 27 member states. Finally, the Treaty Establishing a Constitution for Europe was accepted by the European Council and prepared for the signing ceremony on October 29, 2004, in Rome.

All key propositions of the Draft Constitutional Treaty were accepted in the Treaty Establishing a Constitution for Europe:

- The future legal basis of the European Union was to be one single treaty (Treaty Establishing a Constitution for Europe, colloquially labeled Constitutional Treaty or European Constitution). The confusion with four different legal and protoconstitutional provisions was to come to an end. The so-called Pillar Structure, introduced by the Treaty of Maastricht in order to distinguish between the supranational and the intergovernmental dimensions of the European Union on the one hand and the European Community on the other hand, was to be terminated.
- The preamble of the Constitutional Treaty did not make explicit reference to God but was to recognize the Christian heritage of Europe;[11] the Constitutional Treaty was to introduce the mechanism of a permanently structured dialogue between the EU organs on the one hand and Christian churches and other religious communities in Europe on the other hand (Constitutional Treaty, Part I, Article I-52).[12]
- The Constitutional Treaty was to give legal status to the symbols of the European Union the flag, anthem, motto of "Unity in Diversity", currency, and Europe Day on May 9th, (Constitutional Treaty, Part I, Article I-8).[13]
- The European Union was to gain legal personality (Constitutional Treaty, Part I, Title I, Article I-7).[14] The EU was to consist of one European Union, overcoming the past differentiation between European Union and European Community. Legal personality would allow the European Union to enter into treaty relations with other political entities in the world, including the United Nations. This could be relevant, for instance, for peace-keeping operations under a UN mandate.
- The Charter of Fundamental Rights of the European Union was to be included in the Treaty and thus made judiciable (Constitutional Treaty, Part I, Article I-9; Part II).[15]
- The order of competencies of the European Union was to be considerably simplified (Constitutional Treaty, Part I, Title III, Article I-11 to Article I-18).[16] The Constitution distinguished between exclusive competencies of the European Union, shared competencies of the European Union and its member states, and supporting, complementary and coordinating competencies of the EU.
- The European Parliament was understood to be the co-decision body in

11 European Union, *Treaty Establishing a Constitution for Europe*, op.cit.: 9.
12 Ibid.: 42
13 Ibid.: 19.
14 Ibid.: 19.
15 Ibid.: 19; 46-60.
16 Ibid.: 20-22.

practically all future EU legislation (Constitutional Treaty, Part I, Title IV, Article I-20).[17] The President of the European Commission was to be nominated by the European Council in light of the outcome of the elections to the European Parliament whose majority would have to approve him. The European Parliament was to be given the mandate to express a binding vote of non-confidence against the Commission President and each EU Commissioner (Constitutional Treaty, Part I, Title IV, Article I-27).[18]

- The European Council was to be chaired by a permanent President, in office for two and a half years, renewable once, and appointed by the European Council (Constitutional Treaty, Part I, Title IV, Article I-22).[19] Council formations were to be simplified and made more transparent. The Council was to meet in public when discussing and deciding on a legislative act (Constitutional Treaty, Part I, Title IV, Article I-24).[20] Council decisions on the basis of a qualified majority were supposed to be taken when at least 55 percent of the EU member states comprising at least 65 percent of the population of the EU are in favor of a decision (Constitutional Treaty, Part I, Title IV, Article I-25).[21]
- The European Commission was eventually (by 2014) to be reduced to 15 members or two thirds of the number of EU member states selected on the basis of a system of equal rotation among all member states (Constitutional Treaty, Part I, Title IV, Article I-26).[22] This provision implied that not every EU member state would be any more able to send a Commissioner to Brussels, thus strengthening the political over the national principle.
- Foreign and Security Policy of the European Union was to become more personalized with the introduction of a Union Minister for Foreign Affairs, who at the same time was to be one of the Vice-Presidents of the European Commission and thus also accountable to the European Parliament (Constitutional Treaty, Part I, Title IV, Article I-28).[23]
- The legislative procedures of the European Union were to be streamlined (Constitutional Treaty, Part I, Title V, Article I-33 to Article I-39).[24] They were to be reduced to six: two legislative acts (European laws and European framework laws) and four non-legislative acts (European regulations, European decisions, European recommendations, delegated European regulations). With almost no exception, future legislation in the European Union was to take place on the basis of co-decision between the Council and the European Parliament.

17 Ibid.: 25.
18 Ibid.: 29.
19 Ibid.: 26.
20 Ibid.: 26-27.
21 Ibid.: 27.
22 Ibid.: 28.
23 Ibid.: 29-30.
24 Ibid.: 32-35.

The new executive instruments of "delegated European regulations" and "implementing acts" were intended to strengthen the executive position of the European Commission.

- The participatory dimension of European democracy was to be strengthened by introducing the right of one million citizens to initiate a proposal for a legal act of the European Union (Constitutional Treaty, Part I, Title VI, Article I-47).[25] In case of such a citizen's initiative, the European Commission was supposed to prepare the necessary steps for such a legal act.
- The budgetary procedures of the European Union were to be tightened and simplified, although this complex issue had remained one of the least successful in the dealings of the Convention (Constitutional Treaty, Part I, Title VII, Article I-53 to Article I-56).[26] The European Parliament was practically to be granted the right of co-decision in long-term budgetary planning. Both the Draft Constitutional Treaty and the Treaty Establishing a Constitution for Europe did fall short of introducing a European tax, thus leaving the EU in a situation of "representation without taxation."
- The role of national parliaments in future EU legislation was to be strengthened (Protocol on the Role of National Parliaments in the European Union).[27] Based on the principle of subsidiarity national parliaments were to be enabled to resort to an early warning mechanism in order to judge whether or not their constitutional rights are curtailed by a planned act of EU legislation.
- The European Constitution offered a structured path of exit, provided a country intended to withdraw from the European Union of its free choice (Constitutional Treaty, Part I, Title IX, Article I-60).[28] The mechanism was intended to alleviate the fear in some EU member states that the future path of EU integration might overly curtail their national freedoms.
- Future procedures of constitutional revisions and amendments were explicitly outlined in the European Constitution in order to facilitate additions or changes to the Constitution in a European Union with a growing numbers of actors and confronted with increasingly complex topics that would require a reassessment of the original provisions of the Constitutional Treaty (Part IV, Article IV-443 to Article IV-445).[29]

The signatories of the European Constitution completely underestimated the pitfalls of the ratification marathon that was to follow their signing of the Constitution. In some cases, the ratification pitfalls were considered the last resort to prevent the Constitution from ever coming into force without being directly blamed for its failure. In other cases,

25 Ibid.: 41.
26 Ibid.: 42-44.
27 Ibid.: 211-213.
28 Ibid.: 46.
29 Ibid.: 196-198.

the arrogance of national governments or the cheap Brussels-bashing that has been a sign of parochialism in many political circles across the EU had to backfire. While the majority of EU member states representing the majority of EU citizens ratified the European Constitution, the majorities of citizens asked in a referendum in France and subsequently in the Netherlands said "no" to the proposition of their respective leadership.[30]

2. Resurrection, Second Death and Survival: the Paradoxical Results of a Confusing Reform Decade

For two years, the European Constitution rested in a state of political coma. It goes to the credit of the sophisticated work done in the Constitutional Convention between 2002 and 2003 that most of the essential elements of the Treaty Establishing a Constitution for Europe were rescued for the reconstitution work in 2007.[31] After a self-declared reflection period among EU leaders, the able work of the German and Portuguese diplomacy during the EU Presidencies of their countries in 2007 transferred the political essence of the Constitutional Treaty into the Treaty of Lisbon. This was no longer a readable, slim or attractive text. But it helped to revitalize the constitutional agenda of the first decade of the twenty-first century. In the end, the 2007 Treaty of Lisbon became a compromise between the 2000 Treaty of Nice and the 2004 European Constitution.

On the occasion of the fiftieth anniversary of the signing of the Treaties of Rome on March 25, 2007, the constitution-building process through cumulative treaty revisions was resurrected. The reflection period of the EU ended with the Berlin Declaration, a somber document signed on March 25, 2007, by the European Council, the European

30 The Treaty Establishing a Constitution for Europe was ratified by the following countries: Lithuania (November 11, 2004), Hungary (December 20, 2004); Slovenia (February 1, 2005), Italy (April 6, 2005), Greece (April 19, 2005), Bulgaria (May 11, 2005, as part of the EU Accession Treaty), Slovakia (May 11, 2005), Romania (May 17, 2005 as part of the EU Accession Treaty), Spain (May 18, 2005), Austria (May 25, 2005), Germany (May 27, 2005), Latvia (June 2, 2005), Cyprus (June 30, 2005), Malta (July 6, 2005), Luxembourg (July 10, 2005), Belgium (February 8, 2006), Estonia (May 9, 2006), Finland (December 5, 2006). The European Parliament ratified the Treaty Establishing a Constitution for Europe on January 12, 2005.

31 On the Treaty Establishing a Constitution for Europe see also Mény, Yves, "Making Sense of the EU: The Achievements of the Convention," *Journal of Democracy*, 14 (2003): 57-70; Brimmer, Esther (ed.), *The European Constitutional Treaty: A Guide for Americans*, Washington D.C.: Center for Transatlantic Relations, 2004; Odvar Eriksen, Erik, et.al. (eds.), *Developing a Constitution for Europe*, London: Routledge, 2004; Höreth, Marcus, Cordula Janowski, and Ludger Kühnhardt (eds.), *Die Europäische Verfassung - Analyse und Bewertung ihrer Strukturentscheidungen*, Baden-Baden: Nomos, 2005; Wessels, Wolfgang, "The Constitutional Treaty – Three Readings from a Fusion Perspective," *Journal of Common Market Studies* 43 (2005): 287-306; Jopp, Mathias, and Saskia Matl (eds.), *Der Vertrag über eine Verfassung für Europa*, Baden-Baden: Nomos, 2005; Church, Clive H., and David Phinnemore, *Understanding the European Constitution: An Introduction to the EU Constitutional Treaty*, London: Routledge, 2006.

Parliament and the European Commission. Through the Berlin Declaration they tried to redefine their leadership task in a joint manner, speaking on behalf of the citizens of European Union as a means to move their own obligation forward: "We, the citizens of the European Union, have united for the better. In the European Union, we are turning our common ideals into reality: for us, the individual is paramount. His dignity is inviolable."[32] This sounded quite noble, but the struggle over the wording and its interpretation among the leaders of the EU was rather undignified. Euroskeptics and those trying to rescue the political substance of the European Constitution were united in avoiding the term Constitution. For many citizens, the announcement of the purpose of European integration was a helpless signal contradicted for several years by the difficult daily path toward European integration. Others were frustrated or even considered it a threat to hear what Europe's political leadership had to say about their unity "for the better." As for its substance, the Berlin Declaration was a masterpiece in diplomacy: It declared the European Constitution dead in order to resurrect it. The Berlin Declaration concluded that "we are united in our aim of placing the European Union on a renewed common basis before the European Parliament elections in 2009."[33] These were empty words for most European citizens, but nuances of self-imposed commitment subsequently hung over the leaders of all EU member states as an obligation to act.

It belongs to the paradoxical realities of the European Union that some of the intentions of the Treaty Establishing a Constitution for Europe – colloquially called the European Constitution – had already been implemented without the ratification of the treaty. In 2004, for example, the President of the European Commission was appointed only after he received the vote of the majority in the European Parliament, representing its strongest political party after the elections of 2004. Since 2004, the EU's Diplomatic Service (European External Action Service) has been built up, and so has the European Defense Agency which, however, does not belong to the treaty. The European Union was working and had enlarged in early 2007 to include Bulgaria and Romania, thus becoming a Union of twenty-seven states. Yet, a sense of crisis and stalemate had accompanied the past two years. Since the negative referenda on the Treaty Establishing a Constitution for Europe in France and in the Netherlands in May and June 2005, the reflection period had tamed the usual self-serving rhetoric of many European politicians; they were eager to regain control over the crisis. The reflection period was a wise mechanism in order to postpone final decisions and help healing old wounds. By 2007, new wounds broke out as new governments represented those countries in the EU with new special interests, concerns, or dimensions of Euro-skepticism.

32 European Union, *Declaration on the Occasion of the Fiftieth Anniversary of the Signature of the Treaties of Rome*, Berlin, March 25, 2007, http://eu2007.de/de/News/download_docs/ Maerz/0324-RAA/English.pdf.

33 Ibid.

When the European Council met on June 12-13, 2007, Poland was instantly criticized for being obstructionist, along with the Czech Republic. Ironically, the Polish population was as pro-European as any citizenry in the EU could be at that point in time. Its conservative-nationalist government was fighting against all other EU member states in preventing the introduction of the principle of "double majority" into the new treaty, a decision that had already been included into the Treaty of Nice and also into the Treaty Establishing a Constitution for Europe. During a night-long negotiation, Prime Minister Jarosław Kaczyński called his twin-brother, Poland's President Lech Kaczyński, several times to discuss the Polish position. The surreal scenery ended with a compromise, elegantly brokered by German Chancellor Angela Merkel, then head of the European Council. Poland accepted the principle of "double majority" for the voting mechanism in the European Council as had already been outlined in the Treaty Establishing a Constitution for Europe. The government of the Kaczyński twins represented a new majority in Polish politics different from the pro-European one that had signed the European Constitution in 2004. To accommodate national political changes, which put into question the former majority's signature under an international treaty, was a negative experience for many in the EU. To reach a compromise with Poland's consent was, in the end, a victory for European solidarity and for the continuity of a Europe with one voice and one speed. But the mandate for an EU reform treaty was only a small step. In fact, it was a patchwork and not a contribution to a new level of real reform. The fierce debate in the European Council over the principle of "double majority" for future Council decisions was telling. The mathematical definition of the weighed votes of equal countries with unequal populations echoed the misinterpretation of the EU as a zero-sum operation. In reality, however, the EU could only be successful as long as its decisions turned out to be win-win-constellations for all. The right step into this direction was the comprehensive introduction of a regular legislative relationship between the Council of the European Union and the European Parliament under the framework of co-decision-making. The "double majority" dispute was a dispute of mutual suspicion, reciprocal fear and parochial notions of Europe among its national governments.

By virtue of the EU's calendar, Germany was holding the rotating EU Presidency during the first half of 2007. The German government under Angela Merkel gained much praise across the EU for its steady commitment to revitalize the reform process and to broker a realistic compromise acceptable to all EU governments. The price for this compromise was high: it was the loss of much of the transparency which the Treaty Establishing a Constitution for Europe had promised. The price was also that the EU was giving up on the idea of a single treaty, of the nomination of its first Foreign Minister and of the explicit reference to its symbols – all this happened without any public debate or transparency. Afterwards, nobody could be held accountable and everybody shied away from looking too deep into the circumstances and driving forces that had triggered these revisions behind closed doors. With a certain generalization it is fair to say that the state in which Europe's political leadership found itself at the time of the European Council of June 2007 was the real problem behind the failure of achieving a European Constitution. The obvious confusion and lack of forward-orientation among many of the EU's political leaders echoed the resentments and dissonances among the citizens in several EU member states. Since the full introduction of monetary union, the transfer of sovereignty to the EU level has met more reservation than ever before among the original 15 member states. With the accession of twelve new member states, mostly post-communist transformation societies, European interests could no longer be defined as "business as usual." Under the conditions of globalization, all the twenty-seven member states of the EU and the EU's institutions were exposed to an agenda increasingly defined outside Europe yet impacting the Union's citizens directly. Returning the Constitution of Europe to a legitimate place had to become the main task in order to turn the Constitution of Europe into a consensual text and cornerstone for future progress. Political leaders were hiding behind disconcerted citizens while citizens were ignored by disconerted leaders.

The structural conflict behind the constitutional crisis was perfect material for a thorough reflection on democratic theory: While normally, international commitments of any government can be expected to be binding for the country whose representatives have signed an international commitment, the legacy of the 2004 Treaty Establishing a Constitution for Europe did run counter to this experience of predictability and reliability. The rift between elites and the people that became evident with the results of the referenda in France and in the Netherlands reflected two serious deficits and flaws that had not been properly addressed or resolved before the ratification procedure of the European Constitution was begun:

(a) The EU leaders argued that time had not been ripe for a pan-European referendum representing one single European public sphere. Instead, they embarked on a long and daunting journey of national ratifications under which the negative result in one single nation would hold all other partners hostage.

(b) The EU leaders argued that contingent exercises of national vetoing powers were no longer acceptable if the notion of European solidarity was to maintain its value and meaning. Yet, in order to maintain any meaningful European solidarity and constitution-building consensus, national vetoing pressure and intimidations had to be accepted by all.

When Austria had tried to relaunch the ratification process for the Treaty Establishing a Constitution for Europe under its EU Presidency in early 2006, it was given a cold shoulder by those governments that were either afraid of the treaty being rejected by their own people or by those trying to monopolize the seemingly new trend of popular Euroskepticism. The European Council on June, 15-16, 2005, unanimously decided that the future of the Treaty Establishing a Constitution for Europe was to be resuscitated under the German EU Presidency during the first half of 2007. This led to the Berlin Declaration with its vague commitment and to the European Council on June 21-22, 2007. Here, the European Heads of State and Government officially decided to drop the concept of a comprehensive European Constitution under the framework of a single treaty. Instead, they agreed to negotiate two new EU treaties through amendments included in one text: a Reform Treaty was to amend the Treaty on the European Union (Treaty of Maastricht) and the Treaty on the European Economic Community (Treaties of Rome) was to change into the Treaty on the Functioning of the European Union. The result of this decision and the subsequent negotiation process was the Treaty of Lisbon, signed on December 13, 2007, euphorically labeled "Reform Treaty" by its signatories.[34]

34 The Treaty of Lisbon was signed by Austria: Federal Chancellor Alfred Gusenbauer, Social Democratic Party of Austria (SPÖ), Federal Minister for European and International Affairs Ursula Plassnik, Christian Democratic Austrian People's Party (ÖVP); Belgium: Prime Minister Guy Verhofstadt, Flemish Liberals and Democrats (VLM), Minister for Foreign Affairs Karel de Gucht, Reformist Movement (MR); Bulgaria: Prime Minister Sergei Stanishev, Bulgarian Socialist Party (BSP), Deputy Prime Minister and Minister for Foreign Affairs Ivaylo Kalfin, Bulgarian Socialist Party (BSP); Cyprus (Greek Republic): President Tassos Papadopoulos, Democratic Party (DIKO), Minister for Foreign Affairs Erato Kozakou-Marcoullis, Independent; Czech Republic: Prime Minister Mirek Topolánek, Civic Democratic Party (ODS), Minister for Foreign Affairs Karel Schwarzenberg, Independent; Denmark: Prime Minister Anders Fogh Rasmussen, Liberal Party (VENSTRE), Minister for Foreign Affairs Per Stig Møller, Conservative People's Party (DKF); Estonia: Prime Minister Andrus Ansip, Estonian Reform Party, Minister for Foreign Affairs Urmas Paet, Estonian Reform Party; Finland: Prime Minister Matti Vanhanen, Centre Party (KESK), Minister for Foreign Affairs Ilkka Kanerva, National Coalition Party (KOK); France: President Nicolas Sarkozy, Union for a Popular Movement (UMP), Prime Minister François Fillon, Union for a Popular Movement (UMP), Minister for Foreign and European Affairs Bernard Kouchner, Independent; Germany: Federal Chancellor Angela Merkel, Christian Democratic Union (CDU), Minister for Foreign Affairs Frank-Walter Steinmeier, Social Democratic Party of Germany (SPD); Greece: Prime Minister Kostas Karamanlis, New Democracy (ND), Minister for Foreign Affairs Theodora Bakoyannis, New Democracy (ND); Hungary: Prime Minister Ferenc Gyurcsány, Socialist Party (MSZP), Minister for Foreign Affairs Kinga Göncz, Socialist Party (MSZP); Ireland: Prime Minister Bertie Ahern, Fianna Fáil – The Republican Party, Minister for Foreign Affairs Dermot Ahern, Fianna Fáil – The Republican Party; Italy: Prime Minister Romano Prodi, Democratic Party (PD), Deputy Prime Minister and Minister for Foreign Affairs Massimo D'Alema, Democratic Party (PD); Latvia: President Valdis Zatlers, Independent, Prime Minister Aigars Kalvītis, People's Party, Minister for Foreign Affairs Maris Riekstinš, People's Party; Lithuania: President Valdas Adamkus, Independent, Prime Minister Gediminas Kirkilas, Social Democratic Party of Lithuania (LSP), Minister for Foreign Affairs Petras Vaitiekūnas, Independent; Luxembourg: Prime Minister Jean-Claude Juncker, Christian Social People's Party (CSV), Minister for Foreign Affairs Jean Asselborn, Luxembourg Socialist Workers' Party (LSAP); Malta: Prime Minister Lawrence Gonzi, Nationalist Party (PN), Minister for Foreign Affairs Michael Frendo, Nationalist Party (NP); Netherlands: Prime Minister Jan-Peter Balkenende, Christian Democratic Appeal (CDA), Minister for Foreign Affairs Maxime Verhagen, Christian Democratic Appeal (CDA); Poland: Prime Minister Donald Tusk, Civic Platform (PO), Minister for Foreign Affairs Radosław Sikorski, Civic Platform (PO); Portugal: Prime Minister José Sócrates, Socialist Party (PS), Minister for Foreign Affairs Luís Amado, Socialist Party (PS); Romania: President Traian Băsescu, Independent, Prime Minister Călin Popescu-Tăriceanu, National Liberal Party (PNL), Minister for Foreign Affairs Adrian-Mihai Cioroianu, National Liberal Party (PNL); Slovenia: Prime Minister Janez Janša, Slovenian Democratic Party (SDS), Minister for Foreign Affairs Dimitrij Rupel, Slovenian Democratic Party (SDS); Slovakia: Prime Minister Robert Fico, Direction – Social Democracy (Smer-SD), Minister for Foreign Affairs Ján Kubiš, Independent; Spain: Prime Minister José Luis Zapatero, Spanish

It was a sign of administrative professionalism that the Portuguese government presented a first comprehensive draft on the new treaty text to the EU Foreign Ministers when they formally opened the Intergovernmental Conference on July 23, 2007. At the European Council meeting on October 18-19, 2007, the treaty found political agreement, as usual after intensive negotiations and last minute bartering.[35] To minimize unpredictable public reactions, this time the EU member states agreed that the ratification of the Treaty of Lisbon should be handled like any other international treaty. With the exception of Ireland, ratification through a parliamentary majority would be the appropriate and sufficient way in all EU member states. It was astonishing to see how the political leaders across the EU underestimated the potentially explosive nature of this one referendum. The referenda in France and in the Netherlands in 2005 should have taught them a lesson of people's dissent and frustration. Yet, they closed their eyes, hoping for a gentle approval by one of the economically most successful populations of any EU member state. Hungary was the first to begin the ratification marathon on December 17, 2007, when its National Assembly ratified the Treaty of Lisbon. 325 of 386 members of the Hungarian parliament voted with "yes." Seventeen other national parliaments followed as well as the European Parliament.[36] But then came what had to come: The victory of the "no" vote in the Irish referendum on June 12, 2008. 46.6 percent of the Irish expressed support for the Treaty of Lisbon, 53.4 percent rejected it. The voter's turn out was high with 53.1 percent. The result was powerful: 862,415 of 491 million EU citizens stopped the speedy implementation of the provisions of the Treaty of Lisbon prior to the next election to the European Parliament in June 2009.

The reaction of the political elites in most EU member states and EU institutions was as predictable as their initial ignorance about the possible explosiveness of the situation. They reacted with shock and awe, frustration and the stubborn hope to go ahead anyway with the ratification of the Treaty of Lisbon. In the end, some constitutional guarantees were granted to the Irish government, especially regarding key

Socialist Workers' Party (PSOE), Minister for Foreign Affairs Miguel Angel Moratinos, Spanish Socialist Workers' Party (PSOE); Sweden: Prime Minister Fredrik Reinfeldt, Moderate Party, Minister for EU Affairs Cecilia Malmström, Liberal People's Party (FP); United Kingdom: Prime Minister Gordon Brown, Labour Party, Secretary of State for Foreign and Commonwealth Affairs David Miliband, Labour Party.

35 European Union, "Treaty of Lisbon Amending the Treaty on European Union and the Treaty Establishing the European Community," *Official Journal of the European Union*, C 306/Vol.50, Luxembourg: Office for Official Publications of the European Communities, 2007, http://eur-lex.europa.eu/JOHtml.do?uri=OJ:C:2007:306:SOM:EN:HTML.

36 The Treaty of Lisbon was ratified by the following countries: Hungary (December 17, 2007); Malta (January 29, 2008); Slovenia (January 29, 2008); Romania (February 4, 2008); France (February 14, 2008); Bulgaria (March 21, 2008); Poland (April 10, 2008); Slovakia (April 10, 2008); Portugal (April 23, 2008); Denmark (April 24, 2008); Austria (April 24, 2008); Latvia (May 8, 2008); Lithuania (May 8, 2008); Germany (May 23, 2008); Luxembourg (May 29, 2008); Estonia (June 11, 2008); Finland (June 11, 2008); Greece (June 11, 2008); United Kingdom (June 18, 2008). The European Parliament ratified the Treaty of Lisbon on February 20, 2008.

concerns of the country such as maintaining its restrictive abortion policy and its military neutrality, opened the way for a second referendum. This time, it went well: On October 2, 2009 67.13 percent of Irish voters said "yes" to the Treaty of Lisbon. With 59 percent, voter turnout was higher than in 2008.

The stage was finally set for the EU-wide ratification of the Treaty of Lisbon. A last moment of tension was introduced by the Czech President, Vaclav Klaus, who inisisted on his righ not to sign the Reform Treaty although both chambers of the Czech parliament and the Czech Constitutional Court had accepted it. Eventually, some opting-out clauses were granted to the Czech Republic, especially the right to refuse the legally binding character of the Charter of Fundamental Rights of the European Union. Eventually, Klaus accepted the Treaty of Lisbon and signed. On December 1, 2009, the Treaty of Lisbon entered into force across the European Union.

One experience was evident for decades to come: No future constitutional reform of the EU institutions can hope for public recognition that will not find the support of a majority of EU citizens across all 27 member states. In this sense, a European public sphere is evolving out of the ashes of the double ratification crisis that shocked the EU between 2005 and 2009. In the end, the result of the whole decade of treaty revision was paradoxical: European constitutionalism is advancing without a European constitution. While the EU remains treaty-based, the notion of the EU as a political project has become stronger than ever.

The Treaty of Lisbon consists of 175 pages of text, 86 pages of accompanying protocols, 25 pages of annexes that renumber the articles in former treaties, and a 26 page Final Act that includes 65 separate declarations. To read and decipher the Treaty of Lisbon is no easy task. Depending upon the perspective, the Reform Treaty includes continuity, improvement and backlash at the same time. The perspective depends on whether one takes the Treaty of Nice or the Treaty Establishing a Constitution for Europe as the starting point for the judgment.

Several provisions of the Constitutional Treaty were deleted or revoked with the Treaty of Lisbon. In particular, the following elements require mentioning:

- The idea of a single constitutional text was relinquished and replaced by the idea of two treaties as the future basis of the EU's primary law.[37]
- The European symbols (flag, anthem, Europe Day, currency) were deleted from the text; hence, they will not gain legal and constitutional status although they will, of course, continue to be used across the EU. In a non-binding declaration added to the Treaty of Lisbon, sixteen EU member states have explicitly

37 Ibid.: 10. Article 1, 2(b) of the Treaty of Lisbon reads as follows: "The Union shall be founded on the present Treaty and on the Treaty on the Functioning of the European Union (hereinafter referred to as 'the Treaties'). Those two Treaties shall have the same legal value. The Union shall replace and succeed the European Community." For a comprehensive analysis of the Treaty of Lisbon see Marchetti, Andreas, and Claire Demesmay (eds.), *Der Vertrag von Lissabon: Analyse und Bewertung*, Baden-Baden: Nomos 2010.

declared their allegiance to the symbols as their recognition helps "to express the sense of community of the people in the European Union."[38]

- Highly controversial was the deletion of the commitment to "a free and undistorted" market policy in the pursuit of the EU's internal market (Treaty of Lisbon, Article 2).[39]
- The wording of the Charter of Fundamental Rights of the European Union was deleted from the text although reference was made to the Charter which therefore was to gain legal status (Treaty of Lisbon, Article 6)[40]; in a Protocol to the Treaty of Lisbon, Great Britain, Poland and the Czech Republic were granted the right not to apply the Charter of Fundamental Rights of the European Union in their countries.[41]
- The term Foreign Minister was cancelled and replaced by the introduction of a High Representative of the Union for Foreign Affairs and Security Policy with the same function, including his dual hat mandate, which makes the holder of this office at the same time Vice-President of the European Commission (Treaty of Lisbon, Article 9 E).[42]
- Any reference to the terms "European law" and "European framework law" was deleted in the legislative acts of the European Union.

There was, obviously, a price to pay for a text that should include many of the initial reforms of the Treaty Establishing a Constitution for Europe while avoiding any new public debate. The backdoor arrangements among the EU governments took place without public protocol. Nobody could properly explain why these curtailments of the originally agreed text had happened or what the benefit of the new wording might be. To the credit of the Treaty of Lisbon, several of its essential improvements over the Treaty of Nice made by the Treaty Establishing a Constitution for Europe were upheld. These included:

- Across the text of both treaties, the term European Community was replaced by European Union (Treaty of Lisbon, A. Horizontal Amendments).[43] Therefore, the Treaty Establishing the European Community (Treaties of Rome) was renamed Treaty on the Functioning of the European Union, while the Treaty on European Union (formerly Treaty of Maastricht with amendments made in the

38 Ibid.: 267.

39 Ibid.: 11. The text reads now: "The Union shall establish an internal market. It shall work for the sustainable development of Europe based on balanced economic growth and price stability, a highly competitive social market economy, aiming at full employment and social progress, and a high level of protection and improvement of the quality of the environment. It shall promote scientific and technological advance."

40 Ibid.: 13. Article 6 reads: "The Union recognises the rights, freedoms and principles set out in the Charter of Fundamental Rights of the European Union of 7 December 2000, as adapted at Strasbourg, on 12 December 2007, which shall have the same legal value as the Treaties."

41 Ibid.: 156.

42 Ibid.: 21.

43 Ibid.: 42.

Treaty of Amsterdam and in the Treaty of Nice) maintained its name.

- The three pillar structure, in place since the Treaty of Maastricht, was relinquished. The term "Common Market" was replaced by the term "Internal Market" (Treaty of Lisbon, A. Horizontal Amendments).[44] EU competencies in the fields of foreign and security policy on the one hand, in the field of justice and home affairs on the other hand were enhanced.
- The preamble of the Treaty on European Union made reference to the cultural, religious and humanist inheritance of Europe (Treaty of Lisbon, Article 1).[45] An "open, transparent and regular dialogue" between the European Union on the one hand, and the churches and religious communities on the other hand, was introduced, recognizing the special role of religion in the public life in Europe (Treaty of Lisbon, Specific Amendments, Provisions Having General Application, Article 16).[46]
- The European Union was granted legal personality (Treaty of Lisbon, Article 46A).[47] This should help the EU to get into contractual relations with international organizations, for example with the United Nations on matters of peace keeping. In a rather clumsy way, the important primacy of EU law over national law was confirmed (Treaty of Lisbon, Final Act of the Intergovernmental Conference, Declaration No.17).[48]
- The order of competencies of the European Union was clarified and simplified considerably, although any transfer of competencies remains governed by the principles of conferral, subsidiarity and proportionality (Treaty of Lisbon, Article 3b).[49] The Treaty of Lisbon distinguishes between exclusive competencies of the European Union, shared competencies of the European Union and its member states, and supporting, complementary and coordinating competencies of the EU (Treaty of Lisbon, B. Specific Amendments, Categories and Areas of Competence).[50]

44 Ibid.: 42.

45 Ibid.:10. The new text reads: "Drawing inspiration from the cultural, religious and humanist inheritance of Europe, from which have developed the universal values of the inviolable and inalienable rights of the human person, freedom, democracy, equality and the rule of law."

46 Ibid.: 51.

47 Ibid.: 38.

48 Ibid.: 256.

49 Ibid.: 12.

50 Ibid.: 46-48. The exclusive competencies of the EU include: customs union, the establishing of the competition rules necessary for the functioning of the internal market; monetary policy for the Member States whose currency is the Euro; the conservation of marine biological resources under the common fisheries policy; common commercial policy; the conclusion of international agreement when its conclusion is provided for in a legislative act of the EU. The shared competencies of the EU and its member states include: internal market; social policy; economic, social and territorial cohesion; agriculture and fisheries; environment; consumer protection; transport; trans-European networks; energy; area of freedom, security and justice; common safety concerns in public health matters; research, technological development and space; development cooperation and humanitarian aid. The supportive competencies of the EU include: protection and improvement of human health;

- Although the provisions on the legislative acts of the European Union did not introduce the terms "European law" and "European framework law," a hierarchy of norms was established which distinguishes between legislative acts, delegated acts and implementing acts. The co-decision procedure between the European Parliament and the Council was renamed "ordinary legislative procedure" (Treaty of Lisbon, B. Specific Amendments, Legal Acts of the Union).[51] It was extended to agriculture, fisheries, structural funds, justice and home affairs, thus covering most legislative acts of the EU.
- The European Parliament was reduced to 750 members plus its President and recognized as the regular co-decision body in practically all EU legislation (Treaty of Lisbon, Article 9A).[52] The future President of the European Commission was to be nominated by the European Council in light of the outcome of the elections to the European Parliament whose majority will have to approve him (Treaty of Lisbon, Article 9D).[53]
- The European Council was made a comprehensive EU institution, to be chaired by a permanent President, in office for two and a half years, renewable once, and appointed by the European Council (Treaty of Lisbon, Article 9B).[54] The Council formations were simplified and made more transparent. The Council meetings were to be public when discussing and deciding on a legislative act (Treaty of Lisbon, Article 9C).[55] Qualified majority voting was introduced as the general rule in the Council. Qualified majority voting is defined as a majority of 55 percent of states, representing 65 percent of the population while a minimum of four states is needed to constitute a blocking minority. This provision was to come into force in 2014 and could be blocked until 2017 (Treaty of Lisbon, Article 9C).[56] Only the most sensitive issues were to remain subject to unanimity: taxes, social security, citizens' rights, the seats of institutions, languages, and common foreign, security and defense policies. Enhanced cooperation was to be strengthened (Treaty of Lisbon, Article 10).[57]
- The European Commission was reduced to a number "corresponding to two thirds of the number of member states" as of 2014 (Treaty of Lisbon, Article 9D).[58] This provision (most likely beginning with 20 commissioners for 30

industry; culture; tourism; education, vocational training, youth and sport; civil protection; administrative cooperation.

51 Ibid.: 113. Article 249 A of the Treaty on European Union reads now as follows: "The ordinary legislative procedure shall consist in the joint adoption by the European Parliament and the Council of a regulation, directive of decision on a proposal from the Commission."

52 Ibid.: 17.

53 Ibid.: 20.

54 Ibid.: 17.

55 Ibid.: 19.

56 Ibid.: 18.

57 Ibid.: 22.

58 Ibid.: 19.

member states) implies that not every EU member state would any more be able to send a Commissioner to Brussels, thus strengthening the political over the national principle of representation. The stronger European political parties become, the more this trend toward a politicized European Commission would become relevant. Equal rotation between member states and regions would ensure representation of all interests.

- The general provisions for foreign, security and defense policy were outlined in detail, helping to facilitate the identification of the EU's strategic interests and objectives. The existence of the European External Action Service and the European Defense Agency were formalized (Treaty of Lisbon, Article 10-28).[59] The European Union recognizes a "solidarity clause," thus committing its member states to "act jointly in a spirit of solidarity if a Member State is object of a terrorist attack or victim of a man-made disaster" (Treaty of Lisbon, Article 188R).[60]
- The citizens of the EU were granted the right to initiate legislative processes when one million citizens address the European Council with their signature. In this case, the European Commission must "submit any appropriate proposal on matters where citizens consider that a legal act of the Union is required for the purpose of implementing the Treaties" (Treaty of Lisbon, Article 8B).[61]
- The budgetary procedures of the European Union were tightened and simplified. The European Parliament was granted full parity for the approval of the whole annual budget. The multi-annual budget of the EU would require agreement by the European Parliament (Treaty of Lisbon, Article 272-277).[62]
- The role of national parliaments in future EU legislation was strengthened (Treaty of Lisbon, Article 8c; Protocol on the Role of National Parliaments in the European Union)[63]. Based on the principle of subsidiarity national parliaments would be able to resort to an early warning mechanism in order to judge whether or not their constitutional rights are curtailed by a planned act of EU legislation.
- The Treaty of Lisbon was to offer a structured path of exit, provided a country intends to withdraw from the European Union of its free choice (Treaty of Lisbon, Article 49A).[64] This mechanism is intended to alleviate the fear in some EU member states that the future path of EU integration might overly curtail their national freedoms.
- Future procedures of constitutional revisions and amendments were explicitly

59 Ibid.: 23-38.
60 Ibid.: 100.
61 Ibid.: 15.
62 Ibid.: 123-126.
63 Ibid.: 15-16;148-149.
64 Ibid.: 40.

outlined (Treaty of Lisbon, Article 48) in order to facilitate additions or changes to the Reform Treaty. Conventions shall be the norm of future treaty revisions.[65]

In light of these provisions of the Treaty of Lisbon, politicians could claim that the "political substance" of the European Constitution was rescued. They even added several important new political commitments, including the development of a common asylum and immigration policy (Treaty of Lisbon, Article 62-63)[66], a common policy on climate change (Treaty of Lisbon, Article 174)[67], and a common energy policy (Treaty of Lisbon, Article 176A)[68]. These were important commitments for the development of a Europe of results. But by resorting again to a secretive, non-transparent Intergovernmental Conference for drafting the Treaty of Lisbon, and by deleting several important aspects from the Constitutional Treaty without substantial public and Europe-wide debate, national politicians lost the momentum for a more transparent Europe that could initiate a stronger sense of ownership through constitutional symbolism. Enhancing transparency, efficiency and democracy – that had been the original mandate formulated in the 2001 Laeken Declaration for the institutional reforms ahead. In 2007, the promise of transparency was again curtailed. The decade of treaty reform ended with two steps forward and one step backward.

It was not really a paradox that public opinion took a swing in Ireland in the course of the first ratification camapaign of the Treaty of Lisbon. The only EU member state to ratify the Treaty of Lisbon by a referendum became exposed to all possible interferences and manipulations. Ireland was perceived as voting on behalf of the whole of Europe's citizenry. Most of those who eventually said "no" to the Treaty of Lisbon on June 12, 2008 insisted to be good and loyal Europeans. They claimed a better Europe. They sent a message of disapproval of the backdoor work of EU leaders and, paradoxically, advanced the development of a European public sphere through their negative vote. For the political leaders across the EU, this was no consolation whatsoever. The greatest paradox: Europe's political leadership had given up the idea of a Constitution although more than ever the majority of Union citizens were ready for it. 66 percent of EU citizens expressed their support for a European Constitution in the summer of 2007.[69] The gap between cautious and (especially on matters of power symbolism) divided leaders and ambitious (and on many concrete issues likewise divided) citizens triggered an impasse. The European Union was ever more becoming the governance frame around the key issues of public life in Europe while time was not ripe to present a concise, simple and short constitution for an EU-wide referendum on one single day.

65 Ibid.: 38-41.
66 Ibid.: 60-62.
67 Ibid.: 87.
68 Ibid.: 88.
69 European Union, European Commission, *Eurobarometer 67: Public Opinion in the European Union*, June 2007, http://ec.europa.eu/public_opinion/archives/eb/eb67/eb_67_first_en.pdf.

This is a highly ambivalent situation for those who have hoped for a speedy new political frame around the European Union and for a happy and simple new narrative regarding the rationale of European integration. A decade has obviously not been long enough for the EU to move from incremental and cumulative constitution-building to a proper constitution in name. The European Union has introduced the term European Constitution into the public sphere. But its inner constitution is not prepared to politically implement a European Constitution yet. Nevertheless, the historical momentum has not been lost to complete failure: The European Union is more than ever recognized as a genuine body politic with its inherent constraints, conflicts of interests and slow consensus-building mechanisms. But its political leaders are at the brinks of losing control over a crisis they have triggered in the first place.

For the time being, the European Union has a cumulative constitution based on several treaties and treaty-revisions. The EU will continue to operate on the basis of this cumulative constitution as it has been doing since its beginning, growing and deepening over time. As the first decade of the twenty-first century is coming to a close, it is again time to improve the state Europe finds itself in and to reconnect European integration to the Union citizens its elites claim to serve. The Second Founding of European integration was not as smooth as it could have been. Yet, it is happening and it will continue. The constitutionalization of a united Europe has been brought a step forward. One might counterfactually suppose that the European Constitution could have been rescued in the course of the first decade of the twenty-first century if politicians had waited another year or so before launching a Europe-wide referendum instead of giving themselves a new mandate for a backdoor compromise below the level of a formal constitution. It is, however, not helpful to think too much about incorrect sequencing or bad timing. The wind of change is favoring a revival of Europe. Also, in the future, history will not consider artificial political itineraries or public sentiments its prime determinants. History will only consider the result of politics which has moved to the core of European integration and is defining the European Union more than ever after its initial five decades. In the future, the European Union institutions must be taken more seriously and likewise its citizens must be taken more seriously by its leaders. This will be the only key to close the gap of mistrust that has been spreading across the EU as deeper integration had become more necessary than ever.

3. People's Power: The Role of Referenda in European Politics

The double ratification marathon of the European Constitution and the Reform Treaty has led to a paradoxical result: It derailed the original Constitution and its repair successor but it initiated the first real constitutional debate in the history of the European Union. The double ratification procedure and the subsequent double ratification crisis became part of the emerging European constitutional discourse. This was rather unintended by the political leadership. In fact, the ratification issue was not at all properly prepared either by the Constitutional Convention or the European Council, neither in 2004 nor in 2007. The Treaty Establishing a Constitution for Europe and subsequently the Reform Treaty had to be ratified in all EU member states and in the European Parliament before coming into force. It would have been a sign of political wisdom to properly organize the ratification marathon. One option was that the governments of all countries would have agreed to ratify the initial Constitutional Treaty during the same day or at least during the same week. Not doing so turned out to be a major setback for the process. In the absence of an EU-wide referendum, the ratification method was uncoordinated. Most countries favored the ratification by their parliaments. Others were constitutionally obliged to hold a public referendum. Some just wanted to write history: When French President Jacques Chirac announced his desire to hold a referendum in France he took his EU partners by surprise. This surprise turned into the deepest frustration when it became clear that several other countries were also to hold a referendum. The fate of the Treaty Establishing a Constitution of Europe was no longer in the hand of a European organ or of the political elites running the daily business of the EU. The European Constitution fall prey to national decisions that might be more influenced by domestic considerations than by the content, usefulness and importance of the European Constitution. In the end, it became evident that the European Constitution was held hostage by a minority of member states representing a minority of EU citizens. This was a pilot's error, not a people's fault.

While the favorable vote of the European Parliament on January 12, 2005, could be taken for granted (500 deputies endorsed the European Constitution, 137 voted against and 40 abstained), the parliamentary ratification procedure in several countries did not pose particular difficulties, beginning with the parliamentary ratification in Lithuania (November 11, 2004) and Hungary (December 20, 2004). Referenda were soon announced in Spain, France, the Netherlands, Luxembourg, Portugal, Denmark, Poland, Ireland, Great Britain and the Czech Republic.

Referenda on matters relating to European integration were not a new phenomenon in Europe. Until the signing of the Treaty Establishing the Constitution for Europe in 2004, 40 referenda had taken place about a multitude of aspects relevant for the further evolution of European integration. In some cases a referendum concerned the issue of EU accession or the continuation of EU membership. Some referenda dealt with bilateral relations of a country not wanting to become a member of the EU and yet enhancing its mode of cooperation with the EU. One referendum decided about membership of other countries. Various referenda were held on matters of a constitutional deepening of the integration process, mostly required by national constitutions. Referenda on matters of European integration began in the 1970's. They became more noticeable and contested with the "deepening" of the integration process following the conclusion of the Single European Act in 1986. This was a clear indication of the fact that European integration was increasingly impacting the national political and constitutional system of its member states. It proved that the European system of multilevel governance and pooled sovereignty had reached a new stage of relevance.

A "deepening" of the integration process did indeed take place. The constitutional legitimacy of any new step of European integration can only matter if it will bring about substantial value added and thus substantially "more" political and constitutional integration. The Treaty Establishing a Constitution for Europe was to lay the ground for the further transfer of sovereignty over time. It was therefore not surprising that the need for a referendum was raised in a number of EU member states, while others upheld the authority of their constitutionally elected and authorized parliaments to vote on further matters of sovereignty transfer.

In the past, the results of referenda on European integration had indicated different patterns of voting behavior depending on whether a referendum was binding or non-binding, obligatory or deliberate, and whether it was called upon by a government or an opposition.[70] Until the referenda on the European Constitution became prominent, two cases of past referendum trajectories were noteworthy exceptions from the general rule: The two referenda in Denmark in 1992 and in 1993 on the Treaty of Maastricht and the two referenda in Ireland in 2001 and 2003 on the Treaty of Nice. In both cases, the result of the first referendum did not only affect the country that was practicing its constitutional right of referendum. Its result affected all other EU member states and the EU institutions as well. In fact, they were taken hostage in their pursuit of EU integration. From both the point of view of democratic theory and integration theory it thus seemed plausible that efforts were made by the EU bodies "to repair" the damage caused by the first rejection of the European proposal presented to the people of Denmark and Ireland.

Table 1: Referenda Held on European Integration[71]

Country, Date	*Subject*	*Proportion of "Yes" votes*
France, April 23, 1972	EEC expansion	68.3 %
Ireland, May 10, 1972	EC accession	83.1 %
Norway, September 24-26, 1972	EC accession	46.5 %
Denmark (Greenland included), October 2, 1972	EC accession	63.3 %

70 See Hug, Simon, *Voices of Europe: Citizens, Referendums and European Integration*, Lanham: Rowman&Littlefield, 2002.

71 Sources: Hug, Simon, *Voices of Europe*, op.cit.: 27; European Union, European Commission, *The Accession Process*, https://europa.eu.int/comm/enlargement/negotiations/accession_process.htm.

Switzerland, December 3, 1972	Free Trade Treaty with EEC	72.5 %
Great Britain, June 5, 1975	EC membership	67.2 %
Greenland, February 23, 1982	EC membership	45.9 %
Denmark, February 27, 1986	Common market	56.2 %
Ireland, May 26, 1987	Common market	69.9 %
Italy, June 18, 1989	European Constitution process	88.1 %
Denmark, June 3, 1992	Treaty of Maastricht	49.3 %
Ireland, June 18, 1992	Treaty of Maastricht	68.7 %
France September 20, 1992	Treaty of Maastricht	51.1 %
Switzerland, December 6, 1992	EEA accession	49.7 %
Liechtenstein, December 12, 1992	EEA accession	55.8 %
Denmark, May 18, 1993	Treaty of Maastricht	56.8 %
Austria, June 12, 1994	EU accession	66.6 %
Finland, October 16, 1994	EU accession	56.9 %
Sweden, November 13, 1994	EU accession	52.7 %
Åland-Islands, November 20, 1994	EU accession	73.6 %
Norway, November 28, 1994	EU accession	47.8 %
Liechtenstein, April 9, 1995	EEA accession	55.9 %
Switzerland, June 8, 1997	EU accession	25.9 %
Ireland, May 22, 1998	Treaty of Amsterdam	61.7 %
Denmark, May 28, 1998	Treaty of Amsterdam	55.1 %
Switzerland, May 21, 2000	Bilateral treaties with the EU	67.2 %
Denmark, September 28, 2000	Euro accession	46.9 %
Switzerland, March 4, 2001	EU accession	23.2 %
Ireland, June 7, 2001	Treaty of Nice	46.1 %
Ireland, October 19, 2002	Treaty of Nice	62.9 %
Malta, March 8, 2003	EU accession	53.6 %
Slovenia, March 23, 2003	EU accession	89.2 %
Hungary, April 12, 2003	EU accession	83.8 %
Lithuania, May 10-11, 2003	EU accession	91.1 %
Slovakia, May 16-17, 2003	EU accession	92.5 %
Poland, June 7-8, 2003	EU accession	77.4 %
Czech Republic, June 13-14, 2003	EU accession	77.3 %
Estonia, September 14, 2003	EU accession	66.9 %
Sweden, September 14, 2003	Accession to the Euro	41.8 %
Latvia, September 20, 2003	EU accession	67.0 %
Spain, February 20, 2005	European Constitution	76.7 %
France, May 29, 2005	European Constitution	45.3 %
The Netherlands, June 1, 2005	European Constitution	38.4 %

Switzerland, June 5, 2005	Accession to Schengen Agreement	54.6 %
Luxembourg, July 10, 2005	European Constitution	56.5 %
Ireland, June 12, 2008	Treaty of Lisbon	46.6 %
Ireland, October 2, 2009	Treaty of Lisbon	67.1 %

In the case of Denmark, the European Union recognized some of the Danish citizens' concerns and renegotiated Danish conditions for accepting the Treaty of Maastricht. The four "opting out clauses" according to which Denmark was not obliged to accept future community policies if it did not want to do so caused great concern among integration purists. They added to the worry about a multi-speed EU that was losing inner cohesion. This fear was piling up until the Constitutional Convention began to address exactly this danger. The outcome of the Danish referendum crisis finally opened the way for the introduction of full Economic and Monetary Union and hence the euro in twelve EU member states. This was a consolation for all those who had second thoughts about the politics of "opting-out clauses" that could set a dangerous precedent.

In the Irish case of 2001, EU partners and institutions remained firm and rejected the possibility of a new set of opting out clauses. The unaltered Treaty of Nice was presented again to the Irish voters two years after they had rejected it on the ground that it would intervene too much into their national sovereignty. This unusual procedure caused great concern among democracy purists as to whether or not the repetition of a vote on the same issue would sufficiently recognize the maturity of a democratic people or instead ridicule it. In the Irish case of 2008, EU partners accepted moderate opting-out clauses and, more importantly, rhetoric reassurances that allowed Irish politicians to present the Treaty of Lisbon a second time to their voters for ratification.

Observers of and participants in the ratification marathon on the European Constitution could not take consolation in EU-wide public opinion but had to wait until the ratification procedure was completed in each single country. Yet, opinion polls were comforting for those fearing another constitutional backlash in one of the countries perceived as being euroskeptical. In November 2003, a Eurobarometer poll had shown 67 percent of EU citizens (in all future twenty-five member states) favorable to a European Constitution.[72] In February 2004, after the failed European Council meeting of December 2003, 62 percent of EU citizens (again in all twenty-five future member states) wished that their own governments accepted compromises in order to save the

72 European Union, European Commission, *Flash Eurobarometer 142*, November 10, 2003, http://ec.europa.eu/public_opinion/flash/fl142_convention.pdf.

Constitution from failure; the percentage of those favoring a European Constitution had risen to 77 percent.[73]

Some had suggested a Europe-wide referendum to enhance legitimacy of the European Constitution. As unrealistic as this was, the idea reflected academic arguments concerning the practical implementation of legitimacy considerations.[74] The political reality across the European Union was not yet ready for such an ambitious idea. As a consequence, individual EU member states got veto power over the Treaty Establishing a Constitution for Europe, raising delicate questions of democratic legitimacy in a multilevel governance system.

The first referendum on the European Constitution was held on February 20, 2005, in Spain. 76.7 percent of the voters said "yes" to the European Constitution. Only three days later, in an unusual joint session, the French National Assembly and the French Senate changed the country's constitution to pave the way for a referendum in France. It is ironic that Nicolas Sarkozy, then Chairman of the UMP Party, was among those particularly favoring a referendum. He was joined by President Jacques Chirac who considered Sarkozy his main internal rival in the struggle for the presidential election 2007. Immediately after the way was made free for a referendum in France, domestic disputes completely unrelated to the European Constitution began to dominate the agenda of French public life and politics: Strikes and mass demonstrations of post and bank workers, at airports, among telecommunications workers and academics created an increasingly depressing atmosphere. Their main concern was the future of the French welfare state. Opponents of the European Constitution linked the domestic crisis in France with, as they saw it, "neo-liberal" policies institutionalized by the European Constitution. The support for the European Constitution and for President Chirac dropped – and it was not always clear who of the two became more unpopular. Public debates about the possibly negative effects of globalization began to dominate the debate about the economic policies of the EU. Those supporting the European Constitution with the argument that it would guarantee a more democratic, efficient and transparent EU became a minority. Even the President's support for the European Constitution became counterproductive, and it was perceived as half-hearted. In the end, the negative result of the referendum on May 29, 2005, was beyond any doubt: While 45 percent of those who had gone to the polls said "yes," 54.8 percent rejected the European Constitution. Voter turnout was only 69.2 percent. There is a general consensus that the vote was largely a vote of no-confidence in President Chirac and the policy of his government. Prime Minister Raffarin had to resign. There was little

73 European Union, European Commission, *Flash Eurobarometer 159*, February 17, 2004, http://ec.europa.eu/public_opinion/flash/fl159_fut_const.pdf.

74 See Esposito, Frédéric, "The European Referendum: A Tool to Legitimate the European Integration Process?," in: Nagel, Stuart (ed.), *Policymaking and Democracy: A Multinational Anthology*, Lanham: Lexington Books, 2003: 15-37; also Weale, Albert *Democratic Citizenship and the European Union*, Manchester: Manchester University Press, 2005.

consolation in calling the result a victory of fear.[75] The real loser was the Constitutional Treaty.

Only three days later, the majority of voters in the Netherlands also rejected the Constitution: Only 38.4 percent said "yes" in that country. Voter turnout was only 62.8 percent. The shock wave across the EU and beyond was substantial. A Swiss referendum on June 5, 2005, ended with overwhelming support for a bilateral agreement between the EU and Switzerland for the usually euroskeptical country's accession to the Schengen Agreement on border control (54.6 percent voted "yes"). This was only a small consolation that technical business of an integrative nature was to continue in Europe. But the momentum to ratify the first ever "European Constitution" was lost. The courageous decision of Luxembourg Prime Minister Jean-Claude Juncker to go ahead with a referendum in the Grand-Duchy ended as a personal triumph for one of the most respected European politicians: 56.5 percent said "yes" in Luxembourg on July 10, 2005. Eventually, also Latvia, Cyprus, Malta, Belgium, Estonia (May 9, 2006) and Finland ratified the Constitutional Treaty. Two-thirds of all EU member states (18 of 27) representing a majority of Union citizens had ratified the European Constitution. It did not help.

Great Britain, Denmark, Ireland, Portugal, Poland, the Czech Republic and Sweden postponed their respective dates for ratification, mostly intended to be held via referendum. The European Council of June 16-17, 2005, still under shock after the French and Dutch referenda, declared a period of reflection while accepting the continuation of the ratification process and postponing the anticipated implementation of the Constitution from November 2006 until the summer of 2007. At first, academic reactions described the EU as being trapped by its constitutional ambition.[76] The subsequent positive votes in seven countries did keep the political responsibility alive for finding a formal and substantial solution to the ratification crisis. They served as a barrier against a new tide of Euroskepticism among the public and several governments of EU member states. While some of them had come to power after the signing of the Treaty Establishing a Constitution for Europe, others had capitalized on the ratification crisis by turning more euroskeptical and retreating from their own signature under the original treaty. But the eighteen positive votes could not rescue the Treaty Establishing a Constitution for Europe. France and the Netherlands had held the rest of the EU

75 See Schild, Joachim "Ein Sieg der Angst – das gescheiterte französische Verfassungsreferendum," *Integration* 28.3 (2005): 187-200. After the failed referendums in France and in the Netherlands, the possible options for European policy makers were immediately evident as suggested by this author: a) declaring the treaty dead; b) presenting it again for a second referendum; c) making additions to the text that could console those who were afraid of losing identity, sovereignty and social stability under the conditions of globalization; d) dividing the Treaty Establishing a Constitution for Europe into two treaties, one dealing with the fundamental institutional provisions, the other one covering the contingent policy issues: see Kühnhardt, Ludger, *Erweiterung und Vertiefung: Die Europäische Union im Neubeginn*, Baden-Baden: Nomos, 2005: 151-164.

76 Diedrichs, Udo, and Wolfgang Wessels, "Die Europäische Union in der Verfassungsfalle: Analysen, Entwicklungen und Optionen," *Integration* 28.4 (2005): 287-306.

hostage; some rather reluctant countries were happily hiding behind the French and Dutch results, and altogether the political elite in the EU, for once, had become speechless and disoriented. The political elite in the EU had failed; it had failed technically to better anticipate and manage the ratification process, and it had failed politically to convincingly present the value added of the European Constitution to the Union's citizens in two key countries. It was no consolation to put the blame on French President Chirac alone. The fact that so many Union citizens in some of the most pro-European countries simply did not believe that the Treaty Establishing a Constitution for Europe would bring about more democracy, efficiency and transparency should have been a more serious warning signal for politicians across the EU.[77] In fact, it meant the deepest crisis of confidence and hence legitimacy for the European project. The Union citizens wanted to see political results as a consequence of European integration. Many were worried about the effects of globalization. They were under the impression that welfare state reforms in the EU would only mean a reduction in social security for them personally. They did not believe that European integration as presented by the work of the current political leadership would generate value added for their own lives. Often, they almost felt offended that politicians were putting all their energy into institutional reforms while the citizens of several European countries – most notably France and Germany, the former dynamos of integration – were going through a serious economic recession. They were concerned about migration and radical Islam, not about the weighing of votes in obscure EU organs.

The effect of the first ratification shock was twofold: On the one hand, negotiations about institutional reforms of the European Union were returned to backdoor politics under the framework of an Intergovernmental Conference. The Intergovernmental Conference that opened in July 2007 was mandated to repair the broken promises and achievements of the European Constitution. On the other hand, the negative outcome of the referenda in France and in the Netherlands initiated, in a paradoxical and counter-intuitive way, the first broad constitutional discourse across the European Union. The second ratification shock followed the same pattern and triggered the same initial reflexes among politicians as the first one three years earlier: After the Irish "no" vote in 2008, shock and awe were followed by busy activities to come to the rescue of the Treaty of Lisbon. Blaming the Irish or, even worse, blaming the people of Europe in general could only be counterproductive. Yet, the immediate political reactions in June 2008 were repetitions of the set of reactions in 2005. The most convincing initial answer to rescue the Treaty of Lisbon was the effort to implement useful and consensual elements of the Treaty through secondary EU law. Eventually, and to the surprise of all skeptics, the Treaty of Lisbon was ratified across the European Union and entered into

77 See Niedermayer, Oskar, "Die öffentliche Meinung zum Europäischen Verfassungsvertrag," in: Jopp, Mathias, and Saskia Matl (eds.), *Der Vertrag über eine Verfassung für Europa*, op.cit.: 435-449.

force on December 1, 2009. While the day may come for a concise, short and readeable European Constitution, it will now be on the political leadership in Europe to work for the next years, if not decades under the conditions laid out in the Treaty of Lisbon and to generate substance and results. The Treaty of Lisbon improves governance conditions in the EU. Governance results must be generated by those acting under its umbrella.

Eventually, this will be the only way to reconnect with the people of Europe and to revitalize respect for the EU institutions and procedures. To make a debate about more efficient, democratic and transparent institutions of the EU more interesting and relevant for EU citizens requires their trust in the relevance and impact of this work. More than ever, political leaders will be measured by their ability to base their important and noble work on tangible political options and to present accountable results to the citizens they represent. This will be the only way out of the valley of mistrust in the multilevel system of European governance. In the end, thus is the conclusion of a fascinating but also irritating reform decade: The Union citizens seem to be ahead of their political elites in their quest for a constitutionalized Europe of results. While the first effect is regrettable, the second effect is unprecedented in European constitution-building. In fact, it is encouraging for the ongoing Second Founding of European integration.

4. Cumulative Constitution-Building: From Rome to Lisbon

Ever since the mid-twentieth century, the cumulative evolution of a European Constitution has been part of the integration process on the continent. From the outset, interstate-treaties were the basis for European integration. But the parameters of their purpose and legitimacy, their authority and connection with public opinion have enormously changed and broadened over five decades of European constitution-building. For five decades, a pre-constitution of Europe evolved as product of gradual and cumulative treaty-based integration, moved forward by political will and experience, by crisis and adaptation, by interpretation and judicial review. The cumulative European Constitution, based on consecutive treaties and treaty revisions remains unfinished business. This genuine European method of constitutionalizing the process of integration may well prevail while the European Union is encountering its future beyond the adaptational crisis of its Second Founding. As a point of reference for measuring the legitimacy of European integration, the state in which Europe finds itself will certainly remain more important than the texts that constitute the political order of Europe.

The trajectory has never been set for a definitive constitutional goal since the European Economic Community was founded.[78] Cumulative, gradual and incremental

78 On the path toward the EEC see Loth, Wilfried, *Der Weg nach Europa: Geschichte der europäischen Integration 1939-1957*, Göttingen: Vandenhoeck&Ruprecht, 1990.

constitution-building has accompanied European integration since its beginning. On March 25, 1957, the Treaties of Rome were signed, giving existence to the European Economic Community (EEC) and to the European Atomic Community (EURATOM). Unlike the Treaty Establishing a Constitution for Europe in 2004, the Treaties of Rome (officially called Treaty Establishing the European Economic Community and Treaty Establishing the European Atomic Energy Community) were simply an act of interstate-diplomacy. They were ratified by all six national parliaments concerned and took effect on January 1, 1958.

The EEC Treaty affirmed in its preamble the determination of the signatory states to establish "the foundations of an ever closer union."[79] In reality, a customs union was created. A twelve-year transitional period was agreed upon to abolish tariffs among the six member states of the EEC. As of 1968, all tariffs were in fact abandoned two years earlier than expected. At the same time, the EEC began to establish common tariffs for all products entering the EEC while also framing its notorious Common Agricultural Policy. The European Common Market agreed upon in Rome was in fact exclusively a free circulation of goods. The four principles outlined in the Treaties of Rome – freedom of goods, freedom of persons, freedom of capital, freedom of services – remained limited. A genuine impulse for the Common Market truly worth the name did not come about before the Single European Act of 1986.

The Treaties of Rome established the European Commission as supranational authority with the task of protecting the Treaties of the EEC. The European Parliamentary Assembly remained a representation of delegates from national parliaments without any relevant powers. The Court of Justice was established and grew into a strong supranational force poised to enhance the implementation of community law. The Economic and Social Committee was established and has remained a consultative body to this day. Nevertheless, the Treaties of Rome established a path toward treaty-based integration that was to develop its own constitutionalism. It laid the groundwork for the gradual, incremental evolution of a European pre-constitution to which it also belonged and on which it was based.

The Treaties of Rome were a solid basis nobody really questioned. It had taken more than a decade to implement the original aim of the Treaties of Rome, namely to establish a viable customs union in the European Economic Community. But the first modification – and in fact "deepening" – of the original Treaties of Rome took place only in 1986. In 1985 Jacques Delors had become President of the European Commission, giving this body stronger leadership and bringing to full potential its force to pave the way for the EEC as a whole. Since 1981, French Socialist François Mitterrand had been President of France. Christian Democrat Helmut Kohl had been

79 *The Rome, Maastricht and Amsterdam Treaties, The Treaty on European Union (Treaty of Maastricht) and the Treaty Establishing the European Communities (Treaty of Rome) Amended by the Treaty of Amsterdam: Comparative Texts*, Genval: Euroconfidentiel 1999: 6.

German Chancellor since 1982. These two leaders formed the most successful Franco-German partnership possible. It was the beginning of an exceptionally long period in integration progress guided by strong pro-European leadership with Delors as Commission President and Mitterrand President of France until 1995, and Kohl staying in office until 1998.

Following a decision of the European Council, representatives of the member state governments came together recurrently as of June 29, 1985, in order to negotiate treaty revisions. The format of these negotiations came to be known as Intergovernmental Conferences. After its work was concluded, the Single European Act was signed in Luxembourg and The Hague on February 17, 1986, and came into effect after ratification in the nine EC parliaments on July 1, 1987. This was the most visible effort to properly and thoroughly implement the original EEC goal of a Common Market as a market without frontiers, based on economic and social cohesion, a strengthened European Monetary system and the beginning of Europe as a social area. The Single European Act legalized the European Council as a periodical meeting of the Heads of State and Government, intended to discuss and decide fundamental matters relevant to the EEC. The competencies of the European Parliament – directly elected for the first time in 1979 for a five-year period – were marginally expanded. Measures to better coordinate monetary policies among the member states were introduced. To achieve the objective of regional cohesion, the instruments of Structural Funds, Regional Funds and Social Funds were introduced. The most important achievement of the Single European Act was agreement on concrete measures to progressively implement a common market over a period of five years, concluding on December 31, 1992. Finally, an area with freedom of goods, persons, capital and services was to realize the original goal of the Treaties of Rome. 35 years after its initiation, European integration could move to another level.

During the 1980's, the deplored phenomena of "Eurosclerosis" had become tangible for everybody not shying away from economic reality. Europe was confronted with enormous difficulties to overcome the impact of the oil crises of the 1970's and their long aftermath as well as the burden from welfare states without maintaining a strong base for growth-led productivity. While the European Community enjoyed peace, the base for its prosperity seemed to shrink. "Reaganomics" in the United States gave a strong impulse to the economic recovery of the US, echoed by "Thatcherism" in Great Britain. The economic rise of Japan and the "little Tigers" in Southeast Asia (Thailand, Indonesia, Singapore, Malaysia, Taiwan) was felt as another challenge, if not threat to Europe. It was time to move ahead, out of the perception of being incapable of developing strong, productive and ultimately also communitarian policies, if the European integration project was to have a future.

The commitment of French President François Mitterrand, German Chancellor Helmut Kohl and EC Commission President Jacques Delors to complete the European

Community's Common Market was carried further by their ambition to reinvigorate the institutional and political sides of the European Community. The Single European Act was to be followed by a Political Union and an Economic and Monetary Union.

On June 26-27, 1989, the EC member states agreed to initiate two Intergovernmental Conferences in order to pave the way for the definitive establishment of a monetary union and to give new impulses for the realization of a political union. After the fall of the Berlin Wall on November 9, 1989, German Chancellor Helmut Kohl was determined to couple imminent German unification with further progress toward political integration in Europe. The two Intergovernmental Conferences began their work on December 14-15, 1990. Treaty revisions were, again, to come about as a product of negotiations among government officials, with representatives of the European Parliament and of the European Commission invited to participate.

German unification accelerated the creation of an Economic and Monetary Union, although monetary union was not a precondition for German unification, and German unification was not the cause for achieving monetary union. However, the second Intergovernmental Conference on Political Union was less successful. Fundamental differences about national interests regarding European integration remained irreconcilable. In the context of these experiences, the scholarly analysis favoring the intergovernmental perspective felt confirmed.[80] As already sensed during the path toward the Single European Act, the Treaty of Maastricht (officially called Treaty on European Union) seemed to strengthen the European nation state through mutually recognized common goals. To some analysts, it did not seem to strengthen the supranational ambition of the European integration project. At the end, this perspective turned out to be wrong, or at least insufficient as monetary union led to the biggest transfer of national sovereignty so far experienced during the integration process.[81]

On December 9-10, 1991, the European Council completed the work of the Intergovernmental Conference in Maastricht and agreed on the basics of what was to be called the Treaty of Maastricht. The Foreign Ministers of the European Community officially signed the treaty on February 2, 1992, after some "post-last minute" compromises were reached. Yet, the Treaty of Maastricht ran into difficulties during the process of ratification. The Danish population rejected the treaty in a referendum on June 3, 1992, with only 49.3 percent of the population voting with "yes." The EC Commission and political leaders in all other Community countries were shocked. They had finally agreed on a path toward Economic and Monetary Union and now it seemed a stillborn concept. They began to embark on creative measures on how to reverse the Danish attitude driven by fear to lose national identity and sovereignty with an increase in integration. The myth of an emerging "European Super-State" made headlines,

80 See Moravcsik, Andrew, *The Choice for Europe: Social Purpose and State Power from Messina to Maastricht*, op.cit.

81 See Kühnhardt, Ludger *Europäische Union und föderale Idee: Europapolitik in der Umbruchzeit*, Munich: Beck, 1993.

exaggerated often, but useful whenever "Brussels-bashing" helped to gain domestic political support in constituencies driven more by fear than by lasting hope in so far as the integration idea was concerned. As integration became truly serious, time was needed for many Europeans to properly digest its impact.

The Danish government successfully negotiated four "opting-out clauses": They stated that Denmark was not obliged to participate in fundamental union projects if national interests would think it inappropriate, most notably as far as full monetary union, a Union citizenship, a common justice and home affairs policy, and a common foreign and defense policy were concerned. A second referendum in Denmark, held on May 18, 1993 saw 56.8 percent of Danes voting in favor of the Treaty of Maastricht, revised only for their country. The next stage toward Economic and Monetary Union could begin. The Treaty of Maastricht came into effect on November 1, 1993. Since then, the European Community has been renamed European Union. A new period of European integration has begun and with it the paradigmatic shift from economic primacy to a politicized Union.

The result of the Intergovernmental Conference leading to the Treaty of Maastricht did not satisfy those in the European Community favoring deeper political integration as a necessary complementary measure to prepare for a successful Economic and Monetary Union. The Treaty of Maastricht based the structure of the EU on three pillars, indicating the difference between supranational and intergovernmental elements of the integration process. The first pillar alluded to the Community policies set out in the original treaty and included community policies, economic and monetary policies and the newly established Union citizenship. The second and third pillars outlined the newly emerging yet still intergovernmental policies in the field of foreign relations as well as justice and home affairs. Thus the Treaty of Maastricht began to open the daunting way toward a Common European Foreign and Security Policy. Union Citizenship, introduced by the Treaty of Maastricht, remained a complementary addition granted through the member states of the EU. The Treaty of Maastricht introduced the instrument of Cohesion Funds to EU policies and created the Committee of the Regions as a consultative body.

On March 29, 1996, the European Council initiated a new Intergovernmental Conference. Designed like the first one and often with the same representatives from both national governments and the European Parliament, it drafted the Treaty of Amsterdam, agreed upon by the European Council in Amsterdam on June 17, 1997, and signed by the EU Foreign Ministers on October 2, 1997. The achievements of this next step in European Constitution-building were minimal and the Treaty of Amsterdam was widely criticized as being a failure. It added certain elements to the concept of enforced cooperation in foreign and security policies as well as in justice and home affairs. Both were barely noted by the larger European public except for the creation of the office of a High Representative for the Common Foreign and Security Policy of the EU. Former

NATO Secretary General Javier Solana gave profile to the position that remained constitutionally weak and, in some ways, contradictory to the work of the EU Commissioner in charge of foreign relations.

As in the case of the Treaty of Maastricht, even before its formal ratification, the Treaty of Amsterdam encountered much criticism in all member states for being insufficient as far as the necessary institutional reforms of a lasting functional European Union were concerned. Yet, this time, the ratification procedure went smoothly and on May 1, 1999, the Treaty of Amsterdam went into force and was added to the emerging pre-constitution of Europe.[82]

The Treaty of Amsterdam explicitly opened the way for another new Intergovernmental Conference, realizing the limits of its own work. This Intergovernmental Conference was resumed on February 15, 2000. It was mandated to resolve three critical issues relevant in light of the upcoming and presumably largest enlargement of the EU that had ever taken place: the weighing of votes in the Council, the possibility of expanding qualified majority voting in the Council, and the size and composition of the future European Commission. Its results were presented to the European Council in December 2000 in Nice, leading to the Treaty of Nice agreed upon after the longest ever meeting of the European Council on December 11, 2000. The memory of this Summit meeting of Heads of State and Government casts a lasting shadow over the political leadership of the European Union. More than anything else, their final negotiations were driven by the ambition to raise veto powers rather than by efforts to make the European Union effectively work in anticipation of the upcoming enlargement to a host of post-communist countries of Central Europe. The Nice negotiations and their highly ambivalent result were the culmination of a struggle between two contrasting understandings of European integration: On the one hand, the nation states – and in fact that meant the national governments – wanted to remain masters of the Treaties. Most of them did not want to accept a transfer of sovereignty to the EU level while at the same time the biggest among them did not want to allow for voting mechanisms in the Council that could work to their detriment. France and Germany, locomotives for integration projects in the past, had turned to becoming veto powers scared of their partners and their potential claims and also suspicious among themselves. During the same time, the discourse on a democratic deficit of the integration process took ground.

To prevent the EU, enlarged to twenty-seven or more members, from becoming incapable of deciding, the Commission had proposed to generalize the principle of qualified majority voting in the Council. After long debates, the European Council agreed to expand the mechanism of qualified majority voting in forty cases, most of

82 For the texts see *The Rome, Maastricht and Amsterdam Treaties, The Treaty on European Union (Treaty of Maastricht) and the Treaty Establishing the European Communities (Treaty of Rome) Amended by the Treaty of Amsterdam: Comparative Texts*, op.cit.

them rather technical. The most controversial issues, such as migration, taxes, and audiovisual cultural cooperation remained unanimous. More intricate were the debates about the future weighing of votes. Germany, after unification the EU country with the largest population, intended to re-weight its vote in the Council. France insisted on continuous parity with Germany, not only in the Council, but also in the European Parliament. Other countries followed with efforts to reposition themselves and against others, for instance the Netherlands and Belgium. A highly complicated result was found. It was more a sign of sophisticated mathematics than an expression of solidarity in a common union. It strengthened veto powers to the utmost while leaving in doubt whether this could ever help bring about more efficient decisions in the enlarged EU. In order to pass a motion in the Council, 71.26 percent of votes were said to be necessary while this figure would go up to 74.7 percent in a European Union of twenty-seven countries.

The size of the future Commission was limited to a maximum of twenty-seven commissioners, up from twenty before. This would imply that all countries would have not more than one Commissioner in the future. Should the EU increase to more than twenty-seven member states, a new decision on the number of Commissioners would have to be taken. The Treaty of Nice was the low point of the efforts of the EU Commission to safeguard the community spirit against the prevailing and seemingly increasing bad habit of a veto culture. It also marked the low point of authority of the political leaders in the EU. And it finally questioned the usefulness of further Intergovernmental Conferences as a means to reform the institutions of the Union. The failure of Nice became the beginning of a more democratic and public discourse about the future of Europe. Increasingly, EU citizens realized that European integration was becoming relevant and impacting their lives as well as the political and economic structures of their countries. The fact that the Nice summit had adopted the Charter of Fundamental Rights of the European Union did not reduce the frustration with its results, but rather confirmed the need to tackle the democratic deficit and to bring European integration back into the public sphere if it were to advance further. Constitution-building had to turn from obscurity into the limelight of public deliberation if it were to continue with success.

The results of the Treaty of Nice hardly satisfied anybody in the European Union. It could not come as a surprise that only 46.1 percent of the Irish population said "yes" to the Treaty of Nice when asked in a referendum on June 7, 2001. Unlike those who thought that the Treaty of Nice did not go far enough in outlining the working principles for an enlarged union, many Irish voters considered the arrangements of the Treaty of Nice already too strong an infringement on Irish sovereignty and autonomous national decision-making. Yet, the Treaty of Nice was not revised and Ireland was not offered any opting-out clauses equivalent to Denmark's almost a decade earlier. Instead, the Irish government presented the same Treaty of Nice for a second referendum to its population one year later. On October 19, 2002, 62.9 percent of the Irish voted with "yes." An ambiguous understanding of democratic decision-making rescued the notorious Treaty of Nice from rejection by the citizens it claimed to serve. On February 1, 2003, it came into effect.[83]

The main dilemma of European integration had become more evident than ever before with the whole operation surrounding the Treaty of Nice: The EU was not suffering from an abstract democratic deficit. All its member states were flourishing democracies, the very reason why the Copenhagen Criteria had been formulated in 1993 as measurement for the possible accession of post-communist and other European countries such as Turkey. The main dilemma was the governance asymmetry between the democratic member states of the EU on the one hand and the semi-developed democratic governance structures on the EU level and in the multidimensional web between the EU and its member states on the other hand. While increasingly political authority had to be transferred to the EU level, the EU level was not sufficiently democratized by the EU's member states. They were and continue to be afraid of losing sovereignty and political authority to the EU level of European governance. This constellation has turned into a power struggle over the appropriate balance between vertical and horizontal forms of governance in the European Union. Inevitably, the call for a more substantial institutional reform was to be linked to the question about the state in which Europe was finding itself. From this metaphoric debate it was not a long way to raise the matter of a political constitution in order to frame the future operation of the European Union and all its constituent parts.

Constitutions define political power and limit it at the same time. They echo social developments and claims, and they outline the institutional path to deal with the next phase in social and political evolution. For the European Union, a constitution would always mean the continuation of institutional and constitutional integration while the growth of political identity would primarily be shaped through practical experiences and success-based memories. In 2000, the EU was beginning to refocus its trajectory. It would not go unchallenged to move from a community of organs to a community of fate. This had not been easy in all cases of constitutional-based nation-building in Europe. Yet, there was consensus in Europe that constitutionalizing the European Union would not mean the abandonment of traditional nation states. Europe would remain a compromise between a Union of States and a Union of Citizens.

During the first decade of the twenty-first century, the European Union embarked on further cumulative constitution-building as a step in the process of broadening rule of law through the *acquis communautaire*. In doing so, it also broadened the legal base for the political processes across the EU and its horizontal and vertical institutions. The

83 European Union, *Treaty of Nice Amending the Treaty of European Union, the Treaties Establishing the European Communities and Certain Related Act*, Luxembourg: Office for Official Publications of the European Communities, 2001.

interpretation of the EU's constitution-building might remain the prerogative of academics, lawyers and judges. The ultimate legitimacy test is, however, not different from any democracy participating in the European integration process. Popular support is needed more than ever. No matter the details of any constitutional arrangement, eventually, peoples' power will decide Europe's constitution and the quality of the work of those acting under its umbrella. Some politicians seem to fear the Union citizens while certainly many others are hoping to finally reconcile the Union of States with the interests of the citizens of the Union. The search for a contract between the Union citizens and the Union institutions, and those acting in these institutions, remains a daily necessity. No single European treaty can resolve the queries or skepticism about Europe's political, economic, social or cultural constitution.

With the Second Founding of the European Union, democracy has reached European integration politics in a very direct way. Politics, more than anything else, was to define the future of European democracy in its genuine multilevel governance system. The cumulative constitution-building of European integration is the most visible foundation of the genuinely political character of European integration. Both processes are mutually reinforcing each other. Both, the constitutional and the political dimension of European integration can, so it seems, only advance through adaptational crises that eventually strengthen and deepen European integration. Beyond the most recent experience of a turbulent decade, it remains partly an unresolved promise and unavoidably a continuous challenge for the EU to advance simultaneously democracy, efficiency and transparency and keep all three principles in balance.

5. Interpreting Europe's Constitution

Public interest in European integration has grown faster than ever before as a consequence of the debate over the frozen European Constitution.[84] Public interest in European integration did not necessarily coincide with support for European integration. In fact, a certain fatigue about European integration has been noticeable across the EU throughout the last two decades. Too much has happened in the wider world and too little time has been given to ordinary citizens to digest the secular changes and transformations in Europe. But the stalemate over the European Constitution has been more than a matter of psychological adaptation. It has been a combination of a transforming political culture and of growing ruptures in the traditional conduct of doing political business in the European Union. It has also been an echo of the changing rationale of European integration: With the growing opening of Europe to a global role

84 See for example McGiffen, Steven P., *The European Union: A Critical Guide*, London: Pluto Press, 2005 (2nd ed.). Soon published after the results of the referenda in France and in the Netherlands this is one of many contributions to the debate and to a deepened understanding of meaning, scope and effect of the European Union.

and the unavoidable implications of globalization on Europe's domestic conditions, the constitution of Europe was definitively more than the matter of a formal text. Since the outbreak of the ratification crisis of the Treaty Establishing a Constitution for Europe, the identity of Europe has been debated with more emphasis than ever before. It has become evident that the main reason for the rejection of the European Constitution was not the massive 2004 EU enlargement to Central and Eastern European countries. Exit polls in the referenda in France and in the Netherlands indicated that lack of information about the very content of the constitutional text ranked higher in a list of arguments that favored negative votes. And fear of negative effects of the economic policies of the EU ranked higher than the abstract concern to lose national sovereignty. Finally, at the moment of the referenda in France and in the Netherlands in 2005, concern with the economic situation at home was more important for voters than the abstract hope to achieve a more democratic, efficient and transparent Europe with the help of the European Constitution. The rejection of the European Constitution did not mean that French and Dutch voters had turned against Europe. The vast majority of "no"-voters in both countries expressed their hope that their negative vote would initiate renegotiations in the EU that would make the EU eventually more social and sensitive to economic concerns. A similar demand for better and more convincing pro-European action was expressed in the course of the first Irish referendum on the Treaty of Lisbon in 2008.

Since the early 1990's, two fundamental trends had defined the path of the European Union. With the decision to fully implement a monetary union and with the growing focus on the development of a common foreign policy of the EU, the loss of national autonomy in political decision-making became an overall experience. The end of communism and the subsequent eastward enlargement had burdened the EU with an unprecedented financial and potentially social agenda. Migration was discussed no longer as a contribution to give fresh impulses to the productivity, growth and creativity of aging societies. Instead, a widespread perception saw migration as a threat to identity, affluence and social cohesion. Simultaneously, a certain loss of autonomy in decision-making on critical domestic issues and developments was felt in most EU member states, especially the "old" ones. European integration and, in some cases even more contested, globalization impacted domestic political agendas and citizens' life more than ever before. The idea that a European Constitution could provide the EU with instrument's that would enable Europe to stay in the driver's seat of its own destiny was shunned in favor of the worry that a European Constitution would become a threat to the peoples' identity and national political autonomy. Different degrees of controversy and emotions across the EU left a strong mark among weak governments and strengthened the rather euroskeptical part of the citizenry.

Under these circumstances, three strategies were feasible to cope with the situation:

1. Countries – or their governments for that matter – could exit and "opt-out" of further Europeanization.

2. Countries and citizens could give their concerns and interests a stronger European voice and thus influence the decision-making process on the EU level.
3. Countries and people could accept tacit compliance with the trend of furthering the Europeanization through integration and pooled sovereignty.

No matter which choice one might have preferred, the political elites across the European Union are often united in feeling the limiting effect of the EU on their political scope of action. This does not make them good advocates of a European Constitution. Instead of explaining the ongoing trend toward a more interlocking multilevel system of European governance to their citizens, they often pretend to still be in autarkic control of public life while simultaneously they serve anti-Brussels sentiments. The gains and costs of integration are rarely explained in clear and convincing terms to the citizenry.

The political and constitutional conflicts stemming from this constellation are more differentiated than the term Euroskepticism indicates. Often, it seems as if the national political elites are more critical and skeptical about deeper European integration than their own people. The Union citizens desire, and rightly so, a Europe that works. A Europe that delivers is not simply equivalent to a Europe from which citizens immediately benefit in material terms. For instance, all long-term trends of opinion polls indicate that the majority of EU citizens wish for a stronger foreign policy posture of the EU. This attitude echoes a good sense of horizon and realism in the power of one's own state. This insight into the implications of contemporary trends in world affairs goes hand in hand with the skepticism of many Union citizens whether or not their respective political representatives are still capable of managing national affairs with success, and of properly understanding and managing the dynamics of European Union affairs. Confusing leadership leaves confused citizens behind.

As long as Europe exists, political leadership remains crucial. The absence of a coherent European election law is a strong bottleneck to properly and fully implement a genuine political system across the EU. This is not a philosophical matter about the notion of a European "demos." It is a practical matter about the functioning of a political system. Loyalty and trust can only grow across the EU if the organization of decision-making and representation is recognized as one and all member states and societies comply in the same way.

The debate following the outbreak of the ratification crisis of the Treaty Establishing a European Constitution was telling. It showed more than a growing disconnect between Union citizens and EU politicians on all levels. While national politicians tried to bridge the gap by turning to populist, parochial or outright nationalist policy formulas, their colleagues serving in EU institutions could often communicate with the EU's citizenry only in intermediary ways. In many ways, the EU-wide reflection about the root-causes of the ratification crisis of the Treaty Establishing a European Constitution and about the possible perspectives was equivalent to the first truly EU-wide public constitutional debate. The emergence of a European public sphere has become more obvious than ever in the course of this period of reflection and wound-licking. It was an experience equivalent to the German Paulskirche-Parliament of 1848 as a courageous, yet eventually failed step in developing a democratic political system. For the European Union of the early twenty-first century, the situation is better and worse at the same time. Its actor capacity is already stable and, in many ways, strong. The European Constitution would not have had to initiate European integration and its parliamentarization *per se*. On the other hand, the European Constitution has been written because, in the eyes of many, its time had come in order to prepare the European Union for its role in the age of globalization.

It turned out to be a big deficit that the Convention on the Future of Europe did not properly address the issue of how to organize a comprehensive European ratification scheme for the Treaty Establishing a Constitution for Europe. This clearly was a pilot error on the side of both the Constitutional Convention and, more so, on the side of the European Council. The European Council repeated the same pilot eror after signing the Treaty of Lisbon. It was easy to blame the people while their responsible political leaders could have done much better. For all too long, national governments have been reluctant to open a broad public debate on the future of Europe, linked to the meaning and purpose of the European Constitution. Wherever they were asked in referenda, people began to formulate their own opinion, often coupled with different agendas, frustrations and choices. In 2005, the European Constitution was the eventual loser but not because it was too weak or bad. It lost against an unexpected tide of public discourse because the responsible political leaders were not able to lead the discourse properly. The referenda in France and in the Netherlands became tribunals against domestic governments and the defendants were unprepared. Europe was bashed but the respective national political leadership was the target. The European Constitution became a scapegoat. In 2008, something similar happened to the Treaty of Lisbon in Ireland. To many citizens, the current absence of a concrete common European political project contradicts the ambition of an abstract common European constitutional project.

In the end, the constitution-building crisis of the early twenty-first century came as a blessing in disguise. It opened the gate for a broad reflection about the identity and current state of Europe never heard of before. Across the EU – also in countries that had already ratified the Treaty Establishing a Constitution for Europe – the ratification crisis triggered unique and substantial debates about the future of Europe.[85] Most of these

85 For a good overview see Eschke, Nina, and Thomas Malick (eds.), *The European Constitution and its Ratification Crisis Constitutional Debates in the EU Member States*, ZEI Discussion Paper C 156, Bonn: Center for European Integration Studies, 2006; Niemann, Anna, Sonja Ana Luise Schröder, and Meredith Catherine Tunick (eds.), *Recovering from Constitutional Failure: An Analysis of the EU Reflection Period,* ZEI Discussion Paper C 182, Bonn: Center for European Integration Studies, 2008.

debates were linked to specific national issues. But the EU-wide scope of these discourses and their echo in the media was unprecedented. At long last, the potential for a European public sphere became visible.

This phenomenon was reflected in the trends studied by Eurobarometer opinion polls. The results of the Eurobarometer polls echo the political roller coaster the EU was going through. Yet, it also echoed growing political maturity of the Union citizenry. Eurobarometer published its first findings after the negative referenda in France and in the Netherlands in December 2005. By then, the overall support for European integration had dropped, on average, by four percent across the EU (compared with the data for 2004): Only fifty percent of Union citizens felt that Europe was a good thing. However: The concept of a European Constitution found the support of 63 percent of EU citizens, an increase of two percent compared with 2004 and mid-2005.[86] In December 2006, support for European Union membership had gone up to 53 percent, on average, while only 33 percent of Union citizens thought that the EU was currently going in the right direction. Support for a European Constitution had dropped to an average of 53 percent. It was, however, interesting to note that support for the European Union was highest in Poland (63 percent) and that, on average, 53 percent of Union citizens in the countries that had not yet ratified the European Constitution were in its favor.[87] When the Intergovernmental Conference convened under the Portuguese EU Presidency in mid-2007, the Eurobarometer poll found 57 percent of Union citizens in favor of EU membership – the highest score since 1994. On top of all EU member states stood the Netherlands with 77 percent in favor of EU membership, followed by Ireland, Luxembourg, Spain, Belgium and Poland with 67 percent. As for the idea of a European Constitution, the citizens had risen above their overly cautious and bickering leaders. On average, support for a European Constitution had increased to 66 percent. By then, 68 percent in France and 55 percent in the Netherlands were in support of a European Constitution. In Poland, whose government had the greatest difficulties in accepting a new compromise on the institutional reforms of the EU, 69 percent of the citizens were in favor of a constitution for the European Union.[88]

Time had come for a new contract between the Union citizens and the political elites representing the European institutions. This contract could only be achieved over concrete issues and not over abstract institutional designs. In June 2007, when the European Council decided on the path toward a restructured treaty substituting the European Constitution, 52 percent of Union citizens tended to trust the European Commission, an increase by 4 percent compared with the 2006 poll. According to

86 See European Union. European Commission, *Eurobarometer 64: Public Opinion in the European Union*, December 2005, http://ec.europa.eu/public_opinion/archives/eb/eb64/eb64_first_en.pdf.

87 See European Union. European Commission. *Eurobarometer 66: Public Opinion in the European Union*, December 2006, http://ec.europa.eu/public_opinion/archives/eb/eb66/eb66_highlights_en.pdf.

88 See European Union, European Commission, *Eurobarometer 67: Public Opinion in the European Union*, June 2007, http://ec.europa.eu/public_opinion/archives/eb/eb67/eb_67_first_en.pdf.

Eurobarometer the European Parliament was trusted by 56 percent of Union citizens, also an increase by 4 percent compared with the 2006 poll. Time had come for Eurobarometer to also measure trust in the dealings of the European Council. Being the most influential European institution, yet its most obscure and intransparent one, the European Council was the source of much of the confusion over the past decade. Now it aimed at also being the source of a successful restitution. Nobody could imagine a future of Europe without the nation states and hence without national governments represented in the European Council. The European Council has a great responsibility to generate common European interests – and to communicate them properly to the respective national citizenry. It was unacceptable that several members of the European Council gave the impression that their signature under the Treaty Establishing a Constitution for Europe was not really to be taken seriously. It was also highly problematic that a strong majority of EU member states and EU citizens were held hostage by negative referenda generated by the votes of less than half of the population in a minority of EU member states.

In the end, the real problem was one of democratic theory. It had become necessary to better reconcile the methods, preconditions and effects of generating political legitimacy between the different layers of the EU's multilevel governance system and the citizens of the European Union. The political leaders across the EU have promised a Europe with results that works. As for the Union citizens, they are clear in the description of their priorities. In 2007, they identified the following issues as their main concern: unemployment (34 percent, down from 49 percent in 2006), crime (24 percent), the overall economic situation (20 percent), health care (18 percent), inflation (18 percent), immigration (15 percent), terrorism (12 percent) pensions (12 percent), education systems (9 percent) and taxes (8 percent). The overall economic situation was perceived more positive than a year earlier. While in 2006, only 46 percent of Union citizens stated that the economic situation was good, the "economic feel good factor" had gone up to 52 percent in June 2007.[89] It was more urgent than ever to give the EU back to its citizens by way of clearly presenting political choices they could connect with or reject. The election to the European Parliament in 2009 was not meant to make the EU enter into a form of artificial harmony and self-sustaining stability. It might, however, become the gateway to a new era of European politics and European integration: The political nature of European integration was more obvious and more acceptable than ever before in the history of European integration. The election to the European Parliament in June 2009 can be understood as the belated substitute for an EU-wide referendum on the European Constitution. This election was a judgment about Europe's constitution, about the constitution the European Union was in.

When asked in 2007 to predict the future fifty years from now, the majority of Union citizens envisaged the EU as playing a leading role in the world – as a key

89 Ibid.: 11.

diplomatic power (61 percent), with its own army (56 percent) and with its own directly elected President (51 percent). At least 31 percent assumed that the EU at that point in time would have become a secondary economic power, given the enormous transformations elsewhere and notably in China and India.[90] This minority realism also recognized the undeniable continuity of American economic power in the decades ahead.

In order to regain respect and authority, the "chastened leaders" of Europe need concrete policy successes.[91] They need them not for their sake alone but eventually for the sake of their continent. More than anything else it would require for them to exercise transparent deliberations and honest decisions between the several horizontal and vertical, formal and informal levels of EU governance. In the course of the reflection period on European identity and the constitution of Europe the Union citizens had more than ever documented that they wanted to know what was at stake, wanted to get involved in what would eventually impact their personal destiny and the social structures they are living in, and that they wanted to clearly see accountability attached to those representing them. Pragmatic politics and concrete, measurable success – that is the most likely formula to improve Europe's constitution and to give legitimate meaning to the written constitutional provisions of the European Union.

European integration is about value added, the evolution of common goods and the deepening of mutual solidarity among Union citizens and Union states. At the end of a decade of constitution-building, time has come to reconnect Union citizens and Union institutions both on the EU and on the national level. First and foremost, time has come for the leadership across Europe to define European integration again for its potential and no longer from its limits. Time has come for a Political Union that works instead of mainly being obsessed with fine-tuning its procedural mechanisms and constitutive treaties. In the end, Europe's constitution will be measured by the contribution of the European Union to a better, free and safe world.

90 Ibid.: 42.

91 Thus Moravcsik, Andrew, "Chastened Leaders need Concrete Policy Successes," *Financial Times*, January 27, 2006, http://search.ft.com/ftArticle?queryText=Moravcsik&y=1&aje=true&x=11&id=060126008460&ct=0.

Challenge and Response

III. 1957 – 1979: Institutions Consolidated

1. A New Beginning for Europe

March 25, 1957, was no ordinary day in the history of Europe. A continent twelve years out of the ashes of the worst outburst of violence in its history that had left more than 40 million Europeans dead, many of its cities devastated, its economy in shambles, and the world exhausted after waging a bitter campaign to stop the fighting, still filled with dire suspicion about what might come next, possibly again out of Germany and surely out of the Soviet Union. In 1957, Europe was a continent divided by the forces of a Cold War, which more than anything else echoed the fundamental divide between democracy and totalitarianism as the most contrasting concepts to organize the rule of men over men. One form of totalitarianism – national-socialist racism – had been buried along with Hitler's German Reich. The other form of totalitarian dictatorship – communism – was in full swing, no matter how many hopes were aired with the death of Stalin on March 5, 1953. For some in Europe – certainly in France, Great Britain, Belgium, the Netherlands, also in Spain, Portugal and to some extent even in Italy – the world at large was their point of reference. Colonial rule had been exercised for the past centuries in the most remote places on earth. Wouldn't that be the best way to get away from the intricacies of Europe and to pursue the course as a global power? Many in France thought like this, and even more thought so in Great Britain. The British also felt strong transatlantic bonds with the United States of America. Since World War II – like the Soviet Union on its eastern borders – the US had been firmly established as a European power on the western shores of the continent. In 1957, nothing was yet decided as far as the future of Europe was concerned, neither in terms of geopolitical strategy nor regarding the economic development or the evolution of Europe's political systems. Democracy had become a second chance in the Federal Republic of Germany, colloquially labeled West Germany. France seemed to suffer from the idiosyncrasies of its Fourth Republic, tightly knit with the demise of French colonial glory in Indochina and in Algeria. The battle of Dien Bien Phu in 1954 brought a deep humiliation for the once unbeatable French army. The civil war in Algeria was dragging on and in fact escalating. The weakness of the political system in France was symbolized by constantly changing governments.

March 25, 1957, did not transcend all queries and weaknesses, concerns and uncertainties that were flourishing in Europe. Yet it was to become the founding day, the birthday of a new order in Europe with a new structure for Europe through a new beginning among Europeans. The signing of the Treaties of Rome was accompanied by diplomatic protocol appropriate for the moment. The ceremony under the fresco of the battle of the Horatii and the Curatii in Rome's city hall on its famous Capitol Hill was short and serene. Under the statues of Pope Urban VIII and Pope Innocence X, Belgian Foreign Minister Paul-Henri Spaak and the Secretary General of the Belgian Economic Ministry, Count Jean-Charles Snoy et d'Oppuers, French Foreign Minister Christian Pineau and his State Secretary, Maurice Faure, German Chancellor Konrad Adenauer and the State Secretary in the German Foreign Ministry, Walter Hallstein, Italian Prime Minister Antonio Segni and Italy's Foreign Minister, Gaetano Martino, the State and Foreign Minister of Luxembourg, Joseph Bech, and Luxembourg's Ambassador in Belgium, Lambertus Schaus, and finally the Dutch Foreign Minister, Joseph Luns, and the Director for Montan-Integration in the Dutch Eonomic Ministry, Johannes Linthorst Homan, signed the Treaties of Rome. One treaty established the European Economic Community (EEC), the other one the European Atomic Energy Community (EURATOM).

The future that was now beginning was a long and complex one. Whether it was to be successful was not certain on March 25, 1957. That it should become a success story, and in fact a unique, unprecedented experience in Europe and for the world, was the hope of the signatories.

March 25, 1957, was the beginning of "an ever closer union among the peoples of Europe" as the preamble of the Treaties of Rome solemnly, yet somewhat loftily proclaimed.[1] It was not clear what that could mean or should entail. Political will and personal commitment among the signatories of the Treaties of Rome nurtured hope, but skepticism elsewhere in Europe was probably as strong as ever during the next five decades of European integration. "Those who drew up the Treaties of Rome," Paul-Henri Spaak, Belgian Foreign Minister and one of the signatories on March 25, 1957, was to remind members of the Council of Europe in 1964, "did not think of it as essentially economic; they thought of it as a stage on the way to political union." Walter Hallstein, the first President of the European Commission from January 1, 1958, until June 30, 1965, had already underlined the same attitude earlier: "We are not integrating economies, we are integrating politics. We are not just sharing our furniture, we are jointly building a new and bigger house."[2]

This was easier said than done. Mutual suspicion, the scars of two World Wars, divergent political interests and even more so political, economic and social realities and widely different ideas about how to manage the future defined the public discourse

1 *The Rome, Maastricht and Amsterdam Treaties: The Treaty on European Union (Treaty of Maastricht) and the Treaty Establishing the European Communities (Treaties of Rome) Amended by the Treaty of Amsterdam: Comparative Texts*, Genval: Euroconfidentiel, 1999: 6; see also Trausch, Gilbert (ed.), *The European Integration from the Schuman-Plan to the Treaties of Rome: Projects and Initiatives, Disappointments and Failures*, Baden-Baden: Nomos, 1993; Church, Clive H., and David Phinnemore (eds.), *The Penguin Guide to the European Treaties*, London: Penguin, 2002.

2 Both cited in Urwin, Derek W., *The Community of Europe: A History of European Integration since 1945*, London/New York: Longman, 1995: 76; see also Hallstein, Walter, *United Europe: Challenge and Opportunity*, Cambridge, Mass.: Harvard University Press, 1962; Hallstein, Walter, *Der unvollendete Bundesstaat: Europäische Erinnerungen und Erfahrungen,* ,Düsseldorf: ECON, 1969.

in Europe as the Foreign Ministers of the six founding states sat down in Rome to sign the Treaties, which their representatives had negotiated during an impressively short period of time. The Treaties of Rome stabilized the trend to go ahead with integration projects in the sphere of the economy without losing sight of political ambitions and without overburdening the chosen path with too many expectations, goals and intentions. Yet the Treaties of Rome finally brought a lasting solution to earlier "trials and errors" and cautious efforts to give European history a new, predictable and positive course after decades of bloodshed and hatred. They brought an answer after more than two centuries of antagonizing nationalism and political structures on the continent that were largely defined by a balance of mistrust, an inclination to hegemony and disrespect for the voice of ordinary Europeans. Nobody could expect that such a history, in fact its underlying mentality and the identities it had generated, were to be overcome within a short period of time or by one wise political stroke. Such a view would have been a complete misunderstanding of "the forces of history." They might be unleashed at some point with all the power that turn them into events every school child will later learn and remember. They are the product of processes and developments, often contingent, paradoxical, unclear and contradictory, which remain to be understood and interpreted by historians. But they are and always will be expressed in multidimensional processes that justify different interpretations. Often they had already received different interpretations during the time of their creation, as much contested before they came into existence as among latter-day interpreters. This interpretation does not want to leave any room for doubt: The Treaties of Rome that came into force after ratification in all six parliaments on January 1, 1958, were a new, a happy, and a successful beginning for Europe. They marked a turning point in the history of Europe.[3]

This turning point confirmed Europe's route to supranationality. As new as the word was the concept. "Above the national," the loose translation does not help to clarify the content either. Supranationality – defined as a method of decision-making where power is shared by representatives of member states of a political body and independent actors of a polity above the nation state – has never been a static notion. It was not available in any library as a condensed theory, ready-made as a book waiting for its practical implementation. Much of the debate about "supranationality versus intergovernmentalism" – filling shelves of books by now – has only limited meaning and relevance. It cannot explain why Europe embarked on a path toward supranationality, how at this particular point in time this new reality in the political life of the European continent evolved, and whether or not the reality emerging through the idiosyncrasies of supranationality has become irreversible and lastingly legitimized. The core of the Treaties of Rome is beyond any doubt: The treaties initiated the most innovative pattern the European continent has experienced since the emergence of the

3 See European Commission (ed.), *40 Years of the "Treaties of Rome": Or the Capacity of the Treaties to Advance the European Integration Process*, Brussels: Bruylant, 1999.

modern nation state. The nation state, based on the notion of national identity and the righteous quest for self-determination, is itself the product of a long process. Notwithstanding all transformations, strengths and flaws, the nation state has defined the political evolution of Europe ever since the late eighteenth century, if not since the late sixteenth century. For at least two hundred years, Europeans were not able to think of politics as being separated from the realities of the nation state. The rest of the world followed suit, largely by force of European imperialism and its rejection in the very name of national self-determination. Elsewhere, European settler colonies came to the same conclusion as their European ancestors: Political life ought to be organized through the medium of the nation state.

Supranationality encompasses two thoughts. On the one hand, it implies the continuity of the nation state. On the other hand, it marks an addition that in turn will transform the original nation state. Nobody has claimed the copyright for the word "supranationality." Mostly it will be seen as another social science jargon. Thus, the theoretical academic debates about the supranational quality of European integration have always been more vigorous than the political process would have indicated. In political reality, the evolution of European integration was guided by facts emanating from the Treaties of Rome. The discourse about "supranationality" or about "federalism" has largely been a reflex of this factual evolution. Yet it has always been an inherent element in the political agitation and public interpretation of European integration through the first five decades of its evolution.[4]

The Treaties of Rome were not the result of a sudden culmination of wisdom and super-human insights into the nature of man, politics and Europe. They were rather the down-to-earth result of daunting negotiations, trial and error, bickering and crises that time and again posed the strongest possible challenge to European policy makers. With the signing of the Treaties of Rome, the contested interpretation of their meaning and consequence began. Interpretation became a permanent pattern in the evolution of European integration. The starting positions for those who were chosen to sign the extraordinary Treaties of Rome could hardly have been more different. The different realities they were embedded in did not change with the signing of the treaties. Different interests did not disappear either. But a new reality emerged, an additional element of factual substance and multiple implications that were barely imaginable on March 25, 1957. France, Germany, Italy, Belgium, the Netherlands and Luxembourg began a

4 Among the best literature on the integration history see Dedman, Martin, *The Origins and Development of the European Union 1945-1995*, London/New York: Routledge, 1996; Burgess, Michael, *Federalism and European Union: the Building of Europe 1950-2000*, London/New York: Routledge, 2000; Kanthoor, Willem Frans Victor, *A Chronological History of the European Union 1946 – 2001*, Cheltenham: Edward Elgar, 2002; Gillingham, John, *European Integration 1950-2002: Superstate or New Market Economy?*, Cambridge: Cambridge University Press, 2003; Knipping, Franz, *Rom, 25. März 1957: Die Einigung Europas*, Munich: Deutscher Taschenbuch Verlag, 2004; Dinan, Desmond, *Europe Recast: A History of European Union*, Boulder: Lynne Rienner Publishers, 2004.

journey that was intended to lead them through a customs union to a common market and eventually to "an ever closer union among the peoples of Europe". Possible enlargement beyond the original six founding states was implied.

The ingenuity of then Dutch Foreign Minister Johan Willem Beyen will always be cherished as he was the one who presented a plan for an industrial customs union to his colleagues in the other five founding states of the EEC. His plan had originally been launched as part of the concept for a European Political Community that failed in 1954.[5] The dependency of the Netherlands on international trade did not change with such political failures and thus Beyen's "preoccupation with regional economic integration"[6] was a continuous and reliable element in the search for a new European architecture. Trade barriers were by definition against the interest of the Dutch and their partners in Belgium and Luxembourg. In 1944, still in the midst of war, they had set the tone with the creation of a Benelux customs union.[7] Hardly liberated from German occupation, theirs was to be the nucleus experiment of the customs union that was to emerge in Western Europe at large.

That Germany was to be part of this newly emerging reality was altogether a revolution in European affairs. Under the terrible dictatorship of the National Socialists, totalitarianism, racism and aggression emanating from Germany had burnt Europe down to ashes – and ultimately Germany as well. Unlike in former times, the Western allies that had won the war against Germany did finally decide not to punish Germany by isolating or de-industrializing it. They did not squeeze German resources (for understandable reasons) for purposes of reparation, which almost inevitably would have provoked a German sense of revenge. Germany was to be controlled through integration into a newly emerging structure of Western European and transatlantic institutions, policy mechanisms and economic patterns breaking with the past flirtation of Germany to dominate Central Europe in the pursuit of its power policy that was inherently anti-Western (and fearful of Russia alike).

To be afraid of Germany had been a particular and understandable part of the national psychology of France for long time. Three wars of German aggression in less than one century had left deep scars of suspicion on the French national psyche about their eastern neighbors. France was looking for security from Germany, even after the total defeat of the German Reich in 1945. But security from Germany alone would not generate a lasting and sustainable economic modernization of France. Monnet's idea of bringing coal and steel, the resources of power, under supranational control was still somewhat influenced by this attitude of control. But it also opened the way for a

5 Dwan, Renata, *An Uncommon Community: France and the European Defense Community 1950-1954*, Oxford: Oxford University Press, 1996; Ruane, Kevin, *The Rise and Fall of the European Defense Community: Anglo-American Relations and the Crisis of European Defense 1950-1955*, Basingstoke: Macmillan, 2000.

6 Dinan, Desmond, *Europe Recast: A History of European Union*, op.cit.: 67.

7 Castelain, M.F. (ed.), *The Benelux Economic Union: A Pioneer in European Integration*, Brussels: E.D.J. Kruijtbosch, 1987.

complete and courageous reversal of France's national security strategy: The idea to turn the concept of securing France from Germany into one of security for France with Germany and economic cooperation, even while integration with Germany was the most far-sighted contribution French politics could possibly invent after World War II. Yet France did just that, as highlighted by the plan Foreign Minister Robert Schuman presented on May 9, 1950. No direct path led from the Schuman-Plan to the Treaties of Rome as all other subsequent developments of European integration were not dependent on a predetermined path. But the Schuman-Plan changed the strategic parameters under which the reconstruction of Europe was to develop.[8] It was the plan of a wise, great man. The United States, echoed by Secretary of State Dean Acheson, was more than favorable about this turn of French policies toward defeated Germany. In fact, they had somewhat been pushing for this change. Early on, the US supported the idea of a European customs union and the subsequent common market. Europe was to be a much more solid, even attractive partner for the US if its economy was operating under same standards, at least in the democratic part of Europe. In doing so, it would strengthen the democratic revival in Western Europe and its will to defend the democracies of Europe against totalitarian Soviet rule on the eastern side of the Iron Curtain.

The history from the Schuman-Plan to the creation of the European Coal and Steel Community (ECSC)[9], from the failed European Defense Community and European Political Community, to the Foreign Ministers meeting in Messina, and from the Spaak Commission, the Venice Meeting of Foreign Ministers and the Intergovernmental Conference finally to the Treaties of Rome has been studied and described in much detail. Most important remains this key fact: The Treaties of Rome consolidated the quest for a new supranational architecture in Europe. The first EEC Commission President, Walter Hallstein, did not shy away from calling the Treaties of Rome the constitution of Europe. In light of the long history of European integration, the constitutionalization of this exceptional project has often been underrated. Yet, it is true that without a unique treaty at its inception, the founding of an integrated Europe might not have succeeded. The Treaties of Rome must be considered the first founding of Europe. These treaties laid the groundwork for a successful process of reconciliation among the belligerent nations and states of Western Europe. The Treaties of Rome started a top-down process of integration. This process gave a completely new shape to the state structure of Europe. Over five decades, the political architecture of Europe was to change gradually, yet dramatically. The initial decision for a law-based supranational approach had an unwavering long-term effect. After five decades, the citizens of united

8 Dell, Edmund, *The Schuman Plan and the British Abdication of Leadership in Europe*, Oxford: Oxford University Press, 1995; Fontaine, Pascal, *A New Idea for Europe: The Schuman Declaration, 1950-2000*, Luxembourg: Office for Official Publications of the European Communities, 2000.

9 Gillingham, John, *Coal, Steel and the Rebirth of Europe: The Germans and French from Ruhr Conflict to Economic Community*, Cambridge: Cambridge University Press, 1991; Spierenberg, Dirk, *The History of the High Authority of the European Coal and Steel Community: Supranationality in Operation*, London: Weidenfeld and Nicolson, 1994.

Europe were looking for a new rationale for European integration while the leaders of the EU were still busy framing the institutions that were so solidly running the political business of an integrated Europe. At the fiftieth anniversary of the signing of the Treaties of Rome, time had come to realize that the European Union had embarked on its Second Founding. Still, those who were managing the adaptation crisis of the early years of the twenty-first century owed their compass to the exceptional success and genius of the Founding Fathers of 1957.

2. The Treaties of Rome: Content and Interpretation

The Treaties of Rome created two different communities: The European Economic Community (EEC), geared to achieve a customs union without internal tariffs in three stages within twelve to fifteen years, with borderless freedom of goods, people, services and capital and common external tariffs against third countries; and the European Atomic Energy Community (EURATOM), geared to create a common market for the peaceful use of atomic energy, with free movement of nuclear resources, equipment, experts and information, coupled with joint research in the industrial use of atomic energy, but without surveillance of the military use of atomic energy by the EURATOM authorities.[10]

The structure of the European Economic Community followed the logic of the European Coal and Steel Community: a supranational institution, binding the sovereign rights of all participating countries over those sectors and functions of their economy that were agreed upon by the Treaties of Rome and their subsequent elaboration. The European Coal and Steel Community combined "negative integration" (controlling German coal and steel resources) with "positive integration" (doing it jointly on a European level). Its main feature was the institutional arrangement, establishing the High Authority as its chief executive, the Council as the legislature, the General Assembly, a consultative gathering of deputies from the member states parliaments, and the Court of Justice as the final arbiter in case of conflicting interpretation of the Treaties and their implementation. The Treaties of Rome confirmed this institutional structure with certain variations: Instead of a High Authority they established the European Commission, while the Council, the Parliamentary Assembly and the European Court of Justice were to be in charge of all three communities that existed in parallel until the merger of ECSC, EEC and EURATOM into one EC in 1970. The Treaties of Rome also created a new balance between the role of the European Commission (unlike the ECSC's High Authority it was designed as a looser, less

10 Scheiman, Lawrence, *Euratom: Nuclear Integration in Europe*, New York: Carnegie Endowment for International Peace, 1967; Howlett, Darryl A., *Euratom and Nuclear Safeguards*, London: Macmillan 1990.

powerful executive) and the power of the Council, underlining its primacy in different formations as legislature. Domestic and foreign policy matters became increasingly interwoven in the structures of the Council.

There have been many debates about the relationship between the Council and the European Commission, but only one conclusion stands the test of reality and of time: Both the European Commission and the Council have been, and have remained ever since, supranational organs in their own right.[11] The real debate was always about the degree of power of one over the other – or of both in relation to the emerging European Parliament. Neither a European Commission nor a Council had existed in Europe before that day. The balance remained contested and swings of the pendulum in one or the other direction were more usual than atypical over time. Yet the supranational organizational structure of the European Economic Community was intrinsically a novelty for Europe, unimaginable during the age of nationalism.

Clearly, compared with the High Authority of the European Coal and Steel Community, the European Commission that began its work under the Presidency of Walter Hallstein on January 1, 1958, was more dependent upon decisions of by the Council. This primacy of alleged national decisions gave rise to the theory of a predominantly intergovernmental display of the original EEC, one meant to enhance the national good and interest through community means. This is not altogether a wrong analysis. But it is too limited to understand the entire historical dynamics of the process that began in Rome. While decisions of the European Economic Community were to be taken in the Council, it was the role of the European Commission to prepare these decisions and to oversee their compliance with the provisions of the Treaties of Rome. This was not a small role, supported by the choice for Émile Noël as first Secretary General of the European Commission, who stayed in office until 1986, surviving many national governments and eight Commission Presidents. From the beginning, the European Commission was labeled the "protector of the Treaties" – notwithstanding the important role and independence of the European Court of Justice, another exceptional invention originating in the European Coal and Steel Community and confirmed in its supreme authority by the Treaties of Rome.

The interplay between European Commission – originally consisting of nine commissioners – and Council was a typical struggle over power and its balance between executive and legislature known from the evolution of all national political systems. Since the Council was only able to change proposals of the European Commission by way of unanimity, the Commission grew into a pivotal role as far as the interpretation and normative evolution of the Treaties of Rome was concerned. The treaties only

11 Cini, Michelle, *The European Commission: Leadership, Organization, and Culture in the EU Administration*, New York: St. Martin's Press, 1996; Hayes-Renshaw, Fiona, *The Council of Ministers*, New York: St. Martin's Press, 1997; Sherrington, Philippa, *The Council of Ministers: Political Authority in the European Union*, London: Pinter, 2000; Smith, Andy, *Politics and the European Commission: Actors, Interdependence, Legitimacy*, London: Routledge, 2004.

defined a framework for the development of a customs union and the subsequent common market. Thus it was largely in the hands of the European Commission to actively form the European Economic Community, based on its unlimited right to do so according to Article 235 of the Treaties of Rome.

The decision-making process in the Council was based on a weighing of votes, which was driven by the goal to prevent a marginalization of the three smallest EEC member states: Decisions on matters other than the proposals of the Commission – where unanimity was required – were possible only with the votes of four countries. To this interplay between executive and legislative was added the European Parliamentary Assembly, delegated from national parliaments to oversee the activities of the European Economic Community, the European Atomic Energy Community and the European Coal and Steel Community. The 142 delegate members of the Parliamentary Assembly (36 for France, Germany and Italy, 14 for Belgium and the Netherlands, six for Luxembourg) did not carry legislative powers. They were meant to support the process toward a customs union through advice and control. This was by and large also the role of the Economic and Social Committee, with the consequence that both organs were considered equal for a long time in textbooks about the EEC.

The European Assembly grew into a proper European Parliament. The European Assembly itself coined the name "Parliament" on March 30, 1962. At that moment in time, this decision was received with little respect and even less expectation. Yet, over time the authority of the European Parliament grew. In 1979, the citizens of the then twelve EC member states were able to directly elect their representatives into this unique body in the history of European democracy. Within another three decades, the European Parliament became the partner of the Council in legislative co-decision on practically all relevant matters of the European Union.[12] The European Economic and Social Committee remained the consultative body of the social partners, an expression of consociational democracy and decision-making in Europe, that was by now not only established on the national, but also on the supranational level.

One fundamental difference between the European Commission and the High Authority of the European Coal and Steel Community was the fiscal condition under which they were operating. While the High Authority was able to work with its own financial resources – allocated through levies from coal and steel companies according to their turnover – the European Commission and the European Atomic Energy Community were financed by contributions of each member state, thus limiting the independence of action enormously. On the other hand, this procedure confirmed the traditional relationship of an executive to the legislative body of a governance system.

12 On the evolution of the European Parliament since then see: Corbett, Richard, *The European Parliament's Role in a Closer EU Integration*, London: Harper, 2000; Judge, David, *The European Parliament*, Basingstoke: Palgrave Macmillan, 2003; Rittberger, Berthold, *Building Europe's Parliament: Democratic Representation beyond the Nation State*, Oxford: Oxford University Press, 2005.

The fundamental question therefore was not whether the European Commission should gain the right to an independent budget, but whether or not the Council was the only appropriate legislative body of the EEC. As in the tradition of all modern nation states, also in Europe the rule of law was established before parliamentary democracy came to fruition.

180 million Europeans constituted the six founding countries of an emerging European customs union. Article 8 of the EEC Treaty had envisaged a transitory period of twelve to fifteen years to achieve full customs union for industrial goods. By 1962, intra-Community trade had been doubled. Internal custom tariffs had been reduced faster than anticipated – always based on proposals of the European Commission and decisions taken by the Council. By July 1, 1968, all industrial intra-Community tariffs had been abolished and the gradual introduction of a harmonized and finally common external tariff for imports into the EEC had been introduced. The EEC external tariff was in line with the results of multilateral customs reductions negotiated through GATT in the early 1960's. At this point, the EEC was considered to be a particularly liberal economic grouping as its external tariff was less than 35 percent of US, British and Japanese custom barriers. The first steps toward customs union had been taken successfully – and even before schedule – although non-tariff barriers remained the biggest obstacle to the full creation of a common market for goods and to all outsiders trying to do business with the EEC.[13] They were only tackled with the Single Market project, in EC-shorthand the "1992 project" (to commemorate the anniversary of Columbus discovery of America in 1492), more than two decades later.

During the 1960's, the European Commission succeeded in establishing the notorious full-fledged competition policy of the EEC, but could only coordinate cautious efforts to create an industrial policy as counterpart to the Common Agricultural Policy.[14] By 1968, the EEC had survived its biggest institutional challenge so far. The issue was Common Agricultural Policy, a continuous matter of concern ever since.[15] The context in which the matter of financing the Common Agricultural Policy escalated into a severe constitutional crisis was related to the principle of national primacy over community decisions, which was particularly dear to France under President Charles de Gaulle. The inclusion of agricultural policies into the emerging common market was stipulated by the Treaties of Rome, mainly at the insistence of France, where at that

13 See, for example, Government of Australia (ed.), *Customs Union established by European Economic Community: A Review of Major EEC Activities leading to the Establishment of the Customs Union and some Problems this has created for Australia*, Canberra: Department of Trade and Industry, 1968; Vaulont, Nicolaus, *The Customs Union of the European Economic Community*, Luxembourg: Office for Official Publications of the European Community/Washington, D.C.: European Community Information Service, 1981.

14 Swann, Denis, *Competition and Industrial Policy in the EEC*, London: Methuen, 1983; Papaconstantinou, Helen, *Free Trade and Competition in the EEC: Law, Policy and Practice*, London: Routledge, 1988; Blanco, Luis Oritz, *European Community Competition Procedure*, Oxford: Carlendon Press, 1996.

15 Ackrill, Robert, *The Common Agricultural Community*, Sheffield: Sheffield Academic Press, 2000.

time almost 30 percent of the national work force was occupied in agriculture.[16] Germany, on the other hand, did not have more than 15 percent of its work force in agriculture. It had to import agricultural products and was ready to support the agricultural concern of its neighbor in exchange for a speedier opening of French industrial markets for German products. To transfer divergent national regulations for the agricultural market under one common European agricultural framework was a daunting and complex process. A European Market Order for agriculture was considered the only feasible mechanism to provide for the complete free flow of agricultural products in the EEC. The Common Agricultural Policy (CAP) was designed by Dutch Commissioner (and short-time President of the European Commission in 1972) Sicco Mansholt. The decision of the Council on June 30, 1960, was based on four principles: free trade for all agricultural products within the EEC; a market order with gradual harmonization of guaranteed prices; preference for community products executed through a protective system of variable tariffs vis-à-vis agricultural products from third countries; financial solidarity, that is to say financing of the Common Agricultural Policy through a Community budget.

According to the Treaties of Rome, beginning with the third stage of the customs union on January 1, 1966, most decisions of the Council were to be taken with qualified majority. As of 1970, the financial resources for the Common Agricultural Policy were automatically to be allocated to the EEC budget, consisting of custom duties from agricultural and industrial imports into the EEC. As much as this was in line with French interests, under this scheme the European Commission might have acquired genuine budgetary authority. Instead of waiting until 1970, the European Commission wanted to settle the principle question ahead of time with the beginning of the third phase of the customs union. In April 1965 the European Commission proposed that the introduction of the EEC's own budgetary resources as of 1970 would also require budgetary control by the European Parliament as national parliaments were no longer in control of the allocation process. In combination with the prospect of increased qualified majority voting in the Council, this proposal was unacceptable for French President de Gaulle. He feared that France's agricultural interests could be outvoted by others. He ordered French ministers and officials to leave EEC meetings until the matter was settled. Between July 1965 and January 1966 the French chair remained empty.

16 This was to change much faster than the reform of the Common Agricultural Policy. Between 1949 and 1962 1.8 million French workers left agriculture, almost one third of the total agricultural labor force. They went into those sectors of the economy that began to represent the modernization of French industry: chemicals, metal, manufacturers. Between 1962 and 1972 another 1.3 million workers left French agriculture. Because French government was promoting the concentration of industrial ownership as a strategy to speed up economic modernization, many started to work in large national corporations. In 1960, 8 percent of all industrial turnover of France was in foreign hands, by 1980 this figure had increased to one quarter of the whole turnout, in capital goods and chemicals it had even gone up to 40 percent: See George, Stephen, and Ian Bache, *Politics in the European Union*, Oxford: Oxford University Press, 2001: 171.

France agreed to return to Community business in January 1966. The "empty chair crisis" of 1965/1966 ended with the Luxembourg Compromise. It confirmed continuous application of the principle of unanimity in the Council should vital national interests be at stake. The compromise finally reached on the new financial arrangement included French agreement to a German request according to which all remaining intra-Community tariffs on industrial goods be abolished by June 1968 while France succeeded in establishing the mechanism for a community-financed Common Agricultural Policy. Following the crisis, Walter Hallstein announced his resignation as President of the European Commission ahead of time in July 1967, when the merger of the European Community with EURATOM and ECSC was to come into effect. He had become a target of strong critique by de Gaulle, who rejected the allusion that Hallstein could operate like just another head of government.

This institutional conflict was indeed at the center of the crisis. More than an institutional conflict, it was a constitutional one, covered by the important issue of how France was to achieve its agricultural interests in the EEC. At the end, the outcome of the crisis could have been worse. What would have happened if France had left the EEC? The power struggle over the primacy of decision-making in the EEC cannot really surprise anyone. It would also be insufficient to only analyze it in categories related to the issue at stake and the specific national interests involved. During the first phase of the European Economic Community clashing interests, which quickly could have translated into constitutional conflicts, could have easily undermined the political fabric of the whole construction. Thus at the end, the "empty chair crisis" strengthened European integration as it confirmed the political will and shared interest of all participating countries to pursue the path of supranationality set by the Treaties of Rome, no matter how much the art of compromise was necessary.

Often, the "empty chair crisis" is analyzed as proof of the primacy of intergovernmentalism in European integration. This is a static and almost theoretical conclusion of the complexity of the event and its result. It would be enlightening to broaden the perspective and to recognize that the supranational approach as such did not only survive the crisis of 1965/66, but that in the end it was strengthened with the merger of the EEC, EURATOM and ECSC that also was decided as part of the "package deal" between France and Germany at the Luxembourg summit. The "empty chair crisis" was almost an inevitable conflict of constitutional interests that did not destroy the underlying constitutional claim of integration. In light of the changes in France from the Fourth to the Fifth Republic, a complete constitutional revocation of the Treaties of Rome would not have been unimaginable given French constitutional habits. The fact that it did not happen proved de Gaulle's ultimate commitment to recognize the path taken with the Treaties of Rome.

Moreover, the "empty chair crisis" should also be seen as the first interplay of domestic political preferences and European choices. It was a conflict about political norms and priorities as they occur in any pluralistic democracy. In 1958, such a constitutional battle had occurred in France itself. Over the following decades, the EU would see other constitutional battles, be it the budgetary clashes with Euroskeptic Britain under the Premiership of Margaret Thatcher, disputes over the weighing of votes at the Nice Summit in 2000, or the final quarrels about the voting rights under the European Constitution. These intra-community quarrels express legitimate political and even constitutional disputes as they occur in any nation state. As European integration by definition is a supranational addition to the levels of governance in Europe, traditional national debates and preoccupations, interests and normative conflicts also reach the European level. In fact, domestic politics becomes Union politics – and vice versa. The "empty chair crisis" was a first time experience of this challenge to supranational integration from within the process.

Another experience of later integration processes also became visible during the time of testing of the Treaties of Rome in the 1960's. In sum, European integration and its effects are neither the product of "nebulous visions of European unity" nor of "concrete calculations of national advantages" alone.[17] European integration is as much about an intention-effect-nexus that very often is unpredictable. Its development cannot properly be anticipated and fully outlined in advance. Germany started the path into European integration with the hope for rehabilitation. France began it with the clear intention to dominate European integration. German integration changed from a negative one (controlling Germany through integration) to a positive one (integrating Germany for the benefit of the whole). France changed from a sense of natural superiority and fear of Germany to the recognition of European institutions and procedures that require compromises even on the part of the strongest. By developing common interests, all partners of the integration process gained.[18] But the greatest gains were at the supranational level: The treaty-based European Community was consolidated and strengthened as a unique form of policy conduct.

The Treaties of Rome have opened this new chapter of dynamic experiences in the European polity. In many cases, individual decisions in the European Economic Community – and later in the European Union – were made under circumstances different from those that they initiated. The calculus of the intention that was at the cradle of each decision – no matter how big or small – did not always materialize. In fact, the effects of a decision often changed the original calculation and intention. It seems as if this is the only constant law of politics. In so far as European integration can be interpreted through the lenses of this "law," it proves the quintessential political nature of the process of European integration. This has been the ultimate testimony to the imaginative political wisdom expressed by those drafting, negotiating and ratifying

17 Dinan, Desmond, *Europe Recast: A History of European Union*, op.cit.: xiii.

18 See Wilkens, Andreas (ed.), *Interessen verbinden - Jean Monnet und die europäische Integration der Bundesrepublik Deutschland*, Bonn: Bouvier, 1999.

the Treaties of Rome.[19] The rest became "history," but the making of the Treaties of Rome and thus the beginning of the extraordinary path toward European integration was an extraordinary moment for Europe.

3. Challenge and Response at Work

The wisdom inculcated in the Treaties of Rome did not come about as a law of nature or a gift from heaven. It was rather the reaction to a deep crisis in the effort to reorganize the political architecture of Europe. In fact, it was a combination of three responses to a set of three interrelated, but separate challenges:

- A response to the shock of failed community-building through the means of a European Army and a Common Defense Policy under French control.
- A response to the experimental experiences with a variation of mechanisms to bring about a new architecture for Europe none of which had really gained momentum yet.
- A response to the recognition of continuous trajectories of state behavior, national psychologies of suspicion and political perceptions of mistrust that had to be overcome if Europe was to truly begin anew and consolidate its order under newly emerging external threats and pressures.

The failure to succeed in realizing a European Defense Community and a European Political Community between 1952 and 1954 came as a blow to the hope of many that Europe had finally overcome its divisions and was ready to embark on a common path. With the outbreak of the Korean War on June 25, 1950, French resistance to an early rearmament of the Federal Republic of Germany, only five years after the unconditional surrender of the German Reich, was shattered.[20] The United States were redesigning their global posture and considered a loyal Germany to be an asset. Instead of pursuing suggestions to de-industrialize Germany and keep it demobilized, they calculated with a strong economic recovery and a loyal strategic partner in the Cold War. Within two days of the North Korean invasion, Seoul was taken by their army. Should the same fate

19 For many details see von der Groeben, Hans, *Aufbaujahre der Europäischen Gemeinschaft - Das Ringen um den Gemeinsamen Markt und die Politische Union (1958-1966)*, Baden-Baden: Nomos, 1982; Küsters, Hanns Jürgen, *Die Gründung der Europäischen Wirtschaftsgemeinschaft*, Baden-Baden: Nomos, 1982.

20 Only two days after invading on June 25, 1950, North Korean troops, well equipped with Russian tanks, had occupied Seoul. By September 25, 1950 the North Koreans had been pushed back after a UN Force had been able to defend the city of Pusan and after General MacArthur had succeeded with a seaborne landing at Incheon. In November 1950, South Korea had to suffer a second invasion, this time by Chinese forces. On January 3, 1951 they had again occupied Seoul, only to be pushed back on March 15, 1951 by the US and UN Forces. After a long stalemate, an armistice between the two Koreans was signed on July 27, 1953 in Panmunjom.

not occur on the Rhine, Germany was to rearm, both the Americans and the German government under Chancellor Konrad Adenauer concluded.[21]

Adenauer saw this move also as another step toward full rehabilitation of his country. France could hardly bear the idea to see Germans in uniform again. To do this under the structures of the North Atlantic Treaty Organization (NATO) was another hard demand on the French. NATO was founded in 1949 at the outbreak of the Cold War and soon gained reputation as the single most important expression of a transatlantic community that was to link the US and its European partners in the most successful military alliance ever over the next half century. But in the early 1950's, for France the choice was either a US-led security system for Europe or a European security arrangement ultimately led by France. A Foreign Ministers Conference of September 12-16, 1950, in Washington showed French isolation on the matter of German rearmament. Under this pressure, Jean Monnet, the "father" of the European Coal and Steel Community, conceptualized another plan aimed at transferring the supranational method of the community of coal and steel to the military sphere. His concept was accepted by French Foreign Minister Robert Schuman and Prime Minister René Pleven, who presented it as his plan to the French National Assembly on October 24, 1950. Events in the world, the French Prime Minister stated, would leave no choice but to immediately move from transferring coal and steel under the roof of a supranational community to the communitarization of defense through a common European army.

The next meeting of the NATO Council on October 28, 1950, did not reach agreement whether or not German rearmament should take place under the umbrella of US-led NATO or as part of a European Army largely under French hegemony. The US could accept a European Army if it was to recognize NATO leadership. Neither American skepticism nor the effort of Stalin to seduce the Federal Republic of Germany onto a path toward national reunification under conditions of neutrality (Stalin Note from March 10, 1952) could stop the negotiations among the six European members of the European Coal and Steel Community on the creation of a European Defense Community, coupled with a European Political Community. On May 27, 1952, the treaty of the European Defense Community was signed. The result of focused negotiations among six West European countries was the concept of a European army, consisting of 40 divisions, out of which twelve were to be German. A European executive organ was to supervise all relevant questions, including training and recruitment, military production and selection of equipment. The Court of Justice of the European Coal and Steel Community was to be in charge of protecting the full implementation of the defense union treaty.

21 Giauque, Jeffrey Glen, *Grand Design and Vision of Unity: The Atlantic Powers and the Reorganization of Western Europe, 1953-1963*, Chapel Hill: University of North Carolina Press, 2002.

A fierce German debate on the whole matter ended with the ratification of the Treaty installing the European Defense Community and the European Political Community on March 9, 1953, by the German parliament. France went through difficult political waters: between 1950 and 1954, the country experienced eight coalition governments with seven different Prime Ministers and three different Foreign Ministers. Then came the showdown: Pierre Mendès France, who had been in office as Prime Minister since June 18, 1954, ended a heated and highly controversial public debate about the wisdom of sharing sovereignty over the French army with other European partners, and the Germans in particular, by failing to give a recommendation to the National Assembly in favor of ratifying the Treaty on the European Defense Community. On August 30, 1954, the National Assembly, with a majority of Gaullists, communists and half of the radicals and socialists, decided to postpone the decision on the treaty sine die (319 to 264 votes).[22]

Soon thereafter, Germany was to join NATO in 1955, a step already prepared for during the long time of waiting for the ratification of the treaty on European Defense Community. While public attention at the time – and scholarly work thereafter – mainly focused on the failure of the European Defense Community, the fate of the European Political Community almost fell into oblivion. Efforts made at the time were impressive and did anticipate many of the suggestions that were again generated during the Constitutional Convention in 2002/2003. Already during the inaugural session of the Parliamentary Assembly of the European Coal and Steel Community on September 10, 1952, the six Foreign Ministers had been given orders to develop a concept for a European Political Community. The work of a commission under German politician Heinrich von Brentano presented a draft European constitution, which the ECSC Assembly almost unanimously agreed upon on March 10, 1953. The draft constitution was highly federal, with a two-chamber system, one directly elected by the people of Europe, the other (Senate) delegated by the national parliaments. The European government should serve as the executive, its president elected by the Senate. Together, the two chambers of parliament should have legislative powers. A Council should be the intermediary between the national governments and the European institutions. The Council of Justice would be the final arbiter and protector of the community constitution. ECSC and the newly founded European Defense Community should gradually be integrated under the roof of the European Political Community, which would uphold competences for foreign and security policies as well as for economic and monetary policies and the organization of a common market. In substance, the European Constitution of 2004 and the Reform Treaty of 2007 did not go beyond the original

22 Nock, Paul, *Das Scheitern der Europäischen Verteidigungsgemeinschaft: Entscheidungsprozesse vor und nach dem 30. August 1954*, Düsseldorf: Droste Verlag, 1977; Fursdon, Edward, *The European Defense Community: A History*, New York: St. Martin's Press, 1980; Odul, Véronique (ed.), *Décision et Indécision dans la Querelle de la Communauté Européenne de Defense, 1950-1954*, Paris: Centre d'Histoire de l'Europe du Vingtième Siècle, 2004.

proposals of the 1953 draft constitution. With the failure of the European Defense Community, the draft European constitution of 1953 went into the archives.

Although this happened without too much public row, the shock of the failure of the European Defense Community was rather deep. Stalin's death on March 5, 1953, and the Korean armistice on July 27, 1953, seemed to suggest a certain reduction of international tensions. Yet the failure of establishing a European army did not answer the burning question of how Europe's security was to be organized, if at all. August 30, 1954, was a black day for Europe. It was all the more astonishing that it took only a few months for a new initiative on European integration to appear. All in all, a handful of far-sighted European politicians, like-minded in spirit, but certainly in disagreement on many of the details and the long haul of the path European integration should take, did not give up. In fact, they left a legacy of European commitment, political will and the ability to forge compromises after having suffered defeat with the European defense project.

Jean Monnet has to be mentioned. The agile, creative President of the High Authority of the European Coal and Steel Community was worried that if integration would come to a close the limited effort of the community for coal and steel might be doomed as well. During the immediate months following the failure of the European Defense Community and European Political Community, more than fifty concepts were developed under his supervision in the ECSC.[23] He and his advisers suggested the extension of competences of the High Authority beyond coal and steel to the transportation sector and to the whole energy sector, atomic energy in particular. Since the waiver of atomic secrets by the US government in December 1953, the prospect of a peaceful use of atomic energy had become an interesting concept for Europe to meet the rising energy demand in its period of post-war recovery.[24]

Paul-Henri Spaak, Foreign Minister of Belgium since April 1954 and an ardent European federalist, has to be mentioned. He was ready to support the concepts Monnet would develop and give them the political backing among his colleagues of the six ECSC countries. On April 2, 1955, Spaak opened the new chapter of Europe's integration history with a letter to his colleagues suggesting to convene a conference to cautiously reconsider among them the launching of a new European integration initiative. Jean Monnet would head this conference that was to discuss the prospects of extending the competencies of the European Coal and Steel Community to the sectors of transportation, air transportation included, and the whole of the energy sector, atomic

23 Knipping, Franz, *Rom, 25. März 1957: Die Einigung Europas*, op.cit.: 82.

24 The open question was whether or not natural uranium from French and Belgian colonies in Africa should be used or enriched uranium generated through the fusion technology that had been developed in the US. This suggested again a competition between France and the US over the prospects of German industrial development: Would the French be able to organize atomic energy according to their interests, the Germans would be prevented from embracing American technology for the development of their atomic energy policy.

energy in particular. A new community should be considered to deal with the common use of atomic energy under the roof of one European market.

Johann Willem Beyen, the Dutch Foreign Minister and an internationally renowned expert on financial and economic matters in office since September 1952, should not be forgotten. Already during the debates about a European Political Community he had suggested that a political community could not work without an economic base. Beyond partial integration of certain sectors of the economy, a horizontal integration of the whole of the economy under the supervision of a common executive was essential. In reply to Spaak's letter, Beyen proposed that the three governments of Belgium, Luxembourg and the Netherlands jointly take the initiative to bring about a supranational authority, whose goal would be the creation of a common market.

Last but not least, Konrad Adenauer, German chancellor from 1949 and during those days also Foreign Minister of the young Federal Republic, must be mentioned. Internal debates in his government were imminent – both with Economic Minister Ludwig Erhard, who favored a free trade agreement over any regularized European market, and among the chief advisers of both Adenauer and Erhard. Ultimately, Chancellor Adenauer decided that German industry could regain its traditional pre-war strength only through its incorporation into the world economy by way of an integrated West European economic market rooted in a customs union. Both Monnet and Spaak had considered the proposals of Johann Willem Beyen as too far-reaching and not realistic. In response to Spaak's letter, they learned that the German government would favor an atomic energy market only if it were to be part of a larger common market based on customs union. When the six Foreign Ministers of the European Coal Steel Community met in Messina from June 1 to 3, 1955 – shortly before communal elections took place in this home town of Italy's Foreign Minister Martino – they asked Paul-Henri Spaak to supervise an expert committee studying the option of both a horizontal market integration and an extension of the sector specific, functional integration that had begun with coal and steel.

Between July 1955 and April 1956, a committee of government representatives and experts under the leadership of Paul-Henri Spaak conceptualized the report later named after the Belgium Foreign Minister. Following one more meeting of the six Foreign Ministers in Venice on May 29 and 30, 1956, between June 1956 and March 1957 an Intergovernmental Conference worked out the two founding treaties for the European Economic Community and for the European Atomic Energy Community. The shock of failure in 1954 and the limited experience with the European Coal and Steel Community that could somehow be used helped to reach a success achieved with unexpected speed and permeated with a cooperative spirit. None of this could be considered normal in the mid-1950's. That is and remains the legacy of the "founding fathers" of the Treaties of Rome.

The United States served as "federator" with its dual intention to stay in Europe in order to guarantee its peace and to bring the Europeans together in a spirit of cooperation and partnership. During the 1960's, when European integration began to flourish, the US tried to strengthen its influence over the highly dynamic economy. While the US served as a positive federator, the two crises of 1956 turned it into a negative federator: the nationalization of the Suez Canal, indicating to France and Great Britain the end of their world power status and the new primacy of the US in the Middle East; and the Soviet invasion of Budapest, indicating to all of Western Europe the danger of Soviet expansionism were they not to organize security, stability and affluence together.

Under shock and pressure the six founding countries of the European Economic Community achieved a unique result in the political history of Europe. They were able to connect and integrate earlier debates about the primacy of a free trade agreement versus the concept of a common market; this included the limited effect of the Organization for European Economic Cooperation (OEEC), the experience with the intergovernmental Council of Europe, operating since 1949 as the eldest European institution, and the controversial debates within each of the six ECSC governments. The United States under President Eisenhower and Secretary of State Dulles supported this path explicitly.

The pressure under which the six ECSC governments stood can hardly be measured with contemporary methods. Public opinion polls barely existed and media coverage of the events was both limited and had less impact on policy processes than in later decades. The Treaties of Rome were a sign of political leadership, albeit under the influence of pressure and challenge that made their result, content and outcome more unlikely than likely. Yet the Treaties of Rome were negotiated, decided upon, signed and ratified in due course of time. They became in more than one way a model that later decision-making on European integration matters could not live up to. Yet the circumstances in the mid-1950's were different and indeed special. No matter the failure of the European Defense Community, no matter the limited scope of ECSE, OEEC or the Council of Europe: The biggest challenge of all had been World War II. This most horrible of experiences had been only just a decade behind the European nations and the leaders of the six ECSC countries. All of them had gone through this ordeal and had come out of it with deep convictions about necessary change in the direction Europe was to develop politically, economically and culturally.

World views, causal beliefs and principled beliefs came together in an exceptional leadership generation.[25] Tested by horror and yet fully committed to work for a better Europe, the Founding Fathers of integrated Europe are without any earlier example in

25 On these three dimensions in the conduct of foreign policy see Goldstein, Judith, and Robert O. Keohane (eds.), *Ideas and Foreign Policy: Beliefs, Institutions and Political Change*, Ithaca/London: Cornell University Press, 1993.

the entire history of this old continent. They surely deserve a place in the House of European History to be built in Brussels as a contribution to this exceptional generation and the success of European integration thereafter.

In the end, timing matters in politics as much as interests, principles and power.[26] A challenge that is not dealt with at a certain moment in time might grow into an uncontrollable crisis. A missed opportunity cannot be invented again. Momentum lost might spoil and destroy a long-term effort, no matter how successful it had looked thus far. One of the underlying premises of the Treaties of Rome was the conviction among its signatories that in the future no European integration scheme should be torpedoed and destroyed as the victim of one parliament's decision or non-decision. In later decades, this conviction has been stretched to tame the effect of national referenda in member states on integration matters. As much as this sounds undemocratic – and in fact it is undemocratic if democracy is defined by its most excessive liberal connotation – its practice has become a protective shield against the contingencies, idiosyncrasies and populisms of national democracies, which prevail in Europe to this day.

The making of the Treaties of Rome was not only a brave response to the multidimensional challenge of internal affairs, European experience and national trajectories. It also laid the groundwork for a specific habitual component of the European integration process that was to prevail: The emergence of a specific European "chemistry." European integration is not the least about trust and the emergence of a common history. It is about the specific effort to forge political compromises before formal decisions are taken. As much as the formal weighing of votes has become part of the European routine, the "typical" European political process has always been rather deliberative, consensus-oriented and driven toward conflict reduction. This has been all the more evident the higher the stakes and differences were and the louder the public noise was to become. This habitual pattern of European integration "chemistry" has endured and substantially grown through the first five decades. Programmatic differences crossed national and party boundaries on practically every specific issue on the European agenda. Only after the consolidation of the integration process, and with a structural change in the notion and effect of Europeanization since the 1990's, has the political process become more political and openly divisive. It was argued that this was necessary in order to establish a parliamentary democracy that was far from being at the heart of the considerations leading to the Treaties of Rome.

Yet the defining moments for European integration required highly competent and courageous political leadership, nationally as well as on the European level, to combat inertia, skepticism, embedded interests, fear and prestige. European integration is a specific form of policy-making. It is not secretive or above comprehension. It is not better than most other policy-processes the world knows. It is debatable whether or not

26 See Riescher, Gisela, *Zeit und Politik: Zur institutionellen Bedeutung von Zeitstrukturen in parlamentarischen und präsidentiellen Regierungssystemen*, Baden-Baden: Nomos, 1994.

European decision-making is more or less efficient when efficiency is measured in the time span and the work load of discussions, meetings and the yet further discussions it takes to come to final decisions in single EU member states. But whenever decisions are taken by the EU, they can be considered European political decisions on European political interests, a complete novelty in the course of Europe's history. Moreover, these were decisions taken on the basis of commonly accepted rule of law, embedded in contractual consent and political will.

The history of European integration has been written mostly through the lenses of specific national considerations. Alternatively, rather limited case studies were conducted. Another option is theoretical reasoning, trying to justify the superior logic of one theoretical argument over the other. In reality, European integration has always been a down-to-earth process of political bargaining intended to achieve a common European good. This in itself was unheard of in the past and should not be belittled in the name of abstract notions of efficiency.

"The common market was a Dutch initiative," Martin J. Dedman concluded his fine narrative of its evolution, but the Treaties of Rome "largely reflected French preoccupations."[27] It was to become an enormous success story for all: By 1972, West German GDP per head had grown by 178 percent as compared to the level in 1958, in France it had grown by 185 percent, in Italy by 180 percent. To further put the success in context, one needs to note that in Great Britain – first by staying out of the EEC process and later hindered twice in joining it by France (in 1963 and in 1967) – GDP per head grew by 140 percent over the same time span. The political success of the EEC can hardly be measured by statistics alone because one also needs to balance its economic effects against all the histories of failure and destruction, power and violence that seemed to embody Europe for most of its history prior to the first truly energetic and lasting move to integration.

4. Emerging European Interests

The first period of European integration was marked by an incremental evolution of four distinct European interests:[28]

a) An organic recognition of the European Economic Community as a community of law, which meant the often painful national experience in accepting the primacy of community law over national constitutional and political decisions;

27 Dedman, Martin J., *The Origins and Development of the European Union 1945-1995*, op.cit.: 102.

28 Landau, Alice, and Richard G. Whitman, *Rethinking the European Union: Institutions, Interests, and Identities*, Basingstoke: Macmillan, 1997; Piattoni, Simona, *Clientelism, Interests and Democratic Representation: The European Experience in Historical and Comparative Perspective*, Cambridge: Cambridge University Press, 2001; Elsig, Manfred, *The EU's Common Commercial Policy: Institutions, Interests and Ideas*, Aldershot: Ashgate, 2002.

b) A genuine "community spirit," that is to say habitual modes of action within the community institutions and around them;
c) The ability to develop common positions through compromises although (or just because) the starting points – either because of socio-economic realities or because of political or cultural interests – were different and often seemed non-convertible; and
d) An incessant political will among the political elites, which were involved in the process, to search for a new beginning ("relance européenne") whenever a crisis had obscured the prospects for further integration.

(a) The founding period of the European Economic Community as a treaty-based community of law could not naturally resort to common given interests. Many interests of the countries involved in the evolution of the EEC differed considerably. Within EEC member states, political discourses were also split on many of the important issues and propositions. If anything, that indicated one trend: Europe had again become a lively democracy. It was a limited democracy, however, as far as the dimension of parliamentary democracy on the level of the EEC was concerned. In 1958, the idea of transforming the EEC into a supranational parliamentary democracy was more than far-fetched. The implementation of the Treaties of Rome required patient and steady work through mechanisms both among the EEC institutions and between them and the member states, their governments, parliaments and public discourses on the relevant matters. This created a complex web of awareness, competencies, practice and experience, which was defined by formal policy processes, but was also beginning to shape the informal nature of matters and encounters in the EEC. Both formal and informal procedures were beginning to matter.

The first period in the history of European integration was marked by the gradual development of understanding among the participating members of the European Economic Community that the community was not "the other," but part of one's own policy process and oneself in the newly emerging European political system. European law became the key to foster this recognition. Astonishing enough, from the beginning the creation and role of the European Court of Justice (ECJ) was less contested than any other institution of the EEC. Yet it was to become potentially the most influential one.[29] Two landmark cases in 1963 and in 1964 endorsed the theory of the primacy of EEC law: In the "Van Gend en Loos vs. Nederlandse Administratie der Belastingen" case of 1963, a Dutch trucking firm had brought its case against Dutch customs authorities to the court, claiming that it was against community law to be charged with import duties on products imported from Germany. The European Court of Justice ruled in favor of the company, outlining that the EEC "constitutes a new legal order of international law

29 Granvik, Lena, *The Principles of Direct Effect and Direct Applicability in European Community Law*, Abo: Abo Akademi, 1996.

for the benefit of which the states have limited their sovereign rights". Only a year later, in the case "Costa vs. ENEL" the European Court of Justice had to deal with charges against Italy's leading national electricity supplier. It came to the conclusion that EEC law is superior to national law. Since member states had definitively and voluntarily transferred sovereign rights to the EEC, its law could not be overruled by national law without questioning the legal basis of the EEC itself.

(b) Not only the clubbing of "Eurocrats" in Brussels, with their particular and sometimes overly excessive transnational habits, but also the transformation of relationships among acting politicians and diplomats, through continuous experiences in meeting their community partners, were instrumental in creating this specific "European-ness" in the corridors of EEC institutions. All latecomers to the EEC, and subsequently to the EU, immediately became aware of this particular spirit. Mostly they adjusted rather quickly to the community spirit. Over time, a whole network of lobbying institutions evolved around the formal community institutions, supplemented by a growing number of journalists. Even academics started to be organized in a community context, and it was only a question of time before genuine historical work on European integration began to emerge, sponsored by the EC, but also elsewhere.[30] At the core of this period of "Europeanization" lay the evolution of the *acquis communautaire*, a set of legal and political norms, formal and informal procedures, and, last but not least, modes of behavior in EEC institutional circumstances. The *acquis communautaire* became the door through which every possible newcomer had to go. Membership in the EEC did not become a matter of choice through the renegotiation of the EEC's basic regulations. From the beginning it was – and remains to this day – a matter of adaptation to the European Community – now the European Union – rules and regulations, formal and informal, at best alleviated through certain periodical exemptions. The EC paid a high price for granting "opt-out" conditions to euroskeptical governments in Britain and Denmark. In the end it was an acceptable price to pay for growing into a truly continent-wide operation. But a price it was.

(c) A "community spirit" did not merely evolve because it was forced upon the participants by the European Court of Justice. It was also cemented by the experience that different interests can be brought together toward a commonly defined goal without negative consequences for any of the participants. It was not a simple "win-win" game for all; nor was European integration the product of a simple "spill-over" mechanism as suggested by early theoretical reflection about its trajectory. European integration was much more "trial and error" and time and again the recognition of the need to respond to

30 See, for example, Lipgens, Walter (ed.), *Sources for the History of European Integration (1945-1955) - A Guide to the Archives in the Countries of the Communities*, Leyden: Sijthoff, 1980; Perron, Régine (ed.), *The Stability of Europe - The Common Market: Towards European Integration of Industrial and Financial Markets 1958–1968*, Paris: Presse de l'Université de Paris-Sorbonne, 2004.

an inevitable challenge beyond the means and decision-making powers of the nation state. No major decision in the EEC occurred without controversial national debates. It is therefore insufficient to conclude that countries were pursuing divergent, if not antagonistic positions. Often national political debates cross-fertilized debates elsewhere. The gradual emergence of a multilevel governance system was always ahead of the creation of a multilevel system of policy discourse. But European integration has increasingly become adjusted to this phenomenon according to which party political interests across the European Community serve as an additional layer to the bargaining mechanisms among national governments.[31]

The more the European Parliament rose from a consultative assembly to a directly elected body with more or less impartial co-decision-making powers in the legislative process, the more all of the various actors and layers of a stable, cohesive parliamentary system of governance eventually came together on the level of the EU. The binding glue amidst all difficulties and periods of crisis, adjustment and consolidation of the European Economic Community were the unwavering provisions of the Treaties of Rome: A common market was to be achieved based on the primacy of legally binding decisions. This early contractual promise has remained at the core of European integration ever since March 25, 1957.

(d) The integration path was not only a permanent story of bargaining and bickering. In a more fundamental way, it has been a continuous effort to square the circle – with obviously different effects and sometimes ambivalent success. The key dispute before the Treaties of Rome were able to even come about already indicated the future trend: The idea of beginning European integration with the goal to establish a common market – promulgated in general terms for the first time by French Agricultural Minister Pierre Pflimlin at the Council of Europe in March 1951 – was not enthusiastically shared by all actors involved in the process, not the least in his own country; controlling Germany's production of coal and steel was one thing, but to let them have equal access to the French market was quite another idea. In fact the notion of a common market encountered strong resistance by the representatives of two schools of thought: by those who favored the development of a European free trade agreement and by those who thought that sectoral integration along the model of the ECSC should remain the reference point not to be overburdened by too big an idea.

It seemed widely plausible to spread supranational cooperation to the transportation sector. But the idea of promoting a special agency for atomic energy was not intuitively shared by all other partners. In fact it stemmed from the calculation of Jean Monnet that European integration had to serve the purpose of modernizing the French economy

31 See, for example, Featherstone, Kevin, *Socialist Parties and European Integration: A Comparative History*, Manchester: Manchester University Press, 1988; Jansen, Thomas, *The European People's Party: Origins and Development*, Basingstoke: Macmillan, 1998; Gehler, Michael, and Wolfram Kaiser (eds.), *Christian Democracy in Europe since 1945*, London/New York: Routledge, 2004.

should it be able to catch up with the German economic potential. To force the Germans into a common agricultural market would have to be paid for by a further opening of the French market for German industrial goods. But in order to strengthen France's economic competitiveness, Monnet calculated, it would be vital to increase research on and the practical application of atomic energy, preferably also paid for by France's partners without losing French influence over the process and France's sovereignty on matters of the military use of atomic energy. This position could hardly be matched with the proposal of a horizontal customs union leading to a general common market. There was to be only one solution. All partners had to agree on both approaches at the same time. So they did, and the Treaties of Rome created not only the European Economic Community, but also the Atomic Energy Community.

This arrangement set a precedent; moreover it echoed an unalterable fact: European interests were not to be achieved by simply pooling the resources of the partners of the integration process together. Although they shared the principle goal of peace and cooperation, all of them had to find arrangements that reflected different realities and hence different interests in each of their countries and societies. To achieve and maintain peace in Europe was an easy consensus after World War II, to support European integration in general terms as well. Even the idea to promote an ever closer union among the peoples of Europe was to be agreed upon by all rational politicians who had survived two world wars. But how to do it and with which intention – that remained an incessant conflict out of which robust und sustainable European interests deserving the name emerged only gradually. European interests are only those interests solidly agreed upon by all partners, not only in so far as their content, but also in so far as their intended goal and the practiced means needed to achieve it. Whenever this combination of considerations does not materialize, one cannot speak of European interests.

Politicians of all backgrounds tend to use the term European interests very casually to this day. This is significant in two ways: It speaks to the existence of a European public discourse about the formulation and implementation of these very interests, but it also testifies to the difficulty in properly and eventually bringing them about. The decision of the Intergovernmental Conference of 1956/1957 to agree on the establishment of two different European Communities – in fact adding to the European Coal and Steel Community and not taking into consideration the potential role of the Council of Europe, of the OEEC or of the Western European Union (WEU) – did not add to European cacophony and confusion, as one might have expected. Instead, it was the first application of a specific European way to deal with differences in background, approach, methodology and intention without losing sight of a joint commitment to furthering European integration.

The biggest success in the evolution of a multilevel European governance system during the early phase of EEC development is related to the evolution of genuine community resources for financing community policies.[32] This was no easy path and not an easy issue. Transferring national sovereignty to a supranational body was already hard enough a price to pay for traditional politicians, raised under the primacy of the nation state. Giving up budgetary rights would imply more: It would forfeit a parliamentary right that had grown in all European democracies and had become – rightly so – an embodiment of the legitimacy of parliamentary democracy. How could budgetary rights be transferred to the level of the EEC when the EEC did not operate as a parliamentary democracy – and should never do so in the eyes of ardent believers in the primacy of the nation state? To join forces with European neighbors out of necessity or even in order to enhance specific national interests was acceptable, but to give up budgetary rights to an executive that was not controlled by a parliamentary body on its proper level of operation seemed a non-starter. The final answer could only be: If the European Economic Community was to gain budgetary authority, budgetary rights had to be transferred from member states to the EEC, coupled with parliamentary control on the level of the EEC. But at that moment in time it was evident that neither taxation nor representation was a favorable idea for die-hard proponents of the primacy of the nation state, which they began to caress in the name of its ability to provide and protect democracy.

An equivalent to the battle cry of the American Revolution was not heard in the uniting Europe. Over time, its reverse notion grew louder: "representation without taxation." At least some combination of "taxation and representation" began to develop on the European level, slowly but steadily. But it began by contradicting all rules of parliamentary democracy so well upheld in post-war Europe. Budgetary authority was gradually transferred to the level of the European Economic Community and subsequently even extended during the life of the European Community. Its consequence was that the European Union was finally confronted with the overall issue of how to organize a European tax and no longer if or why such a tax would be inevitable.

The result of the "empty chair crisis" was astonishing, and in a way promising. The community method prevailed, no matter how much France insisted on the right to a national veto whenever vital national interests were at stake. More important for the long term deepening of the integration process was the recognition of a genuine community budget following the introduction of the next stage of the Common Agricultural Policy. While the Common Agricultural Policy was rightly criticized for encouraging overproduction and preventing agricultural commodities from other countries to freely enter the Community, it was incoherent and unfair that people criticized the European Commission. It was not the Commission but the will of the

32 See Strasser, Daniel, *Les Finances de l'Europe: Le Droit Budgétaire et Financier des Communautés Européennes*, Paris: Librairie Générale de Droit et de Jurisprudence, 1990.

member state governments to pursue this policy. The Commission was merely the executive body.

In light of the bitter quarrels of the past years, it was surprising enough that the member states granted budgetary rights over the duties levied for imports into the common market to the Commission. In light of growing tasks for the EEC it was only logical that the debate on an increase in the community budget would continue. By 1969 – with de Gaulle replaced by the more conciliatory President Georges Pompidou and the German Christian Democrats for the first time in opposition, being replaced by a majority of Social Democrats and Free Democrats under Chancellor Willy Brandt – the decision was confirmed to switch community funding from direct national contributions to a system of genuine own resources of the EC. A summit of the Heads of State and Government of the EC in The Hague in December 1969 also recognized the right of the European Parliament to control the spending of the Commission, thus beginning the process toward genuine parliamentary democracy on the European level. Simultaneously, the Hague summit also agreed on the establishment of an independent audit board of the community.[33]

When the merger of the three communities was completed in 1970, the number of EC commissioners increased from nine to fourteen. It would have been wrong to conclude from the "empty chair crisis" that the relevance of the European Commission had been completely undermined. For instance, the Commission was able to succeed in the community-wide harmonization of indirect taxes. The common market would continue to exist with different national tax systems. But the European Commission succeeded in convincing the member states to introduce a common value-added tax (VAT). The General Affairs Council of the EU decided in 1967 that all member states were required to introduce a system of value-added taxes, but left room for different rates. The 1969 summit of The Hague finally agreed that the future EC budgetary basis should consist not only of duties levied on agricultural and industrial imports into the EC. As of 1975, each member state was to pay one percent of its VAT income into the EC budget. Both decisions were confirmed by the Treaty of Luxembourg in April 1970, the first amendment to the Treaties of Rome. A cautious first step toward genuine taxation in the European Community had been taken. This was an important sign of the continuous path of political integration, using the realization of the common market as its vehicle but clearly reaching into particular sanctuary spheres of governance.

In 1989, the European Union extended the financial basis for EU operations by introducing a third dimension into the community budget: National contributions according to the proportional relationship of population and GDP in each member state were introduced, while at the same time the budgetary rights of the European Parliament

33 On implications of the Hague summit see Barre, Raymond, "Perspectives de la Communauté Économique Européenne après La Haye," *Bulletin de la Communauté Économique Européenne* 2 (1970): 9-14; Wilson, Jêrome, "Négocier de la Relance Européenne: Les Belges et le Sommet de La Haye," *Journal of European Integration History*, 9.2 (2003): 41-62.

were extended. Efforts to introduce a genuine EU tax in order to make the EU's source of income more transparent did not succeed at any later stage. With the European Constitution in 2004 and the Reform Treaty (Treaty of Lisbon) in 2007, the co-decision powers of the European Parliament were extended for non-obligatory expenses, including the Common Agricultural Policy and the structural funds. But both the European Constitution and the Reform Treaty fell short of introducing a genuine EU tax. Supporters of such a step had suggested that it would add transparency to the operations of the EU if the citizens of the Union were able to see which resources were allocated for which EU spending operation. The technically complicated combination of import duties, VAT rates and national contributions does not clarify the understanding of the broader public about the sources of the EU budget, which had grown to around 130 billion euros in 2008 (1.03 percent of the GDP of the European Union). The struggle for full parliamentary control over the EU's budget would continue. However, as the share of co-decision powers of the European Parliament had increased from four percent in 1970, 13 percent in 1975 and 47 percent in 1993, to 72 percent by 2009, the steady trend toward parliamentary democracy in the European Union was undeniable.[34] In 1957, this trend had been unimaginable even for the most optimistic Founding Fathers of the EEC.

5. The Cathartic Function of Crises

Crises in European integration have always fathered new initiatives of integration, be they repetitions of the original effort under new circumstances, detours and unintended consequences or simply changes of perspectives and priorities. Sometimes they went hand in hand with changes in national political leadership and thus changes in political priorities, new avenues or compromises among all EC actors involved. But the very history of crisis management in European integration matters reflects the highly political – and often politicized – character of the undertakings. This was evident after the failure of the European Security Community. It was again evident during the "empty chair crisis" and its aftermath. It was also visible during the late 1960's and early 1970's, when the European Community embarked on new and multiple impulses: "Completion," that is to say a resolution of the pending budgetary matters, "deepening," that is to say the advancement from a completed customs union to a European Monetary Union, and "enlargement," that is to say final acceptance of British membership after it had been rejected twice by French President Charles de Gaulle.

The initiation for this triple "relance européenne" took place with a visible sense of leadership during the EC summit in The Hague in December 1969. But its spirit was to

34 Maurer, Andreas, *Die Macht des Europäischen Parlaments: Eine prospektive Analyse im Hinblick auf die kommende Wahlperiode 2004-2009*, Berlin: Stiftung Wissenschaft und Politik, 2004: 34.

prevail into the early 1970's. Yet, one conclusion can be drawn from the study of the subsequent efforts of the EC to implement all good intentions of The Hague: Whenever the integration agenda was overloaded, it had to fail, at least in some of its dossiers. The factor of "time" became a dimension to reckon with in European integration matters – time as far as the available time for certain political constellations among like-minded politicians with a particular strong authority and good personal rapport is concerned, time as far as the overall political climate and the effect of contingent events on European integration matters is concerned, and time as far as the timing is concerned, which is required to gradually implement complex matters.

In 1968, a customs union had been achieved, but this was only the first formal step toward a comprehensive common market. The first ideas about a monetary union and in fact a common currency had already circulated during the proceedings of the Spaak Commission in 1955/1956. Since the first British application for EEC membership in 1962, the European Commission had argued that a European Monetary Union would deepen the integration process in an enlarging EEC. In February 1969, the European Commission submitted a memorandum on the prospects for European Monetary Union, named after its author, the French Vice President of the Commission, Raymond Barre. The Barre Memorandum, Desmond Dinan concludes, "was less a bold initiative for further integration than a cautious call for what the French government now wanted: monetary policy coordination and short-term support for balance-of-payments difficulties."[35]

In August 1969, the French franc was devaluated while in October, the German mark was revalued. Coordinating monetary policies – an essential first step toward a comprehensive European Monetary Union – would not be accepted in France if it would prohibit exchange rate fluctuations vital to maintain the effect of common agricultural prices and thus for the income of French farmers. The fundamental difference in the French and German action concerning the coordination of their currency policies left little room for optimism that the time was ready for further progress toward a European Monetary Union. Again it was the very experience of fundamental differences on a matter of relevance to the common interest in a stable and sustainable common market that opened the avenue for Franco-German reflections about a solution to the dilemma; finally, their consent had to be communicated to the other partners in the EC. This could not, however, deny fundamentally different interests as countries like Germany and the Netherlands with balance-of-payment surpluses did not want to constantly bail out France and Belgium, member states with chronic balance-of-payment deficits.

The Hague summit instructed the Council, in conjunction with the European Commission, to develop a plan during the year 1970 on how to establish a European Monetary Union in stages. Pierre Werner, Prime Minister and Finance Minister of Luxembourg, received the task of drawing the plan that was forever to become linked

35 Dinan, Desmond, *Europe Recast: A History of European Union*, op.cit.: 131.

with his name. The goal defined by the Werner Plan (worked out by a committee with representatives of all member state governments and Commission experts) seemed lucid and simple: Fixed exchange rates, a common monetary policy, and a single monetary authority had to be installed if a European Monetary Union was to be achieved.[36] Finance Ministers and experts among EC member states were deeply split between "economists," largely representing German and Dutch positions and insisting that convergence in economic policies had to precede monetary convergence, and "monetarists," largely representing French and Belgian positions according to which an early monetary union would in itself promote the convergence of the economies and hence of economic policies.

The Werner Plan of October 1970, described as the iron rule for achieving a European Monetary Union, stipulated that parallel progress had to be made on economic convergence and monetary policy coordination. In the final stage, the plan suggested the member states of the EC would revise the Treaties of Rome and establish new institutions on the European level, while transferring more rights to the European Parliament to counterbalance the national loss of sovereignty over monetary and economic matters. In reality, this would lead to further steps of constitutionalizing European integration. French President Pompidou – much in favor of a European Monetary Union that would help his country at the expense of partner countries to gain monetary stability without going through unpopular domestic macroeconomic policy reforms – fundamentally disagreed with the idea of stronger supranationalism as the ultimate outcome of the process toward monetary union. On substantial matters as well as on institutional aspects of a European Monetary Union the two leading member states of the EC were split. The idea seemed stillborn.

Amid domestic and European debates and escalating new tensions everybody had hoped would be overcome with the departure of President de Gaulle, the short-term meaning of the Werner Plan was lost. Not only with regard to the Werner Plan, the meaning of long-term planning in matters of European integration often remains undervalued. If political concepts are not immediately realized, both contemporary media and later historians tend to bury them in the archives. But in the process of European integration, the fermenting power of conceptual planning cannot be overrated as it always sets points of reference for later debates – until the moment and the constellation become ready to begin the implementation, if only gradually. The early call for a European constitution by the Parliamentary Assembly of the European Coal and Steel Community in 1953 can serve as such an example; the Tindemans Report of

36 Steinherr, Alfred, *30 Years of European Monetary Integration: From the Werner Plan to EMU*, London: Longman, 1994; Magnunssen, Lars, and Bo Strath, *From the Werner Plan to the EMU: In Search of a Political Economy of Europe*, Brussels: Peter Lang, 2001.

1975 on European Political Union was to become another example.[37] The most crucial and important issues of European integration were always the meeting point of different national interests and conflicting political majorities with substantial needs for Europe out of which, once they were resolved, grew a new, stronger and deeper integrated supranational reality.

In 1971, an international financial crisis broke out, and it seemed as if this would mean the final end to the dream of a European Monetary Union. Looking back on its ultimate effect on European integration, one must come to a different conclusion. The international financial crisis of the early 1970's, in conjunction with geopolitical conflicts, served as another grave challenge for the EC to which it ultimately had to respond with a new and success-oriented initiative toward deeper integration in matters of both monetary and economic policies. Political will prevailed over all sorts of doubts and skepticism. Europe time and again generated leaders and political constellations that rescued the overall dynamics of European integration, no matter whether or not the momentum was often lost on specific issues. As far as the most relevant turning points of European integration were concerned, at the end of each crisis, period of inertia, or external pressure stood a new, deeper and stronger stage in European integration.

6. The Function of Enlargement: The Need for Deepening

On January 1, 1973 the European Community was enlarged with the accession of Great Britain, Ireland and Denmark. This ended more than a decade of unhappy relations between the EEC and Great Britain, but also a twenty-year saga of unclear attitudes and actions, most notably in Great Britain as far as her position toward participation in European integration was concerned. With the accession of Great Britain, Ireland and Denmark, the alternative European path of a free trade zone through EFTA had practically lost its relevance.[38] While EFTA was factually dead, Britain would become and remain a difficult partner in the EC and so would Denmark. But neither of them was able or willing to alter the fundamental course of supranational integration and rip the supranational glue, the *acquis communautaire*, apart.

An exceptional precondition for British membership in the European Community was a referendum held on the matter in France. In fact, it was the first time that citizens in any EC member states were asked in a referendum by their government whether or not they were agreement with a fundamental decision of the EC. On September 21, 1972, with a weak participation of 52 percent, 68 percent of French voters said "yes" to

37 Named after Leo Tindemans, the outstanding Belgian Prime Minister from 1974 to 1979, this report is a historic document furthering the course of federal integration in Europe: Tindemans, Leo, "Report to the European Council," *Bulletin of the European Communities*, Supplement 1 (1976).

38 EFTA (ed.), *EFTA – Past and Future: A Discussion Paper on Achievements in Free Trade and Future Possibilities*, Geneva: EFTA Secretariat, 1980.

the accession of Great Britain. The question of Turkish membership more than four decades later activated the same mechanism of referendum-based membership in France and elsewhere. Should the result be favorable, it would enhance the popular legitimacy of a controversial decision. Should it be negative, it would not only impact the candidate country, but very likely also the credibility of those politicians who had advocated the enlargement. It was certainly a legitimate means to reassure public support inside the EU for a decision that was considered to be more complex and controversial than usual policy matters inside the Union. It was not astonishing that the same heated debates that erupted in some member states over internal policy decisions of magnitude, such as the introduction of the euro, broke out elsewhere over the question of EC membership of Great Britain and EU membership of Turkey. In all cases, the future cohesion and identity of the integration scheme was a legitimate concern.

Since the first round of accessions, it is one of the favorite topics of the academic and media discourse on European integration to speculate about the relationship between "deepening" and "widening."[39] A widely spread prejudice has it that each widening, that is to say the inclusion of new member states, would undermine the cohesion of the integration scheme and render "deepening," that is to say the pursuit and implementation of new common and supranational elements, almost impossible. In fact, the opposite is true. Since the beginning of serious negotiations about EC membership of Great Britain, the function of enlargements of the European Community – and later of the European Union – was the preparation, if not an anticipated preemption of the enlargement and its potential effects through new ways and means of "deepening." Instead of lamenting about a "crisis of deepening" that was intrinsically interrelated with EC or EU enlargements, it is more appropriate to understand the dynamics of the enlargement process. Practically all enlargements of both the EC and the EU have served as medium to either prepare for new initiatives geared to strengthen and substantiate the integration process or they were instrumental in order to undertake such measures in anticipation of an upcoming enlargement. This does not mean to say that enlargements occurred without difficulties and adaptational requirements. Yet on balance, enlargements have always strengthened and deepened the European community and broadened its horizon in a favorable way for each partner of the process as well as for the overall internal balance.

British membership – along with Denmark and Ireland, while the majority of Norwegians said "no" in a referendum following the successful conclusion of membership negotiations between the EC and the Norwegian government – broadened

39 For a solid and rational assessment of the matter see Wallace, Helen, *Widening and Deepening: The European Community and the New European Agenda*, London: Royal Institute of International Affairs, 1989; Nugent, Neill, *The Deepening and Widening of the European Community*, Manchester: Victoria University, 1991; Laurent, Pierre-Henri, and Marc Maresceau, *Deepening and Widening*, Boulder: Rienner Publishers, 1998.

the horizon of the European Community. Since 1957, the EEC's relations with former French and Belgian colonies had dominated the evolving development policy of the EEC, mainly manifested in the Yaoundé Convention of 1963 and extended in 1969. British membership broadened the perspective toward the members of the British Commonwealth. It did not take too long for the EC to draft one of its most innovative policies, the 1975 Lomé Convention, an arrangement with most former French, Belgian, Dutch and British colonies in Africa, the Caribbean and the Pacific.[40] It could also be argued that the embryonic evolution of a Common European Foreign and Security Policy – beginning with the installation of European Political Cooperation in 1970 – took place in anticipation of a stronger international role the EC would surely want to play once it included another of the leading world powers.

The timing of enlargement encouraged the gradual yet cautious evolution of a common foreign policy. In July 1970, the European Community had received another report, written by a committee under the chairmanship of Belgian diplomat Étienne Davignon, which the summit in The Hague had commissioned in December 1969. The Davignon Report had outlined the need for a common foreign policy beyond a common foreign trade policy. Also in the sphere of politics, the European Community should speak with one voice. It should participate in a more visible way in the management of world affairs. The Davignon Report did not suggest a treaty change, but increased cooperation among the member state governments. Regular consultation and coordination would be an important step toward a cohesive common foreign policy. Unlike in 1954 with the failure of implementing a European Defense Community and unlike in 1962 with the Fouchet Plans on political union, this time the project of a common foreign policy did indeed start. Only few months after Great Britain, Ireland and Denmark had joined the European Community on January 1, 1973, the members of the Council received a second Davignon Report on July 23, 1973, indicating that all member states should firmly commit themselves to avoid finalizing their own position unless the other partners were consulted through the mechanism of political cooperation.

From 1970, the Foreign Ministers of the European Community held two annual meetings; beginning in 1973 the meetings increased to four per year. When the European Council was established in 1974, further opportunities for regular meetings on the highest level of government representatives evolved.[41] The meetings of the Foreign Ministers were prepared by a Political Committee, which since 1973 had brought the

40 Frey-Wouters, Ellen, *The European Community and the Third World: The Lomé Convention and its Impact*, New York,: Praeger, 1980; Lister, Majorie, *The European Union and the Developing World: The Role of the Lomé Convention*, Avebury: Aldershot, 1988; Davenport, Michael, *Europe's Preferred Partners?: The Lomé Countries in World Trade*, London: Overseas Development Institute, 1995.

41 For the early years of the European Council see Hoscheit, Marc, and Wolfgang Wessels, *The European Council 1974-1986: Evaluations and Prospects*, Maastricht: European Institute of Public Administration, 1988.

Political Directors of the Foreign Ministries of the EC together four times a year and additionally whenever need for consultation and coordination arose. Within the Foreign Ministries of the EC, European Correspondents, that is to say representatives of the respective European Departments, were installed to constitute the operational framework of European Political Cooperation. The French proposal to establish a permanent secretariat for foreign policy was not supported by her partners in the 1970's as they had not forgotten the French efforts during the debate on the Fouchet Plans to eventually dominate European foreign policy.[42]

In spite of the fact that the common market grew on January 1, 1973, in spite of the creeping trend toward a more coordinated foreign policy and in spite of the beginning of a new global round on free trade negotiations in September 1973 (Tokyo Round), 1973 was not a good year for European integration. The Werner Plan had not been accepted by the Council during two meetings on November 24 and December 14, 1970, respectively. On March 25, 1971, a lowest common denominator-compromise between German "monetarists" and French "economists" had brought about a vague program of intergovernmental coordination of budgetary, tax, macro economic and monetary policies for the first stage of the possible implementation of the Werner Plan. This was already a strong reduction of the original ambition of the Werner Plan. The dollar crisis that broke out in the spring of 1971 destroyed all hope for an early realization of a European Monetary Union. International capital rushed into the Deutschmark as a consequence of a chronic overvaluation of the Dollar, based on the permanent increase in American payment deficits. When US-President Richard Nixon decreed the end of dollar-gold convertibility and a 10 percent surcharge for imports into the US, it factually meant the end of the Bretton Woods System. The Bretton Woods System had been established in 1944 as the new international monetary system based on fixed exchange rates and dollar-gold convertibility. Instead of agreeing to a joint reaction, the European partners split on how to react to the end of Bretton Woods.[43] For the time being, this was the burial of the ambitious and far-sighted Werner Plan. But Europe was to demonstrate again that like Phoenix rising out of the ashes, crisis could generate the revival of important projects once their time had come.

The 1970's did not end in distress, however. 1979 was a year of revival for the original idea of deepened integration. In March 1979, the European Currency System began to operate, the critical revitalization of the idea of European Economic and Monetary Union. In June 1979, for the first time ever, the direct election to the European Parliament took place. It marked a consolidation of institution-building and a new beginning of deepening European integration by connecting institutions and people in Europe. In 1979, the central institutions of European integration were consolidated.

42 See Knipping, Franz, *Rom, 25.März 1957: Die Einigung Europas*, op.cit.:196.

43 See Krause, Lawrence B., *Sequel to Bretton Woods: A Proposal to Reform the World Monetary System*, Washington: Brookings Institution, 1971; Cavanagh, John, et al. (eds.), *Beyond Bretton Woods: Alternatives to the Global Economic Order*, London/Boulder: Pluto Press, 1994.

They were not perfect and they did not exist unchallenged. But they were in place, the stabilized framework that helped to consolidate and sustain the fascinating idea of an integrated Europe through the means of gradual institution-building and policy formation.

The first period of European integration between 1957 and 1979 has to be assessed objectively and in context. No matter how much criticism arose over the very principle of a Common Agricultural Policy and its effects, no matter how slow many decisions seemed to be, moreover not even really transparent, without parliamentary control and often perceived as poor and shabby bickering among egotistic partners, no matter how many good ideas failed and plans were put to the backburner: European integration had for once begun and, in fact, was consolidated around the organizing idea of a supranational community. This in itself was the most impressive, convincing and fundamental response to the challenge, which two World Wars had posed for Europe.

Between 1850 and 1900, Europe had experienced eighteen inter-state conflicts; between 1900 and 1945 it had experienced nine, and since 1945 not one – before the outbreak of the Wars of Yugoslavian Succession in the 1990's.[44] On the territory of the European Community, peace had never had the opportunity for so long in the entire history of the region as is the case since 1945 and 1957 respectively. During World War II, that is to say during the short period from 1939 to 1945, 40 million people were killed in Europe, on average 18,500 per day. In light of these catastrophes, the European Community was more than an ordinary diplomatic or political success. It had become a cultural success story, an anthropological and morale response to the human-made disaster that Europe had suffered and imposed upon the rest of the world. With the end of two World Wars, the European nation state and its underlying principle of nationalism had lost much of its legitimacy. Yet the modern democratic nation state remained linked to the three modern expressions of state-sovereignty: domestic security, monetary control and foreign security. In all three spheres, the existence and evolution of the European Community had made inroads. No matter the critics and the skeptics, between 1957 and 1979 supranationality had been installed in Europe for the first time ever. It did not begin on March 25, 1957, and end on December 31, 1979. There has never been an autonomous date, a single day to understand the dynamics of integration processes. But all in all, 1957 and 1979 marked the first period of European integration. In the late 1970's, it had become common to understand European integration as more than a visionary idea. It had become an institutionalized political process, based on democratic decisions, rooted in the rule of law and about to generate the evolution of what later would be labeled a "multilevel system of governance."

44 Halpern, Joel M., and David A. Kideckel (eds.), *Neighbors at War: Anthropological Perspectives on Yugoslav Ethnicity, Culture, and History*, University Park, Pa.: Pennsylvania State University Press, 2000.

IV. 1979 – 1993: Economies Integrated

1. Monetary Union at Last

1989 was the year of peaceful revolutions across communist Europe. The symbolic breakdown of the Berlin Wall on November 9, 1989, will forever be remembered as a day of history, comparable to the storm of the Bastille during the French Revolution exactly two centuries earlier.[1] 1989 was a turning point for European integration in yet another sense. Less spectacular, often overlooked, belittled at the time it happened and amid many doubts about its final outcome, 1989 was also a turning point in the evolution of a common European currency. As early as 1955, after Jean Monnet had stepped down as President of the High Authority of the European Coal and Steel Community to become head of a private Action Committee for the United States of Europe, he had already pointed to the usefulness of a common monetary policy. In 1959, and again in July 1961, his committee proposed the introduction of a European Reserve Fund as first step toward a common European currency. Future currency crises should better be dealt with by the EEC. Neither European governments, the European Commission, nor parliamentarians felt a sense of urgency at that time to take the issue further. The world financial system established 1944 in Bretton Woods worked well and as the overall economic recovery of Western Europe seemed without limits, the creation of a common financial market, let alone a common currency, was not an urgent priority.

With the end of the long post-war boom, the mood had begun to change by 1973. But unfortunately European interests and actions in dealing with the global financial crisis were as diverse and contradictory as possible. The break down of the Bretton Woods system between 1971 and 1973, coupled with the consequences of the oil crisis, demonstrated how different economic structures, financial interests, and policy conclusions among EC member states still were. It was only under the pressure of global events beyond their own control that EC leaders developed a sense of urgency to coordinate and if possible to harmonize fiscal, monetary and economic policies. A long journey began when, on March 21, 1972, the EC member states invented the "Monetary Snake" as a first element of joint crisis management. In reaction to the lost certainty about the external value of the dollar, the German government had suggested to its partners that the currencies of the six EC member states should give up their linkage to the dollar. Instead they should float together in order to prevent inflation and to maintain parities among them. The French government, encouraged by the European

1 Kühnhardt, Ludger, *Revolutionszeiten: Das Umbruchjahr 1989 im geschichtlichen Zusammenhang*, Munich: Olzog 1994; Antohi, Sorin, and Vladimir Tismaneanu (eds.), *Between Past and Future: The Revolutions of 1989 and their Aftermath*, Budapest: Central European University Press, 2000; Kumar, Krishan, *1989: Revolutionary Ideas and Ideals*, Minneapolis: University of Minneapolis Press, 2001.

Commission, proposed that the EC currencies should maintain fixed parity with the dollar while introducing a control mechanism to prevent unwanted excessive import of dollars. The French government considered joint floating of EC currencies a factual reevaluation of the European currencies to the detriment of France's economic development. The EC currencies ended up divided in four groups: the Federal Republic of Germany floated freely and accepted a revaluation of the Deutschmark by 5 to 10 percent against the partner currencies; France and Italy imposed different currency import controls; Belgium and the Netherlands floated together.

After the US had accepted an official devaluation of the dollar by 7.89 percent in December 1971 and revoked the additional import surcharge, a new basis for rearranging the international monetary system was found. On December 18, 1971, the finance ministers of the leading industrial countries decided in Washington to end the period of floating and realign exchange rates with a margin of fluctuation of 2.25 percent on either side of the new dollar parity (Smithsonian Agreement). Based on this agreement, the EC members decided to reduce the margin of fluctuation among their own currencies by fifty percent. This was the creation of the "European snake" inside the "Smithsonian tunnel."[2]

Then EC Commission President Roy Jenkins is credited for having been the first to propose the reconsideration of the project of a European Economic and Currency Union in a speech at the European University Institute in Florence on October 27, 1977. French President Valéry Giscard d'Estaing and German Chancellor Helmut Schmidt endorsed the idea and prepared for its formal acceptance in the EC. Their proposal for the creation of a European Monetary System was accepted by the European Council on April 8, 1978, in Copenhagen, reconfirmed along with a detailed schedule by the European Council on July 6, 1978, in Bremen. On March 13, 1979, the European Currency System began to operate. It was based on three elements: an abstract reference currency, the ECU (European Currency Unit, named after a French currency valid between the thirteenth century and 1803), a new system of exchange rates, and interventions and various mechanisms concerning credits and transactions.[3]

The long march toward the euro had only just begun.[4] In spite of its shortcomings, the European Currency System served as an element of discipline helping to return to a period of currency stability and economic growth in the EC during the 1980's, unheard of since 1972. Interventions by central banks and the temporary need for currency parity adaptations did not undermine the European Currency System. When the Dooge Report

2 Aldcroft, Derek H., and Michael J. Oliver, *Exchange Rate Regimes in the Twentieth Century*, Cheltenham: Edward Elgar, 1998; Flandreau, Marc (ed.), *International Financial History in the Twentieth Century: System and Anarchy*, Cambridge: Cambridge University Press, 2003.

3 Grauwe, Paul de, and Theo Peters (eds.), *The ECU and European Monetary Integration*, Houndmills: Macmillan Press, 1989; Ribaud, Jacques, *The Case for a New ECU, Towards Another Monetary System*, New York: St. Martin's Press, 1989.

4 On the early years see Tsoukalis, Loukas, *The Politics and Economics of European Monetary Integration*, London: Allen and Unwin, 1977.

in 1984 initiated a whole series of treaty changes, finally leading to the Treaty of Maastricht and the full implementation of European Monetary Union, it reaffirmed the value of the European Currency System: In times of crisis, it had preserved the unity of the common market, safeguarded stable exchange rates and laid the foundation for the evolution of a currency identity in the EC.

The "1992 project," the path to complete the Single Market, was launched by the new EC Commission President Jacques Delors, in office between 1985 and 1995.[5] His arrival at the helm of the EC followed the beginning of the long Presidency of François Mitterrand in France (from 1981 and 1995) and the even longer Chancellorship of Helmut Kohl in Germany (from 1982 to 1998). In 1983, Socialist President Mitterrand was convinced by his Finance Minister Jacques Delors that France would have to stop socialist deficit spending and resort to a policy of austerity. Otherwise France might be forced to leave the European Monetary System and the Common Market. Mitterrand coupled his decision in favor of an unpopular austerity policy with a consistent commitment to European integration. Chancellor Helmut Kohl had always been an ardent supporter of European integration. Under public pressure against the deployment of new NATO cruise missiles on German territory, his predecessor Schmidt had lost the support of his own Social Democratic Party. Kohl and his coalition of Christian Democrats and Free Democrats resisted the anti-missile protest early in 1983 and received full endorsement for this policy by President Mitterrand. In light of new Soviet threats emanating from their deployment of SS-20 missiles directed against Germany and other West European NATO countries, following the invasion of Afghanistan in December 1979 and the outbreak of a new Cold War, France was adamantly convinced of strong defense. For Chancellor Kohl this attitude confirmed the need for German foreign policy to always couple transatlantic relations with a Franco-German accord. Never should his country find itself in a strategically important situation in which it would have to choose between loyalty to France and loyalty to the US. Helmut Kohl considered this the most important heritage of the policy of Konrad Adenauer. In François Mitterrand, he found his partner for a long period of a constructive Franco-German rapport on the crucial issues of European integration.

Ever since the European Council of Fontainebleau on June 25 and 26, 1984, the two leaders demonstrated the functioning of a Franco-German tandem in European integration matters. Endless initiatives were enacted by the two leaders. Long is the list of compromises they struck on issues of national disagreement. The European Monetary System operated until December 31, 1998, when it was finally replaced by the irrevocable fixing of exchange rate parities among the participants of the European

5 On his interpretation of the events and his presidency in general see Delors, Jacques, *Mémoires*, Paris: Editions Plons, 2003: on his legacy see Endo, Ken, *The Presidency of the European Commission under Jacques Delors: The Politics of Shared Leadership*, New York: St. Martin's Press, 1999.

Monetary Union and the creation of a new exchange rate system between participants and non-participants of the European Monetary Union within the EU.

On June 14, 1985, another agreement with symbolic and practical consequences was signed: The Schengen Agreement, named after a small town on the border of Luxembourg with Germany.[6] Germany, France, Luxembourg, the Netherlands, Italy and Belgium, but also the non-EU member states Sweden, Norway, Iceland, Austria, Spain and Portugal agreed to reduce and eventually completely lift border controls. The implementation procedures lasted an extremely long time, beginning only in 1995. Since 2001, all the signatory states of the Schengen Agreement have abolished border controls and introduced a single visa for all non-EU visitors, who are required to obtain an entry visa into any of these countries. For Europeans, it became a new feeling to cross a border among any of the states of the Schengen Agreement without presenting their passport or seeing a border police officer.

The Single European Act, in force since July 1, 1987, facilitated the way to a coherent political union and called on Europe to reinvigorate its potential and optimism amidst an economic and social crisis.[7] The completion of the Single Market and the realization of full economic and monetary union were the main goals stipulated in the Single European Act, the first noticeable treaty amendment since the Luxembourg Treaty of 1970 on budgetary matters.[8] The EC leaders realized the growing technological and productivity gap between the EC on the one hand and the US and Japan on the other. Europe was in need of a common market and a new initiative toward an integration deserving of this name. Crisis in the financing of the Common Agricultural Policy, necessary measures to implement the project of a Single Market, and the increased need for financial resources to implement community goals were dealt with in a cohesive package (Delors I Package), accepted by the European Council on February 11 and 12, 1988.

Up to this point, the preparatory work for the European Economic and Monetary Union had proceeded speedily. While the public debate was still highly controversial

6 Joubert, Chantal, and Hans Bevers, *Schengen Investigated: A Comparative Interpretation of the Schengen Provisions on International Police Cooperation in the Light of the European Convention on Human Rights*, The Hague/Boston: Kluwer, 1996; den Boer, Monica (ed.), *Schengen, Judicial Cooperation and Policy Coordination*, Maastricht: European Institute of Public Administration, 1997; European Union. European Commission, *The Schengen Acquis: Integrated into the European Union*, Luxembourg: Office for Official Publications of the European Communities, 2001.

7 McKenzie, George, and Anthony J. Venables (eds.), *The Economics of the Single European Act*, London: University of Southhampton, 1991; Engel, Christian, and Wolfgang Wessels (eds.), *From Luxembourg to Maastricht: Institutional Change in the European Community after the Single European Act*, Bonn: Europa Union Verlag, 1992; Swann, Dennis (ed.), *The Single Market and Beyond: A Study of the Wider Implications of the Single European Act*, London: Routledge, 1992.

8 McKenzie, George, and Anthony J. Venables (eds.), *The Economics of the Single European Act*, London: University of Southhampton, 1991; Engel, Christian, and Wolfgang Wessels (eds.), *From Luxembourg to Maastricht: Institutional Change in the European Community after the Single European Act*, Bonn: Europa Union Verlag, 1992; Swann, Dennis (ed.), *The Single Market and Beyond: A Study of the Wider Implications of the Single European Act*, London: Routledge, 1992.

across the EC, and Britain under the Premiership of Margaret Thatcher explicitly opposing EMU, the governments of France and Germany proceeded at full speed toward their common goal, albeit rooted in different interests.[9] They had to harmonize deep differences on the way to achieve this goal – Germany demanding a strong common currency, France requesting the early introduction of the currency by all means. The European Monetary System had shifted European currency relations in favor of the Deutschmark. The other EC member states were increasingly forced to peg their currency to the Deutschmark.

At the peak of German economic and monetary strength, the other European partners were in favor of a common currency in order to liberate themselves from German economic dominance.[10] For Germany, the constellation was more ambivalent. The German government of Chancellor Kohl had to embrace a highly sophisticated policy approach. While it did not want to alienate its European partners, it had to be cautious toward its own voters as far as the idea "to give up the Deutschmark" was concerned. Throughout the 1980's, this was not a popular idea in the Federal Republic.

While Chancellor Kohl signaled President Mitterrand his readiness to create a common European currency, Kohl's Foreign Minister Genscher proposed to establish a "Wise Man's Council" mandated to work out the principles required to create a European currency space with a European Central Bank at its head. Jacques Delors, the President of the European Commission, was designated by the European Council of Hanover on June 27 and 28, 1988, to chair such a council. Under the chairmanship of Delors, the presidents and governors of the Central Banks of the EC member states, a second member of the EC Commission and three monetary experts were asked to draft a manageable plan.[11] The group, by and large, oriented its work on the methods and propositions of the Werner Plan. When the Delors Plan was presented in April 1989, it declared on principle that in a Single Market, in which the movement of capital and goods was no longer under control of national governments, it was essential to harmonize national economic policies and unify currencies.

The member states, the Delors Plan suggested, would execute currency sovereignty together. The common European currency would generate more economic growth and would keep inflation rates low, it would help to strengthen the European economy vis-à-vis the US and would substantially enhance European integration. On June 27, 1989, the European Council in Madrid adopted the Delors Plan on the path toward a common currency. The plan contained three stages: The first one would not yet entail a treaty revision but was supposed to complete the Single Market, coordinate economic policies

9 See Gowland, David, and Arthur Turner, *Britain and European Integration 1945-1998: A Documentary History*, London/New York: Routledge, 2000.

10 On the French position on this matter see Howarth, David J., *The French Road to European Monetary Union*, Houndmills. Palgrave, 2001.

11 On the role and legacy of Jacques Delors see Ross, George, *Jacques Delors and European Integration*, New York: Oxford University Press, 1995.

and monetary cooperation as well as the participation of all EC member states in the exchange rate mechanism of the European Currency System; the second stage was dedicated to the preparation of a European System of Central Banks; the third stage would lead to the transfer of national competences on monetary and economic matters to community institutions, the establishment of irrevocable exchange rates and, finally, a common currency. The Madrid decision of June 27, 1989, reiterated the importance of the parallel developments of the economic and monetary aspects of the endeavor. The beginning of phase one of the European Currency Union was fixed for January 1, 1990. Once the first stage had begun, an Intergovernmental Conference would be summoned to prepare the next and final stages. The decisions of the European Council of June 27, 1989, were the actual turning point toward the European Currency Union. Almost two decades after his promulgation, the Werner Plan was ready to be realized. It would still take until January 1, 2002, for European citizens in 12 EU member states to have a common currency, the euro, in their pockets. For the first time since the Roman Empire – but this time based on voluntary decisions by democratically elected governments, fully and wholeheartedly approved by the European Parliament – Europe had a common currency. Then Spanish Prime Minister Felipe González is credited for having suggested the name euro, divided into cents, which can be understood in all European languages.[12]

The meaning of the decisions taken on European Monetary Union in June 1989 stands out among all other developments of European integration during the second phase of the process. These decisions finally enabled the completion of the Treaties of Rome and restated their intention by a wider, more solid and more meaningful implementation of the prerequisites of a Single Market beyond the formal revocation of tariffs. Finally, they were embedded in a complex web of decisions boosting the evolution of the European governance system and subsequently also the further evolution of a European foreign and security policy.[13]

European Monetary Union at last – that was the result of a long, often daunting and ambiguous process.[14] It required political steadfastness and will, a convergence of very different approaches and attitudes, a survival of crises and the recognition of the basic challenge: If Europe was to compete in the global economy it had to reinvent the concept of the Single Market originally laid out in the Treaties of Rome. It had to complete the project full circle should it not get lost again in the intricacies of executive

12 The decision was taken by the Madrid European Council on December 15 and 16, 1995.

13 See Dinan, Desmond, *Europe Recast: A History of European Union*, Boulder: Lynn Rieffer Publishing, 2004: 239-240.

14 For more detail, see Ungerer, Horst, *A Concise History of European Monetary Integration: From EPU to EMU*, Westport/London: Quorum Books, 1997; Lucarelli, Bill, *The Origins and Evolution of the Single Market in Europe*, Aldershot: Ashgate, 1999; El-Agraa, Ali M. (ed.), *The European Union: Economics and Politics*, New Jersey: Prentice Hall, 2001; Buti, Marco, et al. (eds.), *EMU and Economic Policy in Europe: The Challenge of the Early Years*, Cheltenham: Edward Elgar, 2002.

politics and bureaucratic inertia so often associated with the European integration machinery throughout the 1970's. It was no easy journey to come to sustainable agreements among the proponents of the very same idea. As much as it was a tall agenda the EC leaders had to muster, they have to be credited for not faltering in light of public skepticism and the ever-present British objection.

Among the legacies that surround the common European currency is that of a Franco-German deal in the context of German unification after the fall of the Berlin Wall.[15] In order to obtain French agreement on unification, so a false myth goes, Germany was ready to give up the Deutschmark and share its strong currency with France. Empirical evidence does not support this myth. As empirical evidence shows, the turning point in European integration history in favor of the implementation of a common European currency had been reached before the Berlin Wall came down. It cannot be denied that the whole project, of course, could still have been derailed between 1989 and 2002, but the political prize was too great. It can also not be denied that imminent German unification, and the expectation that a stronger Germany would need more than ever to be integrated into the European community, contributed to the acceleration of the project. But historical evidence must acknowledge the track record of monetary union development, beginning with the Werner Plan of 1970 and continuing with the turning point for the realization of a common European currency at the European Council meeting on June 27, 1989. This is the other significant date in 1989 as a turning point in European integration.

2. Storms over Europe

1973 was not a good year for European integration. When US Secretary of State Henry Kissinger declared 1973 the "Year of Europe," his announcement was perceived among many Europeans as a cynical attack rather than as a promising offer.[16] Parallel to an increasing American disengagement in Indochina, on April 23, 1973, Kissinger proposed a New Atlantic Charter to consolidate and revitalize the Atlantic partnership. Distinguishing between the global commitments of the US and the regional role and ambition of Europe, this approach was bound to receive a critical response. On July 23, 1973, the nine Foreign Ministers of the European Community, obviously under French and British guidance, responded with the claim that it would be time for a proclamation of European independence from the US. In a Document on European Identity, agreed upon at the summit meeting of the Council on December 15, 1973, in Copenhagen, the EC recognized that there was no alternative at this point in time to American nuclear

15 On the context see Knipping, Franz, *Rom, 25. März 1957: Die Einigung Europas*, Munich: Deutscher Taschenbuch Verlag, 2004: 249-253.

16 For his own account see Kissinger, Henry A., *American Foreign Policy*, New York: W. W.Norton & Company, 1974: 165-167 („The Year of Europe").

protection and the presence of American troops on European soil. Yet the relations between the EC and the US had to be put on the basis of an equal partnership. They did not influence the commitment of the EC to act as an independent and distinct entity. When at the end of the debating process the NATO Council recognized the independence of European Political Cooperation and signed a New Atlantic Charter in Ottawa on June 19, 1974, the act was in reality more face-saving than substance. The Americans wanted consultations before the EC decided on a foreign policy matter; the EC insisted to do it the other way around. As neither side was bound to forfeit existing bilateral channels, the New Atlantic Charter was open to a multitude of interpretations. Yet transatlantic relations relaxed again, only waiting for new disputes on, for instance, the issue of European importation of gas from the Soviet Union in exchange for building the pipelines.

1973 was also bad for Europe because of the implications of the outbreak of new violence in the Middle East. The Yom Kippur War of October 1973 was not met with any common European position. Even worse, the increased dependency of the EC on oil imports from the Arab world led to bitter consequences for the EC. Although the EC thought to pursue a highly balanced position on the Middle East, it had to suffer the dire effect of the Arab oil boycott in the autumn of 1973.

In 1958, energy consumption among the six founding countries of the EEC was based on 74 percent coal and only 10 percent oil. As oil got cheaper and access easier, the belief in atomic energy diminished in Europe, and with it the role of the Atomic Energy Community.[17] But as a consequence, by 1968, the EC based its energy consumption on 28 percent coal and 56 percent oil. By 1973, 67 percent of all energy consumption in the EC was based on oil. When all of a sudden oil prices skyrocketed from 2 dollars per barrel in 1973 to 10 dollars per barrel in 1974 and 12 dollars per barrel in 1975 (compared with 54 dollars per barrel in 2004 at the peak of the Iraq crisis) Europe was hit hard. After Arab oil producers imposed an embargo on the port of Rotterdam in reaction to the Dutch government's support for Israel, EC citizens were able to ride with bicycles on highways as their governments prohibited car driving on Sundays in order to save oil. That was the funny side of things otherwise getting worse, and making Europe's leaders realize the energy dependency of the EC.

Although the EU summit in Copenhagen in December 1973 promulgated "a ringing" declaration of European identity[18] – more occupied with the abstract and somewhat obsessive fear of transatlantic dependency of the US than with the effects of

17 EURATOM in itself had been a strange combination of French plans for economic modernization and its anti-American bias. France was favoring the use of a technology for the production of atomic energy based on the natural uranium available in France, in some French overseas territories and in the Belgian colony Congo. The other EURATOM partners rejected this technology and were in favor of enriched uranium, a technology successfully used in the US, cheaper and more advanced. The consequence of this disagreement was the different evolution of European atomic energy technologies throughout the 1960s – in spite of EURATOM.

18 Dinan, Desmond, *Europe Recast: A History of European Union*, op.cit. :153.

the disastrous oil dependency and its impact on the European economy – the EC was not capable of agreeing on a common position on energy matters. Finally, EC member states agreed to join the International Energy Agency (IEA), which had been established on American initiative under the framework of the Paris-based OECD. France refused to join. Finally, in 1974 the Council decided to reduce the EC dependency on oil imports and to establish national oil reserves for 90 days as well as EC-wide coordination in case of supply shortages.

Neither Europe's economic weight nor the ambitions of a coordinated foreign policy could alter the basic parameters of the oil crisis and of Europe's dependency on Middle East oil. Europe's independence was not only challenged by an American quest for primacy in transatlantic relations, but more so by energy dependency on the Middle East in the absence of a strong reciprocal bargaining power. Following the Yom Kippur War, the EC felt left out of diplomatic efforts to bring about a settlement in the Middle East, largely dominated by the US in close collaboration with Israel. In 1974, the EC announced the Euro-Arab Dialogue.[19] During "good weather periods" this might have been considered the most normal thing among regional neighbors. Now, it was almost considered an insult by Israel and the US while it did not substantially alter the power equation as far as European oil dependency was concerned. The US insisted that the Euro-Arab Dialogue would touch neither on the issue of oil nor on matters related to Israel. In 1977, and reiterated in 1980 (Venice Declaration), the European Community outlined its principles concerning a solution to the Middle East conflict: recognition of the right of existence and security for all countries in the region, Israel included, and recognition of the legitimate rights of the Palestinian people. The EC Declaration did not translate into any relevant operational program. When multilateral peacekeeping troops were sent to Sinai and Lebanon in 1981 and 1982, only Great Britain, France, Italy and the Netherlands (only to Sinai) sent individual national contingents. The EC was not a player.

The Middle East quagmire and Europe's helplessness did trigger new forces of self-assertion in the EC; this was also noticeable as far as economic and monetary development was concerned. In the end, various threats came together and merged into an obvious challenge the European Community had to respond to if it wanted to be taken seriously. While the dollar crisis in 1971 was still considered a transitory phenomenon, during the next two years the cumulative impact on the world economy had become evident.

In the field of diplomacy, European Political Cooperation proved most effective, yet hardly decisive. The very first meeting of the six Foreign Ministers of the EC on November 19, 1970, in Munich had already envisaged a possible genuine participation

19 Völker, Edmond (ed.), *Euro-Arab Cooperation*, Leyden: Sijthoff, 1976; Taylor, Alan R., *The Euro-Arab Dialogue*, Washington D.C.: Middle East Institute, 1978; Hallaba, Saadallah A. S., *Euro-Arab Dialogue*, Brattleboro, VT: Amana Books, 1984; Bat Ye'or, Eurabia: *The Euro-Arab Axis*, Madison, NJ: Fairleigh Dickinson University Press, 2005.

of the EC during the upcoming negotiations of the Conference on Security and Cooperation in Europe (CSCE). New hope to end the Cold War was associated with this conference that brought together all European countries, including Albania and the Holy See, as well as the US and Canada. Between July 1973 and July 1975, delegations from 35 countries negotiated in Helsinki until they reached agreement on the Final Act of the CSCE.[20] It became famous for its mechanism of dividing the issues contested in Europe into three baskets: The continent, still living in the absence of a formal peace treaty ending World War II, was jointly looking into matters of security, defense and confidence-building, economic cooperation and technological developments, and human conditions, including improved forms of human contacts and reassurance of basic human rights. Many of the pro-democracy movements opposing communist totalitarianism in Central and Eastern Europe were able to point to the signature of their government under a document clearly reaffirming all relevant basic human freedoms and rights. The CSCE Final Act became an important point of reference for dissidents in their struggle with communist dictatorships. In the European Community, hardly anyone took notice of the fact that the CSCE Final Act could also have served as point of reference for the evolution of a common foreign policy of the EC. On August 1, 1975, Italian Prime Minister Aldo Moro – murdered less than three years later by left-wing terrorists on May 9, 1978 – signed the CSCE Final Act not only as representative of his country, but as acting President of the European Council, also explicitly on behalf of the European Community.

The hard choices were more difficult to muster for the European Community. The economic performance of the EC began to worry many observers during the late 1970's and early 1980's. Japanese technological development impressed the world, the "Little Tigers" in South East Asia emerged, South Korea became a relevant player among industrialized states and the United States recovered under the optimistic leadership of the Presidency of Ronald W. Reagan, who revitalized America's "can do-spirit." Europe in turn became the object of caricature for many media, deprecating obituaries of the EC as the lifeless fossil of a continent burdened by smokestack industries, the inexorable costs of the welfare state, rigid labor laws and even more rigid trade unions. Euro-sclerosis became another term for European integration.

The poor European performance in the global economy was considered to be a function of highly overregulated and inefficient political processes.[21] Between 1950 and 1973, the average annual growth rate per capita GDP in Western Europe had been 4.1 percent on average; between 1973 and 1998 it slumped down to 1.8 percent on

20 Goodby, James E., *CSCE: The Diplomacy of Europe Whole and Free*, Washington D. C.: Atlantic Council of the United States, 1990; Farrell, Henry, and Gregory Flynn, "Piecing Together the Democratic Peace: The CSCE, Norms and the 'Construction' of Security in Post-Cold War Europe," *International Organization* 53.3 (1999): 505-535.

21 See Albert, Michel, and Robert James Ball, *Toward European Economic Recovery in the 1980s: Report to the European Parliament*, New York: Praeger, 1984.

average.[22] The European Community had become the symbol of a huge misallocation of resources at the expense of other parts of the world (Common Agricultural Policy) coupled with increasingly protectionist tendencies, also in the industrial sector, while at the same time incapable of reviving economic productivity and technological modernization, and of organizing its own security. Worst of all, security dependency on the US was linked to a combination of a beggar-thy-neighbor-policy and tides of anti-Americanism. Most importantly, European decision-making procedures were highly dilemma-prone, inefficient, ineffective, and the root cause of the creeping inertia that held the EC hostage.

The second Cold War after the Soviet invasion of Afghanistan in December 1979 reinforced the security obsession in Europe, coupled with fear and an inclination to simply shy away from reform requirements.[23] Yet the global setting, which Europe could not escape and, in fact, even increasingly wanted to shape, was forcing the European Community to wake up to the set of challenges it was confronted with. Between the formal completion of customs union in 1968 and the launching of the Single Market project in 1985, economically the European Community undermined much of the trust and respect it had developed over the first decade of its existence. The Commission had become excessive striving for harmonization, although the root causes were all too often specific economic interests of member states or certain individual companies or sectors of the industry. Yet the stereotypical impression was cemented: That "Brussels" was a bunch of well-fed bureaucrats detached from real life and untamed by any political control. Only the latter aspect was serious, finally giving way to a strengthened role of the European Parliament. Deficits in parliamentary democracy on the level of the EC were exacerbated by the lack of leadership and cohesive orientation on the national level. But this criticism did not pertain to Europe alone. The issue of governability in the Western world during the 1970's and 1980's became a hot topic across the globe.[24]

Under these circumstances, the efforts of Helmut Schmidt and Valéry Giscard d'Estaing to remobilize European insights into the importance of coordinated and harmonized economic and monetary policies were remarkable and laudable exceptions. Progress was to emanate from European integration efforts through crises and pressure, internal and external alike. This had become the rule of experience, affirmed by all possible exceptions. It was also significant that, after all, the political process mattered.

22 See Ferguson, Niall, *Colossus: The Price of America's Empire*, New York: Penguin Press 2004: 240.

23 Heller, Mark, *The Soviet Invasion of Afghanistan: Motivations and Implications*, Tel Aviv: Center for Strategic Studies, 1980; Arnold, Anthony, *Afghanistan: The Soviet Invasion in Perspective*, Stanford: Hoover Institution Press, 1981.

24 Most notable was a Report to the Trilateral Commission: Crozier, Michel, Samuel P. Huntington, and Joji Watanuki, *The Crisis of Democracy: Report on the Governability of Democracies to the Trilateral Commission*, New York: New York University Press, 1975. On the Trilateral Commission and its role see Beverungen, Johannes, *Elite Planning Organizations: Traditionen, Charakteristika, Implikationen der Trilateral Commission*, Baden-Baden: Nomos, 2005.

While the primacy of the market became a global creed, European integration remained essentially a political project, defined by political decisions and not by market forces. No political system under the conditions of democratic rule can overlook the role of the people it pretends to represent. Not only did governments have to exercise the leadership required to keep the European machinery going, European citizens had to be recognized in their desire to have the European Community work to their advantage. By the 1970's, the fear to fall back into nationalism and another war among the EC partners had substantially vanished. Fear of communism remained strong and the Soviet threat a permanent incentive to hold the Western world together. But more and more, concern about the quality of European policy making turned into criticism of a democratic deficit in the EC. Emerging European interests could only be sustained if they would take the people more seriously – not only as part of the process, but as its foundation and purpose.

3. Emerging European Interests in the Spheres of Economics and Politics

The second period of European integration started with consolidated institutions. It came to an end with the refounding of the European Community as the European Union through the Treaty of Maastricht. This period of integration saw the completion of the market integration, the beginning of a steady flow of treaty-based efforts to constitutionalize European integration, and the beginning of the effects of the most fundamental geopolitical changes that occurred with the end of the Cold War. This second phase of European integration experienced the emergence of four new robust and sustainable European interests:

a) A growing understanding that a common market would require a common currency, which would, however, not come about automatically but would be dependent upon intensive processes of harmonization, compromises and legally-binding mechanisms to make it eventually work as a Single Market.
b) An emerging consensus that the common market would need mechanisms of solidarity and resource allocation to develop a better balance among all regions and economic structures of a community whose asymmetries increased with each new enlargement.
c) A solidified agreement that further economic cooperation would inevitably require a consistent development of institutional mechanisms and a steady constitutionalization beyond the original structures laid out in the Treaties of Rome in order to strengthen legitimacy and popular support for European integration.

d) An enhanced awareness that the European Community would inevitably need to raise its international political profile, requiring new initiatives toward political cooperation and eventually the emergence of a common foreign policy.

(a) The path toward European Monetary Union, as outlined above, remained the biggest challenge and the most lasting success of the second stage of European integration. It was achieved only through crises and after phases of failure. But in the end it was achieved. It was coupled with the goal to completely realize the Single Market by December 31, 1992. When European Commission President Jacques Delors presented his program to the European Parliament, he already had in mind that it would take two periods for the mandate of the European Commission to complete the Single Market through the dissolution of all existing barriers. The Single Market Program, as set out in the Commissions White Paper of 1985, constituted the most ambitious and comprehensive supply-side program ever launched under the roof of European integration.[25] The White Paper identified all the existing physical, technical and fiscal barriers, which still justified continuous frontier controls between the EC member states. It then set out a seven-year timetable for getting rid of each of them. British Commissioner Lord Cockfield was in charge of implementing a catalogue of 282 directives as identified in the White Paper. He did it so well that Prime Minister Thatcher became highly critical of him. She accused him of no longer serving his country, but of the worst thing possible: having a European interest. She did not appoint him for a second term to the Commission. Microeconomic as well as macroeconomic barriers had to be abandoned in order to establish a Single European Market. Competition policy became an essential tool to prevent the national re-segmentation of national markets via anti-competition behavior through cartels, state aid, or the abuse of a dominant position. Measures to facilitate the transport of goods at the internal community-borders through technical simplifications of tax procedures and customs control, the dissolution of passenger control at the internal community borders, and simplification of veterinary and phytosanitary control mechanisms at the place of origin of products simplified the operations of the European economy. More difficult was the process of turning the capital markets of the EC into a single one. This process delayed the formal conclusion of the Single Market project at the end of 1992 to a great extent. This was also true with respect to the full implementation of legislation facilitating the comprehensive free movement of people, including the aggregation and portability of pension and social security rights acquired by EC workers. While intra-EC migration in border areas increased by 18 percent between 1987 and 1994 there has never been larger scale migration of labor within either the EC or the EU.

25 European Communities, European Commission, *Completing the Internal Market: White Paper from the Commission to the European Council (Milan, 28-29 June 1985)*, Brussels: European Communities, 1985. On the process toward a Single European Market see Mayes, David G. (ed.), *The Evolution of the Single European Market*, Cheltenham: Edward Elgar, 1997.

Based on the Commission's Social Action Program of 1989, a framework for minimum standards of social policies has been established, for example in the area of health and safety at work, while outright harmonization of social policies has not become an objective of the EU. The Single Market Program accelerated the internationalization of companies in Europe. Consumer interests also became more relevant, although the harmonizing legislation led to mixed results as far as quality criteria and price reductions are concerned. But with the Single Market Program, a new beginning was imminent across the EC, driven by an optimistic prognosis: Freedom of capital, goods, services and people would generate an additional economic growth in the EC of around one percent annually over a period of six years, as estimated by the Cecchini-Report in 1988.

Global economic developments turned out to be favorable for the ambitions of the Europeans. Prices for oil and other natural resources declined. Decisive for the political implementation of the manifold Commission directives was the increase in qualified majority voting with the Single European Act that facilitated decision-making in the relevant formations of the Council. As far as powers to speed up the implementation of the Single Market were concerned, the European Commission was given enlarged competences for issuing decisions, based on Council directives.[26] Across the EU, conglomerates and private businessmen, trade unions and business associations alike, were highly motivated and supportive of the project that returned dynamics and economic growth to Europe and gave focus and new purpose to the integration process.

(b) The technological gap between Europe, on the one hand, and the US and Japan on the other hand, had grown dramatically until the late 1970's. Organizing a community wide technology policy became a new sphere of action for the EC, but this did not seem to produce a turn around. Productivity and technology gaps could not be reduced by new community activities in the fields of telecommunications, biotechnology or information-technology if the framework was not functioning. Non-tariff barriers had survived the creation of customs union and common market. Deregulation was required in many areas, and those who favored this with growing intensity were concerned that new EC initiatives would merely lead to re-regulations while the opposite was the priority of the decade. This general dispute on order concepts was not to vanish without a clear and fresh focus of EC priorities and actions.

Moreover, a European industrial policy and a common industrial space developed only very slowly. Due to the absence of relevant competences in the Treaties of Rome, the EC could only coordinate the industrial measures undertaken by the member states. This was too little to improve their global competitiveness during the 1960's and

26 At the time, the following legislative instruments were in use in the European Community: binding "regulations" with immediate enforcement and "directives" requiring national implementation regulations; non-binding "decisions," "recommendations" and "opinions."

1970's. The European Commission launched a debate on competition policies, another one about the wisdom of public subsidies and it outlined the plan for a European industrial space. While France was favorable to industrial interventions of the EC, Germany, and even more so Great Britain, were against it. The international economic crisis after 1973 forced the EC in some cases to intervene, for example in support of the European ship building, textile and leather industries. During the 1970's, an aggravated crisis in the European steel industry generated the biggest management of industrial matters by the EC thus far. With respect to provisions inherited with the merger of EEC and European Coal and Steel Community, the EC decreed production limitations, negotiated with third countries about limits to their imports into the EC, and in October 1980 announced an "obvious crisis", which gave the EC the right (according to Article 58 of the ECSC Treaty) to impose production quotas on steel companies.

The Hague summit of 1972 initiated support for an EC technology policy. For once, EURATOM was instrumental, as it was agreed upon that its activities should be broadened to cover other high technologies: With the goal to develop controlled thermonuclear fusion as the most promising source of future energy, the first European company, based on Community law, was founded (Joint European Torus). To extend the development of European companies into other spheres proved to be difficult. Labor laws differed too much between the EC member states, and the German model of co-determination between the social partners in large companies led to deep disagreement among EC partners in the early 1970's. The only companies finally operating throughout the EC were American ones, their headquarters mostly based in the US. The European Community was able to promote specialized industrial cooperation, mostly among a few partner states (like Airbus with French, German, Italian and Belgian participation, the European Space Agency, and the two companies involved in the process to enrich uranium, Urenco with German, Dutch and British involvement, and Eurodif with French, Italian, Belgian and Spanish participation). Mergers among companies could not, however, facilitate the creation of a European Shareholder Company (societas europae), which came about only after 2001 – in spite of more than a decade of recognition about its urgency.[27] This new legal form enables European companies to expand and reorganize across the EU without expensive and time-consuming formalities traditionally related to the creation of affiliates. In Germany, the implementation of this European law took until 2005. European companies can now choose between a German management structure with Executive Board and Supervisory Board or the Anglo-Saxon board-model with a Management Board as it also is practiced in France. Co-determination will be regulated through negotiations between the Board and representatives of the employees.

27 Maitland-Walker, Julian, "The Societas Europae: Useful Corporate Vehicle or Political Stalking Horse?," *European Competition Law Review*, 12.3 (1991): 97-100.

Only the project of a Single Market, strategically initiated and popularized by the European Commission, gave European economic efforts a relevant boost, finally launched and legalized as a Community interest by the Single European Act in 1987. The Single Market project, to be completed by 1992, was coupled with various new programs aimed at enhancing cohesion in the European Community. Structural funds, regional funds and cohesion funds completed the list of resource allocation activities of the European Community. They were also a function of the EC enlargement to Europe's south with Greece joining in 1981, Spain and Portugal in 1986.

(c) The institutional design of the European Economic Community established by the Treaties of Rome in 1957 was revolutionary in its time. However, it proved to be insufficient for a community that was growing in relevance, in scope and in size. With the rising ability of the European Community to set norms in an emerging common market, criticism grew about the insufficient accountability for the operations of the European Commission. The need to enhance and streamline the political procedures in the EC became inevitable. The European Economic Community had to grow into the European Community and needed to be reinvented as the European Union. This daunting process required treaty changes that corresponded to the establishment of a European pre-constitution. Throughout this period, national skepticism about the value of increased political coordination, or even integration, remained high. The EC found itself torn between underperformance and over-expectations. It was up to the political leaders of the member states to give a new impetus to the community. European summitry became a new reality in the process of policy making in the EC. It was followed by an ever-increasing quest of the European Parliament to gain a stronger role and to get directly elected in accordance with the democratic principles, which the EC claimed to uphold. Efforts to balance the recalibration of the relationship between the representation of the member state governments and the representation of the community citizens became a permanent feature of power struggles. It turned out to be a gradual, but with creeping advancement toward parliamentary democracy on the level of the EC. The European Commission found itself torn between the role of a neutral protector of the treaties, the motor of further integration, and the object of control by both sides of the emerging double-headed EC legislature.

When the Heads of State and Government of the EC met for their first summits after General de Gaulle had left the scener in 1969 (The Hague) and in 1972 (Paris), they were aware of the fact that the original provisions of the Treaties of Rome had to be revised. An automatic mechanism for the introduction of qualified majority voting had been blocked since the Luxembourg Compromise of 1966. Yet advanced and more focused work was necessary to keep integration on track and deliver the goods that were promised with the emergence of a common market. The Luxembourg Compromise had reduced the role and ambition of the Commission, but it did not eliminate its supranational quality. Yet the Commission President was confronted with difficulties in ensuring his participation in intergovernmental fora, including in the summit meetings and in the European Council that would evolve during the 1970's. It took three decades to find a new balance between the institutions as now outlined in the Treaty of Lisbon. The first decisive steps in this struggle for the power equation and constitutional character of the European Community began in the early 1970's.

On September 14, 1974, the new French President Valéry Giscard d'Estaing invited the Heads of State and Government of the nine EC member states to another summit in Paris. After much skepticism from the side of the smaller EC member states, but backed by German Chancellor Helmut Schmidt, this meeting decided on the permanent procedure to hold regular summit meetings, henceforth labeled the European Council. With the President of the European Commission having the right to participate, the European Council was to meet three times a year, in accordance with the rotating EC presidency across the national capitals. This procedure was amended to two meetings a year in 1985 and later enlarged to four meetings a year, out of which many were held outside national capitals with the intention of showcasing the cultural diversity of the EC.

For the time being, the 1974 decision was executed outside the realm of the Treaties of Rome. It clearly was an intergovernmental operation. Standing outside the EC Treaties, decisions by the European Council could not be bound by the European Commission, the European Parliament or the European Court of Justice. British Prime Minister Margaret Thatcher – arriving on the European scene in 1979 – could rejoice about this intergovernmental structure aimed only at achieving some minimal overlap of national interests by stating in 1981 that "there is no such thing as a separate Community interest; the Community interest is compounded of the national interests of the ten member states."[28] Over time, this rigid perspective had to be replaced by a more differentiated perception according to which an intrinsic amalgamation of national, community and, moreover, political interests evolved in the EC, also espousing the seemingly uncontrolled autonomy of the European Council. With the Single European Act, the European Council finally became a supranational entity, rooted in European law.

The European Council did occupy itself with the widest possible variety of issues. Institutional matters were as much on its agenda as economic and social issues, questions of foreign policy and, of course, monetary policy. "In many ways," Derek Urwin concludes, "the success of the European Council has depended upon the degree of compatibility between French and West German interests."[29] The most important of

28 Cited in Urwin, Derek W., *The Community of Europe: A History of European Integration since 1945*, London/New York: Longman, 1995: 175.

29 Ibid.: 176.

all decisions taken by the European Council was the one of 1978 to establish the European Monetary System.

The Paris summit of 1972, two years before the formal creation of the European Council, had defined as the most urgent and noble goal to transform the relations among the member states of the European Community before the end of the decade into a European Union – although, as then Irish Foreign Minister Garret FitzGerald later recalled, "no one knew what European union meant."[30] It would be inappropriate to describe the relationship between the European Council and the other EC institutions as being one of genetic and permanent antagonism and adversity. The evolution of the European Council did prove the importance and primacy of the member states whenever further "deepening" of the European Community was at stake. The EC was not holding competence-competences. This was the real fact of the matter, yet one which gives a subtler image to a complete story, which was always more than a War of the Roses between the European Council on the one hand and the European Community on the other. The European Council became an organ to shape and, in fact, to advance the European Community before it became a constitutional part of the European Union. This is true; yet, it was never simply "the other," but rather the driving force and the embodiment of the fact that the member states, after all, were the providers of the integration treaties and, hence, also those that largely defined their evolution. This was certainly true in the absence of parliamentary democracy on the European level, which itself was to grow with continuity throughout the 1970's and 1980's.

The founding meeting of the European Council in 1974 decided to enhance the role of the European Parliament. Thus, it initiated the very path toward parliamentary democracy in the EU that would have been unimaginable if the European Council had seen its role primarily as one of opposing the further deepening of European integration. Despite British and Dutch reservations, the first European Council summit also declared a strengthening of the Parliament by granting it more rights in the legislative process of the European Community. Then Commission President François-Xavier Ortoli told the European Parliament in February 1975 that the creation of the European Council "represents a major change in spirit and may, if we are not careful, shake the institutional structure set up by the treaties to their foundation".[31] European Commission and European Parliament became allies in preventing this from happening. By 1976, the European Council was finally accepting the first direct election of the European Parliament. It had gone a long way to achieve this first truly historical success.

For the first time, the European Parliamentary Assembly had demonstrated its will in a more symbolic way in 1958: Against the suggestion of the EEC member states to appoint an Italian candidate – in order to give all member states a share in institutional

30 FitzGerald, Garret, *All in a Life: An Autobiography*, Dublin: Gill and Macmillan, 1991: 132.
31 Cited in Dinan, Desmond, *Europe Recast: A History of European Union*, op. cit. :161.

positions – the very first meeting of the Parliamentary Assembly on March 19, 1958 appointed Robert Schuman as its President. The parliamentarians wanted to honor the work of one of the Founding Fathers of European integration. With his move to organize security and economy not against the defeated Germans, but along with them, he became one of Europe's wise men of the twentieth century. His Schuman Plan of May 9, 1950, was the single most important step on the side of France to change the parameters of conflict in Europe. It was a sign of respect and gratitude that the delegates of the Parliamentary Assembly of the EEC appointed Robert Schuman – who was born in 1886 to a Lothringian father and a mother from Luxembourg, was raised bilingual in German and French, served in the German army from 1914 to 1918, became a French citizen in 1919, was arrested and held by the Nazi secret police (Gestapo) from 1940 to 1942, became French Prime Minister in 1947/1948, a highly respected Foreign Minister from 1948 to 1953 and died in 1963 – their first President.

Later disputes between the European Parliament and the European Council were less dignified. Increasingly, the issues were related to power sharing in a community with ever increasing relevance for public life in Europe. The members of the European Parliament rightly claimed that they are the prime representatives of the European people and hence should get a bigger share in the decision-making process of the European Community. The first direct election to the European Parliament in June 1979 was historic indeed.[32] For the first time anywhere in the world, a multinational parliament was elected by all eligible citizens of a supranational community. No matter how limited the supranational structures and their effect on community life were to be measured, the direct election to the European Parliament was more than just a symbolic act. It was the real beginning of the parliamentarization of European politics, which began with consultation and cooperation rights for the parliament before the mechanism of co-decision opened the door to its full role in the legislative process.

In the process of the evolution of democracy on the level of the nation state, the struggle for parliamentary rights had always been at the center of the quest for democracy, participation and political accountability. While the rule of law was established in most countries ahead of stable parliamentary power, in the end both processes merged, bound together by the budgetary rights of parliament and its right to select a majority-based government. The European Parliament began its journey toward the full realization of this goal with the direct election in 1979. The number of parliamentarians increased sharply from 198 to 410: 81 each for France, Germany, Italy and Great Britain, 25 for the Netherlands, 24 for Belgium, 16 for Denmark, 15 for Ireland and 6 for Luxembourg. A unified election procedure unfortunately did not come about. All in all, the first direct popular election to a European Parliament ever in the

32 Sweeney, Jane P., *The First European Elections: Neo-Functionalism and the European Parliament*, Boulder: Westview Press, 1984; Reif, Karlheinz (ed.), *European Elections 1979/81 and 1984: Conclusions and Perspectives from Empirical Research*, Berlin: Quorum, 1984; Kirchner, Emil J., *The European Parliament: Performance and Prospects*, Aldershot: Gower, 1984.

history of the continent resembled early constitutionalism in Europe's nation states in the mid-nineteenth century.

It should not come as a surprise that the first direct elections to the European Parliament received a lower voter turnout than national parliamentary elections on average in Europe. But the voter turnout of 63 percent on EC average could also be considered fairly high given that the stakes were not yet very high. Why bother to vote for a parliament that had no real decision-making powers? The results reflected the overall party affiliation in the EEC member states, with Social Democrats and Christian Democrats being the two dominant political groupings. The Social Democrats won 27.5 percent (113 seats), the European People's Party – the first EC-wide party established by the Christian Democrats in 1978 in preparation of the direct parliamentary election – won 26.8 percent (110 seats). Together with other smaller groups of the center-right they formed the majority. The French member of the European People's Party, Simone Veil, was appointed the first President of the directly elected European Parliament. The subsequent elections in 1984, 1989, 1994 and 1999 ended with marginal shifts in the political make-up of the European Parliament. While a continuous swing of the pendulum in favor of left of center parties was at first noticeable, in 1999 the European People's Party became the biggest faction.

For the first time, the European Parliament made headlines in November 1984 when it refused to grant discharge of the 1982 EC budget, invoking one of its limited rights. Throughout the first two decades in operation, the European Parliament was largely operating on a consensual basis as both big political groupings were promoting an increase of parliamentary rights. As this was the most important issue in the early decades of emerging parliamentary democracy in the EC, it seemed as if disagreement on policy choices hardly existed. Over time, this made it difficult for EC parliamentarians to gain authority in their respective national debates as they were often perceived as lobbyists for the sake of "their own" cause of strengthened parliamentary rights and less so as parliamentarians lobbying for the citizens' cause. The fact that parliamentarians were seated according to factions – labeled "political families" – and not in national order was significant and a practice since the very days of the General Assembly of the European Coal and Steel Community. The more a parliamentary-based system of European governance evolved – undeniable with the Treaty of Maastricht – the more the parliamentary factions gained in power and relevance in brokering European decisions.[33]

To this ambivalent image of the European Parliament in its early days was added the fact that it was not rare for national political groupings to send politicians into the European Parliament who were not or no longer in the forefront of events in their own

33 Morgan, Roger, and Clare Tame (eds.), *Parliaments and Parties: The European Parliament in the Political Life of Europe*, New York: St. Martin's Press, 1996; Lewis, Paul, and Paul Webb (eds.), *Pan-European Perspectives on Party Politics*, Leiden/Boston: Brill, 2003.

country. While in the past, it was compulsory for members of the European Parliament to be simultaneously a member of their own national parliaments, during the first legislature of the European Parliament still ten percent of MEPs (Members of the European Parliament) held a dual mandate. Even this percentage soon disappeared as the European Parliament grew in stature, and national political parties began to search for more competent and committed candidates to run for the European Parliament.

The emergence of a directly elected European Parliament was an important event in the formation of the European multilevel system of governance. A group of Three Wise Men (Barend Biesheuvel, Edmund Dell, Robert Marjolin) had been requested a year before this election by the European Council to design proposals in order to improve the ineffective decision-making mechanism in the EC. They suggested to (again) strengthen the European Commission and to extend the use of qualified majority voting in the Council. This report was followed by the so-called Genscher-Colombo-Plan, an initiative of the German and Italian Foreign Ministers in November 1981. Along with the European Parliament, they favored the signing of a Single European Act by which the complex institutional system of the EC should be organized in a definitive way around the European Council. It was also to give complete rights of deliberation on all EC matters to the European Parliament. They stressed the need for each member state to explain in writing why a right of veto was invoked on a matter of "vital national interest" in the Council. A Solemn European Declaration in June 1983 confirmed the gist of the Genscher-Colombo-Plan and opened the way to intergovernmental negotiations for the Single European Act.

The Single European Act legalized the European Council as part of the EEC Treaties. This institution had become indispensable, although its specific function and form was not properly outlined. In order to enhance the efficiency of decision-making in the EC, the Single European Act extended the principle of qualified majority voting in the Council on all matters related to the full implementation of the Common Market and in order to initiate new policy fields in the EC. Unanimity prevailed on tax matters and on questions relating to the freedom of movement for workers in the EC. In order to facilitate the work of the European Court of Justice, the Single European Act established a second court chamber of first instance. For the first time, the European Parliament was designated as such in the EEC Treaties. A new legislative method of cooperation between the European Parliament and the Council was established. On all decisions that were to be taken with qualified majority voting in the Council, the parliament was to be able to add proposals for change. If the European Commission agreed with a parliamentary proposal, it could only be rejected by unanimity in the Council. Vital exceptions remained: Common Agricultural Policy, transportation legislation, and legislation on services and matters of capital transfer; in these dossiers, the European Parliament could only express an opinion.

The Single European Act declared that the common goal of the EC was to realize the Single Market by December 31, 1992.[34] The Treaties of Rome were amended (Article 8 a-c) to legally facilitate the full implementation of this new priority of the EC. Some observers were astonished why the EC had to reiterate what seemed to have been the first and foremost goal of the EEC ever since 1957. Freedom of goods, labor, services and capital had been facilitated by the creation of customs union and common market, but a long and daunting process to overcome non-tariff barriers had only begun. It required a new and focused legislative boost by the EC. The Single European Act designed the legal framework to finally do so.

(d) For the first time in the history of European integration, the Single European Act stipulated a common foreign policy as a real community goal.[35] Euroskeptics could hardly believe that this move had ever happened in the first place. During these years, the European Parliament was already struggling to set up a committee on defense policy. At the beginning, they were only permitted to create a subcommittee on defense and disarmament of the Parliament's Foreign Affairs Committee. With the Single European Act, the "most decisive changes in the structure of the EC since its inception" occurred; with them, the member states "were to surprise everyone, including perhaps themselves."[36] This was certainly a fair assessment as far as the future evolution of a common foreign (and subsequently even security and defense) policy was concerned. The method of gradual harmonization of national positions on foreign policy matters was confirmed; over time this should lead to the formulation of common positions. The Single European Act underlined the necessity of regular mutual consultations before national positions on foreign policy matters were finalized. The loose institutional structures of European Political Cooperation, which had evolved since 1970, were legally rooted. Regular meetings of Foreign Ministers (four times a year in the presence of a member of the European Commission), two further meetings in the European Council, further meetings whenever it was considered necessary and, finally, the establishment of a Permanent Secretariat in Brussels to support European Political Cooperation were decided with the Single European Act. Explicitly, the Single European Act confirmed the need of compatibility between the EC's common foreign trade policy and its intergovernmental political cooperation. The European Parliament was to be kept informed about all matters relevant in European Political Cooperation.

34 Button, Kenneth J., et al., "1992 and the Creation of a Single European Market," *Antitrust Bulletin*, 37.2 (1992): 281-335; Garrett, Geoffrey, "The European Community's Internal Market," *International Organization*, 46:2 (1992): 533-560.

35 Crouch, Colin, and David Marquand (eds.), *The Politics of 1992: Beyond the Single European Market*, Oxford, Blackwell, 1990; Pedersen, Thomas, "Political Change in the European Community: The Single European Act as a Case of System Transformation," *Cooperation and Conflict*, 27.1 (1992): 7-44.

36 Urwin, Derek W., *The Community of Europe: A History of European integration since 1945*, op. cit.: 228.

And another innovation: For the first time, the sphere of security was to be included in European Political Cooperation. Although many details were missing, a first solidly rooted step toward a common foreign and security policy had been completed. While tensions with the Soviet Union strengthened transatlantic cooperation and helped to reactivate Franco-German security dialogue in the context of the almost forgotten Western European Union (WEU), it seemed as if a new start for a common foreign and security policy could finally get the consent of all EC partners.

This was a concept far removed from the idea of a Common European Army as debated during the 1950's. Less ambitious, it was nevertheless a realistic approach that garnered general support in the EC, including that of Great Britain and Denmark. Yet Danish Prime Minister Poul Schlüter – chairing one of many minority governments that existed since the early 1970's – had a hard time convincing his citizens about the value of the Single European Act. Only a very slim majority agreed in a referendum in February 1986 to the Single European Act. It came as a warning sign to take euroskeptical citizens more seriously in any further step toward deepened European integration.

Symbolic efforts to popularize European integration would not be enough, although they were useful expressions of the supranational reality that was evolving. A common European flag, the European anthem (Beethoven's "Ode to Joy"), improvements in passenger traffic across the EC, and mutual recognition of diplomas were some of the results stemming from the report written by former European Parliament member Pietro Adonnino intended to accelerate the creation a of "Europe of Citizens".[37] The ultimate legitimacy of European integration would indeed come from a combination of visible and tangible effects on the daily lives of ordinary citizens, and from efficient and transparent decisions of political leaders assigned to act on behalf of strengthening the European public good.

The 1970's and 1980's saw a steady trend toward more stable governance structures, broadened perspectives and a solidification of the path toward European Monetary Union as the overriding priority of these years. No decision on institutional matters had left all actors satisfied. "Satisfaction" was rarely a category to measure success and evolution of EC governance. More important was an insight into the nature of this process: It continued, often balancing former excesses, in the direction favorable to one of the institutions, then again pushing the alternative concept of who should have primacy over whom. But all in all, a balanced governance system was appearing on the horizon of the European Community. Policy evolution and governance development did continue throughout the 1970's and 1980's, but both were never fully cohesive. Instead, each new result left enough frustration to keep the ball rolling toward the next goal.

37 Magiera, Siegfried, *The Emergence of a "Europe of Citizens" in a Community without Frontiers*, Speyer: Forschungsinstitut für Öffentliche Verwaltung, 1989; Bruter, Michael, *Citizens of Europe?: The Emergence of a Mass European Identity*, Houndmills: Basingstoke, 2005.

This remained the nature of how progress was defined in the making of the European Community. Crises had become its best friend.

4. The Deepening Effect of New Enlargement

No matter how incomplete the European integration process was, for more Europeans it became, nevertheless, attractive to apply for membership in the EC. Its performance could not have been so bad after all. Membership questions always spurred emotional debates in the process of European integration. But only two of them were particularly tense: the application of Great Britain and the application of Turkey, which the EU received in 1987. Under mounting public controversy, the European Council decided in December 2004 to open negotiations with Turkey that might last for ten to fifteen years.

In a much easier context, during the second half of the 1970's and until the mid-1980's the membership prospects of Greece, Portugal and Spain were at the center of attention. All three countries were able to gradually oust dictatorial regimes in 1974 and 1975 and establish rule of law-based democracy. As their economies had always been market-oriented, membership in the European Commission seemed to be the logical way to stabilize their domestic situations and to support their course of economic modernization. But what would be the benefit for the European Community to accept them as new members?[38]

When the EEC was founded, such a question had not even existed. The British application had produced resistance in France for reasons of political power and equilibrium. By the mid-1970's, the European Community had largely been transformed in its meaning for many of its citizens. It was no longer the indispensable peace vehichle to prevent the French and Germans from again resorting to destructive nationalism, and no longer a mechanism to decide on French-British struggles for dominance in Europe. It had become a vehicle to maximize affluence. Affluence, however, also generates fear of competition, greed and jealousy. When Greece, Spain and Portugal knocked at the door of the EC, politicians were excited in helping them to stabilize their democracies. Many citizens, however, were worried about the economic and financial effects on their own lives. Spain alone would increase the population of the EC by 20 percent, but its share of the EC's GDP was only 10 percent. Its agricultural land would add 30 percent to the EC's agriculture, and its agricultural work force another 25 percent to that operating in the EC. The country had surpluses in olive

38 Seers, Dudley, and Constantine Vaitsos (eds.), *The Second Enlargement of the EEC: The Integration of Unequal Partners*, New York: St. Martin's Press, 1982; Gibson, Heather D. (ed.), *Economic Transformation, Democratization and Integration into the European Union: Southern Europe in Comparative Perspective*, Basingstoke: Palgrave, 2001; Kaiser, Wolfram, and Jürgen Elvert (eds.), *European Union Enlargement: A Comparative History*, London/New York: Routledge, 2004.

oil and citrus fruits that would be added to the EC surpluses due to the Common Agricultural Policy. It could not come as a surprise that membership negotiations with Spain and Portugal lasted for more than six years. Twenty years later, both countries were among the most dynamic and growth-oriented regions in Europe.

When membership negotiations began with Spain and Portugal, it was already foreseeable that the Common Agricultural Policy would absorb almost 80 percent of the EC budget by the time of Spanish accession. The regional development funds would also come under severe pressure given the size of Spain, but also from the claims of the other two applicant countries. Reform of the EC structures was overdue. In fact, the enlargement process to the "olive belt" facilitated the necessary reform of the EC's Common Agricultural Policy. Production quotas reduced the spending in the Common Agricultural Policy and by 1992 – when the MacSharry reform came into being – the budgetary share for Common Agricultural Policy had gone down to 60 percent of the overall EC budget. This was no breakthrough, but at least a beginning in a sphere of misled community policy that had seemed unalterable. French agricultural labor had gone down to 2 percent of the overall work force of the country, but changes in agricultural reform were as controversial as if the ultimate destiny of the nation was at stake. Other countries exhibited this strange behavior, a fact that can only be explained by the importance of the agricultural vote in elections. The scope for victory had become rather narrow in European countries, mostly producing coalition governments to form a stable majority.

The other controversial issue that was related to Spanish EU membership prospects was its fishery fleet, which was 50 percent of the size of the total EC fishery fleet in 1980.[39] Common Fishery Policy had existed since The Hague summit of 1969, and following the Common Agricultural Policy became the other primary economic sector. As the Common Fishery Policy required changes prior to Spanish accession, the EC agreed on those changes preventing a crisis of its financial position in 1983. This set a precedent however that the Spaniards did not forget and when the EU had to decide on membership of a whole series of post-communist countries in the late 1990's, they made sure not to lose any of the financial privileges they had accrued since the beginning of their membership. Unfortunately, this behavior was a sign of national exploitation rather than a convincing argument for further funds meant to harmonize regional and structural asymmetries in an enlarged EU.

Since the beginning of the European Economic Community in 1958, special funds were allocated to support specific sectors of the EEC: the European Social Fund and the European Agricultural Guidance and Guarantee Fund. The latter one was absorbed by the Common Agricultural Policy. The philosophy behind the European Social Fund was to ensure social cohesion in the EEC with its diversity of economic potential and social

39 See Dedman, Martin J., *The Origins and Development of the European Union 1945 – 1995*, London/New York: Routledge, 1996:127.

cleavages. In 1973, in order to alleviate structural and regional imbalances that were considered detrimental to the big aim of economic and monetary union, the European Regional Development Fund was created. Already before joining the EC, Ireland, Great Britain and Italy had formed an unofficial grouping lobbying for the establishment of this fund. Consequently, they became the greatest beneficiaries of its resources, along with France, and Greece, Spain and Portugal after their accession to the EC during the 1980's.

In 1988, not least because of the consequence of the enlargements of the past years, the EC restructured the operation of its funds and put them on a much more refined basis, thus developing certain elements of an EC welfare state-like policy. This approach – embodied in the creation of the EC's Structural Funds – was never free of controversy. With the implementation of the Treaty of Maastricht the EU Cohesion Funds added a new instrument to the reallocation of EU resources. With the beginning of Cohesion Funds in 1993, the European system of solidarity became more elaborate, but not less controversial. Main recipients of Cohesion Fund resources were Ireland, Portugal, Greece and Spain, but also other regions with income discrepancies and socio-economic deficits substantially below the EU average, including the "new German Länder."

Whether the policies supported by these funds were successful remained a matter of political debate.[40] That they contributed to a strengthening of the role of the European Commission and, through the mechanism of co-decision-making introduced with the Treaty of Maastricht, also a strengthened role of the European Parliament is the institutional dimension of the debate. EC policy instruments were growing as much as they increased the degree of necessary adjustments, corrections, overhauling, and a permanent quest for increased financial resources to be available for the EC in order to be redistributed. Tommaso Padoa-Schioppa, later to become an Italian member on the Executive Board of the European Central Bank, made a convincing case for the importance of enhanced structural funds. In 1987, he stressed "the serious risks of aggravated regional imbalances in the course of market liberalization."[41] While the Southern European countries were hesitant to embrace market liberalization as part of the path toward the Single Market, the northern European countries were skeptical about the wisdom of turning the EC into a welfare state community. After a year of

40 Evans, Andrew, *The EU Structural Funds*, Oxford: Oxford University Press, 1999; Bachtler, John, and Ivan Turok (eds.), *The Coherence of EU Regional Policy: Contrasting Perspectives on the Structural Funds*, London: J.Kingsley Publishers, 1997; Rodokanakis, Stavros, "Fifteen Years (1988-2002) of Structural Funds' Intervention: Critical Evaluation and Impact on Economic and Social Disparities among EU Countries and Regions," *The European Union Review*, 8.1-2 (2003): 65-105; Beugelsdijk, Maaike, and Sylvester C. W. Eijffinger, "The effectiveness of structural policy in the European Union: An Empirical Analysis for the EU-15 in 1995-2001," *Journal of Common Market Studies*, 43.1 (2005): 37-51.

41 Padoa-Schioppa, Tomasso, et al., *Efficiency, Stability and Equity: A Strategy for the Evolution of the Economic System of the European Community*, Oxford: Oxford University Press, 1987: 10.

broad debate among policy makers and experts, the Delors I Package – adopted by the European Council in December 1988 – confirmed the logic of this argument. Another step toward consolidated – and controversial – welfare state mechanics was taken by the EC. The criteria for defining regions or sectors as "lagging behind" and being in need of financial solidarity from the EC was to remain a permanent fixture in EU decision-making, aggravated in the context of the accession of a series of post-communist countries in 2004 and 2007. However, constitutionally speaking, both the Structural Funds and Cohesion Funds clearly had the effect of solidifying the community's supranational profile.

Enlargement had again proven to be supportive of a "deepening" of the integration process rather than being an obstacle to it. This does not suggest that enlargement implications were only win-win situations. But it would also be misleading to assume that enlargements were only a burden on the process. They always had anticipatory, almost preemptive and accelerating functions. In the long run, enlargements always strengthened the community spirit although this might not have been immediately evident. They deepened the sense of identity for all those involved in an ever more visibly, truly European project. They also transferred mechanisms of political interest formation and at times even an aggressive pursuit of specific national or political interests to the European level. But in the end, isn't that what democracy is all about, also under the conditions of each nation state?

The problem for policy making on the European level was increasingly one of accountability and transparency in its underlying institutions. The more the EC became active, the more European citizens realized the reach of its policies. But unlike in each national political system, the political structures in the EC appeared highly bureaucratic. No specific persons, parties or organs seemed to be accountable. All sorts of criticism was increasingly directed in a very general way toward "Brussels." But "Brussels" could hardly be profiled. Institutional reforms were therefore increasingly linked to the intention of making the EC policy process more visible, accountable and effective. Fiscal matters remained, however, a largely technical affair. Moreover, the increasing interconnectedness between national and European policy processes, aside being multidimensional on the horizontal level with the involvement of various European institutions, sharpened the feeling of detachment from the decision-making process. Even experts had a hard time understanding the mechanics of communitarian decision-making procedures. The term "comitology" became more than a short-hand word for a complex web of formal and informal influences, including interest groups, expert panels and pre-decision-making diplomacy. It became a synonym for the Western European equivalent of what Sovietologists meant with the term "Kremlinology," a helpless and hopeless set of speculations about who might be in charge of what.[42]

42 For an effort to bring reason into the system see Wessels, Wolfgang, "Comitology: Fusion in Action. Politico-Administrative Trends in the EU System," *Journal of European Public Policy*, 5.2 (1998):

The expansion of EC policy spheres had to overburden its institutions. Yet, it remained common to blame the European Commission for being overly centralizing, overstaffed and under-competent. This was unfair, not in the least because much of its staff were interpreters or did clerical work. All together, the interpreters included, the size of the European Commission was never bigger than the size of the administration of a larger European city. The real complaint about EC decision-making and policies should have been directed to the national political actors. As long as the EC was evidently able to deliver – that is to say to enhance the well being of the recipients of its actions – it was applauded. Road signs in peripheral regions of Ireland, Portugal and Greece, indicating that the improvement of traffic conditions were financed by the EC, had a positive effect on the attitude of local people about the EC. In countries that were net contributors to the EC budget, the focus was on spending and in support of the prejudice that taxpayers' money be wasted elsewhere. Political leaders did not always contribute to fighting prejudice and defending innocence by explaining the link between contributing to the EC and benefiting from the effects of integration, for example, through an increased import of goods originating in net-contributor countries. The 1980's led to a "monetarization" of EC matters – or better, it led to a materialistic reduction of its purpose. This was not only due to the preparation of the European Monetary Union. The whole EC was increasingly considered to be an operation of spending here and taking there, as an uneven and unfair monetary resource allocation scheme. The rationale for European integration was sometimes threatened so completely that it disappeared amid complaints about too much spending here and too little receiving there.

5. Budget and Politics: The Nasty Side of Enlargements

The evolution of a budget for the European Community and subsequently for the European Union is amongst the most important and yet unresolved matters of European integration. The European Community did increasingly grow into acquiring new tasks, both intended to deepen the integration process and to enhance redistributive programs aimed at consolidating the community through more symmetry in its socio-economic realities. The McDougall report of 1977 concluded that the EC would have to increase its budget to at least five percent of the Community GDP in order to properly perform both its redistributive and stabilizing role. This has not happened over thirty years, in spite of a continuous increase in work and competencies for the EU. The EU budget for

209-234; Christiansen, Thomas, and Emil Kirchner (eds.), *Committee Governance in the European Union*, Manchester: Manchester University Press, 2000; Ballmann, Alexander, et al., "Delegation, Comitology, and the Separation of Powers in the European Union," *International Organization*, 56.3 (2002): 551-574; Bergström, Carl Fredrik, *Comitology: Delegation of Powers in the European Union and the Committee System*, Oxford: Oxford University Press, 2005.

the period 2007-2013 still hovers around one percent of the EU's combined GDP. Such a limited budget cannot give adequate support to the claimed strategic role of the EU. Economic analysis comes to the conclusion that in spite of reforms within the redistributive mechanisms – foremost by reducing the costs for the Common Agricultural Policy – the European Union's budget to this day "simply is inadequate to perform this strategic role."[43]

Budgetary matters have been constitutional issues in all political systems at all times. The European Community is no exception to this rule. Public perception, however, tends to relate budgetary struggles in the EC primarily to political battles and egotistic claims for redistributive advantages at the expense of community solidarity. Both aspects have indeed been intertwined in the history of EU budgetary policy. Yet it must be stressed that first and foremost, budgetary debates and decisions in the EC were – and remain so in the EU – matters of constitutional relevance. This has certainly been the case since the budgetary disputes between Great Britain and her EC partners, embodied in the famous outcry of then Prime Minister Margaret Thatcher "I want my money back."[44] This was a constitutional assault on the very foundation of the EC as a supranational decision-making body with binding consequences for all its constituting parts. Prime Minister Thatcher succeeded in gaining a budgetary rebate for Great Britain. The constitutional implication was looming large whenever the issue was brought up again to be resolved: How substantial shall an autonomous EC/EU budget be as this would ultimately define the supranational character of European integration as a federal system.

The origins of the British quest for rebate are linked to British membership negotiations in the early 1970's. 40 percent of British butter was supplied by New Zealand and most of its sugar came from Caribbean Commonwealth countries. While New Zealand lamb, another commodity dear to British taste and heart, did not produce problems as the EC at the time did not yet have a market organization for lamb, butter did. French and Dutch producers hoped to take over the British share after accession of Great Britain to the EC. Realizing that British membership might not pass the approval of the House of Commons should it be detrimental to the links to New Zealand, France made the EC change the strategy of accession negotiations. Great Britain had originally offered to contribute initially 3 percent to the EC budget, going up to 15 percent in 1977. This was too little anyway, but now the EC insisted that New Zealand butter would be allowed into the EC only if Great Britain would substantially increase her

43 Lucarelli, Bill, *The Origin and Evolution of the Single Market in Europe*, op. cit.:157.

44 For her own account see Thatcher, Margaret, *Downing Street Years*, New York: HarperCollins, 1993: 60-64, 78-86, and 541-545; see also Young, John W., *Britain and European Unity, 1945-1992*, Basingstoke: Macmillan, 1993; George, Stephen, *An Awkward Partner: Britain in the European Community*, Oxford: Oxford University Press, 1998.

contribution to the EC budget. In the end, Great Britain agreed to contribute 8.64 percent in 1973, rising to 18.92 percent in 1977.[45]

With Margaret Thatcher becoming Prime Minister of Great Britain, the distorted budgetary contribution became a permanent and noisy EC topic again. Since Great Britain's agricultural sector was smaller than that of other EC partners, and since the country imported more agricultural commodities from outside the EC than the other member states, the British budgetary contribution was relatively higher while the country regained disproportionately less in return from the EC. Prime Minister Thatcher almost turned the issue into a matter of life and death. But she was not only concerned with the unfair treatment of her country and looking for "financial justice." On principle, she objected to the trend to an ever-increasing autonomous EC budget, which was to become the inevitable consequence of the growing costs for the Common Agricultural Policy and other redistributive policy schemes of the EC. Prime Minister Thatcher threatened to withhold British budgetary contributions, which would have been an illegal act under EC law. French President Giscard d'Estaing and German Chancellor Schmidt ventilated the possibility of relegating Great Britain to second-rank membership, which would have been legally possible. In the end, a compromise was struck in May 1980 in the General Affairs Council of the EC: Budget reform became an issue on the EC reform agenda and Great Britain received a rebate of two-thirds of its contributions over a period of three years.

Mrs. Thatcher's reelection in 1983 and the replacement of Giscard and Schmidt by Mitterrand[46] and Kohl did not make budgetary matters easier. In fact, the conflict stiffened. At the European Council meeting in Fontainebleau in June 1984, a rather permanent and, in fact, all too permanent solution was found: By unanimous agreement, Great Britain gained a permanent rebate of 66 percent each year on the difference between Great Britain's value-added tax contribution to the EC budget and its gains from the EC through its various funds, agricultural subsidies included.[47] If that sounds Byzantine, so it was! But it would be misleading to assume that the matter only concerned agriculture, value-added tax and the like. For Margaret Thatcher, the budgetary issue was the equivalent of what qualified majority voting in the EEC Council had been to French President de Gaulle before he ordered his ministers to move out of EEC meetings in 1965, a matter of principle, objection against further federalism through the backdoor of seemingly secondary issues and developments.

It was no coincidence that the evolution of budgetary matters loomed large again in the EC when the critical juncture of achieving both the Single Market and European

45 On the intensity of this negotiation see Dinan, Desmond, *Europe Recast: A History of European Union*, op. cit.:137.

46 On his legacy see Cole, Alistair, *François Mitterrand: A Study in Political Leadership*, London: Routledge, 1994.

47 See Denton, Geoffrey, "Re-Structuring the EC Budget: Implications of the Fontainebleau Agreements," *Journal of Common Market Studies*, 2 (1984): 117-140.

Monetary Union was reached in 1988. By then, Great Britain – content with its rebate – had been replaced by Spain, Portugal and Greece in the quest for overly excessive fiscal solidarity from their EC partners. Since Spain and Portugal were holding a blocking minority in the EC's Council – one of the reasons why the re-weighing of votes became so heated in the negotiations of the Treaty of Nice in 2000 and ever thereafter – they threatened to accept the Single Market program only if they would receive additional funds to adjust their economic structures to the conditions of tougher competition in the emerging Single Market. For those who still vividly remembered the budgetary disputes with Great Britain, this was a sort of remake under different circumstances. The ultimate issue, again, was not the Single Market, but the constitutional conditions of decision-making in a supranational Community wanting to achieve common goals without being able to resort to "natural" common interests.

Should the stand-off with Spain and Portugal be resolved in a way equivalent to the decision on Great Britain's rebate, and should the EC at the same time become enabled to finance new policies – among them science, technology and development aid – that were added to the Community's tasks with the Single European Act of 1987, an increase in the autonomous budget of the EC was inevitable. The European Council decided in Brussels on February 11 and 12, 1988, on a comprehensive budgetary reform (Delors I Package). The limit for "own" budgetary resources of the EC was set at 1.15 percent of the cumulated GDP of all member states for 1988, increasing to 1.2 percent in 1992. This meant already for the 1988 budget an increase of 20 percent to a total of 45 billion ECU. To the extent this money was not generated through import taxes, levies and the value-added tax share of 1.4 percent per member state, the EC was to receive net-contributions from its member states according to their GDP in proportion to their respective populations. By 1992, the next budgetary cycle was to include further increases. The Edinburgh European Council of December 11 and 12, 1992, concluded that the fiscal framework for the period 1993 to 1999 should begin with a ceiling on the EC's "own" resources of 1.2 percent of the cumulative GDP of all member states and grow to a ceiling of 1.27 percent in 1999, meaning an increase from 69 to 84 billion ECU. These budgetary decisions were already taken in light of the upcoming enlargement with the post-communist countries of Central and Eastern Europe. The pre-accession strategy, intended to help them achieve the standards of the *acquis communautaire*, was already included in these budgetary provisions. Once more, an emerging enlargement had provoked anticipatory extension of the scope of supranationality in Europe.

6. Single Market as Organizing Idea with Political Implications

The organizing idea throughout the second phase of European integration was the goal of completing the original promise of the Treaties of Rome, that is to say a Common Market. The more appropriate term Single Market underlined the deliberate political intention behind the project, which turned into a long and sometimes highly technical, often controversial process. The negotiation of the Treaty of Maastricht in 1990/1991 marked the end of the second phase of European integration. When the Treaty of Maastricht was signed on February 7, 1992, (and even before it eventually came into force on November 1, 1993, after a very difficult ratification process), European integration entered a new phase: So far, economic integration had been at the core of the European integration processes. Increasingly, European integration became politicized and politics Europeanized. The Treaty of Maastricht refounded the European Economic Community as the European Union. This was not only about semantics. It indicated the entry into a new period of European integration, aimed at constantly politicizing and constitutionalizing it.

This transformation into the next period of European integration was linked to another, rather sobering experience: Even legally binding decisions in the appropriate EC institutions did not automatically create new European realities. Most directives of the EC had to be transposed into national legislation. It was here, that European decisions were often halted in an effort to re-nationalize political decision-making. The struggle with this trend turned out to be one of the most time-consuming obstacles to early completion of the Single Market, no matter the extent to which the European Commission argued its case: By December 31, 1992, the Council had decided on 282 proposals from the European Commission. 213 of them had to be transposed into national legislation. Denmark with 189 decisions (88.7 percent), and Greece with only 150 decisions (70.4 percent), marked the upper and lower echelon among the member states' consistency with their own EC decisions. Nevertheless, the Edinburgh European Council of December 1992 declared mission accomplished. On July 6, 1988, Commission President Jacques Delors had stated in an often-cited speech to the European Parliament that in ten years time, "80 % of our economic legislation, and perhaps even our fiscal and social legislation as well, will be of Community origin."[48] In turn, this meant that 80 percent of legislation in member state parliaments was merely a reactive move to implement decisions already taken on the EC level. No matter how accurate Delors' prediction was, no single argument became as famous in order to demonstrate the substance of supranational political realities in the integrated Europe.

Some effects of the Single Market Program were supported by positive development in the world economy. The main result of the Single European Market remains the fact

48 Delors, Jacques, "Speech to the European Parliament, July 6, 1988," *Official Journal-European Communities/Annex*, 2-367 (1988):140.

that companies in EC member states gained access to larger markets, consumers had more choice, and increased competition has improved productivity and profitability. The trade surplus in European Union manufactured products rose from 12 billion euros in 1989 to 169 billion in 1997. Profits in the banking sector rose by 75 percent between 1997 and 2000. Total premiums written by European insurance companies rose by 50 percent between 1995 and 1999. One of the biggest markets that would gradually open up across the EU was that of public procurement. In 1999, it was estimated that the annual market for goods and services purchased by national, regional and local governments in the European Union was in excess of 700 billion euros. The Single European Market produced a considerable increase in intra-EU trade of 3 to 4 percent. GDP and welfare gains were obtained across the EU, although often difficult to calculate exactly. Estimates vary between a 1.1 and 1.5 percent increase in GDP for 1994 alone. Rationalization of production, better use of economies of scale through increased industrial concentration and reduction of price cost margins, were observed across the EU.

The completion of the Treaty of Maastricht (Treaty on European Union) was the culmination of the most successful phase of the Franco-German tandem in the EC context up to that point. Time and again, French-German cooperation proved to be the enabling precondition for progress toward deepened integration. The Franco-German tandem presented initiatives to bring the EC forward, organized compromises, advanced decision-making and achieved consensus results.[49] While the first phase of supranational integration – in spite of its historic beginning – was clouded by French claims of national primacy, France and Germany were confronted during the second phase of European integration with similar British claims, although constructed around different topics. Nevertheless, the principle of supranational political integration survived this period. It did not only survive, but was to become even more deeply rooted with the European Monetary Union and Treaty changes since the Single European Act and culminating with the Treaty of Maastricht. The Treaty of Maastricht opened the doors for a new period of European integration. Since the ratification debate on the Treaty of Maastricht, European integration has become increasingly politicized. Subsequently, politics became increasingly Europeanized. The fall of the Berlin Wall and the end of communist rule over Central, Eastern and South Eastern Europe put the question of imminent European unification on the political agenda of the continent. The issue of Eastward enlargement had many components, but most importantly, it established the primacy of politics in managing the European integration process. The

49 Calleo, David P., and Eric R. Staal (eds.), *Europe's Franco-German Engine*, Washington D. C.: Brookings Institution Press, 1998; Webber, Douglas (ed.), *The Franco-German Relationship in the European Union*, London: Routledge, 1999; Hendriks, Gisela, and Annette Morgan, *The Franco-German Axis in European Integration*, Cheltenham: Edward Elgar, 2001; Colard, Daniel, "Le Couple Franco-Allemand et la Construction de l'Europe," *Questions Internationales*, 11 (2005): 120-123.

Treaty of Maastricht itself initiated controversies about the limits of national autonomy and the primacy of European solutions beyond all experiences in post-War Europe. The controversies over Economic and Monetary Union were no less heated than those over a Common Foreign and Security Policy, and in fact over the very notion of transforming the European Community into a European Union with Union citizenship. European integration received a blow when Denmark rejected the Treaty of Maastricht on June 2, 1992, by less than 50,000 votes. A subsequent referendum in France on September 20, 1992, ended with the marginal support of 51.05 percent in favor of the Treaty of Maastricht. The path toward deepened European integration had become a contentious issue among the citizens of Europe. Following additional negotiations with Denmark, leading to four opting-out clauses for the Danes, the second referendum on the Treaty of Maastricht on May 18, 1993 was successful. The message of this experience was clear: Although the process of European integration seemingly remained a technical economic and bureaucratic operation, the citizens of the EC wanted to be heard and the member states began to see a shrinking of autonomous decision-making powers as a consequence of integration. This was indeed the case, and it was both intended and the logical consequence of deepened and solidified integration. The debate about the Treaty of Maastricht indicated a new transformation from economic primacy to Europeanized politicization. The challenge of absorbing the post-communist new democracies of Central Europe fueled this transformation and consumed EU activities for more than a decade. Often, the unification of Europe was interpreted as the ultimate goal and achievement of integration. But the Maastricht controversy made clear that integration would not succeed if it did not balance a new wave of widening with solid deepening.

The Treaty of Maastricht could not be more than another step in the direction of a political union that would deserve its name in reality. Failures and underperformances, however, also remained noticeable. The deficits in balancing governance structures and making them both efficient and legitimate were beginning to be widely recognized: Suggestions on what to do – as outlined with all clarity in the Tindemans Report in 1975 and in the draft for a European Constitution presented by the European Parliament in 1984 – were ahead of their time. The emerging global role of Europe was definitively lacking focus and substance. To the credit of the EC one has to add that the EC remained not only a prisoner of its own shortcomings, but also a hostage of the Cold War division of Europe – and a continuous beneficiary of American protection.

Parallel with this development, transatlantic relations were flourishing, but they were also going through their own history of progress and regression and again progression. The overriding strategic concern about the security of the Western world dominated the agenda, although the evolution of the global economy superseded in real terms the worries of many of those who were responsible for the maintenance of both stability and affluence, if not stability through affluence, on both sides of the Atlantic. The Second Cold War, escalating with the Soviet Union's deployment of new missiles

(SS-20) targeted at Western Europe, its invasion of Afghanistan in December 1979, and the imposition of martial law in Poland in December 1980, was counter-balanced only by new hope for non-communist dissidents in Central and Eastern Europe through co-operation with the West, and with the right to relate their human rights claims to the provisions of the CSCE Final Act signed by all countries of the continent. Sometimes, the CSCE Final Act was considered the substitute for a formal peace treaty to end World War II and all related claims, particularly claims to change borders in Europe again. For dissidents in Central and Eastern Europe, the Soviet Union included, the CSCE Final Act was only the beginning of a new chapter in their history, the beginning of freedom and the move to a unified Europe. The election of Karol Woytila as the first Polish pope in history on October 16, 1978, was indicative of things to come. During the first visit to his homeland in June 1979, Pope John Paul II, who would arguably become the most impressive, important and lasting among all leaders of the twentieth century, called on his countrymen, on all Europeans and, in fact, on all citizens of the world, not to be afraid, but to go ahead with a life of hope.[50]

50 On the papal visit to Poland and on related events of the peaceful revolutions in Europe see Garton Ash, Timothy, *The Uses of Adversity: Essays on the Fate of Central Europe*, London: Penguin, 1989; on the historical meaning and legacy of this arguably most outstanding personality of the twentieth century see Weigel, George, *Witness to Hope: The Biography of Pope John Paul II.*, New York: HarperCollins, 1999.

V. 1993 – 2009: Politics Europeanized

1. Constitutionalizing the European Public Good

(1) Crisis of Trust as Crisis of Deepening Integration

Surprisingly, the fall of the Berlin Wall on November 9, 1989, turned out to be the biggest challenge to Europe since the fall of Hitler's Third Reich in the same city on May 8, 1945. Instead of rejoicing about the end of Europe's division in happy anticipation of European unification under the banner of freedom, democracy and market economy, skeptical concern, fear and immobility soon filled the air. With German unification imminent as the immediate consequence of the fall of the Berlin Wall, even the very rationale of European integration seemed to have become questionable. Germany might not need European integration any longer, some argued. Other notorious skeptics perceived united Germany as the dominating European power, while some analysts were questioning whether or not Germany would maintain its interest in pursuing European integration at all. Soon, a first set of reassuring answers was given: The government of united Germany under Chancellor Helmut Kohl was reelected twice after the unification of the two German states on October 3, 1990, before he lost his Chancellorship in the 1998 election. At all times during this decade, Kohl's government remained unwavering in its commitment to European integration. German unification and European unity were considered as two intrinsically linked sides of the same coin.[1] Rapid German unification had come about only after formal consent of the four allied powers, who had won World War II against the German Reich. German unification accelerated the path toward the European Monetary Union. It also opened up the possibility of further enlargements to include Central and Eastern European countries: After all, the accession of the German Democratic Republic to the Federal Republic of Germany – based on its traditional internal federal structures with five "new Länder" joining the eleven "old Länder" of the Federal Republic – was the first accession of a post-communist transformation society to the European Community, albeit under different conditions. Joy could have been the overall European attitude.

This, however, did not happen because a second set of answers to the questions raised with the end of the artificial division of Europe was much more difficult to obtain. In fact, it even took EU leaders a couple of years to define the right content of questions following the fall of the Berlin Wall and the end of the Cold War. The fall of the Berlin Wall in 1989 found a first formal answer in the EU membership of ten post-communist countries in 2004, followed by another two in 2007. Further applicant

1 See Szabo, Stephen, *The Diplomacy of German Unification*, New York: St. Martin's Press, 1992; Zelikow, Philip, and Condoleezza Rice, *Germany United and Europe Transformed: A Study in Statecraft*, Cambridge, Mass.: Harvard University Press, 1995.

countries from Southeast Europe and the application of Iceland in 2009 reminded the EU that even the enlargement marathon had remained unfinished business. The 2004 and 2007 enlargement of the European Union to include former communist countries had been the only possible and morally right answer to overcome the division of Europe originating in the Cold War. Before joining the EU, the new member states had to go through a tough period of internal transformation in the course of which they had to adopt the EU's *acquis communautaire*. Through this daunting process, they became formally more Europeanized than most of the "old" EU member states.[2] None of them would have wished to go through the ordeal of a comprehensive review of the EU compatibility of its legal system.

No matter how important the enlargement process was, the other long-term question for the future of the European Union was not raised with the same clarity as the enlargement issue: How to deepen European integration and with which objectives? Eventually, during the 1990's and throughout the first decade of the twenty-first century the idea of what European integration was meant became blurred across most of the EU. Instead of finding joint answers to the question of what European countries and societies could do together, the leadership of many EU member states became obviously more absorbed in preventing the European Union from advancing. They were trying to delineate the limits of European integration. Instead of pro-actively defining and advancing a common European good, they emphasized national interests. The European Union was stumbling from one crisis into the next and from one symbolic exit of a crisis into the next stage of self-doubts. The main question remained unanswered: How could united Europe define common interests and common public goods in order to prevent a permanent stalemate over vested national interests, mutual suspicions and an overall sense of stagnation and loss in the age of globalization? Paradoxically, the potentially positive process of constitution-building that culminated with the signing of the first ever European Constitution turned more into an expression of reciprocal suspicion than of convincing leadership. At its beginning stood the Treaty of Nice, the embodiment of a politics of veto instead of a politics of enabling open doors. At its end stood the Treaty of Lisbon, no bad result given the failure of the European Constitution, but still more the expression of the lowest common denominator than the platform for courageous political action to be taken in the years ahead.

2 See Zielonka, Jan (ed.), *Europe Unbound: Enlarging and Reshaping the Boundaries of the European Union*, Abingdon: Routledge, 2002; Dimitrova, Antoaneta C. (ed.), *Driven to Change: The European Union's Enlargement Viewed from the East*, Manchester: Manchester University Press, 2004; Cameron, Fraser, *The Future of Europe: Integration and Enlargement*, London: Routledge, 2005; Schimmelfennig, Frank, and Ulrich Sedelmeier (eds.), *The Politics of European Enlargement: Theoretical Approaches*, London: Routledge, 2005; Schimmelfennig, Frank, and Ulrich Sedelmeier (eds.), *The Europeanization of Central and Eastern Europe*, Ithaca: Cornell University Press, 2005; Brimmer, Esther, and Stefan Fröhlich (eds.), *The Strategic Implications of European Union Enlargement*, Washington D. C.: Center for Transatlantic Relations, 2005; Grabbe, Heather, *The EU's Transformative Power: Europeanization through Conditionality in Central and Eastern Europe*, Houndmills: Palgrave Macmillan, 2006.

The absence of solid achievements of deeper integration in parallel to the unprecedented enlargement of the EU turned into a crisis of trust in Europe's political leaders. The crisis over the ratification of the European Constitution generated a reflection period which turned, interestingly, into the first reasonable constitutional debate in Europe. The constitution of the European Union, of European identity and of EU policy-making was discussed more than ever before in five decades of EU integration history. In itself, this was a good and reassuring reaction to the crisis in constitution-building. Hopefully, it could eventually turn out to be the beginning of a process bringing about a new contract between Union citizens and EU leadership. If so, the initiation of a new consent about the future of Europe - triggered through crisis, contraction and a cautious new beginning - would be a positive signal for the next stages of the Second Founding of European integration. Amidst the crisis in constitution-building, it became already evident that European citizens were frustrated with their politicians but not with the idea of Europe. The Europeanization of politics in Europe became more widely accepted than ever. In 2007, 66 percent of EU citizens considered issues related to the European Union to be an element of domestic politics and not of foreign politics..[3]

During five decades of European integration, institutional Europe has been established. But, still, Europeans are rare. The end of communist totalitarianism and the divisions of the Cold War opened enormous prospects and opportunities for many societies in Europe. But, surprisingly, amidst the peak of success, the idea of value added through a united Europe became increasingly obscure. While for the first ten years after the fall of the Berlin Wall, the enlargement agenda had occupied the political elites across the EU, the second decade was meant to end with achievements in deeper integration. After the political establishment in the EU had already failed the ratification of the European Constitution of 2004, initially they also failed the ratification of its replacement, the Reform Treaty of 2007. The political establishment in the EU did not very convincingly explain the usefulness of deeper integration to the citizens they claimed to serve.

As a consequence, the majority of Irish voters rejected the Treaty of Lisbon in June 2008. The Irish were asked to vote again in October 2009. This time, the majority of Irish voters accepted the Treaty of Lisbon. One experience stood above all others during these years of trial for European integration: Europe needs to be a Europe of results if its institutions want to regain legitimacy. "A Europe that works," as political leaders began to formulate this insight, would remain the ultimate bench-mark for judging the readiness of the European Union to take its desired place in the world on the basis of a new internal consent among EU citizens and EU leadership. In spite of its grave

3 See *Frankfurter Allgemeine Zeitung*, No. 187, August 14, 2007: 19. With 79 percent, the Portuguese were leading the assumption of this opinion poll, with 46 percent the Belgians were, astonishingly, the people with the lowest support for the thesis of EU affairs being a matter of domestic politics.

adaptation crisis, the European Union would have been ill advised not to look beyond and put the first decade of the new century into a larger context. During this decade, European integration went through a process of redefining its rationale under the conditions of a new world order. It did so by trying to establish a new relationship between the involvement of its citizens and the accountability of its political elites. Together, these fundamental structural trends – a European Union exposed to the world and exposed to its own citizens – epitomized nothing less than the Second Founding of European integration.It was not surprising that the Second Founding of European integration went hand in hand with a massive adaptation crisis.

The enlargement challenge arising from the secular change encapsulated in the fall of the Berlin Wall and the end to communist totalitarianism was handled reasonably rationally and successfully. With German unification in October 1990, the first EU enlargement to include a post-communist society took place. It should have been obvious that somehow the intra-German adaptations would have to be dealt with on a much larger scale in the face of an EU enlargement with a host of post-communist countries. On a much larger scale, socio-economic, political, constitutional and cultural matters needed to be addressed. The psychological and physical consequences of communist rule, and the implications of deep structural transformations, were unavoidable for the EU as a whole once other countries followed the German Democratic Republic (GDR) in joining the European Union. This was not an all too pleasant and comfortable thought for many political leaders in Western Europe. Politicians therefore tried to downplay its implications and continued to celebrate the unification of Europe in the name of freedom and democracy as a symbolic victory. Eventually, together with Malta and Cyprus ten post-communist countries joined the European Union during the first decade of the twenty-first century. In 2004, when the first eight of them entered the EU with a total of nearly 73 million inhabitants, they had a combined GDP of 458.4 billion euros. This combined GDP was not larger than that of the Netherlands with 465.3 billion euros and little more than 16 million citizens.

During the 1990's, the realization of economic differences, fundamental regional asymmetries and daunting long-term questions with respect to the necessary degree of solidarity in Europe began to deeply infect the political joy of renewed freedom in Europe. Across the European Union, imminent challenges connected with its eastward enlargement had been portrayed as being larger than life, while often the opportunities of enlargement were played down – or missed. Polish agriculture with 8.5 million farmers in a population of 35 million alone would have increased the EU budget by 20 percent if currently recognized Common Agricultural Policy provisions would have been granted to them. But instead of reforming the Common Agricultural Policy before Poland was to join the EU, the EU put emphasize on transitory periods to prevent Poland from joining the controversial benefits of the agricultural policy after becoming a full EU member. Double standards of membership were preferred to renewal and deeper integration for the benefit for all. The same phenomenon took place with regard to the issue of labor mobility: While some EU member states welcomed new workers from Central and Eastern Europe, others emphasized transitory solutions in order to protect their domestic labor markets as long as possible. The sense of solidarity disappeared among European societies.

In institutional terms, this myopic attitude was to have immense consequences for the balance of power among the institutions. The net-contributors to the EU budget were afraid to be outvoted by coalitions of the have-nots as they might inevitably gain a majority in EU institutions. Yet the morally fortunate perspective to unify Europe after decades of Cold War, dictatorship and separation could not remain a vision without a commitment. Eastward enlargement had to happen, and for many good reasons, while at the same time the derailing of EU decision-making capacities had to be avoided. The Treaty of Nice in 2000 was the peak of a policy that defined European integration from the perspective of its limits and not from the perspective of its opportunities. It opened the door for a unique constitution-building process in the European Union. Many national political leaders followed this process only half-heartedly. Not surprisingly, their citizens were not properly engaged in any reasonable public communication strategy. In the end, the result of the Constitutional Convention came more as a challenge to many national leaders than as a promise to Union citizens. The national leaders came under pressure to strike a deal and find a compromise. On October 29, 2004, all of them signed the Treaty Establishing a Constitution for Europe. Some of them did it with skepticism and inner reservations. The great vision of a European Constitution was about to come true. But Europe's national leaders did not properly reflect about the ratification hurdles ahead. Although the majority of EU member states representing a majority of Union citizens ratified the European Constitution, two negative referenda in France and in the Netherlands put the project in a coma. The idea to revitalize and reinspire European integration by providing a common constitutional framework around the enlarged EU stalemated. It was an idea ahead of its time, or at least ahead of its political leaders.

(2) The Need for Redefining Common European Interests

Obviously, the European Union needed the dual crisis of deeper enlargement and of trust between citizens and political actors. It initiated two unprecedented processes: the political establishment of the European Union declared a period of reflection, which basically developed into a period of restraint among politicians normally full of grand rhetoric. It also led to unprecedented discourses across the European Union about European identity and other pre-conditions for solidified constitutionalism. Would the European Constitution have passed its ratification marathon without a detour, the debate about European identity and the question in which constitution Europe was finding itself at the beginning of a new century may never have been so broad: The reflection about a European Constitution became a reflection about the condition in which Europe actually was.

The state in which Europe found itself during the first decade of the twenty-first century was deplorable. So was, at least in a formal sense, the result of the constitution-building process. Paradoxically, the public debate about the condition of Europe was as broad as never before. While the politicization of the European Union advanced, the constitution-building retrenched. At the end of the first decade of the twenty-first century, the European Union had deepened its constitutionalism without gaining a constitution. The public interest in the future of Europe was never stronger than during these years of trial.

Table 2: Member States of the European Union

EU Member State	Population (in million, 2005)[4]	GDP (in billion euros, 2005) [5]	GDP per capita (2005, EU average: 100)[6]	Seats in the European Parliament (as of 2009)[7]	Votes in the Council (as of 2009)[8]
Austria	8.2	245	122.7	17 (2.32 %)	10 (2.0 %)
Belgium	10.4	298	117.7	22 (3.01 %)	12 (3.48 %)
Bulgaria	7.8	21	32.1	17 (2.32 %)	10 (2.90 %)
Cyprus	0.7	13	83.5	6 (0.82 %)	4 (1.16 %)
Czech Republic	10.2	98	73.0	22 (3.01%)	12 (3.48 %)
Denmark	5.4	208	124.2	13 (1.78 %)	7 (2.03 %)
Estonia	1.3	11	57.4	6 (0.82 %)	4 (1.16 %)
Finland	5.2	155	112.1	13 (1.78%)	7 (2.03%)
France	60.6[9]	1710	109.0	72 (9.84 %)	29 (8.41 %)
Germany	82.5	2258	109.8	99 (13.52 %)	29 (8.41 %)

4 European Union, European Commission, *Europe In Figures. Eurostat Yearbook 2006-07*, Luxembourg: Office for Official Publications of the European Communities 2007, http://epp.eurostat.ec.europa.eu/cache/ITY_OFFPUB/KS-CD-06-001/DE/KS-CD-06-001-DE.PDF.

5 Ibid.

6 Ibid.

7 European Union, European Commission, Treaty of Nice: A Comprehensive Guide, http://europa.eu/scadplus/nice_treaty/bodies_en.htm#PARLIAMENT.

8 European Union, European Commission, Treaty of Nice: A Comprehensive Guide, http://europa.eu/scadplus/nice_treaty/council_en.htm#VOTES.

9 The figure for France refers to metropolitan France only, it does not include the overseas departments and territories.

Greece	11.1	181	82.2	22 (3.01%)	12 (3.48 %)
Hungary	10.1	88	60.9	22 (3.01 %)	12 (3.48%)
Ireland	4.1	160	137.1	12 (1.64 %)	7 (2.03%)
Italy	58.5	1417	102.8	72 (9.84 %)	29 (8.41%)
Latvia	2.3	13	47.1	8 (1.09 %)	4 (1.16 %)
Lithuania	3.4	21	52.1	12 (1.64 %)	7 (2.03 %)
Luxembourg	0.5	29	247.8	6 (0.82 %)	4(1.16%)
Malta	0.4	4	69.3	5 (0.68 %)	3 (0.87 %)
Netherlands	16.3	502	123.5	25 (3.42 %)	13 (3.77 %)
Poland	38.2	243	49.9	50 (6.83 %)	27 (7.83 %)
Portugal	10.5	147	71.4	22 (3.01 %)	12 (3.48 %)
Romania	21.7	79	34.8	33 (4.51 %)	14 (4.06 %)
Slovakia	5.4	38	55.1	13 (1.78 %)	7 (2.03 %)
Slovenia	2.0	27	80.0	7 (0.96 %)	4 (1.16 %)
Spain	43.0	904	98.7	50 (6.83 %)	27 (7.83 %)
Sweden	9.0	288	114.7	18 (2.46 %)	10 (2.90 %)
United Kingdom	60.0	1791	116.8	72 (9.84 %)	29 (8.41 %)

The European Union has become a household name. Its system of multilevel governance has finally reached the sphere of European society. People have begun to take interest in EU affairs. Obviously, many have been critical with this or that EU policy. Across the EU, they have begun to take an interest in what the EU does because they have realized that it affected their lives. In spite of rejecting reform propositions offered by the poltiical establishement end, the majority of EU citizens also in France, the Netherlands and Ireland claimed to be more pro-European than their bickering political leaders, often involved in tactical games with more than one eye on the domestic perception of their European handling. In the summer of 2007, 66 percent of EU citizens were in favour of a European Constitution.[10] While their leaders abandoned the initial project of the Treaty Establishing a Constitution for Europe (and struggled to make a convincing case for the subsequent Reform Treaty in the only country where a referendum was held on the matter), many EU citizens have realized that the European Union has become an unavoidable part of their daily life and an unavoidable element of their political destiny. The constitution-building process that has taken place during the first decade of the twenty-first century politicized the European Union more than anything before since the signing of the Treaties of Rome. Along with the emotional

10 European Union, European Commission, *Eurobarometer 67: Public Opinion in the European Union*, June 2007, http://ec.europa.eu/public_opinion/archives/eb/eb67/eb_67_first_en.pdf.

debate across the EU about the future role of the United States and the perspective of Turkish EU membership – the most obvious scapegoat debates reflecting anxieties about European identity - the crisis of adaptation broadened the public sphere of the European body politic.

Europe was in need of new roots and new visions. It was in need of redefining the rationale for integration and of refocusing its objectives. This agenda looked taller than ever. Yet, achieving it could not work without common Europe-wide perspectives on what to do together and without a European-wide recognition of what to gain or to loose: Europe could only win together or lose together. Amidst the crisis of trust and confidence during the first decade of the twenty-first century, this insight was gradually returning to the EU. Its citizens seemed to be more open than ever to this insight yet were reluctant to embrace its consequences. Their leaders were having difficulty in conveying the consequences convincingly and worsened the situation by playing down the initial insight of unavoidable Europeanization as the only way forward for Europe.

The underlying principles of European integration had to be advanced and adopted by all applicant countries in Central and Eastern Europe in order to make the community institutions work after its biggest ever enlargement. The degree of adaptational requirements and the possible number of new member states were at the center of EU developments throughout the 1990's and during the first decade of the twenty-first century. These developments overlapped with self-doubts among EU elites about the institutional structures and their efficiency. Their debates, largely technical and self-centered, were coupled with new power struggles and surprising excesses of pride and jealousy among the old EU member states. Often, so it seemed, the EU had become an immobile club of affluent and self-complacent countries trying to safeguard their achievements against unprepared, if not outright "dangerous" beggars from the East. However, the adaptational transformation of the institutional structures of the Union generated a constitutional overhaul, including and most promising a broad reflection about Europe's identity and the state of its integration process that was eventually to have an integrating effect on the political culture across the European Union. It paved the ground for a thorough Europeanization of European politics. The nature of European integration would never be free from controversy. Clashing interests are a natural element of democratic politics. But these controversies were more than ever linked to the European level of governance and hence to the EU as a governance system.

Optimists, therefore, considered the outcome of the first decade of the twenty-first century as primising. The Treaty of Lisbon streamlines the EU governance system by politicizing it and by making it more exposed to public discourse. The European Parliament becomes the co-decision making body in most of European legislation. The co-decision making mechanism is renamed as "regular" legislative process. The European Commission has become more political than ever, as was evident during the hearings in the European Parliament in January 2010 prior to installing the new commission under the old leadership of Commission President José Manuel Durão Barroso.The role of national parliaments in EU decision-making is strengthened – it was now up to national politicians to take the EU seriously. They could not hide any longer behind their respective government and putting all blame for unpleasant European decisions on "Brussels". The European Council received a permanent President: Herman van Rompuy had gained reputation for his conciliatory style as Belgian Prime Minister. Was he, after all, not a better choice for the position of the first ever permanent President of the European Council than any flamboyant and self-serving politician at hand? He would have to coordinate results in the business of the European Council – not a little challenge in order to project the image of an EU that works.

Catherine Ashton, as of 2010 High Representative for the Common Foreign and Security Policy, was instantely labeled "EU Foreign Minister" by the international media. Initially, it was her job to organize the European External Action Service to be operational by 2012. Instead of expecting from her to engage immediately in high politics and travel the world, she had to prepare the European institutional mechanisms for a more coherent global presence. This was no easy and no unimportant task.

Yet, the EU could not take consolation in these institutional achievements at the end of a long and often frustrating decade. The voter turnout in the election to the European Parliament in June 2009 was lower than ever. But it was not the voters to be blamed for it. The voter turnout in elections of the European Parliament was to be low as long as voters would not be presented solid political choices by competing European political parties. Even more so, the direct election of the President of the European Council across the EU would probably do more good for enhancing attraction and authority of EU institutions than all noble yet myopic efforts of fine-tuning European treaties hardly any ordinary citizen is interested in.

(3) The Lisbon Strategy as Failed Modernization from Above

Currency union and eastward enlargement were enormous projects. They attracted attention all over the world. Yet they were only instruments in further deepening and widening the integration process. The glue to make both work, and to keep their effects manageable, was provided by a sequence of treaty revisions, advancing the constitution-building process of European integration. This process opened up new avenues for pursuing the two most obvious challenges that will accompany the European Union beyond the third phase of its integration experience: That challenge will be to stabilize public support for the EU, in light of increasing implications of European integration on the political and social realities in all member states, and to solidify a common foreign and security policy with robust actions and a sustainable and coherent global presence of the EU.

The constitution-building crisis went hand in hand with a deep recession and structural deficits in the modernization of the European Union. The upbeat spirit that accompanied the project of a Single European Market since the early 1980's was absent when the European Union announced its Lisbon Strategy in 2000. In a way, the Lisbon Strategy looked like the logical continuation of the Single European Market agenda.[11] But instead of introducing self-binding commitments to change – as was the case during the Delors years – the Lisbon European Council on March 23 and 24, 2000, had only promulgated preposterously that by 2010 the EU would become the leading economic and technological player in the world, surpassing the dynamic zones in the US and in Asia. Safer jobs across the EU, broad efforts in deregulation, increased spending on big infrastructure projects, such as trans-European highways, and a more productive EU by enhancing the welfare state; these were the noble goals. In reality, in the early twenty-first century the EU was confronted with sluggish economic growth, high unemployment, and lack of economic dynamism. Leading experts and civil servants had warned the EU immediately that the realization of the Lisbon Strategy was about to fail. From 1980 to 2001, the EU growth rate did not climb above 2.2 percent (compared with 7 to 8 percent growth rates in China, 12 percent in Singapore and Hong Kong, 5 percent in Korea and 3 to 4 percent in the US). In 2002, the EU's growth rate even fell to 0.7 percent, compared with 2.4 percent in the US. To reach the Lisbon goals, economic growth should have been around 3 percent. Work productivity per hour had also slowed down in the EU: While in 1995 European workers had produced 87 percent per hour of the outcome of their American colleagues, the ratio had gone down to 82 percent by the end of 2004.

Between 1970 and 1983, unemployment had been lower in Western Europe than in the US. Since then, the parameters had changed. While Western Europe had constant unemployment rates around 10 percent – after enlargement this figure became a reality as an average for all 27 EU member states – the US has had an average unemployment of only 5 percent since the 1990's.[12] Should the EU be able to achieve the goals of the "Lisbon Agenda," it would have had to generate 21 million new jobs by 2010 and increase the employment quota from 64 percent in 2004 to 70 percent in 2010. By early 2005, the new EU Commission under its President José Manuel Durão Barroso reduced the expectations and goals connected with the Lisbon Strategy. Instead of pursuing overly ambitious goals, the EU became more realistic and began to promote pragmatic measures supporting economic growth and employment in rather general terms. It was evident that without enormous investment in future-oriented technologies, such as telecommunications, and in its sluggish education system, the EU would lose the race for competitiveness with the US and the leading Asian countries.

11 See Grin, Gilles, *The Battle for the Single European Market: Achievements and Economic Thought, 1945-2000*, New York: Columbia University Press, 2003.

12 See Ferguson, Niall, *Colossus: The Price of America's Empire*, New York: Penguin Press 2004: 240.

According to the original Lisbon Strategy – but in principle also according to its reduced version of 2005 – EU member states needed much more intensive and focused reforms to stimulate growth and employment, educational and scientific modernization and increased productivity. They were supposed to reform their welfare and tax systems, enhance the integration of older employees, raise the equality among sexes, and substantially improve the quality of education, from kindergarten to the university. Finally, the Single Market was also to be completed in the field of services, the administrative burden had to be reduced across the EU, and competitive innovation needed improvement through increased spending for research and development. All in all, the subsidy-based European intervention and welfare state had to be replaced by a lean state providing the legal framework for socio-economic dynamics. The state quota in Europe would have to be drastically reduced in order to generate sustainable growth and employment. As these achievements seemed highly unlikely, the European economy continued to lose global competitiveness in spite of a strong euro. The American economy was continuously booming through high growth rates, increased productivity and higher employment rates, no matter the US high twin budget and trade deficit. As for the EU, the International Herald Tribune judged in late 2004: "Europe gets failing grade on competitiveness."[13]

Across the EU, it was necessary to reduce the state quota of the GDP, to reduce taxes, to produce incentives for payable work and to integrate the financial markets, which would effect Germany in particular as its banking structure was overly split. To comply with self-declared EU goals would mean to give up traditional socio-economic structures and, most importantly, to cut down the size of the welfare state. This tall agenda defined the overriding conflict for European integration in the years ahead: A conflict of aims between the preservation of a specific European variant of the welfare state – hardly payable any more under conditions of aging populations, slackened productivity and growing generational gaps with not enough children to maintain balanced reproduction rates – and the global pressure on the EU to not only take a stronger political role, but to also serve as a reliable locomotive for sustainable global growth and to absorb higher rates of migration. This conflict of aims was accelerated by the accession of the post-communist transformation economies and their quest for social solidarity by the EU. The necessary completion of the enlargement process in Southeast Europe would sharpen this conflict further. For the interim, the creation of a Central European Free Trade Agreement in late 2006 (between the countries of the Western Balkan, Romania, Bulgaria and Moldova) was a transitory step forward. The

13 Bowley, Graham, "EU Gets Failing Grade on Competitiveness," *International Herald Tribune*, November 5, 2004; on the broader context of the issue see Hall, Ronald, et al. (eds.), *Competitiveness and Cohesion in EU Policies*, Oxford: Oxford University Press, 2001.

comprehensive reconciliation among the people and countries in the region and with Europe as a whole could eventually only happen through full EU membership.[14]

The European Union did not do too well while it was struggling with the implementation of the Lisbon Strategy. Only four member states were able to achieve the employment objectives of the Lisbon Strategy by 2010 (Denmark, Netherlands, Sweden, Great Britain). The competitiveness of the tax system remained a bone of contention in the European Union. Some member states, most prominently Slovakia, made positive experiences with the introduction of a flat tax. Since a flat tax rate of 19 percent was introduced in Slovakia in 2004, unemployment went down from 18.6 percent to 11.1 percent in 2006. The number of enterprises increased by 154 percent, the country's GDP growth rate climbed above 54 percent annually and the state earnings reached record highs.[15] The EU as a whole rejected the idea of standardizing tax systems while making efforts to at least create a common EU-wide corporate tax base. Most of the "old" EU member states continued to struggle with state subsidies for uncompetitive sectors of their economies. Since 2007, the EU Commission was beginning to report in public about the volume and direction of state subsidies across the EU. They amounted to 0.6 percent of the EU's GDP and remained difficult to curtail. After the rejection of the Treaty Establishing a Constitution for Europe in France and in the Netherlands, the EU even introduced a "globalization fund" aimed at helping victims of globalization across Europe. Up to 500 million euros per year were offered to workers who had lost their job as a consequence of globalization. The European Union wanted to be a global player but at the same time protect itself against global trends. Too many vested interests were opposing the socio-economic modernization, which they perceived as turning them into victims. Deregulation remained an EU-wide objective, which was clashing with old and new forms of reticence. While in some countries, such as Germany, EU-induced deregulation seemed to be the only source of reforms, other countries, such as Great Britain, perceived EU legislation as a new form of re-regulation they opposed. The quest to introduce an EU equivalent to the US Regulatory Oversight Office remained unanswered.

It would be unfair to deny achievement. At the end of 2007, the Schengen Area was enlarged to most new EU member states in Central Europe. Eight Central European countries (all new member states except Romania and Bulgaria) and Malta introduced control-free border crossing, the most prominent symbol of shared freedom of citizens across Europe. On January 1, 2008, the Single European Payments Area (SEPA) was inaugurated, providing for cost-free cashless financial transactions across the European

14 See Biermann, Rafael, "Robert Schuman's Perspective of Peace and Stability through Reconciliation: A Legacy of Continuing Actuality Also for the Balkans?," *Ankara Review of European Studies*, 1 (Autumn 2001):45-60.

15 See Schwarz, Karl-Peter, "Mehr Unternehmen, weniger Arbeitslose, gleiche Staatseinnahmen," *Frankfurter Allgemeine Zeitung*, August 26, 2005: 13; Miklos, Ivan, "Das beste Steuersystem der EU," *Frankfurter Allgemeine Zeitung*, September 3, 2005: 13.

Union. Estimates assume that customers will gain 35-70 billion euros annually. Simultaneously, Malta and Cyprus introduced the euro as their legal tender, followed by Slovakia in 2009, thus bringing the member states of the eurozone to sixteen, covering 325 million EU citizens. Only in the course of 2008, the euro gained 13 percent against the US dollar. In less than a decade of existence, the euro's share of world currency reserves had reached 30 percent. When the global financial crisis broke out in 2008, Europeans were increasingly concerned about the strength of their currency. Yet, in spite of nice catchwords such as knowledge economy, technology governance and the expected magic of an "open coordination mechanism" the Lisbon Strategy had to be declared failure when EU leaders replaced it in spring 2010 by a strategy "Europe 2020". For the next decade, the EU was to strive for an intelligent and green social market economy.

The outbreak of the global financial and economic crisis in 2008 posed unprecedented challenge for the EU. Whether in the final analysis the sources of the crisis were state failure or market failure remained a matter of contentious debates on both sides of the Atlantic. While US bank paid the state support back in order to regain their traditional degree of freedom, in Europe the role of the state seemed to exponentially grow again in response to the crisis. The EU did well in coordinating joint EU action in preparing for the global crisis management. The degree of future regulation of financial operations in the EU remained a bone of daunting struggle among market advocates and state internventionists. The strategy "Europe 2020" would eventually be measured by its ability to be more than a source of interventionism and neo-protectionism, the traditional enemies of a common and free European market.

European leaders kept on talking about a fictitious European Social Model while the full realization of the objectives of the Single Market and the requirements of technology-based modernization remained a continuous challenge in the EU. At the beginning of the twenty-first century, only 17 percent of all high-tech companies worldwide came from Europe. US companies spend more than 40 percent more than their European counterparts on research and development. In the meantime, even China had already reached almost 50 percent of European research and development spending.[16] The European satellite project "Galileo" was meant to become a symbol of European pride and prestige. After endless debates between the European Union and private enterprises, the idea of public-private partnership for the satellite navigation system failed in May 2007. "Galileo" became the risk of European taxpayers when the EU decided to built the navigation system purely with public resources (3 billion euros estimated cost). The idea of a European Institute of Technology, much favoured by the European Commission, was also laid to rest over national objections. In fear of losing some of their best researchers to a genuine European institution, nations were clinging

16 See *Frankfurter Allgemeine Zeitung*, "Der Hochtechnologiestandort Europa ist bedroht," November 17, 2005: 13.

to their national institutions and hence accepting an increasing brain drain of young academics to the United States. The limited success of the Lisbon Strategy did not encourage optimism about the forthcoming decade under the umbrella of the strategy for green growth, innovation and education "Europe 2020".

2. Causes and Effects of Consolidated Constitutionalism

The need to deepen European integration during the 1990's and the first decade of the twenty-first century was a response to a threefold challenge posed to Europe: The European Union had to consolidate its economic structures in order to maintain stability for its emerging currency. It had to prepare the EU for dealing with the consequences of enlargement toward post-communist Europe and, in a related matter, for a recalibration of transatlantic relations, neighborhood relations in Southern and Eastern directions, and Europe's role in future global management. Finally, it had to find satisfying responses to the ever-increasing claims that the EC was suffering a "democratic deficit" and was lacking legitimacy, while its Byzantine institutional structures, not transparent and full of inconsistencies, impeded the efficient outcome of EU operations.

The decade after the fall of the Berlin Wall began with the ambitious effort to simultaneously realize the European Monetary Union and a European Political Union. During the European Council meeting in Strasbourg on December 8 and 9, 1989 – under the deep impression of the historical developments in Central and Eastern Europe[17] – the establishment of an intergovernmental conference on European Monetary Union was decided upon. In light of possible resentment in Germany about the loss of the Deutschmark to a common European currency – and certainly in East Germany, where the Deutschmark had only recently been introduced in replacement of the weak Eastern Mark – German Chancellor Kohl pleaded for tactical postponement of the announcement of the date of the Intergovernmental Conference; he had to win the first national elections in a united Germany on December 2, 1990. Finally, the European Council in Dublin on June 25 and 26, 1990, decided to begin the work of an Intergovernmental Conference in mid-December 1990 under the Italian Presidency. The same European Council also agreed on a joint initiative by French President Mitterrand and German Chancellor Kohl to launch a second Intergovernmental Conference on political union, likewise starting its work before the end of the year.

Both intergovernmental conferences conducted their work throughout 1991, finishing complex and sometimes highly controversial negotiations at the European

17 See Helmut Kohl's account of the frosty atmosphere at this meeting, where he was not only welcomed with joy about the fall of the Berlin Wall, but also with concern about the future prospects of a stronger Germany: Kohl, Helmut, *Ich wollte Deutschlands Einheit*, Berlin: Propyläen Verlag, 1996: 194-201.

Council in Maastricht on December 9 and 10, 1991.[18] At this meeting, the main parameters of the Treaty of Maastricht were agreed upon. Its most important decision was the finalization of the beginning of the third stage for European Monetary Union on January 1, 1999. But other aspects of the Treaty of Maastricht regarding the future structure of the European integration process were not less important, including its rather incomplete decisions on political union. The Treaty of Maastricht was the most thorough treaty revision since 1957. It was also the beginning of a series of further revisions that were to continue during the 1990's. The institutional (and, more importantly, conceptual) deadlock reached with the Treaty of Nice in 2000 made EU leaders realize that it was no longer possible to continue with incremental and Byzantine institutional changes. The European Union urgently needed a constitutional overhaul and in fact its refoundation. The Treaty of Maastricht had established the "three pillar" structure of European integration (another sort of Luxembourg Compromise reminiscent of 1966) to cover diverging interests and positions in order to find a new balance between federalists and intergovernmentalists in Europe. The Treaty of Maastricht declared the Common Market – including European Monetary Union – initially introduced by the Treaties of Rome as Pillar One. Foreign Policy matters were dealt with under Pillar Two and Justice and Home Affairs – an important achievement of future union policy – under Pillar Three. Pillar One covered the European Community and its Treaties and legislation, Pillar Two and Three were considered to be the nucleus of an emerging European Union, the overarching name now given to the whole construction. The Treaty of Maastricht was highly incoherent, consisting of 300 articles, 17 protocols and 33 declarations. Yet, it constituted a common framework for the European Union and another step in its economic and political development, though parallel progress had not yet been achieved.

The Treaty of Maastricht strengthened all organs of the EU but left fundamental questions of an institutional balance unresolved. In matters of the Single Market, the Treaty of Maastricht granted the European Parliament the right to co-decision on all matters which the Council was to decide on the basis of qualified majority voting. Throughout the first 25 years of integration, the European Parliament was not allowed to participate in around 70 percent of Community legislation. With the Treaty of Maastricht, this figure came down to around 35 percent.[19] This enormous upgrading of the power of the European Parliament was often underestimated by skeptical academics and national politicians alike. They also underestimated the informal nature of many pre-legislative contacts and negotiations and the psychological importance of an

18 See Dyson, Kenneth, and Kevin Featherstone, *The Road to Maastricht: Negotiating Economic and Monetary Union*, Oxford: Oxford University Press, 1999; Mazzucelli, Colette, *France and Germany at Maastricht: Politics and Negotiations to Create the European Union*, New York: Garland, 1997.

19 See Knipping, Franz, *Rom, 25. März 1957: Die Einigung Europas*, Munich: Deutscher Taschenbuch Verlag, 2004: 217; on the general evolution of EU legislation see Iral, Hubert, *Between Forces of Inertia and Progress: Co-Decision in EU Legislation*, ZEI Discussion Paper C 114, Bonn: Center for European Integration Studies, 2003.

enhanced role of the European Parliament. Decision-making processes among the organs of the EU remained uneven. Most confusing was the structure of the Council, simultaneously serving as legislative organ on matters of the European Union and as executive organ on matters of political cooperation in foreign affairs. The Council of Ministers was identified as the most undemocratic of all EU institutions, convening behind close doors and not even making its protocols accessible to the public in order to understand how individual countries had voted. The Committee of Permanent Representatives (COREPER), which is also a community institution, deals with all matters of the EU; so does the Secretariat of the Council. It seemed as if the European Commission was relegated to the role of a secretariat, "only" preparing legislation on matters dealing with the traditional European Community, but not so in the emerging sphere of foreign policy and justice and home affairs.[20] In reality, however, the European needed to resort increasingly to the expertise of the Commission, albeit often in informal ways, just across the Rue de la Loi in Brussels, where both institutions are located.

The Treaty of Maastricht became somewhat notorious for its introduction of the subsidiarity principle that hardly anybody in the EU understood. Subsidiarity is a principle of ordering social affairs, residing in Roman Catholic social doctrine and introduced in the papal encyclical "Quadragesimo anno," written by Pope Pius XI in 1931 with support of the German Jesuit Oswald von Nell-Breuning: "Just as it is gravely wrong to withdraw from the individual and commit to a group what private enterprise and industry can accomplish, so too it is an injustice, a grave evil and a disturbance of right order, for a larger and higher association to arrogate to itself functions which can be performed efficiently by smaller and lower societies." This is a fundamental principle of social philosophy, the encyclical concluded, "unshaken and unchangeable."[21] In the Treaty of Maastricht, the subsidiarity principle reads as follows: "In areas which do not fall within its exclusive competence, the Community shall take action, in accordance with the principle of subsidiarity, only if and in so far as the objectives of the proposed action cannot be sufficiently achieved by the Member States and can therefore, by reason of the scale or effects of the proposed action, be better achieved by the Community." (Treaty of Maastricht, Article 5). Thus began a long dispute about establishing competences in the European Union, barely settled with the 2007 Reform Treaty.

With the Treaty of Maastricht, European Political Cooperation (EPC) was upgraded to a Common Foreign and Security Policy. This was as limited as any reform could be –

20 The European Commission – besides the college of the commissioners - consists of around 25,000 civil servants, of which only 15,000 are administrators, the rest being employed either in scientific research or as interpreters; the Council secretariat - in charge of both the European Council and the Council in its various formations - consists of around 2,300 staff, a tenth of whom are senior civil servants; the Secretariat of the European Parliament – unlike the other services not located in Brussels, but in Luxembourg – consists of approximately 3,500 administrative and clerical staff.

21 Pius XI, *Encyclical Letter Quadragesimo Anno*, London: Catholic Truth Society, 1946: 31.

Dinan called it "portentous"[22] – under the impression of an obvious revitalization of old habits and national interests across Europe. The failure to organize a common EC position in the Yugoslavian crisis was indicative of the lack of potential for "systematic cooperation", as the Treaty of Maastricht promised. The rhetoric compromises enshrined in the Treaty of Maastricht were ridiculed by the weak and uncooperative policies pursued by various EC partners while the Yugoslavian dissolution escalated. The effect of self-imposed pressure to change a wrong course as consequence of massive internal failures became even more evident a decade later after the agreement on the Treaty of Nice, one of the weakest ever performances of the European Council. French President Jacques Chirac found himself in a dilemma: He was host to the European Council in Nice and thus obliged to chair, coordinate and search for compromises, yet he wanted to gain essential results in favor of France. Most important for him was to maintain parity with a united Germany as far as the number of seats in the European Parliament and the weighed votes in the Council were concerned. The Nice Summit of the EU of December 7 to 11, 2000, ended as the longest ever in the history of integration. It should not be forgotten that it was also the summit that politically agreed to the Charter of Fundamental Rights of the European Union. This Charter had been drafted by a Convention under the chairmanship of former German President Roman Herzog that served as model for the Constitutional Convention of 2002/2003. But on matters of institutional reform, the Treaty of Nice produced the opposite of clarity and sustainable results. It codified the limits of European integration instead of approaching integration from the vantage point of its opportunities. It institutionalized veto capacities that were to burden the EU for the decade to come. The highly complex mechanism found in Nice for the weighing of votes as of January 1, 2005, in the enlarged European Union was the climactic expression of a rather dangerous, if not absurd trend. In past decades, the issue of the weighing of votes had never been of any interest even to most experts on European integration. Suddenly it seemed to be the central "life or death"-question for Europe.

In Nice, the share of votes of France, Germany, Great Britain and Italy, but especially the share of Spain, was increased in proportion to the growing number of smaller and medium-size countries. A qualified majority was introduced consisting of three dimensions: 73.4 percent of weighed votes had to be reached for a decision, the majority of member states must agree and this majority must represent at least 62 percent of the combined European Union population. This was an increase of seats in the European Parliament from 626 to 732 as of 2004 in favor of a stronger German share compared with France,[23] and there was a reduction in the number of

22 Dinan, Desmond, *Europe Recast: A History of European Union*, Boulder: Lynn Rieffer Publishing, 2004: 257.

23 Germany 99, France, Great Britain and Italy 78, Spain and Poland 54, Netherlands 27, Greece, Belgium, Portugal, the Czech Republic and Hungary 24, Sweden 19, Austria 18, Denmark, Finland and Slovakia 14, Ireland and Lithuania 13, Latvia 9, Slovenia 7, Estonia, Cyprus and Luxembourg 6,

commissioners as of 2004 – only one commissioner per country while the number of commissioners would go below the number of member states after the EU will have grown to twenty-seven member states. These issues were also decided during the long and frustrating days and nights of Nice.

In spite of all its flaws and failures, it was remarkable that the Treaty of Nice extended qualified majority voting to asylum policies (as of January 2004)[24] and to decisions on structural funds (as of 2007). Spain accepted this only on the condition that the structural funds it was receiving would remain untouched until 2013 (the end of the fiscal frame lasting from 2007 to 2013), anticipating that the co-decision power of the European Parliament – the automatic implication whenever Council decisions are taken with qualified majority – will favor a gradual reallocation of resources to other policy areas or regions in need.

With the Treaty of Nice, more than ever European integration was defined by its limits and no longer by its opportunities. Yet, the path toward further constitutionalization was unavoidable. The quest did not die in demand for "more" and especially for a "better" European Union. A European Constitution did not come to fruition during the third period of European integration. But more than anybody could have imagined in 1993, politics had been Europeanized when the Treaty of Lisbon entered into force in 2009. The Treaty of Lisbon consolidated two decades of institutional bickering that had turned from promise into nightmare. The solution was not perfect and left constitutionalism in the European Union with a European Constitution. The 2009 Reform Treaty was the the best possible result in the typical sense European integration is moving forward: It produced the highest degree of criticism along with the insight that any other option would be worse. While entering a new period of integration, the European Union kept its idiosyncratic nature.

3. Emerging European Interests as Manifestations of Political Disputes

The third period of European integration started with the Treaty of Maastricht and the effect of the breakdown of communist regimes in Central and Eastern Europe. It was ending with the implementation of the institutional reforms of the Treaty of Lisbon and the breakthrough of the politicization and Europeanization of politics in the European Union. During this third period of European integration, the EU was able to broaden the basis of consent concerning European interests, which, by now, would include the following components:

Malta 5 members; on the European Parliament see also Corbett, Richard, *European Parliament's Role in Closer EU Integration*, Basingstoke: Palgrave, 2001.

24 On EU asylum policies see Rahimi, Ashkaan, *The Evolution of EU Asylum Policy*, ZEI Discussion Paper C 142. Bonn: Center for European Integration Studies, 2005.

a) The primacy of community law was consolidated in spite of strong irritations, at times, about the meaning and substance of a "European spirit," leadership deficits and structural problems in upholding and deepening the treaty-based *acquis communautaire.*[25]
b) Budgetary matters have become an intrinsic element of a community of destiny, bound by the will to maintain the strength of the common currency in a common market; however, no sustainable solution has yet been found to install solid economic governance and fiscal federalism.
c) The impact of European integration on domestic structures in all member states has given a new and larger meaning to the notion of Europeanization; the process of politicizing European integration has increased the need to adapt national traditions, legislature, governance processes and economic structures, which did not remain without critical reactions from the side of EU member states.
d) The right to speak "in the name of Europe" is not the privilege of any institution or member state, and certainly not the privilege of the bigger member states alone, France and Germany in particular; in order to achieve a Single Foreign, Security and Defense Policy it will be necessary for the European Union not to define herself as counter-power to the United States.

(1) Lack of European Solidarity and a Slow Return to the Principle

The worst deficit in European integration during its third period has been the continuous provocation by several member state governments to question European solidarity in the name of national prerogatives. In any solemn speech on Europe, a European spirit is invoked in high tone. In reality, European Union operations and the European spirit were less and less in harmony with each other. It is difficult to identify one single event or one single political leader for being responsible for this trend. The de-solidarization among EU member states has been a creeping trend, which escalated in the course of the failure to implement the European Constitution. It has only recently begun to be revised. It may take as long to overcome the attitude of European integration as a zero-sum game as it has taken to turn this attitude from an exception rather than a rule in EU matters.

Without being too unfair, it may not be exaggerated to argue that the idea of European Union membership as dominantly driven by material self-interests started when then British Prime Minister Margaret Thatcher demanded "I want my money back" at the EU Summit in Fontainebleau in 1984. Here, one government challenged the European spirit, while in 2000 fourteen EU governments except for Austria

25 See Craig, Paul, and Gráinne de Búrca (eds.), *The Evolution of EU Law*, Oxford/NewYork: Oxford University Press, 1999.

challenged the European spirit when they imposed sanctions outside the clearly defined EU rules against Austria, done because of an unwelcome result of the Austrian elections. As for the effects of de-solidarizing on the EU constitution-building the downward spiral escalated at the cradle of the Treaty of Nice when the main obsession of France's political leadership was the fortification of vetoing positions prior to the unloved enlargement to include the Central and South Eastern post-communist countries. This European non-spirit was immediately copied by some of them once they had joined the European Union. Unlike France, the Polish leadership did not get away with tacit respect of their European peers. Poland was publicly put on a rhetorical European trial. As far as respect for the *acquis communautaire* is concerned, Germany's leadership during the late 1990's (supported by France) in the early years of the twenty-first century made a mockery of legally binding EU provisions by disregarding the implications of the Stability and Growth Pact. All EU governments raised a legitimacy matter of grave concern when they signed the Treaty Establishing a Constitution for Europe in 2004 without being able or willing to fully implement their international commitment. When the ratification process was stymied, the EU governments simply declared the positive ratification by eighteen out of twenty-seven EU member states null and void. The implication of this political act on the legal consciousness of European Union citizens as far as international commitments of their respective national governments are concerned, was never properly discussed anywhere in the EU arena. Instead, Europe's political leaders tried to get away with the self-induced fiasco by preparing the 2007 Treaty of Lisbon. When handed over to citizens of Europe for ratification, the Irish voters rejected the Treaty of Lisbon while simultaneously claiming to be pro-European. The best one can say about the relaunching of EU reforms in 2007 was the creeping recognition that the skeptical attitude toward deeper integration and the subsequent path of de-solidarization taken during the past two decades of European integration was wrong. It needed to be gradually reversed by all EU member states in the name, indeed, of a better European spirit than practiced theretofore.

Whether it was Spanish rigidity on budgetary matters, the French position on voting rights in the Council or – together with Germany – resistance to full implementation of the Single Market for services, the French and German attitude toward the Iraq policy of the US or its overly long resistance to implement the agreements on a common asylum policy, Italian resistance against a European Arrest Warrant, the British exploitation of the work of its partners to implement the euro while calmly staying aside, or Polish pathologies in its relationship to history and its German neighbor – all these experiences during the 1990's and the first decade of the twenty-first century were expressions of a lack of European spirit unworthy of an "ever closer Union." By the end of the first decade of the twenty-first century, time had come indeed to interpret Europe again from the perspective of its opportunities.

One significant event on the negative road that thoroughly deconstructed solidarity among EU partner states for all too long had occurred in 2000, when fourteen governments declared sanctions against Austria. In doing so, they were circumventing formal EU procedures and overly exaggerating domestic political developments in Austria for the sake of demonstrating a sense of leadership that ended exactly opposite from what was intended – to the detriment of the vociferous claim that the EU considers itself a community of values.[26] When a new Austrian coalition was formed by the Austrian Christian Democrats and the Free Democrats on February 4, 2000, at the initiative of French President Jacques Chirac sanctions were imposed by a decision of the other fourteen EU governments outside the EU decision-making system. Leading Austrian representatives were not allowed to participate in EU meetings. Even on the popular level, the frenzy was spreading. In the Netherlands, a boycott was organized against music tapes with Austrian children songs. Article 6 of the EU Treaty declared that a member state will provoke grave consequences if its policy is not in line with EU norms and values. Article 7 described the procedure that will be invoked in such a case, including a hearing with the accused member state. None of these procedures were activated by the "EU Group of 14," while they used the EU Commission to advance their policy. Although Article 6 was not legally invoked and hence the sanctions against Austria never constituted EU law, the very idea of the EU as a community of values and strictly relying on its legal norms was brought into question. The Austrian government had not done anything wrong. In fact, it had not even been established that it had when the campaign against Austria started. At the end, the "EU Group of 14" had to renounce their sanctions, hiding behind the findings of a commission of Wise Men in September 2000 (Martti Ahtisaari, Jochen Frowein, Marcelino Oreja) according to which Austria and its government were fully in line with EU values, norms and regulations.

More delicate was the de-solidarizing behavior of France and Germany regarding the implementation of the European Pact for Stability and Growth. The German government under Chancellor Helmut Kohl had insisted on this Pact at the Amsterdam European Council meeting in June 1997. According to the pact, the participating members of the European Monetary Union were obliged to maintain rigid austerity and budget measures in order to ensure the stability and viability of the euro. The annual national budget deficit was not to grow above 3 percent of the GDP. Except for extraordinary reasons, the EU would penalize any member state of the European Monetary Union no longer in compliance with this criterion. France had insisted that the subsequent measures of punishment, including the possible payment of fees to the EU,

26 See Gehler, Michael, "Präventivschlag als Fehlschlag. Intentionen und Konsequenzen der EU 14-Sanktionsmassnahmen gegen Österreich im Jahre 2000;" in: Loth, Wilfried (ed.), *Das europäische Projekt zu Beginn des 21. Jahrhunderts*, Leverkusen: Leske & Budrich, 2001: 352-382; Kühnhardt, Ludger, "Europa als Wertegemeinschaft – Verlierer der Österreich-Krise 2000?," *Wiener Zeitschrift zur Geschichte der Neuzeit*, 1 (2001):73-80; Bischof, Günter, et. al. (eds.), *Austria in the European Union*, New York: Transaction Publishers, 2002.

would require a political consideration of the matter and a subsequent decision in the Council.

This provision rescued France and Germany, but also Portugal, Belgium and Greece to be penalized for their overly excessive budget deficits since 2001. The fact that Germany had transgressed the strict criteria of budgetary discipline it had evoked in fear of other countries more lax attitudes produced "undisguised delight of its EU partners".[27] More shocking was the threat of the German government under Chancellor Schröder simply not to accept an early warning letter of the Commission in February 2002, let alone possible penalties. The Stability and Growth Pact and the role of the European Commission as guardian of EU norms came under severe legitimacy pressure. At the end of 2003, the Council of Finance Ministers (ECOFIN) in the European Monetary Union formally declared the Stability and Growth Pact obsolete by suspending deficit proceedings against Germany and France. In 2005, the EU redefined the Stability and Growth Pact, recognizing contingent national circumstances as temporary excuse to deviate from the rigid norms of the pact. While this was a victory for Germany – for the fourth time in row the slowest growing European economy and breaking the public debt criteria of the Stability and Growth Pact, critics considered it a big defeat for the EU. Many economists had supported the political move to reform the stability pact. They considered the criteria of the stability pact as being too rigid while Germany and other EU member states were suffering recession.[28] But even a reformed stability pact would have to confront the fact that economic growth cannot be planned, no matter the goals of the EU's Lisbon Strategy. The psychological effect of the whole episode was, however, detrimental to enhancing a true and solid European spirit: Representatives of bigger countries seemed to respect community law only if it was in their favor. It did not really help to eliminate this impression when the European Commission dropped its charges against the German government in May 2007 after the country had returned to respecting the Maastricht criteria for public deficit spending.[29]

In spite of these challenges, by and large, the primacy of community law was maintained and thus stabilized during this difficult period of European integration. The role of the European Court of Justice (ECJ) was not only formally strengthened through statutes. Increasingly, the European Court of Justice demonstrated its commitment to full implementation of Union law, which after all was always the result of voluntary political decisions based on rules and regulations of the EC and EU Treaties. In spite of the absence of a European Constitution, the European Court of Justice has become the Constitutional Court of Europe. Whenever the European Commission brings up charges

27 Dinan, Desmond, *Europe Recast: A History of European Union*, op.cit.: 303.

28 See Bofinger, Peter, and Eric Mayer, *The Stability and Growth Pact. Time to rebuild!*, Würzburg: University of Würzburg, 2004; Heipertz, Martin, and Amy Verdun, "The Dog that Would Never Bite," *Journal of European Public Policy*, 11(2004): 765-780.

29 On the European Commission and its overall development during recent years see Dimitrakopoulos, Dionyssis G., *The Changing European Commission*, Manchester: Manchester University Press, 2004.

against member states or individual companies by insisting on competition law provisions, this role of the European Court of Justice is, of course, not welcome by the accused partner country or company. But the clear European vocation of the European Court of Justice has continuously guaranteed the proper implementation of the fundamental regulatory measures of the EU in the context of the Single Market.[30]

The judges of the European Court of Justice have become notorious for being radical proponents of the strict implementation of Union law. Their role as final arbiters of the legal base of the EU has not been challenged on principle by national governments and only partially by national constitutional courts.[31] In fact, their record has grown over time as far as almost revolutionary decisions and subsequently emerging doctrines in favor of extended supranational integration are concerned. Following the early doctrinal decision of "Van Gend en Loos" in 1963 and "Costa versus ENEL" in 1964, the court rulings in the cases "Factortame" (1990) and "Francovich versus Italy" (1991) underlined the primacy of community law over national law. Another track record – beginning with the ruling in the "Isoglucose" case (1980) and leading to the comitology case "Parliament versus Council" (1990) and the Chernobyl case "European Parliament versus Council" (1991) supported the emergence of a legally strengthened role of the European Parliament, considered to be "the biggest beneficiary of the EJC's distinctive approach to institutional relations."[32] The strong role and consistently pro-integrative track record of the European Court of Justice was all the more amazing as none of the judges of the EJC (one per country) would have been appointed – for six years with the possibility of a renewable term – without consent of the national governments. Even the British Law Lords have continuously recognized the primacy of European law.[33]

30 Among eight rulings of the European Court of Justice in 2004 on matters of direct taxation in the EU, two decisions against France and Finland would have lasting effects across the EU: The French taxation of migrants leaving France was considered illegal under EU law. Finland lost the right to double-tax profits made in companies elsewhere in the EU; when they have been taxed in the country of origin, these taxes can be deducted from the overall taxable income in the country of residence. Tax experts identified also 44 German tax rules as colliding with EU law. It could not come as a surprise that the European Court of Justice came increasingly under criticism of those who wanted to maintain the primacy of national autonomy over Europeanized solutions and legal standards.

31 For instance in the case of the German Constitutional Court, which declared in 1993 the Treaty of Maastricht compatible with the German constitution but limited further deepening of the European Union if it would not happen in accordance with decisions of the German parliament that alone was representing the German people; a European people did not exist which the European Court of Justice could invoke to legitimize its claims of a superior European law, the German Constitutional Court stated.

32 George, Stephen, and Ian Bache (eds.), *Politics in the European Union*, Oxford: Oxford University Press, 2001: 275.

33 Ibid.: 281-283 with the example of the court ruling in the "Factortame" (1990) case on a dispute of a Spanish fisherman with the British Merchant Shipping Act of 1988 that was considered a breach of EC law although it was an explicit Act of Parliament, the most revered tradition of British democracy.

All in all, the idea to promote "a Europe of results" or "a Europe that works" indicated the desire to return to European pragmatism, including solidarity wherever needed and being useful. The solidarity clause that was introduced in the European Constitution in reaction to the terror attacks in Madrid on March 11, 2004, was a first indicator of a European Union that is willing to apply solidarity whenever any of its constituent parts needs it. In 2005, Poland heavily critized a German-Russian deal over energy transport through the Baltic Sea (Nord Stream) circumnavigating Poland and leaving the country potentially in the cold. When Russia cut energy supply to Ukraine, also EU member states such as Hungary were affected in their access to natural gas from Russia. Suddenly, the whole EU began to be concerned about energy dependency. The inclusion of the concept of energy solidarity in the 2007 Reform Treaty was a reaction to the realization that the EU as a whole – and not only Hungary or Poland - was dependent upon a steady flow of energy resources from Russia, North Africa and the Middle East.

In turn, the Polish government was reminded that solidarity is not a one-way street. Poland's national-conservative government was also asked to practice solidarity with their EU partners by accepting necessary compromises on matters relevant to relaunching institutional reforms after the Constitution had failed. Obviously, it was unfair to put all the blame on Poland, no matter how difficult a partner its government was at times during the path toward the 2007 Reform Treaty. The European Union as a whole had to be reminded that solidarity is a European principle only if accepted by all in reality and not only on paper.

When Ireland rejected the Reform Treaty in a first referendum in June 2008, the rest of the EU had to be reminded that it would not be in the European spirit of solidarity to put the blame on the Irish alone.The efforts made to rescue the Reform Treaty in Ireland were an indicator of a new sensitivity vis-à-vis smaller member states.

Only returning to the principle of European solidarity will give new impulses to the advancement of a genuine European spirit. European solidarity will have to be a guiding principle in the next long-term period of European integration if this integration is to be sustained. The next period of European integration will have to deal with matters of fundamental relevance to the principle of solidarity, be it in the context of Europeanizing elements of the welfare state, or be it in the context of European peace keeping and other international obligations.

(2) The Frustratingly Slow Revision of Wrong Priorities

The intricacies of budgetary matters are often only of interest to technical experts. Yet budgetary matters are essentially political. The debates on necessary revisions of EU policies, on new reform goals and priorities increasingly reflect this fact. Throughout the first decades of European integration, by and large only the notorious budget for the Common Agricultural Policy attracted public attention. The MacSharry reforms of 1992 finally brought a substantial reform. Named after the Irish Commissioner in charge of the agricultural dossier, this was the first serious effort to curb agricultural expenditures in decades. Under the pressure of the Uruguay Round of the General Agreement on Tariffs and Trade, the MacSharry reforms decoupled agricultural subsidies from production. Instead of paying for overproduction through guaranteed prices, the EU organized agricultural subsidies as direct payments to stabilize and increase the income of farmers. Initially, the reformed Common Agricultural Policy – which also recognized the importance of farmers in preserving the natural landscape of Europe – was more expensive than the earlier structure. This was due to overly generous compensation schemes offered to huge numbers of farmers. In 2003, the initial MacSharry reforms were almost neutralized when France and Germany refused to cut farm spending while agreeing to limit its growth to 1 percent per year after 2006. When the European Union moved toward eastward enlargement in June 2004, almost 50 percent of its budget was still bound by expenditures under the schemes of the Common Agricultural Policy. For the period 2000 to 2006, all in all 307 billion euros were provided for these subsidies, reaching barely 4 percent of the EU's population. For the financial period 2007-2013, 370 billion euros out of a total budget of 862 billion euros (47 percent) were reserved for the agricultural sector. This wrong prioritizing did more harm to the global image of the EU than anything else.[34]

It would have been impossible to extend the commitments and expenditures of the Common Agricultural Policy to the new member states. The proportion of the population living off farming differed in the acceding countries. In Poland 19.6 percent of the workforce were employed in agriculture, in Romania an astounding 37.7 percent, in Hungary only 6.0 percent, in Slovakia 6.6 percent, in Estonia 6.5 percent, and in the Czech Republic 4.9 percent.[35] In spite of protest from Polish and other farmers and their representatives, the EU negotiated transitory schemes for the new member states. During the first seven years of their EU membership, their farmers would receive only 25 percent of the direct agricultural subsidies granted to farmers in the "old" fifteen EU member states. Subsequently, this proportion will rise by 5 percent a year, reaching the full 100 percent by 2013. This "phasing-in" could hardly enhance the hope for a comprehensive "phasing-out" of the entire agricultural subsidy mechanism after 2013.

The EU's structural and cohesion policies is aimed at reducing socio-economic disparities in the enlarged European Union, accelerating economic reforms in response to globalization, and responding to the development of a knowledge-based economy

34 Knipping, Franz, *Rom, 25. März 1957: Die Einigung Europas*, op.cit.:285.

35 The figures of the agricultural workforce for the other newcomers were: Cyprus 5.3 percent, Latvia 15.3 percent, Lithuania 18.6 percent, Malta 2.2 percent, Slovenia 9.7 percent, Bulgaria 10.7 percent. On expectations and implications of EU's eastward enlargement see Barrass, Robert, and Bernard Steunenberg (eds.), *Widening the European Union: The Politics of Institutional Change and Reform*, London: Routledge, 2002; Brusis, Martin, and Janis A. Emmanouilidis (eds.), *Thinking Enlarged: The Accession Countries and the Future of the European Union*, Bonn: Europa Union Verlag, 2002.

while Europe was facing an aging population with its special welfare needs. Prior to the eastward enlargement, the EU had defined those regions lagging most strongly behind the overall economic development with a per capita GDP in the range of 60 to 75 percent. The per capita GDP of most regions in the new member states stood at 30 to 40 percent of the 2004 EU's average. During the 1990's, some EU regions had made significant progress as a consequence of EU support. Irelands per capita GDP increased from 64 percent of the EU average in 1988 to 119 percent in 1999 and 133 in 2004. The five German "new Länder," the former German Democratic Republic, increased their per capita GDP from 38 percent of the EU average in 1991 to 68 percent in 1995, largely due to West German resource transfers of more than one annual West German GDP. It was estimated that structural funds of the EU helped to boost the per capita GDP in Portugal by 4.7 percent and in Northern Ireland by 1.27 percent, and supported the creation of around 800,000 new jobs and the training of 8.15 million people in those regions eligible for EU structural and cohesion funds. Regions such as Lisbon, Northern Ireland, Burgenland in Austria, and Flevoland in the Netherlands surpassed the threshold of an average per capita GDP of 75 percent before 2004, making them no longer eligible for EU support. Yet, the negotiations about phasing-out periods were as rough as they could have been. The gap between the rich and the poor regions in the EU was certainly not to be closed through the mechanism of structural and cohesion funds, no matter their size. The percentage of EU citizens living in regions eligible for EU subsidies increased with the eastward enlargement from 18 to 22 percent, that is to say from 68 to 116 million people. Inner London, the most affluent EU region with 66.744 euros per capita income, achieves 315 percent of the EU average. The Eastern Polish region of Lubelskie, identified as the poorest region with an average per capita income of 6762 euros, achieves 32 percent of the EU average, or roughly one tenth of the income in Inner London. No EU redistribution scheme would ever be able to close this gap. The effects on the service and knowledge-based society on the dividing lines between rich and poor in the enlarged EU remained a matter of controversial interpretation.[36]

Yet, the politicization of European Union politics did not begin with the issue of social justice. It began with budgetary issues as was the case in the classical evolution of parliamentary democracy of the European and North American nation state. For the first time in 1988, the European Community agreed on a longer-term fiscal plan (Delors I Package). The Fiscal Perspective for the period 1988-1992 was followed by the Fiscal Perspective for the period 1993-2000 (Delors II Package). For the first time in integration history, the EU's budget received broad public attention across the EU when the EU's Fiscal Perspective for the period 2000-2006 was negotiated under German EU

36 See Liddle, Roger, and Frédéric Lerais, *Europe's Social Reality: A Consultation Paper from the Bureau of European Policy Advisers* (2007), http://ec.europa.eu/citizens_agenda/social_reality_stocktaking/docs/background_document_en.pdf.

Presidency in 1999 (Agenda 2000).[37] Increasing awareness about the importance of budgetary matters had grown, but in the end it was not proportional to the results of the Agenda 2000. With the first wave of eastward enlargement of the European Union on May 1, 2004, the EU found itself in a paradoxical situation. The new member states from Central and Eastern Europe were not only receiving 40.8 billion euros between 2004 and 2006 to help them modernize their economies and adjust to the Single Market, they were also contributing to the EU budget, the total amounting to some 15 billion euros for the period 2004 to 2006. The distribution of costs and benefits in the enlarged EU left considerable room for controversy. According to the European Commission, in 2004 Poland was receiving 67 euros per capita annually, Hungary 49 euros, the Czech Republic 29 euros, Greece, however, 437 euros, Ireland 418 euros, Spain 216 euros and Portugal 211 euros.[38]

Before their accession to the EU, some of the new members from Central Europe had explicitly criticized the Common Agricultural Policy as an expression of central planning, bitterly known to them under communism.[39] All of them had to scrap their own agricultural subsidies during the 1990's as part of their transition to a market economy. Having joined the EU, their attitudes began to change: They started to appreciate the subsidies from Brussels and were hardly ready to give them up again soon.

The negotiations over the Fiscal Perspective for the period 2007-2013 were initiated with a general positioning of the main net contributors Germany, France, Great Britain, Austria, the Netherlands and Sweden. In a letter dated December 15, 2003, to the then President of the European Commission, Romano Prodi, they declared their will to limit the EU budget for the period 2007 to 2013 to one percent of the Gross Domestic Product of the EU. Until then, the ceiling had been 1.24 percent without ever being reached. The negotiations were long, tough and uncomfortable. They were an expression of the overall crisis of confidence in European integration and the shabby bickering over national interests without keeping a common European good in mind. The European Commission had demanded an increase of the EU budget from 133.5 billion euros in 2007 to 158.4 billion euros in 2013, a total increase of 22.8 percent over the period 2007-2013. Otherwise, the European Commission argued, the growing tasks and expectations for the EU could not be met. The European Parliament supported this position and demanded a total budget (2007-2013) of 975 billion euros. Several rounds

37 See Wittschorek, Peter (ed.), *AGENDA 2000: Herausforderungen an die Europäische Union und an Deutschland*, Nomos: Baden-Baden, 1999.

38 See Fuller, Thomas, "EU Get's a 'Bargain' in Expanding East," *International Herald Tribune*, December 17, 2002.

39 Hungary, for instance, had even joined the "Cairns Group" of countries that favors complete liberalization of agricultural trade. It had to leave the group prior to joining the EU. For an interesting EU-US comparison on agricultural reforms see Moyer, Wayne, and Timothy Edward Josling, *Agricultural Policy Reform: Politics and Process in the EU and in US 1990s*, Aldershot: Ashgate, 2002.

of negotiations in the European Council failed. And when finally a deal was done in December 2005, the European Parliament demonstrated that no longer could its role be underestimated: It refused the result of the European Council. Only after EU member states increased the budget compromise of December 2005 by 4 billion euros, did the European Parliament accept the new inter-institutional agreement on the Fiscal Perspective for the period 2007-2013 on May 17, 2006.

After two and half years of negotiations, the Fiscal Perspective for the period 2007-2013 included the following elements: The overall budget of the European Union would amount to 862.4 billion euros, equivalent to 1.045 percent of the EU's combined GDP. 72 billion euros were meant for competition policies, 308.1 billion euros for structural funds, 370.8 billion euros for agriculture, 10.3 billion euros for justice and home affairs, 50.0 billion euros for foreign, security and development policies, and 50.3 billion euros for administrative expenditures. In 2008/2009 a mid-term revision of the budget structure was to happen. It was no secret that this would lead to another round of hard negotiations. The path to a serious and comprehensive EU Fiscal Constitution was still long and daunting. Should the EU wish to achieve a status in which claims and performance could match each other reasonably well, it would have to enormously increase its budget. Without the introduction of a genuine EU Tax, reasonable fiscal autonomy was not achievable.

(3) Losing Popular Support over a Visionless Europeanization

Since the Treaty of Maastricht, European integration has become a two-way process. On the one hand, establishing European institutions in Brussels continued. They needed cohesion, were to be made more transparent, democratic and accountable, and they had to better focus on topical challenges rather than intra-institutional bickering. On the other hand, European integration had an ever increasing impact on the EU member states, their societies and public policies. The European Union began the process of real Europeanization in the context of properly implementing the objectives and legislation of the Single Market.[40] This process was prepared and managed by competent and committed leadership. The secular process of European unification and the parallel deepening of European integration that was required during the second half of the 1990's and the first years of the twenty-first century required at least the same degree of leadership, vision and commitment. However, during these crucial years, the European Union experienced a decade of weak leadership and a lack of orientation. It was particularly painful that France and Germany, the traditional engines of European integration, were absorbed by domestic crises that turned them inward, helpless and frustrated about Europe. Instead of leading the way beyond the introduction of a

40 See Featherstone, Kevin, and Claudio M. Radaelli (eds.), *The Politics of Europeanization*, Oxford: Oxford University Press, 2003.

common currency in 2002 and the accomplishment of EU enlargement in 2004, they were clinging to parochial domestic debates with a strongly euroskeptical overture.

The unusual introspection in France and in Germany during a difficult decade spread across the EU. Particular noteworthy was the resistance to the full implementation of a Single Market for services, not only in Germany and France, but also elsewhere in the EU. Heated controversies over takeovers of public banks in Italy became as much a matter of national protectionism inside the EU as the requirements of full liberalization of the labor market in French and German service industries. While in reality, more financial integration in the EU was necessary, and the full liberalization of service industries to cheaper labor from Central and Eastern Europe inevitable, governments and EU institutions – confronted with high unemployment and slackening productivity – did not succeed in resolving these bottlenecks to a more dynamic Europe. As the International Herald Tribune put it in spring 2005, the political leadership in the European Union spent too much energy "on trying to decide just how the power will be divided in Europe."[41] Their main concern was not with "a Europe that works."

Germany was a particular focus of concern during the second half of the 1990's and into the first decade of the twenty-first century. The admission of East Germany dismantled and integrated into the Federal Republic of Germany in October 1990 had facilitated the illusion – both in East and in West Germany – that the five "new Länder" were exempted from the dire transformation stress and EU-imposed accession preparation all other post-communist countries had to go through. In reality, the whole of Germany indirectly became a country with the post-communist transformation agenda. On top of this challenge, the effects of German unification camouflaged the general slowing down of reforms in West Germany at the time. It is fair to say that German unification absorbed enormous human energy and financial resources of West Germany. But in focusing on East Germany's development, West Germany lost track of some of the modernization trends its West European partners and the US were undergoing. It could not come as a surprise that around the turn of the century, the country ended in crisis: In its Western part, reforms had been delayed that would have allowed it to catch up with globalization and innovative reforms of deregulation, liberalization and modernization and other reforms in order to muster the Single Market, which had been adopted by various EU partner states. In East Germany, in spite of an enormous transfer of financial resources from West German tax payers, no overall sustainable economic progress had happened. Since 1996, Germany's economic growth was only around 1.0 percent on annual average, half the percentage of the other eurozone countries.[42] The German tax rates were no longer competitive in order to encourage necessary new investments in Germany. A radical and coherent tax reform remained however absent from the radar screen of German politics while the country's

41 Norris, Floyd, "Tough EU Rules?," *International Herald Tribune*, March 22, 2005.
42 See Ferguson, Niall, *Colossus: The Price of America's Empire*, op. cit.:241.

elites were largely complaining about the complaints of their compatriots. A decade after unification, Germany had lost much of its strategic importance of the Cold War era, as far as the economic dynamic, its foreign and security policy posture, and its drive for European integration were concerned.[43] While the Netherlands, Austria and Ireland had unemployment rates of around four percent, Germany continuously had an unemployment rate above ten percent.

Based on purchasing power parities, Germany still had a per capita GDP of 27,000 dollars, compared with Norway, the US and Ireland, Canada, Denmark and Switzerland of around 38,000 dollars. But while, for instance, Ireland had sky-rocketed into the leading group of industrial nations – not in the least due to EC/EU membership effects – Germany had fallen from the leading group of industrialized nations into a backward middle position. Productivity was too low and the potential for economic growth had gone down to 1.6 percent maximum, while the real growth rate was around or below 1 percent. In 2005, for the fourth time in a row, Germany failed to reach the public deficit criteria of the Treaty of Maastricht with 3.7 instead of 3.0 percent of public debt in relation to the country's overall GDP, which was allowed by the Treaty of Maastricht (more than 80 billion euros for 2004 with a total public debt of 1.400 billion euros). Coupled with demographic trends – increased longevity with costs for the social systems on the one hand, an enormous decrease in population reproduction and the weakest desire for children across the EU – and hesitance to embrace the opportunities of more immigration, on the other hand, Germany was trapped by her success and her geographical position. From having been the strategic dynamo for European integration, Germany became "the sick man of Europe."

The change of government in 2005 was not a real liberalization from this burden. The Grand Coalition under Chancellor Angela Merkel simply redefined the starting point for reforms in the country. The government accommodated fear of too speedy reforms with an overall disconnect of the political process from the majority of citizens. The de-politicization of the German public sphere overshadowed the lack of conceptual approaches for the social and political development in Germany. The Grand Coalition, of course, declared itself successful but in reality, many of the structural deficits of the sociological reality of Germany were not addressed at all. Some of the reforms were

43 One of the senior members of the European Parliament and member of the German Christian Democrats analyzed that German net contribution to the EU had continuously gone down from 33 percent in 1994 to 22 percent in 2002 reflecting the economic crisis of Germany. And yet, Europe was criticized in Germany for costing too much. In real term, Germany's contribution had been reduced from 21.3 billion euros to 17.5 billion euros. Fiscal support reallocated by the EU to Germany – mostly for agriculture, structural policies and research policies – amounted to a reduction in net contribution to the EU from 10.4 billion euros in 1994 to 5.1 billion euros in 2002, equaling two percent of Germany's national budget. During the period 1992 to 2002, German export into EU partner countries rose sharply from 161 to 355 billion euros, amounting to 54 percent of all German exports. The trade surplus rose from 12 billion to 84 billion euros during this period, although this enormous benefit from integration was rarely mentioned in German debates: Brok, Elmar, "Der Nutzen wird verschwiegen," *Frankfurter Allgemeine Zeitung*, March 1, 2004.

acknowledged as being positive, although it was debatable whether the reduction in unemployment was the result of certain policies or rather the effects of dire reforms in the private sector, helped by a booming global economy. Some critics considered the reform agenda of the Grand Coalition cosmetic while others became even more radical in their critique: Some labeled the Federal Republic of Germany "GDR light."

In terms of EU policies, one must add, it goes to the credit of Chancellor Merkel that Germany under the Grand Coalition returned to the pro-active European policy the other EU partners had experienced under the Kohl government. For the rest of Europe, the internal stagnation of structural modernization in Germany was not really felt. Therefore, the focus of most German partner countries was different and the relief was obvious about the new, more constructive style of Chancellor Merkel in European affairs. Compared with the Schröder government, she emphasized better relations with smaller EU partner countries and impressed her colleagues with her determination to broker a deal on the Fiscal Perspective for the period 2007-2013 in December 2005. This was followed by an overall successful EU-Presidency of Germany in the first half of 2007. Chancellor Merkel succeeded in de-icing the frozen institutional reform process. She declared the European Constitution dead and relaunched its political substance through the negotiation of the 2007 Reform Treaty.[44] At the same time, Germany's public deficit returned to being in line with the Maastricht criteria. France was also exempted from further EU Commission charges for having failed the Maastricht criteria. The election of President Nicolas Sarkozy in May 2007 gave immediate hope to a new, dynamic France on the European scene. The Franco-German tandem began to pick up speed again, this time in a more constructive way than for most of the past decade. The overall atmosphere improved and provided room for a fresh start of Franco-German cooperation on EU matters. This was certainly not enough to renew both countries internally. But it helped the EU leadership to overcome a frustrating decade of paralysis and self-destructive myopia. Merkel and Sarkozy were considered to be an odd couple. Yet they tried their best to relaunch the almost magic symbolism of the Franco-German tandem as being vital for any sustainable achievement in EU matters. Should the two countries, being so different in spite of all invocation of friendship, say "yes" any deal was considered to be possible for the EU as a whole.

(4) Hesitant Recognition of Europe's Global Presence

During its first decades, European integration had been, by and large, an inward-looking operation. The absence of a stronger political role, let alone a visible global role, was considered European normalcy. Europe preferred to be perceived as a soft

44 On the German EU Presidency 2007 see Marchetti, Andreas, and Martin Zimmek (eds.), *Annäherungen an Europa: Beiträge zur deutschen EU-Ratspräsidentschaft 2007*, ZEI Discussion Paper C 175, Bonn: Center for European Integration Studies 2007.

economic power. With the end of the Cold War, the world returned to Europe and with it hard politics. In the past, failed efforts to develop a common European foreign policy remained largely abstract matters. West European security was guaranteed by the nuclear umbrella of the US and a continuous presence of American ground troops in strategically important partner countries. Efforts to develop a solid European base for foreign and security actions were always perceived as not more than a psychological act of emancipation from the US. It did not really matter. The threat of the Cold War was real and yet abstract. With the end of the Cold War, Europe turned again from an object to a subject of world politics. The initial introduction of Europe as a political factor was coupled with disaster and tragedy: The outbreak of the Wars of Yugoslavian Succession in 1991 brought bloodshed back to Europe. The media coverage was enormous. Millions of Yugoslavian guest workers had been living among West Europeans for decades. Millions of West Europeans had spent holidays on the Adriatic coast. Images of the shelling of Dubrovnik hit their soul. Europe's citizens – whom the Treaty of Maastricht had granted Union citizenship to after all – were demanding action from their politicians in an unprecedented way. Yet the decade of the 1990's was lost for European foreign policy credibility. Legally and politically, the European Union was not ready. The hesitant introduction of a chapter on political union into the Treaty of Maastricht was the only possible expression of commonality. Beyond legalistic rhetoric, time was not ripe for common perceptions of the Balkans, let alone for common policies or actions. Only American military actions could finally force Yugoslavian dictator Milošević to stop the ethnic cleansing after four dirty Wars of Yugoslavian Succession. The European Union was forced to speed up its internal cohesion-building. It had to recognize international responsibility beyond its own borders. The European Council in Cologne on June 3 and 4, 1999, presented the agreement with Milošević to the world, which had been concluded by its emissary, former Finish President Martti Ahtisaari. But without the US bombing of strategic targets in Serbia, this would not have happened.

It goes to the credit of the European Union that its belated process of sharpening the claim to a common foreign and security policy began to take speed unheard of before in this field normally belonging to national prerogatives. The EU learned to accept that it had to project its own stability beyond the borders of the European Union if its citizens and states were to benefit from the fruits of stability, peace and affluence in the long run. A comprehensive structure for crisis management and peace enforcing began to emerge.[45] By 2008, the most sensitive issue following the break-up of Yugoslavia was to be resolved: the final status of Kosovo.[46] This time, the European Union was playing a major role in stabilizing and subsequently Europeanizing an independent Kosovo. In

45 See Quinlan, Michael, *European Defense Cooperation: Asset or Threat to NATO*, Washington D.C.: Woodrow Wilson Center Press, 2001.

46 See Eiff, Hansjörg, *Zum Problem des Kosovo-Status*, ZEI Discussion Paper C 144. Bonn: Center for European Integration Studies, 2005.

1999, such a development was unthinkable and a taboo among EU policy makers. In the meantime, the European Union had taken over policing and military operations in Macedonia, Bosnia-Herzegovina and in Kosovo itself. More importantly, the EU had opened up the prospect of membership to all people and countries in the region at the Thessaloniki European Council in 2003. Slovenia had already joined the European Union along with other post-communist countries in 2004. Croatia and Macedonia had been granted membership status. Membership negotiations with Croatia began on October 3, 2005 but were not expected to conclude before 2011. In 2009, Iceland applied for EU membership. Optimists expected Iceland to join along with Croatia, skeptics recalled the inherent nature of Icelandic politics and society In any case, also on matters of enlargement, a new era had begun: Iceland did not apply in the name of European reconciliation but in order to receive a European umbrella protecting the Atlantic island country against the effects of the world financial crisis. Europe's global exposure was the new rationale for European integration. In this transformation period, the first ever non-European mini-enlargement to the very West of the world passed unnoticed in Europe: After a constitutional change in the Netherlands, the Caribbean islands of Bonaire, St. Eustatius and Saba became regular Dutch municipalities on December 15, 2008 and thus regular parts of the European Union.

The evolution of a Common Foreign and Security Policy and finally of a Common Security and Defense Policy confirmed the old experience: Cooperation and eventual integration work out much faster under the pressure of an inescapable challenge the EU was facing. This experience was also true in the context of achieving a European Arrest Warrant in response to the international wave of terrorism. Since the introduction of the first vague provisions on justice and home affairs into the Treaty of Maastricht, the EU was continuously striving for a more solidified European Space of Freedom, Security and Justice. The European police unit Europol was created, based in Amsterdam and sometimes compared with the FBI.[47] Yet, the EU was not really making progress throughout the 1990's on two essential matters: the introduction of an European Arrest Warrant as key to strengthen the common judicial system and enable court rulings on the basis of commonly agreed standards, and the introduction of an European Asylum and Migration policy, a burning issue across the EU but with different intensity and implication in its member states. The Treaty of Amsterdam, signed on October 2, 1997, as the first follow-up treaty to the Treaty of Maastricht, did not extend co-decision between the European Council and the European Parliament to matters of asylum and migration policies, primarily because of a last minute turn-around by German Chancellor Kohl at the time. Only complicated transition periods for the further evolution of a common asylum and migration policy were agreed upon in the Treaty of Amsterdam. Only weeks before the big eastward enlargement to include the Central

47 See Occhipinti, John D., *The Politics of EU Police Cooperation: Toward a European FBI?*, Boulder: Lynne Rieffer Publishing, 2003.

European post-communist countries on May 1, 2004, the Council of Home Affairs Ministers of the "old EU" was able to agree on the principles of a common migration policy. The ministers did so under a cloud of fear that decisions could be to their disadvantage once the newcomers joined the table.

The external pressure to decide on a common European Arrest Warrant was of an even more spectacular nature: "9/11." The terrorist attacks on New York and Washington accelerated the decision for a European Arrest Warrant and a common definition of terrorism in an unprecedented way. Only weeks after the horrible events in the US, the European Council passed the decision on a European Arrest Warrant on December 11, 2001. The details were designed during the first half of 2002, parallel to the establishment of EUROJUST, the nucleus of a European Attorney General. While the development of a common asylum and migration policy was initially blocked by Germany, a common Arrest Warrant was at first rejected by Italy. It remains a strange example of reactive integration that the EU reacted only to the shocking terrorist attacks in the US with legalistic and policing methods in order to protect the EU from similar crimes. But in doing so, the EU also laid the groundwork for pragmatic and technical transatlantic normalcy that prevailed even during the fierce political rows over Iraq in 2002/2003.

Nevertheless, the self-binding effect of political events on the political leaders in Europe had become a continuous safeguard for an eventual return to rationality in transatlantic relations and subsequently for new progress in European integration. The fact that EU leaders had to be driven more often by external events than by internal consensus-building and anticipatory decision-making might be the nature of politics. It guarantees the continuous evolution of the EU even in times of weak leadership. Nobody can claim the monopoly to speak "in the name of Europe," including France with or without Germany at its side. Europe's voice can only be heard if all EU member states can identify with what it says. To preserve this anti-hegemonic and inclusive understanding of the meaning and scope of European integration was more than ever an emerging common European interest, should the enlarged European Union be capable of deepening the impact of its policies in the course of the decades to come.

4. Effects of "Enlargement Fear:" New Perspectives for Deepening

During the 1990's, the joy over the end of communist rule in Central and Eastern Europe gave way to realism, concern and also resentment in Western Europe. While the post-communist countries were seriously and adamantly struggling to incorporate the EU's *acquis communautaire* into their domestic agenda of transformation, the 15 old EU member states were trying to prevent the transformation also impacting their ways. Speculation about the costs of integrating and reforming Central and Eastern European countries reached by the wildest projections concerning possible flows of migration. A certain increase of illegal migration and organized crime related to the new openness of borders were undeniable, but it seemed as if this was the inevitable prize of freedom. At the same time, the larger markets in Central and Eastern Europe were a golden opportunity for many businesses and companies across Western Europe. More trade with the new participants of the European market substituted for exhausted consumerism and recession in Western Europe. Fear of uncontrolled migration was another dubious prejudice that all of a sudden obsessed Western Europe. A more sober and differentiated analysis about migratory patterns into the EU had to consider two kinds of labor movements originating in the post-communist societies: complementary movement and competitive movement.[48] While the first type was needed in several sectors of the Western European economy that are in need of seasonal manual workers or of cheap temporary workers (i.e. harvesting, construction business), the second one simply required stronger efforts by the economies of "old Europe" to proceed with the evolution of new levels of a modernized division of labor. Some countries of Western Europe were faster than others in recognizing the need for enhanced reforms of their labor markets and welfare systems, their education structures and curricula from kindergarten to university. Others were resorting to protectionist instincts as if new walls would have ever helped anybody in Europe.

Five million people had migrated to Germany alone between 1989 and 1996. Most of them did not come from the EU applicant countries, but from the former Soviet Union. Across the EU, the total number of 850,000 residents originating from another EU member state constituted only 0.2 percent of the population in the old EU. This number was in reverse proportion to the degree of polemic against migration from Europe's center and east. It also has to be mentioned that 600,000 Poles returned home once the communist regime had disappeared in their homeland. As contradictory as the concerns and fears related to migration from Central and Eastern Europe were across the EU, the 1990's saw an increasing debate in the old EU about the need to balance eastward enlargement with new initiatives toward the Southern littoral of the Mediterranean. Should the European Union's stability be projected and exported in order to impact its neighboring regions, the orientation toward the Southern Mediterranean region was compulsory. The mix of arguments, however, for building up a coherent European approach was not consistent at all. Simultaneously, fear and hope were invoked, development intentions and strategies for increased economic interdependencies were presented, security concerns and visions of a cultural dialogue were expressed, ideas of how to deter migrants and how to better involve the economies of North Africa into the Single Market process were aired. The net result was not clear and the strategy resulting from this first initiative of the European Union to look to its

48 See Kühnhardt, Ludger, *Die Europäische Union – Fragen zur Erweiterung*, Berlin: Auswärtiges Amt/Europäische Kommission, 2003 (3rd ed.): 35-37.

immediate South was accordingly incoherent. Yet, the inevitable eastward enlargement also enlarged and widened the perspective of the whole European Union toward its Southern neighbors.

The Euro-Mediterranean Dialogue of the European Union was initiated during the early 1990's. As far as the intention of the EU Commission – and especially of Spain and France – was concerned, it was a response to the eastward orientation that dominated after the end of communist rule in Central and Eastern Europe. France and other Southern EU member states anticipated that the eastward orientation of the EU would largely be to the economic advantage of Germany and other countries in Northern Europe. Along with Germany Great Britain, Denmark, the Netherlands, Finland and Sweden expressed special interest in bringing their post-communist neighbors as soon as possible into the status of full EU membership. Italy found itself in an ambivalent situation. As much as Austria, Italy benefited economically from the newly emerging markets in Central Europe, but was at the same time hesitant to enlarge the EU to the east if it meant a loss of its own influence. Understandably so, the Southern members of the EU wanted to balance the prospect of a new and broader Europe to the East with a strengthened emphasis on partnership with the Southern littoral countries around the Mediterranean. This policy became known as the Barcelona Process, bringing together all EU member states and most Southern Mediterranean countries for the first time on November 27 and 28, 1995, in Barcelona. The simultaneous presence of Israel and the Palestinian National Authority was spectacular. The absence of Libya was noticeable, at that time still scorned as a terrorist state. By the end of 2004, the European Union had not only engaged Libya in the Barcelona Process, it had even lifted its ban on arms sales to Tripoli.

The Euro-Mediterranean Dialogue was suffering a series of flaws in the management of this largely asymmetric partnership.[49] Yet it did not remain limited to the original intention of serving as a counter-balancing program to eastward enlargement of the EU. In fact, both processes were reinforcing each other and engaged all EU member states, including their civil societies.[50] The prospect of partnership and co-operation with the Southern Mediterranean and presumably with further Arab and

49 See Calleya, Stephen, *Is the Barcelona-Process Working?*, ZEI Discussion Paper C 75. Bonn: Center for European Integration Studies, 2000; Maier, Felix (ed.), *Managing Asymmetric Interdependencies within the Euro-Mediterranean Partnership*, ZEI Discussion Paper C 101. Bonn: Center for European Integration Studies, 2002; Jacobs, Andreas, (ed.), *Euro-Mediterranean Cooperation: Enlarging and Widening the Perspective*, ZEI Discussion Paper C 131. Bonn: Center for European Integration Studies, 2004; Calleya, Stephen, *Evaluating Euro-Mediterranean Relations*, Routledge: London, 2005; Marchetti, Andreas (ed.), *Ten Years Euro-Mediterranean Partnership: Defining European Interests for the Next Decade*, ZEI Discussion Paper C 154, Bonn: Center for European Integration Studies, 2005.

50 The Euro-Mediterranean Study Commission (EuroMesCo) was established as network of think-tanks, research institutes and scholars from both sides of the Mediterranean, comprising subsequently also of members from the new EU member states from Central and Eastern Europe as much as their representatives participated in all political activities of EU institutions in the context of the "Barcelona Process," see: www.euromesco.net.

African countries also affected policy makers in Scandinavia, in Poland and the Baltic States, and if only as far as competition over foreign investments was concerned. Portuguese or Maltese policy makers were in turn increasingly involved in the implications of eastward enlargement, including migration and the effects of cheap labor.[51] The Southern orientation of the European Union never gained the degree of emotional reaction as the prospect of eastward enlargement did. It was clear that Egypt, no matter what, would never become a European Union member state. Poland was about to join the EU in 2004. The only Southern country provoking a strong degree of emotions inside the "old" and also inside the enlarged European Union was Turkey. Amidst controversial disputes of Turkey's European character and vocation, the EU eventually opened full membership negotiations on October 3, 2005. The subsequent process was to become more twisted than all previous experiences with Central and South Eastern Europe.

The enlargement process of the European Union that took place during the 1990's finally buried all ideas to design Europe as a free trade zone only. If EFTA had not already been actually dead with the accession of Great Britain to the EC in 1973, the accession of Sweden, Austria and Finland in 1995 limited even the potential of its heir, the European Economic Space. The EU had negotiated this European Economic Space in 1992. It guaranteed that the remaining members of former EFTA accepted the legal provisions of the Common Market without becoming a member of it. For any prospective new member state from Central and Eastern Europe, the EU developed a highly complex pattern of assistance, association and pre-accession schemes involving more experts in EU institutions and a higher degree of civil society participation than in any other enlargement (and in fact in any other policy process) before. On March 31, 1998, the European Commission began formal negotiations with a first group of six candidate countries, followed by the opening of negotiations with the remainder six countries on February 15, 2000. These negotiations were defined by the membership criteria of the EU, known as Copenhagen Criteria: stability of institutions guaranteeing democracy, rule of law, human rights and respect for and protection of minorities; existence of a functioning market economy and the capacity to cope with competitive pressures and market forces in the EU; and the ability to implement all obligations stemming from EU membership, including adherence to the aims of political, economic and monetary union.

These criteria, decided by the Copenhagen European Council on June 21 and 22, 1993, were the basis for a series of progress reports by the EU, reflecting the enormous legal, political, socio-economic and psychological transformation in all candidate countries during the 1990's. The top five candidates for EU accession grew at an average of 3.4 percent over the period 1995-1999 compared with the EU's average

51 See Grabbe, Heather, *The Constellations of Europe: How Enlargement Will Transform the EU*, London: Centre for European Reform, 2004.

growth rate of 2.4 percent. During the 1990's, the total sum of foreign direct investment in Poland had overtaken the sum of foreign investment in Portugal and Finland. The necessary costs to meet EU standards were increasingly becoming a source for attractive economic activities: Poland alone has to spend 6.6 billion dollars to meet EU directives on regulatory and administrative structures. Improving the environment in Central Europe will require enormous investments for decades.

In spite of many efforts across all transformation countries since 1989, stark differences remained obvious when the "big bang" enlargement took place on June 1, 2004. While the US unemployment rate in 2004 stood at 5.7 percent and the unemployment rate in the old EU of fifteen member states at 8.0 percent, it increased in the enlarged EU to 9.0 percent. The difference between 19.1 percent unemployment in Poland, 8.0 percent in the Czech Republic, 5.9 percent in Hungary and 4.7 percent in Cyprus was telling. Most depressing was the high unemployment rate among people under 25 years of age: In Slovakia this rate was 30.5 percent, in Estonia 21.0 percent and in Poland even 40.7 percent, compared with 12.0 percent in the US and 15.4 percent in the EU-15. The Copenhagen European Council had decided to go ahead with a "big bang" enlargement. The European Parliament approved the enlargement on April 9, 2003. After they joined the European Union in 2004, the new member states turned out to be the main engines of the economic growth in the European Union: For 2004 and 2005, their aggregate GDP grew by 4.5 percent, while the aggregate GDP of the 15 old member states grew by only 2.5 percent. Romania and Bulgaria were accepted as EU member states in 2007, however, accompanied by much concern about corruption and tzhe overall readiness of both countries to fully adopt the *acquis communautaire.* Turkey, the most controversial of all applicant countries, was recognized by the EU as candidate country at the Helsinki European Council on December 10 and 11, 1999. The European Council on December 16 and 17, 2004, finally decided to start full membership negotiations with Turkey in October 2005, although somewhat conditional.

Immediately, the Turkish membership issue was twisted by the condition of the European Union and the issue of deepened integration. While in the case of other candidate countries, a shared European identity was rather a matter of encouragement, in the case of Turkey the issue of European identity became the centerpiece of controversy and resentment. The prospect of a Muslim country joining the EU raised questions of religious and cultural difference in secularized Europe more than any other question had done in the past. It seemed that the truly religious parts of European society were more relaxed about the prospect of joining the European house with a Muslim country than many secularized and laicistic Europeans. The overly successful visit of Pope Benedict XVI to Turkey in late 2006 has done more for inter-religious dialogue and understanding than all anti-Turkish claims of modernizers in European politics and intellectual life. It was anticipated that Turkish accession would not come about before 2020, and even then subject to some highly controversial and volatile referenda across the EU. Turkey, one should not forget, participated in the Constitutional Convention and its Prime Minister signed the Treaty Establishing a Constitution for Europe in October 2004.

After Poland, Hungary, the Czech Republic, Slovakia, Slovenia, Estonia, Latvia, Lithuania, Malta and Cyprus – still divided after a majority of Greek-Cypriots had refused the UN-Plan (Annan Plan) in a referendum on April 24, 2004, which would have opened the way to a confederal unification of the divided island - had joined the EU on May 1, 2004, only Norway, Liechtenstein and Iceland were left as members of the European Economic Space. Being a vanishing species became even more evident when Iceland applied for EU membership in 2009. In a strategic assessment of Europe's emerging Neighborhood Policy, the European Commission was contemplating whether or not the European Economic Space could be a viable concept to engage with the remaining Eastern European countries, namely Ukraine, Belarus, Moldova and Russia, possibly also Georgia, Armenia and Azerbaijan, but also the Southern littoral countries of the Mediterranean.

For the time being, the failure to bring about a solution to the Cyprus problem, pending since 1974, was the biggest deficit of the European Union in dealing with its peripheries. In fact, it looked as if the Greek-Cypriots had blackmailed the EU as they had continuously declared that EU membership of the island would help resolve the partition. In the end, it was their vote against the Annan Plan that said "no" to the unification of the island. The Turkish-Cypriots would have accepted the vision of a confederation as outlined in the Annan Plan.

The European Bank for Reconstruction and Development forecasts annual growth rates in the new EU member states of around 4 to 7 percent over a consistent period of time. This would certainly require steady growth in the eurozone member states of the EU, high levels of investments and rapid productivity growth. To "catch up" with the economic standards of Western Europe will take quite a long time anyway. Since the "old EU" will also continue to grow and international investments have already begun to react critically to wage increases in Central Europe, World Bank estimates show that for the most advanced countries of the group, it would take 20 years for Slovenia, and for Poland, Hungary and the Czech Republic 40 years to only reach the EU average incomes of the year 2004. For Romania, the estimate is 80 years.[52]

The real challenge was yet to come, the evolution of a common image of Europe, of a commonly shared vision for Europe. It was easy to invoke Europe as incarnation of freedom and unity. To make use of Europe as the framework for reciprocal forms of solidarity became much more difficult. Nobody was really to blame. After decades of living under communist totalitarianism, the new EU member states from Central and South Eastern Europe went through substantial transformations of their political culture. This was a matter of ideas, but also a matter of generations. It took time to get used to

52 See Grabbe, Heather, *The Constellations of Europe*, op.cit.: 6-13.

the mechanisms, the symbolism and the emotions of European integration. This new reality in the public life of Europe was also a growing challenge in the traditional EU member states of Western Europe. They experienced the effects of European integration and were going through a genuine period of leadership crisis. Citizens across the EU were skeptical about the ability and seriousness of their political leaders. It was time for a new contract between the citizens of Europe and their political leaders. How to reach it, was not clear.

Political loyalties and party structures changed faster and more often than in decades. The overall sense of dissolution, transformation and realignment had reached the EU as a whole. When the constitution-building process took shape in the early twenty-first century, the political landscape of Europe had become grey and vague. In Central and South Eastern Europe, hardly any political party was still present in the circles of power that had overturned communist totalitarianism in 1989. In Western Europe, the dissolution of traditional sociological and hence political loyalties had spread all over. Uncertainty and political skepticism were dominating. The initial idea of a European Constitution that could serve as a political safety belt around the two parts of Europe that were growing together failed. It was overly optimistic, maybe even romantic. Europe was growing together, from bottom to top, and it had to grow together in reality, through a change of generations and through the realities of daily life, before a new European contract and one between Europeans and their European leaders could follow. In light of this frustrating reality, the 2007 Reform Treaty will be judged much more generously.

The roots of this necessary yet difficult realignment of ideas are to be found in the transformation processes of post-communist and post-Cold War societies both in East and West Europe. The consequences were felt in the European Parliament after new representatives from Central and Eastern Europe joined. They were also felt in the deliberations of the European Council, most notably after the constitution-building process was started again in 2007. It was all too simple to blame just one or the other country for the daunting process that was lying behind the EU. For decades, two different parts of Europe had grown into two separate directions. To bring them formally together after the end of communist dominance was a technical process, including EU enlargement. To reach the hearts and souls of Europeans and to bring them into the stream of a common search for joint and mutually reinforcing perspectives for the continent as a whole was to take much longer. Only to those who had never thought about the parallelism of the unparallel did this experience come as a total surprise. The others had to accept the consequences. It would take several more years to define common European objectives. The controversies about the primacy of national interests would prevail. The idea that "European spirit" simply meant to define what could better be done together had to take roots before its fruits could be harvested. Yet, eventually there was no alternative to the return of a "European spirit." In political terms it meant that there was no alternative to deeper integration aiming at the full realization of a political Union. The true enlargement fear was the fear to fail the challenge of deeper integration.

5. Dysfunctional Governance Structures and Growing Politicization

The third phase of European integration europeanized politics in all EU member states and politicized the institutions of the European Union beyond the formal level of Political Union. This third phase of European integration has been defined by the quest of constitutionalizing and politicizing European economic integration in an enlarging and ever more political Europe. Its implications led inevitably to a growing dichotomy in European politics. The distinction between national and European levels of decision-making was not simple and clear any more. European politics has become a web of multilevel governance mechanisms. The European Union has bred its genuine system of governing and rule. As a consequence, the debate between those who preferred the primacy of national autonomy in decision-making and those who favored the evolution of a European public sphere has become pertinent.

EU enlargements were always matters of a particular fascination and broader public attention. They have a dimension of geographical and cultural curiosity. They prove a sense of identity that immediately vanishes when the debate shifts to matters of political cooperation and integration. The fascination of EU enlargement is the fascination with the cultural unity and diverse history of Europe. The breakdown of communist rule over Central and Eastern Europe was of secular significance. It meant the end of the Cold War and the artificial partition of the European continent. Eastward enlargement of the European Union was highly complex due to the scope of the task and due to the fundamental structural and mental, socio-economic and political differences that had become cemented in those countries for decades and generations. Most impressive was the fact that finally the Central and Eastern European countries had liberated themselves. The charisma of Lech Wałęsa, the electrician from Gdansk, and Pope John Paul II, the priest from Cracow, are legend. These two exceptional Polish personalities are symbolic icons of one of the most impressive European narratives of modern times. Their unforgettable contribution to the European journey of freedom, the rule of law and human rights has been of exceptional importance. Yet, following the end of the division of Europe, a consistent "deepening" of the integration process has become essential and existential for the future of the united continent.

The French Member of the European Parliament, Alain Lamassoure, has been the first to suggest that eastward enlargement should take place simultaneously with the election to the European Parliament on June 13, 2004. The direct election to the supranational representation of all Union citizens from Lisbon to Tallinn and from

Tromsö to Nicosia, he argued, would symbolize the new European identity more than anything else. The whole European Parliament subscribed to his idea and it was subsequently approved by the European Commission and by the European Council. This detail shows that the political approach to integration as represented by the European Parliament is not only dependent upon formal constellations of co-decision.It also challenges the widespread prejudice that France was *per se* overly hesitant about EU enlargement to include Central and Eastern Europe. Alain Lamassoure is a Frenchman after all – and France's former Minister for European Affairs. The informal interaction among the actors in the different institutions of the European Union will increase further. It will also have an integrating effect upon the new participants in the process from Central and Eastern Europe. The recognition of this experience is needed more than ever to revitalize the "European spirit" in the decades ahead. It would be regrettable if Europe could find its spirit only by defining its integration as directed against "the other," against others.

The election of 732 members to the European Parliament in June 2004 brought about the following political constellation: European People's Party/European Democrats 268 seats (36.61 percent), Social Democratic Party of Europe 200 seats (27.32 percent), Alliance of Liberals and Democrats for Europe 88 seats (12.02 percent), Greens/European Free Alliance 42 seats (5.74 percent), European United Left/Nordic Green Left 41 seats (5.6 percent), Independence/Democracy 37 seats (5.05 percent), Union of Europe of the Nation States 27 seats (3.69 percent), 29 members did not belong to any faction (3.96 percent). The representatives of 183 national parties came together under the roof of the seven parliamentary groups. The historic 2004 election of the European Parliament[53] was followed by an impressive power struggle between the institutions as part of the overall evolution of a balanced separation of power among them. In 1999, the dethronement of the Santer Commission originated in pressure from the European Parliament, but in 2004 the parliamentary claim for an equal share of power with the European Council received much broader public attention. It was a constitutional conflict that ended in favor of shared power and an enhanced interlocking of the main institutions of the European Union.

53 Not surprisingly, the result was belittled by media commentators who pointed to the relatively low voter's turn out: 44.9 percent in 2004, compared with 49.8 percent in 1999, 56.8 percent in 1994, 58.5 percent in 1989, 61 percent in 1984 and 63 percent in 1979. Compared with American mid-term and even presidential elections, the result was not that bad: 2004: 60.0 percent; 2002: 40.1 percent, 2000: 51.3 percent, 1998: 36.4 percent, 1996: 49.1 percent, 1994: 38.8 percent, 1992: 55.1 percent, 1990: 36.5 percent, 1988: 50.1 percent, 1986: 36.4 percent, 1982: 39.8 percent, 1980: 52.6 percent, 1978: 37.2 percent. The European average voter turnout was 55.6 percent, the US average voter turnout 44.4 percent. On the 2004 elections see Lodge, Juliet (ed.), *The 2004 Elections to the European Parliament*, Basingstoke: Palgrave Macmillan, 2005.

Table 3: Elections to the European Parliament[54]

1979: 410 members from 9 countries

Socialists	112 seats
European People's Party (Christian Democrats)	108 seats
European Democrats	63 seats
Communists	44 seats
Liberals	40 seats
European Progressive Democrats	22 seats
Independents	11 seats
Non-attached	10 seats

1984: 434 members from 10 countries

Socialists	130 seats
European People's Party (Christian Democrats)	110 seats
European Democrats	50 seats
Communists	41 seats
Liberals	31 seats
Movement of European Democrats	29 seats
European Alternatives (Green-Alternatives)	20 seats
European Right	16 seats
Non-attached	7 seats

1989: 518 members from 12 countries

Social Democratic Party of Europe	180 seats
European People's Party (Christian Democrats)	121 seats
Liberal, Democratic and Reform Group	49 seats
European Democrats	34 seats
Greens	30 seats
United Gaullists	28 seats
Movement of European Democrats	20 seats
European Right	17 seats
Coalition of the Left	14 seats
Rainbow Group	13 seats
Non-attached	12 seats

54 See European Parliament, *Composition of the European Parliament. Historial Data,* https://europarl.europa.eu/parliament/archive/elections2009/hist_composition_en_txt.html.

1994: 567 members from 12 countries

Social Democratic Party of Europe	198 seats
European People's Party (Christian Democrats)	156 seats
European Liberal, Democratic and Reform Group	44 seats
Group of European United Left	28 seats
Forza Europa	27 seats
Movement of European Democrats	26 seats
Greens	23 seats
Rainbow Group	19 seats
Europe of Nations	19 seats
Non-attached	27 seats

1999: 626 members from 15 countries

European People's Party (Christian Democrats) - European Democrats	233 seats
Social Democratic Party of Europe	180 seats
European Liberal Democrat and Reform Party	50 seats
Greens	48 seats
European United Left/ Nordic Green Left	42 seats
Union for Europe of Nations	30 seats
Mixed Independent Group	18 seats
Group of European Democracies and Diversities	16 seats
Non-attached	9 seats

2004: 732 members from 25 countries

European People's Party (Christian Democrats) - European Democrats	268 seats
Social Democratic Party of Europe	200 seats
Alliance of Liberals and Democrats for Europe	88 seats
Greens/European Free Alliance	42 seats
European United Left/Nordic Green Left	41 seats
Independence/Democracy	37 seats
Union for Europe of the Nations	27 seats
Non-attached	29 seats

2009: 736 members from 27 countries

European People's Party	265 seats
Progressive Alliance of Socialists and Democrats	184 seats
Alliance of Liberals and Democrats for Europe	84 seats
Greens/European Free Alliance	55 seats
European Conservatives and Reformists	54 seats
European United Left/Nordic Green Left	35 seats
Europe of Freedom and Democracy	32 seats
Non-attached	27 seats

These power struggles advanced the politicization and the constitutionalization of the European Union. Although the European Constitution was never ratified, several of its provisions were implemented even during the crisis of ratification. Among them was the election of the President of the European Commission based on the result of the election to the European Parliament. In disregard of the vote to the European Parliament in June 2004, French President Chirac and German Chancellor Schröder proposed the liberal Belgian Prime Minister Guy Verhofstadt as new President of the European Commission. Their colleagues belonging to the "political family" of the European People's Party disagreed with this proposal. They supported the claim of the parliamentary faction of the EPP that the next Commission President should come from its group, being the biggest one in the European Parliament. After much party political bickering among crosscutting institutional and party-political structures in the European Union, Verhofstadt had to withdraw his candidacy and the conservative Portuguese Prime Minister José Manuel Durão Barroso was nominated by the European Council. He was able to take over his new office after he received the vote of confidence of the majority of the European Parliament. In a remarkable sign of leadership and his claim for a strong Commission, he designated the portfolios of the newly arriving 25 Commissioners without waiting for the national governments to impose their will upon him. Then he convinced some governments to replace their candidates, as he would have failed to win the necessary support in the European Parliament for his team. On November 18, 2004, the first Barroso Commission was confirmed by the European Parliament and immediately began working.

In anticipation of the treaty reform, further innovations and reforms were installed. These included the beginning of a European External Action Service and the establishment of the European Defence Agency. Measures of enforced cooperation were taken in anticipation of the future treaty provisions. This included EU military and policing operations and the progress made in the field of justice and home affairs. With the Treaty of Lisbon ratified and entering into force in December 2009, additional innovations became possible in EU governance, including the right to initiate EU legislature through a popular initiative brought about by 1 million signatures. In the European Council, the principle of qualified majority voting was now extended in practically all matters of justice and home affairs, including border protection, asylum and migration policy and judicial cooperation in matters of civil law. All in all, the decade of constitution-building did not leave the EU decapitated. Even during the frustrating time of trial the scope of action for EU institutions was strong enough: The EU institutions worked at any moment. Eventually, the crisis of ratifying a new EU treaty was not a crisis of integration. It was a crisis in integration eventually to be remedied by a new EU treaty.

During the third period of European integration, the European Parliament became increasingly visible as one of the key actors in European Union politics. Its formal and its informal influence on EU legislation increased noticeably.[55] With the accession of Bulgaria and Romania in 2007, the number of deputies increased from 732 to 785 until 2009. With the help of some of the newcomers from Bulgaria and Romania, a new but short-lived euroskeptical faction "Identity, Tradition and Sovereignty" was formed. The dispute between those who define European integration from the perspective of its limits and those who define European integration by the scope of its ability to achieve a common value added had reached the floor of the European Parliament.

The controversies over the future of Europe were not to disappear. The election of 736 members to the European Parliament in June 2009 produced the lowest ever voter turnout. Only 45.4 percent of eligible voters participated in the elections. This time, the comparison with the US election was devastating for Europe: The election of President Barack Obama in November 2008 had come about on the basis of an exceptional high voter turnout of 63 percent In the EU, the 2009 election campaign had stayed national and no European political party had presented itself with political choices different from its competitors. The European People's Party had expressed support for a second term in office of Commission President Barroso; this signal alone did not turn the campaign into a truly pan-European one. In the end, the Socialists lost, the Christian Democrats stayed the stronger political group – and all of them lost to the rise of populist anti-European groups eventually forming a reasonably strong political group consisting of 54 members.

Until 2014, the composition of the European Parliament was as follows: European People's Party 265 seats (36.1 percent), Progressive Alliance of Socialists and Democrats 184 seats (25.0 percent), Alliance of Liberals and Democrats for Europe 84 seats (7.4 percent), Greens/European Free Alliance 55 seats (7.4 percent), European Conservatives and Reformists 54 seats (7.4 percent), European United Left/Nordic Green Left 35 seats (4.7 percent), Europe of Freedom and Democracy 32 seats (4.0 percent), 29 members remained non-attached (3.8 percent).

55 See Kreppel, Amie, "Moving Beyond Procedure: An Empirical Analysis of European Parliament Legislative Influence," *Comparative Political Studies*, 35.7 (2002): pp. 784-813.

Table 4: Presidents of the European Commission

1958 – 1967	Walter Hallstein
1967 – 1970	Jean Rey
1970 – 1972	Franco-Maria Malfatti
1972 – 1973	Sicco Mansholt
1973 – 1977	Francois-Xavier Ortoli
1977 – 1981	Roy Jenkins
1981 – 1985	Gaston Thorn
1985 – 1995	Jacques Delors
1995 – 1999	Jacques Santer
1999 – 2004	Romano Prodi
2004 – 2014	José Manuel Durão Barroso

Table 5: Presidents of the European Parliament

1979 – 1981	Simone Veil
1982 – 1984	Piet Dankert
1984 – 1986	Pierre Pflimlin
1987 – 1989	Lord Plumb
1989 – 1991	Enrique Barón Crespo
1992 – 1994	Egon Klepsch
1994 – 1996	Klaus Hänsch
1997 – 1999	José María Gil-Robles
1999 – 2001	Nicole Fontaine
2002 – 2004	Pat Cox
2005 – 2007	Josep Borrell
2007 – 2009	Hans-Gert Pöttering
2009 – 2011	Jerzy Buzek
2012 – 2014	Martin Schulz

The most remarkable move of the European Parliament in 2009 was the election of Jerzy Buzek as its President. The former Polish Prime Minister became the first representative of a former communist country to chair one of the EU organs. The European Parliament, as Buzeks predecessor Hans-Gert Pöttering vowed in his program speech in February 2007, "cannot allow itself to be outdone by anybody when it comes to completing the task of unifying our continent."[56] Pöttering emphasized the dignity of

56 Pöttering, Hans-Gert, *Defining Europe's Values – For a Citizen's Europe*, Programme Speech to the European Parliament, Strasbourg, February 13, 2007, http://europarl.europa.eu/president/defaulten.htm?home; see also Pöttering, Hans-Gert, *Von der Vision zur Wirklichkeit: Auf dem Weg zur Einigung Europas*, Bonn: Bouvier, 2004.

man as the basic value of European integration. He pleaded for a dialogue of cultures and underlined that European integration was based on the idea of achieving a community of values. Indeed, if the European Economic Community was the basis for European integration, only the notion of being united in a community of values would provide the sustainable framework for the future of the European Union.

Some claimed that Europe was lacking political leaders. At certain occasions, it seemed that Europe had too many of them. The overlapping and interlocking mechanisms of politics in Europe – between the regional, the national and the European level, but also among political parties and "party families" – often produces inter-blocking situations. This can be confusing and frustrating for actors and observers alike, yet it is the price to pay for a unique experiment in European history: Never ever had the European continent experienced such a highly sophisticated and complex system of a mutually binding political order. It could not come as a surprise that resistance to certain aspects of this system clashed with demands for more and deeper integration.

The ultimate challenge ahead of the political leadership on all levels of the European Union was to prevent the victory of myopic parochialism. This had internal and external dimensions. More than ever the leaders of the European Union are under public scrutiny as far as the quality and effect of their work are concerned. Not apathy with European integration, but rather apathy with the performance of the dominant political elite has become a recurrent theme of popular criticism in the European body politic. The key for the political class in the European Union to maintain or to regain credibility was to fully understand the link between the structures they – or their predecessors – had set up and their factual performance (and all too often under-performance) in delivering European public goods. While politicians were trying to bring balance and perfection into the web of European institutions and procedures, Union citizens were more interested whether or not the many political debates, decisions or postponements of decisions were having a positive effect on their lives. For better or worse, European integration had become part of the reality of ordinary life across the European Union.

The Global Setting

VI. Transatlantic Relations: The Bonds that Hold

1. Structural Change and Lasting Relevance

The solidity of relations between America and Europe is not rooted in harmonious (and boring) similarities but in complementing differences that help to serve as each other's mirror. Similarities are usually invoked to cover differences or to play them down. Differences are rarely touched upon in order to reinforce a relationship, but rather to prove its fragility. None of this is correct and constructive when attempting to identify the strength of transatlantic relations. It would be surprising to have two continents without differences. It would also be strange to describe a relationship using terminology of divorce and confrontation when in fact the interdependence of the two continents is greater than ever.

The United States and the European Union provide for 10.9 percent of the world's population, but hold 36.2 percent of the global GDP and almost 40 percent of world trade. 85 percent of all global capital flows take place between the US and the EU and more than 50 percent of all global resources are consumed by the people of the US and the EU.

Table 6: Transatlantic Comparisons (data 2007)[1]

	United States of America	European Union
Population	301.1 million	491 million
Density	30 / sqkm	115 / sqkm
Life expectancy	78 years (estimate)	78.7 years (estimate)
GDP (PPP)	$13,675 billion (estimate)	$14,953 billion (estimate)
GDP per head (PPP)	$43,444 (estimate)	$28,213 (estimate)
Budget	$2,800 billion	$ 153.27 billion (€ 115.5 billion)[2]
Military expenditure	$548.8 billion	$267.4 billion

The US accounts for about 22 percent of EU trade, and the EU for around 19 percent of US trade. Transatlantic commerce makes up almost 60 percent of the world's trade and investment, worth 2.5 trillion US dollars annually. Even California exports more to Europe than to Japan. In net figures, transatlantic trade grew from 422 billion US dollars in 2000 to 475 billion US dollars in 2004, a 12 percent increase. Unlike trade

1 CIA, *World Factbook 2007*; http://en.wikipedia.org/wiki/EU; http://auslandsjahr.eu/2007/ 03/26/eu-europa-militaer-haushalt/

2 These figures are based on the dollar-euro-parity as on January 1st 2007.

relations with Japan and China, there is no transatlantic structural deficit. Economists estimate that something close to a quarter of all US-EU trade "simply consists of transactions within firms with investments on either side of the Atlantic."[3] Even in the midst of the biggest transatlantic political dispute ever over the right policy toward Iraq in 2003, transatlantic investments increased sharply. US firms put 100 billion US dollars into Europe during that year, a record high. 60 percent of the total US capital outflow of 609 billion US dollars in the decade between mid-1990's and the middle of the first decade of the new century has gone to Europe – 373 billion US dollars. Today, there is more EU investment in Texas than the total US investment in Japan and China together. US investments in the Netherlands alone are bigger than annual American investments in China. In 2003, the worst year for transatlantic relations, European affiliates in the US earned around 44 billion US dollars, a record high, and US affiliates in Europe earned 82 billion US dollars in 2003, a 25 percent increase within one year. "A weaker trans-Atlantic bond," concluded Daniel S. Hamilton and Joseph P. Quinlan, "would render Americans and Europeans less safe, less prosperous, less free and less able to advance their ideals or their interests in the wider world."[4] Around seven million Americans work for European affiliates in the US while more than six million Europeans work for US affiliates in Europe.

EU enlargement to include Central and Eastern Europe in 2004 did not slow down the increase in US-EU economic relations as one might have expected with the post-communist countries only adding 5 percent to the combined EU's GDP. Already in 2003, one year before the biggest ever EU enlargement took place, US investments in Central and Eastern Europe were about 60 percent greater than US investments in China – 16.6 billion US dollars compared with 10.3 billion US dollars.[5] The daily exchange of goods between the US and the EU is above a value of 1.2 billion US dollars. On a daily basis, almost 50,000 air passengers, 1.4 billion e-mails and 1.5 billion US dollars cross the Atlantic. In the course of a year, around ten million Europeans visit the US and 8 million Americans visit Europe, compared to less than half a million in each direction in the 1960's.

The transatlantic market place could work much more effectively. According to the President of the European Commission, José Manuel Barroso, air-transportation liberalization alone could stimulate more than 25 million passengers on transatlantic flights, generate more than 20 billion US dollars of benefits for customers through cheaper tickets and create 80,000 new jobs in Europe and in the United States.[6] Yet, the

3 Baldwin, Matthew, et al., "Trade and Economic Relations," in: Peterson, John, and Mark A. Pollack (eds.), *Europe, America, Bush: Transatlantic Relations in the Twenty-First Century*, London/New York: Routledge, 2003: 31; see also Egan, Michelle, *The Transatlantic Marketplace: Government Policies and Business Strategies*, Manchester: Manchester University Press, 2005.

4 Hamilton, Daniel S., and Joseph P. Quinlan, "We Can't Afford this Trans-Atlantic Squabble," *International Herald Tribune*, November 5, 2004: 9.

5 See Drozdiak, William, "Betting on the EU," *Newsweek*, May 10, 2004: 28-29.

6 Barroso, José Manuel, "Hands Across the Ocean," *International Herald Tribune*, April 27, 2007: 6.

idea of a Transatlantic Free Trade Area (TAFTA) has never tried and even the idea of a transatlantic economic space will take a long time to come to full fruition. It would reduce prices and increase transatlantic trade and consumer satisfaction. It would strengthen the strategic ties between the European Union and the US. During the 2007 EU-US Summit, a Transatlantic Economic Council was initiated, the best way to put the complex issue on a long haul.

Economic interdependency definitely is the backbone of transatlantic bonds that hold. Economic interdependency translates the invocation of commonly shared values – freedom, dignity of man, democracy, human rights – into the realm of commonly shared interests. This does not prevent the regular emergence of conflicts of interests. As normal as this is in any state, it also occurs in transatlantic relations. But unlike the media attention these conflicts get, they amount to not more than five percent of all transatlantic economic relations. Transatlantic economic ties are the strongest source of common strategic interests. Both sides of the Atlantic are also linked by the same threats and dependencies, most importantly as far as energy resources are concerned.

In 2005, the US imported 3,527,696 barrels of crude oil and 99,015 barrels of natural gas. By 2025, US energy imports will increase from one-quarter to one-third of its overall consumption. As for oil, the import rate could grow from 50 to 70 percent, most of it coming from the Persian Gulf. More than ten percent of US oil imports originate from Africa. Although most of America's gas consumption is based on North American production, the trend to import gas is increasing. Trinidad and Tobago has become the largest provider of thermal gas for the US. Although the US hopes to invent hydrogen-based cars by 2020 and replace the current daily oil consumption by hydrogen in 2040, for the time being the dependency on energy import is strong. As for the European Union, the situation is even more serious. Energy imports into the EU might grow from 50 percent of the overall consumption in 2005 to 70 percent in 2025. 45 percent of EU's oil import originates in the Middle East and 17 percent in Russia, from which the EU also imports 40 percent of all of its natural gas. Only Japan's energy dependency is higher with about 80 percent of energy resources to be imported. If only for their energy dependency, none of the leading industrialized regions has an interest in instability, aggressive dictatorships, terrorism, the proliferation of weapons of mass destruction and unresolved regional conflicts around the world.

For fifty years, the Atlantic Alliance has been the most successful alliance in history, winning the Cold War without firing a single shot. Yet, the controversy over the war against Iraq in 2002/2003 was equivalent to an internal Cold War of the West. It symbolized the structural transformation from the traditional Atlantic Alliance – military protection of democratic Europe under US strategic leadership – into transatlantic relations – a joint relationship of partners in the management of global affairs. The Iraq debate was as emotional and controversial as it could have been. It reflected different experiences and perceptions, also power struggles and conflicting political choices. It hit the Atlantic partners hard: It was instigated through external events without any early warning system that could have helped to manage the controversy with smooth diplomatic measures. It was so deep and so painful since it was not only about Iraq. The depth and divisiveness of the controversy demonstrated the growing reality of a transatlantic domestic policy sphere. The European Union claims equal partnership while its internal cohesion depends upon the solidity of transatlantic relations. More than ever, transatlantic relations are increasingly turning the Atlantic civilization into a transatlantic domestic sphere and its controversies into elements of transatlantic governance. In the aftermath of the Iraq controversy, the annual G8 Summits of the leading industrialized nations became the most visible forum to bridge transatlantic gaps, to bring compromises about and to give transatlantic relations a new impulse. Thus was the case during the 2004 G8 Summit under the US presidency, when the future of the Broader Middle East was discussed in a way that helped to bring the warring Western parties together again. Thus was the case during the 2007 G8 Summit under the German presidency when face-saving compromises on the policy to combat climate change were found. They helped to bring the US back into the multilateral process under the umbrella of the UN aimed at finding a successor instrument to the controversial Kyoto Protocol by 2012. With a new President in the White House since Janaury 2009 and confronted with an exceptional global financial and economic crisis, transatlantic domestic policy controversies became increasingly linked to emerging global power shifts – as indicated by the enlargement of G8 Summits to the G20 format in 2009. Also under the Presidency of Barack Obama, conflicting interests influenced transatlantic disputes. In the future, multilateralism had to take into account the interests of non-transatlantic actors. Yet, in spite of their near divorce over the Iraq war, the EU and the US remained the backbone of a reasonable management of global affairs.

One of the insights of Darwinism and other subsequent social anthropology refers to the fact that groups close to each other tend to quarrel more than distant groups. What is true for animals is true for humans as well, and it is true for nations, states and their politicians. This anthropological insight can explain the harshness of the transatlantic quarrels in 2002/2003 and the outbreak of mutual resentments – not only between Americans and Europeans, but no less among Europeans who were of a different opinion on the issue of how to deal with the regime of Saddam Hussein and how to judge the US. It was a dispute over threat perceptions, conflicting moralities and contrasting strategic choices. It was a dispute in the absence of an organizing principle that could have served as a framework and means of orientation for the transatlantic political actors as they were clashing over Iraq.

This clash indicated the unfinished character of a three-fold transformation: the bilateral post-Cold War transformation from Atlantic Alliance to transatlantic relations, the transformation of Europe from being an object of the Cold War under US-protection and support as its federator to a Europe in search of a genuine common foreign policy and pro-active global role, and the recognition by the United States of this Europe's new and increasingly global role. None of these three complex processes had been completed when the Iraq controversy broke out. In fact, the Iraq crisis accentuated the unfinished character of all three transformations. These transformations remain indicative for the new nature of relations between the United States and Europe. The US is no longer Europe's federator and it has to accept that Europe is growing into a global political role. The European Union is incomplete as far as the formulation of common foreign policy strategies and the realization of a common political will is concerned. Yet, while it is continuing to develop such a global profile, it cannot do this successfully with the intention to become a counter-weight or counter-power to the US. In fact, both processes are even more delicate: For a good number of Europeans, the US has turned from a positive federator to a negative federator. For them, the US is no longer the supporter of Europe's integration, but Europe's antidote and antithesis that requires more integration in order to emancipate Europe from America.[7] For a good number of Americans, the European Union is an idiosyncratic, pretentious and overly regulated entity that tries to veto US policies while remaining unable to project itself beyond the role of a regional power with a stuttering, non-dynamic economy. In the absence of a common frame of mind – that is to say, a new common transatlantic project – this differing trend, not surprisingly, did trigger a crisis of perceptions as root of a crisis in cooperation. It has become also a turning point toward new efforts in redefining both the perspective and projection of European integration and the parameters of transatlantic relations for the next decades.

Given their economic and political, strategic and ultimately cultural potential, the United States and the European Union are the key players in the management of global affairs. They are the two leading regions in the world as far as their soft and their hard power is concerned. The projection of their role has a global significance second to none and the expectations of their global role are not matched by any other country or region. This is often more a curse than an asset as it requires consistent attention to the multilateral implications of actions and inactions alike. Not only the United States, but also the European Union – and certainly its main constituent member states – have practiced the selective use of multilateralism.[8] It is simplistic to assume that multilateralism is the weapon of the weak and unilateralism the destiny of the strong, as

7 For example, see Derrida, Jacques, and Jürgen Habermas, "Nach dem Krieg: Die Wiedergeburt Europas," *Frankfurter Allgemeine Zeitung*, May 30, 2003: 33 (as "Europe: plaidoyer pour une politique extérieure commune," *Libération*, June 2, 2003.). The renowned philosophers called for Euro-patriotism as an act of of emancipating Europe from US hegemony and unilateralism.

8 See Pollack, Mark A., "Unilateral America, Multilateral Europe?," in: Peterson, John, and Mark A. Pollack (eds.), *Europe, America, Bush: Transatlantic Relations in the Twenty-first Century*, op.cit.: 115-127; Oudenaren, John van, "E Pluribus Confusio. Living with the EU's Structural Incoherence," *The National Interest*, Fall (2001): 23-37.

Robert Kagan had argued in an overblown essay on the transatlantic dispute of 2003.[9] The use of multilateral options can reinforce a country's strength, assure it and broaden its effect. It can also serve the opposite, namely to organize support for the implementation of interests that cannot be sustained unilaterally. Finally, multilateralism can also reflect the multilateral and multinational character of a problem that does not originate in one specific country or region and cannot be resolved on the basis of voluntary decisions of one or few participants in the global community. Joseph S. Nye has defined international relations as a three-tier chess-game according to which "military power is largely unipolar," that is to say dominated by the US, while on the middle chessboard, where "economic power is multipolar…the United States is not a hegemon and often must bargain as an equal with Europe"; finally, the bottom chessboard is defined by "transnational relations that cross borders outside of government control," a situation in which "power is widely dispersed and it makes no sense to speak of unipolarity, multipolarity, or hegemony."[10] Nye warned the US not to wrongly exaggerate its self-assessment as the "only surviving superpower," to take Europe more seriously, and to understand the changing nature of sovereignty: "The old images of sovereign states balancing and bouncing off each other like billiard balls will blind us to the new complexity of world politics."[11]

In order to understand the complex nexus of continuity and change in the nature and structure of relations between the United States and Europe, it is useful to go beyond the popular discourse about unilateralism versus multilateralism. At least three additional factors of relevance ought to be mentioned:

(a) The United States has served as pacifier and federator of Europe since the end of World War II. In doing so, beginning with the Marshall Plan and the strategic decisions to remain a European power during the rising Cold War, the US has protected the process of reconciliation among old European enemies, supported the construction of the common market and basically encouraged Europeans to learn to speak with one voice in political and security matters. The most recent US support for the reconciliation among Europeans (that is the support of the US for a speedy EU enlargement) clashed with Europe's own timing, goals and procedures: During and after the Wars of Yugoslavian Succession in the 1990's, the EU was not ready yet to act as a security and defense union; the US encouragement for Turkish EU membership was not considered to be helpful for Turkey in the EU; President Bush's support of anchoring the Ukraine and Georgia into the Euro-Atlantic structures was received as un-enthusiastic as the plea of his predecessor, President Clinton, to ultimately even reach out for the EU membership of Russia.

9 Kagan, Robert, *Of Paradise and Power: America and Europe in the New World Order*, New York: Knopf, 2003.

10 Nye, Joseph S., *The Paradox of American Power: Why the World's Only Superpower can't go it Alone*, Oxford/New York: Oxford University Press, 2002: 39.

11 Ibid.: 53.

The genuine American support for the creation of a European common market lost enthusiasm once the European market started to become a competitor to the US. Now, the US insisted on market liberalization. The US even pressed, though in vain, for participation in the creation of a European Economic and Monetary Union. Finally, the US encouragement of one European voice in foreign and security matters has always been based on mixed feelings: The primordial role of NATO as Europe's peace organization and backbone of transatlantic strategic cooperation was not to be blurred. As long as this was predominantly a theoretical debate, the stakes were limited. Once this issue became serious – failing its first serious test in Yugoslavia and turning out to produce vetoing ambitions by France and Germany in the case of Iraq – the American attitude toward European foreign and security policy integration became reserved again.

(b) In the early twenty-first century, Europe's relationship with the United States has become multidimensional. As a consequence of growing European integration, the European Union has become a growing factor in international affairs. Partially, for instance in the area of external trade, direct US-EU relations replaced the role of national European governments and capitals. In other policy areas – mainly in foreign and security matters – diverging national interests among EU member states and political majorities prevented a common European voice. This European deficit encouraged the US to maintain bilateral relations with European countries. The US can hardly be blamed for this attitude in light of Europe's genuine deficit. But, the US did also not avoid exploiting this European diversity whenever it suited its interests. Never was this more strongly felt in Europe than during the Suez crisis in 1956 – which helped to trigger France's acceptance of integration measures with Germany – and during the Iraq crisis of 2002/2003 – which saw the failure of French and German vetoing ambitions, both in bringing the European caucus together and in succeeding to stop the US from taking military action.

(c) During the Cold War, the relationship between the US and Europe was asymmetric in terms of power equations but it was based on a joint organizing idea, the idea of freedom and the protection of the West. With the evolving multidimensional character of the relationship, the organizing idea shifted more to the economy. In the economic sphere, however, the idea of commonality clashed with legitimate and inevitable forms of competition, with trade disputes and economic rivalry. Since the end of the Cold War, the situation was aggravated in spite of the parallel enlargements of NATO and the EU and in spite of the continuous adaptation of strategies and instruments to meet "out of area" conflicts. Global terrorism and the future of democracy in the Broader Middle East did not help to immediately produce a new and joint organizing idea for the Atlantic community. Quite the opposite, it immediately triggered contrasting threat perceptions, mutual suspicion and transatlantic dissent. Gradually, the awareness was unavoidable on both sides of the Atlantic that stability (and hopefully democratic rule of law) in Afghanistan and in Iraq would require the multilateral commitments of all Atlantic partners for many years to come. It became even more evident that the only way to successfully deal with the threat of an Iranian nuclear program could only be based on a common approach. This was likewise true with regard to a long overdue solution to the Middle East conflict. But a new organizing principle guiding the transatlantic partners in the post-9/11 age of globalization has yet to be identified. As part of this process, the European Union needs to fully grow into its new role as a global partner of the US. In doing so, the EU will have to recognize America's primacy in the exercise of hard power, but the US would have to recognize the European Union as a political weight in its own right, with soft and hard power capabilities. Some American analysts were faster than others to do so. Following the reelection of President George W. Bush in 2004, both his administration and European leaders tried to rebuild confidence and common ground in transatlantic relations. Several visits of President Bush to Europe could not turn the widely spread public resentment of his administration around in much of the EU. One advantage of the Bush years in transatlantic relations became increasingly evident: At its core were different political choices and policy controversies. With the election of Barack Obama in November 2008, Europe's favourite candidate, this fact of international politics did not disappear.[12]

The Atlantic Alliance has moved forward to transatlantic relations: While NATO as the embodiment of the Atlantic security alliance prevails and increasingly plays an "out of area" role, the broad spectrum of transatlantic relations will be a mix of cohesion and cooperation, complementary actions and outright competition, if not blunt dissent. Transatlantic relations by definition will be political and therefore regularly controversial. The array of transatlantic attitudes and performances will not be a return to big power rivalry similar to that of the nineteenth century. It will rather grow into a new stage of transatlantic relations, in which the intensive links between governments, business and civil society will impact a new form of transatlantic domestic policy sphere. This has become already evident, inter alia, in debates about each other's education system, health conditions for food security, necessary reforms to enhance economic competitiveness, the disputes about climate change and the controversies over the right strategy in taming global warming. During the current period of recalibration, an excessive positioning of either side will most likely continue. Its resolution will not simply depend upon the personality of the incumbent President in the White House or the political majorities in leading European democracies. No matter how controversial it may get, the disputes of past years have amply shown that neither side could sign a

12 See De Vasconcelos, Alvaro, and Marcin Zaborowski (eds.), *The Obama Momentum: European and American Perspectives,* Paris: The European Union Institute for Securtiy Studies, 2009; for the Bush Presidency see: Jabko, Nicolas, and Craig Parsons (eds.), *The State of the European Union - With US or Against US?: European Trends in American Perspective*, Oxford: Oxford University Press, 2005; Schnabel, Rockwell, *The Next Superpower: The Rise of Europe and its Challenge to the US*, Lanham: Rowman & Littlefield, 2005.

Declaration of Emancipation or an Act of Divorce. Interdependency will prevail as the stronger instinct and rational calculation in transatlantic relations.

Eventually, this insight into transatlantic interdependency may reactivate one of the original ideas of Jean Monnet, dating back to 1948, of linking European integration with some form of treaty-based Atlantic confederation. At that time, Monnet already proposed a "Federation of the West," encompassing the US and Western Europe, along with Great Britain and the British Dominions.[13] Whether or not the *acquis atlantique* that has evolved over several decades can constitute the basis for a broader treaty-based relationship between the United States and the European Union is still unclear six decades later. A treaty-based US-EU relationship could be the logical consequence of the evolution of this relationship. It is not only special and strategic but it also echoes a genuine Atlantic civilization with a colorful yet ambivalent nexus of fascination and distance. "Ever since this part of European mankind ceased to be a colony, framed its constitution, and declared itself an independent republic," the philosopher Hannah Arendt explained this ambivalence to her American readers, "America has been both the dream and the nightmare of Europe."[14] Finding a stable balance among the US and the EU will remain the most important task for the Atlantic partners in the twenty-first century as reality is forcing them into a common global agenda. It must be based on a mutual recognition of common habits and different attitudes, shared values and their different application at times.[15] The institutional structure of their relationship has matured over time. But a constitutional underpinning is still absent. As younger generations grow into the Atlantic civilization, they are encountering its sometimes paradoxical links with globalization. Atlantic leaders will have to give profound answers that are not only contingent on a momentous crisis or an obvious success of "the Western world." At some point, they will have to come back to Jean Monnet's proposal to constitutionalize the Atlantic community. Ultimately, this will be necessary not only to manage global affairs, but also to legitimize their actions before their own publics and link them with the interests and concerns of other participants in the global community.

13 See Duchêne, François, *Jean Monnet: The First Statesman of Interdependence*, New York/London: W.W. Norton & Co., 1994:187; Schwabe, Klaus, "Jean Monnet, die Vereinigten Staaten und die Rolle Europas," in: Wilkens, Andreas (ed.), *Interessen verbinden: Jean Monnet und die europäische Integration der Bundesrepublik Deutschland*, Bonn: Bouvier, 1999: 232.

14 Arendt, Hannah, *Essays in Understanding, 1930-1945*, New York: Harcourt Brace & Company, 1994: 410.

15 See for a brilliant analysis Bark, Dennis L., *Americans and European Dancing in the Dark: On Our Differences and Affinities, Our Interests, and Our Habits of Life*, Stanford: Hoover Institution Press, 2007.

2. *Turning Times in Euro-Atlantic Relations*

(1) The Formative Years

Jean Monnet's original proposal was part of the long debate that finally led to President Kennedy's concept of a Grand Design, outlined in his speech of July 4, 1962, in Philadelphia. It was no coincidence that the President expressed his vision of a transatlantic partnership on US Independence Day at Philadelphia's Independence Hall. Like the American founding fathers, he said, Europe has begun "to find freedom in diversity and in unity, strength." Kennedy made clear that the US was on the side of this fascinating European project "with hope and admiration. We do not regard a strong and united Europe as a rival but as a partner...We believe that a united Europe will be capable of playing a greater role in the common defense, of responding more generously to the needs of poorer nations, of joining with the United States and others in lowering trade barriers, resolving problems of commerce, commodities, and currency, and developing coordinated policies in all economic, political, and diplomatic areas."[16] In order to achieve these joint goals, Kennedy called for a Declaration of Interdependence between the US and the emerging European Economic Community. The importance Kennedy attached to the implementation of his was evident: Kennedy's Grand Design was basically a proposal for an Atlantic Community with the US and a European Economic Community that should include Great Britain as its two poles. The economic pillar of the Kennedy administration, the Trade Expansion Act presented by President Kennedy to Congress on January 25, 1962, was meant to enhance American export to Europe based on the reduction of European custom tariffs. Monnet supported the idea of an Atlantic Community. He had described it as necessary and urgent in a letter of April 7, 1961, to EEC Commission President Walter Hallstein. Common problems required common solutions, he argued. An Atlantic Community could however not be built as long as Europe was divided and compartmentalized. Since Germany and France had begun with comprehensive European integration that could be considered from the perspective of finally aiming to become a second United States, time had come to also begin with the creation of partnership between the US and the European Economic Community.[17] The first EU Commission President Walter Hallstein was more hesitant than Monnet to embrace this idea. While Monnet pursued his idea to institutionally bind

16 Kennedy, John F., *Address at Independence Hall, Philadelphia*, July 4, 1962, http://jfklibrary.org/Historical+Resources/Archives/Reference+Desk/Speeches/JFK/003POF03IndependenceHall07041962.htm.

17 See Hackett, Clifford P. (ed.) *Monnet and the Americans: The Father of a United Europe and his U.S. Supporters*, Washington: Jean Monnet Council, 1995; Winand, Pascaline, *Eisenhower, Kennedy, and the United States of Europe*, Houndmills: Basingstoke, 1997 (2nd ed.); Schönwald, Matthias, "'The same – should I say – antenna'. Gemeinsamkeiten und Unterschiede im europapolitischen Denken von Jean Monnet und Walter Hallstein (1958-1963)," in: Wilkens, Andreas (ed.), *Interessen verbinden: Jean Monnet und die europäische Integration der Bundesrepublik Deutschland*, Bonn: Bouvier, 1999: 289-297.

the US and the EEC, Hallstein rejected a quasi-federal transatlantic construction. He could not anticipate the age of e-mail as binding glue stronger than most political rhetoric. To this day, a Declaration of Interdependence or an outright Transatlantic Treaty is still missing.[18]

The idea of an Atlantic community is surprisingly young. The Rhodes scholar, journalist and member of the US Delegation at the Paris Peace Talks in 1919, Clarence K. Streit, has received credit for having been one of its first active supporters. Following his 1940 book "Union Now," he promoted solidarity with Western European countries under Nazi German occupation and founded a movement under the same name. But he did not explicitly link the idea of an Atlantic community to that of European unity. The Atlantic Charter of 1942 documents the will of the United States and Great Britain to join forces in their struggle to defeat Hitler's totalitarian regime. Also the Atlantic Charter did not make reference to the prospect of European unity. The War Conferences in Teheran, Yalta and Potsdam did not mention the issue of European unity and integration either.[19]

Jean Monnet's conceptual considerations on the future of the Euro-Atlantic world were largely developed during World War II. Although he was in London at the time of French military defeat, he did not join General de Gaulle's Free France Movement, but went on to work on allied economic policies attached to the British Embassy in Washington. In 1943, he met de Gaulle again in Algiers, joined his movement, and in 1946 became head of French national economic planning ("Commissariat Général du Plan"), shortly before de Gaulle resigned from his post as French President. As Desmond Dinan writes, Monnet believed "that capitalism could best be served by judicious government direction of key economic activities."[20] Eventually, the rationale for the Marshall Plan did not really differ from Monnet's concept for European integration. Monnet was an exceptional bridge-builder between the idea of Atlantic solidarity and European unity. Not only for a Frenchman, but by all standards of his time, his attitude was a rare combination of ideas. Monnet wanted to engage the American government in the struggle to defeat Hitler's totalitarian regime. With his American friends he shared the understanding that post-War Europe had to integrate defeated Germany. He did not want Europe to be an American satellite nor did he assume this would always be the American policy toward Europe. When the Marshall

18 See Kühnhardt, Ludger, and Hans-Gert Pöttering, "EU-US: Plädoyer für einen Atlantischen Vertrag," *Integration*, 26.3 (2003): 244-250.

19 For other conceptual planning of the post-War future see Hearden, Patrick J., *Architects of Globalism: Building a New World Order During World War II*, Fayetteville: University of Arkansas Press, 2002.

20 Dinan, Desmond, *Europe Recast: A History of European Union*, Boulder: Lynne Rieffer Publishing, 2004: 31.

Plan was announced, Monnet was delighted. This was the right beginning of Europe's reconstruction that would ultimately turn it into a viable partner for the US.[21]

The years 1947 to 1949 were crucial for the new design of America's policies toward Europe. First the Truman Doctrine and the Marshall Plan, then the realization that France should take the lead to start European integration by engaging defeated West Germany that was turned from three occupied zones into one new democratic state: These were the corner-stones of US European policy under President Harry S. Truman and his Secretaries of State George C. Marshall and Dean Acheson. These policies were to be continued under the specter of a much more dangerous and noticeable Cold War by the administration of President Dwight D. Eisenhower and his Secretary of State John Foster Dulles. But no other President so explicitly defined the Atlantic Alliance as a framework to link US-European partnership with the welcomed integration of Europe as John F. Kennedy. In the end, all post-war administrations pursued their policies out of enlightened American self-interest.

The most relevant change in US policies toward Europe came as a reaction to the emergence of the Cold War. During the War Conferences, neither the US nor the USSR brought up the issue of a regional order in Europe. President Franklin D. Roosevelt was looking for American-Soviet cooperation beyond the immediate cessation of warfare. Stalin was planning to extend Soviet control over as much of Eastern Europe as possible. With the exception of communists, the European exile movements were discussing European integration favorably. But they remained dependant upon the will of the victorious powers.

Churchill's speeches in Fulton on March 5, 1946 ("an Iron Curtain"), and in Zurich on September 19, 1946 ("the United States of Europe"), had a strong impact, although he was no longer British Prime Minister. The winter of 1946/1947 saw a gradual turn-around of the US position from the concept of global cooperation with the Soviet Union to the doctrine of "containment." In March 1947, President Truman outlined what was to become known as the Truman Doctrine by expressing support for stabilizing Greece and Turkey against communist infiltration. At the initiative of Senator J. William Fulbright, the US Congress passed a resolution in the same month demanding the creation of a United States of Europe under the umbrella of the UN (which had been founded in 1945). President Harry S. Truman, Secretary of State George C. Marshall and his Deputy Dean Acheson thought along the same lines. The gradual emergence of the Marshall Plan – announced at the Harvard Commencement on June 5, 1947 – became the most visible expression of this policy change – and its implementation

21 See Monnet, Jean, *Memoires*, Paris: Fayard, 1976: 313-320; Duchêne, Francois, *Jean Monnet: The First Statesman of Interdependence*, New York/London: W. W. Norton & Co., 1994:166-175; Roussel, Eric, *Jean Monnet, 1888-1979*, Paris: Fayard, 1996; Schwabe, Klaus, "Jean Monnet, die Vereinigten Staaten und die Rolle Europas in der Atlantischen Völkergemeinschaft," in: Wilkens, Andreas (ed.), *Interessen verbinden: Jean Monnet und die europäische Integration der Bundesrepublik Deutschland*, op.cit.: 225-252.

under the official title of European Recovery Program the most famous legacy of America's commitment to Europe and its readiness to stay a European power.[22] In the end, under the Marshall Plan 5 percent of US GDP was transferred to Europe – "an unimaginable act today."[23] Economically speaking, recipient governments were able to raise funds in local currency by selling goods supplied through the Marshall Plan. Thus, American aid helped the European economies to generate their own capital, "certainly without returning to the deflationary competition of the 1930's."[24] With the help of the Marshall Plan, the US was serving the interests of its export industry, the containment of Soviet expansion, and the struggle over the "mind of Europe"[25] as it was reconstructing itself as part of the "free world". For the US, this meant that it had become "locked into an enduring European involvement, within which it had a decisive influence upon West European moves toward closer collaboration and integration."[26] Whether or not the Marshall Plan "saved" Western Europe, even critical voices admit that "it certainly helped Europeans chart out a path to a new era of peace and prosperity."[27] And while they did so, the US stayed a European power in all aspects, except for membership in the European Economic Communities.

Most important was the multilateral approach of the Marshall Plan, as it was not directed at individual countries but to Europe as a whole. While the Soviet Union's Foreign Minister soon withdrew his presence "after failing to convince the others to reject the US insistence on a joint European request for assistance,"[28] the Soviet Union had prohibited her newly emerging satellites in Central and Eastern Europe from taking part in the first Marshall Plan conference. This conference was ultimately attended by 16 European countries between July 12 and September 22, 1947, in Paris. The meeting concluded with the estimate of a need of 22 billion US dollars over a period of four years for the near term recovery of Western Europe, the three Western zones of Germany included. The need for US support was estimated at 19 billion US dollars; in the end, US aid amounted to almost 13 billion US dollars. The US had insisted that the Europeans would define their need alone, which forced them to coordinate their policies

22 See Melandri, Pierre, *Les Etats-Unis face à l'unification de l'Europe, 1945-1954*, Paris: Pédone et Publications de Sorbonne, 1980; Isaacson, Walter, and Evan Thomas, *The Wise Man: Six Friends and the World They Made*, New York: Simon and Schuster, 1986; Neuss, Beate, *Geburtshelfer Europas? Die Rolle der Vereinigten Staaten im europäischen Integrationsprozess 1945-1958*, Baden-Baden: Nomos, 2000.

23 Peterson, John, and Mark A. Pollack, "Introduction," in: Peterson, John, and Mark A. Pollack (eds.), *Europe, America, Bush: Transatlantic Relations in the Twenty-First Century*, op.cit.: 3.

24 Dinan, Desmond, *Europe Recast: A History of European Union*, op.cit.:21; see also Maier, Charles S. (ed.), *The Cold War in Europe: Era of a Divided Continent*, Princeton: Markus Wiener, 1996 (3rd ed.).

25 See the interesting booklet edited by Galantière, Lewis, *America and the Mind of Europe*, London: H. Hamilton, 1951.

26 Urwin, Derek W., *The Community of Europe: A History of European Integration Since 1945*, London/New York: Longman, 1995: 13.

27 Hitchcock, William I., *The Struggle for Europe: The Turbulent History of a Divided Continent, 1945 to the Present*, New York: Anchor Book, 2004: 141.

28 Dinan, Desmond, *Europe Recast: A History of European Union*, op.cit.: 21.

and plans for recovery. Industrial war damage, lack of infrastructure and machinery, destruction of agriculture and cities and the enormous human loss during the war defined the starting point for all Europeans. Prognosis was difficult, but not only pessimists assumed that it would take 20 to 25 years for Europe to recover from the war damage and its aftermath. Hardly anybody was expecting the recovery to be "sustained as a long boom through the 1950's and 1960's"[29] as it was to eventually happen. Between 1948 and 1950, the annual sale of washing machines grew from 94,000 to 311,000 in Great Britain and from 20,000 to 100,000 in France. By 1950, foreign trade in Western Europe was already 20 percent higher than prior to the war "and production was rising every year."[30]

The creation of the Paris-based Organization for European Economic Cooperation (OEEC) on April 16, 1948, gave the American support for Europe a multilateral roof. The OEEC was not only mandated to distribute American aid, it was also supposed to develop economic cooperation among Europeans, reduce mutually limiting trade barriers, prepare a multilateral payment system, stabilize European currencies and prepare customs unions or free trade areas. In spite of its relevance, the OEEC did not turn from being a loose intergovernmental structure into one of more integrated cooperation with autonomous competences. As a consequence of American worries after the split in Europe had taken place with the formation of the European Economic Communities in 1957, the OEEC was changed into the Organization for Economic Cooperation and Development (OECD) with the United States and Canada becoming full members in 1960.

This enlargement and readjustment of the OEEC was strongly supported by none other than Jean Monet: While the US had been confronted with payment deficits in their trade with Europe since 1959 and demanded an early reduction of European customs tariffs, Monnet seized the opportunity to again link Atlantic relations to European integration. During a visit to Washington in March 1959 (at the occasion of the funeral of Secretary of State John Foster Dulles) he proposed to American government officials OEEC enlargement through US and Canadian membership. This would alleviate transatlantic trade disputes, link Great Britain (an OEEC member) to the trade policies of the EEC and strengthen the reputation of the EEC as part of a solidified Atlantic relationship. The transformation from OEEC to OECD came as a success for Monnet in style, albeit not in substance, as the OECD continued as a purely intergovernmental transatlantic trade organization (and later grew into a global forum of industrialized countries).[31]

29 Dedman, Martin J., *The Origins and Development of the European Union, 1945-95*, London/New York: Routledge, 1996: 34.

30 Ibid.

31 See Schwabe, Klaus, "Jean Monnet, die Vereinigten Staaten und die Rolle Europas in der Atlantischen Völkergemeinschaft," in: Wilkens, Andreas (ed.), *Interessen verbinden: Jean Monnet und die europäische Integration der Bundesrepublik Deutschland*, op.cit.: 243-244.

The OEEC did not remain the only new institution geared toward the transformation of Europe as part of the evolution of a transatlantic community. Following the US-led founding of the new global financial system at Bretton Woods in 1944 – with the creation of the International Monetary Fund and a monetary system based upon fixed exchange rates, backed by both the US dollar and pound sterling as reserve currencies – twenty-three states signed the General Agreement on Trade and Tariffs (GATT) in October 1947, in Geneva. It immediately began to negotiate over one hundred bilateral treaties affecting half of the world's economy.

(2) The Strategic Imperative

The United States served also as midwife for European cooperation in the field of security. European cooperation was to be a precondition for American participation, State Secretary Marshall adamantly declared. In January 1948, British Foreign Secretary Bevin proposed the creation of a Western Union, using the French-British Security Treaty of Dunkirk (March 4, 1947) as its basis. Belgium, the Netherlands, and Luxembourg, possibly followed by other countries, were to get together. In the wake of the communist coup d'état in Czechoslovakia in February 1948, it took only days to sign the multilateral alliance treaty on March 17, 1948, in Brussels. The Brussels Pact – renamed Western European Union in 1954 and after 1999 gradually incorporated into the European Union – was meant to be valid for 50 years. The pact was driven by fear of Soviet expansionism and uncertainty about a revival of aggressive potential in Germany. Before the Brussels Pact was properly installed, it had become already obsolete: On April 4, 1949, twelve countries signed the Treaty of Washington, establishing the North Atlantic Treaty Organization (NATO). Brussels-based NATO was to become the centerpiece of transatlantic relations and the embodiment of the Atlantic Alliance.

In taking the lead to secure Europe's freedom, the US indirectly and substantially encouraged the process of a focused and rational economic integration as it evolved during the 1950's. The period from autumn 1948 to autumn 1949 was a "turning point" with the Berlin airlift, the creation of NATO and US military commitment to European security and the establishment of two German states. But more than anything else, the outbreak of the Korean War on June 25, 1950 – with more than two million people dead – rapidly accelerated the establishment of integrated transatlantic military structures. Instead of diverting American attention from Europe to Northeast Asia, as Stalin had hoped in his calculation of the North Korean attack, it provoked the opposite. Stalin failed to undermine Truman's resolve. In April 1951, General Eisenhower became the first Supreme Allied Commander in Europe (SACEUR). Western Europe had become part of the Atlantic security strategy of the US. Under this umbrella of protection, in the same month of April 1951 European integration began with the signing of the Treaty of the European Coal and Steel Community. By then, the US had recalibrated its European policy and encouraged France to take the lead in the internal restructuring of Europe instead of Great Britain that remained highly ambivalent about its future role in Europe.[32]

America's priority was security. Out of its 175 divisions, the Soviet Union had 22 divisions stationed in Central and Eastern Europe, compared with two each for the US and Great Britain in West Germany out of a total of 14 NATO divisions. The American nuclear umbrella over Western Europe was a credible deterrent until 1955 when the Soviet Union had developed its own delivery system for atomic weapons with long-range Tupolev bombers. West German rearmament was becoming one of the most important issues for the US in its European policy. The East Germans already had 60,000 "people's police," paramilitaries under weapons and organized in "alert units." Jean Monnet was trying to convince his American interlocutors that, as he was to write in his memoirs, the first new German soldier ought to be a European soldier.[33] After French Foreign Minister Robert Schuman was confronted with the American intention to prepare new German divisions to bolster Western defense – at the Foreign Ministers meeting of September 12, 1950 – Monnet started to apply his economic theory to the sphere of security. His goal was a European army within which German soldiers should find their place. During a discussion with General Eisenhower on June 21, 1951, it is believed that Monnet was able to convince the SACEUR that a European army would be the only way to generate legitimacy for German remilitarization in Europe.[34]

The failed European Defense Community convinced the Americans that in this crucial field French leadership would not serve either European or their own interests. NATO would become indispensable in the absence of a European integration in foreign policy and defense matters. Yet this American strategic and military primacy also contributed to wiping out remaining doubts among French leaders about the rationale for economic integration at the side of its long-time enemy Germany. In conjunction with the failed European Defense Community, the Suez crisis forced France to re-evaluate the European constellation. Even more pressing was the parallel evolution of the events at Suez and the revived Soviet threat that became visible through its brutal crashing of the Hungarian uprising. The Hungarian uprising had begun on October 21, 1956. On October 25, 1956, Russian tanks rolled through the streets of Budapest. On

32 See Schwabe, Klaus, "The United States and European Integration, 1947-1957," in: Wurm, Clemens (ed.), *Western Europe and Germany. The Beginnings of European Integration, 1945-1960*, Oxford/New York: Berg, 1995: 115-135.

33 Monnet, Jean, *Memoires*, op.cit.: 422.

34 See Wilkens, Andreas, "Jean Monnet, Konrad Adenauer und die deutsche Europapolitik," in Wilkens, Andreas (ed.), *Interessen verbinden: Jean Monnet und die europäische Integration der Bundesrepublik Deutschland*, op.cit: 97. Wilkens cites a related conversation between German Chancellor Konrad Adenauer and the US High Commissioner to Germany, John McCloy, on July 5, 1951, when McCloy declared that Germany's defense contribution ought to take place in the context of a European army, not directly under NATO command (97-98).

the same day, the Suez crisis broke out.At its end, France had to realize that it had only one option left if it was to remain the dominant power in Europe: To speedily build economic integration with the Germans while keeping the British "out of Europe."

The Suez crisis was more than the symbolic transfer of global power from the old European colonial empires France and Great Britain to the new world power United States. It was a true "humiliation"[35] of France and Great Britain by their war ally, the US. France had decided to begin with its own military nuclear program in 1956. In spite of defeat in Indochina in 1954 and the outbreak of anti-colonial war in Algeria in the same year, France's world power status, in its own eyes, ought not to be questioned. If on August 30, 1954, the French National Assembly would have voted in favor of the European Defense Community, the world might have seen a common European army two years later, consisting of 40 divisions, among them 12 German ones as outlined in the treaty. But as the National Assembly did not ratify the EDC Treaty of May 27, 1952, France's global role – not unlike that of Great Britain – shrank further. Whether France and Great Britain liked it or not, in matters of strategy and security the United States had replaced all of its European allies as the dominant power. If they were to return Europe to a global role, it would have to be through long-term, steady and convincing means of solid European integration.

The Suez crisis was more than a power quarrel over Egyptian nationalism. It was an unprecedented power confrontation among the Western allies that would find no repetition until the Iraq crisis of 2002/2003. While the Suez conflict demonstrated America's preeminence in the Middle East in political terms, the Iraq crisis confirmed this preeminence in military terms, but left many doubts as far as the political implications were concerned. In both cases, however, conflicting positions between the US and some of its European partners were resolved with "success" for the US: European countries could not stop the US's choice for unilateral action. But both crises also served as a "negative federator" for European integration: In the end, they brought the European caucus closer together, recognizing that this alone would be in the interest of Europe and strengthen its global position while the anti-hegemonic skepticism against the US was affirmed among all those Europeans who were and who are particularly sensitive to this issue.

The Suez crisis had escalated after Egypt's President Gamal Abdel Nasser nationalized the Suez Canal.[36] The canal, built in the 1860's, was the main artery for cheap and speedy transport of Middle East oil to Europe. Some 70 percent of Europe's oil imports passed through the Suez Canal. The British government held 44 percent of the stakes in the Suez Canal Company at the time. Beyond its economic importance, the canal was also part of a chain of outposts projecting British global influence and power.

35 Hitchcock, William I., *The Struggle for Europe: The Turbulent History of a Divided Continent, 1945 to the Present*, op.cit.: 177.

36 For the following account see Hitchcock, William I., *The Struggle for Europe: The Turbulent History of a Divided Continent, 1945 to the Present*, op.cit.: 177-183.

Great Britain was furious about Nasser's decision. The United States called all parties to reason and proposed a series of conferences to resolve the issues at stake, including the creation of some sort of international monitor. These meetings did not succeed and by mid-October 1956, British Prime Minister Anthony Eden was determined to invade Egypt.

Nasser supported the anti-French rebels in Algeria by sending arms and training their cadres. This scandalous behavior brought the French and the British together on the Suez Canal. During a meeting at the Prime Minister's country house at Chequers on October 14, 1956, the leaders of France and Great Britain agreed on a rather crazy, if not outright stupid plan. They arranged for the Israeli government of David Ben Gurion to attack Egypt on the evening of October 29, 1956. The next morning, France and Great Britain would call on Egypt and Israel to stop fighting and withdraw their troops from the Suez Canal zone. Assuming that Egypt would reject this proposal, British and French troops would have an excuse to attack Egypt on October 31, 1956. Thus it began.

But on November 2, 1956, the United Nations called for an immediate cease-fire. With both the US and the Soviet Union in favor of this declaration, France, Great Britain and Israel were totally isolated. Yet, on November 5, French and British paratroopers landed in Port Said, followed next morning by a large naval contingent. Expecting an oil embargo from the Arabs, currency traders had started to exchange pounds sterling for dollars. Since the summer of 1956, British currency reserves had fallen immensely, dropping by 57 million US dollars in September, by 84 million US dollars in October and by 85 million US dollars in the first week of November. President Eisenhower refused to intervene in favor of stabilizing the British pound until the Suez invasion was stopped. On November 6, 1956, British Prime Minister Anthony Eden and his French partner in crime, Guy Mollet, tried to save face by agreeing to a cease-fire. Eisenhower wanted the complete withdrawal of all British and French troops from the Suez Canal and their replacement by UN troops. On December 3, 1956, Britain declared victory and the withdrawal of its troops. Within a week, the International Monetary Fund approved a 561 million US dollar loan for Great Britain. While Great Britain recognized US leadership, the French government drew an opposite conclusion from the Suez crisis: More than ever it was suspicious of the Anglo-Saxons and prioritized European integration without them and, instead, and in spite of all historic feeling, together with the Germans. On March 25, 1957, the Treaties of Rome, constituting the European Economic Community and the European Atomic Energy Community, were signed.

(3) The Economic Calculus

Paradoxically, the US was stabilizing Europe's security through its economic commitment and it was encouraging European economic integration when it dominated Europe's security. After the first experiences in balancing European integration and Atlantic relations, the next phase throughout the 1960's and into the 1970's was defined by strong strategic links and growing economic competition. Since the construction of the Berlin Wall on August 13, 1961, "the Western world" had a defining, formative idea regarding its mission: Freedom first.[37] However, when President John F. Kennedy spoke on US Independence Day 1962 about the need for a solid transatlantic partnership, he did not only echo the common ground defined by shared values in the struggle against communism. He also underlined America's primacy in matters of European security after the EEC partners had failed to achieve political union as outlined by two subsequent Fouchet Plans. He also stressed the need for a true partnership with the intention to reduce European customs tariffs for America's export industry.

The West European economy experienced impressive growth rates during the early years of integration. The difference between the EEC member states and Great Britain, which had opted to stay out, were startling: The EEC's productivity increased by 19 percent between 1957 and 1961, the productivity of the US by 13 percent and of Great Britain by 12 percent. The GDP of the EEC member states increased by 27 percent between 1957 and 1961, compared with 18 percent in the US and 14 percent in Great Britain. The enormous increase in the EEC's industrial output (by over 90 percent between 1950 and 1960 compared with 39 percent in the US and 29 percent in Great Britain) might have been also the logical consequence of post-war reconstruction, and not of integration alone.[38] In any case, it was real, and was backed by the beginning of integration mechanisms. While the EEC was speedily reducing customs duties among its member states – in 1963 by 60 percent compared with the level of 1957 – the US were hoping for a stronger reduction of customs tariffs in transatlantic trade in order to better benefit from the booming European economies.

In parallel to Kennedy's Philadelphia speech, the first "trade war" between the US and the EEC broke out over chicken imports from the US. In the past, these chicken imports had been confronted with, for example, 4.5 cents per pound of German import tariff. Under the unified Common Agricultural Policy they were to pay an EEC tariff of 13.5 cents per pound. After mediation under a GATT panel, the EEC accepted that its policies were discriminatory, while the US accepted compensation payments. This was

37 See Hitchcock, William I., *The Struggle for Europe: The Turbulent History of a Divided Continent, 1945 to the Present*, op.cit.: 213-220. The Berlin Wall also constituted and symbolized the special emotional relationship between the US and West Germany that was to last beyond German unification in 1990 and was only seriously shattered during the Iraq crisis in 2002/2003.

38 For figures and interpretation, see Dedman, Martin J., *The Origins and Development of the European Union, 1945-95*, op.cit: 112.

the beginning of a series of never-ending "trade wars," becoming a constant factor in an otherwise solid trade relationship. A long-term legacy of President Kennedy's Grand Design was the Kennedy Round of GATT negotiations lasting until 1967. It ended with success, all fifty-three members of GATT agreeing to reduce tariffs over a five-year period by an average of almost 40 percent. However, frictions between the US and the EEC became permanent, not only in agricultural products, but also in industrial products. Yet, a remarkable trade expansion prevailed. In the early 1960's, the EEC was already receiving 30 percent of all US exports.

Only a few days before Kennedy's Philadelphia speech, Jean Monnet and his Action Committee for the United States of Europe had called for an overhaul of relations between the US and the EEC intended to gradually bring about partnership. In Kennedy's administration some of Jean Monnet's oldest American friends were in influential positions, most prominent among them Undersecretary of State for Economic Affairs, George Ball. He and others drafted the outline of Kennedy's Grand Design, intended to frame a solid European-American partnership among equals. No matter what else can be said about the Grand Design, its intention to bring Great Britain into the European integration scheme failed when French President de Gaulle vetoed the idea of membership negotiations in January 1963.

This was not the only headache General de Gaulle was causing for the Americans. In his analysis, the Cuban missile crisis had proven that the US "would take its own decisions irrespective of Western Europe's position and views".[39] Therefore, de Gaulle opposed President Kennedy's concept of Atlantic partnership. His alternative concept for a political union in Europe failed however. Much to the frustration of the General, he could not prevent the Germans from limiting his ambition for unification with them if it would have come about at the expense of transatlantic bonds. The issue of establishing Europe as a counter-weight to the US was not invented during the Iraq crisis of 2002/2003. But unlike then, in the 1960's Germany did not opt for Paris or Washington, but stayed the course as good partner and ally of both. When the Elysée Treaty of January 22, 1963, consolidating Franco-German reconciliation and rapprochement, was ratified by the German Parliament on May 16, 1963, the United States was pleased about the resolution passed by the German parliament and attached to the treaty, affirming Germany's commitments to NATO: "It emasculated de Gaulle."[40]

As if to compensate for the frustration with transatlantic relations, France initiated the EEC's comprehensive policy for Africa, that is to say toward former colonies of France and toward other French overseas territories. The Yaoundé Convention, signed in July 1963 by the EEC and seventeen African countries and Madagascar, created a

39 Urwin, Derek W., *The Community of Europe: A History of European Integration Since 1945*, op.cit.: 124.

40 Dinan, Desmond, *Europe Recast: A History of European Union*, op.cit.: 103.

free trade association in agreement with the original provisions of the Treaties of Rome. With the help of a development fund, the EEC started to support its African partners and considered this task no longer purely the obligation of the former colonial empires. Over time, the Yaoundé Convention was replaced by four subsequent Lomé Conventions and – since 2000 – by the Cotonou Agreement, defining the EU's relations with 79 countries in Africa, the Caribbean and the Pacific region. It took the EU four decades to transform its relations with most former European colonies from big power attitude and colonial dependency to partnership. And it took the US four decades to realize that the promotion of regional cooperation in Third World regions is a genuine strategic approach of the EU in support of a multipolar world and not just another peripheral aspect of world politics or a European escape from failed dominance in transatlantic relations. Through five decades of the existence of a European integration scheme, Europeans and the US have continuously struggled to find the right balance of transatlantic relations torn between ideals of partnership and realities of big power competition, notwithstanding their permanently invoked prime role for global management in the twenty-first century.

Over time, it seemed as if the US was more successful in negotiating with a strong European Community than trying to influence its political path. This experience was to repeat itself during the 1990's, when the US and the EU were entertaining a solid relationship as far as mutual trade negotiations based on a recognized partnership were concerned. But whenever, for example, the US promoted Turkish EU membership for strategic reasons, this proposition faced strong counter-reactions as if some Europeans felt offended to engage in a strategic discourse with their American partners, whom they in turn liked to "educate" on environmental issues, the death penalty and the like. Kennedy's Grand Design of a partnership of equals was still charged with emotional sensitivities and lacking a solid and self-assured relationship. Kennedy had been right in his Philadelphia Speech of July 4, 1962, when he called upon the Atlantic partnership not to look inward only, "preoccupied with its own welfare and advancement. It must look outward to cooperate with all nations in meeting their common concern." He was brave enough to conclude by saying that ultimately the Atlantic partnership "would serve as a nucleus for the eventual union of all free men."

(4) Reordering Europe

The final stages of the Cold War and the peaceful revolutions of 1989/1990 leading to European and German unification were a masterful process of Atlantic strength and rivalry. In the end, not only was Germany unified and Europe transformed, but also

41 Kennedy, John F., *Address at Independence Hall, Philadelphia*, July 4, 1962, op.cit.

Europe was unified and the Atlantic Alliance transformed.[42] The leadership role of the US came under increasing pressure in political terms, although US military protection was gratefully accepted, helping Europeans to spend less on defense. In the meantime, the economic relationship of the Atlantic partners had reached the level of equals. Certainly, they were struggling for interests and competing for market shares while recognizing a solid set of rules and norms worth the community of values often recited as a guiding rod of transatlantic relations. Beginning with the "Year of Europe," announced by Secretary of State Henry Kissinger for 1973, US-EC relations began to be somewhat clouded by identity quarrels. Their foundation however was strong enough to sustain these quarrels. The success of NATO was exceptional. Yet America's Western European partners were "deeply suspicious"[43] about Kissinger's proposal for a new Atlantic Charter. Many feared an American demand to increase their contribution to NATO with the US maintaining its leadership role. Others were skeptical about the intention of the US on principle. They were afraid that renewed claims of US leadership in transatlantic relations would undermine, if not derail the European integration process. As this process found itself in a deep stage of inertia, the pressure from the US could only serve as a wake up call for another relaunching of the European integration impetus.

Announcing a "Year of Europe" without prior consultations with the European allies was indeed not very helpful to make the idea truly flourish.[44] Kissinger's classification of the US as a power with global interests and the EC as a regional actor was annoying. The imminent EC membership of Great Britain strengthened the European market. The best outcome of the subsequent diplomatic row was economic, the beginning of the Tokyo Round of global trade negotiations in September 1973. Its results materialized in 1979 with further reductions of tariffs on industrial goods by one third between 1980 and 1987. Except for some special arrangements, the US and Japan had to accept the EC's agricultural policies. To this day, the EU's Common Agricultural Policy has remained the quintessential stereotypical misgiving about European discriminatory policies.

1973 was a bad year for Europe altogether. The immediate effect for Europe of the Yom Kippur War in October 1973 between Israel on the one hand, Egypt and Syria on the other hand, was a sharp increase in the price for crude oil: The price rose from 3 US dollars a barrel in October 1973 to 11 US dollars a barrel in January 1974. By 1980, the crude oil price had increased to 30 US dollars per barrel. The oil price shock had a lasting impact on the European economy. Annual growth rate in the European

42 See Zelikow, Philip D., and Condoleezza Rice, *Germany Unified and Europe Transformed: A Study in Statecraft*, Cambridge, Mass.: Harvard University Press, 1995.

43 Urwin, Derek W., *The Community of Europe: A History of European Integration Since 1945*, op.cit.: 159.

44 See Hamilton, Keith, and Patrick Salmon (eds.), *The Year of Europe: America, Europe and the Energy Crisis, 1972-74*, Abingdon: Routledge, 2006.

Community decreased from 6.0 percent in 1973 to 1.8 percent in 1974 and even to a record low of -0.9 percent in 1975. It never was to achieve American growth rates again. In 1980, the EC's growth rate was 1.0 percent, in 1985 2.6 percent and in 1990 an exceptionally high 3.0 percent. By 2005, the EU's average growth rate was 2.1 percent, while the average US GDP growth rate between 1977 and 1990 was 3.1 percent on annual average, between 1995 and 2005 even 5.0 percent on annual average.

Of course, it was not only the high prices for energy that contributed to the slow down in the long boom that Europe had enjoyed throughout the 1950's and 1960's. Exports decreased, labor relations strained and productivity receded during the 1970's and 1980's. Eventually, the obstacles of an incomplete European market were recognized across the EC. Only when the EC launched the "1992 project" of a Single Market in 1985 did the perception of "Eurosclerosis" slowly give way to new economic dynamism.[45]

In terms of European security, the US continued to provide the necessary nuclear and non-nuclear umbrella. With the CSCE Process, the dawn of communist totalitarianism and of the Cold War began in 1975. It was indicative that the EC participated in the CSCE process for the first time as a political actor. To get used to this European claim for a political positioning of the EC was difficult for many Americans to accept as more or less economic parity with the EC in spite of productivity gaps and the high welfare state costs in Europe. Yet it happened and the trade negotiators on both sides of the Atlantic developed their own community of shared interests and explosive conflicts over trade issues, which the media loved to portray as "wars."

When the communist edifice finally collapsed, the Berlin Wall came down in November 1989 and the Cold War ended, it was unquestionable that the West was led by the US. Many people behind the Iron Curtain had longed for freedom as they saw it represented by the US and for security provided by the US – particularly in the Baltic republics Estonia, Latvia and Lithuania that emerged from the long shadow of the Hitler-Stalin Pact and their submission to the Soviet Union. With their hope for prosperity, the post-communist countries looked to the European Union. At best, they wanted to join both the EU and NATO, which opened its door first.[46] On board a warship off the coast of Malta, US President George H.W. Bush and USSR President Mikhail Gorbachev declared the Cold War over on December 3, 1989. The long way from Yalta to Malta had ended. By 2007, ten former communist countries had become members of NATO and members of the EU.

The outbreak of four Wars of Yugoslavian Succession between 1991 and 1999 confirmed all American skepticism regarding the political weight of the European

45 See Silva, Michael, and Bertil Sjogren, *Europe 1992 and the New World Power Game*, New York: Wiley, 1990.

46 See Asmus, Ronald D., *Opening NATO's Door: How the Alliance Remade Itself for a New Era*, New York: Columbia University Press, 2002.

Union. The semantic refounding of the EC as European Union was not enough. The Treaty of Maastricht initiated a common foreign and security policy, but it was too slow to prevent the first wars on European soil since the end of World War II and it was too incoherent to gain respect in the US. How difficult the shaping of a common European interest would remain became clear at the very beginning of the Yugoslavian crisis: The European partners could not agree on the procedures to recognize the first breakaway republics Slovenia and Croatia in late 1991. They disagreed on the recognition of Macedonia's state name with the Greeks insisting that this new republic be called FYROM (Former Yugoslav Republic of Macedonia), to ensure that it would not be confused with the Greek region of Macedonia. They were not able to resort to military power to stop the ethnic cleansing by Yugoslavian dictator Slobodan Milošević in the Kosovo province.[47] It had to be stopped by American bombings on Milošević's installations of power across Serbia. Only when the subsequent UN-led protectorate over Kosovo was challenged by the unwavering will of the Kosovo Albanians for independence, was the EU finally doing better in the process of finding a status solution for Kosovo: Eventually, the European Union agreed on recognizing the province's desire for independence and by the end of 2007, the EU decided to lead the civilian mission supervising Kosovo's independence in the following year.

From an American point of view, the Yugoslavian nightmare of the 1990's was a repetition of the experiences with Europe during the 1940's and 1950's. Again, the US had to serve as pacifier and subsequently also as European unifier. At first, the EU remained reluctant to recognize the newly emerging republics of former Yugoslavia as EU candidates. Then, the EU remained hesitant to accept the independence of Kosovo. The US was not only pushing for this direction of reordering the territories of the former Yugoslavia. The US was even promoting Turkish EU membership while it remained overly controversial inside the European Union. While the European Union was still debating the ability of Romania and Bulgaria to join the EU, NATO had already taken both Southeast European countries on board as new members in 2004. The same procedure took place in 2008 when NATO invited Albania, Macedonia and Croatia as new member states while the European Union was still hesitant to accept them as EU candidate countries or members. While the US was considering the reordering of Southeast Europe a strategic issue, the EU was approaching the troubling region with cautious reluctance.[48] It goes to the credit of both the US and the EU that the diplomacy of bringing independence to Kosovo eventually became a coordinated transatlantic operation. But at that time, in late 2007/early 2008, US strategists were already looking

47 See Biermann, Rafael, *Schattenjahre: Das Scheitern der internationalen Konflikteinwirkung im Kosovo vor Kriegsbeginn*, Paderborn: Schöningh, 2005; Ahrens, Geert-Hinrich, *Diplomacy on the Edge: Containment of Ethnic Conflict and the Minorities Working Group of the Conferences on Yugoslavia*, Washington D.C.: Woodrow Wilson Center Press, 2007.

48 See Altmann, Rüdiger, and Eugene Whitlock (eds.), *European and US Policies in the Balkans: Different Views and Perceptions, Common Interests and Platforms*, Berlin: Stiftung Wissenschaft und Politik, 2004.

beyond Southeast Europe in order to anchor the Ukraine and the countries of the Southern Caucasus into Euro-Atlantic structures. Visionary strategists like Ronald D. Asmus were stretching the Eastern promise even to the countries of Central Asia.[49] Strategically speaking, the EU was always one step behind, in spite of the evolution of its own Central Asian Strategy that was adopted by the European Council on June 21-22, 2007. This strategy was more of a declaratory nature without a rigid definition of genuine EU interests in Central Asia.[50]

3. The Quest for Global Order

The most important effect of the end of the Cold War for the Atlantic Alliance was its change into transatlantic relations – a transformation underlined by the vast body of literature that was published on this matter throughout the 1990's.[51] Of course, there was no immediate end to the Alliance, as Geir Lundestad rightly reminded all skeptics of the debate.[52] But its most important need was to search for a new organizing idea beyond the traditional security paradigm rooted in the common ideal of defending freedom in the Euro-Atlantic region.[53] In the immediate years after the end of the Cold War, the economy was identified as the new organizing principle of strong transatlantic ties. The Transatlantic Declaration of 1990, the New Transatlantic Agenda of 1995 and

49 See Asmus, Ronald D., "Europe's Eastern Promise: Rethinking NATO and EU Enlargement," Foreign Affairs, Vol. 87.1 (2008): 95-106.

50 Council of the European Union, *Presidency Conclusions of the Brussels European Council*, 21/22 June 2007, http://consilium.europa.eu/ueDocs/cms_Data/docs/pressData/en/ec/94932.pdf.

51 See among many others van den Broek, Hans, et al., *Transatlantic Relations in the 1990s: The Emergence of New Security Architecture*, Washington D.C.: Brassey's ,1992; Lugar, Richard, *The Future of Transatlantic Relations: Euro-Atlantic Community and the Continuing US Role in Europe*, London: HMSO, 1993; Heuser, Beatrice, *Transatlantic Relations: Sharing Ideals and Costs*, London: Royal Institute of International Affairs, 1996; Bronstone, Adam, *European Union – United States Security Relations: Transatlantic Tensions and the Theory of International Relations*, New York: St. Martin's Press, 1997; Dembinski, Matthias, and Kinka Gerke (eds.), *Cooperation or Conflict?: Transatlantic Relation in Transition*, Frankfurt/New York: Campus, 1998.

52 Lundestad, Geir (ed.), *No End to Alliance: The United States and Western Europe: Past, Present and Future*, Houndmills: Macmillan, 1998; Lundestad, Geir, *"Empire" by Integration: The United States and European Integration*, Oxford: Oxford University Press, 1998; Leech, John (ed.), *Whole and Free: NATO, EU Enlargement and Transatlantic Relations*, London: Federal Trust for Education & Research, 2002; Sloan, Stanley, *NATO and Transatlantic Relations in the twenty-first century: Crisis, Continuity or Change?*, New York: Foreign Policy Association, 2002; Sloan, Stanley, and Peter van Ham, *What Future for NATO?*, London: Centre for European Reform, 2002; Sloan, Stanley, *NATO, the European Union and the Atlantic Community: The Transatlantic Bargain Reconsidered*, Lanham: Rowman & Littlefield, 2002; Mahncke, Dieter, et al. (eds.), *Redefining Transatlantic Security Relations: The Challenge Ahead*, Manchester: Manchester University Press, 2004.

53 Brandon, Henry (ed.), *In Search of a New World Order: The Future of US-European Relations*, Washington D.C.: Brookings Institution, 1992; Croci, Osvaldo, and Amy Verdun (eds.), *The Transatlantic Divide: Foreign and Security Policies in the Atlantic Alliance from Kosovo to Iraq*, Manchester: Manchester University Press, 2006; Zaborowski, Macin (ed.), *Friends Again?: EU-US Relations After the Crisis*, Paris: European Union Institute for Security Studies, 2006.

the Transatlantic Economic Partnership of 1998 were more than only inflationary rhetorical ambitions. While the Transatlantic Declaration established regular political encounters of the highest level between the US and the EU, the other two declarations were framework strategies and formulas aimed at installing the market as the core of the transatlantic relationship.[54] This was more than understandable, given the importance of transatlantic economic relations. Although the whole set of transatlantic security and policy relations were mentioned in the New Transatlantic Agenda (from the promotion of democracy to the fight against organized crime), it was primarily perceived as yet another declaratory contribution to manage economic globalization. The biggest flaw with this primacy of the market was not eliminated. By definition, the economy is a competitive sphere in which partnership can certainly transcend national loyalties, but in which conflicts can also easily poison the overall perception of the relationship and its sense of priority and urgency. Every successful transatlantic merger was balanced by the impression of another banana or steel "war" simmering through the media on both sides of the Atlantic.[55] Most importantly, the primacy of market relations left the political sphere absent and along with it the search for a new organizing principle encompassing both political and economic relations. More than ever, the backlash of this deficit was felt after 9/11 as "policy imperatives" resurfaced.[56]

The imminent perspective of a completed Single Market by 1992 and a common European currency produced a long series of proposals for how to reinforce transatlantic economic relations during the 1990's. When transatlantic relations were framed by the Transatlantic Agenda of 1990 and the New Transatlantic Agenda of 1995, the US and the European Union were perceived as "seeking to open a new era in the history of their relationship by committing themselves to a transatlantic partnership."[57] The two largest economies of the world were intensifying transatlantic regulatory cooperation, recognizing that they are "the most active participants in the process of economic globalization…the primary instigators of international economic negotiations and the primary users of the international trade dispute settlement system."[58] Since the mid-

54 See Reinicke, Wolfgang H., *Deepening the Atlantic: Toward a New Transatlantic Marketplace?*, Gütersloh: Bertelsmann Foundation Publishers, 1996; Monar, Jörg (ed.), *The New Transatlantic Agenda and the Future of EU-US Relations*, London/Boston: Kluwer Law International, 1998; Pollack, Mark A. (ed.), *The New Transatlantic Agenda at Five: A Critical Assessment*, Fiesole: European University Institute, 2002.

55 See Busch, Marc L., *Transatlantic Trade Conflicts and GATT/WTO Dispute Settlement*, Fiesole: European University Institute, 2002.

56 See Hensel, Howard M. (ed.), *The United States and Europe: Policy Imperatives in a Globalizing World*, Aldershot: Ashgate, 2002.

57 Gardner, Anthony L., *A New Era in US-EU Relations?: The Clinton Administration and the New Transatlantic Agenda*, Aldershot: Ashgate, 1997: 1.

58 Pollack, Mark A., and Gregory C. Shaffer, "Transatlantic Governance in Historical and Theoretical Perspective," in: Pollack, Mark A., and Gregory C. Shaffer (eds.), *Transatlantic Governance in the Global Economy*, Lanham: Rowman & Littlefield, 2001: 4.

1980's, "the relative economic clout of the United States stabilized to be about equal to that of the European Union."[59]

After World War II, the US national income was greater than the rest of the world's market economies combined. This enormous supremacy of the US was not without reason. During the 1930's, world trade declined by approximately 60 percent. One of the causes of the Great Depression was the effect of the "infamous"[60] Smoot-Hawley tariff that established the highest general tariff structure the United States has arguably ever practiced. European and other states reciprocated and world trade plummeted. US imports fell from 4.4 billion US dollars in 1929 to 1.4 billion US dollars in 1933 and US exports plunged from 5.1 billion US dollars to 1.6 billion US dollars during the same period. The Great Depression was man-made after all. European economies resorted to autarky and political radicalism surged. During the war years, the US economy expanded by 106 percent, while the GDP of Europe's economies decreased sharply: in Germany by 48 percent, in Austria by 43 percent, in Italy by 21 percent and in France by 17 percent.

With the end of World War II, the global economy was expanding again, although at the beginning there was hardly any cross-border investment. As they were reconstructing their war-torn economies, the EEC member states began to catch up speedily with the US. From the late 1950's to the 1980's, the US share of world production dropped from more than 50 percent to just over a quarter. The US began to perceive Europe "as an economic rival as well as an ally."[61] In spite of free trade agreements favoring more transatlantic trade, the largest amount of protective measures were non-tariff barriers. It was estimated that in the 1980's about one third of the manufacturing sectors in the US and in the EU economies were protected by non-tariff barriers. Yet, transatlantic investments began to substantially increase: between 1977 and 1984 from 34.6 billion US dollars to 159.6 billion US dollars.[62] Time was ripe for stronger transatlantic regulatory mechanisms to frame this dynamic interaction.[63]

The bilateral EU-US debate as well as their extension into the WTO context was wavering between liberalization and regulation. Increasingly, US-EU disputes and solutions alone would not make the WTO work, as other countries of the world became stronger in the representation of their own specific interests. This became evident during global trade negotiations in the early years of the twenty-first century. After initial bilateral compromises between US and EU trade negotiators in 2001, the Doha Ministerial Meeting in November 2001 – in the shadow of the terrorist attacks of 9/11 – agreed on a Doha Development Agenda that went beyond much of the original intention

59 Ibid.: 7.
60 Ibid.: 8.
61 Ibid.: 10.
62 Ibid.: 12.
63 See Bermann, George A., et al. (eds.), *Transatlantic Regulatory Cooperation: Legal Problems and Political Prospects*, Oxford/New York: Oxford University Press, 2001.

of the US and the EU to further global trade negotiations. The concerns of developing countries had to be taken much more seriously than ever in order to reach any kind of consensus in Doha. The mandate of the Doha Conference included negotiations on agriculture and services, but also brought interests of developing countries, for instance regarding the protection of their medicine markets, to public attention.

The fact that the EU and the US could no longer dominate the outcome of WTO negotiations became evident in September 2003, when the global meeting of trade ministers in Cancun failed to reach results acceptable to all member states. On trade matters, the EU and the US will have to learn to live with an ever-stronger multipolar and multidimensional world. An example for their failed policies of effective and meaningful change are the continuous subsidies of the US and the EU to their cotton industries while Benin, Chad, Mali and Burkina Faso have submitted a strong proposal to the WTO to stop this practice as it destroys the potential of Africa's main cotton producers. Due to US and EU subsidies in this sector – the US alone was subsidizing a few thousand cotton farmers with 6 billion dollars in 2001 – the income of 10 million people who depend directly on cotton production in the aforementioned African countries has shrunk dramatically. Although the countries of western and central Africa have increased their cotton output by 14 percent between 1999 and 2001, their export receipts fell 31 percent while the world price of cotton has plummeted for over a decade.

Transatlantic economic governance encompasses intergovernmental, transgovernmental and transnational levels. Regular annual summit meetings between the US President and the EU Commission President began with the Transatlantic Declaration of 1990. In endless transgovernmental meetings and negotiations civil servants are working with their transatlantic counterparts; and on the transnational level business representatives, union leaders, civil society activists and academics began to network in innumerable ways.[64] Yet, the primacy of politics was restored when terrorist enemies attacked the US and thus the whole Western world – not only affecting the outcome of the Doha conference, but particularly impacting transatlantic threat perceptions.

The outpouring of European solidarity after the terrible terrorist attacks on New York and Washington on September 11, 2001, was boundless. "Le Monde" titled its front page with "We are all Americans" and the invocation of NATO's Article 5 – the alliance clause – on September 12, 2001, was a doubtless commitment to the reciprocity of Atlantic solidarity by America's European allies. The Bush administration did not make a very wise use of this solidarity. Unilaterally, it prepared to destroy the Taliban-regime in Afghanistan that was harboring the bulk of Al Qaeda terrorist structures. The military operation in Afghanistan began as a unilateral American action on October 7, 2001, although with political support from the European Union. A UN sponsored

64 Ibid.: 17-34.

Afghanistan Conference was held in Bonn between November 27 and December 5, 2001, outlining the new constitutional structures and the framework for power-sharing in Afghanistan. Since August 11, 2003, under NATO command, twenty-three EU member states were providing the largest contingent of 8,500 peacekeeping troops to the International Security Assistance Force (ISAF) in post-Taliban Afghanistan. By 2007, thirty-seven nations were contributing to the International Security Assistance Force. Its more than 18,500 soldiers were supposed to stay in Afghanistan for many years to come. In 2007, the European Union established EUPOL Afghanistan, a civilian mission aimed at consulting and supervising the Afghan police force. The situation in Afghanistan had not become easy or stable. In light of continuous terror attacks and the new recruiting of Taliban terrorists in certain areas of Afghanistan, the potential failure of ISAF had become a permanent political and media issue across NATO countries. NATO and the EU could only succeed together – or fail together. Most troubling was the situation in neighboring Pakistan, which became dangerously uncertain and an increasing cause of concern in Europe and the US.

Disputes about tactics and strategy prevailed between Europeans and Americans, but they were moderate compared to the immediate crisis over priorities in the war against terror that had broken out after "9/11" and the beginning of the Afghanistan operation. The transatlantic controversies had escalated after President Bush's speech to the US Congress of January 29, 2002. His attack on the "axis of evil" (Iraq, Iran, North Korea) as possible targets for further military regime-change triggered a storm of opposition in Europe, unheard of since President Ronald W. Reagan had labeled the Soviet Union an "evil empire" in a speech to the British House of Commons on June 8, 1982. President Bush's speech was more than the announcement of American strength, retaliation and, maybe, unilateral action against further rogue states. In the eyes of many European critics, this was the return of an old testament-like world-view in the sphere of secular politics. A value gap between the US and Europe was noticeable that had obviously been covered and tamed by the common threat of communism and the supremacy of open, pluralistic Western society.

Differing threat perceptions, contrasting interpretations of the usefulness of multilateral actions and conflicting policy choices culminated in clashing moralities. Transatlantic relations reached their all-time low. Internal European relations were as badly hurt as transatlantic trust. The split among EU members and soon-to-be-members was as deep as the transatlantic controversy – and may be even more bitter and lasting.[65]

65 See Bannermann, Edward, et al. (eds.), *Europe after September 11th*, London: Centre for European Reform, 2001; Stemplowski, Ryszard, and Laurence A. Whitehead (eds.), *After the Attack: "Several Europes" and Transatlantic Relations*, Warsaw: Polish Institute of International Affairs, 2002; Wells, Sam, and Ludger Kühnhardt (eds.), *The Crisis in Transatlantic Relations*, ZEI Discussion Paper C 143, Bonn: Center for European Integration Studies 2005; on a special aspect of the situation see Zaborowski, Marcin, and David H. Dunn (eds.) *Poland: a New Power in Transatlantic Security*, London/Portland: Frank Cass, 2003.

Soul searching began on all sides in order to contain or even heal this unique internal Cold War of the West.[66]

On both sides of the Atlantic, efforts were made to repair transatlantic relations. They would not become again as smooth as they once used to be. America's primacy might be inevitable, but its political dominance was to be challenged continuously by a European Union more self-assertive than ever. President Bush had declared a "war on terror" and the majority of American citizens saw their country at war. This feeling was not shared across Europe and it seemed that in spite of many healing efforts, the fight against global terrorism could not properly serve as a new organizing idea for the Atlantic community. From a European perspective, the war on terror would have to be complemented by the readiness of both Atlantic partners to reach out to Muslim societies in a joint fight against radical ideology and terrorist violence, but also in a joint fight against social injustice, negligence and political autocracy. While senior analysts in Europe defined Europe's best interest as "staying close to number one,"[67] the European public was in favor of developing the European Union into a superpower equal to the United States. 71 percent supported this idea in an opinion poll conducted by the German Marshall Fund of the United States. When however challenged with the necessary increase in defense spending this would eventually entail, support for the idea of an independent European superpower dropped to 44 percent.[68] The best approach for the European Union states and citizens had always been and would remain to be "smart allies," as Christoph Bertram put it.[69] In order to have any influence on the American debate and America's policy, Europeans would need to listen to American arguments, to consistently develop internal European cohesion about common interests and they would have to stay loyal transatlantic partners.

Beyond the agenda of the Bush Presidency, Americans were still in the learning process of taking the European Union more seriously. They needed to better grasp the genuine nature of the European Union that had come a long way since the days of Jean Monnet. The fact that President Bush paid his first foreign visit after his second inauguration to Europe in February 2005 was a subtle recognition of this fact. President Bush could never regain the political reputation in Europe that he had lost in the thick of

66 See European Commission. Directorate-General for External Relations (ed.), *European Union Relations with the United States*, Luxembourg: Office for Official Publications of the European Communities, 2002; United States Congress. House, Committee on International Relations, Subcommittee on Europe, *Renewing the Transatlantic Partnership: A View from the United* States, Hearing Before the Subcommittee, June 11, 2003, Washington D.C.: US G.P.O. Congressional Sales Office, 2003; United States Congress. House, Committee on International Relations, Subcommittee on Europe, *The Future of Transatlantic Relations: A View from Europe*, Hearing before the Subcommittee, Washington, June 17, 2003, Washington D.C.: US G.P.O. Congressional Sales Office, 2003; Grant, Charles, *Transatlantic Rift: How to Bring the Two Sides Together*, London: Centre for European Reform, 2003.

67 Bertram, Christoph, "Europe's Best Interest: Staying Close to Number One," *Internationale Politik und Gesellschaft*, 1 (2003): 61-70.

68 *Frankfurter Allgemeine Zeitung*, "Europäer wollen Weltmacht sein," 9. September 2005: 6.

69 Bertram, Christoph, "Europe's Best Interest: Staying Close to Number One," op. cit.: 69.

his policies in Iraq. Barack Obama was Europe's choice. The newly elected US President, in office since January 2009 reached out to a world waiting anew for American commitment to multilateralism. To support this global expectation, he received the Nobel Peace Prize in December 2009 before any lasting and measurable success. President Obama found himself in the midst of a tall and ever taller global agenda: Afghanistan was slipping into violence; the strategies to avoid the Iranian nuclear program did not really succeed; how to cope with a neo-authoritarian Russia was as uncertain as any early resolution of the Middle East conflict. Most importantly for the Obama presidency, however, was the handling of the global financial and economic global crisis that had broken out in 2008. More global governance was necessary than ever and only little was achieved by moving the G8 to a G20 format during summit meetings in London (April 2009) and Pittsburgh (September 2009). The global financial and economic crisis became increasingly interwoven with emerging global power shifts. For the time being, their impact on transatlantic relations remained unclear.

4. Culture and Religion: The Value Gap

Common values were invoked as the foundation of transatlantic relations for almost all too long. Artificial debates proceeded about the relationship between values and interests. With the clash over Iraq and the return of religion as a public category, a "war of Weltanschauung" began to change the cultural fabric of European-American relations. With hindsight, the Cold War helped to make easy and general choices. Even during the Cold War, President Ronald Reagan's use of the term "evil empire" was considered by its critics as a naïve expression of a cowboy-like actor-turned-politician. For a long time, many Europeans did not take "the American spirit" seriously and did not recognize the underlying cultural and religious foundation of the US. As proud as they were to have overcome warfare and hatred by tolerance, secularization and rule of law based civil society, they often failed to understand the religious character of America. Already superficial reading of early European writings about America – such as Alexis de Tocqueville's "On Democracy in America" (1836/1840) – could have helped explain this important matter concerning the American identity. All too often, the stereotypical image of the US as an incarnation of liberalism and freedom of choice in all possible meanings of the word blurred a more differentiated European perception of the US. Religion, after all, had always been a cultural divide between the Old World and the New World. While the ideology and life style of the cultural revolution of 1968 was phasing out both in Europe and in the US, this difference was immediately brought back into the limelight when Islamic terrorism struck.

One of the remarkable features in its aftermath was the almost theological coalition of the "moral majority," America's conservative, largely evangelical Christians, and the American Jewry, traditionally renowned for its liberalism and secularism. Under pressure from Islamic fanatics they joined ranks, declaring that Palestinian violence in Israel was another expression of the same threat, and that basically Jews in the Holy Land and Americans in the US were chosen people with a biblical mission. Wasn't this close to the belief of the "Pilgrim Fathers" of the early seventeenth century? Four centuries ago, Europe had persecuted the "Pilgrim Fathers" and had forced them to leave for the New World. In the early twenty-first century, by and large Europe had become indifferent to a public role of religion. Neither the language of President Reagan nor the terminology used by President George W. Bush found sympathy among many Europeans that had replaced the term "evil" by categories of "social contingency" and the term "sin" by a psycho-sociological language of "preference" and "tolerance." They considered themselves to be the proud acolytes of the age of enlightenment and the American conservatives as figures from the dark ages of Europe's own past.

Deep convictions – and certainly religious creed and strong faith – estranged left-liberal European intellectuals who at the same time did not feel comfortable about Islam either. The matter was complicated by the fact that many European conservatives are not explicitly religious. Whenever they are religious, they tend to be less evangelical and fundamentalist as their American brothers and sisters. This trend is nurtured by the fact that Catholicism is much stronger in Europe (and elsewhere in the world, particularly in Latin America and Africa) than in the US. Catholicism tends to focus on forgiveness and reconciliation, on ecumenical values rather than on rigid dichotomies between inescapable clashes of good and evil. The late Pope John Paul II on the one hand, and US President George W. Bush on the other hand, represented two different political theologies when they disputed the justification of invading Iraq.

Different interpretations of the same values are not a particular phenomenon that divides Americans and Europeans, religious and non-religious citizens alike. Among Europeans one can find as many different interpretations of the same values and moral norms as one can find in the US. What is however a remarkable difference is the relevance citizens of the two Atlantic societies attribute to God, faith and the public role of religion. For 82 percent of Americans, life is meaningful only because God exists. In Europe, all societies have far lower approval rates for this belief. Spain leads with 37 percent of its citizens explicitly saying that life is meaningful only because God exists. Many other people in Europe have less explicit attitudes on faith. Often, the answer to religion is in the negative: 49 percent of Danes, 55 percent of Swedes and nearly 75 percent of Czechs explicitly say that God does not matter to their life at all. Church attendance is substantially lower in Europe than in the US. This is not only a matter of personal faith, but has implications for community-building where churches have always played a crucial role.[70]

On matters of religion and the public relevance of religiosity, Europe had become the exceptional continent. This startling gap in faith and religion not only echoes different personal choices, it has fundamental implications for the public discourse about moral issues and for the public meaning of religion. It also has deep effects on the transatlantic community of values. As religion has become a public matter again in the Western world, these differences impact the smooth evolution of a new organizing transatlantic rationale enormously.

The religious question surfaced at a time when the implications of the cultural revolution of 1968 were slowly vanishing from the center of Western political culture. While 1968 was an uprising of youthful discontent with the political establishment of the time, by the early twenty-first century the protagonists of "1968" had accommodated themselves in the position of establishment. In 1968, the Western world witnessed the evolution of a counter-culture to its established norms and authorities.[71] In the early twenty-first century, the late-culture of 1968 was confronted with the revival of religious claims in public life against its long-standing prognosis of the withering away of religion and faith. Since "9/11," the focus has largely shifted to the question of how to perceive Islam and how to encounter Muslims living in Western societies. The answers given to this burning question are linked to overall religious attitudes in the West. The more inclusive and positive a society is in dealing with the faith of its citizens the less "political correctness" produces zones of taboo, prejudice and fear toward the faith of others. Theoretically, the US and the EU will agree on this assumption, in reality, their societies tend to pursue different attitudes. Whether Islamic terrorism (with the Madrid train bombing of March 1, 2003, killing 191 innocent people) and the presence of fundamentalist Islam in general (after "9/11," twenty times more terror suspects were arrested in Europe than in the US); whether the debate about head scarves in French schools or the brutal murder of a Dutch film director – frivolously critical of Islamic practices against the dignity of women – on November 2, 2004, in downtown Amsterdam; whether the unsatisfactory outcome of the debate about the inclusion of God in the preamble of the Treaty Establishing a Constitution for Europe or the excessively critical reaction to the traditional Catholic position on rejecting homosexual marriages and on women as mothers by Italian cabinet minister Rocco Buttiglione that cost him his career as an incoming European Union Commissioner – the Old World was not better prepared to deal with the return of religion as a public, at times disturbing and controversial issue. As for the transatlantic dimension of this question, it was important whether or not Europe and America would

70 See Ferguson, Niall, *Colossus: The Prize of America's Empire*, New York: Penguin Press 2004: 236.
71 See Suri, Jeremi, *Power and Protest: Global Revolution and the Rise of Détente*, Cambridge, Mass.: Harvard University Press, 2003.

be able to deal with the public meaning of religion and multireligious realities in their societies in a concordant and complementary way. In order to reclaim an organizing idea for the future cohesion of the Atlantic civilization, this remains a cardinal issue if the West does not want to reduce its own identity as simply and primarily being anti-Islamic. It would not help the West or any of its constituent parts to simplify Islam as a non- or even anti-Western religion. To be critical against all forms of radicalism and unclear notions of violence as a political means was important and legitimate. But to define Western identity would need to recognize the historical and contemporary contributions of Judaism and Islam, the two other "Religions of the Book."

The American concept of inclusive patriotism and of civil religion is absent in Europe, let alone in the European Union. Reference to the Christian Occident would not suffice to fill this gap. It would be speculative to project developments on either side of the Atlantic. But the value gap as a gap in the perception of the public meaning of religion had to be bridged beyond diplomatic niceties as an issue on the transatlantic agenda if common ground was to be found again. Until "9/11," Islam in the US was largely perceived as a matter of black empowerment. As a religion, Islam was neither questioned nor considered overly relevant in the US. As for the broader public discourse, it was not linked to the cultural upheavals in the Arab world or to implications for US migration policies. The US had never been perceived as facing particular problems of integrating its Arab-Islamic population, yet the US became the most prominent victim of Islamic fanaticism. Europeans, thinking that they had practiced tolerance with their Muslim migrants and accepted difference since the end of European colonialism, found it difficult to reconcile the uncomfortable awareness of parallel societies among themselves – with thousands of radicals mixing with millions of decent citizens of Islamic faith – and the inescapable proximity to the Arab world with their own advanced level of secularization and claim for laicism, which is to say a strict division between personal faith and public life. More eye-opening should have been the fact that aggression and violence among Muslims is not a matter of good or bad integration; it is a matter of ideology and related to radical organizations with a readiness to exercise acts of terrorism. It would come as a delusion on the matter if the European Court of Justice at some point had to rule on the issue of head scarves of European Union citizens in public schools of the EU. Europe has to learn to live with Islam in its midst, while at the same time it must do the utmost to fight radical and criminal violence perpetrated or planned in the name of this world religion. Europe would also have to contemplate how seriously it wants to return to its own Christian roots again and whether this ought to occur in an exclusive or inclusive manner.

Religion, civil religion and inclusive patriotism not only have theological implications, they also affect the political culture and the economy. So far, the European Union has not been able to generate a viable Euro-patriotism that would not be anti-American or anti-Islamic or anti-Russian, and yet be a defining moment for European citizenship. Timothy Garton Ash, in rightly describing Euro-Gaullism or Euro-nationalism as the alternative to Euro-Atlanticism, has been warning that "the line between Europe as Not-America and Europe as Anti-America is not clearly marked on any map."[72] There is only one way out, he concluded, and that is to strengthen the Atlantic partnership for the sake of a better and freer world: Timothy Garton Ash recalled that many of those in Europe who appear "anti-American" "are often disappointed lovers, measuring America against its own high ideal of itself." A Europe, he concluded, "that likes the idea of America is a better Europe. Indeed, if we confront America with its own better self, we are confronting it, historically speaking, with a vision of a better Europe."[73] Sometimes, to follow this noble perspective seems to be more difficult than squaring the circle. It is difficult for many old and new Europeans alike. Unlike in the US, migration into the European Union is basically not driven by the political or cultural attraction of a European patriotism. It is driven by the political freedom prevailing in Europe, and it is driven by the prevailing welfare state benefits of the European states. No matter how culturally diverse the US is, it is united in a multireligious civil religion, and in a religion-based constitutionalism, which the European majority rejects. It is not surprising that as a consequence of this European secularism and, in fact, global exceptionalism, religious diversity poses stronger problems for most European societies than for the US, where religion remains a strong fact of life amid secular liberalism.

Popular culture and "high culture" have found a good balance and mutual recognition across the Atlantic. Euro-Disney in Paris and classical operas in San Francisco, McDonald's, pop music and Hollywood movies across Europe, growing numbers of French and Italian restaurants in the US and a continuous prevalence of European tourists among Americans – these and related questions touch on the lowest possible level of transatlantic stereotypes and commonalities. Even matters of biologically engineered food, the death penalty or political unilateralism are "merely" of a political nature and can be managed as issues of transatlantic domestic policy. The real transatlantic value gap is about the public role of religion, faith and God. Compared with the days of the "Pilgrim Fathers," cause and effect of the dispute about religion had been reversed. The US was perceived as fundamentalist, Europe as relativistic. No matter the many shades of grey that prevail, religion has obviously become the most divisive matter among many citizens of the Atlantic civilization.

72 Garton Ash, Timothy, *Free World: Why a Crisis of the West Reveals the Opportunity of Our Time*, London: Allen Lane, 2004: 64.
73 Ibid.: 232.

"Who needs a counterweight anyway?" asked Niall Ferguson, only to immediately give the quintessential answer: "Both the United States and the European Union have far more to gain from cooperation than from competition. The bottom line is that they need, even depend on, each other."[74] This does not mean that fantasies of counter-power and suspicion of a hidden European agenda will not prevail. It also does not mean that cooperation could not again give way to competition, and it surely will. The answer lies in the degree of competition and cooperation that is acceptable for transatlantic cohesion. It is ultimately a matter of defining priorities that are essential for the well-being, the freedom and security of all in the Atlantic civilization. The US and the EU will grow into a common global agenda by trial and error only, so it seems. Their contrasting interpretations of fundamental concepts such as national sovereignty, the relationship between soft power and hard power, and their attitude toward the United Nations and other instruments of multilateralism will have to be balanced with their shared interests, increasingly shared threat perceptions and the set of instruments they are ready to entertain in order to achieve their goals.[75]

The differences on migration and integration as discussed above also have implications for the way in which the US and the EU approach matters of global relevance, and certainly the relationship with the Arab world. Europe sits at the frontline of the Western world with Russia to its east and with the world of Islam to its south. None of these experiences confronts the US. Mexican immigration, legal or illegal, is of a substantially different nature and the integration pattern of the largely Catholic population from Latin America underlines the differences of its effects compared with Islamic migration into Europe.

More than for the US, the migration issue has a twofold-meaning for Europe. It is not only confronting Europe with the migration of Muslims – today constituting 3.2 percent of Europe's 491 million citizens (15 million) – but it also confronts Europe with its neighboring Muslim states and their internal situations.[76] During the Cold War, one of the favorite disputes among Atlantic partners related to the question of who understood the Russians best. While Europeans claimed that proximity and historical experiences among neighbors mattered more, Americans insisted on their own strategic competence and personal knowledge of the Soviet Union and its ambitions. The Atlantic Alliance was able to balance both views with its two-fold approach of deterrence and cooperation as outlined in the 1967 Harmel Report. To this day, a similar balance of transatlantic views on the Broader Middle East, and especially on the future relationship with Iran, is still missing. The EU maintains a Euro-Mediterranean

74 Ferguson, Niall, *Colossus: The Price of America's Empire*, op.cit.: 257.

75 See Kühnhardt, Ludger, *Contrasting Transatlantic Interpretations: The EU and the US Towards a Common Global Role*, Stockholm: Swedish Institute for European Policy Studies, 2003.

76 Estimates for the Muslim population in the US vary between 3 and 6 million.

Partnership, NATO manages its own Mediterranean Dialogue but none of these cooperative efforts has been able to either transform the region or to link it in cooperative ways to the West in a new security structure.

One of the promising elements of recent developments has been the creation of the Middle East Quartet. In spite of rivalry and ongoing differences in perception and strategic approach, the US and the EU, together with the United Nations and Russia, were able to work out the Road Map for a lasting peace in the Middle East. This document of April 2003 has become the road map for a sustainable and comprehensive solution to the Middle East conflict.[77] The resolution of the Middle East conflict on the basis of a two-state solution – a secure Israel in recognized borders and a secure Palestine in recognized borders – remains the highest and most pressing priority on the international agenda. Continuous failure in resolving the Middle East conflict will also mean a continuous de-legitimization of both the United States and the European Union to be accepted as honest brokers and mediators. The relaunched Arab peace initiative of spring 2007 has added a new dimension to the search for a comprehensive peace concept. The Middle East Quartet would be well advised to take the Arab League on board and take their new commitment to a comprehensive peace order in the Middle East seriously.

The European Union has been taken more seriously by the United States – and also by Israel – since it has enhanced its robust presence in the region since 2006. At the request of Israel, the European Union has been securing the Gaza border in Rafah since early 2006 (European Border Assistance Mission, EUBAM). With the deployment of about 6,000 European soldiers in Southern Lebanon and in the coastal waters between Lebanon and Israel in 2006, the European Union has become a key player in the Middle East conflict.

The Middle East conflict is inextricably linked to and overshadowed by the rise of Iran as a regional power. The Iranian nuclear ambition has met Western concern and helplessness. Iran's policy has changed the power equation in the Broader Middle East and will continue doing so. Western reactions will remain obfuscated and limited as long as the original Middle East conflict cannot be resolved and taken off the global agenda. No matter the outcome of the specific issues, the Broader Middle East will remain the most difficult region for the United States and the European Union to project their partnership and global role. In order to achieve peace and stability, freedom and prosperity in the Broader Middle East, the US and the EU will have to map out the future for the region in cooperation with all moderate forces in the Arab world. They may try to apply certain experiences from their successful past, most notably the idea of

77 For the context see Musu, Costanza, and William Wallace, "The Middle East: Focus of Discord?," in: Peterson, John, and Mark A. Pollack (eds.), *Europe, America, Bush: Transatlantic Relations in the Twenty-first Century*, op.cit: 99-114.

a multidimensional (and, of course, multilateral) approach to the evolution of a comprehensive peace order.[78]

Beyond the Broader Middle East, the European Union and the United States are increasingly confronted with the painfully unsettled agenda of Africa's development. Africa, after all, is Europe's immediate neighboring continent. Africa cannot be neglected any longer without unpleasant repercussions for Europe itself, including the effects of illegal migration and the spreading of crime. In a sense, Africa as much as the Broader Middle East, are not really "out of area" for Europe. They form an integral element in the shaping of Europe's future.

The term "out of area" began its career as a technical description of engagements of the Atlantic Alliance outside the territory of its partner countries covered by the NATO Treaty. In its variant "out of area or out of business" the term has become an American slogan for judging the strategic competence and readiness for action of the European Union.[79] In historical perspective, "out of area" differences have been the longest standing disputes of the Atlantic civilization. Spanish and Portuguese colonialism in Latin America was followed by the global outreach of Great Britain and France, the Netherlands and Belgium, and belatedly Germany and Italy. After the independence of the Latin American republics following the defeat of Napoleon in the early nineteenth century, the Monroe Doctrine of 1823 declared US dominance over the affairs in the Western hemisphere. Latin America fell under the strategic control of the US. Interventions occurred whenever American interests were at stake. The claim of the United States in the seventeenth century to gain independence from colonial and oppressive European states was followed by genuine American imperialism in the nineteenth century: Haiti, Puerto Rico, Cuba, Guam, the Philippines, "Gun Boat Diplomacy" toward Japan, China, and Korea – the list of imperial American power projections and colonial adventures is substantially shorter than the list of European colonial expansions, nevertheless it exists. Woodrow Wilson's insistence on national self-determination came as a liberating support to the colonized people and the ethnic minorities in multi-ethnic empires in Europe. Yet American power projections did not vanish from the surface of the earth after his the Fourteen Points of his post-war program had been outlined.

Decolonization of the twentieth century has correctly been perceived as the shrinking of Europe's global power. Although this is by and large true, Europe's influence in its former colonies and its interest in their development has not vanished. But the notion and content of power has changed in both directions. Most post-colonial

78 See Kühnhardt, Ludger, *System-Opening and Co-Operative Transformation of the Broader Middle East: A New Trans-Atlantic Project and a Joint Euro-Atlantic-Arab Task*, EUROMESCO Papers No.26, Lisbon: Euro-Mediterranean Study Commission, 2003; Marchetti, Andreas (ed.), *The CSCE as a Model to Transform Western Relations with the Broader Middle East*, ZEI Discussion Paper C 137, Bonn: Center for European Integration Studies, 2004.

79 See Gompert, David, and F. Stephen Larrabee (eds.), *America and Europe: A Partnership for a New Era*, Cambridge: Cambridge University Press, 1998.

elites of the first generation had been educated in Europe and their political socialization manifested European concepts more than anything else. Their new states followed stages of sovereignty not so alien to the internal evolution in Europe itself. The rise of the nation state in the name of national sovereignty, the quest for popular sovereignty and democracy, the antagonism between national integration and political pluralism, and finally the ongoing migration pattern toward the former "colonial centers" linked Europe again with its former colonies, often with growing approval by the indigenous population.[80] Since the beginning of European integration, a new relationship between European countries and their former colonies was part of the evolving European process. Europe's strategic interest became ever more focused, promoting regional cooperation and, wherever possible, integration across the Third World. Moreover, the European Union is the largest donor of development aid to countries in Asia, Africa, and Latin America and often the leading investor in their emerging markets.

The US filled the power vacuum European countries had left "out of area" with their own strategic, military, political and humanitarian presence. The US started its Indochina involvement in 1954 with the participation at the Geneva Conference following French defeat in Dien Bien Phu. Also in 1954, a US-inspired coup overthrew the Mossadeq government in Iran, which started the US presence in a region that formerly belonged to the British sphere of influence. The fall of the Shah in 1979 changed America's strategic position in the Gulf region. Saudi-Arabia became America's most important ally – until "9/11." Since the days of the Suez crisis and intensified with the Arab-Israeli War of 1973, the US has become the dominant external power in the Middle East with strong protective ties to Israel, but also with strong ties to some of the other countries; Egypt and Jordan receive more military aid than any other country in the world except for Israel. European political, and moreover military, influence has shrunk with the withdrawal of troops from the Middle East, from Indochina, from the Indian subcontinent and from many places in Africa – although France maintained its post-colonial big power presence in sub-Saharan Africa as long as it could. With the emerging Common Foreign, Security and Defense Policy of the EU it is not without conceptual reason, historical foundation or political purpose that the European Union is beginning to again expand the projection of its power – both geographically and in terms of instruments and goals.[81] The test case for Europe's global role in the twenty-first century will all in all be in regions where Europe once used to execute colonial interests. In the twenty-first century, Europe returns to global presence. As the European Union, Europe's interests are defined by peace, partnership and development through good governance, by the promotion of rule of law, democracy

80 See Kühnhardt, Ludger, *Stufen der Souveränität: Staatsverständnis und Selbstbestimmung in der Dritten Welt*, Bonn: Bouvier, 1992.

81 See Thiele, Ralph D., "Projecting European Power: A European View," in: Brimmer, Esther (ed.), *The EU's Search for a Strategic Role: ESDP and Its Implications for Transatlantic Relations*, Washington D.C.: Center for Transatlantic Relations, 2002: 67-82.

and regional integration. This is altogether a very different approach and agenda from past projections of European-ness around the world.

Defining the "terms of engagement"[82] on these matters through a continuous transatlantic bargain is without alternative if the US and the EU want to manage global affairs as each other's most important partner during the twenty-first century. US power projection will remain necessary, irreplaceable and inevitable, yet the US needs partners, as became painfully evident not only after the military defeat of Saddam Hussein in Iraq in 2003. On the other hand, the EU, driven by its experience that favors non-military solutions to resolve conflicts and by its genuine focus on conflict-prevention, will need the partnership with the US if it wants to truly succeed in most of the world's intricate conflicts of a new era. The global financial and economic crisis that broke out in 2008 added a new dimension to the quest for global order: Emerging global power shifts that were to affect both the US and the EU more than anybody was ready to admit in the transatlantic sphere.

It is the curse of their common past and the logic of their limits that bind the US and the EU together in building and executing a common global agenda. Whenever possible, they will be well advised to engage other countries and their resources, experiences and perspectives. Transatlantic partnership will increasingly be embedded in a multipolar structure of world affairs. Their primacy in world affairs can only be undermined by their own hands, as became a matter of concern after the outbreak of the global financial and economic crisis in 2008.[83] Amidst its Second Founding, the European Union would continuously need the United States as its indispensable and most reliable partner in the promotion of shared values and common interests. Whether this European insight and creed was enough for revitalizing the Atlantic civilization amidst global power shifts, especially related to the rise of China, was another matter. The United States wanted to remain a global power while the EU was still uncertain of what it meant if the EU would also get one.

82 Lindley-French, Julian, *Terms of Engagement: The Paradox of American Power and the Transatlantic Dilemma post-11 September*, Paris: European Union Institute for Security Studies, 2002.

83 See Kupchan, Charles A., *Power in Transition: The Peaceful Change of International Order*, New York: United Nations University Press, 2002; on the immediate impact of the global financial and economic crisis see: Kurki, Kristian et.al. (eds.), *The Great Regression?: Financial Crisis in the Age of Global Interdependence,* Helsinki: The Finnish Institute of International Affairs, 2009.

VII. Globalization and the Changing Rationale for European Integration

1. Buzzwords as Moving Targets with Limited Explanatory Capacity

Any perusal of the social science literature reveals that "globalization" has become the most important buzzword of the early twenty-first century. To understand and define the current path of the world, scholars seem to assess the processes of globalization as the main driving force of the newly emerging world order.[1] Economists reinforce this assumption of globalization as the most important paradigm of the current development on earth with empirical evidence. Also historical logic seems to lend support to the perspective of an inevitable road toward more globalization, with only the sky as the limit. In the world of politics, more on the left it seems, the logic of globalization is being perceived as the most important driving force for the future formulation of foreign and of domestic policies alike. In spite of the absence of a clear understanding of what globalization truly means and which definition of its character and role can claim consensus, the term "globalization" has achieved greater recognition than any other single word that tries to characterize the post Cold War era.

Although the global financial and economic crisis that broke out in 2008 challenged the deterministic view of globalization as an unlimited phenomenon, usually the term "globalization" refers to science and technology-driven increases in global interdependence and to seemingly limitless trans-border cooperation for the sake of new economic and cultural opportunities. Globalization means the exponential increase in cross-border flows of goods, services and capital and an incessant increase in cross-border exchanges of knowledge. Critics of globalization have described the outbreak of the global financial and economic crisis in 2008 as the end of endless globalization.[2] Globalization is intrinsically linked to an increase in individualization and thus seems difficult to deal with on a political level, as demonstrated by the debates about the "Tobin tax" and other proposals intended to regulate global market developments. Some

1 See Kempny, Marian, and Aldona Jawlowska (eds.), *Identity in Transformation: Postmodernity, Postcommunism, and Globalization*, Westport: Praeger, 2002; Goddard, C. Roe, et al. (eds.), *International Political Economy: State-Market Relations in a Changing Global Order*, Basingstoke: Palgrave Macmillan, 2003; Das, Dilip K., *The Economic Dimensions of Globalization*, Basingstoke: Palgrave Macmillan, 2004; Dinopoulos, Elias, et al. (eds.), *Globalization: Prospects and Problems*, Abingdon: Routledge, 2007.

2 See Sassen, Saskia, and Kwame Anthony Appiah (eds.), *Globalization and its Discontents*, New York: New Press, 1998; Lafougère, Michel, *L'Europe face au défi de la mondialisation: les consequences socials de la reconstruction des économies en Europe*, Strasbourg: Editions du Conseil de l'Europe, 1998; Loch, Dietmar, and Wilhelm Heitmeier (eds.), *Schattenseiten der Globalisierung*, Frankfurt: Suhrkamp, 2001; Sykes, Robert, et al. (eds.), *Globalization and European Welfare States: Challenges and Change*, Houndmills: Palgrave, 2001; Ariès, Paul, et al. (eds.), *L'Europe Globalisée: la fin des illusions*, Paris: Harmattan, 2002; Kurki, Kristian et.al.(eds.), *The Great Regression ?: Financial Crisis in an Age of Global Interdependence,* Helsinki: The Finnish Institute of International Affairs, 2009.

authors have gone so far as to suggest that globalization means the end of politics and thus the end of the established nation state as globalization is unleashing unprecedented forces undermining all notions of territorially-based loyalty and power.

As is the case with all great and thus intrinsically simplistic notions that try to label a whole era, the definition and assessment of globalization will undergo further transformations while its realities and implications unfold. It remains to be seen whether or not globalization will truly define the "Golden Age" of a new global century "beyond modernity," as Martin Albrow has suggested, transcending former notions of time and of space-bound ways to organize human life and society and bringing peace and prosperity, modernization and stability, consumerism and individualism to every corner of the earth.[3] Skeptics have framed the term "globaloney."

So far, the best and most widely spread description of globalization has been provided by journalistic rather than by scholarly reflections of the phenomena involved.[4] This is an indication of the moving character of the target. From all available evidence we know that globalization remains incomplete in its global outreach, contested in many places of the world and challenged in its unique character as far as former experiences or current directions of mankind are concerned.[5]

One should not try to add another definition to the ever-increasing literature on globalization – which in itself might be a symptom of globalizing trends. The most condensed understanding of globalization available in the current academic literature reads as following: Driven by science and technology, a global market place is unfolding, guided by an invisible hand and working to the benefit of all those world citizens ready to accept the patterns offered by globalization and willing to relate their life and work to them. Such a catch-all definition must accept the most fundamental critique of globalization, namely that the market alone does not provide paradise on earth and that globalization therefore is in danger of becoming an ideology, shying away

3 Albrow, Martin, *The Global Age: State and Society beyond Modernity*, Stanford: Stanford University Press, 1997.

4 For example, see Friedman, Thomas, *The Lexus and the Olive Tree*, New York: Farrar, Straus, Giroux, 2000 (rev.ed.).

5 See Fürtig, Henner (ed.), *Abgrenzung und Aneignung in der Globalisierung: Asien, Afrika und Europa seit dem 18. Jahrhundert*, Berlin: Das Arabische Buch, 2001. Besides historians who have studied the transfer of cultures and religions across the continents in former eras of human history, some economists also point to the limited uniqueness of globalization as an expression of borderless economic interaction; see Hirst, Paul, "The Myth of Globalization," in: Vellinga, Menno (ed.), *The Dialectics of Globalization: Regional Responses to World Economic Processes, Asia, Europe, and Latin America in Comparative Perspective*, Boulder: Westview 2000: 23: If globalization ever existed, Hirst argues, it was during the Belle Époque. Several major states had high trade to GDP ratios, and these were not exceeded in the period of rapid growth after 1945 – France's ratio in 1913 was 35.2 percent and in 1973 it was 29.0 percent; Germany's was 35.1 percent in 1913 and 35.2 percent in 1973. Hirst certainly does not analyze the whole picture by only pointing to one single variable and two particular countries. For that matter, even the popularized understanding of the term "globalization" does imply a bigger variety of variables. On other critical aspects the notion of globalization, see Barber, Benjamin, *Jihad vs. McWorld*, New York: Times Books, 1995; Huntington, Samuel P., *The Clash of Civilizations and the Remaking of World Order*, New York: Simon & Schuster, 1996.

from the asymmetries and alienation it (also) produces. No matter how far the processes of global interdependence and homogenization will go, disparities will prevail on a large scale. No matter how far the enormous transformations in communication and the unique spread of technology reach, the number of world citizens who can truly harvest the fruits of the financial markets and trans-border moves of global companies, of scientific and technological interdependencies, of all materiel and immaterial aspects of globalization, remains limited. Some of the debates about globalization seem to be a new variation of the intellectual and ideological quarrels between Adam Smith and Karl Marx and both their acolytes and heirs.

One of the speculations about globalization concerns its implications. Globalization, one analyst has argued, may be understood "as a dialectical process in which homogenizing forces may bring with them a new emphasis on difference and diversity."[6] It is at this juncture that globalization has been linked with Europeanization, referring to the processes of European integration. Peter van Ham has asked whether globalization and Europeanization are parallel processes or parallel puzzles: Does globalization push Europeanization or is it the other way around? The outbreak of the global financial and economic crisis in 2008 has accelerated the need to better understand the relationship between European integration and globalization.

2. European Integration as Forerunner or Latecomer to Globalization?

The relationship between the processes of European integration and globalization is as intricate and complex as the relationship between "globalization" and "Americanization," terms often used synonymously. Sometimes it is said that European integration in itself was a consequence of global developments, if not an early reaction to post-war globalism. The start of European integration in the 1950's cannot be understood without focusing on the role that the United States has played in it. The creation of the Bretton Woods System and the Marshall Plan, the International Monetary Fund and the World Bank were relevant elements in preparing the path to European integration. "The immediate ideas," George Ross wrote, "came from the fertile brain of Jean Monnet, but the constraints which made producing such ideas necessary – American pressure to resolve outstanding postwar economic and political

6 van Ham, Peter, *European Integration and the Postmodern Condition: Governance, Democracy, Identity*, London/New York: Routledge, 2001: 30; see also Wiarda, Howard J., *European Politics in the Age of Globalization*, Fort Worth: Harcourt Publishers, 2001; Roloff, Ralf, *Europa, Amerika und Asien zwischen Globalisierung und Regionalisierung: Das interregionale Konzert und die ökonomische Dimension internationaler Politik*, Paderborn: Schöningh, 2001; Cavanna, Henry (ed.), *Governance, Globalization and the European Union: Which Europe for Tomorrow?*, Dublin: Four Courts, 2002; Barry, John, et al. (eds.), *Europe, Globalization and Sustainable Development*, London/New York: Routledge, 2004; Sweeney, Simon, *Europe, the State, and Globalization*, Harlow: Pearsons, 2005.

differences between the French and the Germans and thus normalize the new Germany and allow it to participate in European defense in the Cold War context – were global."[7]

American scholarship tends to emphasize the US role in laying the groundwork for European integration.[8] From a European perspective, the internal European impetus to reconcile the warring nations of Europe will always be cherished as its own genuine moral rationale for integration. As far as the geopolitical setting is concerned, it is worth debating in which way the origins of European integration were already rooted in a global context or not. As seen from Europe, certainly the oil shock of 1973 had global roots and ramifications, and it convinced political leaders in the European Community to lay the groundwork for a common currency. Inflexible labor markets, welfare state constraints, and insufficient productivity hampered the early realization of this idea, leading to worldwide talks in the 1970's about "Eurosclerosis." In the end, it was overcome by the creation of a Single Market and a common currency. While for Europeans, these developments were logical consequences of an internal rationale, from an American perspective they might be synonymous with "anticipated globalization in one region."[9]

Whether or not this European strife for "anticipated globalization in one region" was truly intentional will remain subject to scholarly debates. Scholarly approaches are often conditioned by the position and perception that one takes to understand the inherent driving forces of European integration. Those who look at it from the outside seem to view Europe and European integration through the eyes of its common foreign trade policy, which represents various national and sectoral protectionist interests. Those who look at European integration from within the EU seem to look at it through the eyes of the *acquis communautaire*: A common European law, supported by the work of the Commissioner for Competition, facilitated the development of a Single Market and continues to shape it through policies of deregulation and market liberalization, along with the creation of common norms. The euro has turned what used to be labeled intra-EU trade into de facto domestic trade. For the members of the eurozone the export share has sunk to around 10 percent of their overall trade, which is close to the export share of the US economy.

No matter the economic focus on the evolution of the European Single Market, it is imperative to recognize that it always has been a policy-induced concept. From its origin, European integration has been a political goal and a policy-led process. The

7 Ross, George, "European Integration and Globalization," in: Axtmann, Roland (ed.), *Globalization and Europe: Theoretical and Empirical Investigations*, London/Washington D.C.: Pinter, 1998:165.

8 See Duignan, Peter, and L. H. Gann, *The United States and the New Europe*, Oxford: Oxford University Press, 1994.

9 Ross, George, "European Integration and Globalization," in: Axtmann, Roland (ed.), *Globalization and Europe: Theoretical and Empirical Investigations*, op.cit: 177; see also Verdun, Amy, *European Responses to Globalization and Financial Market Integration*, Houndmills: Macmillan, 2000; Kokkinos, Theodore, *Economic Structure-Functionalism in European Unification and Globalization of the Economies*, Frankfurt/New York: Peter Lang, 2000.

creation of a common market was the consequence of sector-specific and functional mechanisms aimed at finally achieving a political goal: to bring about peace and a new order on the European continent. Sector-specific and functional integration succeeded, because it followed the logic of the market in an era of ever increasing cooperation, including the use of comparative advantages. However, the European market-building process has been initiated and promoted by political will and political considerations; this explains some of its idiosyncrasies and contradictions. The political imperative does not mean that genuine market forces did not support the creation of a European Single Market. In fact they did, at times even against the creeping skepticism and wavering will of timid politicians. The support of most European business leaders for a Single Market and for the creation of the euro was overwhelming. But it must be reiterated that first and foremost European integration was – and still is – a politically driven process. Globalization, in turn, has been market driven from the outset.

Some of the key characteristics of the strategy to create a European Single Market with a common currency suggest the existence of an inherent parallelism with the processes of globalization. The search for comparative cost advantages, the efforts to support economies of scale and the steady liberalization of markets and labor laws was always intended to project the economic potential of Europe to the global economy as a whole. These dimensions of European integration imply techniques which are complementary to the overall processes of globalization. Nevertheless, the driving principle behind the patterns of globalization and of "Europeanization" has always been different in its most fundamental respect: "Europeanization" was always a political goal, driven by political will, while "globalization" was induced by the market through technological achievements. European integration was based and remains based on the assumption that politics will bring nations and states together. Globalization is understood as a process where the market brings people together. As a consequence of this inherent difference, European integration has always followed a very top-down approach while globalization primarily follows a bottom-up pattern.

Both processes have been criticized for an inherent lack of democratic accountability. As one of the reactions to this critique, European politicians invented the notion of a "Europe of the Citizens." Irrespective of the term, its underlying logic and the efforts to turn it into reality will ultimately succeed in increasing legitimacy and public support for the integration process remains to be seen. Some are inclined to judge the whole effort as populist and as fishing for compliments. As far as the defenders of globalization are concerned, they still have to invent a concept in the first place that could be capable of translating global street protests against globalization into a viable and inclusive goal that can constructively influence the future pattern of globalization.

For academics, the relationship between European integration and globalization might remain a "chicken and egg problem." Ambivalences and disparities are bound to continue, particularly with regard to the political economy of Europe and its exposure to further trends of globalization. To name but a few of them:

The European welfare state will continue to be challenged by the ever-dynamic American economy. Issues of market liberalization – from agriculture to energy and from education and health – will remain a source of transatlantic disputes. They will also be the source of questions of whether or not the EU is dynamic enough to cope with its internal problems of unemployment. This is not to say that EU leaders do not know or understand the problems at the root of the structural unemployment in Europe.[10] But the EU's political economy will have to undergo continuous and probably even stronger changes if it wants to meet the challenges posed by American interests in the application of globalization.[11]

EU enlargement to Central and Eastern Europe has enhanced social and regional disparities within the European Union with lasting consequences for labor relations, disparities of affluence and an incessant search for comparative advantages which in turn will be criticized as "social dumping."[12] The new Central and Eastern European member-states of the EU are not only confronted with internal EU disputes over solidarity and reallocation of resources, they are also exposed to the challenges of the globalized economy. Some of these challenges contradict their needs and hopes with regard to the consequences of EU membership. While they wish to protect their newly established and still developing market economies through EU membership, they are confronted by other emerging regions with strong competitors for direct private investments.[13]

10 Romano Prodi, then President of the European Commission, put the finger into the most pressing European wound: Europe, he stressed in 1999, must find a way of translating competitiveness and efficiency into economic growth which creates new jobs. If Europe today would have the same employment levels in the service sector as the US, the EU would have more than 30 million extra jobs, almost twice the total number of people currently unemployed in Europe: Prodi, Romano, "The European Dimension," *Progressive Governance for the XXI. Century*. Conference Proceedings, Florence, 20 and 21 November 1999, Florence: European University Institute/New York University School of Law, 2000: 8-17; see also Boyer, Robert, and Pierre-Francois Souyri, *Mondialisation et régulations: Europe et Japon face à la singularité américaine*, Paris: Découverte, 2001.

11 See Mueller-Graff, Peter-Christian (ed.), *Die Europäische Gemeinschaft in der Welthandelsorganisation: Globalisierung und Weltmarktrecht als Herausforderung für Europa*, Baden-Baden: Nomos, 1999; Ducatel, Ken, et al. (eds.), *The Information Society in Europe: Work and Life in the Age of Globalization*, Lanham/Boulder: Rowman & Littlefield, 2000; Weber, Steven (ed.), *Globalization and the European Political Economy*, New York: Columbia University Press, 2001.

12 See Amin, Ash, and Nigel Thrift (eds.), *Globalization, Institutions, and Regional Development in Europe*, Oxford: Oxford University Press, 1994; Kindley, Randall W., and David F. Good (eds.), *The Challenge of Globalization and Institution Building: Lessons from Small European States*, Boulder: Westview, 1997; Rodemer, Horst, and Hartmut Dicke (eds.), *Globalisierung, Europäische Integration und internationaler Standortwettbewerb*, Baden-Baden: Nomos, 2000; Bieler, Andreas, and Adam David Morton (eds.), *Social Forces in the Making of the New Europe: The Restructuring of European Social Relations in the Global Political Economy*, Houndmills: Palgrave, 2001.

13 On some of the socio-economic issues involved, see Zloch-Christy, Illiana, *Eastern Europe and the World Economy: Challenges of Transition and Globalization*, Cheltenham: Edward Elgar, 1998; Fernandez Jilberto, Alex E., and Andre Mommen, *Regionalization and Globalization in the Modern*

During the second decade of the twenty-first century, the European Union is going to see more and rather heated debates over resource allocation and the competences for regional autonomy in economic decision-making. It remains doubtful whether the current mechanisms of EU Structural and Regional Funds can be maintained as the main source of resource allocation and as a means to overcome internal disparities within the enlarged EU. It might be difficult to achieve, but the EU is in need of a new mechanism to balance internal solidarity and regional cohesion in economic decision-making with a new dynamics and competition-mindedness to grasp the opportunities of globalization. The EU needs an autonomous source of income. It needs an EU tax.

The more the EU develops as a global economic and political actor, the more it will be confronted with the hopes and interests of developing countries who want a fair share in the overall pursuit of globalization. Whether on social issues, as far as economic demands or questions of cultural identity are concerned, the developing countries of the southern hemisphere are increasingly claiming their proper place in a globalizing world. While for some regions in the southern hemisphere European integration can serve as a model for regional cooperation and integration, other regions are still in the process of "cultural decolonization." They are torn between the quest for autonomous, i.e., non-Western identity-building and their claim of greater economic solidarity from the West in order to achieve their goals of sustainable development.[14] Neither Europe nor the other developed regions in the world can escape the economic consequences and political conflict in the developing world any longer.[15]

The most fundamental question directed at the European body politic is simple and yet irritating: To what extent does globalization limit or even undermine autonomous political decision-making, democratic accountability and the supremacy of law? Is there a different effect of globalization on the individual member states of the European Union and on the European Union as a whole? Given the speed and the primarily autonomous, if not anarchic character of globalization, it is imperative to ask how far any local, national or supranational political entity can tame, frame and direct the path of globalization? The European Union claims to be the answer to the limits of national sovereignty among European nation states by way of pooling sovereignty on a

World Economy: Perspectives on the Third World and Transitional Economies, London/New York: Routledge, 1998; Segbers, Klaus, and Kerstin Imbusch (eds.), *The Globalization of Eastern Europe*, Münster: Lit Verlag, 2000; von Hirschhausen, Christian, and Jürgen Bitzer (eds.), *The Globalization of Industry and Innovation in Eastern Europe: From Post-Socialist Restructuring to International Competitiveness*, Cheltenham: Edward Elgar, 2000; Meier Dallach, Hans-Peter, and Jakob Juchler (eds.), *Postsocialist Transformations and Civil Society in a Globalizing World*, Huntington: Nova Science Publishers, 2001.

14 See Nederveen Pieterse, Jan, and Bikhu Parekh (eds.), *The Decolonization of Imagination: Culture, Knowledge and Power*, London/New Jersey: Zed Books, 1995; Horman, Denis, *Mondialisation excluante, nouvelles solidarités: Soumettre ou démettre l'OMC*, Paris: Harmattan, 2001; Cuyvers, Ludo (ed.), *Globalisation and Social Development: European and Southeast Asian Evidence*, Cheltenham: Edward Elgar, 2001.

15 See Gruber, Lloyd, *Globalization and Political Conflict: The Long-Term Prognosis*, Washington D.C.: American Institute for Contemporary German Studies, 2001.

supranational level. Could this Europeanized sovereignty be hijacked by the processes of globalization before its fruits can properly be harvested?

A case in point is the challenge of migration to the European Union. In the process of forming the Single Market, "freedom of labor" was heralded as one of the four most valuable goals, moral and political in character, economic and cultural in consequence.[16] Since the 1990's, the European Union has experienced external migration which clearly outnumbers the internal migration within the European Union as envisaged by the strategists of the Single Market. The notion of migration within the European Union as a symbol of a post national European identity has turned into a symbol of fear and for some even into an outright threat to Europe's stability and affluence from poor and troublesome peripheries of Europe. This change in the perception of migration poses unprecedented social, economic, and identity questions for the European Union, while at the same time the EU is promoting a "Europe of the Citizens" and its concept of a European citizenship as promulgated for the first time in the Treaty of Maastricht.

Ethnicity – which the member states of the European Union were able to overcome among themselves – has come back as an issue of concern through open borders and migration from outside the EU. With EU enlargement to Central and Eastern Europe, minority matters still prevailing in these areas have been imported into the EU and have become "internal matters" of the whole European Union. But more pressing for the EU is the enormous increase in migration from the peripheries of Europe, notably from territories of the former Soviet Union and from North Africa. Although the issue of migration and integration is also pertinent in the US, it is of a somewhat different character in North America. While ethnicity might be considered a perennial issue in the US, migration has always been linked to the homogenizing identity of America. In the absence of a clarified constitutional identity, Europe is not able to approach the underlying issues of identity, inclusion and difference in the same way as the US. Migration will continue to affect national identities, integration capacities and political parties all over the EU. Among the key players in the world economy, Japan and South Korea are least affected by implications of ethnically heterogeneous migration. While the US is homogeneous as a market and unwavering in its political identity, Japan and South Korea remain ethnically homogeneous with the traditional nexus between nation and state remaining intact. Europe cannot take consolation in either of these experiences as there is no "European dream" into which migrants to Europe could immerse by way of expressing their civic commitment to the European body politic. And long ago, Europe surpassed the homogeneity levels of Japan or of South Korea. The EU must create its genuine immigration policy with an inclusive perspective for immigrants accepted into the EU.

16 The others were the freedom of capital, freedom of goods and freedom of services.

Assessments of the economic implications of globalization on Europe dominate the scholarly reflection.[17] This is not surprising, and shall not be questioned here. Not enough attention however has been given to the political and conceptual consequences of globalization on the processes and prospects of European integration and on key concepts of constitutional democracy. By making reference to two famous books written by Thomas Hobbes in the seventeenth century, it has been suggested that globalization does transform the "Leviathan" into "Behemoth": Globalization could be understood as transforming the autarkic and homogenizing power of the modern nation state, which was described by Thomas Hobbes in analogy to "Leviathan," a monstrous creature symbolizing evil in the Old Testament. Eventually, globalization forces the nation state to retrench. The retrenching nation state no longer capable of exerting all-pervasive power over its citizens and losing its homogenizing capacity was described by Thomas Hobbes in analogy to "Behemoth," the retrenching huge water animal likewise found in the Old Testament.

This argument insinuates that the "winners" of globalization might disconnect speedily from proven patterns of national loyalty while the "losers" of globalization will be excluded from the fruits of globalization without the ability to resort any more to traditional means of national solidarity. Along with the reduced capacity of the old-styled nation state to act, both the rule of law and the mechanisms of welfare solidarity will be undermined by globalization. This argument might be questioned altogether. But it is worth asking whether or not the implied consequences of this perception for the political capacity of action of the individual nation state might include insights into the effects globalization poses to governance in the European Union.

On economic matters, the EU is responsible for about 80 percent of the decision-making of its member states. The question of shrinking capacities for autonomous political action might also be valid in light of the developing Political Union, which will stretch the need for autonomous capacity of action to new policy fields beyond those already established through the formation of the Single Market. The issue is not just about abstract political concepts. It is also one about leadership and the selection of political leaders under conditions of globalization: Will the market outweigh politics and public affairs? What are the consequences for the quality of leadership in public office if the execution of leadership is increasingly more attractive and rewarding in the private sector? Who is interested in public office under the conditions of globalization?

Given the political character of European integration, the EU and its leadership is forced for its own sake to reflect on the needs to make both the Single Market and

17 See Strange, Susan, "Europe's Future in the Global Political Economy," in: Row, Thomas (ed.), *Reflections on the Identity of Europe: Global and Transatlantic Perspectives*, Bologna: Baiesi, 1996: 27-33.

European governance a lasting success. In this context, three aspects are of particular interest as they point to the implication of globalization on governance structures and market mechanisms in the European Union:

a) implication of globalization on the consistency and strength of EU governance;
b) implication of globalization on popular legitimacy and the ability to generate loyalty within the EU; and
c) implication of globalization on the rationale of the European Union.

(a) Many reflections on these matters must naturally remain speculative, but it can be assumed with certainty that the process of European integration will be affected and challenged by an "increasing global exposure," as Jörg Monar has described it.[18] Since the end of the Cold War, Europe has been confronted with a growing demand to increase its international posture. Many actors and observers from within the European Union have stressed the need for a stronger international role of the EU. Challenges from the outside, such as the conflicts in Southeast Europe, but also the evolution of the international trade regime, have increasingly encouraged the European Union to develop a stronger international profile.

The increasing international exposure of the European Union forces the EU to address questions about its political and military will in order to act beyond its own borders. But also the ever stronger interdependence of markets, goods, technologies and even of social developments continuously impacts the scope, the structures and the goals of the multileveled governing processes in the European Union. The European Union is not only exposed to international competition, it also has to make policy choices with systemic consequences on issues which traditionally have been outside of the purview of European integration. This is, for instance, also inevitable with regard to the need of what the French like to call "gouvernance économique": A sustainable euro is not feasible if it is not coupled with a governance system on economic and fiscal matters that echoes tested and proven structures of economic governance within the traditional nation state. Another case in point is education, formerly a taboo for EU regulation. The prerogatives of national cultural identity, federal autonomy and the skepticism about a European education policy have been strong barriers against a visible European Union profile in this policy field. Since the promulgation of the failed Lisbon Strategy of 2000 – and repeated with the strategy "Europe 2020" in 2010 – it has been recognized that the EU should at least coordinate matters of education, developments of curricula and education structures within the EU.[19] The EU has not done enough by

18 Monar, Jörg, "The Future of European Governance," in: von der Gablentz, Otto, et al. (eds.), *Europe 2020: Adapting to a Changing World*, Baden-Baden: Nomos, 2000: 23.

19 See Chisholm, Lynne, "The Educational and Social Implications of the Transition to Knowledge Societies," in: von der Gablentz, Otto, et al. (eds.), *Europe 2020: Adapting to a Changing World*, op.cit: 75-89; Reding, Viviane, *Die Rolle der EG bei der Entwicklung Europas von der*

these standards. Methods of benchmarking have been introduced in order to encourage learning processes on the basis of positive experiences in the education system of other EU partner societies. The standardization of academic degrees in the EU along the line of US norms (the Bologna Process has initiated BA and MA degrees as standard university degrees across the EU) has introduced the first elements of competition and openness in the European education market. This standardazitation has been widely critized for being overly bureaucratic and destroying the academic freedom necessary to combine creativity in research and solidity in teaching.

The most worrying fact remains: An increasing brain drain makes young Europeans leave for the US. There they find the best possible research universities in the world and often an attractive entrance into the job market. Europe is losing its future if it cannot reverse the trend by which almost 80 percent of young European scholars who have done their PhD in the US do not return to Europe. Europe has to dig deeper than changing degree labels and structures. Ultimately, the European Union's education debate has to reevaluate its anthropology as far as the pedagogical norms – from kindergarten standards to education aspirations at the tertiary level – are concerned, if it wants to properly tap the full potential of its children in the age of globalization and if it wants to remain attractive for the brightest of its young adults. Europe needs to offer them opportunities and encourage the development of their talents. This must become the most important matter on the domestic political agenda of the EU.

The European governance debate on this and related matters will continuously oscillate between the advocates of autonomous decision-making on the national or regional or even local levels and those who favor a stronger framework set by the European Union. If Europe wants to develop consistent responses to the quest for a stronger global role, it requires governance mechanisms capable of strengthening and projecting Europe's political choices and strategic decisions in all fields relevant for the formation of the future societies in Europe, including education and research.

So far, the European debate on these matters has been limited by an artificial divide between those who favor centralized concepts of policy-formation and those who ardently support decentralized solutions, rooted in Europe's diversity. Some aspects of the controversies might be withering away once increased realization will spread about the global challenge posed to all EU societies alike. Responses will always leave room for local decisions on matters of education, and they should always encourage competition among European and American solutions. But there can be no doubt whatsoever that the debate is not just about Europe's competition with the US or Europe's desire to balance challenges of globalization with local solutions which preserve cultural – and linguistic – identities. The debate is about EU governance in so far as the ability of its member states is concerned to generate and exert power of

Industriegesellschaft zur Wissens- und Informationsgesellschaft, Discussion Paper C 84, Bonn: Center for European Integration Studies, 2001.

decision-making and policy-implementation in the speedily transforming world of globalization. The strategic importance of education and research is still to be discovered by the EU: Europe also needs to see its Union as one stretching into a common education and research market if it wants to compete with the best forms of teaching, research and development in the US and elsewhere. Not doing so because of national or regional pride would undermine the strength of the European market by undermining the most critical precondition for its continuous success: the evolution of new generations with leadership qualities and competitive skills ready for the globalizing world.

(b) The more the EU agenda is widening and globalizing, the more the EU will have to address the issue of legitimacy among its citizens. A stronger "sense of ownership" has to grow between European Union citizens and European Union institutions. This issue is neither new nor specific to the European Union.[20] It must however worry supporters of European integration that the increase in European legislation and the tendency to European solutions of challenges posed by the post Cold War agenda has not substantially increased popular support for the basic idea of European integration. Whenever hard political choices are necessary, the majority of EU citizens still prefers to rally behind the structures and the power of their own state. This has been even visible, for instance, in the aftermath of the terrorist attacks on the US on September 11, 2001, and in Madrid on March 11, 2004.

As long as cohesive governance structures and robust constitutionalism are still evolving, the European Union can easily be blamed by member state governments and oppositions alike for being either incompetent or penetrating too strongly into national or regional prerogative rights. As long as EU governance structures are less than optimal in terms of coherence, transparency, efficiency and democratic accountability, it will remain abstract to discuss whether EU institutions claim enough, too little or already too much loyalty from EU citizens. Any legitimacy tests must compare the comparable. This is certainly not the case when nation states, whose powers have been developed and exercised over centuries, are compared to the performance of the European Union, which only began to link its ambition of governance to the desires, hopes and concerns of Europe's citizens five decades ago. Legitimacy is a variable of consistent structures that can claim to truly deliver. If they fail to deliver, legitimacy will be endangered. If, however, they are not yet enabled or mandated to act in an appropriate way, they can neither lose legitimacy nor be blamed for underperformance.

Globalization adds a new dimension to the reflection about EU legitimacy. The impact of globalization on the ability of the European Union to maintain and increase its legitimacy (a process which requires a parallel increase in coherent, transparent and

20 See Niedermayer, Oskar, and Richard Sinnott (eds.), *Public Opinion and Internationalized Governance*, Oxford: Oxford University Press, 1995.

efficient governance) will remain a test case to be answered by the degree of recognition of the EU among its citizens in the course of the next decade. The improvement of governance structures is one instrument to achieve this goal, notwithstanding the difficulties of treaty revisions the EU has experienced twice in the first decade of the twenty-first century. Another instrument is the full use of the potential of European citizenship, originally introduced by the Treaty of Maastricht. This concept has yet to be filled with substance, for instance through the introduction of a European-wide referendum or through better means of citizen participation in pan-European parties, but also through technical improvements such as the introduction of a uniform electoral procedure for European Parliament elections or through an EU tax.

The proof of the pudding lies in the eating. In order to increase EU legitimacy, it is important to raise the awareness among its citizens that the EU is about political choices and not only about the execution of bureaucratic norms. To this end, the EU needs political goals and projects, which require strong governance and facilitate the identification of the EU citizens with "their" European Union. This is the only way to inculcate life into the concept of "ownership," which was originally introduced in discussions about "good governance" in developing countries. But it also holds merits for European integration.

(c) The third and most fundamental aspect affecting European integration as a consequence of globalization points to the very rationale of European integration. The raison d'être of European integration has undergone enormous transformations since the 1950's. The idea of internal reconciliation among former enemies – France and Germany in particular – led to a twofold integration: internally, beginning with the six founding states of the European Economic Community and extending to the EU with almost thirty member states in the early twenty-first century; externally, between the EU and other key players of the global economy who at the same time are the most important partners of the EU in pursuing democratic values and pluralistic societies, notably the United States and Canada, Japan and South Korea.

Globalization is pushing the European Union into a comprehensive global role that transcends the original raison d'être of European integration. Internal reconciliation has begun to be broadened by the search for Europe's reconciliation with global contradictions, tensions and constraints. In doing so, Europe is turning from an internally driven object to an externally oriented subject of world politics. More than ever, the global financial and economic crisis has underlined the need for coherent EU policy- coordination. As Europe is becoming more globally oriented than ever, the EU has to ensure that domestic political concerns will not be neglected.

Good governance, legitimacy and clarity on the EU's raison d'être are intrinsically interlinked if Europe is to play the role the euro indicates and the increasing global exposure of the EU insinuates. This is not going to be a simple and easy process. It poses challenges to Europe's identity and to the internal cohesion between local, regional, national and European interests. It challenges loyalties. It must also take into consideration the ever-increasing role of the media, particularly as long as a European public sphere has only incrementally developing. It must reckon with backlashes and must sustain contradictions. It will have to search for recognition among its own citizens – which turns out to be a new version of a "plébiscite de tous les jours," this time on a European level – and for respect and acceptance among its global partners.

As part of the process to adopt European integration to the challenges and opportunities of globalization, the European Union, must redefine the notion of its "border" and its "limits." While the *acquis communautaire* is defining the internal border and frames the political and legal norms for all EU member states, the global projection of European interests requires a reassessment of traditional geographical restraints on the projection of its scope of action. Europe still has to better learn that borders in the age of globalization are no longer, and certainly not only marked by geography. Borders in the age of globalization are defined to a great extent by the political will to conceive and explore what lies behind them.[21]

To define the notion and limits of "borders" as a function of political will and not merely of geography and territoriality becomes inevitable if the European Union wants to maintain its aspiration as a political driven and political led operation in the age of globalization. In order to shape globalization and not only be shaped by it, the European Union must – on all accounts – develop a global posture, a global role. This means nothing less than a redefinition of the rationale of European integration. The European Union will have to turn from an internally driven process intended to overcome divisions and conflicts within Europe to an externally oriented process intended to contribute to world developments and to influence the future path of the earth by sharing experiences and projecting interests.

Until the mid-twentieth century, Europe has had the reputation of an imperialistic and colonial continent, dominating most global developments for more than two centuries. Two totalitarian regimes and two world wars led to the self-destruction of Europe and to the exhaustion of both its ideals and its reputation. During the second half of the twentieth century, Europe was capable of recovering through means of internal reconciliation, law-based democratization, and Euro-Atlantic integration. The process of internal reconciliation is not completed until the enlargement of the European Union has come to full fruition, ultimately defining the geographical borders of Europe's institutions. In parallel with this endeavor, Europe has already begun to redefine its global ambitions and interests.

The global role of Europe can be based on the best experiences in European history during the second half of the twentieth century. Democratic values of an open society

21 See on the matter also van Houtum, Henk, et al., "Borders and interaction," in: Goverde, Henri (ed.), *Global and European Polity? Organizations, Policies, Contexts*, Aldershot: Ashgate 2000: 9-28.

must be matched with legitimate interests in economic cooperation and political order-building with other regions of the world. While the transatlantic partnership will remain the most important pillar in a global role for Europe, the European Union has to develop a much more ambitious profile for connecting with the other regions of the world in shaping the global agenda. European integration is no longer a purpose and function of internal considerations. The rationale for European integration will increasingly be measured by the degree of Europe's cooperation with other regions and by European contributions to global order-building. In this sense, globalization is not limiting European integration. It is forcing European integration to accept purposes and means that lie beyond Europe's territory.

4. Implications of a Broadened Rationale on Key Notions of European Political Theory

Implications of globalization on the process of European integration do not only affect the material composition of the EU. Implications of globalization are also becoming virulent for the interpretation of established key notions of European political philosophy and theory, notably for

(a) The notion of sovereignty.

(b) The notion of democracy.

(c) The notion of universality and order-building.

Globalization and its impact on Europe's rationale for integration is adding new components to concepts of politics, which can no longer be fully understood if only perceived through the lens of static national experience.

(a) Modern Western political philosophy has been state centric. One of its key terms, at least since the Treaties of Westphalia, is the notion of sovereignty. The traditional notion of sovereignty as developed in Western political philosophy consists of two components: state sovereignty and popular sovereignty. Sovereignty as a concept of political philosophy and legal philosophy has been tightly knit to the evolution of the modern nation state. Thus it developed into the guiding principle for the assessment of the confines of territoriality and the political space. It also became the legitimizing engine for the promotion of participation and popular representation. What began as a contradicting conflict between the two concepts of sovereignty developed into a mutually reinforcing cohabitation: State sovereignty became recognized as an important prerequisite for realizing popular sovereignty. Popular sovereignty became embedded in and preserved through state sovereignty. The weaker the state, the more vulnerable is popular sovereignty; the weaker popular sovereignty, the more vulnerable is the state.

The concept of sovereignty was neither static in the West nor did it remain limited to the Western world. In the wake of decolonization processes, it spread all over the world. In the context of emerging new states after the end of colonialism, new indigenous political leaders were all too often inclined to promote state sovereignty and to neglect the demands of popular sovereignty. Often, popular sovereignty was tainted as undermining the newly won state sovereignty.[22] Sometimes, this seemed to be an irresistible argument in the earlier stages of nation-building in the Southern hemisphere. One might wonder whether the European Union is going through a similar and comparable experience while it is struggling to match its quest for sovereignty with its claim to democracy.

Normally, the issue of sovereignty in the context of European integration is discussed by mirroring established Western notions of state sovereignty and popular sovereignty as prerogatives of the nation state with the efforts to pool sovereignty on the supranational level of the EU. European integration runs counter to proven notions of state sovereignty while at the same time it is criticized for being unable to generate and preserve the inherent democratic values of popular sovereignty. While the EU, say the critics, undermines state sovereignty, it cannot deliver sufficient popular sovereignty either. If at all, European integration can therefore only yield legitimacy as long as it is revitalizing the strength of the nation states as its constituent parts. Some analysts define the success of European integration by the degree with which integration can strengthen Europe's nation states.[23] The evolution of the European governance system, including the introduction of the euro and the search for a European Constitution - but also the increasing implications of globalization on European integration - do not support this state-centered analysis. While the European nation state has not turned into an obsolete bystander of European politics, the processes of globalization and of European integration "have certainly deprived the state of its centrality as an autonomous actor."[24] This has consequences for the concept of sovereignty.

It seems to be growing consensus that the European Union has acquired some form of genuine sovereignty (sovereignty sui generis), at least since the pooling of national economic and fiscal sovereignty. Peter van Ham has described the introduction of a single European currency as a "defining moment which has established the EU as a new European sovereign."[25] As long as the political Union lacks a comprehensive character, Europe is unfortunately still incomplete as a complementary form to the nation states, which have created the European Union and remain its constituent parts. The biggest deficit is not institutional but psychological. Europe has been made, by and large, but Europeans are still missing all too often. The European Union is what its name expresses, a Union. As such, the EU has been criticized for its lack of popular

22 See Kühnhardt, Ludger, *Stufen der Souveränität: Staatsverständnis und Selbstbestimmung in der Dritten Welt*, Bonn/Berlin: Bouvier, 1992.

23 See Moravcsik, Andrew, *Choice for Europe: Social Purpose and State Power from Messina to Maastricht*, Ithaca: Cornell University Press, 1998; Milward, Alan S., *The European Rescue of the Nation-State*, London/New York: Routledge, 2000.

24 van Ham, Peter, European Integration and the Postmodern Condition, op.cit.:100.

25 Ibid.: 104.

sovereignty, for a "democratic deficit". The European Union has developed many elements of a functioning and accountable parliamentary democracy, but has still fallen short of projecting the reputation of representing an undisputed notion of popular sovereignty on the European level that is equivalent with, or even a substitute for, the traditional concept of popular sovereignty, which is still primarily bound to the nation state.[26]

This skeptical view might evaporate over time. After all, the problem with most of the critique on Europe's search for sovereignty is its static character: Critics are inclined to see European integration as a phenomenon without political will and drive, run by murky technocratic ambitions which will always fall short of generating substantial results and legitimacy that can compete with the well established norms and notions of political and legal philosophy linked to the nation state. Many analysts tend to equate European integration with the outcome of the evolution of sovereignty in the context of European nation states with their centuries-long history. European integration can only be on the losing edge of the argument since it is just too young a concept and too unfinished a reality to be comparable with nation states created in the course of a long history. In a certain way, it might be more instructive to compare Europe's struggle for sovereignty with the struggle for sovereignty in the countries of today's Third World.

Neither in Europe nor in the Third World was sovereignty achieved over night. Neither in Europe nor in the Third World was sovereignty consistently based on the two mutually reinforcing pillars of state sovereignty and of popular sovereignty. Neither in Europe nor in the Third World did sovereignty always mean the same. Neither in Europe nor in the Third World was there ever a fixed, preconceived notion of sovereignty which served once and for all its purpose in describing realities or forging new ones. As long as the EU is developing, the notion of sovereignty in Europe will develop with it.

Europe will continue to struggle for both territorial sovereignty and for democratic legitimacy, that is to say: popular sovereignty. Whenever the European Union is accepted as a genuine political phenomenon, it also ought to be accepted that this genuine political phenomenon is producing a genuine political theory and norms of political and legal philosophy of a genuine character. The European integration process is still evolving and has not yet created realities that are forever enshrined and frozen in clear and consensual norms and theoretical assessments. European integration will continue to bring about its own categories of political and legal theory. As far as good governance, democracy, sovereignty and identity-building are concerned, the European Union is as developing as any developing country on the face of the earth.

The Westphalian peace order of the seventeenth century initiated and legitimized a state-centered, territorial based notion of politics and of sovereignty which has become all-pervasive in the modern development of the European state. However, it has never

26 See Siedentop, Larry, *Democracy in Europe*, London: Allen Lane 2000.

been an absolute, as demonstrated by any study of European history prior to the seventeenth century,[27] and underlined by the recognition of the many flaws and contradictions in Europe's application of both state sovereignty and popular sovereignty since the Treaties of Westphalia. Globalization and European integration are gradually eroding key notions of the Westphalian order of territory-bound politics and sovereignty. In the twenty-first century, power will increasingly de-territorialize. It has become an excessively multidimensional phenomenon, which can no longer be linked to territorial and state power alone.

Globalization and its impact on European integration will force a continuous reassessment of the equation between power and sovereignty in the European context. In the past, state and nation were bound together with the state being the administrator of the nation. The existence of multinational states such as Switzerland has always questioned the cohesion of this purist view. Legalization of dual citizenship in European states underlines the possibility that individuals can split their loyalties between two states. The introduction of an EU citizenship demonstrates that loyalties can be split between two vertical sets of body politics. Analogous to the notion of dual citizenship between two nations, the EU citizenship introduces the creation of the notion of dual citizenship between a state and the European Union. As a consequence, citizenship need not be linked any longer to one state and one nation alone. This is an important result of five decades of transformation of the notion of sovereignty in Europe. But it can only be the beginning of an enhanced degree of transnational solidarity among Union citizens.

Most of the Central and Eastern European countries that have joined the EU in the first decade of the twenty-first century still have to fully experience the transformation of the notion of sovereignty that has been a purely Western European experience for the first fifty years of European integration. Mostly, they still tend to cling to established notions of state sovereignty. Way beyond the formal accession to the EU, the EU will remain confronted with the implications of a different intellectual past on the mentality and the political culture of people in Central and Eastern Europe. "Nations and other hallucinations," as Peter van Ham put it, will continue to accompany the path of European integration in the decades to come.[28] It is worrying too that a strong degree of these hallucinations of national parochialism have returned to Western Europe.

This transformation period will not help the EU to avoid reacting to the impact of globalization. Globalization forces the European Union to develop its appropriate role as a global power. One of the dimensions highly underestimated in the scholarly reflection about European integration has been the role of European law, and of the

27 Charles Tilly has counted some 500 more or less independent political units in sixteenth century Europe. Compared to this, the current number of nation-states in Europe indicates a clear tendency to absorption and integration in bigger territories with ever changing loyalties and legitimacies - in spite of the breakdown of the European empires which were thriving in the nineteenth and early twentieth century: Tilly, Charles (ed.), *The Formation of National States in Western Europe*, Princeton: Princeton University Press, 1975: 15.

28 van Ham, Peter, *European Integration and the Postmodern Condition*, op.cit.: 15.

European Court of Justice in particular. Since the 1960's the European Court of Justice has applied and developed structural constitutionalism. Whether through the direct effects of its rulings, through the generally recognized supremacy of EU law, the preemption of national decisions as a consequence of the norm-setting standards of EU law or due to the Court of Justice's judicial review: In spite of much criticism and legalistic efforts to draw a line in the sand – as has been done by the German Constitutional Court in 1993 in its decision on the Treaty of Maastricht by stating that the EU should only be considered an "association of states" and that the majority principle in EU decision-making shall remain limited "by the constitutional principles and fundamental interests of the Member States" – the supremacy of European law over national law has been steadily developing along with the evolution of an ever increasing role of the European Court of Justice.[29] The European Court of Justice has been and remains a strong pro-integrative factor inside the EU.

Political will to properly implement European law might sometimes lag behind, but the tendency seems indisputable: The supremacy of European law is increasing. While the territorial state and its law will not wither away, through European legal norms the EU is adding visible and binding dimensions to Europeanized notions of law and of sovereignty, including the definition of citizenship, the place of migrants in European societies and the role of national minorities in EU member states. Instead of artificially questioning whether and to which extent European integration might continuously "take away" rights and prerogatives from the nation states in Europe and how this situation could be handled with a win-win outcome for all layers of the system of governance in Europe, it might be useful to start the debate by recognizing that European integration as a genuine political form has also brought about a genuine category of supranational legal sovereignty.

Sovereignty has always been a relative and a relational notion which remains tied to public acceptance and legitimacy. Sovereignty came to be perceived as protecting a given political unit from outside pressure and as binding a body politic internally on the basis of shared values and notions of authority and public good. Both categories can be applied to the growing experience with European Union efforts to organize the pooling of sovereignty in more and more policy fields. So far this has basically been a top-down approach, pooling sovereignty together on a supranational level, where it generated value added in functional terms, and where it was finally able to gain the status of "operational sovereignty."[30] This is another way of describing pooled sovereignty as "functional," a term with a long history in European integration theory. Beyond the

29 See Weiler, Joseph H. H., "Community, Member States and European Integration: Is the Law relevant?," *Journal of Common Market Studies*, 21.1-2 (1982):39-56; Höreth, Marcus, *Stille Revolution im Namen des Rechts?*, ZEI-Discussion Paper C 78, Bonn: Center for European Integration Studies, 2000; Arnull, Anthony, *The European Union and its Court of Justice*, Oxford: Oxford University Press, 2003.

30 See van Ham, Peter, *European Integration and the Postmodern Condition*, op.cit.: 99.

classical literature on integration concepts, political philosophy might also take note of some findings and categories of recent international relations theory. Robert O. Keohane, one of the pundits in this field, has stated that sovereignty in modern international politics "is less a territorially defined barrier than a bargaining resource for a politics characterized by complex transnational networks."[31] It might be problematic to view European integration purely through the eyes of international relations theory, but it is appropriate for various academic disciplines to take note of each other's findings as much as European integration scholars within Europe have to deal with the perceptions and deliberations of their colleagues from outside of Europe.

The European Union consists of supranational, intergovernmental, subnational and cross-societal elements and modes of governance. European Parliament, European Court of Justice, European Commission, European Council, European Central Bank, Europol, Committee of the Regions, Committee of Economic and Social Affairs – no matter what has to be said on each of these institutions, there can be no doubt that they represent new realities in Europe, transgressing all criteria that forged and legitimized the nation states since the Treaties of Westphalia. The continuous shape of a new reality of sovereignty in Europe can also be seen in the impact on the management of national political institutions. Accumulation of power and the increasing complexity of decision-making on the level of the European Union force its member states to continuously change and adapt to European solutions. European affairs are no longer matters of "foreign policy" in EU member states. European affairs have become a matter of domestic politics in all EU member states.

Without doubt, the European Union has developed into a new and genuine sovereign, demonstrated by the superiority of EU law, by the existing supranational institutions – including fiscal sovereignty which has always been considered a key ingredient of autonomous state sovereignty – and by the complex set of decision-making in EU practice, which is increasingly based on qualified majority voting. The overall system remains incoherent. But it is no longer possible for either legal scholars, political scientists or political philosophers to reject the notion that the European Union has become a unique, yet ever developing sovereign. As such, the EU remains challenged on two accounts to give thorough consistency to this new reality: The EU has to enhance its sense of identity and it has to increase its global profile.

The EU as a new, albeit limited, sovereign has overtaken the formation of proper philosophical notions to sufficiently understand and describe its character. The notion of the European Union as a new sovereign, based on operational – and thus by definition conditioned and limited – sovereignty, in search of constitutionalism, coherent and efficient governance and a global role has to be added to the textbooks of political

31 See Keohane, Robert O., "Hobbes's Dilemma and Institutional Change in World Politics: Sovereignty in International Society," in: Holm, Hans-Henrik, and Georg Sorensen (eds.), *Whose World Order?: Uneven Globalization and the End of the Cold War*, Boulder: Westview, 1995: 177.

philosophy in its own right. It is no longer sufficient to view the European Union through the lenses of a political philosophy whose categories have purely developed with the evolution of the state.

One might also apply the following comparison, recognizing that the evolution of Western political philosophy reflects not only autonomous philosophical reasoning but that it has always been linked to the political development which it both fosters and reflects: The European Union is emancipating itself from the established monopoly of state sovereignty in as much as Marsilius of Padua has reflected about the emancipation of the secular empire from the church in thirteenth century Europe[32] and as much as Jean Bodin has succinctly described the new reality of the autonomous European nation state in the seventeenth century.[33] So far, the European Union has not yet lived up to the demands and aspirations of the notion of popular sovereignty as expressed in the political philosophies of John Locke,[34] Charles de Montesquieu[35] or Alexis de Tocqueville.[36]

(b) European decision-making, which remains strongly executive-driven, heavy-handed and non-transparent, has been compared to medieval European, and particular German, notions of "policy" measures which antedated the concept of politics as it is known by the modern sense of the word.[37] Bureaucratic, "cameralistic" processes of "policy" were widely established in late medieval and early modern Germany as in other European states. They were intended to implement a "good order" from above while preventing social pluralism, which after all could go astray with a questionable effect on the monopoly of the elite powers.[38] Will the EU remain the postmodern expression of a pre-modern, late medieval organism of statehood – increasingly developing its claims for union sovereignty without living up to the idea of popular sovereignty?

For the time being, no scholarly effort can apologetically make the democratic quality of the European Union more plausible and blossoming than it truly is. There can be no doubt whatsoever about the democratic structures and liberal constitutionalism in all EU member states. Democracy, the rule of law and the protection of human rights have been made prime criteria conditioning accession to the European Union. But on the level of the EU, the situation is less perfect. In spite of many achievements over the

32 Marsilius of Padua, *Defensor Pacis*, New York: Arno Press, 1979.
33 Bodin, Jean, *Les six livres de la République*, Paris: Fayard, 1986.
34 Locke, John, *Two Treatises on Government*, London: Cambridge University Press, 1967.
35 de Secondat, Charles, Baron de Montesquieu, *De l'esprit des lois*, Paris: Garnier, 1977.
36 de Tocqueville, Alexis, *De la démocratie en Amérique*, Paris: J. Vrin, 1990.
37 See van Ham, Peter, *European Integration and the Postmodern Condition*, op.cit.: 112-123; Zielonka, Jan, *Europe as Empire: The Nature of the Enlarged European Union*, Oxford: Oxford University Press, 2006.
38 See Maier, Hans, *Die ältere deutsche Staats- und Verwaltungslehre*, Munich: C. H. Beck, 1980 (rev. ed.).

past decades, the European Union is still not fully consistent with standards of democratic theory and popular sovereignty recognized among Western democracies. It must always be reiterated that EU member states themselves are responsible for this deplorable situation as they are not yet ready to properly democratize the EU and its institutional web. The institutional development in the EU since the 1980's has seen a steady increase in the co-decision powers of the European Parliament. But the parliamentary rights have not yet reached the most critical question of parliamentary rule: the right to taxation. Unfortunately, at least so far, European democracy is representation without taxation.

The growing claim of the parliamentary groups in the European Parliament to put their mark on political choices in the EU is without doubt. But more than political rhetoric is necessary for the EU to properly realize the claim of being a functioning parliamentary democracy. Until now, critics still have the upper hand by lamenting about an essential political vacuum in the EU with democracy and citizenship merely "as political derivatives."[39]

The European Union has achieved much in spite of its daunting process of democratization and constitution-building. Ultimately, the EU will need to encourage its citizens to develop a genuine European "constitutional patriotism." Many skeptics find this perspective impossible in light of the continuous existence of nation states that continue to absorb so many loyalties of their citizens. Others plea for patience and suggest a long-term view: A growing culture of European memory, the psychological effects of European symbols and a continuous legacy of success through integration will not remain without effect on Euro-patriotic attitudes. Notwithstanding the content of EU treaties, European symbols do exist in reality, being known to all EU citizens and across the world: a European flag, a European anthem, a European currency, Europe Day – these are relevant elements for the evolution of a genuine Euro-patriotism. The installation of a European Social Service and of a European Peace Corps for young adults, but also the presentation of one European tea, of athletes at Olympic Games, a European Memorial Day for all War Victims of the continent and general use of European textbooks in schools and universities could have enormous symbolic and substantial effects.

Last but not least one should mention the ever-growing number of European Studies as a new interdisciplinary and transnational field in universities inside and outside Europe.[40] The existence of this relatively new field of studies is yet another sign of expanding realities of European integration.

The search for a democratic European Union is under pressure by the implications of globalization on the formation of the European Union, but the European Union is

39 van Ham, Peter, *European Integration and the Postmodern Condition*, op.cit.: 155.
40 See Loth, Wilfried, and Wolfgang Wessels (eds.), *Theorien europäischer Integration*, Opladen: Leske & Budrich, 2001.

also trying to shape the character of globalization on its terms. Globalization has generated a broad set of regulatory mechanisms – from environmental protection to global trade and from law enforcement through the International Court of Justice to multilateral disarmament efforts or the search for sustainable development, to randomly name but a few fields of application. These are ingredients of emerging global governance. The common supranational position of the EU in some of the critical international policy areas – such as world trade negotiations and negotiations on global warming – might have been the result of intergovernmental bickering within the EU, but nevertheless the EU has been able to come up with a cohesive and consensual supranational position. Democracy might be incomplete in the European Union, but whatever has been said about the potential for global governance, its results so far remain even more bureaucratic and executive oriented than decision-making in the European Union. The idea of global governance will continue to have limited recognition and legitimacy as long as many states in the world remain without democratically accountable regimes.

The European Union is confronted with an internal quest for stronger popular sovereignty, for more transparency and democracy, while the development of global governance mechanisms point to executive, regulatory and thus intrinsically non-democratic solutions. It might therefore be argued whether or not globalization could undermine the efforts of democratizing the European Union.

In spite of all the skepticism on these matters,[41] it might be worth embarking on an optimistic path of speculation, given the enormous drive which the global role of the euro will generate for a more streamlined internal structure of the EU. In methodological analogy to the above-cited assessment of George Ross concerning the creation of the euro – "anticipated globalization in one region" – a future political union in Europe could well serve as another contribution to "anticipated globalization in one region." It would have an enormous impact as inspiration for other regions in the world and as an innovative, in fact unique contribution to good governance on the global level.

The order to achieve global democracy and rule of law remains tall. Regulatory mechanisms of decision-making seem, at least so far, to be the only possible option in a world as diverse as it is in terms of regimes, interests and capacities. If at all, regional forms of supranational democracy might be viable. In light of its achievements and potential – certainly since the introduction of the euro – the European Union should have less reason to be as skeptical of its own future as many academics insinuate it should be. Of course, the EU still has a long way to go to match monetary union with full-fledged political union. But it has embarked on the right path, no matter how ambitious it is. The efforts of the European Union to harmonize regional (economic and political) sovereignty with regional parliamentary democracy, rooted in the rule of

41 See van Oudenaren, John, "E Pluribus Confusio: Living with the EU's Structural Incoherence," *The National Interest*, Fall (2001): 23-37.

(European) law, might very well turn out to have an enormous impact on the global agenda concerning good governance.

EU experiences, notions and concepts cannot immediately serve as model for transnational institution-building in other parts of the world. Yet, they find a cautious echo in several of the regional groupings across the globe. In the same sense, European experiences may also be projected to the level of global governance: It is, for instance, astonishing that no scholar studying the European Union has so far proposed a parliamentary chamber for the United Nations, or at least regular meetings of all Chairpersons of Parliamentary Committees on Foreign Affairs parallel to the Annual UN General Assembly. Could a two-chamber system for the UN not support the notion of global political governance complementing economic and scientific globalization? It could also give a partial answer to the popular critique of globalization being undemocratic and not transparent.

The European Union's search for overcoming its own "democratic deficit" by developing a balance between intergovernmental and supranational aspects of governance – which is to say a balance between the Council as its intergovernmental chamber and the European Parliament as its popular and democratic chamber – might be viewed as a farsighted contribution to a better framework for good governance on a global level. It could help to complement economic globalization with a politically driven framework, which is direly needed to tame the effects of globalization, as they have remained outside of the purview of democratic and political control. As much as this might turn out to become a real possibility, European integration would contribute enormously to re-politicized global order-building.

The idea of a democratic EU has to fight against various stereotypes. Besides the notion that Europe cannot develop a democracy because of the absence of a demos, a European people, another veil, which is being put over the debate on "democratizing the EU," is the constant mystification of democracy as a pure and unchangeable concept. Hardly any debate on the "democratic deficit" in the European Union is taking note of the huge literature and public debate regarding the limits of democracy in any contemporary democratic state. Complaints about shrinking citizens' involvement in politics, as seen by reduced participation and a lowering sense of responsibility for public affairs, complaints about the quality of party politics and of the authority of elected leaders: all these charges have accompanied Western democracy for the last two or three decades. Whenever the question of the democratic character of the EU is being raised, one should clearly abstain from overburdening the EU by either expecting too much or by hoping that the EU might rescue democracy from today's national limits.

It has been suggested that the European Union has developed mechanisms of decision-making which correspond to a system of "post parliamentary governance,"[42] a system of governance which puts priority on the executive and on bureaucratic regulations as the seemingly most efficient and competent way in dealing with modern challenges; not the least those posed by globalization. The argument reflects a static view of both democracy as a concept and European integration as a process. While the role of the European Parliament has been increasing in the course of the last two decades of European integration, national parliaments in EU member states were labeled "losers" and "latecomers" in dealing with the implications of European integration on domestic politics and structures.[43] Likewise, the impact of globalization on local democracy has received ambivalent reactions.[44] While Euroskeptics argue that the role of the European Parliament has gained already too much strength with the broadening of its role in the co-decision-making of the EU, empirical evidence demonstrates the diminished role of national parliaments in EU member states even on purely domestic issues. The same holds true for regional or local parliaments. The constitutional provisions on subsidiarity will hardly be able to reverse this trend. Western-type democracies have, by and large, become executive-dominated democracies.

In a world where a unitary public sphere based on citizenship and state sovereignty seems to be evaporating to the advantage of market power, it is conceptually only logical that a changing notion of sovereignty must also affect the notion of democracy. The state is still the main subject in international law in spite of the changing character of state sovereignty. And democracy remains conceptually tied to a state-based notion of a homogenous "demos" in spite of the realization that market forces have partially undermined purist notions of democratic choice. All this remains true in spite of the fact that the loyalty and legitimacy of today's citizens have multiple foci in any democratic nation state, the European ones included. Multilevel governance, multilevel sovereignty, multilevel democracy: Each of these key notions of political theory has been broadened by the experiences reflected in European integration.

Until now, it has been difficult to include the European dimension of democracy into a multilayered concept of democratic theory. Reflection about the democratic character of the European Union has to take into account the challenge of globalization, which inevitably points to a growing role of regulatory mechanisms to the disadvantage of classical political choices and democratic decisions. In as much as this process is unavoidable, one of the suggestions concerning our understanding of the democratic

42 See Andersen, Svein S., and Tom R. Burns, "The European Union and the Erosion of Parliamentary Democracy: A Study of Post-Parliamentary Governance," in: Andersen, Svein S., and Kjell A. Eliassen (eds.), *The European Union: How Democratic is it?*, London: Sage, 1995: 227-251.

43 Maurer, Andreas, and Wolfgang Wessels (eds.), *National Parliaments on their Ways to Europe: Losers or Latecomers?*, Baden-Baden: Nomos, 2002.

44 See Hambleton, Robert, et al. (eds.), *Globalism and Local Democracy: Challenge and Change in Europe and North America*, New York: Palgrave, 2002.

capacity of the European Union has been to shift the focus from concern with the "democratic deficit" in the EU to concern for the democratic process as an interplay with intergovernmental and supranational decision-making with both parliamentary and executive dimensions. It has been argued that the question should not be "whether the EU is democratic or not, but to what extent the EU can handle the traditional concerns of the democratic process, while at the same time solving the effectiveness problems of EU member States."[45] Traditional concerns, of course, mean: accountability, transparency, and primacy of the rule of law. However, it is not only theory but also practical experience which forms our notions of how to understand their interplay.

In light of the debate about political fragmentation, increased loss of social cohesion in the Western world and centrifugal notions of power, it remains remarkable to note the claim of the European Parliament and those who support its cause to continuously advance parliamentary democracy on the level of the European Union. Supranational parliamentary democracy is indeed a novelty both to international relations and to democratic theory. As much as borders and notions of sovereignty have become permeable in a globalized world, notions of democracy and concepts of parliamentary democracy will have to recognize how much they have been permeated by the implications of a new interplay of regional, national, intergovernmental and supranational decision-making procedures, while globalization is also claiming its toll upon democratic norms. Under these circumstances, the European Parliament cannot be lauded enough as a unique historical experiment, and as a substantial contribution to "democratize" the European Union. The "party families" in the European Parliament are increasingly gaining a stronger profile in projecting their choices into the public arena.[46]

The introduction of formal European citizenship in the Treaty of Maastricht has become another factual ingredient of European democracy which responds to the limited decision-making capacities of the traditional nation states and to the quest for a European identity in light of the global exposure of Europe, which is widening its territory and is deepening its political character. European citizenship can foster European identity in the wake of processes of globalization often characterized as undermining any sense of belonging and identity.[47]

The concept of citizenship explicitly demonstrates that all citizenship is limited. Otherwise the world would not be seeing so many variants of citizenship. Their character and connection to territorial entities has changed over the course of time. It would, therefore, be unhistorical to judge the concept of "European citizenship" purely on the basis of its achievements in the short period since 1993. European citizenship

45 Andersen, Svein S., and Kjell A. Eliasen, "Democracy, Traditional Concerns in New Institutional Settings," in: Andersen, Svein S., and Kjell A. Eliasen (eds.), *The European Union: How Democratic is it?*,op.cit.: 253.

46 See Johansson, Karl Magnus, and Peter Zervakis (eds.), *European Political Parties Between Cooperation and Integration*, Baden-Baden: Nomos, 2001.

47 See Beck, Ulrich, *Was ist Globalisierung?*, Frankfurt: Suhrkamp, 1997.

was promulgated with prospective affirmation and not with reference to empirically hardened evidence about its existing appraisal and acceptance among EU citizens. The majority of them might not know Article 8 of the Treaty of Maastricht, which simply reads as follows: "Citizenship of the Union is hereby established. Every person holding the nationality of a Member State shall be a citizen of the Union."[48] The affirmative, normative character of the text does not mean that its claim cannot, over time, evolve into an empirical, descriptive reality, no matter how strong the skepticism might still be at this moment.

The concept of a European citizenship will foster a sense of belonging and can encourage the notion of "ownership." It needs to be filled with clearer notions of transnational solidarity among Union citizens. As much as the EU reflects new dimensions of the notion of sovereignty and of the notion of democracy, this also holds true with regard to the notion of citizenship. Elizabeth Meehan has argued that a new kind of citizenship is emerging in Europe "that is neither national nor cosmopolitan but that it is multiple in the sense that the identities, rights and obligations associated...with citizenship, are expressed through an increasingly complex configuration of common (i.e., EU) institutions, states, national and transnational voluntary associations, regions and alliances of regions."[49] The problems associated with a European citizenship are mostly of the same nature as they are in regard to the contemporary character of national citizenship. Basically, a citizenship is both inclusive and exclusive. The test for the European citizenship whether or not it can substantiate its claim is therefore also twofold: It has to prove that it can generate a sense of "ownership" among EU citizens and it has to find answers to the development of multi-ethnic and multireligious realities within the EU, not the least as a consequence of Muslim migration to Europe.

Both aspects challenge the European notion of identity and solidarity. Most challenging is the fact that with 15 million Muslims living in the European Union, Islam has become the biggest non-Christian religion in Europe. Beyond many problems of practical integration and outbreaks of xenophobic outcries as expressed in the formation of anti-immigration parties in various EU countries, the question can no longer be avoided whether or not the dimension of a "Muslim Europe" has to be added to the traditional notion of European identity as predominantly shaped by Christian traditions, values and habits. Linked to this development is the even more sensitive question whether a phenomenon called "Euro-Islam" can develop in Europe as long as Islam is

48 *The Rome, Maastricht and Amsterdam Treaties: the Treaty on European Union (the Treaty of Rome) and the Treaty Establishing the European Community (the Treaty of Maastricht) Amended by the Treaty of Amsterdam: Comparative texts. 1st ed.*, Genval, Belgium: Euroconfidentiel, 1999: 47.

49 Meehan, Elizabeth, *Citizenship and the European Community*, London: Sage, 1993: 1; see also Hudson, Wayne, and Steven Slaughter (eds.), *Globalisation and Citizenship: The Transnational Challenge*, Abingdon: Routledge, 2007.

not changing its position on secular politics, democracy and the rights of women in core Muslim countries.[50]

The idea that European citizenship can generate a "sense of ownership," and that the EU might be rooted in the hearts and minds of its citizens, touches on a sensitive albeit more traditional topic. Fundamental for a plausible answer to this question is the relationship between rights, European citizens' claim as much as anybody else in the Western world, and duties, which will become inevitable if European solidarity is to work. One expression of the possible controversies ahead is the question of a European tax, which does not necessitate the need for higher taxes but could. It must certainly create a new and coherent notion of a European tax instead of continuing with complicated notions about the various modes of how taxes are either raised by the EU directly or granted to the EU through its member states. "Ownership" of the European citizens might also imply duties, such as a compulsory European civil (social) service for young adults, men and women alike. Such a Europe-wide exchange program might do more good in promoting European identity, as well as a sense of solidarity and citizen responsibility, than all books published on the subject and all conferences held in its name.

"Ownership" of the European Union by the European citizens will not and cannot mean creating a homogeneous and standardized society. Nothing is further from evolving in the EU. But in responding to challenges posed by globalization and the societal developments within the EU, all EU countries are increasingly realizing that the thrust of the bountiful opportunities and daunting challenges ahead is of an increasingly similar, if not identical character. Although the answers will remain local, regional or national, the debate about the content of the answers can certainly be "Europeanized" in spite of language barriers or nationally confined political and media systems. European integration will increasingly be about the conceptual challenge involved in bridging heterogeneous realities in culture, society and politics on the one hand and common discourses about similar challenges on the other hand.

Generating a Europe "owned" by its citizens is a cultural challenge which requires more than teaching languages, creating European media and streamlining European-wide debates on the same topics in the institutions of the European Union and the member states. It is always easier to do so as long as the challenge is of an external nature. It will become increasingly difficult if the challenge implies that established patterns of local or national interest representation have to be changed. A new order of competencies between the EU, its member states and the regions within these member states, will enhance accountability and transparency, while at the same time defining the

50 See Al Sayyad, Nezar, and Manuel Castells (eds.), *Muslim Europe or Euro-Islam: Politics, Culture, and Citizenship in the Age of Globalization*, Lanham: Lexington Books, 2002.

scope of political mandates for each level of the EU governance system in a better way, always in line with the famous notion of "subsidiarity."[51]

The EU has been challenged to complete its internal order-building if it wants to cope with the swift developments and the apolitical character of market lead globalization. The European Union can only live up to this challenge by increasing its focus on what is primarily needed: not a consistent theory of post national political philosophy but an efficient, democratic and transparent structure of governance, not discourse, but decision, not debate, but action. Whenever the EU succeeds, it will also redefine the theoretical notions we have about politics in Europe.[52]

(c) The necessary responses of the European Union to globalization are also impacting the notion of order-building as it has evolved in Europe's intellectual history. In the past, the notion of "order-building" has been understood as building a European order. Since the creation of the modern state system, Europe was its own prime focus. Variations of a state-centric search for balance of power determined Europe's history, its political and legal evolution and the intellectual reflection about it.

In the final analysis, colonialism and imperialism were also functions of the internal European struggle for power and hegemony. Europe's ambitions were projected globally, but they remained their own prime focus of interest for the European colonial states; the impact of colonial glory on the intra-European posturing for power was more relevant than colonialism itself. Bismarck, when being asked to engage more in African affairs, pointed to a European map as "his Africa." This was more than the specific reaction of the German latecomer to colonialism. From the outset, also Spanish and Portuguese, French and British, Belgian and Dutch, Russian and Italian – and hence also German – colonialism were functionally linked to the strife for power and supremacy in Europe. By definition, smaller European nations were left out of this type of order-building. In the end, power politics could neither enable the leading European nations to maintain balance of power among them, nor help them to maintain an unchallenged global role.

After three centuries of a state-centric search for power and many failures to balance it, the second half of the twentieth century has seen the evolution of a truly unique European experiment. Intergovernmental cooperation and supranational integration have developed in an unprecedented way, complemented by the evolution of a transatlantic partnership, which has been substituted for former inter-European reassurance treaties. For the first fifty years of the evolution of this "new European

51 See Ronge, Frank, *Legitimität durch Subsidiarität: Der Beitrag des Subsidiaritätsprinzips zur Legitimität einer überstaatlichen politischen Ordnung in Europa*, Baden-Baden: Nomos, 1998.

52 See also Albrow, Martin, and Darren O'Byrne, "Rethinking State and Citizenship under Globalized Conditions," in: Goverde, Henri (ed.), *Global and European Polity?: Organizations, Policies, Contexts*, op.cit.: 65-82; Murphy, Craig N., "Globalization and Governance," in: Axtmann, Roland (ed.), *Globalization and Europe: Theoretical and Empirical Investigations*, op.cit.: 144-163; Vibert, Frank, *Europe Simple, Europe Strong*, Cambridge: Polity Press, 2002.

order," the underlying premise was to find peace and stability, prosperity and solidarity among former European enemies by way of binding resources, interests, values and goals together in Europe and for the sake of Europe. The post-communist developments since 1989 have stretched the concept of the "new European order" to Central and Eastern Europe. They did not change it structurally. "Order-building" remained Europe centric, although its notions were taken, right from the beginning and if only unintentionally, from the philosophy of Immanuel Kant's essay "On Perpetual Peace."[53]

Kant's proposition of eternal peace requires continuous work and attention. Peace, he argued, must be based on the notion of individual self-realization, the rule of law and a voluntary association of states. His argument remains as universal in its claim as it was when he published his essay in 1795. Europe has applied the basic assumptions and propositions of Immanuel Kant, only two centuries later. Simultaneously, globalization exposes Europe to a new and pressing reflection about the notion of universality, particularly in its connection with the old European ideal of order-building.

With the advancement of technology and science and the enormous increase in knowledge all over the world, concepts of modernity, participation and democracy have become globalized as well. The quest for the universal acceptance of human rights is the most pronounced case of the impact of this transfer of culture and norms. Intellectual challenges to the notion of the universality of human rights, expressed by advocates of cultural relativism, have time and again been challenged and delegitimized by the proponents of human rights on all continents and cultures.[54]

The intellectual debate about universality and Europe's attitude toward universalism has come back full circle to a continent which is showing an increasing tendency of self-complacence about the impressive success in peaceful order-building and reconciliation between former antagonisms inside Europe. Globalization forces Europe to reflect anew about universality as a European call. It challenges Europe to evaluate what in fact distinguishes European concepts of identity from universal ones. It exposes Europe's sense of solidarity to respond to universal demands. It forces Europe to engage in global order-building. It enables Europe to share its experiences with others and to engage in an intercultural dialogue. Finally, it leads Europe to reflect on how much of its identity is European, or how much of it is Western or even universal by definition.

From the days of ancient Greece, Europe was defined as "the other," in alternatively to its peripheries and neighbors. The dichotomy between the Greeks and the Persians, as narrated by Herodotus, the father of European historiography, has remained a *leitmotif* for Europe's definition of its Self against other regions, cultures and countries in the

53 See Kühnhardt, Ludger, *Von der ewigen Suche nach Frieden: Immanuel Kants Vision und Europas Wirklichkeit*, Bonn: Bouvier 1996.

54 See Kühnhardt, Ludger, *Die Universalität der Menschenrechte: Studie zur ideengeschichtlichen Bestimmung eines politischen Schlüsselbegriffs*, Munich: Olzog, 1987; Archibugi, Daniele, et al. (eds.), *Re-Imagining Political Community: Studies in Cosmopolitan Democracy*, Cambridge: Polity Press, 1998; Dower, Nigel, "Human Rights, Global Ethics and Globalization," in: Axtmann, Roland (ed.), *Globalization and Europe: Theoretical and Empirical Investigations*, op.cit.: 109-125.

world. It is not surprising that the latest debate about Europe's Self in the age of globalization has been ingrained with a substantial dose of Anti-Americanism or better: post Americanism. For fifty years, transatlantic commonality has fortified the notion of "the West," while the communist order and the states resorting to it were seen as "the other." With the end of the Cold War, new debates about "Europe or America" or even "Europe against America" have surfaced and put into question the notion of a transatlantic civilization.[55]

Globalization is confronting Europe with two important intellectual choices. The first one relates Europe's assessment of the notion of universality to Europe's perception of "the other." Does identity necessarily need an opposing "other"? Does it require, in the worst of cases, an enemy? Already Aristotle has understood that nothing is more difficult than defining oneself without resorting to adversary notions of "the other." As long as Europe tries to reduce its profile and ambition to that of a global trading state, it evades the challenge this question poses. In doing so, Europe is lacking also honesty in dealing with its most important partner, the United States. Criticizing Americans as resorting to overly simplistic notions of "good" and "evil" when it comes to identifying their place in the world and the threats they are confronted with, does not help either. Europe cannot exempt itself by pointing to the US. All in all, to use Timothy Garton Ash' quip, "Europe is an adolescent son rebelling against an American uncle who was himself originally Europe's daughter."[56] Even after diplomatic reconciliation in the aftermath of the bitter disputes between Europe and the US on Iraq, the problem of transatlantic adversity on the formulation of universal order building and norm enforcement remains salient. As much as democracy and European integration are not ends in themselves, transatlantic relations aren't either. In the age of globalization, the powerful US and the not powerless EU have to synchronize their search for answers to the most fundamental question they are confronted with by the rest of the world: "A power for what?"[57]

To assume that Europe's "other" might not be America, but the Islamic world (or at least its radical forces) opens an ever bigger and more delicate set of conceptual questions, which the EU would have to deal with if it were to give in to this inclination. Different political and economic interests among EU member states and institutions on matters of relations with the Arab world, with the idea of anchoring Turkey in Europe, and with the role of Islam in Europe make it questionable whether a genuine and robust European consensus would emerge even on the notion of a common understanding of

55 On the structural links between Europe and America in the age of globalization and thus on their mutual dependency see Pollack, Mark A., and Gregory C. Shaffer (eds.), *Transatlantic Governance in the Global Economy*, Lanham: Rowman & Littlefield, 2001; Brewer, Thomas L. (ed.), *Globalizing Europe: Deepening Integration, Alliance Capitalism, and Structural Statecraft*, Cheltenham: Edward Elgar, 2002.

56 Garton Ash, Timothy, *Free World: Why a Crisis of the West Reveals the Opportunity of Our Time*, London: Allen Lane, 2004: 106.

57 Ibid.:91.

the issues involved and their possible implications. European discussions after the terrorist attacks of "9/11" (2001) have underlined that for many Europeans the two issues of how to deal with the United States and how to deal with the Islamic world are interwoven and might generate highly emotional responses on both scores. Consistency with regard to a European concept of normative universality has not yet been found by the EU, not even in the aftermath of the terrible bomb attacks in Madrid on "3/11" (2004).

On the intellectual level, the search remains difficult as long as the philosophy of postmodernism and of deconstructionism prevails. These relativistic philosophical modes of reasoning undermine the ability to fundamentally understand somebody else's reasoning by denouncing it as fundamentalist already before it has been analyzed in its own context and reasoning. Postmodern relativism is the intellectual adversary of the development of a proactive European concept of universality in the age of globalization. One of the most critical matters for Europe is the question whether conceptually Europe's normative understanding of universality in the age of globalization "needs" an enemy without endangering Europe from undermining the strength of its own identity. If one prefers to negate the thorny question, one must logically accept a much higher degree of involvement of Europe in the search for coherent global order-building.

This leads to the second fundamental challenge which globalization poses to a Europe that wants to be consistent and proactive in the pursuit of "global normative universality." Europe has to make choices about its own readiness to get consistently and strongly involved in the global dissemination of universal norms if it accepts the underlying premise that order-building has evolved from an intra-European challenge to a global challenge. First of all, Europe has to prioritize its understanding of the content of normative universality. In light of the enormous plurality of value preferences, which exist in Europe today, this is no longer an easy task to deal with. In order to act consistent with Europe's claims to universality of human rights, rule of law, democracy and peace, Europe has to focus its scope of action and enhance its readiness to play a global role. Otherwise the critique of relativism falls back upon Europe: In terms of practical political action, Europe will be seen as parochial, lacking sufficient sense of solidarity and partnership, and unwilling to accept the use of force as the last resort to reestablish peace and stability. In intellectual and moral terms, to talk universally, but to act only regionally, is equivalent to intellectual and moral abdication.

Europe has no choice but to develop a stronger, comprehensive and consistent, multidimensional and proactive global role if it wants to maintain credibility with its charge that norms of moral political behavior ought to be universal. Immanuel Kant's notion of peace exposes Europe finally to the challenge of a global role, which the era of globalization makes both possible and inevitable.

So far, Europe's contribution to universal order-building has been most visible in the regulatory work which has been done to organize global trade and the norms it is based upon. The creation of the World Trade Organization with its mechanism of arbitration has demonstrated Europe's ability to contribute to universal order-building under conditions of self-interest. Whether this can also be achieved in the fields of politics and law remains to be seen. Most difficult to identify is Europe's answer to all possible variations of global disorder which might imply the use of force and subsequent peace building in order to reinvigorate failed states.[58]

Practically, this conundrum can only be resolved by the complete introduction of majority voting in European Union's Foreign and Security Policy. Intellectually, the task remains much more difficult than finding politically workable solutions. In the final analysis, it would require both the citizens and the member states of the European Union recognize the EU's legitimate right to exercise global powers in all respects. This is an intellectual task for which the current European debate is still too narrow. And doubt about the capacities of political leadership in Europe might prevail, even if the EU were mandated to truly and comprehensively act globally on all possible accounts. The inability so far to create a common EU representation on the Security Council of the United Nations is one strong indication of this fact.

Instead of becoming a truly global power, Europe might be more active and outspoken in the years to come in promoting supranational and intergovernmental regionalism along the lines of the EU model. The existing efforts in the ASEAN region, in the MERCOSUR, in the Gulf region, in South Asia and Southern Africa, in the Andean region and in Central America point to the potential. At the same time, the quest for global regionalism remains vague and based on different assumptions of the future character of the states involved, about the relevance of institution-building and constitution-building and of course about the capacity and the resources to learn from European experiences in regional order-building under completely different circumstances.[59] A case in point is the Middle East, where ideas about functional-sectoral integration of the economies have been floating around for years in order to stop the enmity and violence between Israelis and Palestinians. But can a concept based on the experience with the Franco-German tandem as engine of regional cooperation and integration work in the Middle East? What would it require to work? Who would monitor it? These questions link Europe's potential for sharing experiences about regional order-building with Europe's will to participate in global order-building. As partner of the Road Map toward a two-state solution for the Middle East conflict, the European Union is already involved in the Middle East, albeit with a very subdued profile given the proximity to the region and relative to Europe's interest in favoring a peaceful solution in the region. The EU must reassess its potential and will to project itself as a regional pacifier in the Middle East if its claim to play a global role in the

58 See Cooper, Robert, *Breaking of Nations: Order and Chaos in the Twenty-First Century*, London: Atlantic Books, 2003.

59 See Schirm, Stefan A., *Globalization and the New Regionalism: Global Markets, Domestic Politics and Regional Co-Operation*, Cambridge: Polity Press, 2002.

twenty-first century is to be convincing, meaningful and substantial. Failing to do so cannot be blamed on the dominance of the US or the contrasting interests of the regional actors alone.

The Middle East is but one strong and globally visible test-case for Europe's comprehensive commitment to the universality of order-building. The delicate geopolitical situation in North East Asia must be mentioned as the other matter of global concern that should activate a stronger EU readiness to offer its good services and experiences. To this day, the EU is limited in exercising the role many expect it to play because of the limited will of EU member states. Still, this is a stronger internal wall than any of the hopes and fears alike by which the prospective future global role of Europe is perceived around the world.[60]

5. Globalizing Europe as Answer to a Globalized World

By definition, the European Union is a contribution to the building of world order. Whether it can contribute also to intellectual notions and norms, to key concepts about our understanding of universal order-building depends ultimately upon the ability of the European Union to generate a consistent and widely accepted set of new key notions of political theory on permeable sovereignty, multilevel governance and democracy, on ownership and citizenry, and on a commitment to make universal notions of law, peace, and freedom viable. Inside the European Union, the reaction to this challenge remains ambivalent. This coincides with an ambivalent attitude of many Europeans to market-driven globalization. So far, globalization has had a stronger impact on the European economy, and on culture and lifestyle in Europe than on the intellectual discourse about the role of politics under conditions of market-driven globalization. Europe has not yet fully grasped the meaning of globalization as both an opportunity and a challenge to preconceived European notions of state-market relations between political power and the power of the market.[61] Over the past decades, the member states of the European Union have significantly liberalized their economies, but they remain in general much more state-centric than, for example, the United States. While globalization is often perceived as a threat to local cultures, the majority of Europeans is however not in general support of the anti-globalization movement often associated with European skepticism about globalization. According to special Eurobarometer polls taken in 2003 (that is to say before EU enlargement to include Central and Eastern Europe), 64 percent of EU citizens are "rather" (51 percent) or even "totally" in favor (13 percent) of globalization, while only 28 percent were "rather" (20 percent) or "totally" (8)

60 See Goldmann, Kjell, *Transforming the European Nation-State: Dynamics of Internationalization*, London: Sage Publishers, 2001.

61 See Kierzkowski, Henryk, (ed.), *Europe and Globalization*, New York: Palgrave, 2002.

opposed. The strongest opposition to globalization was expressed in Greece and Austria; the strongest support for it was found in the Netherlands, in Germany, and in Ireland. A solid number of EU citizens felt that their country's economy was properly equipped to encounter the global economy (41 percent). A third of EU citizens (31 percent) argued that their country's economy was rather "too closed" compared with 20 percent arguing that their country's economy was "too open" to the effects of globalization. The vast majority of EU citizens (62 percent) expressed believe that globalization can be effectively controlled and regulated, compared with 35 percent who did not think so. In fact, a large majority of EU citizens (56 percent) believes that globalization needs more regulation. 61 percent of EU citizens expressed confidence that the European Union – better than their own country - will guarantee that globalization moves into the right direction, compared with 34 percent not having this confidence in the EU's capacity to act.[62]

The long-term effect of the global financial and economic crisis that hit the world at the end of the first decade of the twenty-first century remains to be seen. The conceptual debate was going on whether state failure or market failure had been the root cause of the worst crisis since the 1930s. It remained subject to historical judgement whether this was a crisis of globalization or a crisis in globalization. The huge rescue packages organized by EU member state governments were perceived as a sign of re-emerging state power across Europe. Whether or not this would truly be a long-term trend or not was to be seen. In any case, nobody could deny any longer that globalization and European integration have become parallel processes, remaining dynamic in their own right and mutually broadening the other's agenda and understanding of the world we are heading for. In the midst of new uncertainties of universal order-building, the unleashing of market forces and a crisis of political authority, Europe is challenged with nothing less than the need to reinvent itself as a global player consistent with the challenge, and coherent with its own standards and claims, aspirations and interests. Europe should do this out of enlightened self-interest. It will be the only workable response to globalization that will allow European societies to flourish.

62 European Union, European Commission, *Flash Eurobarometer 151b*, November 2003, http://ec.europa.eu/public_opinion/flash/FL151bGlobalisationREPORT.pdf.

VIII. The Global Proliferation of Region-Building

1. Assessing Stages: From Decolonization to Globalization

European integration has gained global interest. Increasingly, European integration is perceived as a source of inspiration for processes of regional cooperation and integration around the world. The European integration experience cannot be used as a simple "role model" to be emulated under contingent conditions. On the other hand, symmetric developments in other parts of the world are not a necessary precondition to prove the global relevance of European integration experiences. European integration does not serve as a static model that can be proliferated: Neither European sources nor goals and neither European governance structures nor institutions can be found as identical copies elsewhere in the world. Yet, growing reference is made in other parts of the world to the European integration experience as other schemes of cooperation and integration are being reexamined, streamlined and strengthened. In the course of the twenty-first century this shared experience with regional integration will reflect the global proliferation of regional integration schemes on regional developments, governance structures, cultural identities and – last but not least – world order-building.

The global proliferation of regional integration coincides with a more assertive global role of the European Union. Through EU policies, the European Union supports regional integration efforts elsewhere. Since the late twentieth century, EU policies and instruments of cooperation with other regions have broadened: from trade to economic integration (EU relations with the Gulf Cooperation Council), from developmental aid to association and political cooperation (EU relations with MERCOSUR, the Andean Community and the Central American Integration System), from trade to development and governance issues (EU relations with the partner countries of the Cotonou Agreement in Africa, the Caribbean and the Pacific), from economics to a preferential strategic partnership (EU relations with ASEAN). None of these developments are static or have achieved final results. Over time, some processes of bi-regional cooperation might become more stable, sustainable and successful than others. Some of them are responses to past experiences with bi-regional cooperation or even a remote echo of colonial and post-colonial memories. Others are a reaction to "globalization" and the global role of the United States. Most relations between the European Union and regional integration schemes elsewhere are asymmetrical, with the EU being more politically integrated, more law-based and economically much stronger than most other forms of regional integration. In this context it is also revealing that the two regions with the lowest degree of regional integration efforts – Northeast Asia and the Broader Middle East – are the most difficult geopolitical regions in contemporary world affairs.

And they are the source of many differences, if not controversies between the European Union and the United States.

Academic literature about the global proliferation of regionalism is confusing because of its use of confusing definitions of regionalism. “Open regionalism,” “new regionalism,” “regional cooperation,” “regional integration,” “sub-regionalism” or “regionalization,” these are but some of the terms used to characterize trends and processes of different structures, speed and depth. Those who compare the European Union with other regional cooperation and integration schemes tend to underestimate the relevance and strength of the political and legal character of the EU: regional integration in Europe is more than economic cooperation. Often, the comparison tends to be too static to the detriment of non-European integration efforts, thus failing to sufficiently take into account the dynamics of the evolving character of integration formation outside Europe. It is not convincing to conclude that while no regional integration scheme outside Europe has yet reached the EU level of supranationality, they are doomed to remain flawed and irrelevant. It is also not sufficient to base the comparison on criteria of economic power by concluding that the economic giant EU is incomparable with, for instance, the Caribbean Community because of grossly disparate GDP rates. It has become necessary to broaden the scope of comparative regional integration studies. Global proliferation of regional integration will have to be taken seriously in light of a combination of two sets of experiences. On the one hand, it is important to understand regional integration as a process of contingent historical circumstances, specific combinations of challenge and response and local conclusions and consequences. On the other hand, regional integration is linked to global trends in politics and economics. It is an indigenous response to exogenous challenges as much as it is a local scheme that might echo distant experiences of others. Comparative global regionalism will be a source of useful and valuable new research efforts in the years to come.

This effort will reflect the growing relevance of integration processes in many regions of the world. Area studies will have to be linked with studies about the relationship between democratic transformation and the evolution of regional stability. Research must also consider regional developments of integration or cooperation in light of specific regional economic, social, cultural, political and security challenges. The global proliferation of regional integration schemes has to be put into its specific historical, cultural, socio-economic and political context. It must generate multidimensional approaches of comparative research regarding motivation, structure, function, scope, depth and deficits of regional integration schemes that exist in the world of the early twenty-first century.

Can we talk about the logic of integration?[1] As much as any other historical determinism, the notion of seemingly inevitable path dependencies of regional integration must be rejected. There is simply no law of history that unfolds in a global and universally applicable form. By the same token, it would be misleading to assume that regional integration could be modeled and made suitable for export and implementation elsewhere. Integration can fail (as happened in East Africa in the mid-1970's). It can also endure divergent modes, patterns and processes. It can regain strength after periods of weakness. At least since the turn of the century, global proliferation of regional cooperation and integration has begun to re-map the world. With the end of the Cold War and communist dictatorships, the distinction between a first and a second World has dissolved. The transformation experiences in post-communist countries have substituted geographical and cultural fixations that existed over decades. Realignments such as the inclusion of Central European countries in NATO and the European Union have happened, but also the revival of Russia's Great Power status as a neo-autocracy in the midst of enormous economic impoverishment, and the reemergence of Central Asia as a geopolitical fact. As the transformation agenda for politics, culture and the economy has developed since the last decade of the twentieth century, also the developing world – traditionally labeled Third World – has undergone transformations of great magnitude. The global proliferation of regionalism renders dubious the very idea of a seemingly cohesive Third World. In socio-economic terms, the distinction between "newly industrialized countries," "threshold countries" and "least developed countries," measured by indicators of human development and criteria for good governance, has long since supported a differentiated perception. With the global proliferation of regional integration and cooperation on a continental scale, the very term Third World must be replaced by a new understanding of the world's continents and specific regions on these continents. Regional integration brings geography and proximity, but also culture and identity, back to the study of world politics and developmental issues.

To understand the global proliferation of regional integration, it is useful to distinguish historical periods in the evolution of sovereignty. It is important to reconsider the two faces of sovereignty outside of Europe as much as this has been relevant in order to understand the evolution inside Europe: sovereignty as state sovereignty and sovereignty as popular sovereignty. To link regional integration with the evolution of the sovereign state is one important perspective. To link it with the evolution of popular sovereignty – that is to say with the relevance of democratic governance and rule of law among the participating members of an integration scheme –

1 Mattli, Werner, *The Logic of Integration: Europe and Beyond*, Cambridge/New York: Cambridge University Press, 1999, on the theoretic and methodological connotations of this issue see: Murray, Philomena, "Towards a Research Agenda on the European Union as a Model of Regional Integration," *Asia-Pacific Journal of EU Studies*, 2.1(2004): 33-51.

is the other important European experience that needs to be reconsidered when embarking on global comparative efforts regarding regional cooperation and integration.

As much as sovereignty – both state sovereignty and popular sovereignty – has undergone different phases in its development during the twentieth century, concepts of integration and experiences with integration schemes have been transformed. None of this has followed universal patterns. But it is imperative to link the focus of research across stages of time, conceptual reconfigurations and impacts on complex regional processes. In doing so, it might be helpful to understand two distinct stages in the relationship between sovereignty and regional integration outside as well as inside Europe.

Stage One: Europe emerged destroyed from the ashes of two World Wars and found itself divided along highly ideological and rigid geopolitical lines. Democratic countries began to rebuild Europe through the mechanism of integration. At the same time, the process of decolonization continued, reflecting causes and effects of Europe's "de-empowerment" in the twentieth century. Originally, the newly independent countries of the Southern hemisphere copied European concepts of state-building based on rigid notions of national sovereignty. In many developing countries, the hope for democratic statehood was challenged in the name of national unity. Often, notions of state sovereignty and claims to popular sovereignty clashed in what came to be understood as the Third World. Concepts for regional cooperation and integration often remained a defensive response to the process of decolonization, if not an element of it. They occurred under conditions of weak sovereignty, both in its state and its governance dimension. Weak economies and enormous social pressure due to high poverty levels refocused the priorities of most developing countries. While transnational cooperation and integration were rhetorical invocations, the prime focus was on state-induced socio-economic development and nation-building. The state was considered to be the promoter of nation-building, and the more its capacities were involved in this process, the more it fell short of engaging in regional cooperation, let alone integration. But in the end, neither democracy nor support for trans-national cooperation or even regional integration was achieved in many developing countries.

During the 1960's and 1970's, Europe was still perceived as a (post)-colonial continent while its new reality of democratic integration was still fragile and confronted by many internal challenges and backlashes. The 1980's, and more so the 1990's, brought about two new elements in the relationship between the European integration experience and the evolution of regional integration in other parts of the world: 1. European integration gained speed and substance, increasingly being rooted in a common European law and leading to the implementation of a Single Market with a common currency and the beginning of political union. 2. The Third World began to undergo enormous differentiations with some regions – notably South East Asia and parts of Latin America – improving considerably. Many developing regions began to reconsider national strategies of import-substitution that had dominated much of the "Third World" during the 1960's. Export-oriented integration into the world market, linked with the use of comparative regional advantages began to prove successful. Most prominently, ASEAN became a case in point although ASEAN integration structures initially did not aspire to the European degree of supranationality. ASEAN proved that stronger national sovereignty would benefit from strengthened regional cooperation and integration that in turn would strengthen the national ambitions of economic and political development.

Stage Two: Three developments coincided during the 1990's and into the early twenty-first century. First, the European integration process became serious, while at the same time the perception of Europe in the developing world changed from post-colonial suspicion to the recognition of the EU as model for regional peace, affluence and stability. The EU's constitutionality will bring about continuous empirical and theoretical clarification and new contestations at each level of agreement. This constitutional interpretation and review will continue to transform politics in the European Union from a sphere of negotiated compromises in elite-institutions to a sphere of publicly debated goals. It will continue to politicize the integration process and strengthen the claim that the EU is a community of destiny. The idea of Europe being a community of values increasingly generates a legal framework and becomes a political fact. The European Union has consolidated its law-based role as the expression of political Europe. This new Europe is perceived elsewhere on the basis of attitudinal changes: The Europe of the twenty-first century is recognized for its will to partnership. Second, geopolitical and geo-economic trends usually characterized as "globalization," coupled with the experience of the United States as the dominant power of the world system, led to reconsiderations of both national policies and regional perspectives in all continents. Third, the fall of communist dictatorships and the Soviet Empire brought about a reassessment of the advantage of democratic governance, rule of law and trans-border cooperation in many developing countries. The conditions for successful development and the resolution of regional conflicts were re-evaluated in light of the European integration experience. This was even the case in Russia and in some of the other successor states of the Soviet Union.

These trends have opened the way to a remapping of the world, based on the characteristics of continents rather than on numerical concepts of a "first," "second" and "third" world. It has led to an increase in regional, continental and global cooperation efforts, to regulatory processes and continental structures favoring free trade and necessary arbitration mechanisms (WTO, ASEM, NAFTA, ALCA, Euro-Mediterranean Partnership). This development went hand in hand with a more assertive European Union encouraging developing regions and post-conflict regions to resort to patterns of integration. Finally, these trends have brought about the reinvention of some older cooperation schemes in various parts of the world, often coupled with a trend toward political and economic integration along the line of European experiences. This does not suggest that the economic success of Europe could immediately be copied by other regional arrangements. Neither does it imply that the European response to the challenge of state-building and nation-building under conditions of democratic integration could be transferred to other regions as if European developments of supranational and intergovernmental integration were an export product. The global proliferation of regional integration does not automatically generate a cohesive multipolar world order. Traditional soft and hard power factors linked to nation states in their highly diverse and extremely asymmetrical distribution continue to shape much of the twenty-first century. Yet, more attention should nevertheless be given to the global proliferation of regional integration schemes, including in transatlantic discourses about the emerging world order. The global proliferation of regional integration is relevant for America's understanding of global trends, although the United States as a country of continental dimensions seems to be largely unaffected by the new surge of interest in and support for regional integration. US interests are primarily defined by the concept of free trade without sufficient sensitivity for the psychological, cultural (including geographical) and political components of integration patterns elsewhere, including the European experience.

New mental maps of world politics and international relations are not the linear outcome of one-dimensional trends, no matter how recurring and strong they might be. The global proliferation of regional integration efforts cannot immediately revolutionize notions of sovereignty, international relations, economic power and patterns of state behavior across the globe. Such an assumption would be unrealistic. The degree of its impact is gradual and long-term. With this qualification, the prediction can be made that the twenty-first century will experience a greater surge of regional integration – beyond the formation of free trade zones – in various regions of the globe than during any former time in the history of statehood. As much as this emulates the European experience with regional integration, it also constitutes a revival of Europe's global role. The success of Europe's ability to share its integration experiences does not depend upon linear copies. The most solid and lasting success for Europe might rather occur through indirect and contingent means of an "experience transfer:" An applied local adaptation of European insights into integration will most likely generate highly diverse integration schemes elsewhere. Yet it may emulate the European integration experience and hence express a new global respect for Europe.

Ongoing differences in the economic and social status across the world's regions have to be taken into consideration. Yet, European integration can be an important point of reference, also for island nations in Oceania whose collective GDP is below one percent of Europe's GDP.

Map 2: Global Proliferation of Regional Integration

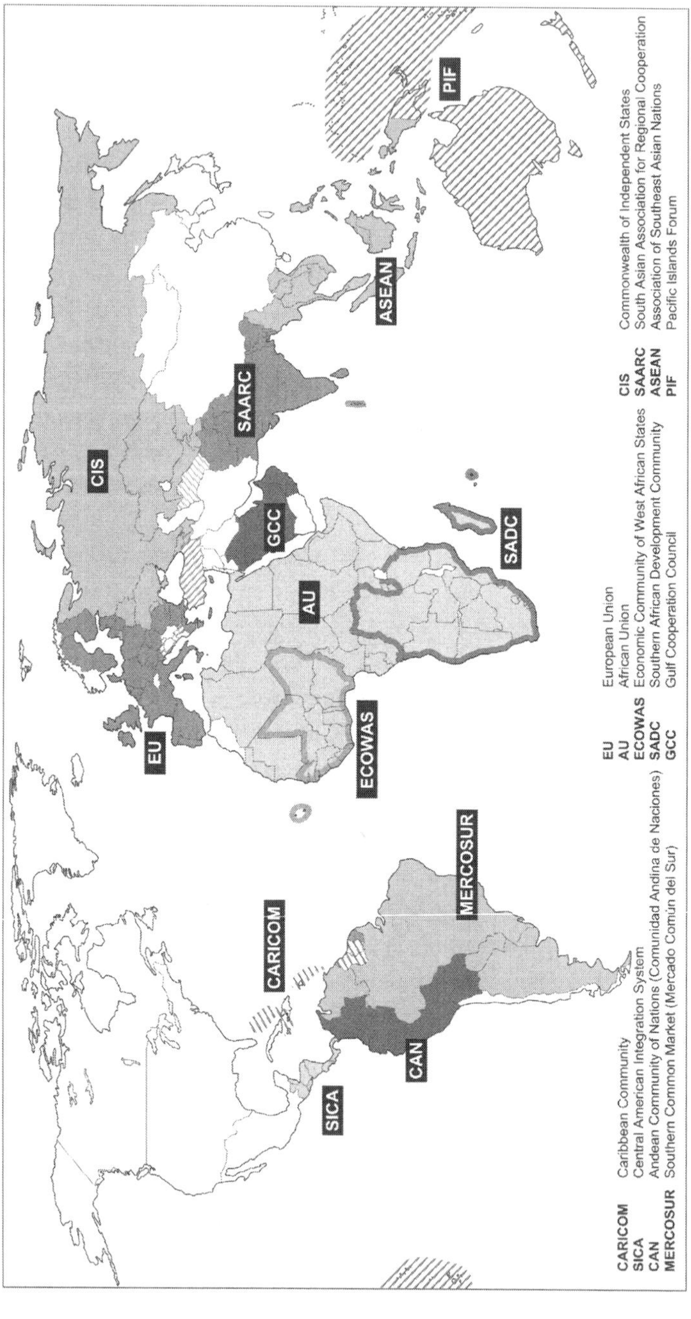

A general insight is valid and noteworthy: As weak sovereignties generate weak integration schemes, anywhere in the world integration can support, if not generate, political stability, socio-economic development and strengthened sovereignty, while at the same time it might begin to forge a new reality of multilevel governance. Empirical evidence suggests that this can be done over time anywhere outside of Europe with similar, yet genuine, effects of multilevel governance, shared sovereignty and multiple identities.

2. An Overview: Region-Building Across Continents

Notwithstanding hundreds of multilateral and regional schemes of cooperation all across the world, this study introduces twelve regional integration processes and discusses them in comparison with the European integration experience. This comparison must be done with caution and in full realization of the fact that each integration approach is different while, at least so far, none of the discussed schemes includes the main dimension that distinguishes the European Union from all of them: supranationality. Yet, structured by continents, schemes of regional cooperation and integration that aspire to emulate the European integration experience include the following regional groupings:

(1) Latin America

(a) Interestingly enough, Europe aside Central America has the longest experience with regional integration efforts. Dating back to the early 1950's, the creation of the Committee of Economic Integration in Central America (CCE) in 1951 and subsequently the Organization of Central American Countries (ODECA) – with the membership of Costa Rica, El Salvador, Guatemala, Honduras and Nicaragua – predated the creation of the European Economic Community in 1957. Inspired by the Spaak Report and the reflection on economic integration in Europe during the early 1950's, but also in view of the fact that Central America had undergone fourteen failed efforts for regional integration since its independence from Spain in 1821, CCE and ODECA laid the groundwork for a successful phase of regional economic cooperation and integration that nevertheless failed in the end. With the General Treaty on Economic Integration in Central America (Tratado General de la Integración Economica Centroamericana), signed 1960 in Managua, the five Central American countries departed from the goal of forming a Central American Common Market (Mercado Comun Centroamericano MCCA), intended to grow into full-fledged customs union with a Secretariat for Central American Economic Integration (SIECA) as its institutional helm. Intra-regional trade increased from 6 million US dollars in 1963 to

1.8 billion US dollars at the end of the 1970's. Sector-specific free trade, the introduction of a common customs procedure leading to a common customs zone, and a joint procedure for dealing with external goods were completed and supported by the creation of a Central American Bank for Economic Integration (Banco Centroamericano de Integración Economica) in 1975. Around 5,000 kilometers of roads were built to improve the infrastructure necessary for a common market. Agricultural products were exempted from customs duties, with the exception of some of the strategically critical goods for each partner country, such as coffee, sugar and wheat. Telecommunications did not lag behind and by the late 1970's, Central American countries managed to build a highly efficient telecommunications system. Inflation did stay below 3 or 4 percent in all of the participating countries and the growth rates over a period of 15 years from the early 1960's until the mid 1970's hovered around 4 to 5.5 percent.

The Golden Age for Central American integration with growth and modernization came to a halt as a consequence of deep sociological changes and subsequent cleavages. They escalated from the "Football War" between El Salvador and Honduras in 1969 into bloody civil wars during the 1980's, primarily in El Salvador, Guatemala and Nicaragua. Uprisings against the political systems and their underlying social orders turned into full-fledged civil wars, coupled with an enormous and tragic refugee plight. The Marxist Sandinista regime in Nicaragua (1980-1990) fuelled political antagonism in the region and provoked US military interventions under the Reagan administration. For a time, regional integration broke down. As part of the pacification process for the region, in 1984 the European Community initiated the San Jose Dialogue with a Declaration, jointly signed by the then nine EC member states, the acceding countries Spain and Portugal and six states of Central America – by now including Panama – in the presence of representatives of the UN, the Contadora Group and the Organization of American States (OAS). This ministerial meeting is considered the foundation of modern European relations with Central America. Political support of the EC went hand in hand with the renewed socio-economic co-operation in the region. Europe claims to have successfully contributed to the reemergence of regional integration efforts in the early 1990's. US efforts in exercising rather hard-power tactics in what is traditionally considered America's sphere of influence contributed to the fall of the Sandinistas and to the reemergence of like-minded democratic political regimes in the region. Parallel efforts of the United Nations and the Contadora Group (Mexico, Columbia, Venezuela and Panama) prevented a spill-over of the conflicts into the broader region. In 1989, the Peace Treaties of Esquipulas ended the most dramatic period in the modern history of Central America.

In 1993, new efforts for regional integration began, largely driven by the desire for peace and the growing understanding of democratic rule as a precondition for security. As per capita income had decreased by almost 70 percent since the early 1970's and poverty had sharply increased (25 percent of the population in Costa Rica, and 70 percent in Guatemala lived now below the poverty line), the pressure of "neo-liberal globalization" and the prospect of the North American Free Trade Agreement NAFTA (since 1990 emerging between the US, Canada and Mexico) forced Central America into new efforts of regional cooperation and subsequently integration. The Tegucigalpa Protocol of 1991 established new institutional mechanisms for regional integration. It was followed by the Guatemala Protocol of 1993. Since then, Guatemala, El Salvador, Honduras, Nicaragua, Costa Rica and Panama, eventually also Belize have formed the Central American Integration System (Sistema de la Integración Centroamericana, SICA).

Institutional arrangements to support Central American integration have mushroomed since then: The highest political bodies are the regular summit meetings of the Heads of State and the regular meetings of the Economic Integration Council, composed of Ministers for Economic Affairs and the Presidents of the Central Banks of the member states. SICA's General Secretariat is based in El Salvador. Its Constitutional Court in Nicaragua has begun to work again after years of being practically closed. SICA's Parliamentary Assembly in Guatemala and its Bank for Economic Integration with branch offices in all five member states of the Central American integration system have been charged with new tasks. A whole set of interregional specialized agencies has been established or streamlined, including an academic organization. As the Central American integration system SICA does not yet contain genuine supranational elements, it has been criticized for remaining too weak to lastingly impact the integration of the region. And decisions taken by the heads of state (450 between 1990 and 1999) were implemented in only 60 percent of the cases.[2]

Nevertheless, certain progress is noteworthy, all the more in light of the long and persistent history of crisis and conflict in the region. In 1995, the members of the reinvented Central American integration system agreed upon common customs tariffs as the first important step toward customs union. In 1996, Guatemala and El Salvador decided to establish full customs union, a proposition joined by Honduras and Nicaragua in 2000 and by Costa Rica in 2002. According to a decision of the Presidents of the Central American integration system, comprehensive economic integration was to be implemented by 2004; this was to include all necessary normative arrangements, full tariff harmonization, the removal of obstacles to trade, a common customs administration and an external trade policy aimed at achieving full customs union. In the meantime, 19 percent of Central American trade is intraregional. While the target date of 2004 was missed for full customs union, the trend seems to be more promising than ever before in the history of the region. In all fairness, one also has to recognize the

2 de la Ossa, Alvaro, "Der zentralamerikanische Integrationsprozess: Ende einer Entwicklungsalternative," *IBERO-Analysen*, Vol.6. Berlin: Ibero-Amerikanisches Institut, (2000): 17; also: Minkner-Bünjer, Mechthild, "Zentralamerika zwischen regionaler Integration und Eingliederung in die Weltwirtschaft im "Schlepptau" der USA," *Brennpunkt Lateinamerika*, No.13, Hamburg: Institut für Iberoamerika-Kunde, 2002: 129-142.

great obstacles to regional integration in Central America, most notably high poverty levels, lack of infrastructure, and strong dependency on the US with which 40 percent of all trade of the Central American countries is conducted while the US remains the most important investor in this region.

18 percent of El Salvador's GDP is based on financial transfers ("remesas") from migrants living in the US. The prospect of the US-driven Free Trade Area of the Americas (FTAA) is not without contradiction to the concept of stronger regional integration, including its prospects of developing supranational elements. The European Union claims to support regional integration in Central America through SICA with about 60 percent of all external EU funds for the region. In 2006, the European Union started negotiations with SICA for a bi-regional association agreement. The economic stake of the EU in the region – Central America represents 0.4 percent of the total external trade of the EU – cannot explain this commitment. It is for political reasons that the EU genuinely encourages Central America to take further steps along the long road toward substantial integration. Compared to where the EU might stand after more than a decade of civil wars and refugee plight, it seems fair to judge Central American integration by the path that began anew after 1991.[3]

(b) Integration efforts in the Andean Region date back to the foundation of the Pacto Andino in 1969. Based on the Treaty of Cartagena, the Pacto Andino marked the beginning of almost thirty years of rather unsuccessful integration as its intention ran practically counter to all national political strategies at the time. Individually, Bolivia, Ecuador, Peru, Colombia, Chile and Venezuela tried to pursue policies designed by "dependencia"-theories about center-periphery-relations in the capitalist world order. Pointing to the fact that American, European and Japanese capital controlled most industrial investments in Latin America, "dependencia"-theorists argued in favor of strict control of foreign investment and import-substitution as elements of a strategy to gain stronger national independence and thus strengthen national sovereignty. This approach was neither cohesive, nor successful, while it paralyzed the hope for regional integration. Furthermore, the geopolitical climate was as unfavorable to sustainable regional integration in Latin America as the recurrent threat of democracy by neo-authoritarian military dictatorships in the region.

The Pacto Andino failed its historic test, and yet aspirations for regional integration in the Andean region reverberated in a new and different global context. With the rise of neo-liberal economics and the return to democratic governance in most of Latin America during the late 1980's and early 1990's, the rationale for regional integration as a tool to enhanced economic well being, and ultimately a stronger political voice, spread

3 See Ulrich, Stephan, *Die zentralamerikanische Integration. Stand und Entwicklungsperspektiven*, Berlin: Deutsches Institut für Entwicklungspolitik, 2000: 30-31; Zimmek, Martin, *Integrationsprozesse in Lateinamerika: Aktuelle Herausforderungen in Mittelamerika und der Andenregion*, ZEI Discussion Paper C 153, Bonn: Center for European Integration Studies, 2005.

anew. After four years of intermission, the Presidents of the Andean countries met again for the first time in 1995 and approved a new strategy of increased regional integration as a response to the challenges and opportunities of globalization. The Cartagena Agreement of 1997 established a new Andean Integration System, transforming the original Pacto Andino into the Andean Community of Nations (Communidad Andina de Naciones, CAN). The Andean Presidential Council, composed of the Presidents of CAN, became its highest body. In addition to the Andean Community Foreign Ministers Council, the Commission of the Andean Community was established, composed of Ministers of Trade and Industry. A General Secretariat was established in Lima, an Andean Parliament as a deliberative body in Bogotá, and a Court of Justice of the Andean Community in Quito. A whole array of institutions was established, covering social partners, banking, investment and academic life in the Andean Community.

The Andean Community of Nations included Peru, Bolivia, Ecuador, Colombia and Venezuela, before Venezuela left CAN in 2006. The populist neo-socialist authoritarian regime of Hugo Chávez in Venezuela had undermined the hope of developing CAN into a solid community of democratic Andean nations as precondition for substantial political integration. Yet, its withdrawal from CAN was also negative and confronted the Andean Community of Nations with its biggest crisis. In the late twentieth century, CAN had survived the civil war in Colombia and never broke apart in spite of weak infrastructure and very limited intra-regional trade. Eventually, CAN also survived the 2006 crisis and announced that Chile would become an associate member.

The European Union recognized the continuous relevance of CAN and started negotiations for a bi-regional association agreement in 2007. The EU's policy toward CAN is aimed at strengthening integration in the Andean region with the ultimate goal of introducing supranational structures. In earlier years, the EU had even contributed to the salaries of the Lima-based Secretariat. Such a policy might be astonishing, given the limited economic relevance of CAN for the EU and the inherent weakness of CAN. EU exports from CAN represent only 0.9 percent of total EU imports, while EU exports to CAN represent 0.7 percent of EU's total global exports. It should not be underestimated, however, that the EU is the largest investor in CAN as it is in the whole of Latin America. The main driving force of the EU's policy is not an immediate economic interest in a regional community with 115 million inhabitants. The rationale of EU policy toward CAN – as it is toward other regional groupings – is grounded in the EU's understanding that sustainable and "real" regional integration can serve as a basis for successful development, democratic governance and a new global order. Supranational orientation is still missing in CAN, although the discussion about its usefulness has grown during the initial years of the twenty-first century. Following the EU model, discussions have begun inside CAN about the possible path toward monetary union, a directly elected community parliament and the creation of Andean citizenship.[4]

Since the new beginning of Andean integration in the 1990's, progress toward complementary economic structures has been made, although incrementally and slowly. While Venezuela, Colombia, Ecuador and Bolivia agreed on common external tariffs as cornerstone of a common free trade zone, Peru preferred to remain absent. The less developed economies of Bolivia and Ecuador received temporary exemptions from complete liberalization of their markets. CAN's goal to implement a free trade zone by 2005 and the subsequent realization of a common market was not implemented in time. Yet, the effort toward free trade and a common market has been more serious during the last two decades of CAN than during three decades of the Pacto Andino. [5]

One interesting feature of this development is the possible implication of increased trade between CAN and the Southern Common Market (Mercado Común del Sur, MERCOSUR), established in 1991 in the Southern Cone of Latin America. 8.5 percent of MERCOSUR imports come from CAN countries, while 10.8 percent of CAN imports originate in MERCOSUR. Both regional integration schemes are contemplating ways toward a bilateral free trade agreement. Sometimes, the possible fusion of both processes under the label MERCOCAN is envisaged.[6] This idea coincides with the eternal and cyclical invocation of the idea of pan-Latin American unity: On December 8, 2004, representatives of twelve Latin American countries signed the Declaration of Cuzco, aimed at establishing the South American Community of Nations.[7] For the time being, the only realistic prospect for unity in Latin America is based on the existing regional groupings. In spite of all their deficits and fragility, they are the only real embodiment of region-building in Latin America. The idea of MERCOCAN or the dream of a South American Community of Nations has to be seen in the context of the debate about advantages and disadvantages of the Free Trade Area for the Americas project. In 1991, the US had proposed the completion of this FTAA (in Spanish: Area de Libre omercio de las Americas, ALCA), a project whose implementation began in 1994 without yet succeeding. Often, skeptics argue that FTAA would only strengthen Latin American dependency on the US economy: The GDP of the US is close to 73

4 See Barrios, Raul (ed.), *Communidad Andina de Naciones: Desafios Politicos y Percepciones de la Sociedad*, La Paz: Friedrich Ebert Stiftung, 1999; Lauer, Rene, *Las Politicas Sociales en la Integracion Regional: Estudio Comparativo de la Union Europea y la Comunidad Andina de Naciones*, Quito: Universidad Andino Simon Bolivar, 2001; Casas Gragea, Angel Maria, *El Modelo Regional Andino: Enfoque de Economia Politica Internacional*, Quito: Universidad Andina Simon Bolivar, 2003.

5 See Le Gras, Gilbert, *The New New World: The Re-Emerging Markets of Latin America*, London: Reuters, 2002; Arnold, Christian, *La Experiencia de la Unión Europea y Sus Anécdotas para la Comunidad Andina de Naciones (CAN)*, ZEI Discussion Paper C 145. Bonn: Center for European Integration Studies, 2005.

6 See Giacalone, Rita (ed.), *CAN-Mercosur a la Sombra del ALCA*, Merida: Editorial Venezolano, 2003.

7 *The Economist* wrote about "fraternity at 3,3000 metres" when refering to the gathering intended to create the "South American Community of Nations": *The Economist*, December 11, (2004): 47.

percent of the combined GDP of all the other countries on the American continent, including Canada, Mexico and Brazil.[8] When the deadline of implementing the FTAA was reached in 2005, most observers argued that FTAA was already dead.

So far, the efforts to transform economic cooperation into political integration remain semantic in CAN and feasible only over the long haul. Yet, the changing attitude in the region, the awareness of the advantages of pooled sovereignties in the European Union, and the pressure not to fall behind in the process of creating a free trade zone for both Americas have exerted new interest in a more coherent economic, and a gradual political, integration in the Andean Community.

(c) Caribbean integration began as a counterintuitive mechanism to its European counterpart. It was meant to be a strategy to tame the inevitable end of British colonial rule over many of the Caribbean island nations that today consist of 34 million inhabitants. The West Indian Federation, founded for the purpose of persevering British influence in the region, failed in 1962. Functional cooperation among some of the Commonwealth Caribbean territories continued, but it remained tainted as a leftover of the failed process of decolonization. The Caribbean development echoed the same trend as other processes of decolonization during the twentieth century: based in the value of state sovereignty, individual statehood was soon followed by difficult processes of nation-building under conditions of development economies, and of weak, often non-democratic governance. A truly post-colonial effort toward regional cooperation and eventual integration was begun in that region only in 1973 – coinciding with Great Britain's entry into the European Community that forced the Caribbean island states to reconsider their strategic interests and market patterns. The original Treaty of Chaguaramas of 1973 established the objectives of the Caribbean Community (CARICOM) and a Common Market as two separate entities of a broader process eventually heading toward the same goal: greater independence from the global economic centers both in Europe and in the US.

The Revised Treaty of Chaguaramas of 2001 came close to refounding the Caribbean Community. While the broad objectives essentially remained the same – economic integration, co-ordination of foreign policies and functional co-operation – the Caribbean Community has launched a reinforced effort to implement its goals. With the incorporation of the Caribbean Community and the CARICOM Single Market and Economy under one legal personality, the Revised Treaty of Chaguaramas resembles European efforts to overcome structures of parallel institutions and mechanisms of "pillars" distinguishing different degrees of integration and cooperation. As a

8 See Fairlie Reinoso, Alan, *Las Relaciones Communidad Andina – Union Europea y la Zona de Libre Comercio del Sur*, Lima: Centro de Investigaciones Sociales, Economicas y Politicas, 2000; Sader, Emir (ed.), *ALCA: Integracao Soberana ou Subordinada?*, Sao Paulo: Expressao Popular, 2001; Vigevani, Tullo, and Marcelo Passini Mariano (ed.), *ALCA. O Gigante e os Anoes*, Sao Paulo: Editora Senac, 2001.

consequence, CARICOM is considered to be "in an advanced stage of transition."[9] The goal was set for a full-fledged Single Market by 2008 with an increased degree of institutionalization that will, however, continue to fall short of introducing elements of supranationality into CARICOM. As in the case of CAN and SICA, the EU strongly supports the evolution of the Caribbean integration experience.[10] In terms of trade relations, the role of CARICOM is rather marginal for the EU: Imports from the region amount to only 0.5 percent of total EU imports, exports amount to 0.7 percent of total imports into the EU.

Membership in CARICOM includes Antigua and Barbuda, The Bahamas, Barbados, Belize, Dominica, Grenada, Guyana – hosting the CARICOM Secretariat in its capital Georgetown – Haiti, Jamaica, Montserrat, St. Kitts and Nevis, St. Lucia, St. Vincent and the Grenadines, Suriname, and Trinidad and Tobago. Associate members are the British Virgin Islands, Bermuda, Turks and Caicos Islands, Anguilla, and the Cayman Islands. Discussion on membership of the Dominican Republic, Puerto Rico and – potentially with the strongest implications – of Cuba has begun, as well as membership for the remaining French, Dutch, British and US territories in the region.[11] The prospect of a Caribbean Community for the whole Caribbean basin might still be a far-fetched vision, but it is no longer inconceivable. In the Caribbean, the European experience of linking a "deepening" and "widening" of the integration process is being carefully studied, supported by the regular CARICOM dialogue with the European Union. [12]

The original CARICOM suffered from weak sovereignties and strong ideological rifts among its member states concerning attitudes toward the US and Europe. The fundamental dilemma of the region has not disappeared with the revision of the Treaty of Chaguaramas: it is the dilemma between "the desire, on the one hand, to enjoy the status of sovereign States, and, on the other, an unwillingness to acknowledge the inadequacy of required capabilities to translate legal sovereignty into a political and economic reality."[13] Increasing reference to the success of European integration is an indication of the continuous soul searching in CARICOM.

The decision to establish a CARICOM Single Market echoed not only the European experience. It also came as a response to the pressure of neo-liberal globalization and the power of the US economy in its immediate neighborhood. The North American Free Trade Agreement (NAFTA), established in 1991 between the US, Canada and Mexico,

9 Pollard, Duke (ed.), *The Caricom System: Basic Instruments*, Kingston: The Caribbean Law Publishing House Company, 2003: 4; see also Payne, Anthony, and Paul Sutton, *Charting Caribbean Developments*, Gainesville: University Press of Florida, 2001; Gonzalez Nunez, Gerardo, and Emilio Pantojas Garcia, *El Caribe en la Era de la Globalization*, Puerto Rico: Publicaciones Puertorriquenas, 2002.

10 See Dearden, Stephen J.H. (ed.), *The European Union and the Caribbean*, Aldershot: Ashgate, 2002.

11 For a Cuban perspective see: Camara de Comercio de la Republica de Cuba (ed.), *Cuba, el Caricom y sus Paises Miembros*, Havanna: Camara de Comercio, 2001.

12 See Payne, Anthony, and Paul Sutton, *Charting Carribean Development*, op.cit.: 197-201.

13 Pollard, Duke (ed.), *The Caricom System: Basic Instruments*, op. cit.: 17.

enhanced the sensation of peripheral neglect in the Caribbean. With the end of the Cold War, the Caribbean was bereft of opting for an alternative model, notwithstanding the continuous Communist regime in Cuba and, increasingly, the regime of Hugo Chávez in Venezuela.

The Caribbean Community has begun to develop a sense of foreign policy identity. CARICOM support for membership of Suriname and Belize into the continent-wide Organization of American States prevented possible escalations of territorial disputes with Venezuela and Guatemala. More important was the positive experience of structured relations with the European Community all the way from the Lomé Agreements to the Cotonou Agreement of 2000. CARICOM considered itself as instrumental for bringing about these widely praised arrangements between Europe and so many countries in Africa, the Caribbean and the Pacific. These agreements constituted "a watershed in north-south relations."[14] In December 2007, the European Union and most CARICOM member states initialed a bi-regional Economic Partnership Agreeement.

The establishment of a Caribbean Commission, an Assembly of Commonwealth Caribbean Parliamentarians, the establishment of a Caribbean Supreme Court in 2005, and the replacement of the Community Council with the Caribbean Common Market Council as the second highest decision-making body in CARICOM were important institutional additions introduced by the Revised Treaty of Chaguaramas in 2001. Contradictions remain, some of which are reminiscent of similar problems the European Union was facing as consequence of "opting-out clauses" granted to Denmark on key policy goals of the EU: The Bahamas are a member of CARICOM and yet they do not participate in the economic structures and goals of the community. As far as the decision-making mechanism is concerned, the Treaty of Chaguaramas introduced interesting reforms. While the principle of unanimity continues to be applied to decision-making in the Conference of Heads of Government, it has virtually been abolished in the other organs of the community. Consequently, this facilitates speedy reactions to the challenges of neo-liberal globalization that require export-oriented, internationally competitive production of goods and services in CARICOM.

It seems likely that the process of incremental yet steady fusion of economic integration with corresponding political processes will continue in the Caribbean. No matter how ambivalent the current character of CARICOM, the history of the Caribbean will no longer only be written with reference to sugar and slavery. Integration has become a new mantra in the region. This coincides with a new sensitivity for democratic governance in the Caribbean. Since American pressure against the revolutionary government in Grenada during the early 1980's, it is also understood in the Caribbean that economic development and democratic governance cannot be

14 Ibid.:20.

separated from a successful integration strategy. The speedy reaction of CARICOM to civil unrest in Haiti in early 2004 was indicative of this realization.

(d) The Southern Common Market (Mercado Común del Sur, MERCOSUR) was founded in 1991 by Argentina, Brazil, Paraguay and Uruguay, signing the Treaty of Asuncion. Originally it was meant to create a common market and a customs union between the participating countries grown out of the experiences of economic cooperation between Brazil and Argentina since the mid-1980's. MERCOSUR proceeded from their sectoral agreements to wide-range liberalization of trade relations. In 1988, Brazil had import tariffs of 51 percent and Argentina of 30 percent. Trade liberalization thus became the first priority in strengthening the partners involved. The Treaty of Ouro Preto of 1994 added much to the institutional structure of MERCOSUR.[15] A transition phase was set into motion with the goal to create a common market by 2006. During the 1990's alone, intra-regional trade jumped up from 4.6 billion US dollars to 20.4 billion US dollars, while foreign investment grew from 22.8 billion US dollars to 32.5 billion US dollars. Since the mid-1990's, officially most intra-regional trade has been free of tariffs; yet more than 800 exceptions remained in place, largely affecting strategic goods and services.[16] In 1996, MERCOSUR established free trade arrangements with Chile and Bolivia, both becoming also associate members of MERCOSUR, followed by Peru (in 2003) and Venezuela as a full but controversial member in 2006.

MERCOSUR remains basically intergovernmental. The Common Market Council (Consejo del Mercado Comun) is its highest body, consisting of the Foreign and Economic Ministers of MERCOSUR member states. The Council meets once a year in the presence of the Heads of State of MERCOSUR member states. The MERCOSUR Presidency rotates and is coordinated by the Foreign Minister in charge. The Treaty of Ouro Preto specified the competencies of the existing organs and added new ones to MERCOSUR: most notable were the Commerce Commission (Comision Comercial del Mercosur), the Common Parliamentary Commission (Comision Parlamentaria Conjunta) and the Consultative Forum for Economic and Social Affairs (Foro Consultativo Economico y Social). A largely technical Secretariat operates in Montevideo. A MERCOSUR Court of Arbitration has been established in Asuncion, so far projecting more good will than judicial power.

In the meantime, MERCOSUR also established a common mechanism for political consultations. Since 2002, like-minded new Presidents in Argentina and in Brazil (Kirchner and Lula da Silva) have rekindled the idea of robust institutional reforms in

15 See Aicardi, Oscar Abadie, *Fundamentos Historicos y Politicos del Mercosur*, Montevideo: Melibea Edicciones, 1999; Becak, Peggy, *Mercosur. Uma Experiencia de Integracao Regional*, Sao Paulo: Editora Contexto, 2000.

16 See *The Economist*, "The Future of Mercosur. A Free-Trade Tug-of-War," December 11, (2004): 46-47.

MERCOSUR: In December 2006, the MERCOSUR Parliament was inaugurated and took its seat in Montevideo. It has started its work as a consultative body, but it might be worth to remember the slow progress in the parliamentarization of the European Community in order to appreciate this effort of MERCOSUR. No matter the establishment of the MERCOSUR Parliament, the weak institutionalization of MERCOSUR remains the Achilles' heel of the project.[17]

Since 1999, the European Union and MERCOSUR have been negotiating a Bi-Regional Association Agreement, so far (2010) without conclusion. Optimistic assessments of an intensified bi-regional relationship refer to the potential of EU-MERCOSUR trade and investment relations. For the time being, MERCOSUR – a market with more than 260 million inhabitants – holds a share of 2.4 percent of total EU imports while the export of the EU to MERCOSUR is 1.8 percent of total EU exports. EU direct investment in MERCOSUR has increased since the mid-1990's, making the EU the largest investor in MERCOSUR as in all of Latin America, except for Central America. The EU is also the largest donor of developmental aid to the region as it is to Latin America in general. The path toward the first Interregional Association Agreement of the European Union with another regional integration process is more than a reflection of the economic importance of that relationship. The EU has always considered MERCOSUR a project of political relevance in accordance with the European desire to strengthen regional integration as an important element in a multipolar world.

Economic liberalization and deregulation, but also a renewed commitment to democracy and an improved rule of law, have contributed to the rise in the importance of MERCOSUR since the end of the 1990's. Next to the US, the EU and Japan, MERCOSUR is the fourth largest economy in the world. It has gained the reputation of being the most advanced regional integration scheme in Latin America, although this is debatable when compared with the structures of SICA, CARICOM and even CAN. MERCOSUR has begun to develop a legal code comparable to the *acquis communautaire* of the European Union.[18] But the gap between obvious potential and political ambition is obvious: The original Treaty of Asuncion included the establishment of common external tariffs. In 1995 the Common Market was supposed to be completed. To this day, MERCOSUR must be considered an incomplete customs union in a free trade zone.

In spite of many obstacles, MERCOSUR is confronted with the need to deepen its structures. Even the possibility of a common currency – a "merco-peso" – and the need for stronger measures to improve co-ordination of macroeconomic policies have been

17 See Caetano, Gerardo, and Ruben M. Perina (eds.), *La Encrucijada Politica del Mercosur: Parlamentos y Nueva Institutionalidad*, Montevideo: Impresora Editorial, 2003.

18 See Haines Ferrari, Marta (ed.), *The Mercosur Codes*, London: BIICL, 2000; Max Planck Institut für Ausländisches und Internationales Privatrecht (ed.), Rechtsquellen des Mercosur, Baden-Baden: Nomos, 2000.

debated in the region. Whether or not MERCOSUR's Customs Union, and the currently incomplete Common Market, will advance through norm standardization and legislative measures to finally become a comprehensive Single Market remains to be seen. Much will depend upon the political will generated in the member states of MERCOSUR, notably in Brazil and Argentina.

In spite of its political shortcomings, MERCOSUR has begun to "discover" the sphere of foreign and security policy as relevant for building more solid regional integration. Joint military exercises between Argentina and Brazil, and meetings of the Chiefs of Staff of both countries, are still light-years away from the depth of Europe's Common Foreign and Security Policy, no matter how incomplete that is. After 150 years of suspicion between Argentina and Brazil, and in the overall context of the history of Latin America, they constitute, however, a promising step forward toward meaningful regional cooperation. The end of military dictatorship in both countries, the decrease in power and prestige of the armed forces and the return to civilian rule in all MERCOSUR member states has been a critical precondition for enhancing the potential of MERCOSUR integration.[19] No matter how limited MERCOSUR still is in regard to supranational elements, it might well grow into a structure beyond free trade and an integrated market. This is certainly the understanding of the European Union and the rationale for its broadening relations with MERCOSUR.[20]

The 2008 global financial and economic crisis raised awareness in MERCOSUR member states to speed up the regional integration process and to give MERCOSUR a stronger role, and ultimately also a stronger voice. The continuous backing of MERCOSUR by the European Union might have added to the understanding in the region that MERCOSUR must use its second chance in order to implement the original goals of the project while at the same time it has to focus on how to turn itself into a "real," viable process of integration – and that also means political and supranational integration.[21]

19 See Diamint, Rut (ed.), *La OTAN y los Desafios en el MERCOSUR: Comunidad de Seguridad y Estabilidad Democratica*, Buenos Aires: Nuevohacer, 2001.

20 See Algorta Pla, Juan, *O Mercosul e a Comunidade Europeia: Uma Abordagem Comparativa*, Porto Alegre: Editorial da Universidade, 1994; Vera-Fluixa, Ramiro, *Regionalbildungsansätze in Lateinamerika und ihr Vergleich mit der Europäischen Union*, ZEI Discussion Paper C 73. Bonn: Center for European Integration Studies, 2000; Zippel, Wulfdieter (ed.), *Die Beziehungen zwischen der EU und den Mercosur-Staaten: Stand und Perspektiven*, Baden-Baden: Nomos, 2002; Diedrichs, Udo, *Die Politik der Europäischen Union gegenüber dem Mercosur: Die EU als internationaler Akteur*, Opladen: Leske + Budrich, 2003; Jaguaribe, Helio, and Alvaro de Vasconcelos, (eds.), *The European Union, Mercosul and the New World Order*, London/Portland: Frank Cass, 2003.

21 See also: Montoya, Carlos Alberto, *Teoria de la Integracion. Los Procesos de Integracion Economica en America Latina*, Medellin: Eafit Fondo Editorial Universidad, 2000; Inter-American Development Bank, (ed.), *Beyond Borders: The New Regionalism in Latin America*, Washington D.C.: Inter-American Development Bank, 2002.

(2) Africa

(a) The African search for regional integration has been torn between the ambition to unite the continent as a whole and the inability to develop existing regional schemes of cooperation into viable success stories. Therefore, a confusing overlap of regional integration efforts coincides with the general underdevelopment of the continent, including the underdevelopment of its regional integration. Nevertheless, both on the regional as well as on the continental level, the idea of integration as the path toward economic success has never vanished from the political agenda, although competing paradigms were pushing toward continental or pulling toward regional solutions. From the creation of the Organization of African Unity in 1963, with the aim of promoting African self-government, to the creation of the African Union in 2000, with the aim of fostering an African Economic Community by 2028, regional efforts in Africa were always considered partial expressions in search of a broader goal, the African Renaissance.[22]

The most ambitious effort to integrate Africa, so far, has been conducted on the continental level. Since the decolonization struggle in the mid-twentieth century, African leaders have had a vision of a united continent. While the Organization of African Unity (OAU) remained incapable of limiting the continent's quest for national sovereignty, it also failed to support economic development and good governance. Moreover, it failed to prevent ethnic conflicts and regional crises that have blurred the reputation of Africa during much of the past three decades.

Africa is by far the poorest continent. Of a total of 765 million inhabitants close to 350 million live below the line of absolute poverty (less than 1 US dollar per day), more than 150 million of them children. During the last decade of the twentieth century, Africa's share in global trade fell to 1.6 percent compared with 4.6 percent in 1980. It was only in light of the recognition of a deep crisis affecting the whole continent – in spite of certain pockets of progress and limited success stories – that leaders from all across Africa made efforts toward a new beginning. The Abuja Treaty, signed at the Summit of the Organization of African Unity in 1991 with the aim of establishing an African Economic Community by the year 2028, and the establishment of the African Union (AU) in 2002, after the required number of 36 ratifications of the founding Treaty signed in Lomé in 2000 have begun to generate fresh impulses aimed at a long-term improvement of the overall prospects for Africa. With all African states participating, the African Union by now is the most comprehensive scheme of continental-wide cooperation. Nevertheless, in structure and goals it is more comparable

22 Thus is the vision Thabo Mbeki has been developing even before he succeeded Nelson Mandela as President of South Africa: Mbeki, Thabo, *The African Renaissance, South Africa and the World*, https://unu.edu/unupress/Mbeki.html; on his thoughts see Ajulu, Rok, "Thabo Mbeki's African Renaissance in a Globalising World Economy: The Struggle for the Soul of the Continent," *Review of African Political Economy*, 28. 37 (2001): 27-42; Cheru, Fantu, *African Renaissance: Roadmaps to the Challenge of Globalization*, London/New York: Zed Books, 2002.

– at least for the time being – to the Council of Europe than to the European Union. In light of the intricate and mutually reinforcing relationship between the two during decades of crisis and uncertainty in Europe, this might not be a bad start for the African Union.

Its Constitutive Act, ratified by all member states of the African Union as an instrument of international law, has established an African Court of Justice, a Pan-African Parliament, the African Commission on Human and Civil Rights, a Monetary Fund and a Central Bank. The AU's Secretariat is based in Addis Ababa. The four institutions of the African Union are: The Assembly, the Executive Council, the Permanent Representatives' Committee, and the Commission of the Union. Although the terminology resembles European experiences, the principal of supranationality has not yet been applied to the structures and competencies of the African Union. It remains an intergovernmental body, "meant to be a pro-active organization to swiftly respond to the Continent's new challenges, especially with regard to promoting and protecting human and civil rights, promotion of self reliance and economic development within the framework of the Union, and the promotion of gender equality, peaceful co-existence of Member States, and their rights to live in peace and security."[23] The ambition of Libya's leader Muammar Al-Qaddafi to create a pan-African defense force and a common market with a common currency has not yet materialized.

The African Union is meant to work as a catalyst to bring various regional schemes of economic cooperation and integration together under the roof of a pan-African vision. The structures of the African Union include mechanisms to deal with human rights protection and to contribute to conflict prevention and conflict resolution on the African continent. In the absence of qualified majority voting as key to efficiency and success of this work, it remains open to long-term judgment how strong the indirect effect of these reinforced commitments on the member states of the "African Union" eventually can be. Self-commitments might garner better results than obligatory efforts geared at formally limiting national sovereignty. The first test case for the new African self-commitment was the outbreak of a human catastrophe in the Western Sudanese region of Darfur in the summer of 2004: It was more than remarkable that the Assembly of the African Union decided on July 8, 2004, to increase the number of AU Observers and to send 3,000 soldiers of the AU Protection Force to Sudan. In stark contrast to the former taboo of non-interference in the domestic affairs of another African country, this AU decision demonstrated the emerging readiness of the AU to exercise continent-wide responsibility. Although this first AU peace keeping operation was too weak to stop

23 Orijako, Desmond T., "Road to the African Union (AU): Opportunities and Challenges," in: African Union (ed.), *The African Union Directory 2002, 1st Heads of State Summit*, Mauritius: Millenium African Communications, 2002: 14; see also Genge, Manelisi, et al., *African Union and a Panafrican Parliament*, Pretoria: Africa Institute of South Africa 2000; Melber, Henning, *The New African Initiative and the African Union: A Preliminary Assessment and Documentation*, Uppsala: Nordiska Afrikainstitutet, 2001; Smith, Malinda S. (ed.), *Globalizing Africa*, Trenton/Asmara: Africa World Press, 2003.

another human catastrophe on the African continent, it was the first and promising sign of a new and focused political will executed by the African Union. By 2007, the AU Peace Keeping Force and a UN Peace Keeping Force were brought together to form a hybrid peacekeeping mechanism for Darfur.

A Peace and Security Council of fifteen member states of the AU, early warning and preventive diplomacy as well as peace-making, including the use of good offices, mediation, conciliation and enquiry, add to the ambitious plan of the AU to mediate open or pending political crises on the continent. The right to intervene in a Member State "pursuant to a decision of the Assembly in respect to grave circumstances, namely: war crimes, genocide and crimes against humanity" (Article 40h of the Constitutive Act) stipulates a new direction in African self-rule and self-criticism. It is not clear whether or not the Assembly of the AU – comprised of the Heads of State and Government – will ever apply the principle of consensus for decisions of this magnitude. The Constitutive Act states that in case the Assembly fails to reach decisions by consensus, a two-third majority will be sufficient to proceed with decisions in the framework of the competencies of the Assembly. Issues of peacekeeping and human rights aside, this includes questions relating to the budget of the African Union. The wording of the Constitutional Act reflects growing sensitivity toward issues of peace and human rights in Africa. Whether or not this can impact state behavior or that of warring forces remains to be seen. Skepticism also prevails regarding the potential of the African Union's Commission to truly turn into a supranational executive analogous to the European Commission.

So far, the same uncertainty applies to the ability of the African Union to promote economic cooperation and development by advancing the gradual merger of existing regional cooperation and integration schemes into an African Economic Community. The African Union has identified the following regional groupings of economic cooperation as the engines for creating a pan-African Economic Community by 2028: the fifteen member states Economic Community of West African States (ECOWAS), founded in 1975; the sixteen member states Common Market for Eastern and Southern Africa (COMESA), founded in 1981 as Preferential Trade Area for Eastern and Southern Africa; the ten member states Economic Community of Central African States (ECCAS), founded in 1983; the ten member states Southern African Development Community (SADC), founded in 1992 as successor institution to the Southern African Development Coordination Conference, which had been created as an anti-Apartheid instrument in 1980, the East African Community (EAC), initially founded in 1967, but factually re-founded in 2000, the five member states Arab Maghreb Union (AMU), founded in 1989, and two other minor groupings. As then EU Commissioner for External Trade, Pascal Lamy, put it at the outset of the twenty-first century: "Recent advances in regional integration in Africa are a clear indication that most African countries have themselves decided to anchor their integration into the world economy through regional economic integration…In the case of many African countries, regional integration can be a stepping stone for their integration into the world economy."[24] No matter how much skepticism prevails in face of past African experiences, the African Union is a promising new and ambitious beginning of a certainly rough and daunting road ahead for the continent.

(b) The oldest among more than a dozen schemes for economic cooperation and integration in Africa is the market-oriented experience of the Economic Community of West African States (ECOWAS). During the critical 1990's, ECOWAS was one of the few regions in Africa that could claim an increase in intra-regional trade. The original Treaty of Lagos, signed in 1975, was revised in 1993 in order to make ECOWAS compatible with the planned African Economic Community. The revised treaty meant nothing less than the actual refounding of ECOWAS. In the meantime, Cape Verde, Ivory Coast, Benin, Burkina Faso, Gambia, Ghana, Guinea, Guinea-Bissau, Liberia, Mali, Mauritania (leaving again in 1999), Niger, Nigeria, Senegal, Sierra Leone and Togo were members of ECOWAS. The total population of 250 million people is experiencing the first effort "to transcend the traditional historical and linguistic cleavages between French, English, and Portuguese-speaking African states."[25] The main objective of ECOWAS, according to its Treaty, is the creation of an economic and monetary union. The plan was outlined in stages, its mid-term goal being the achievement of regional convertibility, before the ten currencies of ECOWAS' member states (nine local currencies plus the CFA franc) could create a monetary union at the end of the process. As a practical step toward the overall goal, ECOWAS traveller checks were introduced to facilitate regional travel and commercial transactions.

Civil wars in Sierra Leone, Liberia and Guinea-Bissau slowed down the prospects for speedy economic integration in the region. At the same time, they widened the agenda of ECOWAS and introduced the first elements of security cooperation. The ECOWAS monitoring group ECOMOG became instrumental in ending the seven-year civil war in Liberia and helped manage the bitter conflict in Sierra Leone. During the 1990's, conflict prevention, peace keeping and the establishment of a Mediation and Security Council went hand in hand with measures to facilitate the free movement of people and goods and the harmonization of economic policies among ECOWAS

24 Lamy, Pascal, "The Challenge of Integrating Africa into the World Economy," in: Clapham, Christopher, et al. (eds.), *Regional Integration in Southern Africa: Comparative International Perspectives*, Johannesburg: The South African Institute of International Affairs, 2001: 15; see also Kühnhardt, Ludger *African Regional Integration and the Role of the European Union,* ZEI Discussion Paper C 184, Bonn: Center for European Integration Studies, 2008.

25 Martin, Guy, *Africa in World Politics: A Pan-African Perspective*, Trenton/Asmara: Africa World Press, 2002: 138; see also Gambari, Ibrahim A., *Political and Comparative Dimensions of Regional Integration: The Case of ECOWAS*, New Jersey/London: Humanities Press, 1991; Lavergne, Real (ed.), *Regional Integration and Cooperation in West Africa: A Multidimensional Perspective*, Trenton/Asmara: Africa World Press, 1997.

countries because the original approach of the economic community was broadened due to security challenges in some of its member states.

Setbacks had already become obvious during the 1980's. Inter-regional trade decreased by 50 percent during that decade; labor mobility was blocked through unilateral measures of Ghana closing its borders in 1982, and of Nigeria expelling 2 million "illegal immigrants," mostly Ghanaians, in 1983. Even with new impetuses and the pan-continental perspective, there is minimal movement of capital within the region.

The original ECOWAS Treaty established a Court of Justice, a Parliament and an Economic and Social Council. With the revised treaty of 1993, the institutions were substantially overhauled and expanded. Most promising is the work of the ECOWAS Parliament and the ECOWAS Court of Justice, both actually in operation only since 2001. The ECOWAS Parliament aims at direct elections across the region. The ECOWAS Secretariat is based in Abuja, Nigeria's capital. Non-compliance of member states with community decisions has been as notorious as problems with budget appropriation. In light of Africa's grave development crisis, it remains noteworthy that ECOWAS can still be considered more of a success than a failed attempt to bring about regional cooperation and integration in one part of Africa.

Of supporting, yet also contradictory relevance for regional economic integration in West Africa is the West African Economic and Monetary Union UEMOA (Union économique et monétaire ouest africaine), a monetary union of eight mainly French-speaking countries in the region. UEMOA countries operate their economies on the basis of a single currency, the CFA Franc. Although UEMOA represents fragile economies with less than ten per cent of inter-region trade, changes since the turn of the century have begun to turn it into a "genuine economic and monetary union".[26] A similar monetary mechanism exists in Central Africa with the Central African Economic and Monetary Community CEMAC (Communauté economique et monétaire d'Afrique centrale) Here, six countries operate their economies on the basis of a common currency.

The two CFA zones are clustered around the concept of the free movement of capital within the respective zone, the pooling of gold and foreign exchange reserves on a common French Treasury account, common rules and regulations for foreign commercial and financial transactions, and free convertibility, at par, of the local CFA Franc, formerly pegged to the French Franc and since 2002 to the euro. The French Treasury continues to supply euros to African Central Banks, which are members of the Franc Zone. "The crucial issue," an analyst argues, "is whether the euro will eventually replace the Franc Zone in Africa, or whether the Franc Zone will remain a crucial link and central element in the system of Franco-African cooperation."[27]

26 Martin, Guy, *Africa in World Politics: A Pan-African Perspective*, op.cit.: 145.
27 Ibid.:151.

Another promising element for the advancement of the goals of the African Union was the Economic Community of Central African States (ECCAS). This ten-nation group, representing 70 million people, and consisting of Burundi, Cameroon, the Central African Republic, Chad, Congo, Equatorial Guinea, Gabon, Rwanda, Sao Tome et Principe, and the Democratic Republic of Congo, aimed to achieve a central African common market and economic community by 1995. Endemic instability and the wars in the Great Lake Region practically ended the activities of ECCAS in the early 1990's.

More promising is the revitalization of the East African Community (EAC). Re-founded in 2000, the East African Community has realized a customs union among its member states in 2005. The EAC, including five member states, strives for ambitious regional objectives in the decades ahead.

(c) Southern and Eastern Africa has been struggling with concepts of regional cooperation and integration in the shadow of decolonization and the long road to overcoming Apartheid regimes in Southern Africa. After ten years of promising activity, the effort to create an East African Community failed in 1977 because of fundamental ideological differences between Socialist Tanzania and pro-Western, market-oriented Kenya.[28] Since the early years of the twenty-first century, the East African Community is trying to re-establish itself as a serious regional grouping. As for other efforts of region-building in Eastern and Southern Africa, the struggle against Apartheid made the front-line states of Southern and Eastern Africa join under the roof of the Southern African Development Coordination Conference (SADCC) in 1980. Angola, Botswana, Lesotho, Malawi, Mozambique, Swaziland, Tanzania, Zambia and Zimbabwe were united in their search to reduce economic dependency on South Africa. In 1992, after the peaceful end of Apartheid, SADCC was transformed into the Southern African Development Community (SADC). Namibia had already joined after its independence in 1990. South Africa joined after the end of Apartheid (in 1994), followed by Mauritius (in 1995), and the Seychelles and the Democratic Republic of Congo (in 1997). Ever since, SADC has been considered to be the most viable engine for economic cooperation and potential regional integration in Southern and Eastern Africa. South Africa has turned from being the unifying enemy of SAADC into the center of power and engine of SADC. SADC countries include 200 million people with a combined gross domestic product of 176 billion US dollars.

The founding Treaty of SADC makes reference to the noble goals of preserving human rights, peace and security, the rule of law, the peaceful settlement of disputes, the development of common political values, systems and institutions and the harmonization of policies, including foreign policy. One of the main organs of SADC is the Inter-State Defense and Security Committee. A regional satellite communications

28 See Potholm, Christian P., and Richard A. Fredland (eds.), *Integration and Disintegration in East Africa*, Lanham: University Press of America, 1980.

network, actions (no matter how vague) against coup makers, peacekeeping training in a Regional Peacekeeping Training Institute, and standardized operating procedures for peacekeeping operations have been among the activities of SADC. In the economic field, SADC aims for a Free Trade Area by 2012, paving the way for customs union and subsequently for a common market. Intra-regional trade has increased and stands at 22 percent, the highest intra-regional trade level in all of sub-Saharan Africa. Progress on the realization of the Free Trade Area – by substantially reducing tariff and non-tariff barriers – has been accompanied by improvement of transport corridors supposed to foster development of the most depressed areas of the region. Since 1995, the region has an integrated power grid "into which the power generated is pooled and allocated to member states as required."[29]

SADC's institutional structure includes the SADC Parliamentary Forum, the SADC Tribunal, the SADC Electoral Commission Forum, the SADC Lawyers Association and various other civil society forums. SADC's Secretariat is based in Gaborone, the capital of Botswana. SADC was confronted with difficult adaptation challenges after South Africa joined. Economically this should not have come as a surprise since South Africa accounts for almost 75 percent of SADC's GDP. The hegemonic potential of South Africa's economy has also affected political cooperation in SADC. A South-Africa-Zimbabwe political conflict over control of SADC organs "stretched it almost to the breaking point."[30] European disputes with Zimbabwe during the 1990's over growing authoritarianism in Zimbabwe did not affect SADC's stance toward its member state. The military intervention of SADC in 1998 in Lesotho caused further disputes among members of the integration scheme. Nevertheless, the potential of SADC remains strong compared to past or parallel efforts in sub-Saharan Africa.[31]

SADC as the engine of regional integration in Southern and Eastern Africa is supported by the activities of the Common Market for Eastern and Southern Africa (COMESA). COMESA was established by a treaty signed in Kampala, Uganda, in 1993 by the member states of the former Preferential Trade Area for Eastern and Southern Africa (PTA), namely Burundi, Comoros, Djibouti, Ethiopia, Kenya, Lesotho, Malawi, Mauritius, Mozambique, Rwanda, Somalia, Swaziland, Tanzania, Uganda, Zambia and Zimbabwe. While Lesotho, Mozambique and Somalia left COMESA, Angola, the Democratic Republic of Congo, Egypt, Eritrea, Madagascar, Namibia, the Seychelles and Sudan joined COMESA after its creation. COMESA's main goal remains the accomplishment of a common market. The target dates for realizing a Free Trade Area by 2000 and a common external tariff by 2004 could not be achieved. Yet, COMESA claims considerable achievement as far as facilitating trade and institution building in

29 Martin, Guy, *Africa in World Politics: A Pan-African Perspective*, op. cit.: 162.

30 Ibid.: 162.

31 See Kösler, Ariane, *The Southern African Development Community and its Relations to the European Union: Deepening Integration in Southern Africa?*, ZEI Discussion Paper C 169, Bonn: Center for European Integration Studies, 2007.

the region is concerned. Headquartered in Lusaka, Zambia, the accounts of COMESA are denominated in the organization's Unit of Account, the COMESA dollar, which is equal to one US dollar.

The main organ of COMESA is the Authority of Heads of State and Government. Its Council, the Court of Justice, the Committee of Governors of Central Banks and other institutional mechanisms resemble European experiences. Yet, the practical performance has not been too impressive. Overlapping membership in COMESA, SADC and ECCAS has been identified as one of the reasons hindering progress toward the implementation of COMESA's goals. The weak development level of most African economies is as much an impediment for early integration as political obstacles resulting from Africa's weak political structures. Weak economic and political sovereignty do not seem fertile breeding ground for rapid regional integration. They clearly do not facilitate the sharing of sovereignty as a strategy for stronger economic and political systems on the national level, and for a strengthening of the overall potential of Africa on the continental level. Yet, Africa has begun to focus on the need for regional and even continental integration more than ever since the beginning of modern independent statehood on the continent.

(3) Asia

(a) Among regional organizations worldwide, the Association of Southeast Asian Nations (ASEAN) is often considered the most favored partner of the European Union. Since its foundation in 1967, ASEAN has indeed put its mark on the world map. The mutually perceived threat of communist expansion in Indochina was the original motive for Indonesia, Malaysia, the Philippines, Singapore and Thailand to form a system of co-operation. A common response to the threat stemming from escalation of political and military events in Vietnam, Laos and Cambodia seemed to be a matter of survival. Over time – not unlike the European integration experience – ASEAN became a magnetic force for the communist countries in Indochina and generated one of the more impressive economic success stories of twentieth century Asia. With impressive growth rates, the "Little Tigers" jumped to the forefront of the world economy. ASEAN also widened its membership. In 1984, Brunei Darussalam joined. With the end of the Cold War, the prospect of an ASEAN comprising all Southeast Asian countries became realistic. Most notable was the accession of Vietnam (1995), Laos (1997) – together with Burma – and Cambodia (1999). Among these three war-torn countries, Vietnam and Laos formally maintained communist regimes in spite of anti-communist revolutions in Eastern Europe. Yet they began to open their economies to market mechanisms. Cambodian membership has indicated an end to the dramatic and horrible history of this pleasant Southeast Asian country and marked the success of ASEAN as a factor of regional stability. The membership of Burma (officially called Myanmar) remains controversial in light of the continuous military dictatorship in the home country of Nobel Peace Prize winner Aung San Suu Kyi.[32]

In economic terms, ASEAN pursues co-operation in "common interest areas" as the Bangkok Declaration – the founding document of ASEAN – has stated the main objective of the group. In four decades of its existence, ASEAN has grown into the largest free trade area in the world with its population of 539 million people, yet it remains the smallest one in terms of actual gross domestic product (659 billion euros). Although ASEAN has expanded its means of co-operation since its foundation, so far it has fallen short of realizing a Single Market: Intra-regional trade has risen to more than 22 percent during the 1990's, demonstrating an increase in complementary production. This figure is small however compared with the EU's internal trade of more than 50 percent. Other Asian countries – foremost Japan, South Korea and China – constitute ASEAN's main trading partners, accounting for 50 percent of its export market and providing the region with 60 percent of its imports. ASEAN's share of world trade has grown from 4.2 percent of imports and 4.9 percent in exports (1980) to 6.7 percent in imports and 8.3 percent in exports (2002). In the early years of the twenty-first century, the EU's share of exports from ASEAN was 3.9 percent, while the EU's import share from ASEAN amounted to 6.3 percent. Intra-regional investment is still limited in ASEAN although it has more than doubled during the 1990's from 12 billion US dollars to 26 billion US dollars. By the early twenty-first century, following the East Asian currency crisis of 1997, ASEAN began to study the feasibility of establishing an ASEAN currency and exchange rate system. Economists argue that ASEAN is comparable to the European Community before the Treaty of Maastricht as far as intra-regional trade, the correlations of aggregate supply shocks, factor flows, integration and symmetry of economic structures are concerned.[33]

Given the degree of tension among the original founding members of ASEAN in the time of decolonization (Singapore was excluded from Malaysia, Indonesia initiated a policy of "Konfrontasi" against Malaysia, the Philippines tried to oppose the very creation of Malaysia) and notwithstanding internal conflicts in the region ever since (dictatorships in the Philippines and in Indonesia, ethnic conflicts in Malaysia, Islamic fundamentalism and terrorism in Indonesia and in the Philippines, military rule in Myanmar, communist rule in Vietnam and Laos, post-conflict instability in Cambodia and economic crises in Thailand, Indonesia and most of the other countries of ASEAN), the success of ASEAN is undeniable. It has grown beyond the original intention of

32 See Gates, Carolyn L., and Mya Than (eds.), *ASEAN Enlargement: Impacts and Implications*, Singapore: Institute of Southeast Asian Studies, 2001.

33 See Plummer, Michael G., "The EU and ASEAN: Real Integration and Lessons in Financial Cooperation," *The World Economy*, 25(2002): 1469-1500.

maximizing economic benefits and has begun to impact regional security and issues of conflict resolution.[34]

During the 1980's and 1990's, ASEAN was able to exert pressure on Vietnam in order to resolve the long-standing Cambodian conflict with the rehabilitation of complete national sovereignty and subsequent accession of both Vietnam and Cambodia into ASEAN.[35] The Cambodia policy of ASEAN has to be seen in the larger context of ASEAN's increasing ambition to project itself as provider of stability and security in the region. In the absence of other regional schemes for security in Asia-Pacific, the ASEAN Regional Forum (ARF) attests to ASEAN's ambition and "pivotal role" in this field.[36] Founded in 1994, ARF is to this day the only security mechanism in Asia. Since the end of the Cold War, various ASEAN political leaders began to challenge the taboo of non-intervention in domestic affairs of member countries. After debates in ASEAN whether the community should favor "intervention" or "flexible engagement" in the face of new regional crises, ASEAN agreed upon the formula "enhanced interaction."[37] The conflict in East Timor (1999-2002) did not see any substantial ASEAN involvement. Difficulties in dealing with the military dictatorship in Myanmar have demonstrated the limits of ASEAN's negotiation capacities in the absence of supranational mechanisms. ASEAN's strategy remains limited to quiet diplomacy and attempts to "mediate or mitigate strained bilateral relations between members."[38] ASEAN does not impose sanctions for the poor conduct of any of its member states. The "ASEAN way" has been described as a set of unwritten norms of interaction and decision-making, thus differing from the rule-based structure of the European Union.[39]

In fact, ASEAN hardly knows any form of institutionalization. It has been suggested that ASEAN member states relate intuitively to a common identity of their region.[40] As much as this is debatable in light of the enormous religious, ethnic, cultural and linguistic diversity of Southeast Asia, the limited degree of institutionalization remains obvious. The original Treaty on Friendship and Cooperation in Southeast Asia of 1976

34 See Yeung, May T., et al. (eds.), *Regional Trading Blocs in the Global Economy: The EU and ASEAN*, Cheltenham: Edward Elgar, 1999.

35 See David, Harald, *Die ASEAN zwischen Konflikt, Kooperation und Integration*, Hamburg: Institut für Asienkunde, 2003: 54-56.

36 Than, Mya, and Daljit Singh, "Regional Integration: The Case of ASEAN," in: Clapham, Christopher, et al. (eds.), *Regional Integration in Southern Africa: Comparative International Perspectives*, Pretoria: The South African Institute of International Affairs, 2001:170; Nabers, Dirk, "Das ASEAN Regional Forum (ARF)," in Maull, Hanns W., and Dirk Nabers (eds.), *Multilateralismus in Ostasien-Pazifik: Probleme und Perspektiven im neuen Jahrhundert*, Hamburg: Institut für Asienkunde, 2001: 89-117.

37 See McDougall, Derek, "Humanitarian Intervention and Peacekeeping as Issues for Asia-Pacific Security," in: Hentz, J., and Morten Boas (eds.), *New and Critical Security and Regionalism: Beyond the Nation-States*, Aldershot: Ashgate, 2003: 43.

38 Ibid.: 177.

39 See Anwar, Dewi F., "ASEAN's Enlargement: Political, Security and Institutional Perspectives," in: Gates, Carolyn L., and Mya Than (eds.), *ASEAN Enlargement: Impacts and Implications*, op.cit.: 31.

40 Acharya, Amitav, *The Quest for Identity: International Relations of South East Asia*, Oxford: Oxford University Press, 2000.

introduced elements of arbitration that remain largely on paper. An ASEAN Secretariat was established in Jakarta, demonstrating the first seeds of supranational potential. The possibility of an ASEAN Parliament has been considered, and some analysts compare the ongoing coordination activity among ASEAN countries to the unwritten constitution of Great Britain.[41]

In the early twenty-first century, more than sixty structures of regional cooperation have been identified in Asia. Formal or informal co-operation is dominant. Continent-wide schemes do not exist. Processes with a continental dimension such as ASEM (Asia-Europe Meeting) and APEC (Asia-Pacific Economic Cooperation) are components of trans-continental free trade cooperation rather than ambitions toward supranational integration.[42] They are responses to globalization and expressions of multilateralism, but they fall short of generating authentic regional integration schemes. While APEC was founded by twelve countries in 1989 at the initiative of Australia, and has grown into a membership of twenty-four countries around Asia-Pacific, ASEM (the Asia-Europe Meeting) is an informal process of dialogue and cooperation between the EU member states and ten Asian countries (Brunei, China, Indonesia, Japan, South Korea, Malaysia, the Philippines, Singapore, Thailand and Vietnam). The fact that not all ASEAN members participate is as indicative for missing political cohesion as it is for the purely economic approach of ASEM. While APEC was founded with the intention to develop into an OECD-like system for Asia-Pacific (including the Pacific countries of Latin America), ASEM – representing 1.9 million people – was largely conceived as a support mechanism for developing global free trade regimes in the context of the WTO.[43] Potentially, ASEAN could be joined by Japan, China, and South Korea – or even a united Korea. Such a prospect for "ASEAN Plus Three" is supported by the increasing participation of the three Northeast Asian economic giants in ASEAN activities. Membership of the three economic giants of Northeast Asia in ASEAN would clearly redefine the rationale of ASEAN: It would "widen" it in a way that would render "deepening" imperative in order to avoid complete dominance by China. In November 2007, ASEAN surprised many of its critics with the signing of the ASEAN Charter.In December 2008, after completing the ratification process, the ASEAN Charter entered into force. Most remarkable, it includes the establishment of a human rights body in the ASEAN region, albeit without binding and enforcing powers.

41 See Wichmann, Peter, *Die politischen Perspektiven der ASEAN: Subregionale Integration oder supranationale Kooperation*, Hamburg: Institut für Asienkunde, 1996.

42 See Ortiz Mena, Antonio, *Regional Integration in the Americas and the Pacific Rim*, La Jolla: California Center for Iberian and Latin American Studies, 1997; Bridges, Brian, *Europe and the Challenge of the Asia-Pacific*, Cheltenham: Edward Elgar, 1999; Chirathivat, Suthipand, et al. (eds.), *Asia-Europe on the Eve of the twenty-first century*, Bangkok: Saksopha Press, 2001; Van Hoa, Tran, and Charles Harvie (eds.), *New Asian Regionalism: Responses to Globalisation and Crises*, Basingstoke: Macmillan, 2003.

43 See Nathan, K.S., *The European Union, United States and ASEAN: Challenges and Prospects for Cooperative Engagement in the twenty-first century*, London: ASEAN Academic Press, 2002.

(b) The Gulf Cooperation Council (GCC) was founded in 1981 as a defensive measure of the conservative Gulf monarchies against the threat of a spill-over of the Islamic revolution in Iran. Cooperation between Bahrain (with a history of tensions between its Sunni and Shiite populations), Kuwait (which also has a Shiite minority), Oman, Qatar, Saudi Arabia and the United Arab Emirates has developed considerably. It is poised to transform into regional integration for a population of 28 million with the implementation of a common currency for the Gulf countries targeted for 2010.

The Gulf Cooperation Council can rely on many commonalities other regional integration schemes fall short of: Its citizens speak the same language, practice the same religion – although with notable variants – they follow comparable social patterns and live with roughly the same structure and standard of economic development. Finally they have similar systems of governments. This might however develop into the biggest obstacle for comprehensive integration as a new wave of transformation and democratization is sweeping through the region. At the same time, the most conservative Arab state, Saudi Arabia, is increasingly exposed to threats from terrorists blaming its regime for being hypocritical and too close to the United States. The dominating role of Saudi Arabia in the Gulf Cooperation Council has always been a matter of concern as the smaller Gulf States seem to be more interested in thorough integration than their big Western neighbor.

At the time of independence of the smaller Gulf States – Kuwait gained independence from Great Britain in 1961 – it seemed possible that all of them might replace British suzerainty with a joint system of statehood. After prolonged negotiations, in 1975 only the seven Trucial Sheikhdoms of Abu Dhabi, Dubai, Sharjah, Ajman, Ras al Khaimah, Fujairah and Umm al Quwain agreed to form the United Arab Emirates, while Bahrain and Qatar opted for independent statehood. The Sultanate of Oman gradually opened up during the 1970's. In 1976 Oman hosted a meeting of the Foreign Ministers of Iran, Iraq, Kuwait, Bahrain, Qatar, the United Arab Emirates, Saudi Arabia and Oman to discuss a coordinated regional security and defense policy. The effort ended without any consent or conclusion among the participants. It took the threat of a spill-over of the Islamic Revolution in Iran of early 1979 to speed up the thrust for cooperation and integration in the Gulf – as a protective measure against one of the potential participants in any logical cooperation around the Arab/Persian Gulf.

After the Soviet Union invaded Afghanistan in December 1979, the geopolitical situation looked increasingly dangerous for stability and legitimacy in the Gulf region. Worsening relations between Iran and Iraq, leading to their protracted war between 1980 and 1988, forced the remaining Gulf States to act. At the initiative of Kuwait, they signed the founding Charter of the Gulf Cooperation Council in May 1981. The Charter refers to the "ultimate aim of unity" (Article 4) and an eventual confederal union emanating from the GCC framework.

The Gulf Cooperation Council consists of the Supreme Council as its highest authority, representing the six Heads of State of the member states. When necessary, the Supreme Council can constitute itself as Dispute Settlement Board. In the Council, where each country has a single vote, unanimity is required to achieve decisions and approve common policies. The Chairmanship in the Supreme Council rotates every year. Below the Supreme Council, the GCC consists of the Ministerial Council, the forum for the Foreign Ministers of the six member states. This is the working policy group of the GCC, supported by other GCC ministerial and expert committees. The Secretariat in Riyadh administrates the GCC and initiates studies reviewing the potential for integration projects. Within the general framework of the Arab world, the GCC has always been perceived as "a force of moderation, conciliation and mediation."[44] The GCC has been involved in mediating several conflicts between the Sultanate of Oman and the then People's Republic of Yemen. After the unification of the two Yemenite states in 1990, forming the Arab Republic of Yemen, efforts of gradual approximation of Yemen to the GCC have been pursued on the level of expert and technical cooperation, leading to a cooperation agreement with Yemen in 1998. The issue of Yemenite membership in the Gulf Cooperation Council remains unresolved, not the least because of the regime difference between conservative Arab monarchies and the socialist Arab Republic. It has become linked to the various, albeit gradual and often incremental efforts of democratizing the conservative Gulf States. As one of the consequences of "9/11," their traditional regimes have come under pressure more than ever, and not the least from the US, their most loyal ally. Across the region, the issue of democratization has spread, not only with encouraging results. Democratization has become an additional dimension impacting region-building in the Gulf.

In earlier decades, the initial strategic and defense rationale behind the creation of the Gulf Cooperation Council led to a spill-over of the integration scheme into the economic sphere. This was more than logical given the rapid modernization of the Gulf region since the 1970's based on its oil exports and the absence of a diversified economy. GCC cooperation soon encouraged the need of oil-producing countries of the Gulf to jointly embark on a strategy of economic diversification in order to strengthen their independence from oil and gas revenues. The member states of the Gulf Cooperation Council hold 45 percent of the world's oil reserves and supply 20 percent of the global production of crude oil. Based on estimates as to the duration of oil and gas reserves, only Kuwait and Qatar might be able to completely rely on oil and gas income for their foreseeable future. Diversification of the economy is a crucial

44 Christie, John, "History and Development of the Gulf Cooperation Council: A Brief Overview," in: Sandwick, John A. (ed.), *The Gulf Cooperation Council: Moderation and Stability in an Interdependent World*, Boulder: Westview Press, 1987: 14.

challenge for all Gulf Cooperation countries in order to make their cooperation sustainable.[45]

In which way the strategic and economic rationale for region-building may be linked to the issue of political and regime transformations remains to be seen. The prime focus has clearly shifted from the original strategic concern about the possible spread of the Islamic revolution in the 1980's to economic considerations and the fear to become too abruptly exposed to the uncontrollable effects of democratization. A new geostrategic dimension arose in the Gulf region in the wake of the terrorist attacks on the United States on September 11, 2001, and the subsequent debate about the stability of Saudi Arabia and the need for the democratic transformation of the Broader Middle East. While some of the smaller Gulf countries embarked on a cautious but steady path toward constitutional monarchy with elements of popular democracy – with local elections as in Qatar, parliamentary elections as in Kuwait, and new constitutional elements as in Bahrain – the difference between the smaller Gulf states and the overwhelming size and impact of Saudi Arabia for the region became even more visible. The constellation remains ambivalent at best.

All GCC countries remain committed to establish a common currency. A GCC summit in December 2009 decided to establish a Gulf Monetary Institute, a clear indication for the sincerity of the project of Gulf monetary union. The geopolitical tensions in the Broader Middle East coincide with severe generational changes across the region.[46] A possible membership of a democratic Iraq could alter the power relations and political priorities of the Gulf Cooperation Council tremendously. In the meantime, the EU has discovered the Gulf Cooperation Council as a preferential partner in the region of such importance for the EU's energy supply and long-term political stability:[47] Eventually, the EU aims at a bi-regional free trade agreement with the GCC.

(c) One of the least functioning regional integration schemes covers South Asia with India as its centerpiece. From its foundation in 1985, the South Asian Association for Regional Cooperation (SAARC) has suffered from the towering power of the largest democracy in the world and from the unwillingness of all its member states to take up controversial issues. The India-Pakistan controversy has been one of the most dangerous regional conflicts in the world for decades. It has therefore come as a surprise

45 See Braun, Ursula, *Der Kooperationsrat am Golf: Eine neue Kraft? Regionale Integration als Stabilitätsfaktor*, Baden-Baden: Nomos, 1986; Nakhleh, Emile A., *The Gulf Cooperation Council: Policies, Problems and Prospects*, Westport/London: Praeger, 1986; Peterson, Erik R., *The Gulf Cooperation Council: Search for Unity in a Dynamic Region*, Boulder: Westview, 1988; Ramazani, R. K., *The Gulf Cooperation Council: Record and Analysis*, Charlottesville: University Press of Virginia, 1988; Al-Alkim, Hassan, *The GCC States in an Unstable World: Foreign Policy Dilemmas of Small States*, London: Saqi Books, 1994.

46 See Fasano, Ugo (ed.), *Monetary Union Among Member Countries of the Gulf Cooperation Council*, Washington D.C.: International Monetary Fund, 2003.

47 See Luciano, Giacomo, and Felix Neugart (eds.), *The EU and the GCC: A New Partnership*, Munich: Bertelsmann Stiftung, 2005.

to many that SAARC never broke down altogether over the contentious issues related to this conflict. Instead, it has continued on a quiet path to consolidated institutionalization with the help of its Secretariat based in Kathmandu. Being itself at the center of violent political controversies since the late 1990's, Nepal has not been able to put visible weight behind the role that the SAARC Secretariat could possibly play. SAARC continues to exist with the membership of India, Pakistan, Nepal, Bangladesh, Sri Lanka, Bhutan and the Maldives. It is the most impossible combination of countries and political regimes, socio-economic realities and ethnic composition, religious and linguistic diversity the world could possibly offer. And yet, the unifying geographical factor has calmed down all possible reservations against the very idea of a South Asian form of regional co-operation and, potentially, integration.

South Asia has a total population of 1.3 billion people. More than 500 million of them live in extreme poverty, representing 44 percent of the poorest of the poor in the world who have to live on less than one dollar per day. South Asia accounts for not more than 2 percent of global GDP and 2.2 percent of the external trade of the European Union is conducted with the region. India is the most important economic factor of the region, receiving 0.4 percent of foreign direct investment stemming from the EU. SAARC was founded – as its Charter says – with the aim of "promoting the well-being of the populations of South Asia and improving their standard of living; this includes speeding up economic growth, social progress and cultural development, reinforcing links between the countries of this area, and lastly, promoting mutual collaboration and assistance in the economic, social, cultural, technical and scientific fields." The ambitions of SAARC stand in sharp contrast to the real power of the integration scheme. From the beginning, decision-making in SAARC was reduced to unanimity. The consultative nature of the process of co-operation was based on the agreement not to deal with controversial issues among the states involved. Given the conflicts in the region – most notably between Pakistan and India, but also those troubling Sri Lanka and Nepal – this founding principle left SAARC practically impotent from its very beginning.[48] With the improvement of political relations between India and Pakistan in the early years of the twenty-first century, new impulses for strengthened integration were proposed by leaders of both countries. One effect of this thaw has been the agreement of Pakistan and India concerning full SAARC membership of Afghanistan in 2006. The other remarkable effect has been the final agreement on a South Asian Free Trade Agreement in 2006, to be implemented within ten years.

In light of the conflicting interests on the South Asian subcontinent, it might be surprising that SAARC came into being at all. Its founding intention, driven by India's diplomacy, was aimed at supporting the policy of non-use of force between India and Pakistan. This was more a negative than a positive definition of region-building. In

48 See Kalam, Abul, *Subregionalism in Asia: ASEAN and SAARC Experiences*, New Delhi: UBS Publishers, 2001.

1988, during the early days of SAARC, India and Pakistan concluded three agreements prohibiting attacks against nuclear installations and facilities and promoting cultural co-operation and the avoidance of double taxation, thus demonstrating the almost bizarre combination of issues driving the agenda of the subcontinent, as SAARC's first Secretary General even admitted.[49] So far, there is enormous resistance in SAARC to revise the original Charter and the working mechanisms of its bodies that include a Standing Committee of Foreign Secretaries, Technical Committees and Committees of Economic Co-operation. Optimistic observers argue that SAARC has induced a certain dynamic of intensified civil society co-operation in the region that could eventually spurn a political reassessment of the parameters of regional integration.[50]

Until today, the disputes between India and Pakistan have prevented SAARC from developing its full potential. Likewise, efforts to create an Indian Ocean Rim Economic Growth Area have been curtailed by these disputes. Instability of some of the regimes in SAARC, most notably in Bangladesh, the struggle with authoritarianism (Maldives), a finally successful anti-monarchic Maoist rebellion (Nepal), uncertain steps to begin the process of constitutionalizing a monarchy (Bhutan), the threat of returning to ethnically induced civil war (Sri Lanka), and first and foremost, the shadow of a failing state (Pakistan) have contributed to a rather negative image of SAARC. These divergent and contradicting regime realities across the region have rendered most constructive initiatives futile, leaving South Asia as "one of the last regions to wake up to the challenge of the new regionalism."[51] Conflict resolution in South Asia, such as the India-Bangladesh scheme to regulate the supply of Ganges waters, or the search for solutions to the civil war in Sri Lanka, took place outside the SAARC mechanism. In order to make meaningful sense, regional cooperation and integration in South Asia requires more regime cohesion among its member countries and a visible increase in complementary economic structures. Unless these fundamental preconditions are achieved, every effort to promote cooperation and trust on the Indian subcontinent will remain hostage of fragile political circumstances. It must however be added that the very existence of the South Asian Association of Regional Cooperation is a recognition of the potential that might be developed further during the course of the twenty-first century. In fact, it might turn out to be the only path to overcome the socio-economic pressure in the region that is mounting, notwithstanding the emergence of a middle class. Eventually, it might be this South Asian middle class that will promote reforms aimed at political and economic complementarity in South Asia as precondition for

49 Bhargava, Kant K., *EU-SAARC: Comparisons and Prospects for Cooperation*, ZEI Discussion Paper C15. Bonn: Center for European Integration Studies, 1998: 7.

50 See Quadir, Fahimul, "Civil Society and Informal Regionalism in South Asia: The Prospects for Peace and Human Security in the Twenty-First Century," in: Hentz, James J., and Morten Boas (eds.), *New and Critical Security and Regionalism: Beyond the Nation-State*, Aldershot: Ashgate , 2003: 113-126.

51 Hettne, Bjoern, "Security Regionalism in Europe and South Asia," in: Hentz, James J., and Morten Boas (eds.), *New and Critical Security and Regionalism: Beyond the Nation-State*, op.cit.: 159.

viable and sustainable regional integration. Still, the path is long and the hope blurred by uncertainties, such as lingering Islamic radicalism in Pakistan that overshadows her transformation from military dictatorship to democracy. For the time being, this poses a new threat to stable regional integration based on democracy and integrated market economies.

(4) Eurasia

The Commonwealth of Independent States (CIS) is the product of post-Soviet geopolitical developments in Eurasia. It has been an instrument in managing the demise of the Soviet Empire without turning into a prospect of sustainable positive region-building. Its original purpose – taming the demise of Soviet power and organizing Russia's new regional base as a global power – was reasonably successful. Going beyond and developing into a new Eurasian regional grouping of solid standing and wide-ranging perspective has remained a vague hope for some and an empty promise for most observers. When the CIS was created on December 8, 1991, its founding members Russia, Ukraine and Belarus stated that the Soviet Union had disappeared as subject of international law and geopolitical reality. On December 21, 1991, CIS was enlarged by admitting Turkmenistan, Uzbekistan, Tajikistan, Kazakhstan, Kyrgyzstan, Moldova, Armenia and Azerbaijan. The CIS committed itself to comply with responsibilities stemming from international treaties signed by the Soviet Union. This included a binding commitment to the common control of nuclear weapons. The CIS stated its support for human rights, the protection of national minorities and respect for the territorial integrity of its member states. On May 15, 1992, a CIS Collective Security Treaty was signed by Armenia, Kazakhstan, Kyrgyzstan, Russia, Tajikistan and Uzbekistan, later also by Azerbaijan, Belarus and Georgia, which joined the CIS in 1993. The Collective Security Treaty reaffirmed the desire of its participating states to abstain from the use or threat of force among themselves. They also promised not to join any other military alliance. In 1999, Azerbaijan, Uzbekistan and Georgia withdrew from the Collective Security Treaty, with Georgia stating that it had been incorporated against its will into the Soviet Union. In 2005 Turkmenistan discontinued its CIS membership and became an associate member. In 2006 Georgia left the CIS military structure and in 2008 – after the Russian-Georgian war in South Ossetia – it left CIS at large, frustrated however of not being immediately invited as a member of NATO and of the European Union.

The Commonwealth of Independent States does not carry any supranational competences. In that regard, it is fundamentally different from the European Union. On the other hand, it is rooted in the long common history of former Soviet republics with their specific form of state-controlled industrialization and an integrated market. This market had broken down as a consequence of the demise of the Soviet Union and its economic imperatives. Yet, traditional mentality and power structures reflecting the highly ambivalent post-Soviet transformation process prevail.

The founding Charter of the Commonwealth of Independent States of January 22, 1993, declared sovereign equality among its member states and recognized each of them as a sovereign member of the international state system. With the signing of the Treaty on Economic Union in September 1993, the CIS embarked on the path to stronger integration, as if by then the European Union was perceived as a distant model.[52]

The Treaty on the establishment of an Economic Union is based on the goal of transforming the interaction of economic relations among CIS member states into a common economic space. It states the principle of free movement of goods, capital, services and workers, thus recalling the original goals of the EC's Single Market. It outlines concerted money and credit policies as well as, tax, customs and foreign economic policies. It defines mechanisms that favour direct production links among CIS countries and a rapprochement of the methods of management of economic affairs. CIS has addressed issues as diverse as transport corridors in its vast territory and common health protection-methods. The proliferation of drugs originating in Afghanistan, for example, has been a concern for the CIS. By remembering the fifteenth anniversary of the Chernobyl atomic power plant catastrophe in 2001 and by coordinating activities commemorating the "Great Patriotic War of 1941-1945" (elsewhere known as World War II), CIS member states invoked a common culture of memory. Unresolved post-Soviet conflicts in Chechnya, Nagorno-Karabach and Abkhazia were as much on the agenda of CIS meetings, for example during a meeting in October 2002, as issues of inter-state TV and radio broadcasting, "in the interest of enhancing mutual understanding and cooperation between CIS member states."[53] In 2003, for the first time a single budget of the CIS was adopted. The full implementation of a free-trade zone – transforming into a single economic space by 2010 – had priority during CIS meetings in the early years of the twenty-first century. Even official documents were forced to recognize that some member states were falling behind the early implementation of measures agreed upon by all CIS member states.

The need for more efficient foreign policy measures was another perennial issue for CIS. The conduct of joint anti-terrorist actions in all CIS countries echoed not only the change in the global arena since the terrorist attacks of September 11, 2001, in the US, but also the ongoing bitter conflicts in the Northern Caucasus region. So far the existence of a CIS Commission on Human Rights has not helped change the direction these conflicts have taken. CIS peacekeeping was developed early on and the first

52 See Leonhardt, Wolfgang, *Spiel mit dem Feuer: Russlands schmerzhafter Weg zur Demokratie*, Bergisch-Gladbach: Lübbe, 1996: 146-151; Strezhneva, Marina, *Social Culture and Regional Governance: Comparison of the European Union and Post-Soviet Experiences*, Commack: Nova Scotia Publishers, 1999.

53 See Meeting of the Leaders of CIS Member States, October 6./7.2002, www.cis.minsk.by/english/meet_cis.htm.

experiences with CIS peacekeeping missions were made in Tajikistan and in Abkhazia.[54]

CIS structures remain intergovernmental. The Council of Heads of State, the Council of Heads of Government, including various ministerial councils, an Inter-Parliamentary Assembly, a joint Council of Commanders of Border Troops and the Secretariat of the CIS are the most important bodies. The Secretariat of the "Commonwealth of Independent States" is based in Minsk, the capital of Belarus. Although its functions were widened over time, like all CIS organs it lacks cohesive orders of competencies. Most important however is the uncertainty about the very concept on which CIS is based. While some countries still consider CIS a mild "divorce" from Russia and a means to protect their fragile sovereignty, Russia considers the CIS as an instrument to project its ambitions of power throughout the post-Soviet sphere. The three Baltic republics, Estonia, Latvia and Lithuania, joined both the European Union and NATO in 2004, the first former Soviet republics with a definitely new geopolitical orientation. The future of the other twelve former Soviet republics remains as unsettled as CIS itself: Between 2003 and 2005, the post-Communist and pro-Russian leadership of three CIS member states – Shevardnadze in Georgia, Kuchma in the Ukraine, and Akayev in Kyrgyzstan – was overthrown in a series of peaceful revolutions. The Ukraine, along with Georgia and in a limited way with Moldova, has taken the strongest pro-Western stance among CIS member states. With the Russian-Georgian war in South Ossetia in August 2008, the claim of CIS to contribute to a post-Soviet peace among all its member states was dead.

Initially, the CIS has undoubtedly contributed to the post-Soviet stabilization of the region. Its contributions to peacekeeping were noteworthy although it has not contributed to resolving ethnic rivalries and conflicts in the Northern Caucasus. The CIS has supported the development of a certain common economic space in Eurasia, but it has not supported the development of the rule of law and democratic governance in a post-Soviet environment in which "democratization is a promise rather than a reality".[55] All in all, the CIS member states have not achieved the ultimate goal of their original endeavor. This fact is however only one element in the ongoing search for a new identity in post-Soviet Eurasia.[56]

All in all, for the first one and half decades of its existence, CIS has remained weak and rather without authority as it has not been able to transform itself into the nucleus of a substantially supranational mechanism. While inter-state borders among CIS member states did not remain impermeable, new visa regimes were established between CIS

54 See Jonson, Lena, and Clive Archer (eds.), *Peacekeeping and the Role of Russia in Eurasia*, Boulder: Westview, 1996; Nazarkin, Yuri K., *Peeace-Keeping Operation in the CIS*, http://ieis.lu/books/future_role_of_russia/nazarkin.PDF.

55 Strezhneva, Marina, *Social Culture and Regional Governance: Comparison of the European Union and Post-Soviet Experiences*, op.cit.: 25.

56 For instance Trenin, Dmitri, *The End of Eurasia: Russia on the Border between Geopolitics and Globalization*, Moscow: Carnegie Endowment for International Peace, 2001.

member states, making freedom of movement more difficult than during the time of the Soviet Union. The quest for strengthened national sovereignty has clashed more than once with the potential of regional cooperation and integration in Eurasia. For the time being, the Commonwealth of Independent States might retain a post-imperial function among its remaining member states in the multiple processes of state-building in Eurasia. In the end, however, CIS might be more comparable to failed post-colonial efforts of federalism exercised by former European colonial powers in the Caribbean or in Africa.

(5) Oceania

The evolution of regional integration has become a global reality. Even most island countries in Oceania have begun to consider the benefits of regional cooperation, and potentially of integration. The Pacific Islands Forum (PIF) is the youngest expression of the global search for region-building. Its development has been driven not least by prospects of a Pacific regional Economic Partnership Agreement with the EU by 2008.[57]

Sixteen Pacific countries and territories are members of the Pacific Islands Forum (PIF): Australia, Cook Islands, Federated States of Micronesia, Fiji, Kiribati, Nauru, New Zealand, Niue, Palau, Papua New Guinea, Marshall Islands, Samoa, Solomon Islands, Tonga, Tuvalu and Vanuatu. They claim to represent "the Pacific Way," a term coined in the 1970's by the first Prime Minister of independent Fiji, Ratu Sir Kamisese Mara. He claimed that "the Pacific Way" would be different from Western ways of conflict resolution: Nobody would be left out, decision-making would always be consensual and the norm of non-interference would be strongly recognized.

Between 1971 and 1999, the precursor to the Pacific Islands Forum was in effect: the South Pacific Forum. Founded in Wellington on August 5-7, 1971, it remained a structure largely dominated by New Zealand, as much as the South Pacific Commission was defined by the strong role of Australia. The South Pacific Forum was by and large a confidence-building measure. It was never institutionalized and had neither legal personality nor a formal voting structure. Decision-making among its members was done by consensus.

The 30th Forum Summit, held in Koror on Palau from October 3-5, 1999, became an act of refounding the basis for regional cooperation and eventual integration in the Pacific. The South Pacific Forum was renamed Pacific Islands Forum. The agreement to establish the Pacific Islands Secretariat was signed on October 30, 2000, in Tarawa, being replaced by a new constitutive treaty at the 36th Forum Summit on October 27, 2005, in Papua New Guinea. This Agreement Establishing the Pacific Islands Forum confirmed the future objectives: "The purpose of the Forum is to strengthen regional

57 See Holland, Martin, *The European Union and the Third World*, Houndmills: Palgrave, 2002; *Neue Zürcher Zeitung*, "Eine 'pazifische Union' am Horizont?," August 9, (2004).

cooperation and integration, including through the pooling of regional resources of governance and the alignment of policies, in order to further Forum members' shared goals of economic growth, sustainable development, good governance and security." (Article II). The ultimate vision is a region "where people can all lead free and worthwhile lives." The Pacific Islands Forum considers itself "an international organization in its own right." It distinguishes between membership, associate membership and observer status.

Beside the Pacific Forum Secretariat and the annual leaders Summit, a Forum Official's Committee was introduced as an Executive Committee. By and large, the Pacific Islands Forum remains a deliberative body, which excludes controversial issues and is short of legally binding mechanisms that would help to implement decisions. This is problematic for development goals as well as for security matters. More rooted in the Pacific island world than ever, an Australian was even able to become its Secretary General. Australia and New Zealand continue to each provide one-third of the budgets of the Pacific Islands Forum. In the meantime, the constructive involvement of New Zealand and Australia in the Pacific Islands Forum is without any doubt. They have become recognized as Pacific countries while their own attitude toward the Pacific islands region has also changed. The fact that the number of Pacific migrants to New Zealand has increased from 3,600 in 1951 to more than a quarter million today has contributed to this change in outlook in New Zealand. As for Australia, the dilemma of being perceived as big brother, yet trying to play the constructive role of a simple partner country prevails.

The Pacific Islands Forum has begun to transform the structures of the former South Pacific Forum into more viable institutions of regional cooperation.[58] In 2001, the Pacific Islands Forum introduced new mechanisms to advance economic cooperation. This was done under Australian pressure and largely in response to the European Union's Agreement with the EU partner countries in the Caribbean, in Asia and in the Pacific (Cotonou Agreement). Australia wanted its island neighbors to advance economic cooperation and not lose its own position in the Pacific. Except for Vanuatu, all Pacific Islands Forum members signed the Pacific Agreement on Closer Economic Relations (PACER), followed by the Pacific Island Countries Trade Agreement (PICTA).[59] PACER is an umbrella agreement, allowing PIF member states to start Forum-wide negotiations no later than eight years after PICTA was to enter into force, but no later than 2011. In other words: In 2011, the PIF countries have to begin negotiations on free trade, which is very much in the interest of Australia. In theory, the PACER agreement allows the PIF member states to negotiate a free trade agreement at

58 Shibuya, Eric, "The Problems and Potential of the Pacific Islands Forum," in: Rolfe, Jim (ed.), *The Asia-Pacific: A Region in Transition*, Honolulu: Asia-Pacific Center for Security Studies, 2004: 102-115.

59 Kelsey, Jane, *A People's Guide to PACER: The Implications for the Pacific Islands of the Pacific Agreement on Closer Economic relations (PACER)*, Suva: Pacific Network on Globalisation, 2004.

their own pace and without external pressure. In reality this sovereignty-friendly promise of PACER was already undermined in 2002 when the PIF member states began to negotiate free trade conditions with the European Union under the Cotonou Agreement signed in 2000. PACER provides for cooperation among the PIF member states on trade facilitation schemes and financial and technical assistance, including trade promotion, capacity building and structural adjustment.

The Pacific Island Countries Trade Agreement (PICTA) took effect in 2003. It focuses on free trade of goods and pursues the goal of trade liberalization over a period of eight years until 2010 for the developing countries of the region and over a period of 10 years for the "smaller island countries" and the poorest countries of the region. The most sensitive industries can be protected in each country until 2016. PICTA does not exclude a later extension of liberalization to the fields of services and investment. The European Union understood PICTA to be a stepping-stone for the negotiation of a Regional Economic Partnership Agreement by 2008. While Australia and New Zealand are left out of the negotiations that have been under way since 2002, they are particularly keen on seeing PICTA and PACER work. They seek to legitimize both regional trade liberalization agreements as genuine expressions of local efforts by the small Pacific island states "to ride the waves of economic globalization without being swept away."[60]

The trade liberalization efforts in the Pacific are a matter of continuous discussion surrounding the relationship between globalization, national autonomy and the social consequences of free trade – not unlike in other regions of the world. The dependency of the small and poor Pacific countries on customs duties is a particular problem in this regard. Customs duties represent a high degree of total tax revenues in the Pacific: 64 percent for Kiribati, 57 percent for Vanuatu, 46 percent for Tuvalu.

Along with the new constituent treaty of the Pacific Islands Forum (Agreement Establishing the Pacific Islands Forum), the 36th PIF Summit on October 25-27, 2005, in Madang (Papua New Guinea) endorsed the Pacific Plan. This is a wide ranging long-term concept for the potential future development of the Pacific Islands Forum. It is aimed

- to enhance and stimulate economic growth;
- to promote sustainable development;
- to enhance good governance; and
- to increase security through regionalism for all Pacific countries.

The Pacific Plan is the most comprehensive outline of region-building ambitions by the Pacific Islands Forum. In principle, the Pacific Plan is non-political, technical and defers to national sovereignty. "Regionalism under the Pacific Plan," it states, "does not imply any limitation on national sovereignty. It is not intended to replace any national

60 Shibuya, Eric, "The Problems and Potential of the Pacific Islands Forum," in: Rolfe, Jim (ed.), *The Asia-Pacific: A Region in Transition*, op.cit.: 113.

programmes, only to support and complement them."[61] The defensive character of this statement is telling. On the one hand, the Pacific island countries are aware of the actual limitation of their sovereignty. On the other hand, their national pride is as strong as their desire to improve real living conditions. The declaratory commitment to national sovereignty and autonomy is therefore coupled with concrete and realistic proposals for pragmatic and functional cooperation. In the end, however, this cooperation will transform the very notion and explicit character of national sovereignty and nationhood. The Pacific region will not be able to escape the universal experience of other schemes of regional cooperation and integration.

3. Europe and the Rest: Comparing Notes

So far, none of the non-European integration schemes has achieved a breakthrough toward supranationality comparable to the European experience. In order to do justice to the limited success of regional integration outside Europe, it is imperative to recall the time-line of the global proliferation of region- building:

- The Central American Common Market (Mercado Commun Centroamericano, MCCA) was founded in 1960 and refounded as the Central American Integration System (Sistema de la Integración Centroamericana, SICA) in 1993.
- The Organization of African Unity (OAU) was founded in 1963 and refounded as African Union (AU) in 2000.
- The Association of Southeast Asian Nations (ASEAN) was founded in 1967.
- The Pacto Andino was founded in 1969 and refounded as Andean Community of Nations (Comunidad Andina de Naciones, CAN) in 1997.
- The South Pacific Forum was founded in 1971 and refounded as Pacific Islands Forum in 1999.
- The Caribbean Community (CARICOM) was founded in 1973 and practically refounded in 2001.
- The Economic Community of West African States (ECOWAS) was founded in 1975 and practically refounded in 1993.
- The South African Development Cooperation Council (SADCC) was founded in 1980 and refounded as Southern African Development Community (SADC) in 1992.
- The East African Community (EAC) was founded in 1967 and refounded after complete dissolution in 2000.
- The Gulf Cooperation Council (GCC) was founded in 1981.

61 Pacific Islands Forum, *The Pacific Plan*, https://.forumsec.org.fj/docs/PPlan/Final%20Draft%20%Pacific%20Plan-%20Sept%202005.pdf.4.

- The South Asian Association of Regional Cooperation (SAARC) was founded in 1985.
- The Southern Common Market (Mercado Común del Sur, MERCOSUR) was founded in 1991.
- The Commonwealth of Independent States (CIS) was founded in 1991.

The life span of all these schemes of regional cooperation and integration is too short to draw conclusions concerning their relevance and long-term impact. Looking back to the history of five decades of European integration, it would have been unhistorical to judge the European Union's ultimate fate by the stage of development of the European Economic Community in 1970, prior to even fully realizing its primary goal of customs union. Nobody can envisage the state of regional integration-formation in Central America by 2020, in the Gulf by 2030, in Asia by 2040 or in Africa by 2050. Yet, preliminary comparative remarks can already be made in the first decade of the twenty-first century. They must have two different approaches: On the one hand, one can ask as to how far key features explaining the success of European integration can be found elsewhere, if only in embryonic form. On the other hand, the current state of regional cooperation and integration outside Europe can be compared in terms of the genuine goals of each scheme and the challenges each of the efforts has encountered so far.

Ten preliminary conclusions can be drawn that invite further research on comparative global regionalism.[62]

(1) There is no universally applicable theory of integration. No law of politics explains inevitable patterns toward regional integration. Contingent combinations of motives, context, goals, interests and potentials define every individual integration process. It is evidently not necessary to begin the path toward integration with supranational elements in order to eventually reach such a stage of integration. With the Pillar Structure of the Treaty of Maastricht, the European Union has shown that intergovernmental cooperation can plant the seed for later supranational integration. The journey along one or the other of the discussed integration schemes might end up taking the same course. Pooling sovereignty over time must not mean beginning with a pooling of sovereignty. One can get there at a later stage. The fact that none of the non-European integration schemes has achieved supranational elements yet does not justify the conclusion that they will never reach that stage. It remains true however that only supranational pooling of sovereignty under the scheme of a common legal order distinguishes regional integration as understood in Europe from cooperative regional integration and other variants of economic and/or political cooperation.

62 For authentic assessments from different regional groupings see Kösler, Ariane, and Martin Zimmek (eds.), *Global Voices on Regional Integration*, ZEI Discussion Paper C 176, Bonn, Center for European Integration Studies, 2007.

(2) The assumption that regional integration continues according to consistent patterns of spill-over must not necessarily be true either. The non-European experience with integration suggests that functional integration takes place notwithstanding the original purpose and orientation of integration schemes. It can, in fact, reach out at any time into a new policy field, depending on political circumstances in a region and decisions taken by regional political leaders (ASEAN, MERCOSUR, SAARC, ECOWAS, GCC, AU). Non-European integration experience also suggests that renewed and intensified integration must not necessarily complete a chosen path along the model of European integration elsewhere. It can leave some integration processes "unfinished", while embarking on a new set of integration policies. Non-European experience also testifies to the fact that integration can fail completely and lead to the dissolution of a seemingly well-established effort (i.e. the East African Community). Non-European experience supports the European experience that processes of "deepening" integration efforts from the logic of economic integration to the sphere of foreign policy and security are not mutually exclusive with means to "widening" the integration community in order to achieve regional membership cohesion (ASEAN, CARICOM, SADC).

(3) All non-European states have originally "copied" the traditional European notion of state-centered sovereignty (the "Westphalian state system"). As much as European states have encountered the limits of this concept and have embarked on the long process to overcome its constraints and flaws, most non-European states – with the United States as a certain exception –encountered the limits of their capacity as single states. In fact, they all contributed to our understanding of sovereignty as "organized hypocrisy" – which contains also a lesson for the United States.[63] Most non-European states concluded the need and usefulness of transnational cooperation and eventual supranational integration as the best possible answer to the limits of the Westphalian model. Motives remain mixed and approaches mostly inconclusive, yet a general experience is evident in non-European efforts toward regional integration: The search for answers to specific economic, political or security challenges is increasingly geared toward regional responses. Formal pooling of sovereignty might come last, but the trend away from rigid state-centered solutions in order to meet the challenges individual states are encountering is obvious in all non-European schemes of regional integration building.

(4) The most important conclusion from the non-European experience with integration building is about the link between regime asymmetry – to be more precise: between a regional commonality of democratic systems – and advanced, trust-based integration with the potential of shared sovereignty and legal norms. The European experience underlines the conditions necessary to embark on the path for viable

63 See Krasner, Stephen D., *Sovereignty: Organized Hypocrisy*, Princeton: Princeton University Press, 1999.

democratic transnational cooperation and supranational integration: Countries are inclined to bind their fate together only if they recognize the political system of their partners as equivalent to their own (GCC, MERCOSUR, SICA). Dictatorships or authoritarian regimes might formally get together with democracies in an intergovernmental organization out of specifically defined common interests, but they will barely tolerate interference in their domestic affairs (ASEAN, SAARC, AU). As this is inevitably the ultimate consequence of pooled sovereignty, they remain reluctant to move from rhetorical integration to real integration. The more partner countries of a given regional integration scheme achieve regime cohesion among themselves, based on democratic governance and rule of law, the more likely it is that the integration process in a particular region can advance toward a better realization of its original ambition and potential. Only cohesion between state sovereignty and popular sovereignty can pave the way to transnational trust and supranational pooling of sovereignties, affecting both state systems and citizens rights. As long as bilateral conflicts nurture mistrust in a region that is also divided by different political regimes, viable integration progress is unlikely (SAARC, ASEAN, SADC). Yet, the seeds of certain integration potential can already be planted, thus recognizing and awakening a growing regional awareness of its desirability and necessity.

(5) The European experience with Franco-German partnership advancing the integration process, while at the same time overcoming historical resentments and balancing ongoing structural differences between the two countries, has been studied in non-European integration schemes. In the rare cases it was applied – even if only indirectly – it generated effects comparable to the European example of Franco-German cooperation (Argentina-Brazil, Thailand-Vietnam). More likely in non-European regions is either the presence of one dominating regional power in the absence of an obvious “lead couple” (Saudi-Arabia, India, Nigeria, South Africa, Russia). Often it is therefore not obvious which countries can play the joint role of a locomotive for regional integration. In the absence of this possibility, regional integration remains largely reactive to challenges the whole region can recognize as common concern. The strong inclination toward excessively consensual decision-making, which is typical in these cases of regional integration, is not supportive of efficient and speedy decision-making.

(6) The pattern of regional integration in a non-European setting does not suggest particular clarity as far as the choice for priorities is concerned. In some cases, defense considerations have generated integration schemes that nevertheless were immediately embarking on economic measures (GCC, ASEAN). In other cases, unfinished economic integration has not prevented partners of a regional integration scheme from starting joint foreign and security policy considerations with their distinct ramifications (ASEAN, SAARC, ECOWAS, SADC, MERCOSUR). The weaker national political or economic sovereignty, the weaker is the inclination – or the ability – to advance pooled

sovereignty on the regional level. Strengthened national confidence, coupled with the recognition of the limits of state-capacity, can support integration efforts. Strong sovereignty in non-European developing countries – as rare as it exists – has not been automatically supportive of the notion of shared or pooled sovereignty with other partners, all the more so if their domestic political system is different or even antagonistic (India, Russia).

(7) The discourse about the relationship between integration and identity has not been limited to Europe. Also outside Europe, geographic proximity and traditional patterns of commerce have been identified as "cultural" elements favoring the logic of integration. Obvious cultural cohesion has been invoked in some cases of non-European regional integration, but it is astonishing that this invocation has not automatically generated stronger integrative bonds (Latin America, GCC). More surprising however is the realization that enormous cultural differences do not necessarily impede the emergence of regional integration mechanisms (SAARC, ASEAN, CIS). They can even transcend into a counterfactual argument favoring the promotion of a regional "consciousness" based on geographic proximity and cultural pluralism. Given their own inclination to define culture exclusively, Europeans might believe that multicultural circumstances are unfavourable to cooperation. Reality elsewhere proves such European perceptions wrong.

(8) Most non-European integration efforts – as was the case in Europe – encountered substantial threats of failure, phases of stagnation, detours and obstacles that enforced a change of direction (SICA, CAN, AU). As in Europe, a stronger focus on regional integration was usually driven by external challenge and pressure. Integration processes always seem to depend, if not "rely" on external pressure. It almost seems as if they can almost hope for a second, externally induced encouragement whenever they exhaust their original internal commitment.

(9) In Europe as elsewhere, processes of regional integration generate multilateral and, moreover, multi-vertical realities – both formal and informal – that impact on the member states of an integration scheme as much as they impact the path of the integration process itself. In Europe, it took several decades before EU member states began to thoroughly experience the impact of integration: Since the 1990's, most of them have begun to increasingly view integration as an intrusion into their domestic political structures. Non-European experiences with integration will most likely go through similar stages. In the end, this mechanism could turn out to be more important than a formal transfer of sovereignty. In fact, it would equal a non-overt, informal transfer of sovereignty. It could lead to pooled sovereignty not by choice, but by implication.

(10) The effects of regional integration on the global state system and on political theory are only gradually emerging.[64] The European experiment has brought about a genuine political form, followed by a genuine notion of sovereignty, of multilevel democracy and governance, of multiple identities and an intuitively multilateral orientation in global affairs.[65] Whether or not these trends will repeat themselves in the context of other regions remains to be seen. The more solidified non-European regional integration becomes, the more it will contribute to the evolution of a multipolar world order, based on the roles of regions and continents, curiously enough with the United States and Canada, and, in a different setting, Australia and New Zealand primarily operating on their own. The global trend of regional integration will also impact our understanding of political theory, most notably about norms of democratic governance, concepts of pooled sovereignty and notions of multiple identities.

The European Union has begun to develop a pro-active policy of promoting worldwide region-building. With the success of European integration, Europe has overcome its image as the colonizing continent. Europe has returned to the world as a partner in cooperation, assistance and multilateralism. This new approach of Europe to world order-building finds an echo in the EU's promotion of region-building.[66] Three dimensions of the pro-active policy of the European Union can be identified:

- Support for existing efforts of region-building.
- Forming of regional groupings by classifying partners through bi-regional negotiations.
- Connecting with the existing and developing regional architectures.

Most comprehensive is the EU's policy toward the countries of Africa, the Caribbean and the Pacific. The EU maintains long-established relations with this group of the poorest countries in the world, the so-called ACP countries. Over time, the 1963 Yaoundé Convention has been replaced by four Lomé Conventions and the 2000 Cotonou Convention, paving the way for regionalized Economic Partnership Agreements (EPA) with various sub-groupings of the ACP countries. The EPA approach has been critiziced for being incoherent and self-serving.

A more political approach has accompanied the EU relations with ASEAN, the Gulf Cooperation Council, MERCOSUR, the Andean Community and the Central American System of Integration. Here, political dialogue has given way to the search for the

64 See also Fawcett, Louise, and Andrew Hurrell (eds.), *Regionalism in World Politics: Regional Organization and International Order*, New York: Oxford University Press, 1995.

65 See Kühnhardt, Ludger, *Constituting Europe: Identity, Institution-Building and the Search for a Global Role*, Baden-Baden: Nomos, 2003: 225-270.

66 See Aggarwal, Vinod K., and Edward A. Fogarty (eds.), *EU Trade Strategies: Between Regionalism and Globalism*, Houndmills: Palgrave Macmillan, 2004; Hettne, Björn, and Fredrik Söderbaum, "Civilian Power or Soft Imperialism?: The European Union as a Global Actor and the Role of Interregionalism," *European Foreign Policy Affairs Review*, 10.4 (2005): 535-552; Telò, Mario, *Europe, A Civilian Power?: European Union, Global Governance, World Power*, New York: Palgrave Macmillan, 2006.

formation of a more broad-based bi-regional association. It is significant for the inner fragility of SAARC and, even more so, of the Commonwealth of Independent States, that the EU has been reluctant to engage in comprehensive bi-regional activities with these two groupings. But all in all, it must be concluded that the EU is in search of bi-regional partnerships and associations across the world. Although only embryonic at this stage, inter-regionalism is becoming a new dimension in global governance.[67]

Interesting, but perhaps not surprising, is the absence of efforts of regional integration-building in those two regions of the world that are at the heart of the most troubling world conflicts and embody the most critical zones of strategic insecurity in the world: the Broader Middle East and Northeast Asia. Both regions reflect the mechanisms of outdated European power struggles (Northeast Asia) and unresolved issues of democratic nation- and state-building (Broader Middle East). Both regions are dominated by a "balance of suspicion," rooted in long-standing conflicts. In spite of North East Asia's share of 25 percent of the global economy, the region lacks a strategic equilibrium based on a common system of cooperative security or on an interdependence-oriented system of economic integration.[68] The Broader Middle East has been "discovered" as a region in the aftermath of the geostrategic implications of Islamic terrorism and the fear of a proliferation of weapons of mass destruction. This regional concept has been framed in response to the absence of democracy and pluralism in the region between "Marrakech and Bangladesh."[69] As in Northeast Asia, neither democratic regime cohesion nor shared understanding, or interest in the potential benefits of regional cooperation and subsequent integration as a path of overcoming regional insecurity and political antagonisms, exists yet in the Broader Middle East.

Instead, a balance of mistrust governs the Broader Middle East and Northeast Asia to this day. And yet, also these parts of the world are at least increasingly perceived as regions. Analysts have begun to discuss elements of comparison between the geostrategic stalemate in Northeast Asia and the European integration experience.[70] The

67 See Farrell, Mary, et al. (eds.), *Global Politics of Regionalism: Theory and Practice*, London: Pluto Press, 2005; Hänggi, Heiner, et al. (eds.), *Interregionalism and International Relations*, Abingdon/New York: Routledge, 2005.

68 See Kim, Samuel S., (ed.), *The International Relations of Northeast Asia*, Lanham: Rowman & Littlefield, 2004; Ludger Kühnhardt, *Northeast Asia: Obstacles to Regional Integration. The Interests of the European Union*, ZEI Discussion Paper C 152, Bonn: Center for European Integration Studies, 2005.

69 Asmus, Ronald D., and Kenneth M. Pollack, "The New Transatlantic Project," *Policy Review*, 115 (2002): 3-18; Kühnhardt, Ludger, *System-Opening and Cooperative Transformation of the Broader Middle East: A New Transatlantic Project and a Joint Euro-Atlantic-Arab Task*, EUROMESCO Papers No. 26, Lisbon: Euro-Mediterranean Study Commission, 2003; Scheffler, Thomas, "'Fertile Crescent', 'Orient', 'Middle East': The Changing Mental Maps of Southwest Asia," *European Review of History*, 10.2 (2003): 253-272; Marchetti, Andreas (ed.) *The CSCE as a Model to Transform Western Relations with the Broader Middle East*, ZEI Discussion Paper C 137. Bonn: Center for European Integration Studies, 2004.

70 See Dent, Christopher M., and David W.F. Huang (eds.), *Northeast Asian Regionalism: Learning from the European Experience*, London: Routledge, 2002; Moon, Woosik, and Bernadette

search to apply EU experiences to integration to a post-conflict Middle East has also generated remarkable proposals while the world is still torn by the ongoing and seemingly irresolvable conflict.[71]

The global proliferation of regional integration has spread the seeds of this process to all corners of the globe. Its ultimate result will not be judged merely by the growth in comparative power of any of these integration schemes, although this will always be an important category for the realistic study of world order. The value of regional integration has to be judged in itself through the prism of the people and countries involved. No matter what the impact of regional integration on global power equations will be, both the people and countries involved own, shape and determine each particular integration process and its effects. It is also in this context that the European integration experience – a Union of states and a Union of citizens – will continue to serve as a precedent for other regions around the globe. At long last, John Stuart Mill's assumption, written back in the second half of the nineteenth century, might find resonance: "When the conditions exist for the formation of efficient and durable federal unions, the multiplication of such is always a benefit to the world."[72]

Andreosso-O'Callaghan (eds.), *Regional Integration – Europe and Asia Compared*, Aldershot: Ashgate, 2005.

71 See Magen, Amichai, and Shlomo Shpiro, *Towards a Comprehensive Security Approach in the Middle East: Lessons from the European Experience in Justice and Home Affairs Cooperation*, Tel Aviv: The Tami Steinmetz Center for Peace Research, 2003.

72 Mill, John Stuart, *Considerations on Representative Government*, Amherst: Prometheus, 1991: 331-332.

Ideas, Norms, Theories

IX. Searching In Vain: Why European Integration did not Work Earlier

1. The Ambivalence between Culture and Politics in Europe

Europe is proud of its civilization. The diversity of European culture is appreciated across the globe. Yet, look at Europe with honesty, close to the pride of culture and civilization lies the legacy of pain and destruction. Europe's history can be written as one of glorious moments in the cultural memory of mankind, but also as a continuous story of power struggles, violence and man-made disasters. Only the very last chapter of European history has brought about peaceful cooperation and political integration as genuine elements of Europe's civility. Obviously, in former times European political culture has been weak as far as the realization of peace and the voluntary pooling of resources of Europe's power were concerned. For most of Europe's long history, culture and politics were apart from each other. Peace and power were antagonistic categories of statehood in most of Europe's history. One notable exception, medieval Christendom, was more religious than politically uniting. Another exception, the medieval Hanseatic League, while economically and legally effective in its own right, was limited to Northern Europe, was missing a political framework and did not address the issue of European identity. To use the economy as an important tool in linking the people of Europe, and the order their elites manage politically, was always a good idea in itself, but it did run counter to other, more dominant ideas about how to organize power and politics across the continent. Peaceful economic and, subsequently, political integration as part of European civilization, is a new reality for Europe. It became a reality only after Europeans realized through pain and destruction that their civilization could only be preserved by means of peaceful and democratic integration. It took Europe more than two thousand years to peacefully establish a pluralistic European political order and to recognize Europeans as citizens of their own united yet diverse continent.

Of course, manifold ideas and concepts of how to integrate Europe existed in former times.[1] In fact, they have accompanied European history. But they never materialized in a peaceful way, based on mutually recognized legitimacy among all European people and political units. The continent is older than its contemporary nation states. The current territorial delineation of European nation states is a relatively new method of ordering Europe's geography. While these territories are the dominant factor of public political reference for the citizens of Europe and for the world in its relations with

1 See Bussière, Eric, et al. (eds.), *Europe: The European Idea and Identity, from Ancient Greece to the twenty-first century*, Antwerp: Mercatorfunds, 2001; Pagden, Anthony (ed.), *The Idea of Europe: From Antiquity to European Union*, Washington D.C.: Woodrow Wilson Center Press, 2002.

Europe today, they are relatively young and have dominated European history only for the shortest period since its civilization began to manifest itself.

The borders of Europe have always been as troublesome as the continent's political identity.[2] Europe's eastern borders have changed over time and cannot claim natural logic. For Greek geographer Eratosthenes, head of the Alexandria library in the third century before Christ, Europe stopped at the Bosporus, a concept also shared by Greek historian Herodotus. During the time of the Roman Empire, the whole Mediterranean basin was considered European. In the Middle Ages, the Bosporus and the river Don were considered to be the eastern borders of Europe, and fifteenth century maps show Europe without Anatolia. In 1730, the Russian court accepted the delineation of Swedish geographer Philip Johan von Strahlenberg, according to whom the Ural Mountains and the Kum-Manych Depression, which divides the Russian plain from the Northern Caucasus, constitute the borders of Europe. Strahlenberg's definition legitimized Russian expansionism and it became widely accepted by scientists – not however so by the Russian government, which also claimed sovereignty over the Northern Caucasus, and of course over the whole of Siberia, and does so to this day.

Europe as a product of history has always been shaped by its topography and climate: a mild climate, a highly diverse and well structured physical environment, naturally dividing Europe into regions and sub-regions. Its well-developed infrastructure originates in streets related to Roman military endeavors and in the networks of Christian monasteries, impacting on legal norms, educational structures and economic trajectories. Yet as striking as its geographical compactness and its natural environment is, Europe is habitat to a highly diverse population, expressing itself in at least 40 languages. Migration has been a continuous feature of Europe, voluntary as well as enforced in character.

The bodily characteristics and features of Europeans "normally" distinguish them from the people of Africa, the Middle East and Asia – although even this stereotypical argument is weakening as Europe has become home to people from all over the world. Yet among themselves, Europeans are continuously inclined to distinguish fellow Europeans not only by language, but also by facial outlook, size or hair-color, mentalities and habits, dress code and life style, religious confession and political conviction.[3] There are more stereotypes about differences among Europeans – and even jokes – than about their commonalities compared with other people in the world. Yet the term "European" clarifies origin. Often it might also define attitudes, behavior and opinions, if not imagined perceptions and full-fledged world-views. The perception of Europeans is as confusing as the self-assessment of Europeans amid their diversity.

2 See Heath, John Everett, *Place Names of the World: Europe – Historical Context, Meaning and Changes*, Basingstoke: Macmillan, 2000; Groenendijk, Kees, et al., *In Search of Europe's Borders*, The Hague: Kluwer 2003.

3 See Kelley, Judith, *Ethnic Politics in Europe: The Power of Norms and Incentives*, Princeton: Princeton University Press, 2004.

The public order under which Europeans are living never completely corresponded to their ethnic or linguistic composition. If not for human differences, Europeans were always striving for territorial clarity. Claims for territory are as old as European history. It is not astonishing that Europeans are different from each other. But it is astonishing that Europeans took so long to realize the advantages of cooperation – more or less – over the inclination to fight each other and, if possible, to go it alone. The European continent has seen long periods of religious homogeneity, long periods of economic cooperation and long trajectories of fruitful cultural exchange. Yet, even the height of Christianity in Europe did not bring about a stable political order that would have been able to recognize linguistic and ethnic diversity, let alone different theological interpretations of the same Christian faith. European students were probably more mobile in the twelfth century than they are in the twenty-first century. The continent has experienced long periods in which the same or at least comparable political systems existed side by side. Yet they did not pool their resources, let alone the paraphernalia of their respective claim to national sovereignty.[4]

European unity has always been more than a political matter of war and peace, as important as this is. European unity has ultimately been a philosophical, if not an anthropological issue. As everywhere else in the world, people in Europe are searching for freedom and protection to pursue a life of happiness in accordance with their identity. They look after their families and reach out to other groups that constitute and share their own identity. Distancing oneself from others and opposing their claims of identity, interests and principled world views is as much part of the human experience as the desire to communicate, relate and cooperate with others for the sake of mutual enhancement of interests. Everywhere this anthropological basis of human society has always been linked to historical and intellectual experiences. As form in movement, Europe has entered the world's history and has prevailed as such to this day. Balancing the human quest for freedom and security with a variant of order and authority has not been a European burden alone. But Europe has given the world manifold variations of answering this obviously eternal struggle of man with him- and herself, with other human beings and with nature surrounding them all.

European history has been a history obsessed with territory and territorial claims. It has experienced all possible and impossible forms of power and political order, has tried to tame or to rewrite its history and has pretended to master its future or even redefine future's destiny. Europe has tested its borders – both in a territorial sense as well as a category of the human experiment with the given resources of nature and civilization. Progress and decline, renaissance and breakdown: Europe has always been a combination of an inward-looking search for a balance between stability and dynamics

4 See Barraclough, Geoffrey, *European Unity in Thought and Action*, Oxford: Blackwell, 1963; Arts, Will, et al., *The Cultural Diversity of European Unity: Findings, Explanations and Reflections from the European Values Study*, Leiden/Boston: Brill, 2003.

and of an outward-looking attitude of curiosity toward others and, at times, aggressive, universal claims and projections of its own norms.

Traditionally, European dynamics has affected all spheres of life and has been diverse and competitive, even antagonistic. Development costs have been externalized in the history of Europe – serfs ploughed the land for their feudal owners, masses paid for churches and palaces, resources were collected across the world from people falling under European colonial rule. But for centuries Europe was also the most innovative and creative part of the world – art, often commissioned by ruling nobility or the clergy, medical progress and educational structures, trading patterns and technological achievements of all sorts are part of the European heritage.

Europe cannot be understood without its Christian heritage and its prevailing Christian realities. Yet Christianity did not originate in Europe and Jesus Christ obviously was born a Palestinian Jew. European identity has grown as a diverse combination of elements and many of its ligatures are *a priori* contradictory.[5] Whichever ideas were bred in Europe, one can surely find others, which are contrasting and challenging. Pursuing interests has not been alien to Europeans across the continent, but how to balance them lastingly with those of one's neighbor has been absent in Europe's history of ideas, let alone in Europe's political history. Competition and suspicion were only superseded by pride and prejudice in favor of one's own community, no matter how it was defined in terms of framework, borders, and goals.

The cultural development of Europe has often been supported by the political powers of a given time. But political culture as a mode of behavior defining methods, goals and means of public policy has only developed most recently as a scientific concept and concern. Europe seems to be driven by the impossible combination of Leonardo da Vinci's vision to fly across any valley there is and Blaise Pascal's fear of the stars in the dark sky at night. Endless optimism and depressing skepticism accompany Europe's intellectual evolution. No intellectual step has ever been taken in Europe without outside influence reflecting earlier positions of thought, and no theory discussed in Europe could ever claim uniqueness without being challenged by new experience and insight. Yet uniqueness is what Europeans and non-Europeans alike tend to attribute to the results of Europe's complex and idiosyncratic path through history. No matter how unique Europe has become as a product of its cultures and civilizations, for more than two-thousand years it has not been able to forge a single political entity based on the free will of its people, the pooling of its material resources and the definition of unquestionable European interests.

Why has Europe not achieved this advancement of its potential prior to the second half of the twentieth century? Why did it build ideas and institutions only as contrasting and not as integrating patterns? Why did it fail for so long to link the three potentials

5 See Bussière, Eric, et al. (eds.), *Europe: The European Idea and Identity, from Ancient Greece to the twenty-first century*, Antwerp: Mercatorfonds, 2001.

Swiss historian Jacob Burckhardt has defined as the most important sources of all statehood: culture (and notably religion), politics, and the economy?[6] The archaeology of European integration can trace many noble concepts and idealistic proposals that have tried to do so. But never before the second half of the twentieth century were the goals of European unity linked to viable methods and sustainable means enabling their implementation. Whenever integration was pursued in Europe's long history, it either remained a spiritual and intellectual effort or it was executed by force and coercion, and in doing so, immediately limiting itself, as it was such behavior that was provoking national, if not nationalistic counter-reactions. Any effort to define European integration as the prime European interest leads to a large body of literature. But as far as its reality is concerned, it has to build on the limited legacy of the past fifty years of European integration. All earlier aspects or elements might be considered preparatory steps, but often they were no more than that. Europe's struggle to balance diversity and unity cannot project a solid and proud past into the unknown future. But this struggle should not be misjudged by past failures either, as it has advanced since the second half of the twentieth century with remarkable speed based on new arrangements between ideals and material contributions, goals and methods of integration, means and ends of European Union.

2. The Archaeology of European Integration

Europe's history is the history of contested borders and challenged concepts of order. The European space has been pressed together from the outside, leaving its delineation continuously imprecise and it has been in movement and under uncertainty from within.

Europe has also been a continent with its people constantly on the move, voluntarily or forcefully.[7] Efforts to unify Europe have often been executed with violence. This fatal error had to fail as it inevitably provoked resistance from within Europe's diversity. It is surprising enough that amid the experience of cultural and linguistic diversity, Europeans have time and again tried to bring about unity.[8] They have done so for different reasons and with different degrees of success. But before the second half of the twentieth century they never achieved unity for a relevant period through a mutually

6 Burckhardt, Jacob, *Weltgeschichtliche Betrachtungen*, Stuttgart: Kroener, 1978 (12.ed.).

7 See Hoerder, Dirk, et al. (eds.), *People on the Move: Migration, Acculturation and Ehtnic Interaction in Europe and North America*, Providence: Berg, 1993; Leboutte, René (ed.), *Migrations et Migrants dans une Perspective Historique: Permanences et Innovations*, Bruxelles/New York: Peter Lang, 2000; Moch, Leslie Page, *Moving Europeans: Migration in Western Europe since 1650*, Bloomington: Indiana University Press, 2003 (2nd ed.).

8 See de Rougement, Denis, *The Idea of Europe*, New York: Macmillan, 1966; van der Dussen, Jan, and Kevin Wilson (eds.), *The History of the Idea of Europe*, New York: Routledge, 1993: Murray, Philomena B., and Paul B. Rich (eds.), *Visions of European Unity*, Boulder: Westview Press, 1996.

recognized, law-based legitimate political system as it is now constituted by the European Union. Ten reasons can explain why Europe never achieved unity and integration earlier:

(1) The notion of Europe is rooted in mythology and religion. In its origin, it was not linked to a political concept for a clearly defined territory and a diverse people. It was rather a notion to justify European difference and authenticity in contrast to the dominating cultures in the region today called the Middle East. Through mythology and religion Europe is linked to the eastern shores of the Mediterranean: The semantic root of the term "Europe" refers to the Semitic word "ereb," meaning dark, or where the sun is setting. According to Greek mythology, the beautiful girl "Europa," daughter of the Phoenician king Agenor, was kidnapped by the Greek god Zeus, disguised as a bull, and hijacked from Tyros to the island of Crete. There, "Europa" became the mother of the Minoan dynasty, Europe's oldest political formation. In Crete, one can sense the geographical features of Europe, its natural climatic mildness and physical structures contrasting with the vast and unfocused deserts in the Phoenician hinterland, today's Middle East. It might have been the physical difference that is almost sensually present on this small island that the Greeks wanted to identify with their world in contrast to the Levant.

Greek philosopher Aristotle defined Europe as form in being. For him Greeks and Scythians were "the Europeans" in contrast to Asians.[9] His compatriot Plato saw Europe as the mirror of an idea, a heavenly image in pure material form. Christianity entered Europe through Anatolia, today's Turkey. There, the term "Christians" was used for the first time in their first church outside of Jerusalem, in a cave above the city of Antioch (56 AD). Christianity spread with great speed, but it did not carry a political program to form Europe's identity. The biblical origin of Europe relates to chapter nine and ten of Book Genesis: According to this text, Noah sent his three sons Ham, Seth, Japheth in all directions to create the nations of the world and to ultimately unify them. Japheth reached Europe and became the founding father of all Europeans, a legend that remained vital in Christian Europe until the tenth century.

(2) Centers of gravity changed in Europe. For the first millennium – beginning with ancient Greek civilization and ending with the Germanic destruction of the Roman Empire – Europe was built around the Mediterranean. The earliest expression of Europe was protected by the Limes of the Roman Empire that cut the British Isles and mainland Europe from the North Sea to the Black Sea. This Europe was defined by Roman law and became increasingly Christian. Greek political concepts also added to this period of

9 Aristotle, *Politeia* VII/1327b, The Scythians are people from the vast grassland and steppe between China and what is today's Ukraine. According to Greek historian Herodotus, in the 5th century BC they had moved from the river Don to the Carpathian mountains.

European formation. Most importantly, yet without lasting impact, were the notions of democracy and of political federation.

The split between Western Rome and Eastern Rome became as constitutive for the second period of European development as the transfer of power to the North Alpine regions – that is to Franconia and the Franks that later split in order to become the nucleus of the German and French nations. Their leaders claimed to be the legitimate heirs to the Roman Empire, which found political expression in the Holy Roman Empire of the German Nation. Its development began with the coronation of Charlemagne on Christmas Day, 800, by Pope Leo III.[10] Charlemagne developed his imperial cult in his favorite capital, the city of Aix-la-Chapelle, which could, however, never compete with Rome as the center of Europe. Constantinople as center of Eastern Rome, that is Byzantium, made a stronger imprint on the mental map of Europe than Aix-la-Chapelle, until Western Europeans tended to exclude it from their mental map of Europe altogether when the city was conquered by the Ottomans and renamed Istanbul in 1453. The split between Latin and Byzantine Christianity in 1054 had already sent a shock wave of spiritual rift across Europe, superseded by the conquest of its South Eastern region by another religion. The split between Latin and Orthodox Christianity has never become irrelevant as far as mental and socio-political differences among European Christians are concerned.[11] With the enlarged European Union in the early twenty-first century, the presence of Orthodox Christianity has increased in the European Union while Orthodox Christianity is struggling with concepts of modernity and social ethics that have long since become normality among Latin Christians.

The shifting centers of Europe were followed by the trading patterns of the Hanseatic League, the emerging strength of Western European sea powers Spain and Portugal, by the rising Muscovite state claiming to be the "third Rome" after the fall of Constantinople, and by the emergence of imperial powers on the British Isles, in France, and in Austria under the Hapsburgs. The spiritual, neo-imperial unity of central Europe could not hold. After the religious split in the age of reformation it escalated into political quarrel and destruction. With the Thirty Years War, the center of medieval and early modern Europe – today's Germany – came under the influence, if not the control of its neighbors.

(3) Greek and Roman political and legal notions were unable to find wide recognition across Europe. Although both ancient "super-powers" were largely perceived as self-complacent or outright imperial by fellow Europeans, they did lay the

10 On his legacy for "Christian Europe" see Morissey, Robert, *Charlemagne and France: A Thousand Years of Mythology*, Notre Dame: Notre Dame University Press, 2003; Becher, Mathias, *Charlemagne*, New Haven: Yale University Press, 2003; Story, Joanna, *Charlemagne: Empire and Society*, Manchester: Manchester University Press, 2005.

11 See Gallagher, Clarence, *Church Law and Church Order in Rome and Byzantium: A Comparative Study*, Aldershot: Ashgate, 2002.

foundation for the formation of political theory and terminology in Europe. Since the eighth century B.C. ancient Greeks distinguished between "amphiktionia," a spiritual union of states, "symmachy," a contract based defense system under the leadership of a hegemonic state with federal organs, a federal council, its own court, currency and army, "isopoliteia," mutually recognized and legally defined citizenship rights, and "sympoliteia," a permanent federation of city states and tribes with a definite administrative structure and a common citizenship. The dichotomy between autonomy of city states and peace for all in one system of protection was already evident during Greek history.

The Roman Empire knew two types of federal contracts: The "foedus aequum," an inter-state contract among equal economic and military partners, while the partners had to renounce their independent foreign policy and had to provide Rome with additional troops. The "foedus iniquum" was an inter-state treaty with Rome dominating its partners. After these partners had become provinces of the Roman Empire, their citizens received Roman citizenship. By the end of the 4th century AD, Rome accepted foreign troops on Roman soil. But they also had to accept the secession of an increasing number of former federal partners, which were changing loyalties in favor of Rome's Germanic enemies.

The Roman Empire is often idealized as the expression of a successful political and cultural unity in Europe. It was a city-centered Empire, yet based on agriculture and the increasing production of metals and construction materials. Its languages were Latin and Greek. Its imperial cult did not overcast the binding written law. The Roman Empire introduced a common calendar, a common currency based on gold and silver throughout its territory, and built not only representative public monuments but – more importantly – streets across Europe that helped to unify the empire as a market. Yet the north alpine world, dominated by Germanic and Scythian people, did not embrace the Roman concept of Europe. Partly nomadic, partly sedentary in wooden villages, their trading system was based on barter. Agriculture was limited to small areas near forests, not on the Roman type of huge pastries ("villae"). Tribal diversity was echoed in linguistic diversity. Conflicts of power and primacy of pagan customs were alien to the theologically refined Christianity of the Mediterranean basin.

(4) Christian universalism was a highly mobilizing religious force, but it did not stimulate a consensual political order in Europe. Christian faith and Christian culture transformed Europe not only as far as its religious landscape was concerned, but also in all possible aspects of civilization and the arts. From Christian church spires to educational institutions, from the impact of the monastic culture across Europe to works of arts, painting, music and literature, European civilization has received its strongest mark from a millennium of Christian faith and religiosity. From the debate about the Christian duty to refuse military service in the Roman Empire, to the famous concepts

of European unity expressed by Dante Alighieri in the early fourteenth century, the Christian contribution to uniting Europe was always morally powerful but politically weak. In his book "De monarchia" of 1308, Dante described the Pope as envoy of God and hoped for European unity under the leadership of an Italian emperor and the Roman nation. Dante was followed by Pierre Dubois, crown jurist of French King Philip the Fair, who considered a unitarian federation with arbitration court and a council of kings and dukes the right basis for a European federation (in "De recuperatione terrae sanctae"). His concept was heavily influenced by the crusades in order to liberate the tomb of Jesus in Jerusalem from "Muslim occupation."

At the time when Bohemian King Georg Podiebrad (1420-1471) sent an envoy to the Pope to negotiate his concept for a European Union of Kings, he presented to the French king the text for a Treaty on a Confederation between King Louis XI of France, King Georg of Bohemia and the High Council of Venice to resist the Turks. While the Hundred Years War between England and France marked the beginning of national wars in Europe, the concept of European unity was largely legitimized as defense against Muslim Turks. The Grand Design of Henri IV, drafted in 1638 by the French King's friend, the Duc Maximilien Béthune de Sully, postulated a Christian republic as a European confederation, consisting of 15 members: The hereditary monarchies France, England, Lombardy, Sweden, Denmark and Spain, the five electoral monarchies Bohemia, Hungary, the Holy See, the Holy Roman Empire of the German Nation, and Poland, and the four republics Venice, Switzerland, the Italian Union and the United Netherlands. The concept of the Duc de Sully was quite detailed: He suggested a Council with 60 members mandated to create a European international law. He envisaged a joint army with 250,000 infantry, 50,000 horsemen, 200 canons and 120 war ships. Overcoming war among European states was as strong a driving force behind his concept as the desire to deter and eventually beat the Ottoman Turks. Neither his nor related ideas were translated into political actions. They moved to the archives of European integration archaeology. Yet, they embody much of what has become EU reality in the twenty-first century.

(5) The universalism of the age of enlightenment was as limited as its Christian precursor.[12] While the material interests of European powers were driven by imperial conquest and the desire to strengthen global sea dominance, national identities, pride and difference were rising among the ruling elites across Europe. The enormous success and technological achievements that went hand in hand with the global rise of European power contributed to a rational world view among European intellectuals. But this rarely generated insights into the usefulness of cooperation and political unity among Europeans. The "Republic of Letters," as the Age of Enlightenment was called, advanced the conquest of nature, critical rationalism, the notion of progress and the

12 See the classical study by Berlin, Isaiah, *The Age of Enlightenment*, Boston: Houghton Mifflin, 1956.

value of science. It increasingly de-legitimized the monarchical and feudal political orders, most notably in France. But it did not constitute a shared new social norm favoring European political unity.

William Penn's "Essay towards a present and future peace in Europe" of 1692 promoted the idea of a League of Nations and a Council of Europe as the cooperative union of Europe's monarchs.[13] The secretary of the French delegate to the Peace Congress of Utrecht in 1713, the Abbé Charles de St. Pierre, proposed a European Federation among the Christian rulers of Europe. The Peace Congress in Utrecht sanctioned the principle of the balance of power, which lasted until the Congress of Vienna in 1815 as the dominating European state system.[14] The pentarchy of its five leading powers (England, France, Prussia, Austria and Russia) was based on mutual recognition of individual power, on mutual suspicion and on the negligence of the interests of smaller nations. None of these influences could advance political unity in Europe.

Charles de Montesquieu – one of the architects of the concept of separation of powers – remained rather apolitical in his "De l'esprit des lois" of 1748 as far as the relationship between the individual society and its future attitude toward the state and the continent was concerned. He confused notions of federalism and confederalism and remained silent on specific institutional provisions for a Europe that he wished to see designed as a "society of societies."[15] The obvious political pluralism in Europe was neither accommodated under a religious nor under a political and legal umbrella. In this, Montesquieu was not alone. Hardly any concept or effort between the sixteenth and eighteenth century was more advanced and focused. The "Republic of Letters" did not help the development of European identity and a common European interest, although leading intellectuals of the time were more respected than ever and became corner stones in the evolution of political and general philosophy to this day.

(6) If at all, European countries made a bad use of the common cultural heritage of the continent. Although each era of national literature, each architectural style or periods of composition found equivalents in other countries, the specific contributions of national artists were by and large used to underline identity differences instead of promoting European commonalities. Whether Shakespeare is British or a genuine expression of European civilization is as interesting as the question to whom Beethoven or Mozart, Voltaire or Goethe, Calderón de la Barca or John Milton, Henri Matisse or Christopher Wren belong. Quintessentially, they are all leading European personalities, but in the age of nationalism, culture was largely misused against its potential ability to

13 See Dunn, Richard S., and Mary Maples Dunn, *The World of William Penn*, Philadelphia: University of Philadelphia Press, 1986.
14 See Sheehan, Michael, *The Balance of Power: History and Theory*, New York: Routledge, 1996.
15 See Shackleton, Robert, *Montesquieu: A Critical Biography*, London: Oxford University Press, 1961.

shape a sense of European commonality. The heroes of Europe's culture were nationalized, often beyond recognition.

Ideational solipsism also prevailed as far as the development of conceptual notions of the modern European state is concerned. Concepts of statehood and differentiations between unitary and federal states were largely shaped as reflection of the rising importance of the individual nation state. The guiding notion of national sovereignty, preeminent since the 1648 Treaties of Westphalia, reduced the horizon of state theorists to the national level.[16] The evolution of legal dogma followed suit. To this day it is one of the last domains of the prevalence of nation state superiority over European integration. This is surprising in spite of the enormous contribution of European law to the shaping of an integrated Europe.

Immanuel Kant's contribution of 1795, namely to organize a European peace order on the basis of republics, and his recognition of the primacy of law, was an extrapolation of his domestic struggle for the rule of law, but not yet a concrete concept of how to transform European antagonisms into viable political unity.[17] The search for peace in Europe seemed to remain eternal. Victor Hugo's plea for the creation of the United States of Europe at the Paris Peace Conference of 1849 was a frustrated echo of Kant's vision, having to recognize that rule of law based democratic rights were not advancing as consequence of the 1848 revolutions.[18] They were rather regressing. This did not help to support the visionary concept of the United States of Europe.

(7) Astonishingly absent from practically all debates and publications on European unity were links between state theories and moral claims on the one hand and a discussion of the role of the material world, that is to say the economy. Neither Johannes Althusius' social federalism of the sixteenth century[19] nor Pierre-Joseph Proudhon's "left federalism" of the nineteenth century, or Constantin Frantz' "conservative federalism" of the nineteenth century, reflected sufficiently about the impact of the most critical economic developments in Europe on the political structure and nature of the continent. Neither the enormous increase in trade and the evolution of the modern banking system, nor the agrarian crisis of the sixteenth century, or the breakthrough of the modern industrial mass society with its social upheavals and

16 On the legacy see Craxton, Derek, and Anuschka Tischer, *The Peace of Westphalia: A Historical Dictionary*, Westport: Greenwood, 2002.

17 Kant, Immanuel, *Perpetual Peace*, translated by Benjamin F. Trueblood, Washington DC: American Peace Society, 1897; see Schwarz, Wolfgang, *Principles of Lawful Politics: Immanuel Kant's Philosophical Draft „Toward Eternal Peace"*, Aalen: Scientia, 1988; Kühnhardt, Ludger, *Von der ewigen Suche nach Frieden: Immanuel Kants Vision und Europas Wirklichkeit*, Bonn: Bouvier, 1996.

18 Hugo, Victor, *The United States of Europe*, Boston: World Peace Foundation, 1914.

19 On this forgotten theorist of federalism see Hueglin, Thomas, *Early Modern Concepts for a Late Modern World: Althusius on Community and Federalism*, Waterworld, Ont.: Wilfrid Laurier University Press, 1999; from his own pen Althusius, Johannes, *Politica Methodice*, with an introduction by Carl Joachim Friedrich, New York: Arno Press, 1979.

increasing monopolizing trends of capital and power accumulation led theoreticians of the European dream to sufficiently contemplate the role of the European economy.[20]

(8) European history is full of efforts to impose hegemonic rule over neighboring countries in order to advance national power, pride and resource-based interests. From the dominating claim of the Holy Roman Empire of the German Nation to the Napoleonic Wars, and from Hitler's racist and aggressive conquest to Stalin's class-ideology driven totalitarian answer, Europe has suffered from hegemonic aspirations. They excessively transposed national claims of homogenous and impermeable sovereign control over one people and territory to the European level. This provoked immediate resistance, and lastingly destroyed trust among Europeans. Once the binding glue of a common religious creed was broken in the age of reformation, Europe was in search of ways to prevent civil war. It did so by mutually recognizing the religious creed of its rulers and their people. Roman-Catholicism and the many variants of Protestantism began a long and still unfinished process of ecumenical understanding of their unity in reconciled diversity. Whenever this quest for ecumenical harmony was challenged in later times, it was rather by secularization than by missionary zeal of either confession.

(9) One of the longest and strongest legacies of European history is the definition of oneself in contrast to some "other." Greek historian Herodotus was the first to identify Greeks in antagonistic difference to the Persians, the losers of the sea battle of Marathon. The longest lasting notion of "the other" in Europe is related to the Muslim world. Since territorial losses to invading Arab troops in the eighth century in Spain and, albeit temporarily, in France, Islam is more feared than understood in Europe. France became the nucleus of a universalistic, Christian state in opposition to Muslim Arabs. In 732 AD, an anonymous author, in pursuing the chronicle of Bishop Isidore de Seville about the battles of Tours and Poitiers, mentioned "Europeans" as the other force in these battles. Here, for the first time, the term "European" was used. As Christian Europe, the concept of a continent in opposition to the Muslim world was further rooted during the long and daunting period of the crusades, lasting from the eleventh to the thirteenth century. After the Ottoman Turks conquered Constantinople in 1453 and renamed it Istanbul, the notion of "the other," and often in fact the notion of an outright enemy, found its new focus in Western Europe. Although not Arabs, the Turks became the antidote of new waves of European identity formation, contributing to this perception with the assaults on the Hapsburg Empire and the conquest of large parts of South Eastern Europe.

20 Archaelogists of European integration claim that for the first time the term "integration" in its economic sense was applied by Gaedicke, Herbert, and Gert von Eynern, *Die produktionswirtschaftliche Integration Europas: Eine Untersuchung über die Aussenhandelsverflechtung der europäischen Länder*, Berlin: Junker und Dünnhaupt, 1933.

Abbé Dominique Dufour de Pradt, Napoleons' chaplain, was the first to describe the emerging opposition between Russia and the United States, a topic Alexis de Tocqueville was to pursue in his 1840 book "On democracy in America." In reflecting upon these new geopolitical concepts, Europeans were quick to define themselves either against Russia or against America or against both. The notion of Europe as being "the other" of Russia found confirmation after the Bolshevist revolution of 1917, a clear rupture with the mainstream of political and economic development of Europe. The aggressive totalitarianism of the Soviet Union helped to forge European and trans-Atlantic integration structures. This last and most successful use of the notion of an enemy as a driving force for European unity cannot conceal the fact that similar impulses did not achieve analogous results in past centuries. The most important reason for this difference is related to the role of the United States as European federator after World War II. In past centuries, Europeans might have been united against the Russians, the Turks, the Arabs or whomever else. But they were always as much split among themselves and not ready to recognize leadership by any of their own. However, such leadership was required to advance the degree of unification that became possible only after World War II with the US as European federator.

(10) Europe as an imagination and concept remained weak in light of the dominance of the nation state that had emerged since the sixteenth century. Authority and rule were linked to a specific territory. The control of territory legitimized the claim of sovereignty and sovereignty became the ultimate source of power and pride in Europe. The first lobby group to change this equation in favor of European integration was the International League for Peace and Liberty, founded in 1867 in Geneva with Garibaldi and Bakunin among its members. In 1868 they published a newspaper, "Les Etat-Unis d'Europe," which circulated until 1919. With the Franco-German War of 1870, its orientation became less federal and more partisan. Later ideological splits among socialists, anarchists and national republicans limited its scope and relevance.

Charles Lemonnier, one of the founding members of the International League, proposed the Swiss or the American model for the future evolution of Europe. He conceptualized a European federation with France, Germany, Italy, England, Spain, Austria, Greece, Belgium, the Netherlands, Switzerland, Denmark and Sweden. A federal core, consisting of Italy, France, Switzerland, Belgium and England should begin the first steps toward federation, he hoped. The European federation should run its own army, maintain a supreme court and develop an economic and social union (sic) in order to dissolve national boundaries and to promote a European sense of togetherness.

Federal theories were also developed in Germany, but largely in order to understand and develop the German Empire as a federation. From Samuel von Pufendorf and Ludolph Hugo in the seventeenth century to Georg Jellinek in the nineteenth century, German legal philosophy was largely driven by the notion of shared sovereignty between imperial rule and autonomy of individual territories within the German Empire.[21] This tradition of shared sovereignty ("duplex regimen") was to prevail in many normative contributions from Germans once European integration started in the second half of the twentieth century. Authentic German contributions to the search for a European integration concept in the nineteenth century followed French and other voices. Arnold Ruge in the Paulskirche Parliament of 1848 or Julius Fröbel in a 1859 book ("Amerika, Europa und die politischen Gesichtspunkte der Gegenwart") suggested the United States as model for European integration. Neither of them offered how to do so and by whom it could be done.

3. Errors Turn into Catastrophes

The quest for European unity remained torn between idealistic constructions of intellectuals and few politicians on the one hand and the myopic, finally self-destructive political actions dominating the European state-system throughout the nineteenth century. The hegemonic cultural aspiration of the French Revolution – that is to say, its universal claim for freedom, equality and brotherhood – was destroyed by its own hegemonic political succession under Emperor Napoleon.[22] The aggressive ambition to transform Europe under his dominance into a messianic embodiment of French universalism failed, provoking nationalistic counter-reactions of the strongest nature. Instead of embracing the values of the French Revolution, most of Europe preferred to copy French nationalism as protective shield against the aggressive universalism of revolutionary and post-revolutionary France. The age of the French Revolution coincided with a socio-economic revolution, opening the door toward industrialization while not being able to find a reasonable balance between economic empowerment and social concern. Poverty aggravated as much as the dynamics of industrialization grew. Social theories analyzing these developments turned into social movements and political parties. Moreover, they turned into ideologies, thus adding to those fabricated in the aftermath of the political consequences of the French Revolution.

Nationalism and socialism, egalitarian democracy and the battle cry for civil and social rights began to define the social parameters of Europe's societies. In political terms, Europe encountered the limits of a peaceful use of balance of power-mechanisms. With the Congress of Vienna, it embarked on a path toward competitive

21 See Jellinek, Georg, *The Rights of Minorities*, London: P. S. King & Son, 1912; Carr, Craig L., *Samuel Pufendorf: The Political Writings of Samuel Pufendorf*, New York: Oxford University Press, 1994.

22 See Baker, Keith Michael, *The French Revolution and the Creation of Modern Political Culture*, Oxford: Pergamon Press, 1987; Aston, Nigel, *The French Revolution, 1789-1804: Authority, Liberty and the Search for Stability*, Houndmills/New York: Palgrave Macmillan, 2004; Campbell, Peter R., *The Origins of the French Revolution*, Houndmills/New York: 2005; Haas, Mark L., *The Ideological Origins of Great Power Politics, 1789-1989*, Ithaca: Cornell University Press, 2005.

power plays, exacerbated by mistrust, nationalistic pride and aggressive prejudices among the leading powers of Europe. The rise of democracy failed in the 1840's, but the failure of integrating Europe's emerging mass societies into a stable social order was only second to the failure of turning balance of power-suspicions into a stable political order. A combination of imperial, nationalistic and economic tensions turned the unstable equilibrium generated by the Congress of Vienna into a disastrous sequence of wars. Their global effect was a precursor to the global loss of power for Europe's colonial states. Inside the continent and on a global scale, Europe's errors ended in Europe's catastrophes.

Four factors were of a particularly destructive nature: Territorial primacy, ideological rigidity, excessive power considerations, and the undemocratic nature of the political systems involved. From the "Republic of Letters" to the gas chambers of the Nazis and the Gulags of the Soviets, Europe underwent the biggest possible self-destruction of its moral credibility as cradle and protector of civilization. Walter Hallstein was right when he described Europe not as a new creation, but as a rediscovery. The traumatic breakdown of culture and politics, in fact of humanity itself, that Europe was experiencing at the height of the age of ideologies and totalitarian perversion of politics was certainly not anticipated, not even intended by the early architects of the nineteenth century order of Europe.

Unworthy of all traditions of civility on the continent, only the complete failure of ideology-driven power politics opened the gates for a new and solid realization of the old idea of European unity. Now it was on Europe, against all experience with its own history, to prove that it had learned the most crucial lesson of history.

In many ways, the French Revolution and Cartesian rigidity of rationalism had marked a new beginning. Old certainties had broken down in Europe, yet they were not replaced by new stability and consistency. Old myths and new realities began to coexist next to old realities and new myths: For instance, the myth of human self-emancipation and the reality of a lasting struggle for constitutional liberties, the myth of national unity and the search for a balance between nation and democracy, the myth of social fraternity and the just effort to relate individual identity and social cohesion. As far as the European order was concerned, three trends caused lasting and ultimately irreversible challenges: The increasing ideological orientation of national politics in all of Europe, the extrapolation of power politics and struggles for dominance across the continent, and the myopic reduction of political thought into national, if not outright nationalistic categories. In terms of foreign policy, nineteenth century Europe thought in the parameters of coalitions and alliances. In terms of domestic policies, nineteenth century Europe's political elites focused on how to prevent participation of the mass society and the introduction of democratic rule.

The Congress of Vienna was able to create a security system of a certain balance, which was probably optimal for its time. But it could not generate sustainable confidence and cooperation. Its paradigm of securing oneself against the evil that is the other was projected as measurement for the pursuit of domestic policies against those demanding a stronger political participation. What has been labeled Europe's bourgeois era was a European phenomenon indeed, but never in harmony with itself. The internal transformation with deep social upheavals nurtured more ideological notions of politics, new categories of distinguishing enemy and friend and de-legitimized national order and international cooperation alike.

Most unfortunate for the development of nineteenth century politics in Europe was the growing ideological character of most debates. Two features were dominant: The myth of the nation, integrating and excluding at the same time. And the myth of human equality, limiting freedom and yet always remaining incomplete as long as human diversity prevails. Starting from these ideological premises, political thought in Europe created new concepts based on hope (and sometimes only the myth of hope) for social, cultural, economic and even biological integration, but it did not contribute to the formation of a human "European-ness."

The effort to frame transforming realities into new terminology produced a whole set of ideological notions, including nationalism, socialism and communism, Darwinism and racism. Human imagination formed a new sphere of artificial ideologies implying endless potential for progress if properly applied. Ideological thinking evolved in the biggest possible human acquisition and domination of the world without actually providing proof of its solidity or even its sheer practicality.

Socio-cultural, demographic and economic upheavals were phenomena across Europe. Political efforts to handle them remained confined to the borders of each state or empire. The quest for internal homogeneity dominated and the rigid use of sovereignty and balanced power in foreign affairs secured the illusion that social homogeneity (through banning other races or eliminating other classes) could be a solution to all the evils of modernity. In the end, ideological messianism created unimaginably more problems, even beyond the horrible suffering of millions of human beings. In the nineteenth century, neither the social nor the national question found adequate European responses. In fact, Europe was considered to be a problem and a reality of the past, incarnated in feudal and absolutist structures that did not give way to the overall recognition of national sovereignty and social equality. Freedom and equality became domestic and foreign policy categories. But emphasis on social stability and international cohesion, of cooperation inside borders and across boundaries of ethnicity, race, language and class was poor.

Neither Napoleon's aggression in destroying the old order in Europe or Metternich's effort to restore monarchical legitimacy and a system of balanced power with the recognized hegemony of a few states could lead Europe into an era of peace with itself. In terms of power politics, the German question – on the agenda since the Thirty Years War – was on the mind of almost all leaders in Europe. In terms of social evolution, the fear of democratic mobilization and economic participation of the masses in an emerging age of industrialization was on their minds too. Europe was missing coherent and complementary domestic institutions and it was missing truly European institutions to deal with the foreign policy fall-out of the big transformation into nineteenth century modernity. Rule of law as a guiding principle for the domestic and the international order was still an alien concept and the more one of the orders tended to move into the direction of rule of law, democracy and cooperation, the more national antagonism and anti-liberal foreign policy flourished. The demographic explosion Europe was experiencing in the first half of the nineteenth century exacerbated the social and political crisis.

It remains surprising that in the midst of an increasingly nationalistic century the first small effort to organize European economic cooperation came about: Danube navigation was confirmed as the right of all ships by the 1836 Paris Peace and the Rhine Navigation Convention of October 17, 1868 – declaring free navigation for all ships in the Rhine – looks almost like a happy yet limited precursor of twentieth century European economic cooperation.[23] Beyond this singular convention, the nineteenth century did not produce a European legal order. It also did not generate European democracies that could advocate political legitimacy linked to European inter-state legality. Yet the constitution-building history in Europe throughout the nineteenth century was to become another forerunner for political Europe in the early twenty-first century. Rooting political orders in constitutional provisions – limiting power by distributing it – was an early hint at what European integration was to achieve should it be lastingly rooted in legitimacy.

While the European power states led by undemocratic elites remained bound by mutual struggle, they reached out for a projection of their respective powers across the world. Imperialism was a continuation of the internal European quarrels by other means in different venues. The gradual retreat of the Ottoman Empire from its hold over South Eastern Europe – a long process between 1683 until 1913 – opened this region for other European empires to pour in, guided by their own no less imperial interests. Balance of suspicion under the umbrella of one civilization became the main feature of Europe.

National romanticism attributed to the social rooting of this distortion of all processes of civilization in Europe always geared toward interaction and mutual inspiration. To saturate one's own national identity, mythology was activated and enmity toward others became acceptable. Identity was transposed from a category of individual psychology to a driving force of social and political processes. Most artificial

23 See Wentholt, Wyger, *A Study of Monetary and Economic Situations in International Relationship: Freedom of Navigation on the Rhine as a Western European Interest*, Amsterdam: W.Wentholt &Co., 1957.For the follow-up to the original "Rhine Navigation Convention" see Convention to Amend the "Revised Convention for Rhine Navigation" signed at Mannheim on 17 October 1868. Strasbourg, 20 November 1963, London: H. M. Stationary Office, 1967. The free navigation principle for the Danube was revoked in 1948, when the "Belgrade Convention on Danube Navigation" declared the river open only for ships belonging to one of the riparian countries.

expressions were generated by the German and by the Italian national movements. The European movement toward freedom and democracy of 1848 ultimately failed. It could neither tame power politics nor turn domestic priorities from the illusion of national homogeneity under authoritarian rule into hope stemming from the priority of civil rights. Parliamentary democracy had to fight a tough fight before it was established alongside the rule of law. Although the economic and social trends of the time were basically Europe-wide in nature and effect, they did not trigger political movements supporting them through a new domestic and foreign policy order for the continent. Growing interconnectedness – always felt in the sphere of European culture – did not automatically generate new political norms. It did not even facilitate new social norms as increasing nationalism, a mixture of pride and prejudice, demonstrated.

The biggest tragedy for Europe was the prevalence of warfare as a legitimate category of politics in a continent increasingly populated and filled with high-technology weaponry. The search for a system of coalitions and alliances and for a balancing of power almost seemed far-sighted and promising in light of the atavistic vices that led a long life as heroic virtues. Without national solidarity there could be no balance among European states, so the rationale seemed to suggest. But the idea of lawyers such as Pasquale Mancini in Turin (who became Italian Foreign Minister in 1881), according to whom international law was to be based on nations and no longer on states as basic units of Europe, was both insufficient and premature. Insufficient it was, because it did not recognize multinational states as acceptable and viable units. And it was premature – or rather one-sided – as it did not reckon with the prevalence of both forces – the state and the nation – that had to be accommodated if Europe were to find peace and inner calm. There was much more suffering to endure before the European Union was to statute Europe as a Union of states and citizens.

The best to hope for in the heated atmosphere of the nineteenth century was rational and realistic power politics. Before cooperation or even integration, Europe had to exhaust all variants of balance and alliance formation. What the continent did not tame was the rising power bloc in its center. The German question was to give a blow to all nicely knit versions of Realpolitik and rational balance. The German dualism between Prussia and Austria did not solve the problem either. More so in Prussia, the consciousness of newly acquired power escalated into a harsh will to power, perceiving France even as a more dangerous competitor than Austria. Honor and prestige, pride and prejudice, balance and suspicion, could never grow into more than fragile inter-state relations and poisoned inter-people perceptions. Political liberalism did not translate into concepts, let alone strategies for a new beginning in Europe.

Instead, the political arena in Europe began to radicalize with these dynamics, unleashing in the Crimean War of 1854/1855. According to British historian Alan J.P.Taylor, this was a war not based on mutual intention to attack but on mutually reinforcing fear, characteristically echoed in the fact that the war aims were "defined in the negative."[24] The same assessment could also be made about the path into World War I and, moreover, the path to stop it. As for the Crimean War, the ambition of the Russian Tsar Nicholas I, to exert influence over Ottoman Turkey and to gain control of the Dardanelles, provoked British counter-measures. The local Russian-Turkish War escalated into a war among Europe's powers when the Western powers entered the Black Sea after the Turkish fleet had been destroyed. This was a flagrant violation of the 1841 Treaty on the Dardanelles between France, Great Britain, Austria, Prussia and Russia and declaring the Straits closed to all but Turkish warships in peacetime. Now, the conflict actually became a Russian-British war with French, Turkish and Lombardi support for the British. The seizure of Sebastopol nevertheless took more than a year before it finally fell to the British in September 1855. The Treaty of Paris of 1856 prevented the escalation of the Crimean War into a full-fledged European war, a possibility looming on the horizon for a long time. A limited war ended with a limited peace.

The Treaty of Paris – with the first inclusion of the Ottoman Empire into the European state system and public order – left a power vacuum that became a precondition for the central European national wars of the next two decades.[25] As much as the Holy Alliance between Austria and Russia was rational, its mysterious dissolution triggered new leadership quarrels among the European powers. The principle of balanced power was inevitably to collide with the nationality issue that was to destroy the rationale of the entire European state system. The rise of Prussia – beginning with the German-Danish War of 1864, and escalating with the Franco-German War of 1870/71 and the humiliating coronation of the first German Emperor in the Versailles castle on January 30, 1871 – was accompanied by an elaborate system of secret diplomacy. Chancellor Otto von Bismarck established an alliance with Austria in 1879, an alliance with Austria and Russia in 1881 and an alliance with Austria and Italy in 1882. Encircled by France, Great Britain and presumably Russia, Bismarck thought in categories of concentric circles. Moreover, he thought in categories of suspicion, fear and security in order to stabilize his new power state in Europe's geographical center. Not even the seed of Europe as a legal community could be laid under these circumstances.

24 Taylor, Alan J. P., *The Struggle for Mastery in Europe, 1848-1918*, Oxford: Clarendon Press 1954:65. The diplomacy of the Crimean War was dominated by the famous French-Austrian "Four Points:" According to them "stable relations could not be established between Russia and Turkey unless (1) the Russian protectorate of the principalities were replaced by a European guarantee; (2) the navigation of the Danube were 'freed'; (3) the Straits Convention of 1841 were revised 'in the interests of the Balance of Power in Europe'; (4) the Russians abandoned their claim to a protectorate over the Christian subjects of Turkey and instead the five Great Powers obtained from the Turkish government security for the Christians." (ibid).

25 Its main provisions: Great Britain safeguarded Turkish independence and achieved the neutralization of the Black Sea. The Danube Duchies remained under Turkish suzerainty with guarantee of the European powers.

When the Ottoman Empire gradually withdrew from the Balkans, "Balkanization" began to manifest itself: Rising partition and secession of hardly viable nation states, claiming to symbolize the quest for national integration after dreadful periods of oppression and rightful secession from the imperial forces.[26] European efforts were absent to balance the dissolution of the first European Empire – others were to follow – with collective forms of cooperative management of European affairs. Instead, with the exception of the multinational Russian Empire, the heydays of national sovereignty flourished across Europe after the 1870's.

Then and now, only Switzerland showed an alternative way for European states: Since the Federal Constitution of 1848, Switzerland has been a stable multilingual and multinational state, a nation above nations.[27] It is amazing that parallel to this unique European state-formation, under the flag of colonial expansion, a thoroughly different concept grew into reality: Global empires under the flag of European powers. Rivalries among them did not escalate within Europe but were executed in their hectic struggle for overseas possessions. European power rivalries gained a global dimension. They also served as a premature and highly controversial form of globalization. But first and foremost, European colonial expansion was a continuation of inter-European power struggles on a global scale. Politics of national, exclusionary unification and power politics went hand in hand in Europe's highly dynamic and unbalanced nineteenth century. As over-stretched as it was, this order of Europe was to suffer self-destruction, beginning with the outbreak of World War I in 1914.[28]

26 "Balkanization" meant the continuous division of territory liberated from Ottoman rule among contending people in the region: In 1859, for example, Moldova and Walachia shared a common duke, in 1861 they were united as Romania, at the Berlin Congress in 1877 Romania received full independence, along with Serbia and with Montenegro. Serbia formed an independent principality, but turned itself into a Kingdom in 1882. In the Treaty of San Stefano, which ended the Russo-Turkish war on March 3, 1878, Bulgaria was recognized as autonomous under the Ottoman emperor. The Berlin Congress of July 1878 reduced the size of Bulgaria. In 1908, Bulgaria became independent, followed however by two "Balkan Wars" with its former allies Greece and Serbia, in which Bulgaria lost Southern Dobruja to Romania and large parts of Macedonia to Serbia and Greece, which in turn provoked Macedonian nationalism. Albania became independent in 1913. Bosnia-Hercegovina was put under Austro-Hungarian control by the Berlin Congress and became part of Yugoslavia after World War I. On the legacy of "Balkanization" see Zwerin, Michael, *A Case for the Balkanization of Practically Everyone: The New Nationalism*, London: Widderwood House, 1976; Thio, Li-Ann, "Battling Balkanization: Regional Approaches toward Minority Protection beyond Europe," *Harvard International Law Journal*, 43.2(2002): 409-468.

27 See Gruner, Erich, "Die Schweizerische Eidgenossenschaft von der Französischen Revolution bis zur Reform der Verfassung," in: Schieder, Theodor, (ed.), *Handbuch der Europäischen Geschichte*, Vol.5, Stuttgart: Klett-Cotta, 1981: 968-986.

28 See Joll, James, *The Origins of the First World War*, London: Longman, 1984; Macmillan, Margaret, *Peacemakers: Six Months that Changed the World*, London: John Murray, 2001; Marwick, Arthur, et al., *Total War and Historical Change: Europe 1914-1955*, Buckingham, PA.: Open University Press, 2001; Hamilton, Richard F., and Holger H. Herwig, *The Origins of World War I*, Cambridge, Mass.: Harvard University Press, 2003; Jukes, Geoffrey, *The First World War*, New York: Routledge, 2003; Neiberg, Michael S., *Fighting the Great War: A Global History*, Cambridge, Mass.: Harvard University Press, 2005.

Two components of a new arrangement inside European states and among them began to appear with irretrievable force in the European arena: The universal claim to national self-determination, expressing itself for the first time with the breakdown of the Russian Empire in 1917, the Austro-Hungarian Empire and the German Empire in 1918, and the Ottoman Empire in 1919; and the claim for universal democratic self-determination, overcoming the relicts of imperial order through republics (or at least through constitutional monarchies), no matter how weak or contested democratic rule of law was to remain in their midst.

The Europe of power politics and monarchical imperialism was not replaced peacefully and its substitutes were immediately contested in the name of conflicting ideologies. From 1914 to 1945 Europe was going through a dire and daunting civil war, its second thirty years war.[29] Fragile concepts of democratic rule of law were struggling with socialist-egalitarian concepts, nationalistic authoritarianism and racism. Each of the dominating ideologies in Europe during that period was related to the primacy of the nation state. Each of them gained power in excluding itself from any other sphere and reality. 1917 was indicative of things to come: With the entry of the United States into the European war theater and with the Bolshevik Revolution in Russia, Europe was torn apart and became increasingly dependent upon the two peripheral powers. In geopolitical and in normative terms they challenged each other and tore Europe further apart. But ultimately Europeans themselves were dismantling their continent from a subject to an object of world politics. The de-empowerment and self-destruction of Europe was the deed of Europeans. Hitler's and Nazi Germany's aggression became the culminating expression of this tragic and horrendous path toward nihilism and dehumanization. Hitler's war was followed by Stalin's victory, no happy alternative for those who were to suffer its consequences.

Europe as a Europe of powers had failed. It had also failed as a Europe of weak democracies and fragile rule of law. Reconstituting Europe after thirty years of war over internal and external principles of public order could only succeed if domestic democracy and cooperation among democracies were to be linked. Ideological politics inside the nation state could only be tamed through solid rule of law. Power politics among nation states could only be tamed through a community of law. This was a tall order indeed. But in the midst of the failure of the old, fragile and futureless order, there was no alternative should European self-esteem, and the very civilization the continent was so proud of, be rescued.

The treaty system ending World War I in 1919 constituted new neurotic aggression among the losers of the war. The terms "Versailles" or "Trianon" became battle cries

29 See Liddle, Peter, et al., *The Great War, 1914-1945*, London: HarperCollins, 2001.

for revisionism.[30] The rejection of the US Congress to join the League of Nation made this brain-child of US President Woodrow Wilson a still-born framework to constitute a new order in Europe. Wilson's 14-point declaration of January 8, 1918 became the birth certificate for new nation states in Central Europe and the point of reference for decolonization movements that were to succeed a generation later. In his time, Woodrow Wilson's vision for a new Europe, a Europe free from hegemonic forces and nationalism, fear and terror, oppression and suffering, was not well received. Yet his legacy clearly is one of the noble founding stones of a new Europe. "What we demand," Wilson outlined his post-war concept, "is nothing peculiar to ourselves. It is that the world be made fit and safe to live in; and particularly that it be made safe for every peace-loving nation which, like our own, wishes to live its own life, determine its own institutions, be assured of justice and fair dealing by the other peoples of the world as against force and selfish aggression."[31]

4. Turning Times: The Final Awakening

Among the most surprising discoveries of the early years of the twentieth century is the enormous increase in economic interdependence among European societies and states. However, the worst disaster for the continent was yet to come. The most widely cited explanation refers to the absence of a political framework ordering the growing exchange of trade and ensuring its stability above political upheavals among the countries and societies involved. A Franco-German rapprochement based on economic cooperation failed after World War I. The creation of a European Coal Commission in 1919, to co-ordinate coal production and distribution in Europe, did not succeed, because it "lacked sufficient authority."[32] A French initiative based on the idea of a bilateral Franco-German rapprochement brought about a steel cartel and the "short-lived"[33] Franco-German Commercial Treaty of August 1927. The world economic crisis of 1929 destroyed all hope for deepened economic co-operation, although at this point nothing would have been more appropriate. Instead, economic regulation and decisions about policy preferences were completely left in the hands of national politicians. No

30 The academic debate lasted throughout the twentieth century, see Jessop, T. E., *"The Treaty of Versailles": Was it Just?*, London: Thomas Nelson, 1942; Boemeke, Manfred B., et al. (eds.), *The Treaty of Versailles: A Reassessment after 75 Years*, Cambridge: Cambridge University Press, 1998.

31 Wilson, Woodrow, *January 18, 1918: President Woodrow Wilson's Fourteen Points*, http://lib.byu.edu/index.php/President_Wilson%27s_Fourteen_Points.

32 Dedman, Martin J., *The Origins and Development of the European Union 1945-95*, London/New York: Routledge, 1996: 32.

33 Ibid: 33.

matter how evident economic rationality was, political priorities, prejudices and pressures prevailed – with disastrous consequences.[34]

Ten reasons are relevant to better understand why Europe finally awoke to reorganize public and inter-state life:[35]

(1) Geopolitical considerations: With the rise of the Soviet Union and the United States, no European country was any longer able to pursue its traditional policies of hegemonic aspiration, imperial conquest and power struggle among neighbors. The political elites in all European states, even the most autarkic and seemingly strong, had to realize the limits of their ambitions. The wars of 1914 and 1939 had been unleashed by Germany, but their effect had turned out to be disastrous even for the winning parties. The geopolitical context also recalibrated the character of future political regimes in Europe. Western European countries had resisted Nazi totalitarianism, but not all of them had successfully rejected authoritarian rule. Faced with the challenge of an aggressive and expansionary Soviet communism, their choice became crystal clear: Preserving freedom was not only a matter of national independence and sovereignty, it was also a matter of domestic democracy and self-determination. America's support for a viable democratic future was the most important and encouraging commitment they could have hoped for. It triggered new reconsiderations of strategic and national interests, but, all in all, it set into motion the establishment of the "Western world," the "free world" as it became known under the impact of the Cold War.

(2) The negative memory of total destruction:[36] Combined with a loss of global relevance, it contributed to the transformation of ideas about European unity into social norms favoring their realization with certain urgency. This was, of course, a gradual process, not yet focused immediately after World War II, but traceable in many places

34 On the effect of World War I and the development of European ideas during the interwar period see Stirk, Peter M. R. (ed.), *European Unity in Context: the Interwar Period*, London/New York: Pinter, 1989; Stirk, Peter M. R., *A History of European Integration since 1914*, London/New York: Pinter, 1996; Spiering, Menno, and Michael Wintle (eds.), *Ideas of Europe since 1914: the Legacy of the First World War*, Basingstoke: Palgrave Macmillan, 2002.

35 On the whole history see Lipgens, Walter, *A History of European Integration*, Oxford: Clarendon Press, 1982; Krebs, Gerhard, and Dieter Oberländer, *1945 in Europe and Asia: Reconsidering the End of World War II and the Change of the World Order*, Munich: Iudicium, 1997: Alting von Gesau, Frans A. M., *European Unification in the Twentieth Century*, Nijmegen: Vidya Publishers, 1998; Stirk, Peter M. R., and David Weigall (eds.), *The Origins and Development of European Integration: A Reader and Commentary*, London/New York: Pinter, 1999; Kanthoor, Willem Frans Victor, *A Chronological History of the European Union, 1946-2002*, Cheltenham: Edward Elgar, 2002.

36 See Smith, M. L., and Peter M. R. Stirk (eds.), *Making the New Europe: European Unity and the Second World War*, London/New York: Pinter, 1990. The worst side of the destruction in Europe was, of course, the annihilation for millions of human beings for purely ideological, mainly ethnic reasons. Unfortunately, this horrendous drama did neither begin nor ended with World War II. See Naimark, Norman, *Fires of Hatred: Ethnic Cleansing in Twentieth-century Europe*, Cambridge, Mass.: Harvard University Press, 2001.

and among people of highly different backgrounds across Europe. European unity as an ideal had a long history, but always a weak popular and even a weaker political backing. Once the idea of European unity had been translated into the necessity for European integration, this new social norm was soon to become a cultural foundation for operational political choices.

The first visible steps toward this goal were taken on the level of what later was to be called "civil society." Most prominent were the efforts of Count Richard Coudenhove-Kalergi, based on his 1923 book "Paneuropa."[37] Seeing Europe threatened after the break-down of the Austro-Hungarian Empire and the Bolshevik Revolution in Russia (renamed Soviet Union in 1922), he pleaded for a renewal of the continent through a political and economic union of all European states from Poland to Portugal. Their union should be based on mutual security guarantees, a common alliance against the Soviet Union, a customs union and eventually a United States of Europe. The list of members joining his Pan European Union ("Paneuropa Union") before and after its first congress, held in 1926 in Vienna, was impressive: among them were French Prime Minister Léon Blum and his minister of works and social welfare, Louis Loucheur, the President of the German Parliament, Paul Löbe, Erich Koch-Weser, chairman of the German Democratic Party and for some time Minister for Justice, Konrad Adenauer, then mayor of Cologne and President of the Prussian State Council. In 1927, Aristide Briand became Honorary President of the Pan European Union. It was almost the natural precursor of the plan he designed three years later as French Prime Minister and that carries his name; it became the first truly political concept for an integrated Europe.

Economic facts after World War II were more powerful than all former well-meaning efforts: According to a UN Commission, 100 million Europeans were living on less than 1,500 calories per day, which is to say they were starving. The immediate post-war period caused further severe economic damage everywhere. Agricultural output in Western Europe in 1947 was only 70 percent of the pre-war level. In the same year, to name but one example, industrial production in Belgium, the Netherlands and Luxembourg was still 30 to 40 percent below the level of 1939.

(3) New understanding of the role of the economy: This was essential in bringing about a transformation of European integration from an abstract ideal into a socially recognized norm. In fact, it was the driving force for many as they analyzed the prospects for economic recovery after the destruction of two World Wars that went hand in hand with enormous inroads into the economic production and its very material base across Europe. Was Europe to be reconstructed and were European citizens to ever reach the shores of new affluence, they had to reverse the nationalistic, autarkic and

37 Coudenhove-Kalergi, Richard von, *Paneuropa*, Vienna: Paneuropa-Verlag, 1923 (in English the book was published as *Paneurope*, New York: Alfred Knopf, 1926).

war-industry driven character of their economies – and they did.[38] This rational calculation coincided with the logic of newly institutionalized political relations in Europe.

The first steps were taken by industrialists and in fact had been taken by them already before the outbreak of World War II. In 1924, business leaders and economists founded the International Committee for a European Union, among them the banker Paul van Zeeland, who was to become Belgian Prime Minister, and the French banker Edmond Giscard d'Estaing, father of Valéry Giscard d'Estaing, who was born in Coblentz in the French occupied Rhineland in 1926.

In this very year, steel industries from France, Belgium, Germany and Luxembourg created a steel cartel, pushed by Luxembourg industrialist Émile Mayrisch, who was an ardent supporter of Franco-German reconciliation. In 1927, steel producers from Hungary, Austria and the Czech Republic joined the cartel, intended to regulate and better distribute steel resources in Europe by eliminating the open market that had turned into aggressively nationalistic competition. Almost half of European steel production fell under the cartel, although at the expense of customers. Yet it reduced nationalistic tensions particularly between French and German producers striving for a new military buildup in their countries.

(4) Fear of falling back into destructive patterns of ideology-driven politics: This can be grouped together with the wide-spread fear of losing many people to the siren songs of simplistic political ideological pragmatism that dominated among the newly emerging political elites. Many among the ruling personalities and political parties during the formative years after World War II had a strong anti-totalitarian background and were eager to see their nations and the whole continent take a very different course.[39] Their idealism-based political realism grew at the right time. It would have hardly been imaginable to repeat it if the critical decisions toward European integration had been postponed for another decade or so because of leadership inertia. As much as ideals about European unity often had been formulated too early, now it was the hour of courageous, wise leadership decisions, which, by the same token, was the most obvious path to enable their people to embark on a better future.

Aristide Briand, Édouard Herriot, head of the Radical Party, cabinet minister and author of a book about the United States of Europe[40], Paul Löbe, Konrad Adenauer, Edvard Beneš, long time Foreign Minister of Czechoslovakia, and Ignaz Seipel, Austria's Catholic post-World War I Chancellor, were among the members of

38 See Foley, Bernhard J. (ed.), *European Economies since the Second World War*, Basingstoke: Macmillan, 1998.

39 For documents see Lipgens, Walter (ed.), *Documents on the History of European Integration*, Vol.3 (The Struggle for European Union by Political Parties and Pressure Groups in Western European Countries 1945-1950), Berlin/New York: Walter de Gruyter, 1988.

40 Herriot, Édouard, *The United States of Europe*, London: George Harrap, 1930.

Coudenhove-Kalergi's "Pan Europe Union."[41] Their pro-European attitudes were shared by other members of the political elites in the inter-war period and by members-to-be in post-war Europe. It was no coincidence that Adenauer came from the West German Rhineland, a highly contested region, but more open for collaboration with Germany's Western neighbors than many other regions in his country; Robert Schuman had a French father, was born in Luxembourg, remained a German citizen until 1918, immediately afterwards becoming a member of the French National Assembly in 1919 and finally French Foreign Minister from 1948 until 1953; Alcide de Gasperi came from the region of South Tyrol, representing the Italian minority in the Austro-Hungarian parliament before World War I and becoming Italian Prime Minister after World War II. These post-war leaders knew the fate of border areas and of ethnic or linguistic minorities and had a genuine sensitivity for cooperation in Europe. A generation later, Helmut Kohl, Chancellor of German unity in 1990, did not get tired of recalling the impression it had made on him as a young man from the French occupied city of Ludwigshafen to be forced by French soldiers to use the other side of the sidewalk; this motivated him to participate in the movement to tear down border posts between France and Germany. Other post-war leaders had suffered totalitarianism in concentration camps or as prisoners in war camps. They had looked into the abyss of war and the nihilistic destruction it had caused in Europe. They wanted, once and for all, to see Europe change its course. Their idealism defined the rationality of their policies in favor of European unity and integration.

(5) A changed notion of security: Once the weapons of World War II had come to a halt, it became increasingly obvious that security could no longer be conceived as a zero-sum game according to which one participant's gains would translate into somebody else's losses. Security was no longer the best form of defending one's nation by deterring others. Security was now understood as a common interest of societies that were organized by like-minded political systems and economies. Rapidly, security also became a common concern against expansionist, communist totalitarianism. It is debatable and controversial to this day whether European unity started more out of fear of Soviet hegemony or out of hope for a better, peaceful and affluent future among former enemies. In the end, both factors converged.

The solutions found for Europe's security after World War I had been completely unsatisfactory. The system of the peace treaties signed in various suburbs of Paris remained bilateral, germinated new conflicts as it was based upon revenge for the winners, and supported the tendency toward re-establishing power-politics and the

41 Coudenhove-Kalergi, Richard von, *Crusade for Pan-Europe: Autobiography of a Man and a Movement*, New York: G. P. Putnam's Sons, 1943; Zurcher, Arnold J., *The Struggle to Unite Europe, 1940-1958: An Historical Account of the Development of the Contemporary European Movement from its Origin in the Pan-European Union to the Drafting of the Treaties for Euratom and the European Common Market*, Westport: Greenwood, 1975.

agony of balancing mutually suspicious alliances. France maintained its fear of Germany and hoped for new hegemonic status in Europe; Great Britain was vacillating between its role as a world power and its commitment to Europe; Germany felt humiliated, and its new rise was to become the precondition for ferocious revisionism. The European repercussions of the breakdown of the empires in Vienna, Petersburg and Constantinople were not dealt with in the Versailles system. President Wilson's idea to internationalize and universalize European affairs through the League of Nations (with finally sixty-three member states) was good, but it could not work with the US withholding its participation, the Soviet Union only joining in 1934 and again being expelled in 1940 after its attack on Finland, and Germany joining in 1926 but withdrawing in 1933 immediately after Hitler had come to power. The sanction mechanisms of the League of Nations failed completely.[42] The vacuum of power in Europe was topped by the vacuum of legitimate rule in Europe, turning the continent into a continuous geopolitical nightmare as World War II was to prove.

German defeat in 1945 forced the leading powers to construct a new political framework, both inside Germany and for Europe. The new instability that followed the crushing defeat of Adolf Hitler and his regime was coupled with a fundamental fragmentation of Germany and – with the emerging Cold War this became undeniable – of the whole European continent. The peripheral powers took Europe's destiny into their hands. For the Soviet Union, this meant advancing the installation of Soviet-type regimes in their sphere of influence.[43] As for the American dominated zones of occupation, the matter was one of installing or reinstalling democratic rule, market economy and a new foreign policy arrangement that was able to harmonize American, British, French and other Western European interests.

Germany was also linked with the overall European development as far as the terrible plight of refugees was concerned. In 1945, thirteen million "displaced persons" were counted across Europe, ten million of them enforced laborers in Germany. While their return was arranged, West Germany had to absorb over 9 million refugees from its former territories in the East. Between 1950 and 1961, when the Berlin Wall was erected, another 3.6 million refugees moved to West Germany. A quarter of its population was by then recently displaced in the area they finally settled.[44]

42 For an early critical assessment see Sarolea, Charles, *The Policy of Sanctions and the Failure of the League of Nations*, London: International Publishing Company, 1936.

43 As far as East Germany was concerned see Naimark, Norman, *The Russians in Germany: The History of the Soviet Zone of Occupation, 1945-1949*, Cambridge, Mass.: Harvard University Press, 1995.

44 See Dyshnyck, Walter, *Refugees are People: The Plight of Europe's Displaced Persons*, New York: America Press, 1947; Danylyszyn, Daniel William, *"Prisoners of Peace": British Policy towards Displaced Persons and Political Refugees within Occupied Germany, 1945-1951*, London: University of London, 2001.

(6) A changing notion of power: The transformed global order forced reflection about what was important to one's own identity and what was not. Discovering "neighborly-ness," not as an antagonistic danger, but as a potential asset for the enhancement of one's own well-being, was a surprising novelty among Europeans. Yet once the first effects of this redefinition of patterns of behavior and policy choices became evident, the results were more convincing than most theories had ever assumed.

Among many groups resisting the military hegemony of Nazi Germany over Europe, concepts of a democratic integration were already discussed throughout the war.[45] Most prominent became the Ventotone Manifest of July 1941 by Ernesto Rossi and Altiero Spinelli, who later was to become a communist member of the European Parliament and the initiator of the draft constitution for Europe, which the European Parliament was to pass in 1984. Other resistance movements in Czechoslovakia, France, Poland, the Netherlands, Yugoslavia, but also in Germany (Kreisauer Kreis) developed federal concepts for a new beginning in Europe. Many of these groups met in July 1944 in neutral Switzerland and presented a declaration, mainly arguing for a federal restructuring of state relations in Europe: A constitution was to provide the framework for a European government directly responsible to the people of Europe and not to national governments. Except for delegates from Denmark and Norway, all other delegates from resistance movements endorsed the paper. In December 1946, 40 national movements from 16 countries created the Union of European Federalists, by far the biggest European lobby group for a federal Europe, existing to this day.[46] Also in Great Britain, federal ideas circulated, and Churchill's son-in-law Duncan Edwin Sandys chaired the United Europe Movement, founded in March 1947 and promoting a Commonwealth-like structure for Europe. This was a response to Winston Churchill's famous speech at the University of Zurich on September 19, 1946, in which the British opposition leader and war hero explicitly called for the formation of the United States of Europe: "Why should there not be a European group," he asked, "which could give a sense of enlarged patriotism and common citizenship to the distracted peoples of this turbulent and mighty continent."[47]

Besides the many private groups and government bureaucracies, political parties took on the challenge to renew the idea of Europe through concrete steps of integration. Christian democratic movements – emerging on the European level under the heading of the Nouvelles Equipes Internationales, founded in March 1947 – were to become a distinctive new feature of the European landscape, particularly favoring a federal

45 For documents see Lipgens, Walter (ed.), *Documents on the History of European Integration*, Vol.1 (Continental Plans for European Union, 1939-1945), Berlin/New York: Walter de Gruyter, 1985; Lipgens, Walter (ed.), *Documents on the History of European Integration*, Vol.2 (Plans for European Union in Great Britain and in Exile, 1939-1945), Berlin/New York: Walter de Gruyter, 1986.

46 See May, Alex, *Europe at the Crossroads: The European Union of Federalists and the Process of European Integration, 1946-54*, London: South Bank European Papers, 1997.

47 Cited in Hitchcock, William I., *The Struggle for Europe: The Turbulent History of a Divided Continent, 1945 to the Present*, New York: Anchor Book, 2004: 7.

integration of the continent as part of its necessary moral renewal. A Socialist Movement for the United States of Europe was founded in June 1947. The breakthrough of a new reality was imminent.

(7) Europe's loss of global preeminence: The loss of managing internal European affairs without interference from the peripheral powers, the US and USSR, had a double effect that turned out to be extremely favorable for initiating European integration. Fear from communism and the expansionist character of Soviet policy helped to bring together the "Western" camp. Most importantly, it resolved the issue of the prospective future of divided Germany. The stronger the Soviet Union was preparing for a Soviet-type model of rule in its satellite states, East Germany included, the faster the US favored turning negative control over West Germany into positive control by integrating West Germany into the newly emerging Euro-Atlantic security structures and means of economic cooperation.

All in all, the United States became the most important federator for Western Europe. Intellectually and as far as the normative reorientation of Europe was concerned, many in Europe looked to the US. Jean Monnet had studied most of the mechanisms and potential effects of his functional, sector-specific method of community building while in exile in Washington. He was not only strongly influenced by American federalism, but also able to connect with many high-ranking officials of the Roosevelt administration while living in Washington. It is almost ironic how America had influenced a Frenchman who was to become the most venerated "god-father" of European integration. It was also indicative that the fifth congress of the Pan European Union took place in New York in March 1943. Count Coudenhove-Kalergi proposed a Council of Europe with a Supreme Court that would entertain binding powers to resolve legal conflicts among its members and with armed forces to implement its decisions.

From May 1945, US commitment to European recovery and reconciliation through integration became a strategic interest and goal for the Truman administration. The Truman Doctrine, geared at containing Soviet expansionism, and the Marshall Plan, directed at economic recovery of Europe out of enlightened self-interest, became the cornerstones for US post-war policies. Along with the continuous troop deployment in Western Europe, the United States played an active, encouraging and supportive role to implant the ideas of reconciliation, recovery and integration in the best suitable and most lasting form. Economic rebuilding and the strategic imperative to contain and deter the expansionist Soviet Union were only to become successful if liberal democracies in Western Europe would be able to show economic success. Without an expanding market, this was as impossible as it would have been to build democracy without committed democrats.

(8) The changing meaning of national sovereignty: The classical idea of national sovereignty had become somewhat abstract after two wars and a cycle of destructive violence that was only stopped through outside, that is say non-European, intervention. Along with sovereignty, other key concepts of how to define power and relate resources to political processes and goals were reassessed. The search for new mechanisms favored what was to be labeled "functional, sector-specific integration," intended to break the gap between the ideal and reality by facilitating instruments and means through which integration could turn into social and political reality.

Under the pressure of military defeat by Nazi Germany in 1940, Great Britain had offered France a Union between the two countries. Winston Churchill's cabinet proposed to their French counterparts a common British-French citizenship and joint organs to lead the war. The French leadership under Prime Minister Paul Reynaud was hesitant and preferred to search for an armistice with Germany as their partner to maintain national sovereignty. The British proposal, beyond demonstrating the readiness to increase Britain's link with continental Europe, was a substantial rejection of all traditional theories of sovereignty. Interestingly enough, it had been developed by a group around Jean Monnet, de Gaulle and members of the British Federal Union movement, among them historian Arnold Toynbee and Permanent Undersecretary Robert Vansittart. At first, Churchill seemed to have been reluctant to embrace such a far-fetched proposal. When he finally proposed it to his French colleague Reynaud, the French cabinet rejected the idea on June 16, 1940, with a 13 to 11 vote. The same evening, Reynaud resigned and was replaced by his rival, General Pétain, who immediately offered Hitler an armistice. But the debate in France about new concepts for Europe was only beginning, as indicated in a letter sent by Léon Blum – in 1936 the first socialist (and Jewish) French Prime Minister – from a prison of the Vichy government, strongly advocating powerful international organizations once this war was over. Otherwise, he feared, this would not have been the last war in Europe. In spring 1944, de Gaulle's "Free France" proposed the integration of Western Europe, including Great Britain – this time without gaining too much British attention.

In November 1940, the leader of the Polish government in exile, General Władysław Sikorski, and the head of the provisional Czech government, Edvard Beneš, expressed their intention of creating a Polish-Czech Confederation once the war was over and their countries were free again. In 1942, Sikorski organized a London conference of governments in exile with representatives from Poland, Czechoslovakia, Norway, Belgium, the Netherlands, Luxembourg, Greece, Yugoslavia and the committee Free France. The participants agreed on the creation of a "European Community" after the traumatic war had ended. The literature outpour during the Second World War on the issue of Central and Eastern European federation was immense.[48] In Western Europe, the Belgian Foreign Minister in exile, Paul Henri Spaak, suggested a Union of Belgium, the Netherlands and Luxembourg with France.[49] Based on the resources of their respective colonies, this union would be able to play an independent global role. Other voices from the same region were more limited in their aspirations and some already reached out to their German enemy. Former Belgian Prime Minister Paul van Zeeland, in London the exile in charge of dealing with Belgian refugees, recommended a West European customs and currency union. Louis de Brouckère, former President of the Socialist and Labour International proposed to include German industrial resources into any future West European cooperation.

A precursor of integration trajectories to come was established on September 5, 1944, with the Benelux-Treaty. The governments of Belgium, Luxembourg and the Netherlands came to agree on the establishment of a customs union once the war activities came to a halt. The abbreviation Benelux to this day remains synonymous for the readiness of smaller countries in Europe to advance the concept of a federal pooling of sovereignty and resources for the advantage of all.

After 1945, France was still searching for security against Germany. But instead of seeking revenge, Germany was searching for rehabilitation after the millenary moral and political humiliation it suffered with the defeat of Hitler's "Third Reich." France was able to begin reassessing the relationship between sovereignty and security in a new light as its own victory could not generate economic recovery unless geo-economic parameters in Europe were recalibrated.

(9) The notion of territoriality was redesigned:[50] Although it was too early to tell, European integration would certainly affect the sacrosanct principle of "non-interference in domestic affairs," one of the cornerstones of classical state sovereignty. Yet the race between the fear of losing sovereignty and the fear of losing economic means to rebuild the war-torn societies gave in to pragmatism. When the matter turned again into one of rigid principle – notably during the empty-chair crisis of 1965/66 provoked by French President Charles de Gaulle – the European integration mechanism had already developed so much authenticity and autonomy that it could not be destroyed and buried completely.

During the inter-war period, European governments were obsessed with redesigning borders or ensuring their permanency against revisionist pressure. When the Locarno Pact in 1925 guaranteed the Western borders between Germany, Belgium and France,

48 See Sworakowski, Witold S., *Bibliography of Books, Pamphlets, and Articles in Periodicals, Dealing with Federation Plans for Central and Eastern Europe, developed during the Second World War*, Stanford: Stanford University Press, 1964.

49 On the historic role of this ubiquitous man see Huizinga, Johan M., *Mr. Europe: A Political Biography of Paul Henri Spaak*, London: Weidenfeld & Nicholson, 1961.

50 See Murray, Philomena B., and Leslie Holmes (eds.), *Europe – Rethinking the Boundaries*, Ashgate: Aldershot, 1998.

with Italy and Great Britain as guaranteeing powers, this seemed to be a breakthrough in overcoming the quarrel for territory. But an "Eastern Locarno" did not emerge as far as Germany's borders with Poland and the Czech Republic were concerned. Hungary was another European country that felt it was treated extremely unfairly at the Peace Conferences post-World War I. While for the Germans, the battle cry of revisionism was "Versailles," for Hungarians – who lost two thirds of their territory compared with the 10 percent loss of Germany – the battle cry was "Trianon." It was no coincidence that the final resolution of German unification in 1990 was also dependent upon the comprehensive recognition of the German-Polish border, while the issue of Hungarian minorities in Romania and Slovakia, but also the relationship between Austrians and their neighbors and between Italy and Slovenia, were matters that stayed on the European agenda even beyond the divisions of the Cold War. But the form in which these issues were debated after 1989/1990, and the efforts to resolve them in the context of European integration among democracies, were light-years more moderate than the aggressive quest for each square meter of territory that had Europeans obsessed, almost bewitched, during the nineteenth and the first half of the twentieth century.

(10) Politics reclaimed responsibility for ordering public life in Europe: The re-establishment of democratic rule in Germany and its consolidation in other Western European states – with the deplorable absence of Spain and Portugal and a bitter struggle in Greece – was a political act. So was the re-designation of the European state order. The partition of Europe in the Cold War was not a natural process but the consequence of normative differences between democracy and totalitarianism. This normative quarrel superseded the great power struggle between Russia and the United States, to which some far-sighted analysts had already made reference to in the nineteenth century, long before the ideological component existed. European integration as a process to unite like-minded democracies in Europe was the deepest possible rehabilitation of legitimate politics on a continent that had been the traumatic victim of ideological and violent politics. No matter what method was to be chosen, no matter which priorities were pursued, and no matter which technicalities might pose as hurdles on a long path, politics claimed to be in charge of ordering a disordered continent. In doing so in a peaceful, democratic and integrative way, it rehabilitated the legitimacy of its own sphere among highly skeptical and frustrated populations.

When French Prime Minister Aristide Briand presented his concept for European integration to the other governments of the continent on May 17, 1930, he proclaimed the primacy of a political order over the reorganization of the European economy.[51] His comprehensive plan for a European order came at the wrong time. His German interlocuteur Gustav Stresemann, the liberal and conciliatory Foreign Minister with

51 See Ferrell, Robert H., *Peace in their Time: The Origins of the Kellog-Briand Pact*, New York: W. W. Norton, 1969.

whom Briand had negotiated the Locarno Pact and received the Nobel Peace Prize in 1926, had unfortunately died in 1929. In light of the world economic crisis, Briand proposed a political framework that could protect the interests of the strong as well as the weak states of Europe. A European Conference as main organ of a loose confederation should come together on the basis of an annually revolving presidency, chosen among European member states of the League of Nations. A Permanent Political Committee was planned as the executive organ that implemented decisions of the European Conference. A Secretariat was to coordinate administrative tasks. The scope of competences was intended to entail economic, financial and structural matters, also transportation, the health sector, exchange of academicians and parliamentarians, the rationalization of bureaucracies, and the coordination in the policies of the member states toward external powers and the League of Nations.

When Briand reported the reactions to his plan at the eleventh session of the General Assembly of the League of Nations in September 1931, a study commission was installed to look further into the matter. This was the death kiss for Briand's plan. The first truly honest political initiative for European integration moved into the archives. Along with the Kellogg-Briand Pact of 1928 – named after Briand and US Secretary of State Frank B. Kellogg formulating a strict renunciation of violence as political means among European states – Briand's plan for Europe nevertheless gave testimony that responsible politicians were looking for alternative paths as the continent's radicals were preparing for the ultimate self-destruction of Europe, its moral credibility and political power.

5. Constructivism at Work

1945 was not a "zero hour" for Europe. As much as many pre-War realities prevailed, it became increasingly clear that most post-War innovations were already planned, if not designed and created during the horrible years of fighting and destruction.[52] This also held true for political concepts that attempted to re-create the European continent in a new manner: Shifting from power struggles to cooperative and integrative means, and moving from fragile or authoritarian governance to democracy. This was the perspective for Western Europe at last, while the Eastern half of the continent unfortunately came under increasing pressure from the Soviet Union to follow its social, political and strategic model. On March 5, 1946, British opposition leader Winston Churchill, who had suffered a startling defeat in April 1945, proving democracy as vital reality in Great Britain, spoke of the "Iron Curtain" that was dividing Europe. In the presence of US President Harry S. Truman, his speech, in Fulton in

52 See Stirk, Peter M. R., and David Willis (eds.), *Shaping Postwar Europe: European Unity and Disunity, 1945-1957*, New York: St. Martin's Press, 1991.

Truman's home-state Missouri, was to give the new era one of its most widely known phrases.[53] For historians, the "Cold War" – another phrase to describe the next five decades of geopolitical antagonism between "the West" and "the East" and the normative struggle between freedom and totalitarian rule – was not to begin before the failed Foreign Minister's meeting of the four victorious war powers in London on December 15, 1947. But the formative period for a whole new era and the emergence of a completely new face of Europe was already in full swing a year and a half earlier.

In addition to efforts of resistance movements and political intellectuals across Europe, "Free France" under the leadership of Charles de Gaulle had proposed the integration of Western Europe, along with Great Britain, as early as spring 1944.[54] Paul-Henri Spaak echoed these ideas with similar concepts in the autumn of 1944. The end of the war would also bring an end to colonial dominance. It would leave Europe with no choice but to rebuild itself as some sort of a "third force" between the United States and the Soviet Union. India's independence on August 15, 1947 – about a year earlier than planned by the British because of the pressure of the independence movement under Mahatma Gandhi – was symbolic for things to come. Europe would lose its global power base and would have to reconsider internal matters thoroughly were it to reemerge as a relevant factor with a reconstructed, morally and materially sound home base.

Interests among Western Europe's leading countries were obvious. Great Britain had elected the Socialists to power only few weeks after the war had ended, outvoting the conservative social policy of the 1930's and defeating War leader and hero Winston Churchill. For the next six years, until the conservatives under Churchill were reelected in 1951, the socialization of key industries and intensive welfare reforms were national priority. Beginning with India's independence in 1947 and ending with the Suez crisis in 1956, the British Empire was in steady decline. The necessity of properly connecting its fate to that of Europe grew, but remained uncertain and contested. In France, the Fourth Republic, established via referendum in 1946 – after the Allied landing in Normandy, the defeat of the Vichy regime, but against the will of de Gaulle, the military leader of France's war resistance – was but in name a renewed Third Republic with its inherent flaws: weak legislature, strong executive, fragmented political parties. Remarkable was the effect of the economic recovery in France. Between 1949 and 1957, its GDP grew by 49 percent. Just as remarkable was the political instability: The country experienced twenty-five different governments in twelve years before de Gaulle

53 See Gilbert, Martin, *The Origins of the "Iron Curtain" Speech*, Fulton, Missouri: Winston Churchill Memorial/Westminster College, 1981; Harbutt, Fraser J., *The Iron Curtain: Churchill, America and the Origin of the Cold War*, New York: Oxford University Press, 1986; Larres, Klaus, *Churchill's Cold War: The Politics of Personal Diplomacy*, New Heaven: Yale University Press, 2002.

54 See Pattison de Ménil, Lois, *Who Speaks for Europe?: The Vision of Charles de Gaulle*, New York: St. Martin's Press, 1978; Hitchcock, William I., *France Restored: Cold War Diplomacy and the Quest for Leadership in Europe, 1944-1954*, Chapel Hill: University of North Carolina Press, 1998; Jackson, Julian, *Charles de Gaulle*, London: Haus, 2003.

installed the Fifth Republic under his leadership. It also failed in its colonial policies: 1954 was the watershed-year with crushing military defeat in Indochina (Dien Bien Phu) and the outbreak of civil war in Algeria. Parliamentary democracy itself came under increasing pressure in France.

For defeated Germany, the perspective was quite different. Its democratic prospects and credentials could only grow, at least in the three Western sectors of the divided country. With the establishment of the Federal Republic of Germany and the German Democratic Republic in 1949, the process of ideological and geopolitical partition climaxed. The defeat of Nazi totalitarianism and the full record of its horrendous crimes brought about a deep loss of moral credibility for Germans. It also turned the occupied country into the battlefield for the newly emerging Cold War. American, British and French post-war plans for Germany were increasingly overshadowed by the challenge stemming from expansionist Soviet communism. The Federal Republic of Germany under its Christian Democratic Chancellor Konrad Adenauer seized the opportunity to lay the groundwork for its remarkable economic recovery during years of an economic miracle ("Wirtschaftswunder"). It also helped in turning negative control over West German sovereignty into positive control of Germany through its participation in the emerging "Western" structures of integration and cooperation.

Italy's post-war development was ambivalent. With the beginning of the Anglo-American invasion of Sicily in July 1943, the country was torn between either resisting Hitler or Mussolini or the Allies. King Victor Emmanuel III ousted the country's dictator Mussolini immediately and sought a separate peace with the Allies. German forces seized Rome and helped Mussolini to establish himself as head of the "Italian Social Republic" on the shores of Lake Garda. The King declared war on Germany. The first elections after the Allies had liberated Northern Italy from both the Germans and Mussolini's forces were won by Alcide de Gasperi, the leader of the newly created Christian Democrats. He immediately established solid relations with the Anglo-American military authorities. In 1947, the communists had to leave his government when Italy became recipient of Marshall Plan aid. The country had made a turn-around and became a pillar in the Western security calculation. It also became a "natural" participant in the emerging European structures of economic cooperation.

As for the Netherlands, the end of World War II was followed by the immediate declaration of independence of her colony Indonesia on August 17, 1945, after liberation from Japanese occupation. The Dutch view that colonial rule should be reestablished, underestimated the strong nationalistic feelings in Indonesia, but also the unwillingness of Great Britain – who had liberated the archipelago from Japanese occupation – to cooperate to this end. After a failed military intervention by the Dutch, Indonesia and the Netherlands agreed on the transfer of sovereignty in 1949, followed by years of tension. In 1957, all remaining Dutch citizens had to leave Indonesia, followed by the nationalization of all Dutch enterprises in 1958. Parallel to this humiliating end of Dutch colonial power, World War II had caused enormous economic damage in the Netherlands. Political life fragmented again along the pre-war lines between religious and liberal or socialist parties. In 1948, Queen Wilhelmina was forced to abdicate, feeling bitter about post-war developments both in Indonesia and at home after liberalization from German occupation. Between 1946 and 1958, the Netherlands were governed by a coalition of the Catholic People's Party and the Labor Party under Labor leader Willem Drees. The Dutch struggle with natural disaster during the terrible flood of 1953 did not derail the overall success of economic recovery supported by Marshall Plan Aid. Supporting European economic cooperation and integration was a natural and consensual idea shared in the Netherlands.

In Belgium, with the end of German occupation, internal lines of controversy reemerged between the Walloons and the Flemish: the Flemish, by and large Catholic, were in favor of a return of the Belgian king, who had been transferred by the Germans to Austria in 1944, while the Walloons, like Socialists and Liberals in general, were against it. A referendum in 1950 showed 58 percent of all Belgians in favor of the return of the king, but in the Walloon country it could have signalled civil war. In August 1950, King Leopold appointed his eldest son, Prince Baudouin, to temporarily rule in his place. In 1951, King Leopold formally abdicated, and his son officially assumed the throne as King Baudouin I. As in the Netherlands, post-war policy in Belgium was also dominated by the decolonization issue, in the Belgian case it was the issue of the Belgian Congo. Belgium also debated the recovery of the mixed economy, the matter of regional autonomy, including issues of education and language, and Belgium's role in the emerging new postwar international and supranational organizations. After a miracle recovery in the late 1940's, Belgium was heavily affected by declining investment rates and strongly reduced growth rates, beside the burden of the aging Walloon heavy industry. The prospect of participating in a wider European customs union was cherished across all political and regional camps in Belgium.

Iron ore had largely made the fortune of modern Luxembourg. During German occupation of neutral Luxembourg as of May 1940, Grand Duchess Charlotte and her cabinet fled abroad. After Allied troops liberated Luxembourg in September 1944, the grand duchy was soon to join the United Nations and, also as one of its founding members, NATO. In 1948 its revised constitution abolished perpetual neutrality. Given its involvement in the European coal and steel industry and its geographical location, it was more than natural that Luxembourg joined the efforts to establish a European Coal and Steel Community, and subsequently the European Economic Community. Luxembourg has always been among the most active and respected partners in the European integration process.

In September 1946, members of various federalist groups from fourteen European countries met in Hertenstein, Switzerland, and decided to form a European roof organization. Under the leadership of Hendrik Brugmans from the Netherlands, the

European Union of Federalists was founded in October 1946. The Hague Congress of May 7-10, 1948, was the most powerful demonstration of civil society pressure for a united Europe so far. It was attended by representatives from politics, the economy and culture from all over Europe, representing the dream of different generations to turn the page in Europe's history once and for all. Konrad Adenauer was among the participants, as well as François Mitterrand, to name but two prominent representatives of two different generations and political camps.

As far as the big geo-political picture was concerned, the wartime Alliance between the US, France and Great Britain on the one hand and the Soviet Union on the other hand had already begun to dissolve rapidly during the year prior to the Hague Congress. President Truman's speech to the US Congress on March 12, 1947, defined the doctrine that became paramount for the years to come: The US was to remain committed to European recovery and security, while the USSR was to be contained wherever necessary. Anti-Soviet considerations and pro-federal idealism, new geostrategic realities and wavering democracies, Christian and Socialist, liberal and humanist traditions converged in the notion and concept of the "Western world." When US Secretary of State George C. Marshall addressed Harvard University's Commencement on June 5, 1947, nobody was able to foresee the results of the rising West. Yet his offer to help war-torn Europe was a turning point of unprecedented importance. It would commit the US to stay a European power although the subsequent Marshall Aid program – the European Recovery Program – did not turn into an institution able to manage economic relations among European states. In December 1947, the US Congress agreed to a first aid package for Europe in the amount of 522 million US dollars for France, Italy and Austria. In total, the Marshall Plan aid grew into 13 billion US dollars between 1947 and 1952.[55]

Concepts for the restructuring of Europe remained confusing during the immediate post-war years. Whether emphasis should be on the political reorganization of Europe or on the economic recovery was as much open to debate as the question of leadership: Should the new Europe be Atlantic or European, should it be a third force in world politics or a junior partner of the US in the emerging conflict with an expansionist Soviet Union? How should the prospects for a peaceful and democratic reunification of the European continent be upheld and what would be the role and position of divided Germany? The period between 1945 and 1955 was truly one of trial and error. The new Europe grew as a social and political construction.

Constructivism does not mean the absence of rational roots or the lack of consensus. But it means that not only political, but also military and economic leaders and leading intellectuals contributed to the emergence of a whole set of Euro-Atlantic institutions.

55 For this figure see Knipping, Franz, *Rom, 25.März 1957: Die Einigung Europas*, Munich: Deutscher Taschenbuch Verlag, 2004: 53. Martin Dedman gives the figure of 22 billion US-dollars for the same period: Dedman, Martin, *The Origins and Development of the European Union, 1945-1990*, op.cit.: 48.

At no point in time was the success or failure of any of them self-evident. All efforts were without precedence. Basic ideas had been outlined throughout the long struggle of Europe's failed history. But details and linkages, effects and implications, were disguised under the veil of an altogether uncertain, yet possible future. Compared with the horrors of totalitarian tyranny and cruel warfare, compared with the secular tragedies of the Holocaust and the prevailing Gulags, the construction of a new political and economic Europe was almost an easy task. Its main difficulty stemmed from the inevitable need to redefine security concepts and future economic and political trajectories in accordance with the values of reconciliation, renewal and cooperation. Wherever this was achieved, all early efforts to reconstruct Europe deserve a dignified place in the historic account of these formative years.

Since 1947, American politicians had supported the creation of regional institutions in Europe. Marshall Aid supported the reconstructing of the widely destroyed infrastructure in Europe. At the same time, discussions among European leaders focused on the prospects of a customs union on the one hand, and a political mechanism for a new European order on the other hand. On April 16, 1948, the convention of the Organization for European Economic Cooperation (OEEC) was signed by sixteen countries; West Germany joined a year later. The OEEC under its French Secretary General Robert Marjolin[56] became the framework for the implementation of American aid to Europe while the final control of the use of the means remained in the hands of the "Economic Cooperation Administration" of the US government. The Marshall Plan did not generate a supranational institution in Europe, but it was the starting point for a new economic beginning in Europe under democratic auspices.

The next step, again supported by the US, focused on the security situation. After the communist coup d'état in Czechoslovakia in February 1948, Great Britain, France, Belgium, the Netherlands and Luxembourg agreed within a few days on a multilateral defense treaty with reciprocal assistance obligations. The Brussels Pact was to exist for 50 years. Later, it grew into the Western European Union (WEU), but it never became more than a coordinating element for the Western European caucus in NATO. NATO was founded on April 4, 1949, by twelve countries – the US, Canada, Great Britain, France, Belgium, the Netherlands, Luxembourg, Norway, Denmark, Iceland, Portugal and Italy, in 1952 enlarged by Greece and Turkey and in 1955 by West Germany – and immediately turned into the backbone of transatlantic security assurances. When NATO celebrated its 50th anniversary in 1999, it had all the reason to be proud of being the most successful defense alliance in human history; it had brought the Cold War and the division of Europe to an end without a single bullet being shot. As for WEU, it was

56 See Ouin, Marc, *The OEEC and the Common Market: Why Europe needs an Economic Union of Seventeen Countries*, Paris: Organization for European Economic Cooperation, 1958; Marjolin, Robert, *Architect of European Unity: Memoirs 1911-1986*, London: Weidenfeld & Nicholson , 1989; Griffiths, Richard, *Explorations in OEEC History*, Paris: Organization for Economic Co-Operation and Development, 1997.

absorbed by the efforts of the European Union to establish not only a Common Foreign and Security, but also a Common Defense Policy.

British Labor Foreign Minister Ernest Bevin is given credit for the proposal of October 1948 to establish the Council of Europe. French Foreign Minister Robert Schuman, holding office since July 1948, immediately agreed, although he would have preferred the name "European Union." In accordance with the European movements as outlined at their Hague congress he suggested it to be a parliamentary assembly. Great Britain accepted, provided each country was independent in selecting its members and could define the agenda of the Council. Future debates about the scope of national autonomy over supranational institutions and their decision-making were beginning to loom on the horizon. When the Council of Europe met for the first session of its consultative parliamentary assembly in August 1949 in Strasbourg, all national parliaments sent leading politicians to attend. The first President of the parliamentary assembly of the Council of Europe was former Belgian Prime Minister Paul-Henri Spaak.

The goal and purpose of the Council of Europe, its early declarations said, was the formation of a European political authority with limited functions, but real competences.[57] The Council of Europe was to gain its main success with its support of human rights: The European Convention on Human Rights, signed in 1952, and the Strasbourg-based European Court of Human Rights are widely acclaimed success stories to this day. As the first ever European regional institution, the Council of Europe was to become a reference point for all democratic states on the continent. With Greece and Turkey joining immediately in 1949, the Council of Europe also proved its potential as bridge-builder among conflicting states. When the Iron Curtain finally fell in 1989/1990, all post-communist countries were eager to join the Council of Europe. But by then, the orientating function of the Council of Europe had turned into a sort of waiting room for early membership in the European Union. In 1949, it would not have been conceivable to see the Council of Europe struggling for its future identity while the path toward economic integration had finally also taken precedence over all other European efforts to forge a political Europe.[58]

The creation of the Council of Europe did not stop reflections among European governments concerning a customs union. US Secretary of State Dean Acheson urged French Foreign Minister Robert Schuman to take the leading role. France maintained strong interest in preventing the revival of untamed German economic strength. It had to accept the need to include Germany in all future considerations concerning European

57 For the overly optimistic beginnings see Hurd, Volney, *The Council of Europe: Design for a United States of Europe*, New York: Manhattan Publishing Company, 1958.

58 On the first fifty years of the Council of Europe see Holtz, Uwe (ed.), *50 Jahre Europarat*, Baden-Baden: Nomos, 2000; for the account of one of its former Secretary Generals see Schwimmer, Walter, *Der Traum Europa: Europa vom 19. Jahrhundert in das dritte Jahrtausend*, Berlin/Heidelberg/New York: Springer, 2004.

economic integration while simultaneously maintaining its dominant position among Western European states. For a British-US-French Foreign Minister's meeting on May 11-13, 1950, Acheson and Bevin were preparing to resolve the limitation of German steel production that was fixed with 11.1 million tons per year. Along with the prospect of an easing of the occupational status for Germany, France became worried. Churchill, in a speech to the British Parliament, had even proposed to establish a German troop contingent as part of a European army. France had to act, and Schuman acted. After receiving support from German Chancellor Adenauer on May 8, 1950, the next day he proposed to place the complete French and German steel and coal production under a common high authority. This would mean rehabilitation for Germany and security for France. It also meant a completely new experience for Europe. When the treaty for the European Coal and Steel Community was signed on April 18, 1951, nobody could anticipate what was to follow. Constructivism had succeeded in just another form to revive and unite Europe. The outcome – short-term or long-term – was still clouded. Integration was a big goal, a normative plea as the work of the Council of Europe was demonstrating. But with the Schuman Plan – the brainchild of Jean Monnet – European integration was to find its means.

Constructing Europe anew was based on the combination of several factors. The mutual realization of the costs of non-integration was coupled with the awareness that integrating Europe's economies or even political institutions would not require that any partner had to give up something relevant. It meant that each partner would gain something instead. The mutual recognition that differences and contrasting interests would prevail was coupled with the understanding that they should be managed in a completely different way than before. The pressure of geopolitics and interdependence – even felt amid the post-war economic hardship and the pressure on democratic rule – was echoed by the voice of civil societies across Europe aimed at stopping the destructive path of European politics. Integration did not become the natural consequence of an invocation of norms. It became the daunting, often difficult and tiresome process of the slow and sometimes all too slow implementation of procedures. The sober functional translation of a great idea did not strip it off its dignity. In fact, it made its realization possible.

European integration began as a foreign policy exercise, pressed by political groups and voices from European citizenry, but largely driven by the politically responsible elites in democratic governments. The role of the United States as federator cannot be overvalued. Yet autonomous European decisions turned the corner from their devastated and demoralized continent. The scope of the new methods, which were established to manage European affairs, was limited and not overly ambitious. The means were focused, the instruments sustainable. The prospects for deepened integration and widened participation were implicit in the new endeavor. Most important was the prevailing spirit of reconciliation. This helped to navigate through the economic, political and security agenda of the late 1940's and early 1950's without ever losing sight altogether.

Compared with Europe's past, this was a revolution. It was a thorough revolution in thoughts and a silent revolution in deeds. Sharing sovereignty and pooling resources was to transform the European body politic. It was to accelerate the path to unprecedented affluence and stable democratic rule. It was to broaden the circle of states joining this experiment and gradually, it was turning from experiment into a new normalcy.

X. "For the Sake of Europe": Prevailing Normative Disputes

1. No Monopoly on the Definition of Europe's Interests

In Europe, Europe is everywhere and every EU citizen is a European. There is no need to participate in the political institutions of Europe to be recognized as European citizen. There is no need to go to Brussels in order to be in a European city. Yet, the political form of Europe is the sum of incremental consensus-building. As much as nation-building or integration-building is a constructivist phenomenon, interest-formation is a genuine and rather daunting phenomenon in Europe. Here, the role of the institutions and of centralized policy-making becomes relevant. In the absence of naturally evident, historically tested and comprehensive political European interests, their evolution is and will remain a process of ideational debate, political bargaining and public interpretation. When it comes to defining common political interests, the European Union is stretched between two opposing poles: Inside the EU, no country or institution can claim the monopoly to define what is "in the interest of Europe." Looked at the issue from the outside, the expectation for Europe to define and project its interests is much higher than the performance of the EU and its self-acclaimed targets can be. European interests have to grow within a culture of consent that has evolved in more than five decades and yet has not achieved its final contours.[1] How to turn consent into new and commonly acclaimed power and authority remains a persistent struggle for the EU. As a consequence of Europe's affluence and its rhetorical claims to uphold values that most reasonable people in the world can share in abstract terms, the European Union is expected to strengthen its capacity for action beyond all realistically available means and instruments. How to turn abstract and all-pervasive expectations into a coherent and sustainable projection of Europe's interests remains a permanent pressure on Europe's authority and power, both worldwide and as far as loyalty among its citizens is concerned.

Power is a function of ambition and will, of goals and resources, of strategies and tactics. For the European Union to execute power requires highly complex processes of formulating consent. This can undermine the EU's immediate claim to authority, but might eventually increase its potential power once a consensual decision has been found. As not all issues exercise the same degree of relevance and impact, one has to be

1 On this issue in general and in the context of organized interest representation see Cini, Michelle, *European Union Politics*, Oxford: Oxford University Press, 2003; Greenwood, Justin, *Interest Representation in the European Union*, Houndmills: Palgrave Macmillan, 2003; Green Cowles, Marie, and Desmond Dinan (eds.), *Developments in the European Union*, Houndmills: Palgrave Macmillan, 2004; de Búrca, Gráinne, *EU Law and the Welfare State: In Search of Solidarity*, Oxford: Oxford University Press, 2005; Dinan, Desmond, *An Ever Closer Union: An Introduction in the European Integration*, Houndmills: Palgrave Macmillan, 2005 (3rd ed.); Richardson, Jeremy, *European Union: Power and Policy-Making*, Oxford: Oxford University Press, 2005 (3rd.ed.).

highly specific about this matter. One general critique is unavoidable: The European Union often tries to square the circle by linking consensus and power with the claim that they mutually reinforce each other. Usually, the perception of the EU from inside and the perception of the EU from the outside differ substantially: EU citizens grant legitimacy to EU decisions if they reflect a consensual point of view. Europe's external partners expect the efficient use of the projection of EU resources and power.

It is not easy to identify the intersection between the two ends of the equation. It is relatively easy on matters of foreign trade policy where international consent expects the EU to act but domestic political reticence prevents it from doing so. The seemingly eternal quarrel over EU agricultural subsidies is a case in point. Sometimes, the opposite occurs: European Union citizens claim action, but their leaders cannot decide on what the action should be and which course they should pursue. The legacy of the failed intervention of the EU to stop the outbreak of the four Wars of Yugoslavian Succession during the 1990's was such an example.[2] Finally, relations between power and consent can have reverse effects when EU consent seems to sharpen a powerful weapon which in fact is undermined because certain member states do not accept the implementation of a common decision or stretch it to the point of sabotaging a commonly agreed to policy. Manifold examples across the EU demonstrate this bottleneck of implementing EU authority in the context of the realization of the Single Market.[3] The only chance for the European Commission to enforce the implementation of commonly agreed law is the invocation of the European Court of Justice. This is a dramatic step. If such a step has to happen and if the final ruling of the European Court of Justice is accepted, eventually the result of such power conflicts has been the recognition of the supremacy of European law over national law and the primacy of European Union consent over dissenting national interpretations. But to get to this result can be a seemingly endless operation, binding human and fiscal resources on many levels and putting time and again the original authority of EU decisions in jeopardy.[4]

2 See Hammond, Andrew, *The Balkans and the West: Constructing the European Other, 1945-2003*, Aldershot: Ashgate, 2004.

3 See Furlong, Paul, and Andrew Cox, *European Union at the Crossroads: Problems of Implementing the Single Market Project*, Wyberton: Earlsgate Press 1995.

4 In 2001, EU member states agreed to reduce the number of Single Market regulations, which were not yet adopted into national law, to 1.5 percent of the complete body of Single Market regulations. In 2004, the share of non-implemented regulations was 4.1 percent in France, 3.9 percent in Greece, 3.5 percent in Germany, 3.2 percent in Luxembourg, 3.1 percent in Italy, 2.8 percent in the Netherlands, 2.1 percent in Belgium, 1.9 percent in Portugal, 1.8 percent in Sweden and 1.7 percent in Austria. Only Finland with 1.3 percent, Ireland with 1.2 percent, Great Britain with 1.2 percent, Spain with 0.8 percent and Denmark with 0.7 percent had complied with the criteria agreed upon by all 15 governments. According to the European Commission, more than 3,000 EU-norms were still pending in order to completely realize the Single Market. In many cases where member states have refused to implement the commonly agreed law, the EU Commission had to open an infringement procedure at the European Court of Justice. In 2004, 149 cases were pending against Italy, 125 against France, 104 against Spain, 94 against Germany, 79 against Greece, 77 against Belgium, 58 against Great Britain, 55 against Ireland, 53 against the Netherlands, 52 against Austria, 44 against Portugal, 39 against Luxembourg, 28 against Finland, 28 against Sweden, 24 against Denmark. All

Like many norm-giving decisions on matters of the Single Market, other components of the *acquis communautaire* continue to be reinterpreted differently in different EU member states and among different social and political groups.[5] The interpretation of EU policies has been echoed by the continuous process of amending the EU treaty system. Only through such epistemological exercises does political authority takes deeper roots in Europe. There is no other way in the absence of naturally ingrained comprehensive European interests. Traditionally defined common interests that could turn interests immediately into habitual and intuitive patterns of European behavior remain weak. As long as this is the case, the EU's multilevel governance polity will often appear to be suboptimal. Although it is not appropriate to measure authority, purpose and value only on the basis of rational categories of efficiency, the effectiveness of EU decision-making will remain an ongoing challenge for European policy makers.

All too often, European politicians claim that their personal position or the policy goal of their respective party is "in the interest of Europe." "For the sake of the EU," they often pursue certain political choices or actions, but all too often, these public pronouncements cannot be taken at face value. At best, they are contributions to an ongoing European debate. As long as these legitimate expressions of interest are conducted within EU institutions, nobody is irritated. Presenting them to the broader public through speeches, interviews and the like has become an integral element of public policy-bargaining in the EU. Still, the audience often needs clarification whether it listens to a mere pronouncement or to a relevant and binding decision. Most irritating is the promulgation of conflicting choices or ambitions outside the EU, where one might find it particularly difficult to distinguish between decision, promise and a tactical positioning for domestic reasons.[6] In spite of these confusing and often frustrating

in all, around one tenth of EU regulations on matters of the Single Market was not applied yet when eastward enlargement took place: See *Frankfurter Allgemeine Zeitung*, July 27, 2004.

5 See Dobson, Lynn, and Andreas Follesdal, *Political Theory and the European Constitution*, London: Routledge, 2004; Church, Clive H., and David Phinnemore, *Understanding the European Constitution: An Introduction to the EU Constitutional Treaty*, New York: Routledge, 2006.

6 Three examples from the field of foreign and security policy within one month only illustrate the attitudinal difference between fact and desire. The first example was the announcement of French President Chirac during a visit to China in November 2004 that the EU would dissolve the arms trade embargo to China, while in fact the EU had not decided on the matter yet and was deeply divided on the position favored by the French President. During an EU-China summit only weeks later, the acting Dutch EU presidency had to tell the visiting Chinese Prime Minister that the time for a decision to lift the arms embargo was not ripe yet. The second example followed immediately after Chiracs China visit, when all EU leaders met their colleagues from ASEAN in Hanoi and clashed over the demand of German Chancellor Schröder to support Germany's bid for a seat on the UN Security Council. In the absence of a common EU policy on the matter, Italy and Poland did not want to support the German bid and prevented the issue from being discussed in the final communiqué of the meeting. The third example occurred in early December 2004, when Germany's Chancellor announced that his country would send military support to the peace mission of the African Union in Sudan while regretting that this could not happen as a EU action. It was left to the observer to judge whether the German government had ever tried to turn their interest in participating in the Sudan mission of the AU into an EU policy action.

experiences, the European Union is exercising self-binding attitudes among its member states. As a consequence of the slowly emerging habitual consent on the primacy of European interests over petite national or even domestic party political considerations, it must be expected that individual member states of the European Union will continue to resort to unilateral (but doubtfully more effective) activities.

As a pluralistic, multilevel structure the European Union will have to live with these idiosyncrasies.[7] Continuous shades of confusion are the price for multilevel and consent oriented decision-making. It is not tolerable, however, when EU member states or EU institutions try to undermine, reinterpret and water down decisions they originally had agreed upon. When confronted with the national impact of certain of their decisions, some political leaders hide behind the EU as if it were an alien beast. They cite anonymous "EU pressure" they had not been able to prevent – although they were part of the decision-making process. Sometimes, they try to redo an EU deal in face of their own national constituents. This double-speak is possible only as long as decision-making in the Council is not transparent.[8] Whether or not solid revisions for its working procedures will suffice to change this habit could only be judged after a reasonable period of time. The daunting search for a common denominator will most likely prevail for a long time, along with contrasting political preferences.

This obstacle to coherent European governance affects all aspects of European politics. No segment of the European body politic is exempt from the ongoing and incomplete struggle to define European interests. Over more than five decades, the European integration process has accrued an impressive set of commonly agreed upon norms, habitual interests and shared positions that are no longer object of repetitious contention among new majorities or due to sudden reconsiderations of specific national or institutional interest. The *acquis communautaire* is the institutional, legal and political structure of norms, the form and function of European integration.[9] The term

7 See Hooghe, Liesbet, and Gary Marks, *Multi-Level Governance and European Integration*, Lanham: Rowman & Littlefield, 2001; Nugent, Neill, *The Government and Politics of the European Union*, Houndmills:Palgrave Macmillan, 2003 (5th ed.); Bomberg, Elizabeth, and Alexander Stubb (eds.), *The European Union: How does it Work?*, Oxford: Oxford University Press, 2003; Bache, Ian and Matthew Flinders (eds.), *Multi-Level Governance*, Oxford: Oxford University Press, 2004; on specific aspects of multi-level governance see Marginson, Paul, and Keith Sisson (eds.), *European Integration and Industrial Relations: Multi-Level Governance in the Making*, New York: Palgrave Macmillan, 2004; Rato, Helena, *Europeanization Impact on Multi-Level Governance in Portugal: Patterns of Adaptation and Learning (1988-1999)*, Oeiras: Instituto Nacional de Administraçao, 2004; Hix, Simon, *The Political System of the European Union*, London: Palgrave Macmillan, 2005 (2nd rev.ed.); McCormick, John, *Understanding the European Union: A Concise Introduction*, Houndmills: Palgrave Macmillan, 2005 (3rd ed.).

8 See van Grinsven, Peter, *The European Council under Construction: EU Top Level Decision-making at the Beginning of a New Century*, The Hague: Netherlands Institut of International Relations, 2003.

9 See Pescatore, Pierre, *The Law of Integration: Emergence of a New Phenomenon in International Relations, based on the Experience of the European Communities*, Leiden: Sijthoff, 1974; Snyder, Francis, *The Europeanisation of Law: The Legal Effects of European Integration*, Oxford: Hart Publisher, 2000; Bankowski, Zenon, and Andrew Scott, *The European Union and its Order: The Legal Theory of European Integration*, Oxford: Blackwell, 2000.

acquis communautaire, however, is not very political and helpful for popularizing the interests of the European Union. As European integration is law-based, political in nature and exercised through institutions with a limited reconnection to the overall European public, it is essential to expand the sense of ownership of European integration among EU citizens. It will not suffice to merely broaden the scope of citizen's rights by giving the Charter of Fundamental Rights of the European Union a legal character to strengthen the sense of ownership with the EU and to raise loyalty to EU norms and procedures. As long as politicians and journalists, academicians and lawyers refer to a technical *acquis communautaire*, this will remain a hopeless exercise. Its reach will not go beyond the boundaries of Brussels. In order for European Union citizens to identify with the European Union and to exert loyalty to the European Union, they must be able to also emotionally share the sense for and the experience of common European interests.

The formulation of European interests requires a translation of European values and preferences into permanent answers to the question "Europe, why?". The continuous interest-formation does not and will not exclude political debates about the right answer to any problem on the future path of Europe. It cannot mean taking forever for granted what has once been agreed upon under specific circumstances. Interests might change and with them their European connotation. Yet, the understanding of European interests will have to continuously grow as a set of intentional and habitual attitudes and as a body of formal norms and functional instruments. In the meantime, the *acquis communautaire* of the European Union includes a broad set of acquired memories, although they may not be explicit in their origin or in their original purpose. The growth of European political identity is linked to the purpose of European integration. Both have developed and continue to develop in contingent correlation to the evolution and broadening of Europe's political agenda and experience.

Some key European interests have been identified in this study. So far, they constitute the acquired memory within the institutions of the European Union. They are a self-referential source of identity, certainly recalled in times of conflict and trouble. Whenever the representatives of the European Union fail to find agreement on crucial issues, it is most likely that one or the other of these principles will be invoked "for the sake of Europe," which is to say to safeguard Europe from a divided and indecisive leadership:

- A genuine "European spirit"[10] as a habitual and intuitive mode of action recognizing the need for European solutions in cases of conflicting national or political preferences.
- Recognition of the European Union as an organic community of law with the

10 It is remarkable and sad that literature on the "European spirit" is only available for the immediate period at the end of World War II; for example, see Jaspers, Karl, *The European Spirit*, London: SCM Press, 1948; Reifenberg, Benno, *Does the European Spirit Still Live?*, Hinsdale, Ill.: H. Regnery Co., 1948.

primacy of EU law over national law, including national constitutional law.

- Compromise-building abilities in spite of different starting points and expectations, based on a synchronization of different methods satisfying different approaches, starting points and expectations among member states and other institutional actors.
- Dedicated political will among the main political actors that can be revitalized in creative ways with the help of refocusing topics, methods and instruments in case of deadlock.
- Growing consent as far as the protection of the European Single Market and the welfare state systems in Europe ("the European Social Model") depends upon permanent processes of balancing local, national and EU-wide solutions that can grow into coherent and thus powerful new political realities in which social cohesion and liberal competitiveness are rooted.
- Recognition of the principles of solidarity and cohesion that require resource allocation in favor of the more backward regions and structures of the European Union in order to lower the political prize of integration in member states where reasonably large population segments feel marginalized or even victimized by European decisions.
- Understanding that a common monetary and fiscal policy requires not only economic cooperation, but in the end, the evolution of a European economic government.
- Awareness that the European Union needs to sharpen its international political profile through the coherent implementation of a common foreign, security and defense policy.
- Taking budgetary matters more seriously to consolidate the preconditions for the strength of the euro, the competitiveness of the European economy and the credibility of European politics.
- Confronting the impact of European integration on domestic constitutional, political, socio-economic and legal structures in a forward-looking way and recognizing European integration as opportunity for reform rather than as threat to national traditions.
- Accepting that all constituent parts in the European Union have the same right to contribute to the evolution of European interests and that no constituent part of the European Union can unilaterally claim to express by its own will a common position "for the sake of Europe."

These are essential elements of consensually acquired European interests. The sad fact is that all these principles and common interests have been violated at some point by one or the other of the constituent actors of the European Union. This frustrating experience does not prove them wrong. It demonstrates the relative weakness of the implementing powers of the EU and the prevailing residual powers of national or

political resilience to accept self-proclaimed principles and interests on the European level. In order to come to terms with the ever-existing chasm between self-defined claims and objective realities, undoubtedly prevalent in all political systems in the world, it is helpful to categorize different levels of normative disputes and conflicting interpretations of self-proclaimed consent in the EU. One has to apply proportionality in order to judge the level of importance, the scope of a breach of acquired interests or the inability of constituent actors within the European Union to pursue the course toward new common interests. One has to put the contingent debates into broader perspective in order to understand their meaning and potential implication, or the lack of them. Finally, one has to apply mechanisms of differentiation in order to better judge the level of compliance or non-compliance of a given act.

On a different level, continuous disputes about principled beliefs, norms, political choices and integration goals have to be dissected according to their inherent quality and imminent plausibility. In the absence of a Europeanized media structure, this is one of the most difficult tasks for professional analysts of the European integration process. For ordinary EU citizens, the matter is even less transparent. They are charged with the heavy task to ultimately judge the legitimacy of the European Union while they can hardly understand the degree of implication of a certain issue, the connectivity of issues, the different policy preferences and choices with their respective impacts, and the scope of influence of a certain constituent part of the European Union. Lack of accountability is the biggest obstacle to an enhanced sense of public ownership and citizen loyalty to the EU. The issue of accountability is not only a matter of constitutional transparency and the ordering of competences: In the European body politic, it is inherently linked to the perception (and misperception) of political priorities and the absence of them.

2. "Bogeyman Debates" and Necessary Symbolism

The built-in degree of deliberative democracy, which is constituent for the European Union as a consensus-driven multilevel system of interlocking powers and shared modes of rule and authority ("consociationalism"), is often a hindrance for clear-cut media coverage that helps to transmit transparency and accountability.[11] For a comprehensive public perception of EU matters, their origin and context, their implication and relatedness, the situation is even more daunting. Such is the genuine fate of all democratic political systems. For the European Union it is even more delicate, because its political performance is still not free from suspicion about its very structure and scope of authority, power and rule. In the absence of consensual clarity about these

11 See Fishkin, James L., and Peter Laslett (eds.), *Debating Deliberative Democracy*, Malden, MA.: Blackwell, 2003; van Aaken, Anne, et al. (eds.), *Deliberation and Decision: Economics, Constitutional Theory and Deliberative Democracy*, Aldershot: Ashgate, 2004.

key determinants of a body politic, the EU has not only to cope with genuine conflicts of interests, power struggles and conflicting interpretations of its interests. The EU also has to cope with matters of illusion and symbolism.

Some political debates about European integration tend to resurface permanently although it seemed that they had long been laid to rest. This includes the question of whether or not the European Union is a genuine polity. This phenomenon also includes the consistently resurging dispute about "intergovernmental" versus "supranational" elements of integration.[12] More elementary is the dispute whether or not the European Union is a federation, should ever become one or will ("hopefully," for some cynics) always fail to achieve federal qualities. This question is often linked to the matter of "political finality." Any politics of fear is confronted with resurging phenomena: The fear of dissolution of the very EU structure (less and less articulated as far as the EU is concerned); the fear of integration overstretch (mostly articulated in the context of the geographical boundaries of the European Union, but also as far as its boundaries of political will, authority, power and rule are concerned); and the fear of too high costs of inefficiency (beginning with the matter of the costs for interpretation that amount to 140 million euros and for document translation in the EU of over 800 million euros, which after all comes down to not more than 2 euros per EU citizen).

Most European debates fulfill two symbolic and policy functions: They are usually directed toward a national audience that likes to support or oppose, according to prior positions and attitudes. Debates on the European level are also directed toward one's own political clientele, mainly party loyalists and supporters. Many of them are "bogeyman debates."[13] In light of the stability of the EU's policy-making processes, both formal and informal, it is overly exaggerated to assume than any debate – no matter how controversial – could either derail the whole integration process or redirect it substantially and immediately. No theoretical academic research or static historical comparison can help to find the right degree of measurement to assess the nexus of formal and informal, symbolic and substantial, national and European elements of any European policy-process. Each European debate and each EU policy-process has to be understood in its own right. This in itself demonstrates the intensity of European governance.

Invocations of a political finality of European integration (and the absence of it) will prevail. But rather than providing a norm, this rhetoric fulfills a functional purpose. Normally, this will promote a new momentum of integration – or just warn about the

12 See Sandholtz, Wayne, and Alec Sweet-Stone, *European Integration and Supranational Governance*, Oxford: Oxford University Press, 1998; Tallberg, Jonas, *European Governance and Supranational Institutions: Making States Comply*, London: Routledge, 2003.

13 To use Brendan Donnelly's term which he applied to the contention that the European Union would eventually lead to a "federal superstate": Donnelly, Brendan, "After the European Council, a Referendum to Win," *EU Constitution Project Newsletter*, July 2004, www.fedtrust.co.uk. Since 1994, Routledge is dedicating a complete academic journal (Journal of European Public Policy) to reflect on European public policy and related debates.

impact of any such move. They might contribute to putting the development of the European Union in a larger historical context, but that will always have limited effects on the daily operations of the EU. It seems as if the European Union will always have to live with the actual finality reached by any given stage of integration, followed by a period of digesting it, and a creeping surge of new claims to deepen European integration on specific matters. There is no other reasonable way in coping with the notion of political finality in an infinite and "un-finishable" world.

Politicians apply a logic and rationality to their actions and decisions that is not always in accordance with their own goals and intentions. Should European Union citizens develop a stronger sense of ownership for the EU, they must certainly identify with its operations.[14] Symbols define not only political toys and gadgets, but are essential for the rooting of a political identity. The flag, the anthem, the holiday, the passport, the currency – these are more than just paraphernalia of European integration. These are symbolic incarnations of the idea of a common political destiny and a shared polity. The symbolic tokens of identity are not only virtual ones. Still virtual, however, is the European capital: Most institutions of the EU are located in Brussels, including all diplomatic missions to the EU, the media and, increasingly, many lobbyists.[15] For good reasons, the European Court of Justice in Luxembourg and the European Central Bank in Frankfurt are located outside Brussels in order to underline their physical and legal independence. It is much more difficult for law-makers and bureaucrats with executive functions to influence the proceedings and operations of a powerful institutional body that is based outside the city in which legislative and executive government work takes place.

More paradoxical and not helpful for the growth of Europe's symbolic identity is the strange split in the location and operations of the European Parliament. Parliamentarians and their staff might be used to roaming around like political gypsies between plenary sessions in Strasbourg, twelve times per year, plenary and committee meetings in Brussels, and a secretariat based in Luxembourg. If it wants to be recognized once and for all as the prime co-decision maker and co-power-shaker of the European Union, the seat of the European Parliament has to be moved to Brussels. Before reaching such a decision, it would certainly be necessary to compensate France, and the city of Strasbourg, for the imminent loss. It would be worth to turn this issue from one of honor and pride into a much more pragmatic one. The matter of formalizing the capital of the European Union is of highest symbolic importance for the rooting of a European

14 See Bellamy, Richard, and Alex Warleigh, *Citizenship and Governance in the European Union*, London: Continuum, 2001; on the prevailing primacy of national loyalties see Bellamy, Richard, et al. (eds.), *Lineages of European Citizenship: Rights, Belonging and Participation in Eleven Nation-States*, Houndmills: Palgrave, 2004.

15 On this last aspect see van Schendelen, Rinus, *Machiavelli in Brussels: The Art of Lobbying in the EU*, Amsterdam: Amsterdam University Press, 2005 (2nd ed.).

political identity and it will have consequences for the increase in a sense of ownership among EU citizens.

Only after a final decision on Brussels, not only as the seat of the EU's legislative and its executive institutions but as the EU's actual capital, will the city gain the momentum to develop architectural features that can contribute to a European political identity. Such a development can be supported by the construction of a House of European History in Brussels with focus on the common traces in Europe's culture, the tragic failures to live up to the values in its history and the evolution of integration as a substantially new fact of Europe's political reality and identity. It is somewhat outlandish that regional representations are establishing palace-like offices in Brussels while the European Union presidency – that is to say the President of the Commission, the President of the European Council and the President of the European Parliament – cannot use representative buildings appropriate for their role. The overall structure and outlook of the "European quarter" in Brussels would certainly gain by a decision to grant the city the status of what it actually is: the capital of the European Union.

Strasbourg was symbolic for the first phase of European integration, organized around the notion of reconciliation between France and Germany. The reconciliation not only of France and Germany but practically among all European nations has been accomplished since the end of the Cold War. Strasbourg's traditional political symbolism has been outlived by the changing rationale of the European Union with its growing political role and increasing global relevance. Strasbourg is no longer the necessary symbol of inter-European reconciliation. Now, Strasbourg could become a symbol of harmonious cultural diversity in Europe, and hence the symbol of the dialogue among cultures and religions. In this spirit, Strasbourg would remain the perfect seat of the Council of Europe and its European Court of Human Rights. It could also make better use of its parliamentary architecture beyond the regular sessions of the Council of Europe. The parliament building in Strasbourg could be used as seat of a worldwide Parliament of Cultures. A Strasbourg-based Parliament of Cultures, initiated by the European Union, could perfectly institutionalize a universal cultural dialogue as one of the main priorities of the European Union and of the Council of Europe. Strasbourg could become a global household name for the dialogue of cultures.

3. The Institutional Balance: Self-Referential or Real?

Most EU citizens do not take interest in the institutional developments of the European Union. Primarily, these have been matters of relevance for the involved political class. Issues of institutional balance between the three main EU institutions will remain a permanent element of EU development. In reality, they have reached a new level of quasi-equality, if not in a formal, at least in informal sense. There can be no doubt about the relevance of an institutional balance between the main institutions for the input-legitimacy of the European Union. As an object of governance studies, institutions will always be attractive to scholars. The fine-tuning of the EU's institutional balance will also remain a legitimate matter of dispute among the institutional actors. But for the majority of EU citizens, the intricacies of institutional balancing are not only beyond their experience, they are simply outside the horizon of their interests and expectations.

This does not belittle the importance of matters of institutional development and balance. But more than during past decades, European politicians have to be sensitive not to confuse their specific institutional, if not personal interests with the interests of EU citizens in integration. More importantly for EU citizens than abstract debates about institutional balances between Council, European Commission and European Parliament are the actions and effects of relevant EU decisions. There is ample room to make these processes more attractive and to reconnect them to the overall public interest in political output. It would help in this effort if debates in the European institutions would become more attractive to the media and hence to the European citizenry at large. It would, for instance, be worthwhile to install an annual State of the European Union Address of the President of the European Commission, the President of the European Council and the President of the European Parliament, all delivered to the European Parliament. Dozens of foreign presidents and many other dignitaries have taken the floor of the European Parliament. They have inspired generations of European parliamentarians, but they have remained rather unheard of among the broader European public. Time has come that European leaders try better than in the past to inspire the European public. The European citizens have a right and a transnational interest to be kept informed about the state of affairs in Europe as seen by the leaders of the three main EU organs. An annual State of the European Union Address would certainly make it on the front page of most relevant newspapers in Europe and onto prime-time television news channels. This would strengthen "the face" of European integration and give more public meaning to the EU's political discourse and the choices at stake.

During past decades, institutional disputes have largely been interpretations of the character of European constitution-building with the intention of achieving amendments in the inter-institutional balance between European Parliament, Council and European Commission. The time has come to realize the political and thus controversial character of the work in the three decisive institutions of the EU. Strengthening transparency and accountability of the European institutions will only work if European voters can acquire a sense of meaning in the pertinent debates on the future of Europe. Such debates must definitively go beyond the mechanical matters of governance, competencies and inter-institutional balances. The political debates among the three European institutions must deal with policy options and preferences on the key questions relevant for the future of Europe. If the European debates cannot make practical sense for Union citizens, their interest in debates of the European institutions will continue to diminish.

It would be of interest to initiate a regular public discussion between the constitutional organs of the European Union, that is to say between the President of the European Commission, the President of the European Parliament, the President of the European Council and, perhaps as well, the President of the European Court of Justice. Such a regular public debate about the purpose and goal of European integration could nurture further deliberations about constitutional patriotism and the importance of public ownership in the European Union.

Often, European integration suffers from linking the right answers to the wrong questions. Never have loyalty, patriotism and public ownership in any state of the world been measured on the basis of the degree of the logic of its traffic order or on the absence of street lights. It would therefore be misleading to measure the degree of legitimacy of the European Union by the quality of EU decisions on technicalities of the Single Market. A fairer element of measuring loyalty, public ownership and constitutional patriotism in the European Union is the degree of voter turnout during elections to the European Parliament.[16] As this is the standard measurement for ownership in national politics, one should not judge the degree of acceptance and loyalty to the EU by additional and, possibly, artificial norms alien to any such judgments on a national level. Voter turnout in the elections to the European Parliament will remain largely a function of the perception of whether or not elections really matter. The degree of relevance of EU decisions cannot be measured by the minutiae of evolving parliamentary powers and the idiosyncrasies of institutional balances. In the age of practical co-decision between European Parliament and Council on most relevant policy matters, the combined legislative powers will be judged by the ability of both the European Parliament and the Council to project their effectiveness to European voters.

For the future of the European Parliament this implies the pursuit of one priority: Projecting its will, ability, and continuity in increasingly shaping the EU budget. No parliament in the world has ever gained authority and power over time without crystal-clear budgetary rights. Even the European Constitution of 2004 would not have broadened the budgetary responsibility of the European Parliament in a substantial way. The European Parliament will continuously have to prove its claim to more budgetary authority through effective and visible actions: It has to demonstrate on the all possible European issues that it can represent the citizens of Europe through a competent,

16 On the evolving role of the European Parliament and supranational political parties in the EU see Kreppel, Amie, *The European Parliament and Supranational Party System: A Study in Institutional Development*, Cambridge/New York: Cambridge University Press, 2002; Steunenberg, Bernard and Thomassen, Jacques (eds.), *The European Parliament: Moving Toward Democracy in the EU*, Lanham: Rowman & Littlefield, 2002; Corbett, Richard, et al., "The European Parliament at Fifty: A View from the Inside," *Journal of Common Market Studies*, 41(2003): 353-373; Lodge, Juliet (ed.), *The 2004 Elections to the European Parliament*, Basingstoke: Palgrave Macmillan, 2005.

assertive and effective handling of its budgetary powers, no matter how limited they are. Beyond the existing framework of budgetary competences, the European Parliament will have to advance the legislative accountability of the EU budget. This could include an annual coherent presentation of a complete European budget, big enough as far as the grown tasks of the European Union are concerned, with a clear sense of those priorities that will define the future strength of the European Union and with realistic sense for political and economic possibilities. Even in the absence of complete budgetary competences, the European Parliament could advance the quest for budgetary autonomy of the European Parliament in complete co-decision with the Council. This could include permanent and fine-tuned proposals for the gradual dissolution of those fixed parts of the EU budget which are bound by subsidies without any convincing effect for the competitiveness of the EU. As early as 1984, the European Parliament presented its complete draft for a European Constitution.[17] Ever since, the European Parliament has proven its authority as the leading proponent of deeper and constitutionalized integration. The commitment of the majority of members of the European Parliament to a full European Constitution prevails beyond the constitution-building roller-coaster of the first decade of the twenty-first century. In the years ahead, the European Parliament needs to advance the public understanding for the usefulness of a European tax with full budgetary rights for the European Parliament in co-decision with the Council.

This is not an issue about raising taxes. It is a matter of streamlining the existing methods of tax allocation and distribution under the label of one European tax. This would enhance transparency and accountability, and moreover the principle of connectivity between tax allocation and spending procedures. For the time being, this connectivity is totally obfuscated under the current budgetary system of the European Union. What is necessary is a budget of scales that can demonstrate the value of common spending over divided (and thus duplicated) budgetary lines among the EU member states. Preventing tax harmonization remains one of the last resorts of formal national sovereignty in Europe. However, also this national prerogative has come under pressure by the logic and the impact of European integration. Any change in the European tax law requires unanimous decision among all EU member states. The European Union does not yet have the authority to grant itself taxing competencies. It depends on the consensual acceptance of this idea by all member states. *De iure*, this limits the realistic potential for a harmonized tax policy in the foreseeable future. It might even make it unrealistic. One should recall that the United States can also live with different tax systems across its 50 states (and one federal district). There are plausible arguments to use tax policy as an instrument of competitiveness across the European Union.

17 See Capotorti, Francesco, *The European Union Treaty: Commentary on the Draft Adopted by the European Parliament on 4 February 1984*, Oxford: Clarendon Press, 1986.

The new EU member states from Central and Eastern Europe enjoy lower tax rates than most "old" EU member states. Although economists argue whether these capital costs or rather the implied low labor costs are more to their advantage,[18] they show little interest in harmonizing taxes in Europe if that would force them to increase the tax burden for their people. In light of this situation, the European Commission has suggested to introduce a code of conduct for capital gains tax. It also has proposed measures to synchronize the level of taxable income.[19] Instead of promoting the idea of direct European tax harmonization, the European Commission is emphasizing the concept of enforced cooperation allowing the Commission to propose more intensive cooperation in certain policy areas with at least eight member states supporting such a move. So far, however, this constitutionally approved principle has never been applied in tax matters. Eventually, this might lead to interesting rulings of the European Court of Justice affecting the last classical prerogative right of the European nation state.

With the growing impact of European integration on the political and socio-economic, but also legal-constitutional structures of the member states of the EU, the role of the European Court of Justice will certainly come under stronger scrutiny than in the past. It must be the unwavering role of the European Parliament and of the European Commission to support the claim of the primacy of European law over national law, even if this becomes an uncomfortable issue at times. The stronger the role of the European Court of Justice as final arbiter in constitutional and legal matters is, the more it can exercise the role of the ultimate protector of the European *acquis communautaire*. The less this role of the European Court of Justice is questioned, the less one has to worry about the role of the European Commission in the institutional triangle with European Parliament and Council. As the executive of a Union of citizens and a Union of states, it will always try to support compromises. It can hardly take a principled side with the European Parliament against the Council. The European Commission should also be freed from the superficial presumption that it is merely a secretariat, which it is not. As the institution with the right to initiate EU legislation and the obligation to help resolve differences by way of inter-institutional compromises, the role of the European Commission can at times conflict with its obligation as final arbiter of the *acquis communautaire*.[20] Therefore, its makes sense to relieve the European Commission of its

18 Labor costs are growing in Central and Eastern Europe and they are increasingly exposed to global standards of comparison and competition. While a direct investment of one million euros generates 70 jobs in Poland, 60 in the Czech Republic and 50 in Hungary, it generates 150 jobs in China. Lack of investment in Western European economies comes from a combination of high labor costs and high capital costs while an overly high state quota of the GDP also burdens these economies. Differences however prevail within the EU: While the state quota in Ireland is 33.6 percent it is overly high in Germany with 48.4 percent, in France with 53.8 percent and in Sweden with 58.5 percent compared with a US state quota of 35.3 percent.

19 See *Frankfurter Allgemeine Zeitung*, "Einstieg in die EU-Steuerharmonisierung," September 13, 2004: 19.

20 See Nugent, Neill, *The European Commission*, Houndmills: Palgrave Macmillan, 2001.

original role as ultimate protector of EU law by the European Court of Justice, the Supreme Court of Europe.

4. Conflicts of Aims as Test Cases for the Authority of Rule

Conflicts of aims are about the organization and distribution of public goods. They demonstrate democracy at work. Contested priorities and ambivalent implementations, resisted decisions and restricted scope of actions are inalienable elements of any pluralistic political system. As such, they are not unusual, abnormal or unacceptable. Yet, the outcome of all conflicts of aims is relevant for the legitimacy and authority of a political system. The resolution of conflicts of aims reorganizes and redistributes power and the authority to rule. Conflicts of aims are a continuous pattern in the multifaceted, multilevel and multidimensional process of European integration. Arguably, their results matter more to the European Union than they matter to single or multiple European nation states.

It must concern all actors of European integration that the process of reforming the Common Agricultural Policy has been under way almost since the beginning of its implementation. Prejudice against and outright rejection of the seriousness of the European Union as a modern, competitive and trustworthy global partner for the advancement of free trade spread much faster than any serious effort to limit, redirect or even reduce the highly ambivalent amount of EU budgetary resources spent for agricultural subsidies. Criticizing Europe's Common Agricultural Policy has become one of the most widely spread stereotypes about presumed self-complacency and egotistic stubbornness of Europe. Common agricultural finances have continuously been used as the prototypical example of the inability of the European Union to correct bad policies and to increase the EU's global competitiveness. Moreover, the fact that for decades around 50 percent or more of the EU budget has been spent to subsidize 4 percent of the EU's population rightly questions the ability of the EU to properly define priorities even under the pressure of its overly limited budget.[21]

The assumption that the Common Agricultural Policy is primarily about agriculture has long been replaced by the understanding that it is primarily about the misallocation of EU fiscal resources. To be more precise, the Common Agricultural Policy of the EU is a French, and to a lesser extent, a German, Italian and even Danish budgetary rebate: France receives around ten billion euros annually in return for its farmers through the EU budget. This amount of money alleviates substantially the net contribution of France to the EU budget. This is the main reason why France has steadily insisted to continue

21 On the perspective of European farmers see Hennis, Marjoleine, *Globalization and European Integration: The Changing Role of Farmers in the Common Agricultural Policy*, Lanham: Rowman & Littlefield, 2005.

the basic parameters of a common market in agriculture, happily supported by other net recipients, no matter what they declare in public about the irrationality of the Common Agricultural Policy.

Also its policies of structural and regional cohesion puts the European Union experience on a permanent collision between expectation and performance. There is little doubt about the positive effects of structural and regional cohesion measures as they have been executed by the European Union ever since these policies came into existence with British EC membership in 1973. However, enormous regional asymmetries prevail.[22] In fact they have grown to unprecedented degrees since the eastward enlargement of the European Union during the first decade of the twenty-first century: When the first ten post-communist countries entered the EU, their per capita income was between 30 and 40 percent of the average of the former fifteen EU member states.[23] This meant an overall reduction of the EU's per capita income by 12 percent. Taking a more revealing perspective, the GDP per capita in the EU member states ranged from 215 percent (above an average of 100 percent) in Luxembourg, 133 percent in Ireland and 123 percent in Denmark to 41 percent in Latvia, and 30 percent in Bulgaria and Romania. No structural or regional cohesion scheme will ever be able to level these differences by way of public reallocation of resources. Some asymmetries are the consequence of centuries of European economic history. Others, more short term, come from decades of state-planned mismanagement under communist rule.

Regional disparities also reflect the dichotomy between urban and rural regions that has not been transcended in the age of instant communications. Most prerequisites to generate production and productivity remain tied to conglomerations with at least relatively high population densities. This situation generates trade-offs, for instance as far as energy consumption, environmental protection and urban planning are concerned. Yet it is no surprise that the most dynamic zones in the European Union are those with advantages of population conglomeration and long-standing infrastructures that facilitate trading patterns, commerce and investment. The European Union's policy of enhancing the availability of trans-European networks – that is to say high-speed trains and a well-functioning infrastructure – is a plausible contribution to fostering cohesion in the EU. However, compared to the challenge, the speed of implementing the EU's infrastructure and transportation policy is excessively slow.[24] Even the issue of

22 See Scott, Joanne, *Development Dilemmas in the European Community: Rethinking Regional Development Policy*, Buckingham: Open University Press, 1995; Terluin, Ida J., *Rural Regions in the EU: Exploring Differences in Economic Development*, Utrecht: Koninklijk Nederlands Aardrijkskundig Genootshap, 2001; Adshead, Maura, *Developing European Regions?: Comparative Governance, Policy Networks and European Integration*, Aldershot: Ashgate, 2002.

23 On the implications see Hardy, Sally, *An Enlarged Europe: Regions in Competition?*, London: Regional Studies Association, 1995.

24 See Johnson, Debra, and Colin Turner (eds.), *Trans-European Networks: The Political Economy of Integrating Europe's Infrastructure*, Houndmills: Palgrave Macmillan, 1996; Turro, Mateu, *Going Trans-European: Planning and Financing Transport Networks for Europe*, Amsterdam: Pergamon, 1999; European Union, European Commission, *Trans-European Network: Implementation of the*

"roaming" with personal cell phones has not found a convincing European consumer friendly solution yet, although in the early summer of 2007 the search for an interim compromise has brought the undeniable relevance of the European Parliament in EU decision-making into the limelight. The slow path toward flexible, consumer-friendly and competitive solutions is all the more regretful as the density and speed of modern communications technology is the European variant of physical mobility in the United States of America, where people are much more ready to physically relocate in order to find new economic opportunities.[25] In Europe, they need to travel fast and telephone cheap in order to connect with new opportunities.

The conflict of aims between EU pronouncements and effective performance is also undeniable as far as the projection of the global role of the European Union is concerned. Foreign and security matters as defined by the ambitious security strategy of the EU require both an increase in effective spending on foreign and security matters and an efficiency-driven increase in pooled resources. The EU's foreign, security and defense policies will also force the EU to reassess the details of its Single Market harmonization. For decades, the primacy of the completion of a Single Market was promoted with the argument that only the Single Market would be the unalterable band that could hold the EU and its common interests together. As the EU aspires to increasingly add foreign and security policy consensus to its list of genuine European interests, it can become more relaxed on matters of overly strict market harmonization. More than five decades after European integration was begun, the process will not derail because of, for instance, the instrument of "co-financing," which might be introduced to enable agricultural subsidies at the level each country likes without burdening the EU budget. The gap between expectation and performance in matters of foreign, security and defense policy continues to question the ability of the European Union to project global authority through its mechanisms of power and rule. It is the utmost credibility test for the EU.

The continuous budgetary dispute between the European Commission and net-contributors among the EU member states is largely one between a top-down approach pursued by the European Commission and a bottom up-approach favored by the net-contributors. While on budgetary matters the European Commission argues for a more assertive policy posture of the EU, the member states with the highest contribution to

Guidelines 1998-2001, Luxembourg: Office for Official Publications of the European Communities, 2004; European Union, European Commission, *The Trans-European Transport Network: Revised Proposals on Guidelines and Financial Rules 2004*, Luxembourg: Office for Official Publications of the European Communities, 2004.

25 See Reid, T. R., *The United States of Europe: The New Superpower and the End of American Supremacy*, New York: Penguin Press, 2004: 205. Reid talks about the new generation of young Europeans as "Generation E" and describes them as loving to travel fast: on trains or by car, crossing the Channel or the Oresund, passing through France or Germany, Italy or Scandinavia, meeting in Prague or in Budapest. For them, Europe is a living reality, a life style, even without knowledge of too many of Europe's languages and without the need to dislocate physically to another country for work and to settle.

the EU budget argue from a position of austerity, fiscal caution and national economic consideration. While the European Commission wants to apply more effectiveness to the self-proclaimed goals of the EU, the net contributing countries insist on efficiency and want to streamline and better focus its spending. This conflict has been at the core of more than two years of negotiations (2005-2007) over the European Union's financial perspective for 2007 to 2013. The next conflict between net-contributing member states, EU requirements and global expectations is inevitable as long as the EU does not have the right to define its autonomous budgetary sources. In order to produce public goods effectively and accountably under the roof of the European Union, in the long run there is no alternative.

5. Political Priorities and Leadership Effects

If all this was not already enough of a tall order, the European Union is torn between claims to increase its scope of organizing public goods in Europe while at the same time having to deal with its constituent nation states being confronted with the radical reduction of supposedly unalterable public goods. This is not a zero-sum game according to which the nation state is losing in competences over the generation and distribution of public goods whereby the EU is gaining. The dispute overlaps the debate about the relationship between de-regulation and re-regulation. On one end of the debate, proponents of deregulation argue that the continuous maintenance of deregulatory liberalization is essential to support market forces that are vital for the reproduction of affluence. They claim that a shift of regulatory activities from the nation state to the European Union would only push the problem one step up while the key challenge is the need to substantially liberalize, deregulate and limit the interference of public institutions in the development of the market. Some member states of the EU have been quite forthcoming with deregulatory reforms during the last fifteen or twenty years and are afraid that re-regulation would undermine the success they have generated. On the other side of the spectrum, proponents in favor of European-wide re-regulatory initiatives usually argue that the need for re-regulatory measures derives from the parameters of global competition that require the European Union to harmonize its market conditions in order to strengthen the global performance of all European market participants. Moreover, they argue, certain member states would never have started even minimal reforms without the pressure of the EU.[26] Germany, for instance, would hardly have experienced de-regulation and liberalization in the fields of postal communication and telecommunications, and in other net-based industries

26 See Eliassen, Kjell A., and Marit Sjovaag (eds.), *European Telecommunication Liberalisation*, London: Routledge, 1999; Koenig, Christian, et al. (eds.), *EC Competition and Telecommunications Law*, The Hague: Kluwer, 2002; Buigues, Pierre A., and Patrick Rey (eds.), *The Economics of Antitrust and Regulation in the Telecommunication Sector*, Cheltenham: Edward Elgar, 2004.

(energy and water supply) and the railway system, if it had not been for EU-decisions and their eventual imposition. Further and stronger reforms of the structures of the welfare state and, even more so, of the public service state are a matter of urgency should the European model of social cohesion be preserved under conditions of ageing and shrinking populations and declining productivity. The domestic welfare state is no longer capable of generating the necessary resources and managing a fair distribution without undermining its own base. As the national welfare state inevitably shrinks, it needs – at least – additional European contributions to welfare and social cohesion.[27]

This is one of the fundamental programmatic disputes that will prevail in the European Union. For 750 (plus 1) members of the European Parliament and 6,900 members of its twenty-seven national parliaments – not to mention deputies in regional and local parliaments as well as other party officials – the potential for political declarations on these and other matters related to the shaping of European policies is enormous. While members of the executive act, politicians pronounce. This is a legitimate and reasonable element in the process of agenda-setting, policy-formulation and the deliberative discourse preceding political decisions. It often however leaves voters confused about the level of discourse, the imminence of a decision and the seriousness of its implications. The spectrum of interests involved in these matters has grown exponentially without the same degree of knowledge proliferation about the mechanisms and the mechanics of Europe's multilevel polity. National interests and party preferences on the national level are increasingly mixed with European party interests and other considerations of the European institutions. At work is not a simple "principal-agent-mechanism."[28]

The European discourse not only occurs between the EU institutions, but also takes place within them. Not only, but most obviously, this is the case with the European Parliament, where party preferences and national interests coexist among the political groups. It also happens in the Council, in the European Commission and between the different actors on the national level involved in formulating EU policies. The borderline between national considerations and Union interests is not as clear as any static view of these institutions would suggest. Often, political actors can hide behind a veil of complexity instead of defending their original position or decision. The complex picture of agenda-setting, policy-formulation and decision-making makes transparency a sophisticated science and hence ownership of the process by a larger percentage of European Union citizens rather unlikely.[29] Whether or not one has to go so far as to

27 See Bonoli, Giuliano, et al. (eds.), *European Welfare Futures: Towards a Theory of Retrenchment*, Cambridge: Polity Press, 2000.

28 See Pollack, Mark A., "Delegation, Agency, and Agenda Setting in the European Community," *International Organization*, 51.1 (1997): 99-134.

29 See Peterson, John, and Elizabeth Bomberg, *Decision-Making in the European Union*, London: Palgrave, 1999:4-30.

criticize politicians for living in houses without windows,[30] the quality of persuasion has become a core aspect of their credibility. This is not a specific matter for the European Union, but relates to other polities as well. Yet, as long as the European Union is under continuous scrutiny as far as its legitimacy is concerned – no matter whether or not this critique is justified – it requires particular commitment and leadership among European politicians to project the legitimacy of their actions. They simply must be as good and may be better than those of other political bodies in Europe in order to cope with the continuous suspicion of skepticism as far as their competences are concerned.

Leadership in the overly consociational system of power and rule of the European Union is not an easy talent to find. Projecting leadership beyond the internal sphere of party politics, national discourse and the European amalgamation of the two is a demanding job. Moreover, projecting one's attitude, one's action and its consequences to a broader European public is almost beyond an individual politician's capacity. At best, they manage to permanently reconnect with the voters in their constituency. For the power-brokers, for instance in the leadership of the factions of the European Parliament, the matter is one of permanent balance between formal and informal processes of networking, argumentation, persuasion, application of policy-processes, and the pursuit of a cohesive path through manifold deliberations before sustainable decisions and results can be achieved. Never is only one topic on the mind and calendar of policy-makers. The management of time is certainly an art that is overly underdeveloped in the structures of European politics. Output-legitimacy of the overall process is influenced by this deficit, whenever issues of public interest surface without finding immediate political response and answer. Explaining the complexity of institutional procedures can easily be perceived as apologetic.

An obvious difference exists between matters of a regulatory nature related to economic issues and those related to foreign policy questions. Economic issues normally do not invoke immediate political action and decision. The competences of democratic politics are limited to only framing market operations. This rarely happens under time pressure. It often takes too long for viable political decisions to emerge, yet the results might not stand any reality test. The legacy of the EU's Lisbon Strategy to make the EU the most innovative and dynamic knowledge-based economy in the world was a good example. The Lisbon Strategy of the EU was outlined in 2000 and presented with pomp and circumstance. Its main content: To increase the EU's employment rate from 60 to 70 percent; to fight poverty and social exclusion; and to improve gender equality, all as instruments to increase economic growth and social cohesion; to enhance innovation by dedicating 3 percent of the EU's combined GDP to research and development; to conclude the Single Market by minimizing bureaucracy and

30 Thus Vernon Bogdanor in his critique on the European Constitution Treaty: Bogdanor, Vernon, "A Constitution for a House Without Windows," *EU Constitution Project Newsletter*, July 2004, www.fedtrust.co.uk.

simplifying tax systems; and to enhance the EU-wide implementation of the Kyoto Protocol, meant to facilitate ecology-friendly sustainable growth. A mid-term review in late 2004 had to conclude with devastating results: The EU was about to completely fail in realizing its goals, an expert group of high ranking officials to the Economic and Finance Ministers of the EU stated. Productivity, economic growth and the creation of new jobs were still lagging behind, both compared with the US and in light of the EU's own targets. In order to reach these targets, the annual growth of the EU's economy was supposed to reach 3 percent per year. Full employment was to be reached on the basis of an employment rate of 70 percent, requiring the creation of 21 million new jobs. On average, the EU had grown only by 1.2 percent during the first half of the decade. The employment rate was 64.3 percent and productivity between European and American workers remained markedly different: In 1995, Europeans had produced 87 percent per hour of the work of their American colleagues, by 2004 this figure had gone down to 82 percent. The main reason for this slowdown of Europe's economic ambitions was the reluctance to implement sustainable and effective social and economic reforms in the leading economies of the EU. The reasons for this enormous underperformance of the EU were failures in national governance and not a market failure. They were also indicative of the absence of comprehensive economic governance on the EU level.[31] In early 2005, the recently installed EU Commission under José Manuel Durão Barroso was forced to correct the original ambitions of the Lisbon Strategy and plea for a new start under the overall imprecise heading of a "plea for growth and jobs."[32] Again, the EU had demonstrated that it was better in announcing its goals than in declaring how to implement them: New policy proposals promised to generate 3 percent economic growth and six million new jobs by 2010. How to achieve these goals amidst high unemployment rates across the EU, debt-ridden public budgets, and an ever-increasing productivity gap with the US, remained a secret even after the Lisbon Strategy's mid-term review.

Optimists might have hoped that inevitable economic decisions by the European Union might benefit from postponement. Economic policies are rarely projected as a matter of urgency although the European economic situation indicated otherwise. But, obviously, on economic matters politicians always find time for another complex analysis or go through endless deliberations on yet again the same matter. While the market or the voters and the media might lose patience, the speed of the process of socioeconomic decision-making is all too often disconnected from the urgency of the matter. This is also the case in matters of long-term political planning in external relations, such as foreign trade negotiations, development policies, global environmental issues. Crisis in foreign affairs however accelerate time and press for

31 See Kok, Wim, *Facing the Challenge: The Lisbon Strategy for Growth and Employment*, Luxembourg: Office for Official Publications of the European Communities, 2004.

32 European Union. European Commission, *A New Start for the Lisbon Strategy*, www.europa.eu.int/growthandjobs/index_en.htm.

immediate action.[33] Mostly, foreign policy is about events and too seldom about structures. After a serious terror attack, amid the escalation of a civil war or in the immediate aftermath of a power conflict stemming from election fraud in a neighboring country, the European Union – as all foreign policy actors – will be forced to react immediately. There is no time for scientific analysis and increasingly less room to justify the absence of a EU position with missing constitutional provisions to act, as was the poor excuse for not committing the EU in stronger ways to prevent the outbreak of the four Wars of Yugoslavian Succession during the 1990's.

It is not surprising that the logic of foreign policy can accelerate the speed of decision-making, provided the political will exists. Examples were the mediating role of the European Union in the Macedonian crisis of 2001 and in the Ukrainian crisis of 2004. However, the EU policy toward the grave humanitarian crisis in Sudan's Darfur province in 2004 again was an ambivalent combination of pronouncements, diplomatic mediation and resurging passivity. As foreign policy crises are also a matter of imminent media coverage, the pressure upon the EU not only to act, but to act both effectively and with sustainable results, is enormous. It is therefore appropriate that the European Union needs to massively increase its human resources and planning capacities if it truly wants to become a major actor in the foreign and security policy field perceived as acting with sustainable effects. Unlike efforts to generate economic growth, foreign policy answers must be immediate and cannot be relegated to some office dealing only with statistics. It is all the more astonishing how unfocused the budgetary implications of the increasing aims and tasks of the EU are in matters of foreign and security affairs.

So far, the European Union has not been able to appropriately convince the European media to project itself as efficient and as a powerful contributor to European solutions. This cannot simply be blamed on the media. Whenever the European Union has been widely perceived as contributing to the solution of a genuine problem of our time, the media reaction was favorable. Whenever the EU performance is fuzzy and blurred, the media reacts accordingly. In order to reconnect the European idea and the institutions of Europe with the Union's citizens, EU actors in leadership positions have to perform in a way that makes people proud of being European and enhances their claim in the ownership of the European integration process.[34] The overall media coverage of European Union events and developments increased across the EU, but the

33 See Zielonka, Jan, *Paradoxes of European Foreign Policy*, The Hague: Kluwer, 1998; Cafruny, Alan, and Patrick Peters (eds.), *The Union and the World: The Political Economy of a Common European Foreign Policy*, The Hague: Kluwer, 1998; White, Brian, *Understanding European Foreign Policy*, Houndmills: Palgrave Macmillan, 2001; Tonra, Ben, and Thomas Christiansen (eds.), *Rethinking European Union Foreign Policy*, Manchester: Manchester University Press, 2004; Mahncke, Dieter, et al. (eds.), *European Foreign Policy: From Rhetoric to Reality*, Brussels/New York: Peter Lang, 2004.

34 See Ward, David, *The European Union Democratic Deficit and the Public Sphere: An Evaluation of EU Media Policy*, Amsterdam: IOS Press, 2002.

image projected by the media about the work of the European Union is still highly ambivalent. Media coverage of EU actions has a strong impact on the perception of the EU's efficiency and effectiveness. Spectacular political conflicts – such as the resignation of the Santer Commission in early 1999 or the failure to ratify the European Constitution in 2005 – were properly reported and triggered rising media interest in EU matters. But it remains difficult to turn this media interest toward "positive" news. Disputes in the European Council over the weighing of votes in the Council in the constitution-building process of the early twenty-first century were power struggles among diverging national interests. Rulings of the European Court of Justice are usually reported as expressions of the primacy of EU law and defeat for the national governments involved. But the less spectacular matters that regularly evolve from the thick web of multilevel governance and shared competences are hard to report on at all, let alone in categories of power conflicts or rule. So far, European policy makers have not developed a genuine culture of controversy that would enable the media to report about clear policy choices without linking it to the usual stereotypes about EU underperformance or EU irrelevance. Whenever the matter is serious and affects the life of many EU citizens – such as the issue of the service directive in 2006 or the question of roaming prices for cellular phones in 2007 – the European Parliament is correctly presented as a genuine and increasingly relevant power-broker in EU affairs.

Often, it remains difficult to relate winners and losers of a certain policy process to a specific EU institution. Based on their national experience with democracy, the media are inclined to prefer such a constellation over the widely used deliberative and consensual decision-making in the EU. The quintessentially political nature of policy processes in the multilevel and interlocked governance system of the European Union is still a secret world to many of Europe's media.

The media coverage of European integration is a political but also an economic issue. Unlike in the US, in Europe print and electronic media are inevitably linked to the linguistic plurality of the continent. Over 600 TV channels with national coverage are one of the indicators of how intensive media consumption in the EU is. The revenue turnover of radio and television companies, approximately 62 billion euros annually, signifies the economic factor. Yet, European wide media, such as "EuroNews" with EU subsidized programs, and newspapers such as "EUReporter" or "The European" have never been able to challenge the market leadership of national programs and newspapers. As a consequence, the process of European integration can only gradually penetrate the established media scene in order to reach normal EU citizens. Leadership by persuasion and with patience becomes pivotal.

As far as the level of political actors in the EU is concerned, leadership by persuasion and with patience is not only a question of convincing principled beliefs, solid arguments and the ability to organize majorities across national borders and within and across party lines leadership by persuasion also requires the ability to synchronize divergent expectations, interests and goals, the mechanisms of the national and of the European level, a balance between symbolic and substantial politics. This has always been a constellation of "give and take," a bargaining process in which short-term and long-term gains need not be symmetrical. The more the bargaining mass of EU matters has grown, the less zero-sum-games have to occur, or even be looked for. Today's minor loss need not be weighed against a relational gain on the next day as there will always be other occasions and different priorities and constellations in the decision-making process.

Strategic thinking is required if leadership is to be more than the tactical mastery of decision-making. The highly strategic nature of the EU Commission Presidency of Jacques Delors has often been lauded.[35] He knew how to combine progress in specific areas and issues with concrete timelines to turn goals into reality without getting lost in the mayhem of daily political bickering. This method was applied to pursue the creation and subsequent implementation of the Single Market (labeled "1992 project"). It was ultimately also applied as the successful strategy to implement the common European currency. Timelines to enter the next stage of the Monetary Union were linked with highly specific criteria defining the readiness of each member state to join full monetary union.

Dense and trust-based cooperation between then French President Mitterrand and German Chancellor Kohl left other EU partners without any doubt that this path and strategy was a serious matter and would not be abandoned by either the German or the French government amid public discontent about the idea, its speedy implementation, or doubts about the solidity of its foundation. Finally, the common European currency came about, pushed by a common European interest of the two leading economies of the EU, although rooted in highly different reasons and expectations: While France was interested in sharing the strength of the German currency as soon as possible, Germany was interested in a strong common European currency. In the end, they agreed to a speedy implementation based on strict criteria for future fiscal policies laid out in the EU Stability and Growth Pact.[36] All the more astonishing was the abandonment of the EU Stability and Growth Pact by a later German government in 2003/2004 in factual breach of European law. The content of the EU Stability and Growth Pact and its strict criteria as far as national fiscal and budgetary policies were concerned, was not only a matter of legitimate economic reasoning concerning the credibility of rigid criteria, such as the 3 percent mark for public deficit, which was not allowed to be reached without the consequence of a penalty. First and foremost, it was a matter of political credibility and reliability of EU law. Therefore, it was not astonishing to note that in other EU member states – both in euroskeptical countries and in smaller ones that often felt

35 See Drake, Helen, *Jacques Delors: A Political Biography*, New York: Routledge, 2000.

36 See Brunilla, Anne, et al. (eds.), *The Stability and Growth Pact: The Architecture of Fiscal Policy in EMU*, Houndmills: Palgrave, 2001.

"lectured" by the dominating economies – expressed grave disappointment about the obstructionist cherry-picking of Germany as far as its unwavering commitment to European law was concerned.

On March 23, 2005, the EU reached a highly ambivalent compromise. Amidst the third year in a row with German public debt above the 3 percent limit of the Maastricht Criteria, and all in all ten out of twenty-five EU member states failing to reach the deficit limit of the Stability and Growth Pact, the strict application of the pact was softened. The new definition provides EU member states with a long list of exemptions, excusing them if they break the 3 percent budget deficit limit of the Stability and Growth Pact. The list includes increased aid spending in developing countries and many other exemptions, but mostly relevant was the recognition of the additional costs of German reunification, covered as costs for the overall European unification. Germany's government had insisted that the country's net transfer from West to East amounts to 4 percent of the country's economic power. While former German Finance Minister Theo Waigel, one of the architects of the original Stability and Growth Pact of 1997, criticized the softening of the Pact, and particularly his country's change of attitude, a "shame," the International Herald Tribune simply concluded that the reforms "effectively kill the EU's growth and stability pact."[37] EU leaders, notably the obstructionist German and French governments, had to explain to the world their economic logic according to which debts could create sustainable jobs. By losing its economic anchor, the EU was slipping into a serious crisis. A leadership crisis on the national level of the two biggest EU member states was beginning to turn into a crisis of confidence for the EU project as a whole.[38] European integration was defined by its limits and no longer by its opportunities – to the detriment of all.

It took the German parliamentary election of September 2005, and the French presidential election of May 2007, to somewhat turn the corner. The German Grand Coalition under Chancellor Angela Merkel was not the choice of the majority of Germans. It managed national politics by simply redefining the agenda. What had been a national disaster before the elections became an opportunity and a sign of hopeful change after the formation of the Grand Coalition. In European affairs, Chancellor Merkel demonstrated that she was a genuine successor to Helmut Kohl. With erudition and sensitivity she handled most European dossiers and gave new respect to the many smaller partners of Germany in the European concert. The first result was widely

37 Bowley, Graham, "EU bends fiscal rules with treaty in trouble," *International Herald Tribune*, March 23, 2005; also see Feldstein, Martin S., *The Euro and the Stability Pact*, Cambridge, Mass.: National Bureau of Economic Research, 2005; Annett, Anthony, et al. (eds.), *Reforming the Stability and Growth Pact*, Washington D.C.: International Monetary Fund, 2005.

38 See Paton, Nic, "Europe's Crisis: It's Not Just the Politics, it's the Leadership," *Management Issues, News and Research*, 24 June 2005, www.management-issues.com/display_page.asp?section=Research&id=2273, and it was even covered in Pakistan, see Wajahat, Ali, "Europe's Leadership Crisis," The Daily Times, 24 August 2005, www.dailytimes.com.pk/default.asp?page=story_29-6-2005_pg3_5.

lauded: The budgetary compromise in December 2005 enabled the EU to initiate its next budget cycle for the period 2007-2013.

The global economic upswing helped the German government. In the course of 2006, the atmosphere in the country turned positive for the first time in a decade. The unemployment rate went down to 9.1 percent, the increase in the state deficit was cut significantly and by June 2007, the European Commission declared that all charges against Germany for breaching the Stability and Growth Pact would cease. By the end of 2007, only Portugal, the Czech Republic, Romania, Hungary and Poland were seen as breaking the Maastricht Criteria of a 3 percent state deficit. Germany was lauded for an economic growth rate of around 2.5 percent in 2007 and in 2008, the highest since German unification. Unemployment across the European Union came down to less than 7 percent in 2008, the best figure in years, while the inflation rate was not expected to go above 2 percent. The economic improvement across the EU came almost parallel to the election of Nicolas Sarkozy as new President of France in May 2007. All over, the economic upswing helped to re-launch the political project of European integration and especially the negotiations that led to the Treaty of Lisbon in December 2007.

Then, the global financial and economic crisis broke out: The immediate and almost restless search for solutions ended with huge rescue packages for systemic banks and quasi-state control over key companies. State intervention became a creeping trend across the world. European Union organs did their best to coordinate, while national governments returned to the center-stage of European economic and financial politics. However: The sound policy of the European Central Bank on lowering interest rates to an all-time low was essential for framing the overall political efforts across the EU.

In a broader context, the global financial and economic crisis that escalated in 2008 and 2009 exposed the European Union more to the effects – and deficits of globalization- than ever before. Defending European citizens against unexpected consequences of globalization – thus EU politicians, especially on the national level, tried to formulate a new attitude of protectionism and state-interventionism. While the global financial and economic crisis unrfolded, it became increasingly linked to debates about global power shifts.Whatever their implication might be, the European Union was not exempted from streamlining its coordination of economic politics and safeguarding its principles of sound fiscal policies. Eventually, the neo-etatist upsurge that followed the outbreak of the global financial and economic crisis of 2008 and 2009 could merely be the sign of a transitory period toward more and deeper integration.

6. National Drawbacks Overcast Input-legitimacy

It cannot be denied that the language of European constitutionalism raises concern and fear among a good number of citizens across the European Union. For different reasons, they air resentment or caution as far as further integration is concerned. Skepticism about the European idea, fear of overly centralized European harmonization, outright nationalism, parochialism and fear of losing one's local identity to anonymous and faraway forces, frustration with efficiency and effectiveness of European policy procedures, general resentment against the political establishment, anti-politics and populism with multiple possibilities of content, object and presence are common reactions.

Across the European Union, the question of how to deal in a coherent and synchronized manner with matters of xenophobic populism and anti-European nationalism remains unresolved.[39] It is the most explicit challenge to both European integration and European democracy so far. Not handled with sensitivity and caution, it includes the potential to unravel some of the integration threads and some components of the democratic political culture that the European Union is always swift in defining as its underlying values.

A delicate case challenging the normative and legal cohesion of the European Union has surfaced after the 2004 election to the European Parliament. Along with the national conservative Union for Europe of the Nations that has existed since the 1999 election, the new formation Independence/Democracy has become the most outspoken advocate of Euroskepticism inside the European Parliament. After Bulgaria and Romania joined the EU in 2007, the number of members of the European Parliament was extended from 732 to 785 for the remainder of the election period 2004-2009. Paradoxically, both euroskeptical groups found further support among the new Bulgarian and Romanian members of the European Parliament. For a short period in 2007, even a far right, neo-fascist group was in existence (Identity, Tradition, Sovereignty). After the 2009 election to the European Parliament, euroskeptics and populist nationalists consolidated their

39 Across the European Union, similar trends occurred since the 1980s, although the local context differed in each particular case. To mention only the most prominent examples: "Front National" in France gained 15 percent of votes as of 1984, and during the presidential election in 2002, its candidate Jean-Marie Le Pen received 17 percent, reaching the second round of voting against incumbent President Jacques Chirac; "Vlaams Blok" in Belgium was renamed "Vlaams Belang" in 2004; by then it had become the third largest political force in Flanders with 18 percent of votes, gaining most votes during the communal elections in Anvers and Mechelen in 2000; Italy's "Lega Nord," together with the countries neo-fascists entered the central government under Prime Minister Silvio Berlusconi in 1994, and again in 2001; Austria's "Free Party" under Jörg Haider was able to join the government as junior partner after it had gained 26.9 percent during the national elections in 2000; in the Netherlands, the "List Pim Fortuyn", named after its slain leader, achieved 17 percent in the 2002 national election, becoming the second biggest political force in the country; in Denmark, the "Danish People's Party" under the leadership of Pia Kjärsgaard joined the government after it gained 12 percent of votes in the 2001 national elections; in Germany's free state Hamburg, the party "Offensive rule of law" under its leader Ronald Schill joined the cities government in 2001 after gaining 19.4 percent of votes; one should also mention the Norwegian "Progress Party" gaining 15 percent under its chairman Carl Hagen in the 2001 national election and the Swiss "People's Party" under Christoph Blocher, who joined his country's government in 2004. The main topics overlapping among the highly diverse national-populist parties in the EU are: anti-immigration, law and order, anti-EU and social populism in the age of globalization. See Baus, Thomas, *Rechtspopulistische Parteien*, Sankt Augustin: Konrad Adenauer Stiftung, 2005.

position in the European Parliament, at the heart of the EU institution always cherished for being the most pro-integration and pro-European. Along with a strong contingent of representatives of the far left, the skeptical positions on parliamentary democracy and on European integration have never been as loud in Brussels or Strasbourg as they have become since 2004. Given the prevailing resentments across the European Union, euroskeptical, anti-immigration or anti-parliamentary, positions will most likely continue to be heard in the European Parliament for many more years to come. The 2009 election of the European Parliament confirmed this unpleasant yet inescapable dimension of democracy in Europe.

The different signs of national drawbacks from the cause of European integration are variants of the same topic. The future of the nation state in the age of European integration and overall globalization has become unclear and clouded. A reconfiguration of the role and relevance of the nation state has become inevitable and it does not happen without tensions in practically all member states. Mostly, the contested issues are variants of welfare state reforms necessary to reduce the scope of state intervention. Historically speaking, the welfare state has been the sibling of the nation state. With the process of European integration, the European nation state has been transformed and europeanized. The welfare state in Europe has not yet been europeanized. This produces the tensions visible across the EU. It has become necessary to recalibrate the role of individual responsibility and the scope of trans-national European-wide social solidarity. The issues are vexing and the debates controversial. They will remain so for many years to come. These debates are intensified by the consequences of migration into the European Union, notably of people of Islamic faith and with non-European background. The related challenges are complex. They cannot be resolved by politics of fear, but certainly also no longer by politics of denial.

For many decades, West Europeans had become used to perceiving politics as the way toward fulfilling their claim rights. The state was the service-agency that guaranteed continuous affluence. Obviously, this traditional role of the nation state has come to an end. As the nation state has come under pressure to redefine its role and purpose, it can no longer deliver the socioeconomic means of security, with which it became inextricably associated. Its old role as guarantor of national security has long been replaced by its role as guarantor of economic security. Not being able to fulfill this role anymore is frustrating for national political actors and generates political discontent in many EU member states. Yet, it is the right and best way ahead to position Europe in the age of globalization. Europeanization impacts traditional constitutional and political prerogatives of the nation state, while the EU member states are simultaneously losing powers and loyalty to the level of regions within their own states. Sometimes, the quest for a reinvigorated national patriotism can be heard. Increasingly, this quest becomes a hollow phrase if it is not connected to the simultaneous process of developing European constitutionalism.

In Central and Eastern Europe, the situation has been of a reverse logic from the trends in Western Europe. The effects, however, are not all too different. As in Western Europe, the communist state with its planned economy was largely perceived as guarantor of economic security, albeit in the absence of prosperity and political freedom. As this economic security went hand in hand with political repression, the legitimacy and credibility of all public order came increasingly under pressure. Since the end of communism, the Central and Eastern European states have been trying to recalibrate the role of the state under conditions of pluralism. The credibility of leadership and political parties has remained severely strained. The enormous and almost permanent changes in the structures of parties and parliamentary majorities since 1989 indicate a fragile and still transient political culture.

With EU membership of many post-communist countries, Western European states started to encounter Central and Eastern European states amidst a common situation of deep uncertainty about the future path of their societies. This constellation has exponentially enhanced the leadership problem for Europe as a whole. Many old concepts of how to guarantee stability and modernization under external pressure do not work anymore. New concepts might undermine either the stability or the leadership it takes to manage the challenging transformation and modernization. The European Union cannot resolve this dilemma on behalf of the European nation states. The European nation states encountered each other during a new period of European unification. Unresolved matters of loyalty, dilemmas of identity, and socio-economic uncertainty were visible across Europe during the first decade of the twenty-first century. The joy of overcoming the division of the continent has been replaced by an unresolved agenda of uncertainty. Across the EU, people have to learn again that uncertainty might be the inherent nature of pluralism and of the diversity Europe can enjoy today in freedom and peace. With an intuitive reflex, many people both in the old West and in the new West of Europe try to preserve structures that have become dear to them. By avoiding change, they might realize too late that this can only end in stagnation and stasis. The current destiny of the European nation state is the management of societal change, not the fulfillment of big visions, theories or ideologies. In the management of change and transformation, all European nation states will benefit from the exchange of experiences, from joint efforts and a common search for new horizons. To facilitate this process is the promise of European integration. It neither rescues the nation state nor makes it obsolete. European integration has become an indispensable partner of the nation state in managing the Europe-wide social change and cultural and political implications. The European Union is part of the solution and not part of the problem that the nation state is facing amid a recalibration of its purpose and reach.

"For the sake of Europe" the European nation states need to be supported by the European Union in redefining their purpose. Otherwise, nationalistic parochialism could further grow. The European nation states have lost much of their credibility in the age of imperialism and nationalism. They overstretched their competition and antagonisms to the point of self-destruction. They have lost the capacity to pursue independent national policies. The logic of economic interdependence has facilitated the recognition of permeable national political structures as economic interdependence generated unprecedented affluence. Yet, across Central and Eastern Europe, the nation state remains the fulfillment of national aspirations of freedom. For those European states that were prevented by totalitarian rule from participating in the earlier West European experiences of shared sovereignty, the aspiration toward prosperity has been a legitimate motivation for joining the European Union. Neither in their case nor in the case of the Western European EU member states has the issue of the future purpose of the nation state been resolved successfully.

The ordering of competencies in the European multi-level system of governance will be a matter of continuous reconsideration of loyalty, legitimacy, and democratic accountability in Europe. Its interpretation will also keep the European Court of Justice busy. Ordering competencies in a complex multilevel system of governance is a daunting and complex process and not a matter of one venerable pronouncement. Competencies require not only transparency and accountability in legal terms. They require successful practical actions. The legitimacy of the newly emerging European order of competencies will be decisive for the lasting recognition of the European body politic. The successful use of constitutionally defined competences is the crossroads where output-legitimacy and input-legitimacy of the European body politic do meet.

7. The Problem: Not European Integration, but Post-modern Democracy

At its core, the dilemma European integration is confronted with is not just about integration. The seriously relevant normative disputes over the evolution of the European body politic and its order of competences are not caused primarily by the structures of European politics. Their resolution is relative to the structures of European politics. The core of the normative disputes over the public order in the European body politic is about democracy, its claims, opportunities and demands and, most importantly, its limits.

During the eighteenth and nineteenth century, the European nation states developed as the framework to protect, strengthen and support the nations of Europe through the means of their state. During the twentieth century, this process repeated itself wherever a European empire dissolved – in the German, the Austro-Hungarian, the Ottoman and the Czarist Russian cases. The process of national harmonization in clearly defined and uncontested boundaries has been completed as far as the various successor states of the German and of the Austro-Hungarian empires are concerned. It has not yet been completed among the successor states of the Ottoman and Tsarist Russian Empires. In these regions, more than in Western Europe, supranationalism is sometimes perceived as an outright threat. And unfortunately, the immediate national neighbor is often still a source of fear.[40]

Simultaneously with the transformation of empires into nation states under full sovereignty, the claim for democratic rule of law, separation of power, and popular participation grew throughout the nineteenth and twentieth century. Popular sovereignty and national sovereignty became intrinsically linked concepts. The nation state became the guarantor of national sovereignty and popular sovereignty alike. The convincing strength of this concept could not be destroyed by totalitarian rule either under the Nazis in Germany or under communism in Central and Eastern Europe. With the end of European dictatorships during the second half of the twentieth century and into the first decade of the twenty-first century, the nexus between national sovereignty and popular sovereignty was reconfirmed in each single case. In the meantime, however, both the nation state and the concept of popular sovereignty and democracy have undergone enormous transformations. European integration has permeated the homogenizing claims of the nation state and has initiated a voluntary, in fact a democratic, process of pooling of sovereignty on the European level. Democracy based on the idea that only the nation state can serve as the protector of the internal freedom of each nation has been enlarged and includes a European dimension: The European Union also protects those civil rights that legitimize its nation states.

Europe has been exposed to unprecedented levels of emigration unrelated to the original notion of any of the European nations and their condition. The reasons were manifold: Ironically, citizens from former colonies migrated to the lands of their former rulers; ethnic minorities migrated to the centers of their nation once their own state allowed them to do so; economic migration turned guest workers into permanent citizens; refugees from all over the world requested civil rights; and legal and illegal pressure has build up in recent years as a peaceful, welcoming, affluent and stable European Union has become a magnetic force particularly for people from the former Soviet Union and from North Africa. Original patterns of migration have changed and new ports of call have become prominent: In 2003, out of 1.6 million migrants into the EU, 594,000 went to Spain, followed by Italy with 511,000. Germany, in 2002 still the country with the highest number of migrants, received 144,000 new people, Great Britain 103,000, and France only 55,000.[41]

40 See Kupchan, Charles A. (ed.), *Nationalism and Nationalities in the New Europe*, Ithaca: Cornell University Press, 1995.

41 See Eurostat. European Demography in 2003, August 31, 2004, http://epp.eurostat.ec.europa.eu/cache/ITY_PUBLIC/3-31082004-BP/EN/3-31082004-BP-EN.PDF.

While Europe was traditionally a continent of emigrants, it has become a continent of immigrants.[42] European democracy has not stayed in step with this development, whereas European integration has done so, albeit in a highly ambivalent way: Long-term studies indicate that European citizens increasingly consider non-Europeans, and no longer co-Europeans from other EU member states, as "the other:" As of 1988, for 63 percent of Germans, the Turks were perceived as "the other," 56 percent of the French pointed to Arabs, 45 percent of Britons mentioned Asians as "the other." The more homogeneous a migration group, the stronger is the ethnocentric reaction of indigenous Europeans.[43] In Great Britain, for instance, numerically the Irish were the biggest group of foreigners in the 1980's. But Asians and not the Irish were perceived as "the others." Unlike earlier boundaries among European nations across Europe during the first half of the twentieth century, in the early twenty-first century Europe perceives non-European migrants and no longer co-Europeans as "the others." This corresponds with a usual pattern of polity-formation:

Table 7: Muslims in the European Union

EU member state	Muslim population	Percentage of Muslim population[44]
Austria	372.800	4.2 %
Belgium	382.870	3.7 %
Bulgaria	950.000 – 1.000.000	12 – 13 %
Cyprus	210.000	22 %
Czech Republic	20.000 – 30.000	2 – 3 %
Denmark	151.500	2.8 %
Estonia	5.000 – 10.000	0.36 – 0.72 %
France	5.000.000	8.1 %
Finland	21.000	0.4 %
Germany	3.400.000	3.9 %
Greece	372.600	3.5 %
Great Britain	1.591.000	2.7 %

42 For a broader perspective see Pooley, Colin G., *Migrants, Emigrants and Immigrants: A History of Migration*, New York: Routledge, 1991; Geddes, Andrew, *The Politics of Migration and Immigration in Europe*, London: Sage, 2003; Cuschieri, Marvin Andrew, *Europe's Migration Policy Towards the Mediterranean: The Need for Reconstruction of Policy-Making*, ZEI Discussion Paper C 168, Bonn: Center for European Integration Studies, 2007; Ina Hommers, *Die Migrationspolitik der EU*, ZEI Discussion Paper C 196, Bonn: Center for European Integration Studies, 2009.

43 See Riketta, Michael, and Roland Wakenhut, (eds.), *Europabild und Europabewusstsein: Bestandsaufnahme der europäischen Forschung und sozialpsychologische Forschungsperspektiven*, Frankfurt/London: IKO Publishers, 2002:46–54.

44 See Zentrum für Türkeistudien, (ed.), "Euro-Islam: Eine Religion etabliert sich in Europa," *ZfT Aktuell*, 102 (2004): 41-42.

Hungary	3.000	0.02 %
Ireland	10.000	0.2 %
Italy	705.000	1.2 %
Latvia	3.000	0.12 %
Lithuania	7.000	1.9 %
Luxembourg	7.500	1.6 %
Malta	3.000	0.8 %
Netherlands	750.628	4.6 %
Poland	4.000	0.005 %
Portugal	40.000	0.4 %
Romania	90.000	0.4 %
Slovakia	10.829	0.2 %
Slovenia	30.247	1.6 %
Spain	402.000	1.0 %
Sweden	305.500	3.4 %

A dividing line between "we" and "them" has been the usual trajectory as a line of demarcation for building political order and political identity. Across the European Union, Muslim migrants are often considered to be "foreign." In the meantime, many of them have become EU citizens or obtained the right to permanent residency. This trend has brought forward the religious issue beyond the simple division between "we" and "them."[45] Debates about the Islamic veil are but a superficial expression of the new uncertainty across Europe about how to cope with a new dimension of plurality and minority. The implications for integration policies, for issues of citizenship, language, religion, including religious service and education, but also for matters of foreign policy, including the war against terror and the struggle with Islamic fundamentalism, are enormous. They obviously challenge the traditional cohesion and basis of European democracy, although their figure does not exceed 3.5 percent of the overall EU population. Yet, Islam has become the second largest religion in sixteen EU member states. A possible EU membership of Turkey would increase the percentage of Muslims in the EU to 15 percent (that is to say to a total of 90 million people). It is noteworthy that the Muslim population in the "old" fifteen member states of the EU has grown from 6.8 million in 1982 to 15.2 million in 2003. The European Muslim community is younger than the non-Muslim communities in Europe, thus adding to the sense of uncertainty among many non-Muslims in the EU.

45 See Kroes, Rob, *Them and Us: Questions of Citizenship in a Globalizing World*, Urbana: University of Illinois Press, 2000; Siedentop, Larry, *Democracy in Europe*, London: Penguin Books, 2000: 189-214 ("Europe, Christianity and Islam"); Garton Ash, Timothy, *The Free World: Why a Crisis of the West Reveals the Opportunity of Our Time*, London: Allen Lane, 2004: 62-63.

These migration trends have grown in size and presence while European democracy itself has undergone a second fundamental transformation beside the process of integration. European democracy, by and large, has become value-free, if not value-relativistic. The controversial debate 2003/2004 about the inclusion of a reference to God in the Constitutional Treaty has demonstrated the dominance of liberal humanism and laicistic notions of statehood over the recognition of a public role for religion in today's EU, and the dominance of individual choice over authority, and of post-modern culture over traditionally binding norms. These cultural patterns, however, did not help the European Union in dealing with its new Muslim citizens and their religious creed and vitality. Since the end of World War II – the most massive moral assault on Europe's identity, triggering a moral and also religious rejuvenation immediately after 1945 – religiosity has continuously decreased across Western European Christian societies. Among strong segments in all Western European societies, religious creed, habits and knowledge have been replaced by secular notions of ethical conduct and liberal humanism. With the end of communist oppression, most societies of Central and Eastern Europe have begun to undergo similar processes of self-secularization.

Muslim communities, in turn, do not tend to follow this pattern of European secularization. Their culture has always been religious-based, if not dominated. As they look for self-assertion in a foreign environment, many Muslims while living in Europe resort to stronger, even radical and violent variations of Islamic teaching. Since the Islamic issue has become a permanent topic of fear and concern for terrorism in the West, this trend has accelerated. The legacy of "9/11" has generated fear among many secular Westerners and an undeniable radicalization of Muslims living in the West, no matter how many others build brave bridges and support the Europeanization of Islam.[46] This has led to cataclysmic eruptions challenging most European notions and illusions about multiculturalism. In fact, Europe's variant of multiculturalism never took shape under the organizing umbrella of a civil religion and a constitution-based patriotism as in the United States. Europe's variant of multiculturalism was defined by an excessive primacy for tolerance, parallel life styles and a weak, if not naïve concept of political integration. The challenge of fundamentalist Islam has shocked many European citizens and forced a good number of proponents of Europe's variant of multiculturalism to confront reality.

In Europe, Muslims do not struggle with pious Christians. They struggle with the concept of liberal secularism and libertarian humanism that tries to define their religiosity and tradition as pre-enlightenment and hence in need of correction. The idea of religious tolerance in Europe grew with its valuable meaning after the religious wars on the continent. Not all its subsequent developments ended in outright secularization.

46 See Al Sayyad, Nezar, and Manuel Castells (eds.), *Muslim Europe or Euro-Islam: Politics, Culture and Citizenship in the Age of Globalization*, Lanham: Lexington Books, 2002; Leggewie, Claus, *The Emergence of Euro-Islam?: Mosques and Muslims in the Federal Republic of Germany*, Bad Homburg: Herbert Quandt Stiftung, 2002.

But the dominating zeitgeist of Europe as it encounters fundamentalist Islam in the early twenty-first century is one of secularization, defensive Christianity and cultural liberalism. Europe of the twenty-first century has one of the least religious populations in the world. In Malta, 95 percent of the population believes in God. In Estonia the figure is as low as 16 percent. According to a 2005 Eurobarometer, the other EU member states range in between.[47] "A continent that is full of ancient churches and religious shrines," an observer sadly wrote, "is increasingly empty of practicing religion."[48] In France, Great Britain, Germany, Belgium and the Netherlands regular church attendance has gone down to around or less than 10 percent of the population. Some Mediterranean catholic countries present higher numbers. Church attendance in Scandinavian or Central European countries is even lower. Strange enough, in its active non-religiosity, Europe has become exceptional.

Many Muslims migrated to Europe in order to escape state oppression or poverty in their homelands. In Europe, an increasing number of Muslim migrants practice a strong, often rigid form of Islam that helps them to maintain their inner stability and personality. The Europe they encounter is not simply a Europe of tolerance that has allowed them to enter its territory. It is not even a world that is different in its own religiosity.

Table 8: Belief in God in the European Union[49]

Malta	95 percent
Cyprus	90 percent
Romania	90 percent
Greece	81 percent
Portugal	81 percent
Poland	80 percent
Italy	74 percent
Ireland	73 percent
Slovakia	61 percent
Spain	59 percent
Austria	54 percent
Lithuania	49 percent
Germany	47 percent
Luxembourg	44 percent
Hungary	44 percent
Belgium	43 percent

47 European Union, European Commission, *Eurobarometer 225: Social Values, Science and Technology*, June 2005, http://ec.europa.eu/public_opinion/archives/ebs/ebs_225_report_en.pdf.

48 Reid, T. R., *The United States of Europe: The New Superpower and the End of American Supremacy*, op.cit: 215.

49 European Commission, *Eurobarometer 225: Social Values, Science and Technology*, June 2005, op.cit.

Finland	41 percent
Bulgaria	40 percent
United Kingdom	38 percent
Latvia	37 percent
Slovenia	37 percent
France	34 percent
Netherlands	34 percent
Denmark	31 percent
Sweden	23 percent
Czech Republic	19 percent
Estonia	16 percent

From their point of view, many Muslims have entered a continent that they perceive as a-religious and agnostic. For them, Europe is relativistic, but highly radical in the claim that liberal humanism is the ultimate stage of human progress. Political liberalism is the laudable and noble philosophy that limits power and rule in Europe. Libertarian cultural liberalism, however, has developed into another variant of fundamentalism in Europe. Self-critique is said to be part of its strength, but in its dealings with matters of religion and personal morality, libertarian cultural liberalism is rigid, and often insensitive if not bluntly ignorant of other people's principled beliefs. As libertarian cultural liberalism is skeptical about the value of principled belief in the first place, its proponents find it difficult to draw limits on their self-proclaimed right to criticize others or to force self-critique upon themselves.

The problem of value-relativism is not new to Europe. It has been intensified with the emerging challenge, if not outright threat of Islamic fundamentalism. As long as Europe's liberalism was only under threat from the absent enemy of communism on the other side of the Iron Curtain and from the absent enemy that is Europe's history with Nazi totalitarianism and religious warfare that came from within, the discourse was highly academic and without practical relevance. In face of the presence of radical Islam in Europe, the issue has begun to put Europe's democratic cohesion and the argument for it under pressure.

There has always been overt consensus that European integration could only have happened among democratic European countries. Democracy was always understood as the founding stone on which, and only on which, European integration could come about and flourish. No integration without democracy: This logic started as a principle of ordering the relations among Europe's states until it finally stretched to become the guiding principle for ordering the internal structures of the integration process. In overcoming the democratic deficit, European integration was assumed to reach its ultimate and indestructible peak. Proponents of this argument rarely reflected on the underlying rationale and the binding glue of democracy, the sources and roots of its meaning and sustainability.

Libertarian liberalism has become a challenge to the logic of the edifice on which Europe has been built. This affects Europe's Christian identity, but as a consequence also the public space of other religious identities in Europe. Cultural liberalism and value-relativism cannot produce and regenerate the moral resources and foundation that it takes to root democracy and help it to be better linked to European integration. The discourse about the relationship between European integration and European democracy has found consent: Without a proper establishment of parliamentary democracy, European integration will undermine the foundation upon which it is built. As for the relationship between European democracy and its very foundation and source, this discourse has not been focused yet, let alone has it generated potential consent. But there can be no doubt that the concept of secular, liberal humanism is not sufficient to root European democracy and Europe's emerging constitutional patriotism. Europe needs to rediscover its public religious space.

European constitutional patriotism – either in the national context or on the level of the European Union – cannot blossom through the sheer invocation of its name. One of its most indispensable roots has to be addressed again in Europe, the re-evaluation of the moral, that is to say pre-institutional, roots of democracy, including the role of religion in public life. Religion can gain a public space to the benefit of European integration as has been demonstrated by the first inter-religious dialogue organized jointly by the European Commission, the European Parliament and the European Council in May 2007. This event showed the right way ahead in order to make use of the moral resources of religion for the secular project of European integration.

Civic sense is among the essential virtues rooted in Europe's long tradition. Reinvigorating civic sense or making it grow is not a matter of political decision and its executive implementation. It has to grow from within a society and will always be related to the sense of purpose and the degree of loyalty it can generate. Whether or not a combination of the many specific national civic senses and one common European civic sense may come into life, remains the most critical normative test case for Europe's nation states and for the European Union alike.

XI. Academic Evaluation: Theorizing European Integration

1. Coming Full Circle: Federation as Union

Finally, the European Union ought to be recognized for what it always was intended to be: a federation. The European Union is a distinctively federal structure with a wide array of functions that are best described as multilevel governance in a European polity encompassing states and citizens alike. The European Union is more than the combination of its parts. It is a body politic in its own right, a composed federation with ambivalent combinations of strong and weak federal qualities. Yet it is more than a moot phenomenon that can only be defined in antithesis to existing states. The European Union, for all intents and purpose, is what its name says, a Union. This reflects its genuine political character and ambition and hence its difference to other existing forms of political authority, be they states, nations or empires. The purpose of the European Union has to be recognized as political – as was the original idea of the Founding Fathers of European integration after World War II. Although purpose and goal of the EU are constitutionally defined as political, its method of policymaking has by and large remained functional. The impulses for the advancement of the EU are a combination of social constructivism, formal and informal political lobbying through legally established institutions based on principled beliefs of the political actors involved, and external pressure.

Federalism is the territorial variant of pluralism, as Karl Loewenstein aptly argued decades ago when discussing "the original telos of federalism as the vertical control of political power." Together with individual rights, federalism and pluralism execute "the function as a sort of shock absorber within the power process," he wrote.[1] Any social grouping that generates, executes and claims authority over people requires legitimacy, loyalty and purpose. A political Union has to be manifest in its constitutional character. A Union is not a contingent political promise, intended to last until limited interests are consummated. A political Union needs to be rooted in shared values, goals and commitments that are accepted by all participants of the Union to last potentially for an unlimited period of time. A political Union cannot be conceived without a set of permanent institutions with decision-making competences, without a territory defined by boundaries, and without a political purpose expressing interests and projecting ambitions, if not power. There can be no doubt that the European Union possesses all these qualities that identify it as a Union. As a Union, by definition, it is a federation.

The traditional use of the terms "federation" and "confederation" was intended to distinguish between strong and weak forms of federal unity. This distinction, invented

1 Loewenstein, Karl, *Political Power and the Governmental Process*, Chicago: University of Chicago Press, 1965 (2nd ed.):286.

in the nineteenth century, long before the European Union came into existence, began as a useful instrument of political theory to better understand the different depth and intention among federal political systems within single states. As far as the theoretical reflection about the character of European integration is concerned, the distinction between federation and confederation, Murray Forsyth rightly argues, "has tended to become frozen into a rigid antithesis...and preoccupation with the antithesis has the unfortunate effect of deflecting the eye from the common union element in federal systems, and also from the more subtle gradation in the strength and weakness of unions."[2]

Parallel with the process of European integration, the body of literature dealing theoretically with this new phenomenon of Europe has grown to fill shelves. Although purpose and meaning of some of this literature are not always evident, a huge mass of thoughtful insights and stimulating reflections have been added to the overall social science literature. Some of the academic literature on European integration claims to offer a comprehensive theory as to how it ought to be understood. Others declare integration theory dead, obviously in light of an ever more complex process of integration that has gone out of control for one-dimensional theory-building. The approach of the academic literature on European integration is as diverse as it could be. Some texts are normative, others are prescriptive. Some build on social science theories, others on empirical research that is dealing with hard-core facts of integration. Some focus on "history-making" events, such as treaty formation and treaty revision, others look into the daily operational mechanisms of the EU's institutions and their decision-making patterns. Some claim to be authoritative on "path-dependencies" in European integration, others object to such a deterministic view, or even question the very character of the EU as a genuine body politic. Some theoretical work truly builds on earlier efforts and conducts a serious academic conversation, other academic contributions are, sorry to say, autistic and self-referential.[3]

Remarkable paradigmatic changes have occurred in the course of five decades of academic occupation with European integration. According to Thomas Kuhn, paradigms constitute the defining categories of research. They assume ontological evidence about social and other realities that can be used to deepen our epistemological understanding. The matter of something seems clearly and objectively evident, and it is a question of knowledge growth that allows better understanding of its meaning and purpose. Scientific work continues until it reaches a point of accomplishment and exhaustion. It will be challenged by what Kuhn labeled a "scientific revolution," which

2 Forsyth, Murray, "The Political Theory of Federalism: The Relevance of Classical Approaches," in: Hesse, Joachim Jens, and Vincent Wright (eds.), *Federalizing Europe?: The Costs, Benefits, and Preconditions of Federal Political Systems*, Oxford: Oxford University Press, 1996: 32.

3 For a good overview of the theoretical approaches see Cini, Michelle, and Angela K. Bowne (eds.), *European Union Studies*, Houndmills: Palgrave Macmillan, 2006.

subsequently leads to the establishment of a new paradigm.[4] As the old paradigm in its time, the new one will be rooted in shared common beliefs of those scholars building their work around this new supposition.

As far as academic work on the processes of European integration is concerned, there have been a series of scientific revolutions and even revolutions within revolutions. While some of the literature has been outright dissident, questioning the premises of preceding arguments in the scholarly community, other texts have contributed to the overall search with variations and specifications of a given paradigm, yet amounting to a factual change of perspective. Most of the academic literature on the processes of European integration is inclined to begin by stating in an almost ritualistic way that European integration is not about state-formation. Some authors say this with distinctive normative clarity, definitely wanting to prevent state-formation through the EU. Others say it almost unintentionally, as if to offer an excuse for delving into the sphere of a Union, which still is all too often under legitimacy scrutiny among scholars that study its deliberations and decisions. Turned around, the obsession with defining the European Union and its underlying integration process as definitely not leading to a state (or a "super-state," as the more despicable expression of the same critical feeling goes[5]) indicates the obvious importance of European integration and the pressure under which the traditional state-centrism of most political and social science has come.

In fact, there is no objectivity in the study of the European integration process. Presupposed and more or less principled beliefs of scholars in the field are as common as the prejudice of scholars about the character of principled beliefs among actors that make the European Union work and advance. One commonality is striking among practically all the different schools and trends of academic reasoning about European integration: Most of it takes the functions and procedures of the European Union (in earlier decades: of the European Economic Communities or the European Community) as starting point and framework for its own premises and deductions, conclusions and prescriptions. Either "history-making" events – that is to say treaty revisions – or regular operational mechanisms of policy-making – agenda-setting, policy-formulation, formal and informal negotiations, bargaining and the logic of compromises, finally policy implementation and assessment of policy implications – are perennial topics that surface in the academic work on European integration. None of this is questionable, let alone illegitimate. All of it has contributed to our understanding of European integration as a process and a polity. But for most of the time, the question "how?" has overshadowed the question "why?". We can say a lot about how the European Union operates, advances, turns cycles and advances again. But we have often been confused why it happened, or why it happened notwithstanding powerful arguments of logic and

4 Kuhn, Thomas, *The Structure of Scientific Revolutions*, Chicago: University of Chicago Press, 1962.
5 See Morgan, Glyn, *The Idea of the European Superstate: Public Justification and European Integration*, Princeton: Princeton University Press, 2005.

scholarly reasoning. The academic reflection on European integration has largely been defined by the functional method used by political actors to generate integration. It has almost become a victim of this primacy for function – as the integration process itself often became.

The history of European integration gives many examples of how European integration was advanced at critical moments or relaunched after periods of stasis, of stagnation or even regression. Always, a new beginning was made possible because of political choices, political leadership and political commitment. Time and again this has supported the assumption that European integration first and foremost is a political operation. Surprisingly enough, social and political science studies on European integration have often been less political than the issue of their study, no matter its deficiencies. "The underlying technicity" of European integration, as Murray Forsyth calls it,[6] has also shaped the succeeding academic reasoning about it. The choice made by Jean Monnet, by Robert Schuman and in later decades by the authors of the Single European Act, or those drafting the Treaties of Maastricht, Amsterdam, Nice and Lisbon did define the scientific paradigm on which European integration theory thrived. The functional logic has been successful and a lot has been achieved on this basis. The functional logic has framed the academic discourse, no matter the paradigmatic changes. Whether liberal intergovernmentalism or multilevel governance, whether application of rational choice theory or whether international relations insights into the rising importance of transnationality: The underlying premise of practically all relevant theoretical contributions over five decades has been the functional logic of the integration process itself.[7] This, by the way, is also the main reason for the reluctance to qualify most academic contributions about European integration as elements of a general and objective integration theory. By and large, they are theories about the integration in Europe, which is an altogether different thing.

Usually, they offer theories about the functional side of European integration in a given time, and that is fair enough. But they often remain silent on the political intention and notion of functional integration, on the underlying constitutional principles of the institutional development, and on the framing of integration policies. The primacy of function, its root causes and their effects, produced different sets of arguments, all worth considering. As the integration process itself, they tended to underestimate or neglect the political and constitutional side of the process. Political actors have focused all too often on institution-building matters as if that was a goal in itself. Policy-formulation, decision-making and policy-implementation had their time, of course, and also their

6 Forsyth, Murray, "The Political Theory of Federalism: The Relevance of Classical Approaches," in: Hesse, Joachim Jens, and Vincent Wright (eds.), *Federalizing Europe?: The Costs, Benefits, and Preconditions of Federal Political Systems*, op.cit.: 26; see also Beach, Derek, *The Dynamics of European Integration: Why and When EU Institutions Matter*, Houndmills: Palgrave Macmillan, 2005.

7 See Brenner, Michael J., *Technocratic Politics and the Functionalist Theory of European Integration*, Ithaca, N.Y.: Center for International Studies, Cornell University, 1969.

corresponding academic literature. Ultimately however, the process and its purpose were political, as has increasingly become evident. European integration was never meant to only produce an affluent and peaceful continent for the sake of affluence and peace. The original intention was to redesign Europe in order to position it anew in the world. The prime focus on economic integration – and as a consequence economic theories of integration[8] – was always meant to be a tool in order to reach political goals at last. Detours, loss of time and the relaunching of initiatives could never obscure this fundamental intention and purpose of European integration. The European Union is a political construction, remains a political purpose and can only be properly understood by recognizing its political ambition to be an actor of global reach. Two fundamental phenomena accompanied the integration process and the academic conversation about European integration with startling consistency: the ritualistic dispute about the non-state quality of European integration, and the atrophic, often cemented debate about federalism.

These astonishing facts are obviously related to the function of discourses – political as well as academic – about the finality of European integration. These discourses never fulfilled the purpose of advancing the integration process toward its very finality. Often, that was not even their prime intention. They rather tried to frame the debate about epiphenomena and matters relevant in their own right, but they were immediately and highly charged if associated and contextualized under the banner of "political finality." From theology, the highly secular European Union could learn that finality is not of this world. Instead, along with growing secularization many political actors try to increase the faith in political terminology. For example, the use of the term "irreversible" – meant to indicate that the European Union cannot be dissolved any more – fulfills functions of political metaphysics. No political institution on earth has ever proven to be "irreversible," so far with the exception of the Roman-Catholic papacy, the oldest public institution in the world. The invocation of the term "irreversible" in the context of European integration has always had the function of exonerating a given result of the integration process by exorcising those ghosts that dared to express a contrary intention to its content and effect. These were and remain largely ritualistic exercises. Seldomly can they properly contribute to advance, reverse or reinvent European integration at any given stage.

The main reason for the astonishing ritual that has accompanied the notion of federalism throughout the history of European integration and its academic reflection goes beyond any serious and necessary dispute: The normative discourse, but even more so the gut feeling attributed to many aggressive debates about the meaning and goal of the European Union, is contradictory. It often tries to cloud the fact that federalism has

8 See, for instance, Molle, Willem, *The Economics of European Integration: Theory, Practice, Policy*, Aldershot: Ashgate, 2001; El-Agraa, Ali M. (ed.), *The European Union: Economics and Policies*, London/New York: Prentice Hall, 2001; Verdun, Amy, *The Euro: European Integration Theory and Economic and Monetary Union*, Lanham: Rowman & Littlefield, 2002.

long been established in Europe. It has been established with the original decision of the Treaties of Rome to constitutionalize the process of European integration, thus taking it away from the unpredictability of political cycles and fashions, logic and illogic.

As much as European integration has been a process ever since, it remains one beyond the fiftieth birthday of the Treaties of Rome in 2007. As much as the evolution of the European federation has been an unending process, it still remains so. It is a federation in permanent making, as all other federations in the world are. The fact that this federation is properly called the European Union is consequential only in so far as the political intention, structure and meaning of the European federation-building process is concerned. The European Union's purpose is a political one. Its institutions are multiple and permanent, its boundaries defined and its policies legally binding for all EU citizens.

Federalism has never been a static concept or a dogmatic matter of one-size-fits-all. It simply is "the theory or advocacy of federal political orders, where final authority is divided between sub-units and a center."[9] Federalism is a concept about shared authority, power and rule. It describes a political structure without formalizing its content, functions, scope and depth. Content, function, scope and depth of any given federation might change in the course of time as empirical evidence from all federations indicates. Yet, federations are distinctively different from unitary arrangements of authority, power and rule. For this simple reason, it is appropriate to call federalism the territorial variant of pluralism. Such a lose definition of federalism leaves enormous space not only for its development, but also for the interpretation of its constituent parts, functions, inner dynamics, decision-making processes and implications. Yet, the concept of federalism was never intended to be different – which is also true for pluralism as its conceptual equivalent. Its application to the process of European integration has a fundamental advantage so much missing and searched for by most of the scholarly conversation, a fixed starting point of reference and a dependent variable.

Having in mind the lose notion of federalism as territorial pluralism and a divided order of authority, power and rule, Carl Joachim Friedrich, one of the distinguished political scientists of the twentieth century, was an early advocate of a paradigmatic shift in federal studies. Already in 1968, in light of the emerging early success of European integration, he suggested to move the discourse about federalism further. He proposed to shift the focus from an analysis of federalist structures – as opposed to unitary, and notably to totalitarian structures of authority, power and rule – to an analysis of federal functions and federalizing tendencies. While federal structures had received sufficient attention throughout the modern history of political philosophy, the empirical-based study of federal functions and processes would be more fruitful, Friedrich argued with firm commitment to the value of European federalism: "We have

9 Follesdal, Andreas, "Federalism," *Stanford Encyclopedia of Philosophy*, http://plato.stanford.edu/entries/federalism/.

federalism only if a set of political communities coexist and interact as autonomous entities united in a common order with an autonomy of its own;" and, "Federal relations are fluctuating relations in the very nature of things. Any federally organized community must therefore provide itself with instrumentalities for the recurrent revision of its pattern or design."[10] This paradigmatic change in the focus of scholarly work on European integration did occur, and it did so with such empathy and effect that, increasingly, definition and meaning of the structure of this process were neglected. To make matters worse, the structure of the process – its constitutional framework – was often absorbed and incorporated as a sub-set of its very functions and hence as any other functional component. The prefigured structure of European integration was not only neglected, but also redefined as one element among other theories about the integration function. This is how "federalism" became a passing theory in the huge and growing edifice of academic reasoning about European integration, while in fact it was and remains the starting-point and root cause of all subsequent theorizing about European integration. With the breakthrough of the political character of European integration and its overall public recognition, the huge corpus of academic reasoning about European integration ought to be understood as a wide and pluralistic set of functional expressions about the federal structure of the European Union.

Five decades after the early work on federalism,[11] there is growing need to again locate all theories and theoretical interpretations of the European integration process into a broader historical picture. It would not require a paradigmatic shift in the sense of Thomas Kuhn's scientific revolution. It only would require a recalibration of the relationship between the original theory of federalism, and secondary and predominantly functional theories about specific stages of European integration. This would not devalue the rich contribution to the academic field of theoretical literature about European integration. But to accept the European Union as a federation in form would be helpful for the focus of research on many pragmatic and practical aspects on European integration as function – research on the EU's inner mechanics, its way and means of generating and distributing power, competences and resources; its ways and means of agenda setting, policy-formulation, decision-making and policy implementation; its impact on member states and Union citizens, its deliberative networks and policy-communities; its transnational and transgovernmental modes of operation, the role of leadership in the EU, the growing scope of policy-issues covered by the EU, and the balance between its institutions; and the increasing role of the EU as an actor in international relations and the effect of European integration on the evolution of political theory, particularly on notions of democracy, sovereignty, and order-

10 Friedrich, Carl Joachim, *Trends of Federalism in Theory and Practice*, New York: Praeger, 1968: 6-7; also see Friedrich, Carl Joachim, and Robert R. Bowie (eds.), *Studies in Federalism*, Boston: Little, Brown, and Co., 1954.

11 See also Macmahon, Arthur W. (ed.), *Federalism: Mature and Emergent*, New York: Russel & Russel Inc., 1962.

building in a world, in which states - either unitary or federal - and supra-national federations obviously co-exist and form a weak new balance of world order.[12]

Without turning the bulk of theoretical literature on European integration artificially upside-down: In the final analysis, practically all of it can be categorized as a contribution to the continuously evolving federalism theory of the continuously evolving European Union. Federalism is the encompassing framework under which the most diverse combinations of theories and the most diverse theoretical debates about the European integration process take place. Federalism is not just one of the many theories about European integration, it is the constitutional framework under which other theoretical considerations could begin to flow and will continue to do so. Without a federal starting point – that is to say with the early political commitment to ultimately achieve federal Union – the European Union would never have come into being. Without the early decision for federalism as the organizing principle of a new order for Europe, theories about European integration would not have evolved and flourished.

This argument might sound provocative. Its central point is not stressed to denigrate five decades of valuable theoretical contributions to social sciences. But time has come – due to the very evolution of the European Union – to recalibrate the theoretical reflection about European integration. All theory is relational, as are all key terms of political philosophy. Federalism is a relational term. It relates to specific forms of divided authority, power and rule. As a consequence, federal structures will always be highly diverse in their specific functions. Federalism also relates to specific assessments of the functions of a federal structure of authority, power and rule. The more the political character of the European Union has been established – according to the original intentions and ultimate aspirations of the Founding Fathers of European integration – the more its character as a federation ought to be recognized. The huge set of theoretical literature on European integration has been weak on authority, power, and rule. This has largely been the consequence of the weakness of the European Union (and its predecessors) as far as its claim to exert authority, its ambition to generate power and its operations concerning the struggle for rule were concerned. An unfocused Union must produce an unfocused body of literature about it.

The European Union is not a state – and has never ever claimed to be one.[13] Such assumption was either wishful thinking, or a product of fear or an effort of slandering, or a little bit of everything by those not wanting to apply rational analysis and judgment to the evolutionary process of the EU. No legal dogma, no political majority or philosophical law requires a federation to be a state. But that all federations represent different expressions of the one original federal decision to create supranational institutions, no matter how incomplete and weak, should be recognized. It is also worth

12 See on the overall context also Dinan, Desmond, *Encyclopedia of the European Union*, Houndmills: Palgrave Macmillan 2005 (2nd. rev.ed.).

13 See Leonard, Dick, and Mark Leonard (eds.), *The Pro-European Reader*, Houndmills: Palgrave Macmillan, 2002.

recalling that the concept of federalism is older than the concept of statehood. It would facilitate further growth of theoretical knowledge about the functions of the European Union if consensus would be reached, at last, on its structure as one quintessentially being federal.

By its very nature, European integration is a process and will remain a process, as all political structures do. The idea of "integration theory" is in itself questionable as its content must change with the development of integration itself. This does not render earlier theoretical contributions obsolete, naive or false. A theory of European integration independent of and in contrast to the recognition of its structure as federal is however a-historical and ultimately apolitical. Proponents of an autonomous theory of European integration must at least accept that their theoretical endeavor is contingent and relational, not only as far as their topic is concerned, but also with regard to the time-line of their propositions. To recognize the European Union as a federation finally recognizes the dependable variable Ernst Haas was looking for to anchor his analysis of European integration. In the 1950's, his theoretical explanation of the early beginnings of European integration became famous under the heading "neo-functionalism." In a way, neo-functionalism became the authoritative theory of European integration.[14] Two decades later, Haas declared integration theory dead: "The task of selecting and justifying variables and explaining their hypothesized interdependence cannot be accomplished without an agreement as to possible conditions to which the process is expected to lead. In short, we need a dependent variable."[15] The dependent variable Haas called for did not yet exist in 1971. The European Community lacked focused political profile and recognizable ambition. In the early twenty-first century, the reality of the European Union cannot longer justify this reluctant and skeptical perception of purpose and scope of European integration: The question of the structure of the European Union has been resolved while the reasoning about its functions remains.

Integration as process will go on. But integration as structure has created a federation called the European Union. This European Union as a European federation will prevail as the dependent variable for further research and academic dispute. Its functions will continue to shape the understanding of integration, but this can hardly add anything else to the understanding of its structure. Therefore, more promising seems to be further research on the authentically political nature and function of the European Union, on its mechanisms of decision-making, the inter-connectedness between the European level and the national levels of government, the impact of European integration on the constitutional systems of its member states, party politics,

14 Haas, Ernst B., *The Uniting of Europe: Political, Social and Economic Forces, 1950-1957*, Stanford: Stanford University Press, 1958.

15 Haas, Ernst B., "The Study of European Integration: Reflections on the Joy and Anguish of Pretheorizing," in: Lindberg, Leon N., and Stuart A. Scheingold (eds.), *Regional Integration: Theory and Research*, Cambridge, MA.: Harvard University Press, 1971: 18.

EU bureaucracy, and organized interest and public opinion.[16] It will be productive to broaden the research agenda as far as the European Union as international actor is concerned. The role of a supranational federation in the shaping of world order-building will require fresh methodological and empirical work.[17] The future of the nation state, of course, is the other big issue emanating from the rise of European integration.

Theoretical reflection about the future path of the European Union remains important. It will enhance our understanding of its inherent processes and it will give inspiration to deal with further adaptations and improvements of the EU's institutional mechanisms, policies and operational modes. As administrative science, the theoretical occupation with EU integration might have its best time yet to come. As policy analysis, the study of the European Union as Europe's federation will deepen our knowledge about procedures and effects of integration. The more this is linked to the categorically fundamental notion of all political science – authority, power and rule – the more it will be truly political and not only functional. Five decades after its beginnings in an atmosphere of trial and error, the European Union does not need to be linked any more to the question of whether or not it is a state or will become one. It is also of limited insight to compare the European Union to former phases of Europe's history, such as the Austro-Hungarian multinational Empire, or alluding to the idea that the EU could develop into a new Byzantium with the US as the new Rome.[18] Finally, it is of limited heuristic value to give in to the formula that the European Union is the first post-modern form of organizing politics.[19] This is true as much as post-modern philosophy is true – and limited with its limited value to relate form and norm. Postmodernism does not answer normative or moral questions along the line of "why?" or "what for?." Assessing integration on this philosophical basis will be confronted with the same limits of its reasoning as its underlying postmodern philosophical methodology. It seems much more convincing to return to a classical, yet timeless understanding of basic structures of ordering the public sphere by recognizing the European Union as a federation in search of a global purpose and in need of a refined constitutional patriotism.

This decision will not overcome the idiosyncrasies of the EU. It will not limit or even eliminate the procedural character as epitomized in the perennial use of the term "European integration." This remains an open-ended saga, and surely the best one in the history of Europe as far as territorially defined authority, liberal modes of power and consociational mechanisms of rule are concerned. Yet, it is appropriate to finally grant

16 See, for instance, Richardson, Jeremy J. (ed.), *European Union: Power and Policy-Making*, London/New York: Routledge, 1996.

17 See Murray, Philomena, "Towards a Research Agenda on the European Union as a Model of Regional Integration," *Asia-Pacific Journal of EU Studies*, 2.1(2004): 33-51.

18 Ferguson, Niall, *Colossus: The Price of America's Empire*, New York: Penguin Press, 2004: 227-257 ("Europe between Brussels and Byzantium").

19 Cooper, Robert, "The Post-Modern State," in: Leonard, Mark (ed.), *Re-Ordering the World: the Long-Term Implications of September 11*, London: The Foreign Policy Center, 2002: 11-20.

the European Union the status of what it has become since it began to grow into something it could only end up with: Europe's first ever, and therefore exceptional, supranational federation. This breakthrough in academic reasoning about European integration will sharpen the theoretical instruments, methods, approaches, and concluding hypotheses with which to study future policy-processes and the impact of the European Union.

2. Functional Prerogatives and the Intergovernmental Proposition

By and large, the academic discourse of the past five decades about European integration reflects the inherent evolution of the integration process. As European integration began with functional and sectoral integration of key economic activities among six founding members of the European Economic Communities, it was plausible to echo this approach in the theoretical reasoning about European integration. Functionalism became somewhat the authoritative theoretical line of the study of European integration. Functionalism was contextualized in the broader genre of international relations theory. This was appropriate as the Treaties of Rome were an international arrangement among sovereign states and as such an element of the formation of international organizations and international law. The assessment of the long theoretical journey of academics parallel to the development of European integration requires clarification in its own context. Each theory normally begins with a basic perception of social realities in a given time and under conditions of available or selected knowledge of the phenomenon it is reflecting about. All theoretical contributions to better understand European integration have made subjective choices about content, scope and intention of their analysis. Often, they were focused, poignant contributions to academic battles taking place in scholarly circles. Their strengths and weaknesses were revealed only over time and with considerable distance to the actual writing of a certain theoretical text.

It is surprising to see how often the work of David Mitrany is mentioned in the reflection about functionalism as lead theory on European integration. With his emphasis that functionalism only knows one logic, which is "the logic of the problem,"[20] he offered insights into the prospect for "a working peace system." His focus was not on Europe, and in later writings he has been highly critical of European regional integration: It is still territory-based and hence doomed to repeat the old mistakes of the state-system. His writing had a surprisingly un-institutional dimension. Mitrany considered himself to be writing in the tradition of social engineering. He was an advocate of rationality and considered all human beings capable of creating the conditions for a lasting peace. This should be done through the merging of social

20 Mitrany, David, *The Functional Theory of Politics*, London: Martin Robertson & Co., 1975: 258.

functions, thus preventing the radicalization of competitive ideas or realities erupting into new conflicts and even wars. Mitrany's discussion of rational and technocratic methods was rooted in a normative approach of how to prevent war and make peace. Mitrany was highly critical of the primacy of national sovereignty among states. He advocated a view of states defined by what he called their "material interdependence."[21] With this premise, he pleaded for the fusion of some of their functions and suggested that this would happen almost as a natural process, as it would "merely rationalize and develop what is already there."[22] Mitrany never explicitly outlined the necessary political actions and processes it would take to engage states in the functional transfer of competences. In the final analysis, he also left unanswered the question as to whom these competences should be transferred. The beginning of European integration was criticized by Mitrany as a path following a territorial logic and not a functional one. In the end, the most powerful states would dominate the EEC. Mitrany saw European integration potentially as replicating state-like functions without the cohesion of the state. With this argument, ironically, he introduced both the leading theoretical guideline for the subsequent understanding of European integration and its strongest critique: The process was one of functional transfer of sovereignty and competence and at the same time, as it seemed to copy the traditional European state, it would fall short of the strength of the state.

Not surprisingly, Ernst B. Haas has criticized Mitrany's concept of a social, if not natural, automatism toward the functional fusion of states. It reminded him of Marxist-Leninist aspirations to replace the rule of man by the "administration of things."[23] Ironically, the inherently apolitical nature of Mitrany's work tried to achieve an extremely political goal, namely global peace. This surprising disconnect from the real sphere of politics as a process of rule did not happen in the theoretical work of Ernst B. Haas. His study of the early stages of European economic integration was labeled "neo-functionalism." While he shared Mitrany's insight into the rising interdependence, converging political preferences and the positive effects of the merger of state functions on the supranational level, he undertook a thorough empirical study on the specific circumstances that would most likely enable the EEC to build on the experience of the European Coal and Steel Community and to reach compromises between differing national interests in Western Europe. His 1958 study "The Uniting of Europe" – published at Stanford as other important theoretical works on European integration were in later decades – defined the parameters of empirical-based theoretical research on European integration for a long time. With the European Coal and Steel Community, "the decomposition of old nations can be systematically analyzed within the framework

21 Mitrany, David, *The Progress of International Government*, New Haven: Yale University Press, 1933: 101.

22 Mitrany, David, *A Working Peace System*, Chicago: Quadrangle Books, 1943: 81.

23 Haas, Ernst B., *Beyond the Nation State: Functionalism and International Organization*, Stanford: Stanford University Press, 1964: 9.

of the evolution of a larger polity – a polity destined, perhaps, to develop into a nation of its own."[24] The European Coal and Steel Community had become the successful blueprint for the emerging European Economic Communities, "because it offered a multitude of different advantages to different groups."[25] Haas proposed the most evident application of the use of the principle of functional integration, namely the introduction of a new and larger polity. It took almost five decades of theorizing on European integration to achieve more or less consensus among scholars in the field on this early characterization of the European Union. For Haas it was not spectacular or doubtful, but empirically evident what took other scholars five decades to discover after much pain and through much controversy.

Haas systematized what he considered insights into the evolution of the emerging European integration process. Integration should begin with cautious steps in fields of less importance and controversy; a high authority needed to be established to oversee the process outside the control of national interests; the integration of specific economic sectors would enhance the functional need to integrate related economic spheres among the participating states; social groups would gradually shift their loyalty to the emerging supranational structures; deepened economic integration would create the need to stronger institutionalize the process and enhance the regulatory requirements; and finally, political integration would become almost inevitable. His theoretical clarity was the most precise lightning rod for the early years of integration studies – and probably remains closest in reconnecting the theory of European integration to the original relationship between the political idea of federalism as a structure of rule and the technical idea of functionalism as a method of implementing and advancing it.

In his very learned study about the evolution of theories of European integration, Ben Rosamond has reconstructed the context in which the study of Ernst Haas could evolve. The behavioral school in American political science – at Stanford most notably represented by Gabriel Almond[26] – was emerging with ever increasing impact. "The behavioral movement," Rosamond wrote, "directed scholarship toward the analysis of political behavior and, therefore, closer to the study of political processes than earlier forms of political analysis which had been heavily institutional and constitutional in their focus."[27] This development in political science methodology coincided with the origins of the "Monnet method" of European integration. Thus Haas's proposition to consider European integration as the expression of a neo-functionalist process became

24 Haas, Ernst B., *The Uniting of Europe: Political, Social, and Economic Forces, 1950-1957*, op.cit.: xi.

25 Ibid.: xiii.

26 See the classic study of Almond, Gabriel, and Sidney Verba, *The Civic Culture: Political Attitudes and Democracy in Five Nations*, Princeton: Princeton University Press, 1963.

27 Rosamond, Ben, *Theories of European Integration*, Houndmills: Palgrave, 2000: 54; also see Nelsen, Brent F., and Alexander Stubb (eds.), *The European Union: Readings on the Theory and Practice of European Integration*, Houndmills: Palgrave, 2003 (3rd ed.); Wiener, Antje, and Thomas Diez, *European Integration Theory*, Oxford: Oxford University Press, 2004.

rooted both in empirical politics and innovative academic methodology. This did not render institutional and constitutional approaches obsolete. With almost cyclical permanence, other methodologies and "schools" of theorizing about European integration followed. But until the early 1970's, none was more influential than neo-functionalism.

Its findings were further rooted in economic theory by the work of Leon N. Lindberg, whose theory of "spill-over" effects within neo-functionalist processes of integration became something of a mantra for generations of students of the European project. His theory – like Haas's published at Stanford – tried to further develop the proposition of Haas that integration breeds integration. The establishment of economic integration in one sector would automatically entail integration of other sectors, Lindberg argued. In accordance with Haas, he defined integration as a process. Following the classical logic of federal notions of shared authority, he understood delegated decision-making as "a basic precondition in shared decision-making." And he concluded: "The processes of sharing and of delegating decision-making are likely to affect the governmental structure in each state involved."[28] Formal and informal means of decision-making and the inevitable development of central institutions would generate an inherently expansive character of European integration functions. "Spill-over" would become the inevitable consequence. "In its most general formulation," Lindberg wrote, "'spill-over' refers to a situation in which a given action, related to a specific goal, creates a situation in which the original goal can be assured only by taking further actions, which in turn create a further condition and a need for more action, and so forth."[29] Lindberg's almost deterministic concept of "spill-over" as a continuous pattern of widening integration was criticized as often as it failed in reality. Yet soon thereafter it again was proven correct as, exactly because of earlier failures, new dimensions were added to the substance of European integration, its growing institutions and expanding functions. What ought to be added is the fact that the "original goal" also expanded: From the original purpose of reconciliation (under enormous internal pressure) among European nations and former state enemies, it slowly and gradually grew into the projection of the European Union as a global provider of peace and stability (though only under enormous external pressure). Lindberg also underestimated the ability of the partners in the European integration process to organize detours in order to reactivate the process once it became hopelessly stuck.

Forgotten and yet highly relevant for any contemporary reflection about the functionability of EU institutions is Lindberg's insight about the "integrative impact of the central institutions": In accordance with general research on organizational

28 Lindberg, Leon N., *The Political Dynamics of European Economic Integration*, Stanford: Stanford University Press, 1963: 6.
29 Ibid.: 10.

sociology, he proposed that the relevance of the institutions of the European integration process "will depend in part upon the competencies and roles assigned to them. Much, however, depends upon whether or not the institutions make full use of their competencies and upon how they define their role."[30] This was a clear reference to the importance of an actor's behavior, recognizing the issue of leadership and the role of policy-communities, formal and informal networks of delegation, consultation, agenda-setting, shaping policy-decisions and supervising their implementation. Further theoretical work on the European integration process generated valuable studies. Philippe Schmitter, to mention but another Stanford political scientist, aimed at sophisticating neo-functionalism by breaking his actor strategy of European decision-making down into characteristics such as: spill-over, spill-around, buildup, retrench, muddle-about, spill-back, and encapsulate.[31] This jargon added valuable insights into actors' behaviors and their preferences under conditions of complex policy-making processes. However, such theories did not answer questions about the structure of European integration. More and more, neo-functionalism reached its limits, as it did not "spill-back" to its federal starting premise and subsequently to constitutional studies.

Ernst Haas wrapped up the result of more than a decade of debate and theoretical reflection when in 1971 he declared neo-functionalism merely a pre-theory, lacking a dependent variable as the ultimate reference point of its reasoning. As long as the final course of European integration remains blurred, he argued, the explanatory power of any pre-theory, including neo-functionalism, will be limited. Integration theory could no longer pretend to explain something that did not yet exist and was proceeding without coherent knowledge about its final cause. For Haas, as he stated in an article in 1975, integration theory had become obsolescent.[32] He left the stage to the rising paradigm of intergovernmentalism. Ultimately, this new theoretical approach of assessing European integration was another variant of functionalism. One could label intergovernmentalism the flip side of federalism, although its proponents preferred to be considered ardent opponents of federal theories.

Yet, theirs was not a theory of the structure of European integration. It was another theory of the functions of integration in light of the political events of the mid-1960's. At the beginning of their theoretical reasoning was not a paradigmatic revolution, but rather General de Gaulle. The General's veto on British EEC membership in early 1963 was the first strong indication of the ongoing primacy of national interests over the necessary community spirit. When the French President insisted on the continuous application of unanimity in EEC decision-making in 1965, this had a strong impact on all realists of international relations who had already been suspicious of the normative

30 Ibid., p. 8.

31 Schmitter, Philippe, "A Revised Theory of European Integration," in: Lindberg, Leon N., and Stuart A. Scheingold (eds.), *Regional Integration: Theory and research*, op.cit.: 242.

32 Haas, Ernst B., *The Obsolescence of Regional Integration Theory*, Berkeley: Institute of International Studies Working Paper, 1975.

perspective of turning the structure of European state-relations from a realistic system of balance of power to a federal system of shared sovereignty. De Gaulle's policy of "empty chair" filled their plate with strong and seemingly convincing arguments. The intergovernmental paradigm survived the integration crisis triggered by de Gaulle. It even survived the overcoming of this crisis as indicated by the continuous pooling of sovereignty that has evolved since the promulgation of the 1986 Single European Act. It required the introduction of the European currency, the deployment of European Peace Keeping Forces across the globe and increasing European inroads into matters of justice and home affairs to shift the underlying assumption of many theories of integration to the sphere of institutional and constitutional considerations. Only in recent years has the basic decision for a federal Union begun to serve with plausibility as the "dependent variable" in the debate on integration theories.

Decades ago, Stanley Hoffmann was the first who had offered a sharp and concise argument in favor of accepting the ongoing role and obstinate reality of the European nation state. He argued, in the mid-1960's, that European unification as a call for "national self-abnegation" had become the victim of the prevalent strength of the nation state as the single most important factor in international relations.[33] Eloquently, he underlined the logic of realism in the theory of international relations: "As the super-powers compete ... the nation state becomes the universal point of salience."[34] For Hoffmann, European integration was only conceivable as a regional subsystem of the global international political system. As such it would always remain limited in its claim to redirect state relations. This holds true as far as the neo-functional theory of spill-over effects is concerned: "The model of functional integration ...is essentially an administrative model, which relies on bureaucratic expertise for the promotion of a policy defined by the policy authorities, and for the definition of a policy that political decision-makers are technically incapable of shaping."[35] Beyond his sharp critique of neo-functionalism as basically apolitical, Hoffmann also took issue with the very idea of European integration as a federalizing process. He challenged the goals, methods and results of the approach taken by Jean Monnet in the 1950's. In questioning their ability to achieve a federal structure, he was starting with the assumption of absolute losses and absolute gains that were at stake. Should a federal structure be established, the nation state would only lose. He understood the functional approach of Monnet as the effort to change the structure of the nation state by circumventing an outright assault on its core. Comparing the process with the method of peeling an artichoke, Hoffmann concluded: "As the artichoke's heart gets more and more denuded, the government's vigilance gets

33 Hoffmann, Stanley, "Obstinate or Obsolete? The Fate of the Nation-State and the Case of Western Europe," *Daedalus: Journal of the American Academy of Arts and Sciences*, 95.3 (1966): 866.
34 Ibid.
35 Ibid.: 887.

more and more alerted."[36] Nation states would never accept that the heart of their sovereignty be taken away by European functionalists or, even worse, federalists.

Moreover, Hoffmann argued, the Founding Fathers of the European Economic Communities never agreed on whether they wanted to create a "security community" in order to pacify Europe after its long history of warfare, "or whether the main goal was the creation of an entity whose position and might could decisively affect the course of the Cold War in particular, of international relations in general." The idea that European integration could lead to a new European polity as more than a contribution to international relations was rejected by Hoffmann: "If we look at the institutions of the Common Market as an incipient political system in Europe, we find that its authority remains limited, its structure weak, its popular base restricted and distant."[37] This was certainly a fair argument in 1966, but it could not exclude later developments that proved skeptics wrong as far as limited authority, weak structure and restricted popular base of the integration process are concerned. Hoffmann discussed the possibilities of parliamentary politics with a weak executive in which short-term political bargaining with a focus on immediate advantages prevails over long-term planning. As this was already a sorry reality in France's Fourth Republic, he did not want to see the method repeated in the Common Market, as he called the EEC. Hence, he concluded, the promise of European federalism had failed.

Normatively, his criticism of federalism was a fair point in light of the European realities of 1966, but it could not give a definite answer in face of an open future of European integration. Yet, Hoffmann initiated influential research based on the assumption that the EEC is not more than an intergovernmental structure in the international order. Democratizing and constitutionalizing the EEC, as Hoffmann rightly asked for, took almost four more decades. Yet in the end, it did happen. Referring to Hoffmann's position in the academic debate, Andrew Moravscik – like Hoffmann at Harvard – refined the theory of European intergovernmentalism to perfection. He understood every aspect in the evolution of European integration from the Messina conference to the Treaty of Maastricht as a chain of intergovernmental bargaining, presumably proving once and forever that the federal proposition was wrongly applied to European integration. It would however have been more correct to simply state that the democratic and parliamentary aspiration was still missing in the integration process, while it was rightly considered to be essential in order to legitimize European integration as federal.

Andrew Moravcsik's influential study "The Choice for Europe" became the quintessential expression of what was to be labeled "liberal intergovernmentalism" in the field of theorizing academics. Recognizing that the European Community was a "unique, multileveled, transnational political system," Moravcsik understood European

36 Ibid.: 884.
37 Ibid.: 885.

integration as it had evolved until the Treaty of Maastricht as the result of three factors: "patterns of commercial advantage, the relative bargaining power of important governments, and the incentives to enhance the credibility of interstate commitments."[38] He accepted that national sovereignty had been transformed to the European level, but was adamant in concluding that this phenomenon had not limited the primacy of the nation state in the bargaining process for economic gains through European channels. Moravcsik focused his study on the "grand bargains" that have paved the way for European integration, ultimately leading to the Treaty of Maastricht. The gradual, though creeping process of transferring sovereignty to European institutions was recognized by Moravcsik. Yet, for him the European Community remained an international organization and not one level of a federal structure: "Choices to pool and delegate sovereignty to international institutions are best explained as efforts by governments to constrain and control one another – in game theoretical language, by their effort to enhance the credibility of commitments. Governments transfer sovereignty to international institutions where potential gains are large, but efforts to secure compliance by foreign governments through decentralized or domestic means are likely to be ineffective."[39] Moravcsik's findings corresponded to the influential historical research of Alan Milward, who explained the beginning of the European Economic Communities as the "rescue of the nation state."[40] This "apparently paradoxical claim"[41] was concomitant with the international relations theory of neo-realism, most aptly articulated by Kenneth Waltz.[42] Rational state behavior – such was the common denominator between their theoretical premises – does not emerge from principled beliefs, fixed premises or pre-figured international norms. Instead it is the result of dynamic internal policy processes intended to maximize the national interest. Based on this assumption, European integration must always remain a zero-sum game, where one's country's gain is another country's loss. However, if European integration was only about short-term economic gains, one was left to wonder why it had become necessary at all as economic gains could well have been organized outside a new political structure. And if European integration was only another organizational component of a realist, that is to say, state-based international order, one was left to

38 Moravcsik, Andrew, *The Choice for Europe: Social Purpose and State Power from Messina to Maastricht*, op.cit.: 1-2.; also see Moravcsik, Andrew, *Negotiating the Single Act: National Interests and Conventional Statecraft in the European Community*, Cambridge, MA: Minda de Gunzburg Center for European Studies, Harvard University, 1989; Moravcsik, Andrew, *Why the European Community Strengthens the State: Domestic Politics and International Cooperation*, Cambridge, Ma: Minda de Gunzburg Center for European Studies, Harvard University, 1994; Moravcsik, Andrew, *De Gaulle and Europe: Historical Revision and Science Theory*, Cambridge, MA: Minda de Gunzburg Center for European Studies, Harvard University, 1998.

39 Moravcsik, Andrew, *The Choice for Europe*, op.cit.: 9.

40 Milward, Alan S., *The European Rescue of the Nation State*, London: Routledge, 1992.

41 Rosamond, Ben, *Theories of European Integration*, op.cit.: 138.

42 Waltz, Kenneth, *Theory of International Politics*, New York: McGraw Hill, 1979; Mark A. Pollack, *International Relations Theory and European Integration*, Fiesole: European University Institute, 2000.

query why the EU – but this was already evident in the days of the EEC and the EC – put so much emphasis on the evolution of a common law and, increasingly, a parliamentary rooting of its decision-making.

Ultimately, intergovernmentalism in all its variants was helpful in explaining the behavioral patterns of national governments as far as their input into the European integration process is concerned. Intergovermentalism was also successful in deciphering the link between the European bargaining of national governments and the effect of social interest groups on national political choices. But it remained unclear why intergovernmentalism became the counter-theory to the one defining European integration as a gradually increasing "supranational" phenomenon. Instead of arguing in an either-or attitude, it would have been more reasonable to consider both theoretical contributions as two intrinsically related elements of a complex web of structures and functions, preferences and interests, implications and modes of bargaining in multilevel policy-making. It is reasonable to perceive intergovernmentalism and supranationalism as the two inevitable and indispensable sides of each federal structure which includes and yet exists above the nation state. After all, a federal structure does not imply the dissolution of either the higher or the lower level of authority, power, and rule. In fact, a political structure can only be named "federal" if it comprises both. European supranationalism requires intergovernmentalism as its corresponding feature – and vice versa – in order to label its basic structure "federal." Otherwise, Europe would be a unitary entity. The simple fact is that it cannot become a unitary entity because it is designed as federal.

Variations of the theoretical debate about intergovernmentalism and its effect on European integration were offered by Wolfgang Wessels and Fritz W. Scharpf, two German voices in a debate with a strong American input. Wessels presented a "fusion hypothesis" to argue that integration dynamics is a process over time in which governments seek integration in order to achieve common goals for shared problems.[43] Scharpf was not enthusiastic about the interlocking nature between governmental decisions and EU decision-making. Joint problems would be resolved, but the outcome was rather sub-optimal as both levels were trapped in the nature of joint decision-making: "The arrangement represents a 'local optimum' in the cost-benefit calculations of all participants that might have the power to change it. If that is so, there is no 'gradualist' way in which joint-decision systems might transform themselves into an institutional arrangement of greater political potential."[44]

Three assumptions were essential to the intergovernmental paradigm: State actors are rational; their principal goal is economic gain; and cooperative arrangements with other state actors lead to conflict-resolution in the context of international relations.

43 Wessels, Wolfgang, "An Ever Closer Fusion: A Macropolitical View on Integration Processes," *Journal of Common Market Studies*,.35.2 (1997): 267-301.

44 Scharpf, Fritz W., "The Joint-Decision Trap: Lessons from German Federalism and European Integration," *Public Administration*, 66 (1988): 271.

While the rationality, consistency, coherence and tenacity of state actors came under growing academic scrutiny, the economic primacy of European integration came under increasing pressure with the Treaty of Maastricht. Intergovernmentalists described the Treaty of Maastricht as the culminating proof of their theory. The Treaty of Maastricht was certainly a paradigmatic turning point and the undeniable breakthrough of the political nature of European integration. It was no coincidence that it took place simultaneously with the beginning of the reunification of Europe at the end of the Cold War. The pending question about the territorial scope of Europe had always been an additional obstacle for unequivocally recognizing the federal nature of integration as its dependent variable. With the imminent path toward the inclusion of former communist countries in Central and Eastern Europe, another condition for federal Unions was about to be met: clarification of its territorial boundaries. The impact of the Treaty of Maastricht demonstrated the continuously evolutionary nature of European integration, increasingly turning to its original political goal. As Thomas Risse-Kappen, a third German voice in the debate, argued, time had come to reconcile international relations theory with the findings of comparative policy research if any new insight in the character and function of European integration was to be found.[45] Comparative policy analysis was increasingly focusing on the relationship between EU member states and the effects of European integration, but also on the governance character of the established set of EU decision-making modalities.

One of the best and most helpful assessments of the complex nature of European integration was also one of the most simple: William Wallace from the London School of Economics distinguished between formal and informal integration. Formal aspects, he argued, are related to the outcome of integration – such as institutions, policies, legislative changes – whereas informal aspects of integration have penetrated the whole web of political and public interactions in Europe "among previously autonomous actors."[46] Informal transnational activities, not only horizontal between analogous institutions, but also across the boundaries of institutions, have increasingly added weight to the EU decision-making process. The weight of these contacts is difficult to measure empirically as it often contributes more to the necessary consensus-building process about ideas than to the nitty-gritty mechanics of formulating details of legislation. It is however undeniable that inter-institutional relations matter more than is evident if the European Union were only to be measured by the outcome of formal meetings of Council formations, European Parliament sessions or European Council summits. This is true in a vertical sense between the EU institutions and the whole array of national institutions. And it is true in a horizontal sense among the actors inside EU

45 Risse-Kappen, Thomas, "Exploring the Nature of the Beast: International Relations Theory and Comparative Policy Analysis Meet the European Union," *Journal of Common Market Studies*, 34.1 (1996): 53-80.

46 Wallace, William, "Introduction: The Dynamics of European Integration," in: William Wallace (ed.), *The Dynamics of European Integration*, London: Pinter, 1990: 9.

institutions, both in a formal and informal sense, and as far as official negotiations and the wide web of unofficial encounters among political actors and between them and representatives of the private sector, civil society, the media and academia are concerned.

3. Integration and Theory In Light of a Genuine European Polity

The academic reflection on the governance quality of the European Union has seen an exponential growth in the aftermath of the Treaty of Maastricht. Finally, a central category of state sovereignty was pooled on the European level. There could be no doubt that the emerging Single European currency was not only an economic event and a sign of "low politics," as academics like to belittle the daily business of European integration. A common currency was a fundamental political act and it required taking the EU more seriously. Relativizing Ernst Haas's 1958 remark about the polity-character of the European Coal and Steel Community, Leon Lindberg and Stuart Scheingold suggested in 1970 that the European Community should be defined as "Europe's would-be polity."[47] With the emergence of the European Union in 1993, those relativistic qualifications could not hold any more. The European Union had become a polity, as Haas had already anticipated in the earliest moments of the path European integration had finally taken.

Lindberg and Scheingold "anticipated the themes of the later multilevel governance literature"[48] and looked into the dynamic nature of the functioning of European integration. They did not offer yet another integration theory. Being influenced by system theory, they developed a concept according to which the political structure of the European Community was not defined by static norms, but by permanent "system change."[49] They connected the "demand" for integration, the existing functional scope of the European Community, its institutional capacities and the degree of systemic support with the politically important issue of leadership. If the details and implications of European integration were properly assessed, academic research would have to look into the notion of "system change." Until the 1990's, European governance was identified as the moveable, independent variable of a process that was still lacking recognition as far as its dependent variable was concerned. But the multilevel governance approach that emerged and finally began to dominate the academic literature on European integration in the early years of the twenty-first century was recognizing the original flexible variable as analyzed in Ernst Haas's theory of neo-functionalism: The European Union was granted the status of a polity in its own right.

47 Lindberg, Leon N., and Stuart A. Scheingold, *Europe's Would-Be Polity: Patterns of Change in the European Community*, Englewood Cliffs, N.J.: Prentice Hall, 1970.
48 Ben Rosamond, *Theories of European Integration*, op.cit.: 90.
49 Ibid.: 114.

This had multiple implications. It opened research about the actor-ness of the European Union, which is to say its international role and its effect as a genuine actor in international relations. It brought about a variety of insightful studies about agenda setting, policy-making, decision-making, policy networks, delegation and the rational choice-based concept of principle-agent-relationship.[50] It supported the urgency to come to terms with the "democratic deficit" of the European Union, whatever that term meant to different minds. And it required a closer study of the implications of European integration on the institutional and constitutional structures and functions of the member states of the European Union. All in all, academic research on European integration throughout the 1990's was defined by "theoretical renewal," as Ben Rosamond put it.[51]

The focus on governance meant that the European Union was recognized not as yet another international organization operating on the basis of intergovernmental bargaining. In finally recognizing the polity-character of the European Union and its genuine status as law-making and law-executing political entity Italian scholar Giandomenico Majone labeled the EU a "regulatory state."[52] Government bargaining was put in perspective as the European institutions were increasingly impacting the shape of European law and national legislation. As part of the realization of a Single Market, regulatory efforts to harmonize standards, norms and practices became all-pervasive. They added to the regulatory claims in the spheres of competition policies and anti-trust policies. The new consideration of institutional issues in their generic historical evolution by academic research (soon labeled "historical institutionalism") recognized the political dimension of the integration process. Although the European Union had remained primarily a market union during the 1990's, it was beginning to project its claim to also be a political union.

As any other polity, the European Union had become an increasingly complex structure with multiple functions and often idiosyncratic procedures. Academics, who focused on the governance character of the European Union, were confronted with two challenges: Addressing and outlining the complexity, and deciphering the main trends within this complex web. This required studying the institutional development, the decision-making mechanisms, policy-setting, policy-making and policy-implementation, the role of member state governments, of political parties and,

50 See, for instance, Pollack, Mark A., "Delegation, Agency, and Agenda Setting in the European Community," *International Organization*, 51.1(1997): 99–134; Sandholtz, Wayne, and Alec Stone Sweet (eds.), *European Integration and Supranational Governance*, Oxford: Oxford University Press, 1998; Hooghe, Liesbet, and Gary Marks, *Multi-Level Governance and European Integration*, Lanham: Rowman & Littlefield, 2001; Pollack, Mark A., *The Engines of European Integration: Delegation, Agency and Agenda Setting in the European Union*, Oxford: Oxford University Press, 2003.

51 Rosamond, Ben, *Theories of European Integration*, op.cit.: 98.

52 Majone, Giandomenico, "The Rise of the Regulatory State in Europe," *West European Politics*, 17.3 (1994): 77-101. For a discussion of environmental policies as an expression of the regulatory character of the EU see Kelemen, Daniel R., *The Rules of Federalism: Institutions and Regulatory Politics in the EU and Beyond*, Cambridge, Mass.: Harvard University Press, 2004.

increasingly, of the European Parliament, of interest groups, of the European Court of Justice, and questions related to the perception of the integration process, notably the role of media in Europe and the effect of public opinion. With the Treaty of Maastricht, the elite-driven character of European integration came under public criticism. Eventually, the academic discourse about the EU's "democratic deficit"[53] was transferred from a scholarly construct in the context of the debate about legitimacy in European integration into a public catchword that was not allowed to be excluded in public speeches by European political leaders of all parties.

In the context of the governance discourse, John Peterson's attempt to structure the decision-making process of the European Union on different levels was most innovative. Each level would require the application of a different theoretical tool to understand it. On the "super-systemic" level, history-making decisions such as treaty revisions are taken. This level can best be understood by the application of macro-theories such as intergovernmentalism or neo-functionalism. On the "systemic" level, EU policy-setting takes place. Here, the insights of "new institutionalism" can best help to understand the operations. On the "meso level," Peterson argued, policy-shaping was at home. Its developments can best be understood by applying policy network analysis.[54] His proposal, said Ben Rosamond, "could be read as an attempt to partition EU studies into a further series of sub-disciplines, each with its prevailing 'normal science'."[55] Such a development would only reconfirm the original recognition of the European Union as a genuine polity requiring multifaceted academic methodologies and discourses in order to grasp the widely spread meaning and impact of its functions. Yet it would remain bound by the parameters of studies of integration functions and would not put in doubt the original assumption that the European Union is a federal union in so far as structure and normative goals regarding the dependent variable are concerned.

The academic study of European integration institutions is not only a matter of penetrating the working mechanisms of constitutionally defined institutions. It also entails reflections on institutions as norms and as norm-setting bodies, both in a formal and in an informal way. Rational choice methods were applied to the study of European integration in order to better understand the "structure-agency" and the "principal-agency" nexus. An important stream of literature dealt with the emerging European policy networks and the increasing meaning of trans-national party structures, economic interest groups and even the role of think-tanks in the European integration process.[56] The focus on policy-lobbying, agenda-setting, policy-making, and policy-

53 See Born, Hans (ed.), *The 'Double Democratic Deficit': Parliamentary Accountability and the Use of Force under International Auspices*, Aldershot: Ashgate, 2004.

54 Peterson, John, "Decision-Making in the European Union: Towards a Framework for Analysis," *Journal of European Public Policy*, 2.1 (1995): 69-94; Peterson, John, and Elizabeth Bomberg, *Decision-Making in the European Union*, London: Palgrave, 1999.

55 Rosamond, Ben, *Theories of European Integration*, op.cit.: 113.

56 See Boucher, Stephen, et al, "Europe and its Think-tanks: A promise to be fulfilled," *Notre Europe*, October 15, 2004, www.NotreEurope.asso.fr.

implementation could not reach ultimate answers to the most burning questions of all: What was to be the purpose of European integration for the next decades to come and where are the limits of European integration?[57]

Functionalist academic work, dealing with transaction costs, path dependencies, externalization of policies, network communities, deliberative methods of policy-formulation and the like had to come back to the ideational issues that lie at the core of European integration: Europe, why? It was no coincidence that with the study of deliberative methods of preparing political decisions in Europe, and with the focus on policy networks and actor-based models, such as epistemic communities or policy communities, original insights by one social science theory arose again; it returned to the field of European governance studies that had long been forgotten, but had stood at the cradle of the European Economic Communities: The transactionalist or communications approach to international integration. Initially, this theoretical work has been associated with the studies of Karl W. Deutsch and his research team in the 1950's. In the book "Political Community and the North Atlantic Area," Deutsch, a Sudeten-German emigrant scholar at MIT, Yale and Harvard, had argued that successful integration as defined by the absence of violent means of conflict resolution requires the establishment of pluralistic and amalgamated security-communities. Such communities would be defined by three principles: Compatible principled beliefs and values, the capacity of political groups to respond to each others' interests through the evolution of a sense of community, and the predictability of the partner's political, social and economic behavior. "The kind of sense of community that is relevant for integration," Deutsch argued, turned out in the course of his studies "to be rather a matter of mutual sympathy and loyalties; of 'we-feelings', trust, and mutual consideration; of partial identification in terms of self-images and interests; of mutually successful predictions of behavior, and of cooperative action in accordance with it – in short, a matter of a perpetual dynamic process of mutual attention, communication, perception of needs, and responsiveness in the process of decision-making."[58] These thoughts have not lost any of their meaning as far as the search for European constitutional patriotism is concerned.

Deutsch, whose intention it was to establish transatlantic relations as well as to promote European integration, characterized two types of integrated communities. The first type he labeled "amalgamated," meaning "the formal merger of two or more previously independent units into a single larger unit, with some type of common government after amalgamation." The second type he called "the pluralistic security-

57 See Howell, Kerry E., *Discovering the Limits of European Integration: Applying Grounded Theory*, Huntington, N.Y.: Nova Science Publishers, 2000.

58 Deutsch, Karl W., et al., *Political Community and the North Atlantic Area: International Organization in the Light of the Historical Experience*, Princeton: Princeton University Press, 1957: 36.

community," in which the legal independence of its constituent parts will be retained.[59] Of course, Deutsch could not foresee the development of NATO as a transatlantic pluralistic security community or of the European Union as Europe's "amalgamated" community. But his emphasis on continuous social learning in order to safeguard, transfer and revive the original structures once established has not lost any of its relevance for both the transatlantic community and the European Union five decades after first being formulated.

His work was quite prophetic, and at least premature, if we would apply his general theoretical understanding of social learning processes to the internal dynamics – both formal and informal – that has evolved in the European Union by now. The underlying habits that constitute a sense of community can only be learned, Deutsch noticed, "in the face of background conditions which change only slowly, so that they appear at any moment as something given – as political, economic, social, or psychological facts that must be taken for granted for the purposes of short-range politics. The speed and extent of this learning of habits of integrative political behavior are then influenced in each situation by these background conditions, as well as by the dynamics of the particular political process – the particular movement toward integration."[60] In 1968, Deutsch criticized federalist positions concerning European integration as advocating "premature overall amalgamation."[61] In 1993, with the Treaty of Maastricht in place, the focus increasingly broadened from economic integration to the study of political integration. It was not only about semantics that since the Treaty of Maastricht the name was changed from "European Community" to "European Union." Alberta Sbragia was one of the first to again recognize federalist theory as offering useful analytical tools to understand the new dynamics of European integration. After all, she argued, federalism is "an exercise in institutional creativity … not necessary a replication of existing institutional designs."[62] Surely, the debate on federalism was not over.

With the Treaty of Maastricht and the subsequent development of European Union politics, the issue of democratic legitimacy entered the center of the academic as well as the public discourse on European integration. The summary of the findings of Karl W. Deutsch and his team are still worth considering some five decades later as far as key criteria for assessing future success or failure of the European Union as a federal structure are concerned. The list of Karl Deutsch's criteria for judging success and failure in regional integration included:

- Mutual compatibility of main values.

59 Ibid.: 6.

60 Ibid.: 37.

61 Deutsch, Karl W., *The Analysis of International Relations*, Englewood Cliffs N.J.: Prentice Hall, 1968: 198.

62 Sbragia, Alberta, "Thinking about the European Future: The Uses of Comparison," in: Sbragia, Alberta (ed.), *Euro-Politics: Institutions and Policymaking the "New" European Community*, Washington D.C.: Brookings Institution, 1992:261; see also Kühnhardt, Ludger, *Europäische Union und föderale Frage: Europapolitik in der Umbruchzeit*, Munich: C.H. Beck, 1992.

- A distinctive way of life.
- Expectations of stronger economic ties or gains.
- A marked increase in political and administrative capabilities of at least some participating units.
- Superior economic growth on the part of at least some of the participating units.
- Unbroken links of social communication, both geographical between territories and sociological between different social strata.
- A broadening of the political elite.
- Mobility of persons, at least among the politically relevant strata.
- A multiplicity of ranges of communication and transactions.
- A compensation of flows of communications and transactions.
- A not too infrequent interchange of group roles.
- Considerable mutual predictability of behavior.[63]

Advocates of social constructivism, one of the most recent brands of theory on European integration, took some of the original suggestions of Deutsch further by referring to "identity-shaping effects on national agents," "shift in actor loyalty," "group dynamics," "social norms," "social mobilization" and "social learning."[64] One of the interesting features underlining the growing importance of social mobilization in the process of European decision-making is the fact that the number of transnational interest groups in Brussels has continuously increased since the founding of the EEC in 1957: Five decades later, 60 percent of around a thousand EU associations had their seat in Brussels, along with 250 European companies with their own lobbying office, and 285 consultancy companies.[65] This is not much compared to 23,000 registered non-profit sector organizations in the US or 1,700 organized groups in Denmark, but it indicates a trend.[66] It might also be a matter of measuring, because more than 10,000 lobbyists were registered in Brussels, although most of them only represent a single company or are their organization's only representative and thus do not qualify as a transnational interest group.

None of the European lobby groups would however have any lasting impact on Europe if their work were not related to the evolution of political institutions with

63 Deutsch, Karl W., et al., *Political Community and the North Atlantic Area*, op.cit.:58.

64 Thus Checkel, Jeffrey T., "Social Construction and European Integration," in: Christiansen, Thomas, et al. (eds.), *The Social Construction of Europe*, London: Sage Publications, 2001: 50-64; also see Wind, Marlene, *Europe Towards a Post-Hobbesian Order?: A Constructivist Theory of European Integration, or How to Explain European Integration as an Unintended Consequence of Rational State-Action*, Fiesole: European University Institute, 1996; Hermann, Peter (ed.), *European Integration Between Institution Building and Social Process: Contributions to a Theory of Modernization and NGOs in the Context of the Development of the EU*, Commack, N.Y.: Nova Science Publishers, 1999; Delanty, Gerard, and Chris Rumford, *Rethinking Europe: Social Theory and the Implications of Europeanization*, Abingdon: Routledge, 2005.

65 *Frankfurter Allgemeine Zeitung*, "Stadt der Lobbyisten," February 5, 2005: 17.

66 See Peterson, John, and Elizabeth Bomberg, *Decision-Making in the European Union*, op.cit.: 26.

legitimate decision-making powers. Only through institutions with the power to execute binding law will social norms continue to lead to habits of behavior, to economic discourses and institutional learning, to the ongoing search for institutional balance, and to growing repercussions of European integration within the structures and functions of its constituent parts, the member states of the EU. At the end of the 1990's, the European Commission estimated that about 30,000 participants annually attend meetings organized by the Commission in preparation for legislative initiatives or decision-making.[67] It is not surprising that the majority of them are civil servants from member states. But they contribute to the increasing nexus between formal and informal integration processes.

The functions of multilevel governance in the European polity will evolve in a continuously dynamic interplay with the evolution of the functions, old and new, of the EU member states, its civil societies and its social partners in an exponentially incomplete Single Market. Efficiency and effectiveness of the European Union will remain under academic scrutiny. The results might never be perfect and can only be relational to other possible options of organizing public life in Europe. Markus Jachtenfuchs has argued that the completion of the struggle over the polity-status of the European Union and the paradigmatic shift to governance analysis has two important implications: "It considerably broadens the field of inquiry and invites contributions from other sub-disciplines of political science, most notably from comparative politics, policy analysis and increasingly from political theory." The second consequence, according to him, is "a certain disjuncture between American and European scholarship, with the former focusing on classical integration theory and the latter more on the patterns and transformation of governance." He cites "differing degrees of exposure to the object of inquiry" as the main reason.[68]

This is a debatable argument. So far, most of the influential contributions to European integration theory were written by American scholars, with and without a European background. While the field of research broadens, as Jachtenfuchs rightly says, the range of comparative transatlantic academic research is also broadening. Recent scholarly contributions already give testimony to this potential. They contextualize research about the European polity and about multilevel governance in the European Union in a larger and increasingly unavoidable comparative framework: That of federalism and the prevalence of federal political structures on both sides of the Atlantic Ocean.[69] Comparative constitutional federalism will certainly add to and enrich

67 Ibid.

68 Jachtenfuchs, Markus, "The Governance Approach to European Integration," *Journal of Common Market Studies*, 39.2(2001): 255.

69 See Lenaerts, Koen, et al. (eds.), *Two Hundred Years of U.S. Constitution and Thirty Years of EEC Treaty: Outlook for Comparisons*, Brussels: Story-Scientia, 1988; Cappelletti, Mauro, et al. (eds.), *Integration Through Law: Europe and the American Federal Experience*, Berlin/New York: W. de Gruyter, 1995; Nicolaidis, Kalypso, and Robert Howse (eds.), *The Federal Vision: Legitimacy and Levels of Governance in the United States and the European Union*, New York: Oxford University

the increasing literature on "transatlantic governance."[70] It will cover a broader spectrum of issues and developments and by its very nature it will have to be more trans-disciplinary than ever, incorporating the perspectives of legal, economic, political and social scholarship on both sides of the Atlantic.

This might also help political philosophy to be reinstalled in its own right. The recognition of the federal character of the European Union as a category of political philosophy would mean a serious broadening of its perspective. The key terminology of political philosophy and democratic theory has matured parallel to the evolution of the modern European nation state. As the European nation states are increasingly – both constitutionally and habitually – amalgamated with the process of integration under the roof of the European Union, a genuine Europeanized political philosophy is yet to emerge.

It is surprising to see how ambivalent the adaptation of social science theory to new realities of European integration has been. While some academic forerunners have launched paradigmatic revolutions with the formulation of a new, mostly normative conceptual framework for the understanding of a given stage of European integration, others have been working on this paradigm way too long and were taken over or at least absorbed by a new stage of integration, which in time produced a new scientific paradigm as to how to assess this new stage of reality. However this cannot be a particular charge against academic contributions to understanding European integration. Often, also the actors who shape European integration have difficulties in staying their course, changing gears or refocusing the whole operation. Therefore it remains highly important to distinguish between the function of integration and its structure. The academic function will always be contingent on changing rationalizations, challenges, responses, priorities and crises. Academic literature reflected these trends throughout the first five decades of European integration. The federal structure and purpose of European integration was often invoked, either with energizing or skeptical intentions. Yet it succeeded in remaining constant and finally has become the "dependent variable" of European integration. In the meantime, the European Union is becoming what the Treaties of Rome initiated when they outlined the prospect for "an ever closer union": a European federation of unity in diversity.

Press, 2001; Fabbrini, Sergio, "Transatlantic Constitutionalism: Comparing the United States and the European Union," *European Journal of Political Research*, 43 (2004): 547-569; Gehler, Michael, et al. (eds.), *Towards a European Constitution: A Historical and Political Comparison with the United States*, Vienna: Böhlau 2005.

70 See Pollack, Mark A., and Gregory C. Shaffer (eds.), *Transatlantic Governance in the Global Economy*, Lanham: Rowman & Littlefield, 2001.

4. Union as Federation: The Logic of Structure

In spite of rudimentary beginnings, of detours, periods of stagnation and ever present crises, the process of European integration has advanced considerably since the signing of the Treaties of Rome in 1957 and the formal beginning of the European Economic Communities on January 1, 1958. More than fifty years of experience with the growth of European integration has been a continuous experience with expanding functions, changing ambitions and creeping, yet inescapable effects. The structural analysis of its functions was part and parcel of the integration process. Yet it was a structural assessment of functions and not of its foundation. Functional analysis did cover a wide range of issues – including ideas about integration goals, its method and its effects. It stretched into all possible policy spheres and finally approved the European Union as a polity, a body politic. Functional analysis also asked about the norms guiding the process, the principled belief of integration actors, the meaning of ideational memory, and the like. As Risse-Kappen put it: "If we want to understand the processes by which norms are internalized and ideas become consensual, we need to leave behind the logic of rational utility-maximizing actors, and incorporate the logic of communicative action."[71] Yet even this necessary change of perspective was mainly functional and followed functional intentions. It is no tautology to say that functionalism was the starting point of integration research because the starting point of integration was itself functional. Within the parameters of this technical approach to integration and the academic reflection about it, the notion of the underlying political structure was left outside the purview. So many actors and analysts alike were struggling with the notion of federalism because they confused structure and function. They tried to influence or explain functions of integration and their consequences by adding or preventing the addition of a label – "federal" – that neither explains these functions nor preempts the need to discuss it as a constitutional design "to indicate a number of devices which have, as their general object the relegating of certain subjects to the central government, and the leaving of other subjects to the state government," as one of the speakers in the Australian constitutional debates said.[72] No matter whether or not it is consensual to label the institutions of the European Union "government," de facto they constitute a centralized political regime. It is a polity with legally-rooted authority in norm-setting, consolidated power in norm-implementation and delegated yet stratified rule over the 491 million citizens of the European Union.

It has been a sad intellectual self-blockade of European integration theory to relate the idea of federalism only to the notion of the modern nation state. Federalism as concept and reality is a much older social and intellectual reality than the nation state. The nation state will not disappear because of supranational federalism. Nor can the

71 Risse-Kappen, Thomas, "Exploring the Nature of the Beast," op.cit.: 69.
72 Cited in Forsyth, Murray, "The Political Theory of Federalism," op.cit.: 31-32.

nation state remain the same with the consolidation of supranational federalism. Both experiences have been established in Europe. This is exactly the reason why functional research has defined the functional outcome of the process of integration, establishing the European Union as a polity and the mechanisms of the internal structure of the functions of the European Union as multilevel governance. None of this, however, undermines, eliminates or redefines the structure in which the European Union exerts its manifold functions. By measuring it with the help of established criteria emanating from the history of political ideas, the European Union must be called a federal structure.

Murray Forsyth has introduced three theoretical approaches to federalism. The first one, best expressed in Immanuel Kant's 1795 essay "On Perpetual Peace," is a moral theory of federalism. Kant's concept of a federal union of republics in Europe was based on his normative proposition to eliminate the root causes of war. The second stream of federal thought relates the federal structure among units of authority, power and rule with the idea of popular sovereignty and participatory self-rule. Authority, power and rule ought to be as close to the people as functionally advisable and possible. This was the thrust of thinkers as diverse as Jean-Jacques Rousseau, Pierre-Joseph Proudhon, the Anti-Federalists, and Pope Pius XI, who established the catholic social doctrine's principle of "subsidiarity" in his 1931 social encyclical "Quadragesimo anno," authored by the German Jesuit Oswald von Nell-Breuning in face of growing totalitarian and centralizing tendencies in many states of Europe.[73] The third current of thought is related to the work of the authors of "The Federalist Papers," promoting the adoption of the American Constitution drafted in Philadelphia in 1787. Forsyth credits Alexis de Tocqueville as having introduced this first concise theory of political federalism into European thought with his 1835 book on "Democracy in America." Political federalism, according to Forsyth, is simply "a phenomenon produced by the pulls and pressures of the political world, with its own logic distinct from that of the unitary state or the world of international relations. Here, federalism is the ensemble of structures and processes whereby a union of states or a union of polities is created and sustained, whether such a union results from a unitary system disaggregating itself, or from a number of political units coming together, or from a simultaneous movement in both directions."[74]

A federal union has to be characterized by arrangements that draw a line between insiders and outsiders – as the EU exercises its concept of European Union citizenship – with a permanent set of institutions – as the EU practices – and by an explicit will to go beyond conventional, treaty-based cooperation. A Union, he argues, has to be constitution-based in order to be called a Union. "The union," Forsyth argues, "does not abolish the constituent members, but rather exists alongside them." However, their right

73 As for the difficulties to implement subsidiarity in the EU see Wakonen, Jouko, *Implications of Federalism and the Principle of Subsidiarity in the Case of Science and Technology Development in Europe*, Turku: Turun yliopisto, 1995.

74 Forsyth, Murray, "The Political Theory of Federalism," op.cit.: 35.

to act internally and externally is "retained in certain spheres." This is equivalent to what Calhoun has labeled "reserved powers" in the context of US constitutional history. Its effect constitutes a union that "implies the co-existence of two such discretionary legislative powers, one at the center, one in the parts."[75] This analysis can also be used to characterize the European Union.

That fact that it is a federal union does not mean that the European Union must – or should – ever become a federal state. But its character as a Union makes the EU a federal entity. The debate about the term "federal" has often been heated among European actors and analysts alike. One of the reasons is misunderstanding and confusion about structure and function as related to the use of the term "federal." It is a semantic battle. In the German political tradition, "federal" means the rights of the constituent parts of a Union to uphold their prerogative, reserved rights. Therefore, the idea of European federalism resonates positive German experiences. In the British (or, for that matter, American) political tradition, "federal" means centralization at the expense of the constituent parts. Therefore the reproduction of the American experience in Europe is anathema to many British observers (and not only to British observers). But the semantic battle, de facto, is more than a semantic one. It is also a battle over limits of power, delegation of authority and the scope of rule. It is a genuine political battle. In fact, the term "federal" and the notion of federalism are often used to propagate or prevent certain concepts and policies directly related to the scope and limits of authority, power, and rule. The semantic component is relational to the political core of the debate. In fact, it is of secondary importance. It has nothing to do with the analytical core of the assessment that a union must be a federal structure in order to be a union. The British debate about the "f"-word is proof of the inherently federal character of a union that can, of course, be in endless disagreement over specific variants of authority, power, and rule without losing its structurally federal character.

The recognition of the European Union as a federal structure makes it easier to contextualize the functions and modes of operations of its institutions. Instead of remaining trapped in the old dichotomy between seemingly irreconcilable notions of intergovernmentalism versus supranationality, it will be analytically helpful to assess institutions of the EU as functional under the overall structure of a Union. This is, for example, relevant for the perception of the role of the Council. Often, the Council is considered an intergovernmental institution, almost naturally in opposition to the supranational institutions, European Commission and European Parliament. If that dichotomy would hold true, nobody could answer why EU member states have never curtailed and cut-back the legitimate power and authority of the European Court of Justice.[76] De facto, it is the most powerful authority that can rule on institutional and

75 Ibid.: 38.
76 See Frey, Bruno S., and Reiner Eichenberger, *The New Democratic Federalism for Europe: Functional, Overlapping, and Competing Jurisdictions*, Cheltenham: Edward Elgar, 1999.

even constitutional matters both horizontally among EU institutions and vertically within the member states of the European Union. The European Court of Justice, as Liesbet Hooghe and Gary Marks summarized it well, "does not merely act as an agent in adapting member state agreements to new contingencies. Through its rulings, it has engineered institutional changes that escape, and transcend, treaty norms. Supranational authority in the ECJ deepened from the 1960's, as a result of Court rulings, not because of treaty language. The constitutionalization of EU treaties is the product of Court activism, not of national government preferences."[77]

The reason for not trying to cut back the role of the European Court of Justice is rooted in the nature of the political character of integration politics. As in any law-based, parliamentary and democratic federal union, the actors assembled in the Council – and also those assembled in European Council summits, which is also a federal EU institution and, like the Council, is supported by a huge secretariat in Brussels that in turn is often asking the EU Commission, operating across the street, for support[78] – advocate political solutions, and if necessary, changes instead of redefinitions of the powers of the European Court of Justice. They recognize the law-based character of the European Union as a political federation. Yet, each of them – and as an institutional composite – considers law-making the political right of the Council. As much as this right is executed in co-decision with the European Parliament, conflicts of interests and battles over content and outcome of political bargaining are among the most normal events in a democratic parliamentary political system. The Council, Forsyth concluded, does "express an authentic federal principle, which is realized in all federal unions, whether in the form of diets, congresses, senates, or even conferences of premiers, namely the representation of the member units at the center of the union."[79]

The evolving extension of qualified majority voting in the Council underlines its character as a part of the federal structure of the EU. The EU is limiting rule not through the principle of separation of power, but the principle of interlocking powers. The proportion of unanimous votes in the Council has steadily decreased: from 49 percent under the Treaties of Rome to 45 percent under the Single European Act, to 35 percent under the Treaty of Maastricht. It rose again to 37 percent under the Treaty of Amsterdam, while with the Constitutional Treaty (and thus with the Treaty of Lisbon) this figure has gone down to 28 percent.[80] The Luxembourg Compromise of 1966 is

77 Hooghe, Liesbet, and Gary Marks, *Multi-Level Governance in the European Union*, op.cit.: 11.

78 It is interesting to note that according to an internal accounting of the European Commission in 1998, only an estimated five to ten percent of legislative proposals were created immediately inside the Commission. 35 percent of legislative proposals were the result of international treaty obligations, 25 to 30 percent amendments to or codifications of existing law, 20 percent requests from other EU institutions, national governments or interest groups and another ten percent obligations stemming from prior treaties: cited in Hooghe, Liesbet, and Gary Marks, *Multi-Level Governance in the European Union*, op.cit: 13.

79 Forsyth, Murray, "The Political Theory of Federalism," op.cit.: 40.

80 See Maurer, Andreas, *Die Macht des Europäischen Parlaments: Eine prospektive Analyse im Blick auf die kommende Wahlperiode 2004-2009*, Berlin: Stiftung Wissenschaft und Politik, 2005: 34.

often cited as the quintessential manifestation of the intergovernmental character of the structure of European integration. But also the Luxembourg Compromise was a transient phenomenon. Between 1966 and 1981, it was invoked less than a dozen times in order to block a decision by claiming vital national interests that made unanimity indispensable. The Luxembourg Compromise was invoked for the last time in 1985.[81] In other words, since then qualified majority voting or informal decisions based on gentlemen's agreement are the rule.

Technical-functional and federal-constitutional aspects of the European governance system are intrinsically linked and mutually impacting each other. Yet they are distinct analytical categories and describe different realities. Academic research will have to focus more on the dimensions that give life and meaning to any federal union: Matters of authority, power and rule. This includes, for instance, studies on the role of individual Commissioners, on Parliamentary Committees or the parliamentary factions in their interplay with national political parties. Although the European integration process has always been a highly political process, such quintessentially political questions have not found exhaustive attention in past academic considerations of European integration. As methodological and normative guiding devices, they must support research on policies, decision-making methods and administrative components of the European Union.

Unlike in the United States, the role of the executive – that is to say the government – is strong in most European countries. European governments are normally also stronger vis-à-vis their parliaments. Nobody would question the structure of, for example, German, Austrian or Belgian federalism because of this form of separation of power. It should therefore come as no surprise that the European Union also practices executive-dominant federalism. Another consequence of the European diversity and its overly pluralistic societal structures can be detected in the European revision of the classical notion of separation of power. Ironically, the European Union practices this longest standing principle of democratic theory exactly in the reverse order of the original proposition by Locke, Montesquieu and others: The European Union is a polity based on mutually interlocking powers. No law of nature has ever postulated that its effect might be different or less legitimate than the idea of an aseptic separation of powers, which is hardly practiced in any country in the world.

Federal structures will always vary from each other. Yet, the fundamental reasons in favor of this pluralistic arrangement for the practice of authority, power, and rule are constant: Fostering peace, promoting economic prosperity, protecting diversity, facilitating joint commitment, projecting stability and enhancing the joint influence of the constituent parts of the federation. There will always be discussion and dispute about the appropriate degree of how authority, power, and rule are distributed in a

81 See Hooghe, Liesbet, and Gary Marks, *Multi-Level Governance in the European Union*, op.cit.: 17-18.

federation. An efficient maximization of preferences cannot take into account only short-term gains, the time allocated to reach agreement and decision, and the legitimacy of input and of output factors as far as the process of agenda-setting, deliberation, policy-formulation, policy-decision and implementation is concerned. Academic research on "fiscal federalism" tries to identify the optimal allocation of authority, the organization of preferences and the distribution of resources.[82] Unitary political structures might always be advantageous as far as speed and implementation of norms and law is concerned. This cannot serve as an argument for strengthening the central decision-making and norm allocation in the European Union. Neither is it a protective argument for any of her constituent member states to advocate national primacy on principle. As far as the crucial indicators for a successful political entity are concerned, a continuous balancing of options will prevail. Loyalty of EU citizens will remain the primary source of stability. Only dynamic economic trends and the application of the principle of subsidiarity will enhance the allocation of authority. Only an inclusive yet normative and attentive democracy will be able to cope with the challenges of cultural diversity and normative pluralism. These are some of the topics to which research on European governance will have to direct itself.[83] They are relational as are all topics of democratic theory and order-building. The more the focus of research is directed toward the question of how the European Union deals with such challenges, the more the European Union will be characterized as an ever-stronger normalcy among the states and nations in Europe and within the global community.

In light of the missing consensus about the recognition of the European Union as a federal union, it is astonishing how far the empirical integration process has come. This nurtures the suspicion that the structural concept of federalism also has a tactical and thus a functional meaning. It is used in favor or in outright rejection of specific policies, methods of bargaining or conflict-resolution that might not only give an answer to a genuine matter of dispute, but also can change the parameters of power, authority and rule. The "empty chair crisis" between the France and her partners on the European level of multilevel governance was an early example. The "rebate debate" between the European level of multilevel governance in Europe and Great Britain was another example. The dispute about the weighting of votes in the Council between different European countries, with France and Germany in the leading veto seat, was a third example. None of these prevented the European Union from gradually and consistently constitutionalizing itself. The ultimate test case of EU recognition and legitimacy will not stem from the coherence of its basic treaties. The ultimate test case of recognition

82 See, for instance, Stehn, Jürgen, *Towards a European Constitution: Fiscal Federalism and the Allocation of Economic Competences*, Kiel: Institute of World Economics, 2002; Baimbridge, Mark, and Philipp Wyman, *Fiscal Federalism and European Economic Integration*, New York: Routledge, 2003.

83 See Follesdal, Andreas, "Federalism," op.cit: 7-8.

will be the degree of loyalty EU citizens express. Their sense of ownership – or the lack of it – will remain a "plebiscite de tous les jours," permanently mirrored and measured by results of Eurobarometer and other opinion polls. But it will also need to be studied through more long-term trends, voting patterns included. Backlashes remain inevitable, but each new achievement will reinforce the original promise of a new order for Europe through peace and freedom, affluence and solidarity, open to the world and ready to again shape the global order with the means acquired by the EU. Over time, this complex, contradictory and ever incomplete process will reinforce the "federalizing tendencies" Carl Joachim Friedrich had in mind when he called for a paradigmatic change in the study of European federalism that finally has come full circle as the European Union has matured into a federal union.

Prospects

XII. Toward European Patriotism?

1. Europe, Why?

The Second Founding of European integration has only begun. Since 1957, the project of European integration has been set against the mainstream of European history. Europe's political history was one of divisions and particularities. Integrating Europe has always accompanied this process as a cultural antithesis. It never became a viable political concept before the mid-twentieth century. European integration as it began with the signing of the Treaties of Rome has become the most successful utopia turned to life of the continent. At its heart, the constitution-building crisis that escalated in 2005 was the single most important adaptation crisis the European Union has gone through so far. The adaptation crisis of European integration is equivalent to its Second Founding. Its beginning cannot be identified with one single event or one single date on the calendar. Its outcome will not be identifiable either with one single event or one single date on the calendar. The unification of Europe post 1989 brought with it an enormous "widening" the integration of the continent. The need for a symmetric process of "deepening" European integration could hardly fail to follow suit. The immediate effort to frame European integration by the first ever European Constitution came too early. Yet, the constitution-building process that formally ended with the Treaty of Lisbon will continue as a factual process of ever deepening European integration through the deeds generated by the EU governance system.

The context of the Second Founding of European integration is important: Since the late 1980's, political leaders in many EU member states have increasingly defined the prospects for European integration by its limits and no longer by its opportunities. They were joined in this negativistic attitude by several leaders of new member states that joined the EU in the early twenty-first century. European integration was increasingly presented as a zero-sum-game, defined by the degree of national fiscal advantage: The more possible gains of others could be prevented, the better the own situation would be. This gross lack of solidarity and of an attitude of common interest did not remain without effect on many Union citizens. In the end, they were blamed by many of their own politicians for being euroskeptical or, at least, hesitant about deeper integration. As for the constitution-building process of the European Union, the results of the first decade of the twenty-first century were disappointing. Instead of implementing the visionary innovation of the first ever European Constitution, the EU experienced a growing gap of consensus between the political elites and the citizens of the EU. The sober repair work embodied in the 2007 Reform Treaty was nothing but a vague consolation for those advocating political union. While EU leaders blamed their own citizens for not understanding the matter properly, they returned to non-transparent backdoor diplomacy, thus undermining the encouraging experience with the Constitutional Convention of 2002/2003. And yet, as European integration went through a difficult period of re-calibrating its rationale, a new contract between Union citizens and Union politicians was to come about through a European Union that works, that is a European Union that is convincing by its success.

As the first decade of the twenty-first century came to a close, it was obvious that the European Union would only slowly regain momentum and dynamics. Years of defining integration by its limits could not be replaced overnight by a new attitude of opportunity and inspiration. It would take years, enormous political input and sustained success to make European integration as attractive as it could be. Reacting to the leadership confusion about the value added of European integration, many Union citizens had become hesitant to embrace a pro-active integration attitude. And yet, both political actors and ordinary citizens knew that there was simply no reasonable alternative to further and deeper integration. A positive, enabling response to the simple question "Europe, why?" had to reckon with the after-effects of a decade of mistrust and de-legitimization. Yet, in order to manage the consequences of the age of globalization, the European Union needs to prepare for a more coherent and effective projection of its global role. This, in turn, could only come about on the basis of a vibrant and dynamic European Union supported by its citizens. With this redefinition of the rationale for European integration, the question of democracy and transparency in EU decision-making has gained a new dimension. More than ever, the degree of ownership among its citizens had become the ultimate source of legitimacy for the continuation – and the deepening – of European integration in the further course of the twenty-first century. To permanently respond to this challenge is at the heart of the Second Founding of European integration.

Europe, why? This simple question can generate the most irritating set of answers:

- Europe as a leadership project, a Europe of conferences.
- Europe as a peoples' project, a Europe of its citizens.
- Europe as means to strengthen the nation states of the continent.
- Europe as partner to the world.
- Europe as a global power.
- Europe as the weak continent, obsessed with soft power that has forgotten the power of evil and destructive forces outside its own territory.
- Europe as synonymous with welfare-state democracy.
- Europe burdened with new social cleavages.
- Europe as engine of innovation.
- Europe as obstacle for socio-economic dynamics in its societies.
- Europe as museum and tourist destination.
- Europe as net contributor to the advancement of mankind.
- Europe as self-complacent protector of its unique stability and affluence.

- Europe as the advocate of an inclusive universalism, including the norms of morality.

This list may be extended. Each answer echoes perceptions, experiences and concerns. Each answer will find a corrective counter-answer. Europe, why? The adaptation crisis of the last decade of the twentieth and the first decade of the twenty-first century has not resolved the form and function of the political and legal constitution of the European Union.

Nobody would define Europe in the early twenty-first century as the exceptional continent or as the indispensable embodiment of global hope. The European Union was far from perfect or even coherent in form and performance. Yet, the interest of the world in the effects of European integration requires Europeans to reconsider the global meaning of their internal experience and ambition. With global economic, political and security activities, the issue of universal norms has returned to Europe. It used to be a matter of interest to European philosophers in the age of imperialism. It has become a challenge to Europeans coping with globalization and trying to understand it beyond simple layers of the economically evident: If globalization is not identical to Americanization, how can Europe relate globalization to universal norms as favored by Europeans? And how does Europe react to global threats against civilization emanating from asymmetrical warfare, terrorism in particular, failed or failing states, but also emanating from poverty, alienation, and social exclusion?

European integration has come a long way during its first five decades. Yet it is, not for the first time, confronted with resurging waves of doubt among the European citizenry why this project should proceed at all and how speedy and far-reaching it really should be. In the more abstract sphere of academia, this issue is framed as a matter of legitimacy of the European integration experience. In the sphere of politics and public opinion, the question – Europe, why? – is primarily answered by the ability of European politicians to deliver public goods to their voters. For academics, legitimacy is an abstract notion, combining elements of input-legitimacy and output-legitimacy. For most voters, legitimacy of a political system depends primarily on the outcome of a political system and process. Both approaches are not mutually exclusive, but they emphasize different priorities, reflect different perceptions, and are likely to receive different answers by political actors and academics.

For centuries, Europe dominated the world. Of course, Europe was not dominating "in the name of Europe" as Europe was never united in this endeavor. Individual European nations, countries and leaders were exploring the corners of the world to enhance the honor of their states. More than anybody before them, they put their mark on the world and organized the first wave of globalization. Exploration and conquest, colonial rule and colonial settlement, missionary work and geopolitical struggle – the legacy of the European quest for global dominance was as powerful as the rejection it provoked over time. When European nationalism reached its peak in the late nineteenth century, European countries were dominating the globe while at the same time embarking on the worst possible path to self-destruction. World War I was a turning point in world history when in 1917 two peripheral European powers emerged, the United States of America and Russia, soon to be the Soviet Union. While the US got involved in the war and hence became a European power, the communist revolution in Russia changed the ideological and strategic composition inside Europe dramatically.

Nationalism escalated into fascist rule in Italy, Spain and elsewhere. It escalated into racist, totalitarian rule under the National Socialist party in Germany, which ultimately destroyed most of Europe and Germany itself. Communist totalitarian rule in the Soviet Union represented the other undemocratic structure of politics with its own geopolitical ambitions and antagonisms.[1] World War II left all of Europe more powerless than ever, at the mercy of the peripheral powers, shaken to its ground and without any moral credibility in most of the world. The strongest European colonial powers, France and the United Kingdom, but also the smaller ones such as Belgium, the Netherlands and Portugal experienced the loss of colonial legitimacy. The European mission that had accompanied and justified centuries of global dominance had come to an end. The age of decolonization emerged with the independence of Indonesia in 1945 and of India and Pakistan in 1948. Other countries followed suit. While the United Nations was founded on October 24, 1945, by 51 countries (Poland joined later that year and became an original founding member), it grew to 192 member states by 2008. This was the result of European "imperial contraction"[2] and the global rise of independent states, most recently also on the fringes of integrated Europe.

(1) Reconciliation through Contraction

The process of decolonization occurred parallel to the emergence of European integration, and surpassed it at the end of the twentieth century. The global contraction of European empires was a reflection of European self-destruction, and at the same time the precondition for a new, post-imperial beginning in Europe. It turned out to be the opening chapter for a renewal of democracy in Europe and the emergence of European integration as a successful post-national experience of pooled sovereignty and shared political destiny.

It is important to understand the relationship between global contraction from colonial power and the rise of democracy inside of Europe. This dual process repeated itself with the demise of the Soviet Empire during the last decade of the twentieth

1 See Arendt, Hannah, "On the Nature of Totalitarianism: An Essay in Understanding," *Essays in Understanding 1930-1954, Hannah Arendt*, New York: Harcourt, Brace and Company, 1994: 328-360; Gleason, Abbott, *Totalitarianism: The Inner History of the Cold War*, New York: Oxford University Press, 1995; Herf, Jeffrey, *Divided Memory: The Nazi Past in the Two Germanys*, Cambridge, Mass.: Harvard University Press, 1997.

2 Abernethy, David B., *The Dynamics of Global Dominance: European Overseas Empires 1415-1980*, New Haven: Yale University Press, 2000: 325-344.

century. Europe had to become democratic in order to become anti-colonial. By becoming anti-imperial, it could become democratic. And it had to become anti-colonial and anti-nationalistic in order to learn the benefit of pooled sovereignty and shared political interests. The process of reconciliation that brought about this painful experience was the prelude to European integration. It was no surprise that European integration had to begin gradual and functional: it could not begin otherwise due to the asymmetrical experiences of its constituent member countries. Europe always maintained a certain degree of difference regarding the value and meaning of integration, mainly due to different historical experiences in the understanding of its peoples. While for all of Europe World War II had a defining meaning, for many decades the mind-set of many Europeans also remained influenced by the parameters of the age of nationalism and colonialism, of ideology and exclusivity. While World War II came to an abrupt end, the colonial legacy only gradually phased out until the 1980's. It is more than a historic accident that the end to colonial power in Namibia in March 1990 – the country had been under UN administration since 1966 – coincided with the breakthrough of democracy in Europe on a continental scale and the evolution of the strongest ever move yet toward pooled sovereignty in the EC with the Treaty of Maastricht aiming at Monetary Union and founding the EU.

The process of internal European reconciliation was not easy after two centuries of antagonistic developments that had not only defined the path of Europe's history but also the mind-set of most of its peoples. Overcoming national pride, exclusivity and hatred was as difficult for some Europeans as it was for others to give up the sense of exceptionalism, which had gone hand in hand with their countries' colonial power status. Reconciling with oneself, coming to terms with one's own history as well as with the perceptions of the others – without resorting to new variants of antagonistic reactions – was a daunting process indeed. During the second half of the twentieth century, hardly any European nation was spared this experience.

Reconciliation was the rationale of European integration when it began in 1957. Indeed, twelve years after the end of World War II, the founding countries of the European Economic Community wanted to change the dark course of European history. The price for non-integration was considered higher than any possible obstacle on the way to integration. Integration was not just about gentleness and friendly feelings. The seeds of integration were ingrained with mistrust and extremely disparate interests about the stake of the operation and the possible achievements ahead. Most notable were the differences between France and Germany. While leaders of both countries agreed to integration as a means to generate lasting peace, their motivations and interests could not have been more apart from each other: France wanted to maintain control of a defeated and divided Germany while both West and East Germany were looking for new recognition as civilized European countries, for a break with Germany's nationalistic and imperial path and for rehabilitation after the moral humiliation

National Socialist totalitarianism had brought about for the whole German nation with the Holocaust and World War II as its most horrible incarnations. The Eastern part of Germany was forced to do this in the communist orbit, the Western part of Germany opted for a policy of anchoring into the West. The smaller countries promoting European integration knew very well from the history of their geographic position between France and Germany that they could only benefit in stability, identity and affluence if their two contesting neighbors would embark on a future of peace, cooperation and ultimately integration. They could only win in a European federation, no matter how incomplete it was. The nationalistic and imperial overstretch of the bigger European countries helped to strengthen their positions in the newly emerging European order.

For a second time, the understanding of European integration as a means of reconciliation resonated strongly after the demise of communist totalitarianism in 1989/1990. The countries that had been forced to live behind the iron curtain claimed their European-ness and requested integration into the European Union to ensure and guarantee their moral claim. The search for reconciliation was of specific relevance for Germany and most post-communist countries as practically all of them had been conquered by Nazi Germany at some point during World War II, handed over to the Soviet Union, like the three Baltic republics Estonia, Latvia and Lithuania, or had become Soviet satellites as a consequence of Hitler's war and Stalin's victory. After 1990, the idea became popular in Germany that a similar effort ought to be initiated between Germans and Poles as had happened between Germans and French after 1945: The "Weimar Triangle" was established, a formal and informal set of links between France, Germany and Poland. It was aimed at providing a supplementary mechanism for policy consultations and societal activities between France, Germany and Poland. The "Weimar Triangle" was considered a means to support the Polish claim for EU membership while strengthening the commitment of France for the accession of Poland and other post-communist countries and getting Germany more strongly involved with its new democratic neighbor in the East.[3] The success of the "Weimar Triangle" remained limited, however. Most disappointing, the "Weimar Triangle" could not prevent new controversies among Europeans, including its three partners, during the Iraq crisis in 2002/2003, could not facilitate the ratification of the European Constitution in 2005, and was not helpful during the budgetary battles of 2003-2005. True and sustainable reconciliation ought to link bilateral efforts of reconciled neighborhoods with EU-wide efforts to promote common perceptions on main issues and common interests on key goals.

3 See Kühnhardt, Ludger, Henri Menudier, and Janusz Reiter, *Das Weimarer Dreieck*, ZEI Discussion Paper C 72. Bonn: Center for European Integration Studies, 2000.

(2) Renewed Self-Esteem through Integration

To balance interests was a precondition should the noble idea of reconciliation work among European nations. This was the logic of functional sector-specific integration and it remained its logic beyond the completion of a European common market. The participating European states transformed into a new form, thus contributing to a new European reality. Reconciling with neighbors that had been perceived as enemies for a long time meant to break from the nationalist past. Balancing interests with competitors in a European market and with rivals in the pursuit of geostrategic interests meant breaking from the primacy of sovereignty as manifested in the Westphalian state-system since the end of the Thirty Years War.

The Westphalian state-system had come about on the basis of two principles, transformed into two goals: The nation state should be sovereign while its internal political system became immune to any external criticism or challenge. On this basis, respectful co-existence could grow in parallel if no antagonistic developments in the political system of the participating states emerged, and there was no breach of the founding principles. This is why the Westphalian system was not challenged by war or contesting political systems for a long time. Paradoxically, conflicts and confrontations did, in fact, reinforce the original Westphalian system. The most fundamental challenge to the Westphalian state-system occurred after World War II and it occurred through peace and democracy.

The Westphalian state-system was the product of the Thirty Years War of the seventeenth century. The European integration experience as epitomized in the evolution of the European Union is the product of the Thirty Years War of the twentieth century. As much as there were intermissions from fighting between 1618 and 1648, the period from 1914 to 1945 was more than a period of two unrelated wars with global consequences: 1914 to 1945 constituted a second Thirty Years War with ideological, territorial, geopolitical and socio-political dimensions of unprecedented consequences. The most important cultural consequence for Europe was the discovery of the benefits of integration.

This discovery began before the war had ended. Historical research on the origins and early developments of European integration post-World War II suggests that the governments involved supported integration because they considered this as the best possibility to advance their national interests.[4] Among a bundle of political, economic and social interests, all European governments were interested in the speedy recovery of their economies. To foster a new social consensus did not require democratic governance alone, but also social progress, both for the industrial and agrarian sectors of the society. In the case of France, the interest to contain Germany remained strong, while for West Germany to regain recognition and respect was of the highest interest. The launching of the European Coal and Steel Community in 1952 provided the best

4 See Milward, Alan, *The European Rescue of the Nation State*, London/New York: Routledge, 1992.

possible win-win situation for all participating countries. German coal and steel production was put under supranational authority, giving France access to the German natural resources it needed for its own recovery, while West Germany was again gaining respect on the European level. A win-win situation also developed for other participating countries. When Belgium's steel industry, the country's main employer, ran into problems in the late 1950's, the restructuring plan launched by the European Coal and Steel Community involved large sums of subsidies to retrain workers and modernize the industry.

The early success of sectoral economic integration enabled the governments involved to present themselves as representing the key interests of their nations. The eagerness of Great Britain to join the European Economic Community during the 1960's was based on the assumption that the United Kingdom would require partnership with Europe beyond the existing trade links through the European Free Trade Association and the Commonwealth. At a later stage, Greek, Spanish and Portuguese EU membership were perceived as a contribution to the full recovery of national self-esteem after their respective dictatorships were overthrown. The same argument gained prominence in post-communist countries applying for EU membership beginning in the early 1990's. EU membership was not only considered a necessary precondition for successful socio-economic transformation, but also a state strategy to enhance the self-esteem of the respective nations and their external reputations.

Motivation for European integration was always as multifaceted as the interests of those engaged in the process. The continuous acceptance of the integration logic was striking as its nature was changing over time. Reconciliation among post-communist countries based on the notion of free democratic rule and reconciliation between them and the countries and societies of Western Europe was a plausible and laudable endeavor after 1989. It was not intuitively self-explanatory why the countries of the "old" European Union should wish to pursue further integration now that they had achieved the original goal of reconciliation among themselves. But they did, and they even pushed the integration process to a higher level while preparing for the accession of post-communist neighbors. In doing so, the structure of European integration began to change.

(3) A New Global Role through Self-Transforming Europeanization

It is important to look back to the origin of early motivations and driving forces of integration. It is likewise useful to connect the experience of Western Europe with the hopes of Central and Eastern Europe in order to understand the dynamics of a new phase of integration that unleashed after the fall of the Berlin Wall. European reconciliation could only be completed with all those European states and nations joining the EU who wanted to do so. While this process was in parallel to the emergence of a European currency, it became evident that the dynamics of integration would be brought to another level. This process already indicated that the logic of integration would not come to a close with the completion of inner European reconciliation. This goal remains valuable although incomplete as long as parts of South Eastern Europe are left out and the question of ultimate territorial borders of the European Union is unresolved. But from these pending questions, it was evident since the 1990's that the rationale of European integration had already begun to go beyond the original logic of reconciliation.

Increasingly, European integration began to be perceived as a project of political integration, shaped by the underlying identity of a community of values. European integration also began to aim for a more comprehensive and pro-active foreign and security policy, thus underlining the prospects of a new global role of Europe. This would not be a revival of the European role as it was known during centuries of exploration, colonialism and imperial glory. Europe was growing into a different global meaning and had already begun contributing to a new understanding of world order. While Europe's legacy of exploration, colonial conquest and imperialism echoed much of the internal social and political forces of Europe during that particular period of time, the evolution of Europe's global role during the twenty-first century was to echo the new internal trajectories of Europe, the socio-political underpinnings and the political culture of the European Union.

Europeanization gained a twofold meaning. On the one hand, it meant the continuous process of forming structures and policies of integration, be it supranational or intergovernmental – it meant "building Europe;" on the other hand, EU member states became aware of the impact of these very structures and policies on their domestic political systems and the social and economic life in every member state.[5] While the first wave of the integration process was happily supported by national politicians as they could convey the successful effects of "building Europe" to their constituencies, the second wave of Europeanization challenged the rationale for

5 See Ross, Georg, and Andrew Martin, *European Integration and the Europeanization of Labor*, Madrid: Centro de Estudios Avanzados en Ciencias Sociales, 1998; Schout, Adrian, *Internal Management of External Relations: The Europeanization of an Economic Affairs Ministry*, Maastricht: European Institute for Public Administration,1999; Börzel, Tanja A., and Thomas Risse, *When Europe Hits Home: Europeanization and Domestic Change*, Fiesole: European University Institute, 2000; Harmsen, Robert, and Thomas M. Wilson, *Europeanization: Institution, Identities and Citizenship*, Amsterdam: Rodopi, 2000; Smith, Mitchell P., *Who are the Agents of Europeanization?: EC Competition Policy and Germany's Public Law Banks*, Fiesole: European University Institute, 2001; Jordan, Andrew, *The Europeanization of British Environmental Policy: A Departmental Perspective*, Basingstoke: Palgrave Macmillan, 2002; Gehler, Michael, *Zeitgeschichte im dynamischen Mehrebenensystem: zwischen Regionalisierung, Nationalstaat, Europäisierung, internationaler Arena und Globalisierung*, Bochum: Dieter Winkler, 2001; Behning, Ute, *Trends of Europeanization in Social Welfare Politics*, Wien: Institut für Höhere Studien, 2002; Featherstone, Kevin, and Claudio M. Radaelli (eds.), *The Politics of Europeanization*, Oxford/New York: Oxford University Press, 2003; Cini, Michelle (ed.), *European Union Politics*, Oxford/New York: Oxford University Press, 2003; Jones, Alun, and Julian Clark, *Europe and Europeanization*, Abingdon: Routledge, 2007.

integration and the legitimacy of the whole process. The more EU structures grew in importance, the more they were questioned – sometimes because of the inherent uncertainty over their final destination, sometimes because of the loss of autonomous decision-making they brought for the individual nation states. At the turn of the twenty-first century, the benefits of integration did not find the same level of advocacy as used to be in the 1980's and early 1990's. Depending on how one interprets this trend, one could say it was proof that integration had become serious and was affecting more citizens than ever.

Since the 1990's – and, of course, not across the whole EU – the concept of pooled sovereignty has begun to be perceived as threat to autonomous national decision-making. Sharing resources was increasingly portrayed – by timid politicians, parochial media and static academics – as a means for losing national resources to a bureaucratic EU that might reallocate these resources outside of the criteria of efficiency and transparency. The connection between Europe and "the rest of the world" made the strongest impression on this debate and its underlying uncertainties. While the introduction of a common European currency was criticized as undermining national sovereignty and decision-making, it won support as an expression of a stronger European role in the global economy. Threat perceptions due to events outside the EU remained crucial to advance the common foreign and security policy of the European Union.

None of these trends took place unchallenged. Whenever European integration came under public or political pressure, its proponents were quick to refer to the benefits while skeptics were quick to point to the costs and risks.[6] This was an ongoing discourse in which the media often took the side of "risk-sensitivity" over "integration-opportunity." Academic research did gradually begin to reflect the two-dimensional character of "Europeanization," largely focusing on the impact of liberalization on internal economic structures due to EU policies. While in some countries – for instance as far as transportation systems in the United Kingdom and in the Netherlands are concerned – EU initiatives followed domestic liberalization efforts, in other countries the EU triggered adaptational pressure of unprecedented nature.[7] Largely, this trend went beyond the completion of the common market and had a growing effect on political decision-making in many policy sectors. The economic giant was finally overcoming its status as a geopolitical dwarf.

In the context of the completion of the Single Market, it has been argued that it had become superfluous to maintain twenty-seven national economic ministers with an EU

6 See Taylor, Paul, *The End of European Integration: Anti-Europeanism Examined*, Abingdon: Routledge, 2007.

7 See Green Cowles, Maria, et al. (eds.), *Transforming Europe: Europeanization and Domestic Change*, Ithaca: Cornell University Press, 2001; Schild, Joachim, "Europäisierung nationaler politischer Identitäten in Deutschland und Frankreich," *Aus Politik und Zeitgeschichte*, 3.4 (2003): 31-40.

responsible for more than 80 percent of economic legislation in Europe (In 2009, the German Parliament assessed that by then only 31.5 percent of German legislation originated in EU decisions). In the context of the EU's Common Foreign and Security Policy of the EU optimists began already to wonder how long it would take to raise the question of the need and legitimacy of 27 national European foreign ministers. In factual terms, a long way would have to be gone in order to achieve this formalized level of Europeanized foreign and security policy. But the "ghost" of intensified and irretrievable supranationality could not be returned to the bottle, even if the strongest proponents of continuous primacy of national sovereignty tried to do so.

2. Layers of a European Public Sphere

The emergence of a European public sphere is a multidimensional and complex issue. The argument that Europe does not have one people, one demos, and therefore it cannot produce either a public sphere or a political system has turned out to be too simplistic. The European public sphere is certainly not growing in quantum leaps and without the continuous role of the public sphere in each of the member states of the EU. Yet, a European public sphere is emerging. The question "Europe, why?" has been taken to political elites across the EU. They are involved in formal and informal debates, often linked to institution-building inside the EU. The issue "Europe, why?" has also been grasped by larger parts of the Union's public. Media and other sectors of civil society, but also the European Union's citizenry at large have begun to accommodate EU matters in their daily lives. The emerging transformation of the character of political, socio-economic and cultural aspects of identity in Europe has become noticeable in many strata of political and public life. The continuation of these trends – and there cannot be any doubt that they are continuing – will remain and, in fact, will increasingly become elements of an evolving constitutional patriotism in Europe. Undoubtedly, a communicative space is in the making.[8]

(1) A Community of Recollections

Translating collective memories into permanent and lasting political commitments is one key to failure or success of the European Union. Collective memories alone will not suffice to define the identity, strength and future direction of the European integration process. But it will remain an important element in this process. Europe will always

8 See Fossum, John Erik, and Philip R. Schlesinger (eds.), *The European Union and the Public Sphere: A Communicative Space in the Making?*, Abingdon: Routledge, 2007; see also Bellamy, Richard, and Alex Warleigh, *Citizenship and Governance in the European Union*, London/New York: Continuum, 2005; Herrmann, Richard K., et al. (eds.), *Transnational Identities: Becoming European in the EU*, Lanham: Rowman & Littlefield, 2005.

continue to ponder its past and only gradually discover its future. Increasingly, the shared memories of Europe – be they divisive or unifying – are turning into a solid normative building-bloc for the EU's claim of being a community of values.

Europe's global projection during the age of imperialism and world wars had ultimately led to moral disdain and political failure. During three centuries, Europe's ideological battles had provoked political and military battles all of which Europe was losing in the end. Europe cannot build a good future by trying to fence off the continent against the uncertainties of globalization and the contingent demands from all over the world. The desire of Europe's citizens to live in peace and to pool resources in order to enhance their collective stability and individual affluence cannot work by neglecting external realities. Europe cannot become an archipelago in the midst of the real world of the twenty-first century. Europe has always been part of global developments and will remain so, for better or worse.

Europe, why? – raising this question is more than the invitation to a friendly discourse about European culture and identity. The question about the purpose of European integration must invariably broaden Europe's view and recognize its role in the world at large. During the period of decolonization, the European nation state had become the model for people in the whole world. In many cases, nation-building followed the act of formal independence and ended in ambivalence. Failing states instead of nation-building began to be a matter of concern for the world. But struggling with the Westphalian state-system was more than an option for other countries. In spite of most recent trends to learn from the European integration experience, independent statehood has become an overall global reality. Other regions have begun to define their own mechanisms of regional integration, but Europe should not simply resort to pride in this proliferation of its latest innovation. It was well advised to learn from others as far as the preconditions of social and political dynamism are concerned. The nature of world affairs and the consequences of the global economy forced Europe to broaden the rationale of integration. The European Union's claim of being a community of values was to be linked both to Europe's past and to Europe's future global presence.

John Stuart Mill talked about the "community of recollections"[9] that will inevitably shape any political identity. Common history and memory cannot be dissolved. Nobody can run away from the cradle one is born into, and we all are linked to the unborn whether we like it or not. Memory can be painful and joyous, focused or obscured. It will always return and never be forgotten. The idea that a society can conceptualize itself anew and fresh as if embarking under a veil of historical ignorance can hardly be maintained. Most people, places and regions in the world are confronted with too much history to digest and only few can translate historical memory into the successful

9 Mill, John Stuart, *Considerations on Representative Government*, Amherst: Prometheus Books, 1991:308. On the meaning of memory for community-building see Booth, James W., "Communities of Memory: On Identity, Memory, and Debt," *The American Political Science Review*, .93.2 (1999): 249-263.

encounter of the future. Memory can entail debt to the past and its actors. It can nurture guilt and shame, pride and happiness. Never can memory be reduced to limited notions of truth if it is to stand the test of time. Europe's memories are defined by great hours and dark times. Since the age of the nation state began, they were mostly brought down to the next generation taking for granted one's own memory as being different from the memory of one's neighbor.

This is why the noble effort to write a common European history book is met with fascination and skepticism. It will take some more time before a common European history book may finally be accepted for higher education all over Europe.[10] Historical research has shown that the correct notions and interpretations of historic events and processes are still distorted by the legacies of national bias. Yet, most Europeans relate to the same images of history even if they have extremely different interpretations. At the outset of the twenty-first century, an analysis of school text books from Albania, Austria, Belarus, Belgium, Bosnia-Herzegovina, Bulgaria, Croatia, Czech Republic, Denmark, Finland, France, Germany, Greece, Great Britain, Hungary, Ireland, Italy, Latvia, Lithuania, Macedonia, Moldova, Netherlands, Norway, Poland, Portugal, Romania, Russia, Sweden, Switzerland, Serbia, Montenegro, Slovakia, Slovenia and Spain has identified the most widely repeated paintings and photographs across Europe, even beyond the European Union, a telling proof of some defining images in Europe's self-interpretation:

- John Trumbull, The American Declaration of Independence (July 4, 1776).
- Jacques-Louis David, The Oath at the beginning of the French Revolution, (June 20, 1789).
- Eugène Isabey, Session of the Congress of Vienna (1815).
- Eugène Delacroix, The massacre at Chios (1822) and Greece on the ruins of Missolunghi (1826).
- Anton Alexander von Werner, The proclamation of the German Empire at Versailles castle (January 18, 1871).
- William Orpen, The Signing of Peace in the Hall of Mirrors, Versailles (June 28, 1919) or a related photography of the event.
- Photography: Lenin talks to Red Army soldiers (May 20, 1920).
- Pablo Picasso, The bombardment of Guernica (April 26, 1937).
- Photogprahy: The Yalta Conference (February 4-11, 1945).
- Photography: The Soviet flag over the German parliament in Berlin (May 2, 1945).

10 One excellent effort is the work edited by Delouche, Frédéric (ed.), *Illustrated History of Europe: A Unique Portrait of Europe's Common History*, London: Cassell, 2001.

- Photography: Fall of the Berlin Wall (November 9, 1989).[11]

Every student will draw individual conclusions from looking at these pictures and photographs. But some collective consequences can be identified as plausible outcomes of the collective power of these images. They constitute fundamental elements of the "community of recollection" that has evolved in Europe:

- Rejection of imperialism.
- Rejection of totalitarianism.
- Sensitivity to hegemonic dominance.
- Primacy of human dignity and human rights.
- Appreciation for freedom and solidarity.
- Confidence in rule of law and multilateral political processes.

These elements help define Europe as a community of values. They originate in the collective memory of Europeans. 1789, 1945 and 1989 were outstanding turning points on the mental map shaping European identity and constitutionalism. But also the idealism of the American independence, the struggle of liberalization from the Ottoman Empire and the totalitarian terror of communism are inscribed into the psychology of Europeans across the continent. While the legacy of the French Revolution remains contested among historians, its creed of liberty, equality and solidarity is alive as a European mantra. While the legacy of early national constitution-building and parliamentary rule has found widespread resonance in Europe, the Europeanization of the processes of 1848 has not yet attracted sufficient public appreciation. While 1945 was not an hour zero, it marked the end of horrible experiences of war and destruction across Europe. While the peaceful revolution of 1989 was more relevant for Central and Eastern Europeans, the rise of freedom and democracy across the Central and Eastern part of Europe has become a constitutive element on the mental map of all Europeans.

From the fall of the Bastille in Paris to the fall of the Wall in Berlin, Europe has acquired a long and solid thread of memories that have entered the collective memory of the continent. Among these memories were the most evil abysses mankind could possibly look into, notably the Holocaust. Among these memories were uplifting signs of courage, notably the peaceful revolution for freedom in Central and Eastern Europe. Europe as "community of recollections" is a combination of good and bad memories. When they are transformed into an obligation for shaping Europe's future, they are transformed from mere facts of history into meaningful elements of a "community of recollections" that wants to be recognized as a "community of values." The grand historical narrative of Europe serves as fertile ground for the contemporary evolution of

11 See Popp, Susanne, "Auf dem Weg zu einem europäischen "Geschichtsbild": Anmerkungen zur Entstehung eines gesamteuropäischen Bilderkanons," *Aus Politik und Zeitgeschichte*, 7.8 (2004): 23-32.

European identity and interests.[12] The last chapter of this narrative was written during the Wars of Yugoslavian Succession in the 1990's. While European diplomacy and politics were reluctant to engage and stop the violence in Yugoslavia, the European public increasingly demanded action on behalf of European values betrayed in the killing fields of Yugoslavia.[13] Ultimately, the ethnic cleansing in Kosovo in 1998/1999 became a turning point in the European reaction to the legitimate use of force. Before ethnic cleansing in Kosovo, most European societies were extremely reluctant to use military actions on behalf of European values and interests. The Kosovo tragedy helped to turn this perception: Now public opinion demanded military action because of Europe's long history of warfare. The European community of recollections has begun to turn into a community of values.

(2) Rooting of Common Experiences

The European integration experience began as antithesis to Europe's history of nationalism. As a counter-historical process it has generated its own history of shared experiences. These experiences with European integration have been added to the collective memory of Europeans. In many societies of Central and Eastern Europe, the original experience of Western Europe has been reiterated and reconfirmed in the course of the peaceful revolution of 1989. Most evident is the freedom to travel. While European borders were rather open before World War I, they had been sealed off increasingly over the century, only disappearing in their most evil form after 1989. Freedom to travel as embodiment of individual freedom has turned from a silent longing of many into the most normal activity for all European citizens.

Living with common European institutions has become normalcy and shared experience. EU citizens may be skeptical about the conduct of these institutions; they may have limited knowledge about how they operate and they still may consider their national political and legal institutions as prime expressions of rightful and legitimate processes of law making. Yet, European institutions have become an element in the collective reflection of Europeans concerning politics and the law impacting their lives. Differences in the degree in which these institutions were felt as imposing their will powerfully and immediately were obvious between Western Europe and the new post-communist member states. In Western Europe, European institutions were experienced

12 See Wilson, Kevin, and Jan van der Dussen (eds.), *What is Europe?: The History of the Idea of Europe*, London/New York: Routledge, 1995; Pagden, Anthony (ed.), *The Idea of Europe: From Antiquity to the European Union*, Washington D.C.: Woodrow Wilson Center Press, 2002.

13 See Naimark, Norman, *Fires of Hatred: Ethnic Cleansing in Twentieth-Century Europe*, Cambridge, Mass.: Harvard University Press, 2001: 139-184 ("The Wars of Yugoslavian Succession"); Biermann, Rafael, *Schattenjahre: Das Scheitern der internationalen Konflikteinwirkung im Kosovo vor Kriegsbeginn*, Paderborn: Schöningh, 2005; Ahrens, Geert-Hinrich, *Diplomacy on the Edge: Containment of Ethnic Conflict and the Minorities Working Group of the Conferences on Yugoslavia*, Washington D.C.: Woodrow Wilson Center Press, 2007.

as gradually emerging since the 1950's. So was the law they generated. European Community law gradually became the focal point for experts, yet only rarely for ordinary citizens. Post-communist democracies were confronted with the European institutions as they had emerged by the late 1980's. The people of post-communist Europe had to learn that in order to join the EU, they would have to accept and absorb European Community Law, the *acquis communautaire*. Their experience was not one of gradual phasing in. European law and European institutions became immediate forces of strong power and external pressure once the post-communist countries had decided to apply for EU membership.

A similar experience for people in twelve EU countries was the introduction of the euro. They had heard of the project of a common currency, of course. But the phases leading to the complete introduction of the euro were not used for broad public reflection, no matter how strong some of the debates about further advancement of the project were. For most Europeans, the introduction of the euro as legal tender came overnight on January 1, 2002. The adaptation to this new reality had to follow later. The euro became the most important element of a practically shared experience in European integration.

Public opinion remains a debatable criterion on which to base the understanding of the legitimacy of the integration experience. Yet, it is widely considered an important element for "measuring the pulse" of European citizens. In 1973 the European Commission introduced the Eurobarometer survey in order to better understand public opinion in the Community. Ever since, Eurobarometer surveys have become an institution of their own.

Among the most basic questions continuously asked is the one inquiring whether or not membership in the Common Market/European Community/European Union is perceived as a good thing, a bad thing, or neither a good nor a bad thing for one's country. The 1974 Eurobarometer poll found that 59 percent considered EC membership of their country a good thing, 18 percent had no opinion and 14 percent found it a bad thing.[14] In 1984, 55 percent of EC citizens found their country's membership a good thing, 11 percent found it a bad thing and 27 percent remained neutral.[15] The all time high of support for EU membership was polled in spring 1991 with 72 percent of citizens of EU member states in favor of it. In 1994, 54 percent expressed satisfaction with their country's membership in the European Union, 13 percent found it a bad thing and 27 percent found it neither a bad nor a good thing.[16] In 2004, 48 percent considered EU membership a good thing, 17 percent found it a bad

14 European Union. European Commission, *Eurobarometer No. 1*, July 1974, http://ec.europa.eu/public_opinion/archives/eb/eb1/eb1_en.pdf.

15 European Union. European Commission, *Eurobarometer: European Election Special*, May 21, 1984, http://ec.europa.eu/public_opinion/archives/eb/eb21/eb21_en.pdf.

16 European Union. European Commission, Eurobarometer No. 41, July 1994, http://ec.europa.eu/public_opinion/archives/eb/eb41/eb41_en.pdf.

thing and 29 percent were neutral.[17] By the end of 2009, 53 percent considered EU membership of their country a good thing, 15 percent found it a bad thing and 32 percent were neutral.[18] The figures given by Eurobarometer require methodological clarification as their results never add up to a neat and clean 100 percent. But more importantly, they reflect a continuous trend of support for EU membership, echo the skepticism (in no EU member states can a majority be found that would be against membership of their respective country), but also rather widespread neutrality about the EU. Comparing the European data with patterns of public opinion in other stable democracies one may conclude that all in all this data indicates normalcy in the citizen's experience with EU realities.

The Eurobarometer polls support the assessment that gradually a European sphere of communication is emerging. Satisfaction and dissatisfaction with European integration are measured not only as far as the general question of support for integration or dislike for it is concerned. During more than three decades of operation, Eurobarometer surveys have increasingly developed sophisticated modes of polling opinion on all relevant issues of European politics. In doing so, Eurobarometer surveys contribute to the evolving European constitutionalism.

The most critical argument against the possibility of political union in Europe relates to the absence of a European people, a European demos. However, the very reference to the concept of demos as criteria for measuring the EU's legitimacy shows the limits of this charge: There have been many fundamental empirical developments and conceptual transformations in the notion of demos from ancient Greek city-states to modern nation states. Instead of focusing on the static dimension of existing nations, it would be more useful to consider the evolution of the European public sphere as the underlying ferment of an evolving political identity of Europe – and vice versa.

The practical absence of homogenizing European media and the multilingual character of Europe should not lead to short-sighted conclusions concerning the nature and impact of Europe's public sphere. The Age of Enlightenment was a pan-European phenomenon notwithstanding language barriers and the absence of a European body politic. In the same sense, a public sphere has emerged in Europe since the beginning of the European integration experience. This public sphere is made up of peculiarities stemming from its overriding character as being "a composite rather than a homogenous public sphere." Yet, a public sphere has emerged in Europe, rooted in a "history of transfers and links between national public spheres."[19]

17 European Union. European Commission, *Eurobarometer Spring 2004: Public Opinion in the European Union*, July 2004, http://ec.europa.eu/public_opinion/archives/eb/eb61/eb61_en.pdf.

18 European Union, European Commission, *Eurobarometer 71: Public Opinion in the European Union*, September 2009, http://ec.europa.eu/public_opinion/archives/eb/eb71_std_part1.pdf

19 Kaelble, Hartmut, "The Historical Rise of a European Public Sphere," *Journal of European Integration*, 8.2 (2002): 10.

The most evident and least controversial fact relates to the language plurality in Europe. Often, it is cited as the quintessential barrier preventing the evolution of a sphere of communications in Europe. Caution would be recommended in dealing with this argument. Not only Switzerland demonstrates the possibility of multilingual democracy in Europe. Language barriers have come down significantly since the process of European integration started in the 1950's. At that time only around 10 percent of Europeans spoke a foreign language. Five decades later about half of all Europeans speak a foreign language, and among the younger generation of Europeans, two thirds do so. Most of them consider English as the most convenient and useful foreign language, followed by French, German and Spanish. Notwithstanding the debate about cultural homogenization and the fear to lose knowledge of and interest in other languages due to the dominating use of English, the practical value of this development is significant. It is not only the social elite that is able to communicate across Europe. As language is both a means of communication and a gateway to another culture, the practical value of a common international foreign language as means of Europe-wide communication should not be underestimated as a contribution to the evolution of a European public sphere.

(3) Future as Common Destiny

Pooling sovereignty and sharing resources has helped Europe to overcome the grave crisis of power, internal self-esteem and global reputation it had been dragged into during the nineteenth and twentieth century.[20] During the second half of the twentieth century, Europe was able to overcome much of this in the name of rule of law, post-nationalistic democracy and regional integration. In many ways, Europe still remains tied to its past as it is defining its priorities for meeting its common future. Europe cannot escape from its past. But even less so can it escape its future. Based on accumulated common experiences, the European Union will continuously learn how to define a common destiny and, moreover, how to shape a joint future. This will not simply entail symbolic actions about fundamental principles and notions of how to manage the world. First and foremost it will require the management of a European Union accountable to its citizens and their daily lives. Europe as community of values must be a community that works.

Against all prejudice, European Union citizens have a clear idea of the necessary priorities of the EU, even amidst the lingering ratification of the Reform Treaty: According to Eurobarometer findings, by the end of 2007 they were identifying the following issues as the main test-cases for stronger and more successful European integration: unemployment (27 percent, down from 40 percent in autumn 2006),

20 See Bracher, Karl Dietrich, *Europa in der Krise: Innengeschichte und Weltpolitik seit 1917*, Frankfurt/Berlin/Vienna: Propyläen, 1979.

inflation (26 percent, up from 16 percent in autumn 2006), healthcare system (21 percent, up from 16 percent in autumn 2006), overall economic situation (18 percent, down from 21 percent in autumn 2006), immigration (15 percent, down from 21 percent in autumn 2006), pensions (14 percent, up from 10 percent in autumn 2006), terrorism (10 percent, down from 15 percent in autumn 2006), the education system (9 percent, up from 7 percent in autumn 2006), taxation (9 percent, up from 7 percent in autumn 2006), housing (8 percent, up from 5 percent in autumn 2006).[21] How to translate these concerns into specific policy strategies is, of course, another matter.

With remarkable clarity, Union citizens are able to identify policy priorities they want to see tackled and resolved on the European level. According to Eurobarometer polls conducted in 2009, Union citizens are expressing the following order of priorities: fighting terrorism (81 percent), promoting democracy and peace in the world (81 percent) fighting organized crime (78), cooperating in research and development (78 percent), protecting the environment (77 percent), securing energy supply (76 percent), managing major health issues (72 percent), promoting equal treatment of women and men (72 percent), ensuring food safety (70 percent). 22 percent of EU citizens consider the EU the best choice for coping with the global financial and economic crisis while only 19 percent prefer their national government and 18 percent the G20 grouping.[22] If for only one thing, these Eurobarometer findings underline the need for a Europe that works.

European Union citizens expect their political leaders to use the governance structures of the EU to bring about clear results and concrete success. The more this experience is recognized, the higher support for European integration will be. If this success is missing, political scientists talk about problems of output-legitimacy. Ordinary Union citizens will probably talk about frustration with their political representatives. Political leaders in turn should be worried about Europe losing worldwide relevance.

As far as its internal constellation is concerned, Europe was "returning to its normal history," as David P. Calleo has described the process of transformation starting with the end of the Cold War.[23] In past centuries, he argued, Europe was plural and interdependent with several interacting centers of power before this "normalcy" was frozen during the Cold War. While embarking on a new chapter of its development, Europe was meant to resume history, Calleo argued. But the next chapter of European history would primarily be defined by the effects of integration. As much as this was a

21 European Union, European Commission, *Eurobarometer 68: Public Opinion in the European Union*, December 2007, op.cit.

22 European Union. European Commission, *Eurobarometer 71: Public Opinion in the European Union,* September 2009, op.cit.; European Union. European Commission, *Eurobarometer 72: Public Opinion in the European Union,* November 2009, https://ec.europa.eu/public_opinion/archives/eb/eb72/eb72_first_en.pdf.

23 Calleo, David P., *Rethinking Europe's Future*, Princeton/Oxford: Princeton University Press, 2001: 3.

new phenomenon in European history, Europe was distancing itself from its own history. As much as it meant that Europe was beginning to claim subject-status again after half a century of strategic dependency on the fringe powers defining the European state order after World War II, it would imply that Europe also needs to renew its global role. The renewal of a global role would be a clear break with any imperial connotation of the nineteenth or early twentieth century. In the age of globalization, the challenge for Europe in positioning itself in the wider world was very different: losing relevance or projecting genuine European interests in global affairs.

In doing so, Europe cannot expect to only encounter the sunny side of international cooperation. No matter its own experience, outside Europe conflicts and fighting continues. Most Europeans might prefer to make them disappear by simply referring to their own historic evolution. They have to learn that this is not the way world affairs are developing and history is evolving. Asymmetric threats make the rational assessment of global developments even more complex. No matter what Europeans are thinking about the global leadership of the United States, they are beginning to understand the challenge of the new era also as a challenge to their own affluence and democratic peace. They begin to realize that to meet these challenges requires mutual solidarity and reciprocal readiness to support common solutions, if necessary based on compromises.

After the terrorist bombings in Madrid on March 11, 2004, the EU invoked a solidarity clause that was not even in place legally. The readiness to invoke solidarity in confronting a common threat that had risen in Europe, no matter the details of political response and controversy, was remarkable. The realization of energy dependency on Russia triggered another dimension of solidarity across the European Union in 2007, most notably in favor of Poland: Eventually, a common energy policy aimed at the security of the energy supply in the whole European Union became a principle of EU energy policy, "in a spirit of solidarity between Member States" (Treaty of Lisbon, Title XX, Article 176A).[24] Solidarity means shared destiny. In the course of escalating disputes over the formulation of the 2007 Reform Treaty, the Polish government was also reminded by its fellow European partners that solidarity is not a one-way-road: Their EU partners expected Polish readiness to compromise on the pending issue of weighing of votes in the Council in return for an inclusion of the principle of energy solidarity across the EU in the final text of the Reform Treaty. Eventually, all sides moved to the benefit of the EU's steady development.

Most intellectual discourses in Europe are still centered around respective national media, books and public voices. National political debates gain stronger attention than European Parliamentary debates. Yet, EU decisions no longer are dispensable from national media coverage. The EU is increasingly present in the media of all EU member

24 European Union, "Treaty of Lisbon Amending the Treaty on European Union and the Treaty Establishing the European Community," *Official Journal of the European Union, C 306/Vol.50, Luxembourg: Office for Official Publications of the European Communities*, 2007, http://eur-lex.europa.eu/JOHtml.do?uri=OJ:C:2007:306:SOM:EN:HTML.

states. Knowledge of other places in Europe and appreciation for the cultural diversity in Europe has grown for millions of tourists and business-people. With the absence of border controls among most EU countries, for Europe's youth this dimension of "returning to normal" has lost practically all excitement. In political terms, the notion of non-interference in domestic affairs has lost most of its meaning in Europe. European political matters are increasingly understood as being part of one's own body politic.

Communication in Europe is not organized in the way the national public sphere has come to be organized over a long period of fertilization. Yet, it would be misleading to believe that the idea of European integration only depends upon the existence of centralized media or a centrally institutionalized public discourse across the EU. In fact, the majority of Europeans consider themselves simultaneously as members of a nation and as Europeans, no matter how far away they are living from the centers of politics in Europe. An unstructured and un-institutionalized notion of "European-ness" exists all over Europe: You don't have to be in Brussels in order to be in Europe and to encounter Europeans. Yet, "Brussels" is synonymous for the EU as institution.

It was mainly the work of the European Commission as the executive wing of European integration that has put Brussels on the mental map of most European citizens. It should not have come as a surprise that the image of "Brussels" was negative. "Brussels" was time and again tainted as the incarnation of a highly bureaucratic regime. No nation state would have maintained public legitimacy if its claim to democracy would have only been answered by the visibility of its bureaucracy. This is why it made perfect sense to question the democratic deficit of the European Union as a deficit in public control and democratic leadership in EU legislation. "Brussels" as bureaucracy was mainly controlled by national interests as long as the European Parliament could not establish itself as the counter-balancing power in an interlocking system of governance.

Brussels, by and large, is solidifying itself as the capital of the European Union. The second biggest agglomeration of journalists in the world after Washington, a growing presence of interest groups side by side with diplomatic missions from all over the world, permanency of European Council meetings and a massive new building for the European Parliament in a European quarter: These facts are signaling the role of Brussels as the center of EU politics. It is ironic that the official seat of the European Parliament is still Strasbourg and its meetings are being split between Strasbourg and Brussels. The effect would be enormous should the EU formally recognize Brussels as the capital of political Europe. Such a move would clearly provide for a sense of belonging and certainly it would contribute to the architectural development of Brussels. Visibility and accountability of "Brussels" would be strengthened. These are exactly the reasons why many member states of the European Union are still reluctant to formally recognize Brussels as the EU's capital. The meaning of such a decision would be more than symbolic. It would be tantamount to reconciling the pooling of sovereignty that has been going on in Europe for five decades with the geographical focus it takes to make a body politic truly visible and hence accountable for its actions. It would constitute another element in the formation of the European Union as an incomplete federation.[25] One day, it will have to happen.

It is remarkable that the first EU-wide movement tantamount to the quest for a referendum is calling for a decision to make Brussels the formal seat of the European Parliament. Establishing Brussels as the capital of Europe would immediately falsify the assessment that the EU still is an elite project. As much as it is elite-driven (which is the case with all democratic political systems) it would help its citizens to identify with the EU if they can get visible access to its center of power. Their parliament therefore should be permanent at the center of power instead of remaining a rotating circus. It will also help to form a European political identity if a creative and interactive "House of European History" will be opening its doors in Brussels. It will undoubtedly attract many of the more than two million visitors coming annually to the EU institutions. The Museum of American History on the Mall in Washington D.C. serves as a source of inspiration. It was a promising first step when the then President of the European Parliament, Hans-Gert Pöttering, formally suggested the establishment of a House of European History in his inaugural speech of February 2007: "It should not be a dry, boring museum," Pöttering said, "but a place where our memory of European history and the work of European unification is jointly cultivated, and which at the same time is available as a locus for the European identity to go on being shaped by present and future citizens of the European Union."[26] In the meantime, the preparation for the opening of a House of European History is under way. Its doors are supposed to open in 2014, hundred years after the outbreak of World War I.

Any decision to strengthen the symbolic meaning of Brussels for the EU as body politic would add to the already quite impressive list of other publicly exposed symbols of European integration: the EU's flag with twelve golden stars on a dark blue background, hanging increasingly at public buildings all across the EU, often side by side with the national flag; the euro, the European passport and the European anthem. Declaring May 9 "Europe Day" has not made this day – in memory of the declaration by French Foreign Minister Robert Schuman on May 9, 1950, initiating the European Coal and Steel Community – as meaningful as Memorial Day in the US or national holidays in Europe's nation states, but it adds to the composite and multiple identity increasingly shaping Europe.[27] While the Constitutional Treaty of 2004 included the European symbols and wanted to grant them legal status, the 2007 Reform Treaty

25 See Pommerin, Reiner, "Die europäische Hauptstadt," in: Salewski, Michael (ed.), *Nationale Identität und Europäische Einigung*, Göttingen: Muster-Schmidt-Verlag, 1991: 18-31.

26 Pöttering, Hans-Gert, *Defending Europe's Values – For a Citizens' Europe*, Program Speech to the European Parliament, Strasbourg, February 13, 2007, http://www.europarl.europa.eu/president/defaulten.htm?home.

27 For a highly positive assessment of "Europe Day" see Reid, T. R., *The United States of Europe: The New Superpower and the End of American Supremacy*, New York: Penguin Press, 2004: 43.

renounced any reference to the European symbols. Without any meaningful public debate, this curtailing of a constitutional achievement has been a diplomatic concession obviously granted to euroskeptical governments in the final processes of backdoor diplomatic bickering and horse-trading. This turn of facts could not leave European federalists without frustration. They could take consolation in the fact that the European symbols would, of course, continue to exist without being referred to in the Reform Treaty. The European Parliament, inspired by its then President Hans-Gert Pöttering, introduced the innovative practice to welcome Heads of State with their own national anthem, played along with the European anthem. This was probably only a small step for the political Europe, but it contributes to the lasting elements in the formation of European identity and a European public sphere.[28] It would also be useful to add the European motto "Unity in Diversity" on the euro bank notes. For the time being, seven distinct European architectural periods are designed on the euro notes: classical Greco-Roman on the 5 euro note, Romanesque on the 10 euro note, Gothic on the 20 euro note, Renaissance on the 50 euro note, Baroque-Rococo on the 100 euro note, Iron and Glass on the 200 euro note, twentieth-century Postmodernism on the 500 euro note. Europe's political identity is growing step by step. The images on the euro bank notes support the sober assessment that, at least so far, European institutional union has been achieved, but, by and large, Europeans are still a rare species across the EU.

3. Citizens' Europe, Citizens' Choices

While the European Union has entered the second half of its first century of existence, conflicting trends have to be reconciled. The nation state remains present across the European Union. Regional asymmetries are stronger than ever. Transfer of sovereignty is contested although the insight is prevalent that only the pooling of resources can generate the strength and dynamics Europeans would like to see attributed to their continent. A public sphere is emerging, yet a common European discourse is still rare. The European Parliament has become more or less equal partner of the Council in EU decision-making, yet the absence of a fiscal constitution matching the political representation is striking.[29] Consensual moral claims are articulated in Europe, yet they do not automatically transpire into European interests, let alone the formulation and implementation of a balanced and comprehensive policy that is based on ideas and interests alike. While entering the second half of its first century as an unfinished federation, Europe remains a laboratory.

28 See Odermatt, Peter, "The Use of Symbols in the Drive for European Integration," in: Leersen, Joseph Th., and Menno Spiering (eds.), *National Identity: Symbol and Representation*, Amsterdam: Rodopi, 1999: 217-240.

29 See Kühnhardt, Ludger, "An EU Constitutional Twist: No Representation Without Taxation," *European Affairs*, 4.2 (2003): 76-81.

The development of legitimacy for European integration remains linked to the perception of political will and the degree of success by which it is organized inside the European Union. The European Parliament – as much as the Court of Justice – has often been underestimated in its potential to generate the necessary political focus as embodiment of the European public sphere. Recent scholarly studies have begun to recognize the power of the European Parliament. Andreas Maurer distinguishes between five different functions of the European Parliament: its function to shape the constitutional and institutional system of the EU; its function to elect the EU leadership; its function to shape EU policies; its function to control the EU executive; and its function to articulate policy preferences and interact with EU voters. In all regards, the role of the European Parliament has definitively been strengthened since its first direct election in 1979. The European Parliament has been firmly established as one of the key centers of power in the EU.[30] As Europe is emerging from early constitutionalism to constitutionalism, it is also emerging from semi-parliamentary democracy to parliamentary democracy. One of the key features of this development is the evolution of the party groups in the European Parliament since its first direct election in 1979.[31] Parliamentary democracy in its specific European variant ("party families") is increasingly politicizing EU decision-making. In contrast to traditional concepts of limiting power through the separation of its institutional centers, the EU is operating as a system of interlocking powers. This is a genuine system of limiting and controlling powers, obviously more appropriate to the diverse nature of the European Union.

The evolution of European integration will not become a copy of the experience with the European nation state. The EU will not substitute for the nation state either. Yet it is worth looking into the conditions it took to develop the European nation state. The European nation state was a construction as much as the EU is sometimes criticized for being a construction. The European nation state across the continent has been a product of history and of specific historical circumstances. After the dissolution of unity between the political and the religious bond of legitimacy and loyalty in Europe – embodied in pre-reformation Christianity and the Holy Roman Empire of German Nation – Europe was in search for a new form based on a new legitimacy. State structures developed as outflows of past bureaucracies by and large already available across Europe. It was rare to relate emerging states to already firmly established nations as incarnations of the cultural root and identity of any of Europe's states. In many cases, the European nation state became a product of the romantic appraisal of difference and

30 Maurer, Andreas, *Die Macht des Europäischen Parlaments: Eine prospektive Analyse im Blick auf die kommende Wahlperiode 2004-2009*, Berlin: Stiftung Wissenschaft und Politik, 2004; Scully, Roger, *Becoming Europeans?: Attitudes, Behaviour and Socialization in the European Parliament*, Oxford: Oxford University Press, 2005.

31 See Steunenberg, Bernard, and Jacques Thomassen (eds.), *The European Parliament: Moving Toward Democracy in the EU*, Lanham: Rowman & Littlefield, 2002.

exclusivity that followed and preceded various movements toward centralized political power in Europe.[32]

In the nineteenth century, German philosophers like Johann Gottlieb Fichte (1762-1814) and Johann Gottfried Herder (1744-1803) made a comprehensive plea for identity-formation through the creation of a homogenous nation.[33] They promoted the rise of romantic and exclusive nationalism. As the German nation did not exist in reality, it had to be constructed. Following the German example of belated nation-building, multi-patterned societies around the world have looked for exclusive statehood at the end of European colonialism. But also the traditional nation states of Europe – rooting the nation in a law-based state – were not free from embracing the notion of romantic and exclusive nationalism, albeit at earlier stages and with different degrees of ideological intensity. Following the age of colonialism, all around the globe statehood shaped the nationhood it pretended to serve. Thus, non-European countries followed the European experience. In practically all of Europe, the state brought about the nation. Whether or not some nations were more advanced than others, belated in the nineteenth century or still in the midst of achieving state-nation-confluence in the early twenty-first century does not matter. As variations of the same theme, European nation-building and Europe's state-building were and are mutually reinforcing processes. As "imagined communities"[34] all of Europe's nation states grew in strength and gained loyalty only over a long span of time. There is no rational argument to believe that over time the same effect could not grow in the European Union.

In the nineteenth century, Alexis de Tocqueville saw an alternative to state-formation and nation-building on the American side of the Atlantic Ocean.[35] He was fascinated with the American experience. Identity was formed through public discourse and consent in the body politic, based on religious commitment and a civil religion transcending all differences in creed and cult. The body politic worked best on the local level. But also on top of the American system, political identity and cultural identity were confluent. Identity was not defined as a moral charge but practiced as a political call. Identity was not bestowed upon citizens by a government. It was not even artificially created by a government. It came into being as "invention" of civil society. Thus it became the American ideal.[36]

In Europe, Herder's romantic ideal grew into rigid realities. Political loyalty and moral claim went hand in hand. Language was used as a formative instrument and

32 See Hroch, Miroslav, *Das Europa der Nationen: Die moderne Nationsbildung im europäischen Vergleich*, Göttingen: Vandenhoeck & Ruprecht, 2005.

33 Fichte, Johann Gottlieb, *Der geschlossene Handelsstaat*, Hamburg: Meiner, 1979; Herder, Johann Gottfried, *Philosophical Writings* , Cambridge/New York: Cambridge University Press, 2002.

34 Anderson, Benedict R., *Imagined Communities: Reflections on the origin and spread of nationalism*, London/New York: Verso, 1991.

35 Tocqueville, Alexis de, *Democracy in America*, Chicago: University of Chicago Press, 2000.

36 See Huntington, Samuel P., *American Politics: The Promise of Disharmony*, Cambridge, Mass.: Belknap Press, 1981.

simultaneously as a means to underscore the exclusivity of every single nation-building process. Multilingual societies were challenged in their composition. The challenge to plurality could even reach out against multireligious community life. Overly dominating was the state-centeredness of the European nation-building process. The state was seen as provider and protector of national identity. Since the emergence of the Westphalian state-system in the seventeenth century, the state in Europe "increasingly came to occupy and, indeed, create the national space of modern European countries."[37] Until the mid-twentieth century the state "orchestrated"[38] nationhood, national aspirations and nationalistic fervor. It did so until both the state and the nation were facing overstretch.

Today, the European Union is confronted with contrasting charges and perspectives as far as the role of politics in the management of social affairs is concerned. The EU will remain torn between aspirations for redistributive resource allocation in favor of welfare solidarity on the one hand and the quest for rigid liberalization in pursuit of the common market principle and a precondition for innovation necessary to gain dynamics under conditions of globalization on the other hand. This clash of concepts regarding the order of state and the notion of security will absorb the internal dimension of the idea of European solidarity and it will bind resources of the European Union over many years to come.

At the same time, the EU will have to address the continuous ambiguity between the claim to democracy and the struggle for efficiency. Whether effectiveness in delivering public goods could appease the quest for stronger elements of participatory democracy is an open question.[39] Whether effectiveness may be generated through modes of deliberative democracy with emphasis on transparency and discursive deliberations is even more questionable. The European body politic will continue to evolve in incremental steps, gradual, with flaws and its specific idiosyncrasies. Yet it will evolve by constitutional and parliamentary means. Therefore the question of political leadership is of primordial importance to the future authority and consistency of European political identity.[40]

Patriotism does not develop as natural consequence of political processes and decisions. It is not a simple reaction to the existence of a constitutional text. It cannot be

37 Dunkerley, David, "The Nation-State in Europe," in: Dunkerley, David, et al. (eds.), *Changing Europe: Identities, Nations and Citizens*, London/New York: Routledge, 2002: 27.

38 Ibid.: 28.

39 Maurer shows that empirically the EU's co-decision procedure, implying equal rights of the European Parliament with the European Council, takes less time than decision-making procedures without involvement of the European Parliament. More than the European Parliament, the European Council is responsible for slowing down decision-making in the EU: Maurer, Andreas, *Die Macht des Europäischen Parlaments: Eine prospektive Analyse im Blick auf die kommende Wahlperiode 2004-2009*, op.cit.: 22.

40 See Vibert, Frank, *Europe Simple Europe Strong: The Future of European Governance*, Cambridge: Polity Press, 2001. Vibert speaks of Europe as an epistemic society and suggests "knowledge-based governance," considering "moral and social standards as subjects of learning just as much as any other aspect of choice" (218).

rooted in constitutional provisions and institutional arrangements alone. In fact, it may not even need the existence of a formal Constitution to advance. European constitutional patriotism is certainly a function of the best possible performance of the law-based organs and institutions of the EU. In the absence of a formal European Constitution, the EU's *acquis communautaire* needs to serve as a substitute body of constitutional law. But beyond any written text or unwritten tradition, ultimately, constitutional patriotism will depend upon the degree of recognition of the European Union by the people and the states constituting it. It will depend on the degree of "ownership" Union citizen's feel for the EU. Whether or not cultural and human resources can be activated to enhance constitutional consent and even constitutional patriotism will largely depend on one single most important experience of EU citizens: How strong are they convinced that the EU is capable to deliver public goods. It will also depend upon the readiness of the member states of the European Union to advance common policies and thus the sense of an ever-closer common destiny, if necessary at the expense of autonomous national decision-making.

(1) EU Citizenship

The introduction of EU citizenship by the Treaty of Maastricht has added an important dimension to the search for European identity. The formal creation of the category of a Union citizenship not only helps to recalibrate the relationship between the EU as a Union of States and a Union of Citizens, it has also brought the level of judgment of EU legitimacy to a much higher level of expectation. It has carried the common market into the sphere of politics and constitutional law.[41]

European citizenship has not created an immediate civic sense or strong European constitutional patriotism. But the very development of European citizenship has focused the discourse about these ideals. The evolution of EU citizenship also indicates the specific historic circumstances in which EU integration takes place. The origins of citizenship and the development of its meaning in the context of the modern nation state followed three stages:

1) The evolution of civil rights in eighteenth century Europe granted individual protection against unjustifiable state interference, defining civil rights largely as negative and defensive rights. This first phase in the evolution of the concept of citizenship led to the recognition of the rule of law.

41 See Shaw, Josephine, *Citizenship of the Union: Towards Post-National Membership?*, Jean Monnet Working Paper Series No.6/1997, Cambridge, Mass.: Harvard Law School, 1997; Holmes, Leslie (ed.), *Citizenship and Identity in Europe*, Ashgate: Aldershot, 1999; Meehan, Elisabeth, *Citizenship and the European Union*, ZEI Discussion Paper C 63. Bonn: Center for European Integration Studies, 2000; Kostakopoulou, Theodora, *Citizenship, Identity, and Immigration in the European Union: Between Past and Future*, Manchester/New York: Manchester University Press, 2001; Guild, Elspeth, *The Legal Elements of European Identity: EU Citizenship and Migration Law*, Boston: Kluwer, 2004.

2) The evolution of political claim rights during the nineteenth century broadened citizens participation in the political process, turning political rights largely into positive claim rights. This second phase in the evolution of the concept of citizenship led to the breakthrough of democracy as organizing principle of legitimate government.
3) The evolution of social rights during the twentieth century strengthened social cohesion by way of granting labor related rights to citizens as workers, making social rights largely a claim to social and inclusive democracy. This third phase in the evolution of the concept of citizenship led to the constitutional recognition of social and welfare rights as democratic claim rights.

So far, the evolution of the concept of citizenship in the context of European integration has followed a reverse order:

- During the first phase in the evolution of the notion of citizenship the citizens of the participating member states were defined as workers and participants in the emerging common European market, distinctively relating this phase to the evolution of economic rights. This phase led to the evolution of the concept of the four freedoms originally set out in the Treaties of Rome, mainly in the context of labor rights.
- During the second phase in the evolution of the notion of European citizenship the EU was defined as a Union of States and a Union of Citizens, granting political participatory rights to the national citizens of EU member states. This phase evolved gradually with the Treaty of Maastricht.
- During the third phase in the evolution of the notion of European citizenship EU citizens are defined as holders of basic civil and human rights guaranteed by the Charter of Fundamental Rights of the European Union. Its inclusion in the 2007 Reform Treaty indicated that, eventually, this Charter is intended to be judiciable in European courts, including the European Court of Justice. This phase is recalibrating the relationship between national rule of law and European rule of law; thus it is also enlarging the concept of European democracy and constitutionalism.

As the European Community was initially and primarily concerned with market issues, it could not come as a surprise that citizens were perceived primarily as economic actors. European legislation referred to "workers" and not to "citizens." The notion of "freedom of labor" in the Treaties of Rome was intended to support the free movement of workers in an emerging European market. The social rights of migrant laborers were to be protected. Although this concept referred to both internal migrants from within the community and those from outside the community (people from Turkey, North Africa, the Caribbean, South East and South Asia in particular), it did not carry any political dimension. The first reference to European citizenship was made at a meeting of the Heads of State and Government of the European Community in 1974.

They launched a study to look into the possibilities under which the citizens of the nine Member States could be given special rights as Members of the Community.

In 1979, the European Commission presented a Directive regarding the right of residence for EC nationals in the territory of other EC member states regardless of economic activity. Consensus had developed that the concept of free movement of persons could not be realized without the permanent right of residence in another EC member state. The promulgation of this right came to be regarded as the first step in establishing a European citizenship. In 1986, the European Commission issued a report on "Voting Rights in Local elections for Community Nationals." In the same year, the Single European Act reiterated the goal of completing a single market where "free movement of persons, goods, capital and services is ensured." The Single European Act used the term "persons" and not only the term "workers." This was more than a matter of wording. It was a contribution to turn the common market into a common political space.

The Intergovernmental Conference preceding the formulation of the Treaty of Maastricht engaged in an intensive discussion about the meaning of a "Europe of the Citizens." The idea to grant all citizens of EC member states the right of free movement, residence and access to work was coupled with the need to also grant them voting rights in local elections in order to make the integration idea more democratic. The question as to how far this right could include access to specific social prerogatives in EC member states remained heavily contested. At the initiative of the European Parliament, the final provisions on European Citizenship in the Treaty of Maastricht included voting rights for citizens of the European Community – renamed European Union – not only in local elections in all EC member states, but also in elections to the European Parliament in their country of residence. Eventually, the Treaty of Maastricht established the "Citizenship of the Union" (Article 8).

EU Citizenship was only granted to national citizens of EU member states. It was therefore criticized for not giving an answer to the civil status of more than ten million legal residents of the EU without national citizenship.[42] Critics argue that the introduction of EU citizenship would only reinforce the role of the nation state as it would maintain ultimate control of access to, enjoyment of, and even forfeiture of the right of citizenship.[43] This perception did not have a full grasp of the dynamics involved in the evolution of European citizenship, which has come quite some way since its modest beginning. It might also have overlooked the fact that European citizenship – as much as European integration in general – was not intended to replace the nation state

42 See McLaren, Lauren M., *Identity, Interests and Attitudes to European Integration*, Houndmills: Palgrave Macmillan, 2006: This data-based study argues that xenophobia strengthens identity among Europeans more than abstract cost-benefit-analysis of European integration.

43 See Howe, Paul, "A Community of Europeans: The Requisite Underpinnings," *Journal of Common Market Studies*, 33.1 (1995): 27-46; Kostakopoulou, Theodora, "Why a "Community of Europeans" could be a Community of Exclusion," *Journal of Common Market Studies*, 35.2 (1997): 301-309; Benhabib, Seyla, "On European Citizenship," *Dissent*, 45.4 (1998): 107-109.

but rather to complement it. It would be a-historical to assume that the concept of citizenship would fully incorporate all residents in all EU member states. One should not forget: Already Roman law distinguished between Roman citizens and foreigners. Even the United States, proud in being a country of migrants, is harboring millions of residents, both legal and illegal, which are not citizens of the US. Nowhere does residency make for nationality.

The evolution of the concept of European citizenry from social and worker rights to participatory and general civil rights – no matter how limited – is without precedence in the history of Europe. For the time being it is incomplete and even inconclusive as a complementary concept to national notions of citizenship. Yet, "citizenship as provider of legitimacy"[44] has become part of an all-out development of multiple identities in Europe to which was also added the Charter of Fundamental Rights of the European Union.[45]

(2) EU Civil Rights

The Charter of Fundamental Rights of the European Union was initially agreed upon by the European Council in 2000 as a political document and has been referred to in the Treaty of Lisbon in 2007. Thus it is poised to eventually become a judiciable element of the *acquis communautaire* and will certainly lead to interpretations by the European Court of Justice. The Charter aroused controversies on various grounds. It was questioned whether or not another human rights charter would truly be needed in Europe and could add anything to the very protection of human rights already existing under the provision of democratic constitutions in Europe, the European Convention on Human Rights promulgated by the Council of Europe in 1950, or the body of human rights provisions of the United Nations, beginning with the Universal Declaration of Human Rights.[46] Proponents in defense of the EU Charter argued that only through this

44 Garcia, Soledad, "Europe's Fragmented Identities and the Frontiers of Citizenship," in: Garcia, Soledad (ed.), *European Identity and the Search for Legitimacy*, London: Continuum International Publishing, 1993: 25; also see Jensen, Ole B., and Tim Richardson, *Making European Space: Mobility, Power and Territorial Identity*, London: Routledge, 2004.

45 The Treaty of Lisbon states the following in Article 6: "The Union recognizes the rights, freedoms and principles set out in the Charter of Fundamental Rights of the European Union of 7 December 2000, as adapted at Strasbourg, on 12 December 2007, which shall have the same legal value as the Treaties," "Treaty of Lisbon Amending the Treaty on European Union and the Treaty Establishing the European Community," *Official Journal of the European Union*, C 306/Vol.50, Luxembourg: Office for Official Publications of the European Communities, 2007, http://eur-lex.europa.eu/JOHtml.do?uri=OJ:C:2007:306:SOM:EN:HTML, op.cit.: 13.

46 See Betten, Lammy, "The EU Charter on Fundamental Rights: A Trojan Horse or a Mouse?," *International Journal of Comparative Labour Law and Industrial Relations*, 17.2(2001):151-164; Kühnhardt, Ludger, "Europe's View of Man under Pressure," in Kühnhardt, Ludger (ed.), *Constituting Europe: Identity Institution-Building and the Search for a Global Role*, Baden-Baden: Nomos, 2003: 47-54.

Charter would EU institutions be held accountable to civil rights standards as laid out in the EU Charter.

Various provisions of the Charter came immediately under scrutiny and criticism as part of the legitimate process of constitutional review. If anything, criticism directed at one or the other provision of the Charter of Fundamental Rights of the European Union was a reconfirmation of its relevance and a further contribution to the evolving European constitutionalism. Most conspicuous is the absence of a clear definition of a view of man. The Charter lacks anthropological firmness. It represents the common denominator of a secular humanism that has become synonymous with the European understanding of values as a foundation of politics. The values invoked by the European Union relate to the most basic notions of liberal democracy, rule of law, protection of minority rights and support of market economy. While no relevant political force was questioning these values, it was difficult to identify what among them could be considered "typical" European.

The Charter of Fundamental Rights of the European Union is not a text without contradictions. While it upholds national interpretations of basic human and civil rights provisions, it is debatable whether or not the explicit provisions of the Charter might in reality reduce the scope of some national human rights provisions. This question was, for instance, raised in the context of the notion and protection of the family. It was also evident regarding the most contentious matters in the human rights debate emerging in the early twenty-first century: definitions regarding the beginning of life and the end of it. The striking absence of any religious rooting of Europe's self-proclaimed secular humanism was beginning to haunt Europe's claim to be the prime defender of human rights and human dignity in the world.

Clashing moralities do exist across the European Union about abortion, euthanasia, stem cell research and other issues related to technical developments in medicine. It is at least a matter of consideration how Europe could uphold the claim for value leadership in the world while it is confronted with clashing moralities among its citizenry on most basic norms impacting the legitimacy of the rule of law. Over three centuries, a moral consent had developed in Europe on the basic principles and applications of political, civic and socio-economic rights. Whether or not the same might happen over time regarding a consensual moral interpretation of human dignity, including the beginning and the end of human life (or when life legitimately could be brought to an end for medical reasons) is a matter of doubt. Controversial debates in Europe about conflicting moral claims do not suggest that this would be an easy task. In fact, these debates only underline the insight of democratic theory that democracies need to be based on notions of morality they cannot reproduce themselves.

Conflicting moral norms not only trigger controversial political debates. They will most likely spurn decisions by the European Court of Justice. The European Court of Justice has the potential of further growing into the EU's Supreme Court, not least on matters relevant to the interpretation of civil rights and basic interpretations of human rights and human dignity. Ever since its work began, the European Court of Justice has played a strong role in advancing European integration through the effects of its rulings. This pattern was largely left outside public attention as the Court was promoting the full completion of the common market agreed upon by all member states. With the growing focus on political union, and strengthened by the incorporation of its statute into the *acquis communautaire* in 2000, the European Court of Justice will increasingly proceed as agent of integration.

Moral and ethical issues are recognized in twenty-first century Europe as part of a common identity. This certainly holds true with regard to collective and abstract concepts such as democracy, freedom, justice, solidarity, the rule of law and the market economy. But it is much less consensual whether or not such collective and abstract notions with ethical implications are rooted in moral resources they cannot generate themselves. At the root of all political and social concepts of ethics are value decisions concerning the very nature of man. Anthropology, philosophy and religion provide insights and offer norms for our understanding of the nature of man, our notion of man and his dignity as an individual and a social being. In Europe – as in many other parts of the modern world – it is far from consensual as to how to define the very cultural and moral positions that relate to our view of man. Europe's striking religious exceptionalism – Europe's overly high degree of secularism – does not facilitate coherent and satisfactory answers to this search.

Two examples show the consequences of the contemporary absence of a consensual view of man in Europe, if not the degree of contradictions on the matter of human self-assessment and self-understanding. The Charter of Fundamental Rights of the European Union states in Article 1 the inalienability of human dignity.[47] Article 2 reaffirms the right of life as an implicit consequence of the inalienability of human dignity.[48] Nevertheless, the Charter does not explicitly recognize a specific view of man as the basis for these postulates. Concerned observers worry about the possible implications of redefining the dignity of human beings as a hierarchically graded and layered concept. Challenges to a comprehensive concept of human dignity are particularly relevant in the context of biogenetic developments, most importantly in light of the consequences of new methods of reproductive medicine. It is also relevant for the context of definitions concerning the end of life and the debate about active euthanasia. These controversies have become particularly pertinent in light of several political and legal decisions taken in Europe at the beginning of the twenty-first century:

- The British Parliament opted in favor of therapeutic cloning.
- The French Court of Cassation recognized the right of a handicapped man not to

47 "Human Dignity is inviolable. It must be respected and protected." (Part II, Title 1, Article II-61) European Union, *Treaty establishing a Constitution for Europe*, op.cit: 48.
48 "Everyone has the right to life." (Part II, Title 1, Article II-62), ibid.

have been born in the first place.

- The Dutch Parliament and the Belgian Parliament passed legislation recognizing active euthanasia. (The Dutch law was soon thereafter criticized by the Human Rights Legislation Committee of the United Nations as not being free of the potential for misuse by those who might put pressure on patients to end their lives.)

Contemporary biopolitical controversies in Europe and throughout the world are an expression of the plight of freedom. Human dignity and human rights are not issues for soft and consensual round table talks. They refer to the totality of human existence. The biopolitical controversies are reflecting the potential of new bio-political ideologies. In his book, "Novum Organum," published in 1620, Francis Bacon defined a theory of ideological thinking. He described the fundamental difference between empty and fact-based opinions ("Placita quaedam inania et veras signaturas atque impressiones factas in creaturis"). Protagonists of French Enlightenment in the eighteenth century used the term "ideology" for the first time, meaning a theory of ideas. Later, the relationship between ideology and utopia was interpreted intensively. The common denominator of many ideological concepts and notions – no matter changes in the specific content and the historical context – was the same: They were united in the goal to overcome a "false" consciousness or a "false" reality in order to serve "progress." Karl Dietrich Bracher, the leading European historian on the fall of the Weimar Republic and on intellectual history in the twentieth century, reminded his readers that the question of ideology remains virulent even beyond the ideological battles of the nineteenth and twentieth centuries: New (and false) promises of a paradise on earth could always surface again, he wrote, and again they could justify violence against human life and the destruction of free communities.[49] In his last homily before being elected Pope Benedict XVI, Joseph Cardinal Ratzinger spoke of a "dictatorship of relativism" as the seemingly "only attitude that can cope with modern times," a way of life "that does not recognize anything as definitive and whose ultimate goal consists solely of one's own ego and desires."[50] It is not surprising that the controversies about the beginning and the end of life are leading to new coalitions between human sciences and natural sciences. This holds true for both directions of the argument. Utilitarian as much as person-centered views of man reflect certain positions in human sciences and natural sciences. Some of them are variations of the same theme. The fundamental conflict between utilitarianism and an integral, comprehensively personalized view of man cannot be "researched away" in the laboratories of biologists or "written away" at the desks of philosophers or lawyers. The core of the controversy is about fundamentally different notions of human

49 Bracher, Karl Dietrich, *The Age of Ideologies: A History of Political Thought in the Twentieth Century*, London: Palgrave Macmillan, 1984: 189-277. ("De-ideologization and Re-ideologization").

50 Ratzinger, Joseph Cardinal, Homily "Pro Eligiendo Romano Pontifice," Vatican April 18, 2005, www.vatican.va/gpll/documents/homily-pro-eligiendo-pontifice_200.

dignity, one ultimately rooted in human decision-power, the other rooted in natural law above a human right to interfere.

(3) EU Civil Society

The evolving European civil society will be primarily Brussels-focused as far as its political ambitions are concerned. By and large, this is a reflection of interests geared at gaining influence on matters of EU legislation. All possible civil society representatives follow this trend and have turned Brussels into the second biggest venue for lobbyists next to Washington, D.C. The Christian churches in Europe noted with satisfaction that the European Union will engage with them in a genuine "structured dialogue" in recognition of their specific status in and for European society. Church representatives and religious leaders across the EU have considered the recognition of their special status in many EU member states by the Constitution and the prospects of a regular encounter with the political leadership of the EU as the most reassuring element in underlining their claim to a public role of religion in Europe, no matter how secularized the continent has become.

In order to strengthen European civic sense, it would be useful to establish an EU-wide civil service. More than ever it seems to be not only useful but increasingly important to help younger people to learn social responsibility in an environment mainly defined by claim-rights. An EU-wide civil service for young adults would do good to balance this cultural reality. Why could a young Spanish adult not do service for a year or so in a Polish home for aging people? Why could a young Swede not help in an ecological project in Italy? Why could a young Estonian not work on a social project for children in Spain? An EU-wide Civil Service could be open for young men and women alike. It may be compulsory or voluntary, but instead of questioning its overall feasibility, it would be worthwhile to just begin at some point and in some places: What could be more promising than a civil service of young adults under the flag of the European Union? It would also contribute to the recognition and reputation of the European Union if the EU were to establish an EU-based Peace Corps for activities in developing countries, most notably in Africa, Europe's neighboring, yet all too forgotten, continent.

In order to raise the internal European sense of ownership and to enhance the global projection of Europe's civil society, the establishment of a joint European Union team for the Olympic Games would be the perfect idea: One single team representing the EU in the world's most prestigious sporting event would certainly send a strong message across the globe and would find a great response in Europe. All European athletes could march into the Olympic Stadium behind the EU flag. They could wear their national flag and label and would divide for the competitions into their respective national teams. Even as long as national interests and moreover national pride will render impossible the formation of a common EU team at the Olympic Games tournaments, the joint introduction and presentation of all EU athletes behind the EU flag during the opening ceremony could do an enormous service to the idea of European identity and global presence.[51]

The divided Koreans entered the Olympic Stadium in Sydney 2000 and in Athens 2004 with one team united behind one flag. Afterwards, both teams competed in the various Olympic disciplines on their own. If such a move was possible among the most heavily antagonistic countries on earth, why could the Korean model not be a good formula for the EU countries to begin with? Had the European Union member states presented a single team during the 2008 Summer Olympics in Beijing, its success would have been unbeatable: The EU team would have won 87 gold, 101 silver and 92 bronze medals. China with 51, the US with 36, Russia with 23 and Australia with 14 gold medals would clearly have been surpassed. Except for Malta, Luxembourg and Cyprus, all other EU member states were able to win medals in Beijing. Why did all athletes of the European Union not enter an Olympic Stadium behind the European Union flag before they return to compete in national teams? After the fierce disputes about China's policy in Tibet, this would have been a strong political demonstration of the European athletes without completely alienating their Chinese hosts. The 2008 Olympic Games in Beijing were missed as perfect opportunity for the EU to show its young athletes to the world as "united in diversity." The 2012 Olympic Games in London would be the next opportunity to do so and to demonstrate for Great Britain to finally be "at the heart of Europe."

(4) EU Political Parties

The evolution of a genuine European civil society obviously takes longer than the creation of its formal legal or political framework. Nevertheless, with the emergence of interest groups on the European level, a substantial step forward has been taken. But the biggest deficit prevails: European political parties are only gradually emerging. Political groups or factions have been well established in the European Parliament, yet they are hardly visible in the national political discourses of most EU member states. The missing link between the formation of European interest groups (and interests in general) and viable party politics on a European level (and being reconnected with EU citizens across the Union) will only come about after the implementation of a common European electoral law. Although elections to the European Parliament have been direct and based on universal suffrage since 1979, they have not yet been truly "European": Each EU member state continues to define the rules and regulations for these elections.

51 Also see Bairner, Alan, *Sport, Nationalism, and Globalization: European and North American Perspectives*, Albany: State University of New York Press, 2001.

This makes it difficult to orchestrate election campaigns across the European Union based on shared party principles within the "political families," as the groupings in the European Parliament have come to be called. But one should not underestimate their role and relevance, increasingly recognized also by academic research.[52] A European electoral law would facilitate a stronger personalization of election campaigns, including the presentation of local candidates from other EU member states. In spite of the difficulties in formal constitution-building, the accountability of the President of the European Commission to the European Parliament has grown steadily. Like each Commissioner, his or her election requires a supportive decision by the majority of the European Parliament. Although the European Council will maintain the right to nominate the respective candidate, it should become normal practice that the political parties in the EU enter the election campaign to the European Parliament with the presentation of their respective candidates for the office of the next Commission President and the leading Commissioners.

European political parties are confronted with similar problems as national political parties. Their inclination to be "catch-all parties" is even stronger than on the national level given the differences in political culture and policy formulation across the EU. Yet, political parties they are, and as such, they serve as a transmission belt between Union citizens and the decision-making centers of the EU. Their work will be recognized the more the European Union as a whole will emerge as political union – and vice versa. For most EU citizens, political identity means affiliation with one or the other concept of politics advocated by the political parties in Europe. Given the particular tradition of party politics in Europe, it is likely that programmatic considerations will continue to play a relatively strong role in the formation of party allegiance and loyalty on the European level. But as is the case in practically every national political context, European politics will increasingly be a matter of personalization and thus a matter of leadership. The higher the degree of personalization in European politics, the more likely it is to convey the Europeanized political discourse to the citizens of Europe through the appropriate media channels.[53]

Internal debates in political parties across the EU represent – or at least are part of – the European public sphere. As much as this holds true for national political parties, it is also a European experience. Much more attention should therefore be given to the internal discourses in the European "party families." As they basically represent normative political loyalties, their internal debates echo the spectrum of existing

52 See Nessler, Volker, *Europäische Willensbildung: Die Fraktionen im Europaparlament zwischen nationalen Interessen, Parteipolitik und Europäischer Integration*, Schwalbach: Wochenschau Verlag, 1997.

53 See Emanuel, Susan, "A Community of Culture?: The European Television Channel," *History of European Ideas*, 21.2 (1995): 169-176; Hodess, Robin B., "The Role of News Media in European Integration: A Framework of Analysis for Political Science," *Res Publica*, 39.2 (1997): 215-227; Semetko, Holli A., et al., "Europeanised Politics, Europeanised Media?: European Integration and Political Communication," *West European Politics*, 23.4 (2000): 121-141.

programmatic roots and of changing or contested political considerations in the European body politic. Various political paradigms can be identified across the EU: the Christian Democratic, the conservative, the Social Democratic, the Socialist, the Liberal and the Ecological paradigm. Regional parties contribute to the diversity of party politics in the EU. Finally, Euroskeptics of all sorts have entered the political arena of the EU. 372 political parties competed for the sixth direct elections to the European Parliament in 2004. Eventually, 183 parties and party groups were elected. According to European traditions of the importance of party politics as expression of social pluralism, this huge number of contesting parties reflected the diverse social fabric of Europe's society. It did not help, however, to focus a politically driven constitutional patriotism in Europe. The election of almost 50 percent of all parties running for the European Parliament is an extremely high rate compared to national elections across the European Union. The formation of seven political factions in the European Parliament after its 2004 election only partially helped to sharpen the profile of each group. An unofficial "grand coalition" between the European People's Party (Christian Democrats and Conservatives) and Social Democrats prevailed in order to obtain the solid two-thirds majorities that are necessary to overrule decisions of the Council. Both groups also agreed on rotating the Presidency of the European Parliament during the period 2004-2009. In doing what seemingly was inevitable at the moment, they did not really help to bolster their political character as competitors based on different conceptual ideas about the future of Europe.

Since democracy has succeeded in post-communist societies, these countries have seen more political realignments during less than two decades than Western Europe has experienced during five decades. Since 1989, many new parties have appeared and disappeared in Central and Eastern Europe. Many gave themselves names that were difficult to associate with traditional party names (and political meaning) across the political spectrum of "old" Europe. It would nevertheless be incorrect to assume that "new" Europe would set the trend for the whole continent. With EU membership, the new representatives of Central and Eastern Europe were confronted with the choice to join one of the "party families" operating in the European Parliament. Most alignments had already taken place before the first election of the European Parliament in a EU with 25 member states in June 2004. No matter their local name, program or orientation, ultimately the parliamentarians from all EU member states came together under the roof of seven factions in the European Parliament.

Whether or not the European Union will ever recognize common – that is to say supranational – decision-making on matters relating to military missions outside Europe will be the ultimate hurdle, for "European solidarity," a defining momentum. So far, sending young Europeans into situations of physical threat to their lives remains the prerogative of national parliaments and in some cases the respective national government. Rightly so, this reflects the historical evolution of the European nation state as protector of civil rights and arbiter of civil duties. Transferring this right to the level of the European Union might come as one of the last building-blocs in the construction of the EU edifice. It would undoubtedly be a defining moment for constitutional patriotism in Europe. For the time being, it seems an unthinkable proposition for the majority of EU citizens and politicians to give the EU the right to send European troops overseas. However, along with the issue of a possible European tax, the incremental advancement of the security discourse is in itself already part of an evolving European consensus on these matters of highest relevance for the evolution of European constitutionalism.[54] This discourse is stretching the frontiers of political will as the basis of EU policy consent further, no matter how strong the resistance, how daunting the path,and how incremental the implementation still is.

4. Claiming Patriotism for Europe

Constitutional patriotism is neither a new concept nor is it confined to any geographical framework. In a famous application to the national discourse in West Germany about the value and meaning of its democratic post-World War II constitution, political philosopher Dolf Sternberger introduced the concept of constitutional patriotism in the 1980's to contemporary Europe.[55] In doing so, he reclaimed "patriotism" as a republican virtue reaching beyond its national, let alone ethnic interpretation. He recalled that patriotism is older than nationalism and, in fact, older than the complete organization of Europe along the line of nation states. The concept of patriotism and even "fatherland" was related to the republican notion of state and constitution in its ancient Roman sense. Freedom of citizens under a constitution – this Roman ideal remains the point of orientation for any useful definition of "constitutional patriotism." With Sternberger's interpretation, patriotism was stripped of its mythical, dark interpretation, often linked to the age of nationalism, and returned to its root of freedom and citizenship. There is no reason to doubt that this type of patriotism, based on the idea of freedom and the value of law enshrined in the European Union's treaty-based *acquis communautaire,* could over time evolve in the European Union.

Sternberger cited Cicero to underline his argument that democratic legitimacy goes beyond loyalty to basic rights and constitutional provisions. In "de legibus" Cicero distinguished two fatherlands: one we have by nature, the other one by citizenship ("unam naturae, alteram civitatis").[56] Patriotism could only remain vivid as constitutional patriotism, Sternberger argued. Rule of law and freedom must pave its way and continue to be the core of its expression over time. Why should it not apply to

54 See Weiler, Joseph H. H., and Marlene Wind (eds.), *European Constitutionalism Beyond the State*, Cambridge: Cambridge University Press, 2003.
55 Sternberger, Dolf, *Verfassungspatriotismus*, Frankfurt/Main: Insel Verlag, 1990: 17-53.
56 Cit. ibid.: 33.

the European Union, what has been valid not only for post-War Germany but already for the ancient Roman republic? As the European Union embarks on its journey as a contract-based constitutional order, gradually its citizens will have to give substance and meaning to a European constitutional patriotism. They will have to defend the "European Constitution" if it is to prevail.

An emerging European constitutional patriotism needs to be shaped by the loyalty of its citizens while emerging European constitutionalism will largely be subject to constitutional interpretations by experts.[57] Public goods will have to be delivered by European politicians but public recognition for the European Union will largely depend upon the attitudes of European citizens. Some academics are concerned that a growing sense of constitutional patriotism in Europe could strengthen the difference, if not the frontiers between Europe and other parts of the world. The opposite is closer to reality: The more Europe becomes confident about its political and constitutional identity, the more reliable it will become as a global partner, certain of its interests and ideals in pursuing a cohesive and predictable global role.

The technical construction of the European demos will remain dependent upon the procedures and results of European parliamentary democracy. The emotional glue necessary to solidify this construction must continuously evolve inside the European body politic; it is here that European patriotism must be reclaimed as the virtue of a new European Republic. The European Union will remain both a Union of States and a Union of Citizens. Its long-term legitimacy will be judged by the degree of the "European spirit" it can acquire and project. The European Union will be tested by the degree of civic sense among its citizens to make Europe work. This is not a metaphysical concept. European spirit and European civic sense can largely be defined by the willingness to contribute to the evolution of the EU in recognition of the benefits of European integration. As much as there is no "naturalistic determinism of the boundaries of nations,"[58] there is no naturalistic determinism of the limits of European integration. The limits of the European Union will be defined by its ability to generate lasting purpose by turning the meaning of integration into sustainable benefits for its citizens. Increasingly, the quest for purpose exposes the EU to a more robust global role. The post-imperial definition of a global role for Europe means nothing less than the return of Europe to the global stage.

Whether or not the European Union as a Union of States and a Union of Citizens will be able to give itself a lasting purpose shared inside Europe and accepted by the world into which Europe is reintegrating as an indispensable partner after a century of imperialism and contraction, of division and self-destruction remains to be seen. No historical model or method exists for Europe to take stock and to measure its ambition.

57 For a critical assessment see Haltern, Ulrich, "Pathos and Patina: The Failure and Promise of Constitutionalism in the European Imagination," *European Law Journal*, 9 (2003): 14-44.

58 Gellner, Ernest, "Nationalism and the Two Forms of Cohesion in Complex Societies," in: Gellner, Ernest (ed.): *Culture, Identity, and Politics*, Cambridge: Cambridge University Press , 1987: 8.

The “old world” is continuing to reinvent itself, a quality normally not associated with Europe. And yet, the ongoing European integration experience is among the most innovative and promising of processes Europe has ever encountered in its long history. European institutions have been established. During the next decades, it is time to inspire the creation of genuine Europeans populating a revitalized and unified continent. Their European patriotism would not be directed against anybody, any other country or region, culture or religion. It would become a patriotism of self-declared tasks and duties for a Europe engaging in the wider world as a partner in freedom.

XIII. Defining Europe's Global Interests

I. Exploring the Seas of the World

(1) Navigating with Caution

As far as the evolution of its global interests is concerned, the European Union acts like a modern version of Prince Henry the Navigator. Carefully, the Portuguese Prince was stumbling his way into the discovery of the world beyond the coasts of Europe. In 1418, the ships he had commissioned traveled for the first time from the coast of Portugal to Madeira. In 1427, they reached the Azores. In 1435, on Henry's behalf, the courageous captain Gil Eanes sailed round Cape Bojador – across the Canary Islands on the African coast – and reached the highly feared "Sea of Darkness." By 1444, in the name of Henry the Navigator Portuguese ships reached the Capverdian Islands, Senegal and Gambia. By 1446, they reached Guinea. It was not until 1487 that Bartolomeu Diaz sailed around Cape of Good Hope. By then, Prince Henry the Navigator had already been dead for 27 years.

With the Treaty of Maastricht, entering into force on November 1, 1993, the European Union was created. Since then, the EU has been pursuing the development of a Common Foreign and Security Policy (CFSP, Treaty of Maastricht, Title V). In the course of less than two decades, the ominous Second Pillar of the Treaty of Maastricht has grown into a wide spectrum of foreign, security and defense policies of the European Union. After the completion of its Economic and Monetary Union, the creation of a Common Foreign and Security Policy has become the main integration project for the EU. In the post-Cold War world, the global presence of Europe has become the main rationale for European integration. New security challenges and foreign policy opportunities occur out of area. They force the EU to either become a global player or remain a regional subject of world affairs. The EU had no choice but to overcome the limits of its self-perception as a civilian power. As a global player, the EU needs to contribute to global governance and world order in all aspects possible.[1] In the meantime, the global presence of Europe entails a wide array of instruments and is covering a broad ground from peace-keeping operations to development aid and democracy promotion. The EU's global presence is far from being comprehensive, robust and sufficient. But the EU has gone a long way from the days of the signing of the Treaty of Maastricht. Security is defined in broad terms, including military and civilian aspects. Politically, the most decisive move in the development of a European

1 See Carlsnaes, Walter, et al. (eds.), *Contemporary European Foreign Policy*, London: Sage, 2004; Marsh, Steve, and Hans Mackenstein (eds.), *The International Relations of the European Union*, Edinburgh: Pearsons, 2005; Telò, Mario, *Europe: A Civilian Power?: European Union, Global Governance, World Order*, Houndmills: Palgrave Macmillan, 2006.

Security and Defense Policy (ESDP) as a major element of the Common Foreign and Security Policy of the EU was the Franco-British agreement of December 4, 1998, in St. Malo. Without France and Great Britain, the concept of a common security and defense policy of the EU would have remained a dead-born theory. The leading military powers among EU member states decided to develop a common and independent European defense capacity. Often, France and Great Britain differed on the usefulness of an independent European defense capacity. While France has always favored it, Great Britain emphasized the primacy of NATO. In St. Malo, the leaders of both countries struck a compromise. This was of central importance for all other EU member states. What France and Germany have been to the achievement of the euro, France and Great Britain are to the achievement of a common European army and defense structure: the pivotal European states.

The breakthrough of a European Security and Defense Policy under the overall framework of a Common Foreign and Security Policy of the EU owes its relative speed to the deep frustration and anger across Europe over the four Wars of Yugoslavian Succession during the 1990's. The European Union was incapable to stop the first wars on European soil since the end of World War II. It neither had a legal mandate nor the military instruments, or the political will to prevent the Yugoslavian tragedy. The decisions in St. Malo were a step in the right direction. The ultimate breakthrough among EU member states followed the Kosovo war in the summer of 1999. Never before had failed crisis management of the European Union triggered such a speedy set of actions and a comprehensive policy approach: The office of the EU High Representative for the Common Foreign and Security Policy had been legally established with the Treaty of Amsterdam (signed on October 2, 1987, entered into force after ratification on May 1, 1999). Former NATO Secretary General Javier Solana took up this almost impossible job under the roof of the European Council in October 1999 (original budget 40 million euros). He began to exercise it with diplomatic skills, enormous commitment and steadily growing success. Gradually, military-political coordination and decision-making structures were established in Brussels. The Helsinki European Council of December 2000 decided the "2003 Headline Goals" according to which the EU was to initiate an operative military component of 50,000 to 60,000 soldiers for possible crisis management. A Capabilities Commitments Conference in November 2000 had registered the readiness of EU member states to provide up to 100,000 soldiers, 400 fighter planes and 100 marine ships for future military crisis management of the EU. This nucleus of an EU military unit should be staffed from existing armies, "without any major commitment to more soldiers or more equipment."[2] One exception was related to the lack of adequate transport planes, being one of the

2 Reid, T.R., *The United States of Europe: The New Superpower and the End of American Supremacy*, New York: Penguin Press, 2004: 182.

fundamental deficits of the EU: The EU agreed to produce a fleet of new troop transport aircraft, to be built by Airbus.[3]

Frictions between EU and NATO slowed down the ambition of a substantial EU commitment in military crisis management, no matter the elegant diplomatic rhetoric. In the end, arrangements between the EU and NATO in December 2002 on the use of common structures and capacities ended prolonged debates about the dangers of "duplication" and "decoupling." The terrorist attacks of September 11, 2001, halted the initial effort of an integrative approach for a European Security and Defense Union. For the time being, the idea of a collective European defense union, including a European army, was put aside. Following an American request for burden sharing, and under the impression of the need of crisis management in an age of asymmetric warfare, Europe began to concentrate on a small and flexible structure for EU military our of area crisis management. In 2004, EU member states agreed on the establishment of a European Rapid Reaction Force of around 60,000 soldiers, structured in units of 1,500 soldiers in reinforced battalions ("Battlegroups"). These Battlegroups were ready for action in 2007. In a non-formal sense, joint military operations by British, Spanish, Italian and Polish troops in Iraq had been of an anticipatory nature. The EU Battlegroups were to combine peacekeeping and humanitarian tasks. They would operate in harmony with the concept of a NATO Rapid Deployment Force being developed simultaneously. Whatever the ultimate fate of these Rapid Deployment Forces may be, with the development of a European Security and Defense Policy the EU was adding hard power to its global role. The European Union could not afford to simply remain a benevolent soft power. The complex nature of modern security concerns require a definition of security that entails military and civilian, environmental and developmental, policing and order-building aspects. The evolution of EU policies and instruments happened with laser-like speed compared with other integration projects. In light of the even faster transformation of global security challenges following the terrorist attacks of "9/11," the incremental and cautious development of EU policy instruments in foreign, security and defense matters was still reminiscent of the gradual global outreach of Portuguese seafarers in the fifteenth century.

One of the interesting paradoxes of the evolution of a Common Foreign and Security Policy of the EU has been a surprising reversal of form and function. During the Wars of Yugoslavian Succession, then EC leaders were hiding behind the absence of legal instruments that would enable the European Community to take action. Less than two decades later, the European Union is advancing its foreign, security and defense instruments ahead of legal clarifications. The 2004 Constitutional Treaty proposed the establishment of a European Diplomatic Service ("European External Action Service") in support of the High Representative for the Common Foreign and

3 See Giovanni Grevi et.al. (eds.), *European Security and Defence Policy: The first 10 years (1999-2009),* Paris: The European Union Institute for Security Studies, 2009.

Security Policy who was to be renamed Foreign Minister. While the constitutional debate was still going on and the ratification crisis over the European Constituton escalated, the European External Actions Service was already beginning to take shape in Brussels. In the 2007 Reform Treaty, its future competences – by and large remaining of an intergovernmental nature - were outlined in detail (Title V, General Provisions on the Union's External Action and Specific Provisions on the Common Foreign and Security Policy).[4] However, the prestigious title of an EU Foreign Minister was scrapped – much to the regret of those who wished for a stronger EU profile in global affairs. The proposed future title High Representative of the Union for Foreign Affairs and Security Policy was even clumsier than that of its predecessor. When Catherine Ashton was appointed to the post, she was welcomed with a combination of skepticism and curiosity. On top of being the EU's first Foreign Minister in all but name, she was also appointed Vice-President of the European Commission, thus replacing the Commissioner for External Affairs. Whatever the eventual judgement of her term in office may be, this connection of the two main posts dealing with external affairs had to be considered as a sign of strengthened authority of the EU in foreign and security affairs. More than formal treaty provisions, political realities would shape the future EU's global projection.

The same phenomenon had already occurred with regard to the first military and policing operations under the banner of the EU (that is to say as intergovernmental, cooperative actions coordinated by the Council Secretariat). Even before proper military structures were organized, the European Union initiated its first out of area peace-keeping actions. An EU-led civilian police mission in Sarajevo with 500 police officers from 30 countries in January 2003 was followed by "Operation Concordia" in Macedonia. Between March and December 2003, the EU led a civilian police operation of 300 men from 27 countries to implement the EU brokered peace-plan for Macedonia. In 2004, this mission was followed by the civilian police mission "Proxima," unfortunately lacking a robust mandate to implement the peace accord by fighting corruption and organized crime in Macedonia. In 2003, for the first time the European Union operated as peace-keeper in Africa. "Operation Artemis" in the north-eastern Congolese region of Bunia was aimed at providing security and order as precondition for improving the humanitarian situation in Bunia. "Operation Artemis" "provided the operational template"[5] for EU's future Battlegroups. It came to a successful end in September 2003. In December 2004, "EUFOR" (European Union Force) with 7000 soldiers under EU command replaced NATO's Stabilization Force SFOR in Bosnia-

4 European Union, "Treaty of Lisbon Amending the Treaty on European Union and the Treaty Establishing the European Community," *Official Journal of the European Union*, C 306/Vol.50, Luxembourg: Office for Official Publications of the European Communities, 2007, http://eur-lex.europa.eu/JOHtml.do?uri=OJ:C:2007:306:SOM:EN:HTML, 23-38.

5 Lindstrom, Gustav, *Enter the EU Battlegroups*, Chaillot Paper No. 97, Paris: European Union Institute for Security Studies, 2007: 9.

Herzegovina. This operation, code-named "Althea," was the biggest military mission of the European Union yet. The stabilization of the Western Balkans remained the first priority for the EU, but it could no longer avoid operations with a global reach.[6]

Other operations followed, including the EU support to the Palestinian Civil Police (EUPOL COPPS), the Aceh Monitoring Mission in 2005, monitoring the implemenetation of the peace agreement on the Indonesian island, the monitoring of elections in Kongo in 2006 under a UN mandate, and the training of judges, investigating magistrates and senior policy officers in Iraq since 2005 (EUJUST Lex). The most spectacular mission in terms of world politics so far came about with the EU presence at the border post between the Gaza Strip and Egypt in Rafah, which started in November 2005 (European Border Assistance Mission, EU BAM). After Israel and the Palestinian National Authority had agreed to reopen the Rafah crossing, the EU was asked to provide border assistance. After a decision in the EU General Affairs Council on November 21, 2005, it took only until November 25, 2005, for the first European police officers to appear at Rafah. The mission was immediately staffed with 77 police officers. Soon, the original mandate was prolonged until at least 2008, but its execution remained subject to the overall situation in the unruly Gaza Strip. Following the war between Israel and Hezbollah forces in Lebanon in the summer of 2006, the European Union stepped up its engagement in the Middle East: More than 6,000 soldiers were stationed in Southern Lebanon and in the waters between Lebanon and Israel. Although the soldiers were of individual national backgrounds, the whole operation was considered to be the biggest military involvement yet of the European Union in search for a lasting and stable peace in the Middle East.

Until December 2009, when the Treaty of Lisbon of Lisbon entered into force, the European Union had engaged in 21 military and policing missions all over the world. Formally, the Treaty of Lisbon confined the European Union's foreign and security policy to intergovernmental consent and national committment: Yet, the global exposure of the EU was a strong sign of anticipating action that would eventually also undermine other prevailing national prerogatives. For the time being and in spite of the establishment of a coherent set of institutions in Brussels – namely the Political and Security Committee, the Military Committee, the Military Staff and the EU Operations Center – the European Security and Defense Policy had not yet become a proper supranational operation. Only in matters of external trade and, partially, in matters of development policy can the European Commission represent Europe directly. This confusing gap of cohesion may slightly be bridged over the years with realities being shaped by Catherine Ashton and her successors in their doubled-hatted role as High Representative of the Union for Foreign Affairs and Security Policy and as Vice-

6 See Tocci, Nathalie, *The EU and Conflict Resolution: Promoting Peace in the Backyard*, Abingdon: Routledge, 2007; O'Brennan, John, *The EU and the Western Balkans: Stabilization and Europeanization Through Enlargement*, Abingdon: Routledge, 2007.

President of the European Commission. Eventually, the real relevance of the position will not be a matter of treaty provisions but of personal authority. After all, since 2010 the High Representative is chairing all meetings of the EU Foreign Affairs Council.

Progress in projecting the interests of the European Union in the field of foreign and secuirity cannot be denied. Any European military or policing presence would have been unimaginable only a decade ago, in 2000. Now, even Israel wants the EU to get involved in the Middle East with more soldiers and a more robust mandate. By all accounts, the new trends in the Middle East were the most dramatic turn in the global recognition of the European Union as an honest mediator and peace broker. Since 2003 the EU is participating in the Middle East Quartet that had outlined a Road Map to a viable peace based on a two-state solution. Only now, with a stronger military and policing profile, has the claim of the European Union to serve as an honest and impartial broker of peace in the longest standing and most tragic conflict on earth gained momentum.

The police mission of the EU in Afghanistan (as of June 2007 the fifteenth EU mission under the European Security and Defense Policy) and the civilian mission monitoring the independence of Kosovo after the province's formal independence on February 17, 2008 have been logical continuations of a trend that had started with extreme caution and hesitance: During the first decade of the twenty-first century, the European Union has advanced its global ambition by a gradual and creeping approximation to this challenge comparable to the approach of the Portuguese seafarers sent to discover the oceans of the world by Prince Henry the Navigator almost six centuries earlier.[7] While the United States of America has been familiar with geostrategic and global thinking at least since the late nineteenth century, the European Union was incrementally forced by new geopolitical and geo-economic realities to follow a similar direction in the early twenty-first century.[8] The EU is increasingly contributing to global governance.[9] This has also become evident in the field of climate policy. The European Union wants to be understood as a "world player".[10] However, EU citizens remain ambivalent about the role their political actors should play. While 70 percent of Europeans want to see the EU as a world power like the United States, only 44 percent support additional defense spending if that should be the unavoidable consequence of their claim to global involvement.[11]

7 See Geographica Slovenica (ed.), *Political Geography in the twenty-first Century: Understanding the Place, Looking Ahead*, Ljubljana: Institute of Geography, 2001.

8 See Brimmer, Esther (ed.), *The EU's Search for a Strategic Role: ESDP and its Implications for Transatlantic Relations*, Washington, D.C.: Center for Transatlantic Relations, 2002; Rühl, Lothar, *ESDP and Intervention Strategies in Reaction to US and NATO*, ZEI Discussion Paper C 137. Bonn: Center for European Integration Studies, 2004.

9 See Ortega, Martin, *Building the Future: The EU's Contribution to Global Governance*, Chaillot Paper No. 100, Paris: European Union Institute for Security Studies, 2007.

10 See European Union. European Commission, *A World Player: The European Union's External Relations*, 2004, http://ec.europa.eu/publications/booklets/move/47/en.pdf.

11 See *Frankfurter Allgemeine Zeitung*, "Europäer wollen Weltmacht sein," September 7, 2005.

(2) The EU Security Strategy

Beyond immediate crisis management, the EU tried to stabilize its global outreach by way of creating intermediary structures between its own sphere and its hemisphere: Membership of the European Commission in the Council of the Baltic Sea States, the Barents Euro-Artic Council or the Black Sea Economic Cooperation Organization are some examples of how of the EU bridged Europe's surrounding shores. Build on these experiences and realizing the limits of possible enlargements in its vicinity, the EU began to develop a more or less cohesive Neighborhood Policy. Before the underlying concept of this projection as regional power had been concluded, the EU was already beyond the immediate discovery of geography and had entered the world of geopolitics. In December 2003, for the first time in its history, the European Union published a comprehensive Security Strategy.[12] Considered as a European response to the National Security Strategy of the US of September 2002 – which was controversial in Europe primarily because of its justification of "pre-emptive strikes" against states posing a fundamental threat to the security of the US[13] – it was a remarkable document nonetheless given the EU's traditional reluctance to go global and claim to be a strategic power.[14]

The emerging global outreach of the EU's strategic horizon took place in the shadow of the United States. It was largely driven by the new geopolitical approach of the US in its "War on Terror," pronounced by the Bush Administration in the aftermath of the terror attacks of September 11, 2001. The EU document could not hide lingering disputes among EU member states on fundamental threat perceptions, and moreover on subsequent policy conclusions. National and ideational attitudes had to be brought to consensus. The EU Security Strategy was a contribution to reconcile threat perceptions of the US and the EU after the painful disputes over the war in Iraq. It surely was only the first and by no means the last strategic outline of EU's global projection.

Under the title "A Secure Europe in a Better World," the EU Security Strategy analyzed the main threat scenarios for Europe in the early twenty-first century and reflected on the strategic imperatives Europe saw itself confronted with:[15]

- Also in the twenty-first century, Europe remains confronted with security threats and challenges. A European Union with twenty-seven member states, 491

12 European Union, *A Secure Europe in a Better World: European Security Strategy*, Paris: European Union Institute for Security Studies, 2003

13 U.S. National Security Strategy: *A Balance of Power that Favours Freedom*, http://usinfo.state.gov/journals/itps/1202/ijpe/pj7-4rice.htm.

14 On the immediate reactions to the EU's Security Strategy see Everts, Steven, "Two Cheers for the EU's New Security Strategy," *International Herald Tribune*, December 9, 2003; for a deeper analysis see Reiter, Erich, "Die Sicherheitsstrategie der EU," *Aus Politik und Zeitgeschichte*, 3-4 (2004): 26-31; Biscop, Sven, and Jan Joel Andersson (eds.), *The EU and the European Security Strategy*, Abingdon: Routledge, 2007.

15 European Union, *A Secure Europe in a Better World: European Security Strategy*, op.cit: 5-9.

million citizens and a share of 25 percent of the global gross domestic product inevitably has to act as global player.

- Recent developments in international affairs have raised the awareness that non-state actors and new security risks can threaten the stability of Europe. Terrorists with religious extremism as their ideology and the readiness to use violence have chosen Europe both as their target and their base. The dependency of Europe and thus Europe's vulnerability have increased with the latest developments of globalization.
- Security is a precondition for development. Between 1990 and 2003, four million people have died in warfare. The proliferation of weapons of mass destruction, particularly in the Middle East, and progress in the bio-sciences, which can lead to a dangerous use of chemical and radiological material, expose Europe to growing risks. But likewise, hunger and malnutrition, AIDS, the impoverishment of sub-Saharan Africa, the competition for natural resources – with consequences for global warming – and the energy dependency of Europe, are dangerous trends.
- State failure, bad governance and the collapse of states are alarming phenomena that undermine the goal of global governance and increase regional instability.

In light of the terror attacks of September 11, 2001, the European Union declared its readiness to confront the new global challenges and presented its relevant achievements:[16]

- The EU has contributed to the global fight against terrorism with the introduction of a European Arrest Warrant and other measures to stop financial transfers to terrorist groups.
- The EU supports the policy of preventing proliferation of atomic weapons and demands universal recognition of multilateral measures and treaties in support of this goal.
- The EU supports the end of regional conflicts and wants to contribute to the rehabilitation of failed states. This includes the EU's efforts to reintroduce good governance in all countries of Southeast Europe.
- The EU is pursuing a policy of enhanced security in its neighborhood. Integration of further European states into the EU – in particular in Southeast Europe – will enhance security and stability in the EU's vicinity.
- The EU supports a solution of the Arab-Israeli conflict. This is considered to be a strategic priority of the EU. The EU remains committed to a peaceful solution based on two states and declares its readiness to provide resources until the conflict is resolved.
- The EU considers the Mediterranean as a region which requires increased and

16 Ibid.: 10-13.

effective cooperation in economic, security and political terms. The EU also underlines its desire to increase its engagement with the Arab world.

On the basis of these principles and experiences, the EU's support for an effective multilateral order is considered a high priority as the adequate global frame to resolve the new strategic challenges:[17]

- The EU declares its commitment to the preservation and development of international law. Strengthening the role of the United Nations is a priority for the EU. However, international organizations, regimes and treaties have to comply with international norms, and international organizations have to be ready to act whenever international norms are breached.
- Transatlantic relations remain one of the core elements of the international system. Strengthening them is not only in the bilateral interest of the EU and the US, but according to the EU it will strengthen the international system in general. The EU will continue to support the development of regional cooperation and integration schemes. ASEAN, MERCOSUR and the African Union are explicitly mentioned.
- The quality of the international system depends on the quality of the governments that form this system. Therefore it remains essential to continue the EU's policy of improving governance elsewhere through means of support and cooperation, but limited by conditionality in the EU's relations with external partners, and targeted trade measures. Countries that prefer to opt out of the orbit of international norms must realize that they will have to pay a price for this norm-breaking behavior.

As far as policy challenges for the EU are concerned, the European Union drew the following conclusions from its security analysis: [18]

- The EU will pursue its goals in a more active manner by using the whole spectrum of its instruments of crisis management and conflict prevention.
- The EU expressed its desire to develop a strategic culture in Europe supportive of early, speedy and if necessary robust interventions.
- The EU intends to strengthen its capacity to act based in a systematic pooling and effective use of available defense resources. The EU is aware of its need to achieve greater cohesion and better coordination in all policy fields that are vital for the strengthening of the global weight of the EU. In this regard, transatlantic relations with the US are considered irreplaceable.

Prince Henry the Navigator was a theoretician who is said to have only once touched the planks of a ship. In a similar sense, the Security Strategy of the European Union was primarily a theoretical construction that was waiting to stand the test of practice. Over time, it indeed lived up to the practice. Although the EU document

17 Ibid.: 14-16.
18 Ibid.: 17-21.

avoided the term "preventive attack," it did recognize that in light of new threat potential the first line of defense might often be outside Europe. In response to a possible combination of totalitarian Islamic ideologies, the readiness of fanatics to resort to terrorism and the proliferation of weapons of mass destruction in undemocratic and hence unpredictable states "we should be ready to act before a crisis occurs."[19] Slowly, but inevitably (and not unlike Prince Henry the Navigator and his captains), the European Union was sailing toward the most dangerous currents and unknown cliffs of twenty-first century world politics.

(3) The Broader Middle East and Neighborhood Strategies

The Broader Middle East was identified both in Europe and in the US as the first main post-Cold War challenge. Due to uncertainty, backwardness and the absence of pluralism in most Arab societies, the Broader Middle East included a whole list of potential threats to Western security. Since the Bush Administration had declared reforms, if not the outright transformation of the Broader Middle East, its priority in the war against terrorism, the European Union had to catch up with reality in broadening its theory of how to deal with challenges that were considered more of a threat than an opportunity. More important than the semantic quarrel over whether the zone of instability between "Marrakech and Bangladesh" (as US strategists Ronald D. Asmus and Kenneth M. Pollack put it)[20] should be labeled Greater Middle East or Broader Middle East was the issue of goals, means and instruments to be used in order to encourage freedom and democracy on the southern Islamic borders of the West. By all accounts, the region is essential for peace and well-being of Europe and the United States. In the early twenty-first century, 15 of 22 Arab states were governed in an authoritarian or dictatorial manner. Islamic fundamentalism was not only threatening the West, but also various Arab regimes. Permanent terror attacks, most notably in Saudi-Arabia grew the awareness of the inherent problematic character of Arab regimes – and the dilemma that radical religious alternatives might not be any better, and in fact probably even much more anti-Western.

It was important to note that while Prince Henry the Navigator was driven by a desire to fight the Moors – that is to say, all non-Christians – the European Union of the early twenty-first century constantly warned against the danger of a clash of

19 Ibid.: 11; on the complexity of the matter see Kühnhardt, Ludger, *System-Opening and Co-Operative Transformation of the Greater Middle East: A New Trans-Atlantic Project and a Joint Euro-Atlantic-Arab Task*, EUROMESCO Papers No. 26, Lisbon: Euro-Mediterranean Study Commission, 2003; Pflüger, Friedbert, *Ein neuer Weltkrieg? Die islamistische Herausforderung des Westens*, Munich: Deutsche Verlags-Anstalt, 2004; Marchetti, Andreas (ed.), *Ten Years Euro-Mediterranean Partnership: Defining European Interests for the Next Decade*, ZEI Discussion Paper C 154, Bonn: Center for European Integration Studies, 2005.

20 Asmus, Ronald D., and Kenneth M. Pollack, "The New Transatlantic Project," *Policy Review*, 115 (2002): 3-18.

civilizations and religions. Overshadowed by legitimate controversies over Israel's policies in the occupied territories, the democratic character of Israel and the legitimate security needs of Israel did not always find the appropriate recognition in Europe. It could therefore not come as a surprise to the EU that controversies over Israel exacerbated its disputes with the US. Often, the EU was perceived as being more interested in the Euro-Arab diplomatic dialogue than in more controversial matters of promoting democratic governance in the Arab world. Whether or not this was a correct and fair perception, it did not help to facilitate the evolution of a common Western strategy toward the Broader Middle East and mutual trust between the West and the Islamic world. Americans and Europeans also had to learn that a reform-oriented opening of political conditions in the Arab world ruled by autocratic regimes for all too long could produce Islamic trends, including radical ones, suppressed in the past. Hamas' victory in free and democratic elections in Palestine in January 2006 triggered a new round of frustration, chaos, and radicalization, including the violent take-over of power in the Gaza Strip in June 2007 by Hamas. In the end, it was impossible to simply boycott the Hamas government if a new all-out escalation in the Middle East was to be avoided. But how to deal intellectually with Islamic concepts of politics if they find democratic legitimacy would remain the even bigger challenge for the West for many years to come. The voyage around Cape Bojador had never been without risk.

Following the formulation of its first ever Security Strategy on December 12, 2003, the European Union complimented its new strategic assertiveness on May 12, 2004, with a Strategy Paper of the European Commission on European Neighborhood Policy. The goal of the EU's policy toward its neighbors in the East, the Southeast and the South was defined as "a set of priorities, whose fulfillment will bring them closer to the European Union."[21] This statement was followed by a cascade of good intentions: "Political dialogue and reform; trade and measures preparing partners for gradually obtaining a stake in the EU's Internal Market; justice and home affairs; energy, transport, information, society, environment and research and innovation; and social policy and people-to-people contacts."[22] The ultimate goal would be to share with the neighboring countries in the East, the South East and the South the advantages of the

21 European Union. European Commission, *European Neighbourhood Policy: Strategy Paper*, May 12, 2004: 3, http://ec.europa.eu/world/enp/pdf/strategy/strategy_paper_en.pdf. For an analytical assessment of the matter see Dwan, Renata (ed.), *Building Security in Europe's New Borderlands: Subregional Cooperation in the Wider Europe*, Armonk, N.Y./London: EastWest Institute, 1999; Gillespie, Richard, and Richard Youngs (eds.), *The European Union and Democracy Promotion: The Case of North Africa*, London: Frank Cass, 2002; Batt, Judy, et al., *Partners and Neighbours: A CFSP for a Wider Europe*, Chaillot Papers No.64. Paris: Institute for Security Studies, 2003; Dannreuther, Roland (ed.), *European Union Foreign and Security Policy: Towards a Neighbourhood Strategy*, London: Routledge, 2004; Marchetti, Andreas, *The European Neighbourhood Policy: Foreign Policy at the EU's Periphery*, ZEI Discussion Paper C 158, Bonn: Center for European Integration Studies, 2006.

22 European Union. European Commission, *European Neighbourhood Policy: Strategy Paper*, op.cit.: ibid.

enlargement of the European Union to post-communist Central Europe in 2004, "in strengthening stability, security and well-being for all concerned."[23]

The vision of the Neighborhood Policy of the European Union "involves a ring of countries, sharing the EU's fundamental values and objectives, drawn into an increasingly close relationship, going beyond co-operation to involve a significant measure of economic and political integration."[24] East of the EU and around the borders of the Mediterranean, the EU intends "to promote a ring of well governed countries with whom we can enjoy close and cooperative relations."[25] For the fiscal period between 2007 and 2013 the European Union provides 11.2 billion euros of aid through the new European Neighborhood Instrument. For the Eastern European partner countries (Ukraine, Moldova, Armenia, Azerbaijan, Georgia) the EU thus provides an average support of 3.64 euros per head. For the Mediterranean partner countries the EU provides 3.36 euros per head. In absolute terms, this financial instrument seemed almost ridiculously low. But the EU insisted that the appropriate use of its support would eventually trigger structural reforms across Europe's neighborhood. Concrete projects include, for instance, the support of a European-Maghrebinian Energy Market as part of a "strategic energy partnership" with the Maghreb region.[26] Neighborhood cooperation in the field of energy must indeed be of particular interest to the EU as its energy imports will grow from 50 percent in 2004 to 70 percent in 2030. The EU also announced support in Southern Mediterranean countries for the establishment of independent regulatory authorities and the opening of markets for fixed telephone and for advanced services such as the internet.[27] The main obstacle to the EU's Neighborhood Strategy: It could not remain a cohesive, single strategy beyond the moment it was to take into consideration the vast differences between the belt of neighbors as diverse as Morocco or Ukraine.

Moreover, the Neighborhood Strategy of the European Union did not even try to answer the question as to how the EU would be able to generate the necessary resources for the implementation of its Neighborhood Policies. The result of budgetary negotiations for the fiscal period 2007–2013 in December 2005 was disappointing for European foreign policy experts. Out of a budget of 862.3 billion euros, a sum of only 50.0 billion euros was attributed to Foreign and Security Policy, including for Development Cooperation. This means a decrease from 7 to 5.8 percent of the budget total compared with the period 2000-2006. Nobody was able to explain how the EU should be able to meet growing duties with shrinking means. This did not seem to be less easy than the Portuguese effort in the fifteenth century to find the right sea route to

23 Ibid.
24 Ibid.: 5.
25 Ibid.: 6.
26 Ibid.
27 Ibid.: 19; see also *Frankfurter Allgemeine Zeitung*, "Mehr Geld für Europas Nachbarn," December 5, 2006.

India. Some of the naval ships that Prince Henry the Navigator had sent to sea in order to find the fastest sea route to India ended up exploring the Northern Artic Sea. The EU's Northern Arctic Sea was a frozen budget for its neighborhood ambitions.

Nevertheless, at least conceptually the EU has already taken the next step in its discovery of the world. On June 23, 2004, the European Commission and the European Council presented their final report on a Strategic Partnership of the EU with the Mediterranean and the Middle East. The paper stated that common interests should be pursued among the partners of the EU's Neighborhood Policy. Common challenges should be dealt with together. The partner countries south of the Mediterranean should be recognized in their diversity and be dealt with in a differentiated manner. Reforms could only succeed if they would grow out of the partner societies; they could not be imposed from the outside.[28]

The paper was lacking a precise description of common European interests. It was also vague on the instruments and means the EU might be ready to use in order to consistently pursue its normative goals. The term "conditionality" was used in a rather unclear manner, leaving more questions open than it was able to answer. As far as the rationale for the EU's Neighborhood Policy and its attachment to the Mediterranean is concerned, the paper was astonishingly lacking in detail. The EU itself has a Mediterranean coast and yet it seemed as if for the EU the "Mediterranean" only meant "Southern Mediterranean" – and more precisely, the Arab and Islamic Mediterranean. The attachment of the EU to those states and societies, according to the Strategy Report, originates in the presence of a growing number of inhabitants and citizens of the EU with roots in the Southern Mediterranean and in the Middle East. Geographic proximity creates interdependencies. In recognizing this simple fact, the EU Strategy Report was already looking beyond the next corner and called for the need to gradually develop partnership with the countries of the Gulf region. In spite of the general desire for partnership, the EU could not overlook that regional conflicts, terrorism, the proliferation of weapons of mass destruction and organized crime had grown into new security challenges. Partnership with the EU would give all partners of the EU the ability "to move at a pace in accordance with their willingness to engage."[29] The agenda for democratic reform and pluralism in the Broader Middle East could not have been wrapped in a more elegant diplomatic language, totally blurring the purpose and intention of the original meaning of the exercise of engagement. It added to the confusion about long-term strategy and EU coherence when the new French President Nicolas Sarkozy launched his plan of a Mediterranean Union in 2007 without initially

28 European Union, European Commission, *EU Strategic Partnership with the Mediterranean and the Middle East: Final Report*, June 23, 2004, http://ec.europa.eu/external_relations/euromed/publication/2004/euromed_report_78_en.pdf.

29 Ibid.: 4; on the broadening horizon of the EU see Kühnhardt, Ludger, *The Lakes of Europe*, ZEI Discussion Paper C104, Bonn: Center for European Integration Studies, 2002; Aydin, Mustafa, *Europe's Next Shore: The Black Sea Region after EU Enlargement*, Occasional Paper No. 53. Paris: Institute for Security Studies, 2004.

engaging all his EU partners and clarifying links between a Mediterranean Union and the Euro-Mediterranean partnership existing since 1995. Eventually, the European Council of March 2008 unanimously decided on the establishment of the Union for the Mediterranean. By then, the French project had become a joined EU initiative, aimed at giving the Euro-Mediterranean partnership a new strategic perspective.

(4) Migration and Demographics as Common Concern

The mutual interests of Europe and the Broader Middle East have not been conclusively clarified by the EU's Strategy Papers. Common interests can be pursued only if they are based on a common understanding of purpose and goal about the journey toward reforms. The EU could hardly believe that only the Arab Middle East would have to embark on reforms while the EU, by virtue of being politically and economically more advanced, would be exempted from the exercise of reforms. Democratic deficit, socio-economic modernization, and the need for cultural dialogue – these topics could have also applied to any internal EU agenda for reform and modernization. They remained vague in the EU's papers as far as their applicable content for the countries of the Broader Middle East was concerned.

Most ambivalent for Europe is the issue of migration. While the Strategic Paper pursued an approach of normative equidistance, it could not be denied that for the majority of Europeans, increased migration from the Arab-Islam south of the Mediterranean has become a matter of concern, if not of fear and prejudice. Since 2002, Spain has become the EU member state hosting the largest number of migrants per year. From 1.6 million people migrating into the EU in 2003, 594,300 came to Spain. This was more than twice the migration Germany (144,900) and France (55,000) experienced combined. Italy is the second largest recipient of migrants in the EU (511,200 in 2003). Among the migrants to Spain and Italy were and are not only legal and, moreover, illegal migrants from the Maghreb and Africa, but also migrants from Latin America, Eastern Europe and Asian countries such as India, Pakistan, and China.[30] Many Europeans worried about these immigration streams. Yet, in face of a weakened productivity of its economy and confronted with an aging population, Europe will hardly be able to maintain its level of affluence if it does not accept further migration from both the South and the East of its borders. In the absence of sufficient fertility among European citizens to reproduce the EU's population, this seems to be the only viable alternative to maintain the necessary productivity for stable and sustainable welfare state structures in Europe. Opposing both children of one's own and migration from neighbors – who all of a sudden turn from "neighbors" into "aliens" once they convert into migrants – is an alternative Europe cannot sustain. A Strategy Paper of the

30 See Eurostat, *European Demography in 2003*, August 31, 2004, http://epp.eurostat.ec.europa.eu/cache/ITY_PUBLIC/3-31082004-BP/EN/3-31082004-BP-EN.PDF.

EU dealing with the definition of its neighborhood policy toward the Middle East is certainly not the venue to reflect about the link between these issues. But as it claimed honesty and true partnership, it should not have shied away from a superficial analysis of the matter either. It is beyond any doubt that the European Union is in dire need of a more coherent and pro-active migration policy.[31]

According to the Green Paper on Demographic Change launched by the European Commission in March 2005, the EU will have 18 million fewer children and younger people in 2030.[32] Roughly two active people between 15 and 65 will have to take care of one inactive person above the age of 65 as far as pension claims and health costs are concerned. By 2030, according to the European Commission, the EU will lack 20.8 million people of working age. The overall EU population will fall to 468.7 million in 2030. Malta and Cyprus will be the only EU member states with growing populations. On the other hand, the US population will increase by 25 percent between 2000 and 2025.

By 2020, Arab countries will have to generate 100 million new jobs for their young and growing populations. In the absence of any realistic ability to achieve this, millions of young Arabs will have the intention to migrate to Europe, responding to the social pressure inside their own societies. More worrisome for an aging Europe should be the growing age gap between Europe and the Arab world. In 2050, the average Yemenite will be 32 years younger than the average European. While the latter is contemplating health and pension matters, the Yemenite will still be concerned about his own productive future and that of his children. He will continue to ask for his right of a future. How will Europe deal with the implications of these issues that are inextricably interwoven into its partnership web with the Broader Middle East?

It is also astonishing that EU Strategy Papers usually do not dedicate a single sentence to the question of religion. Beside vague reference to totalitarian Islamic extremism, the Strategies of the EU remain silent on the matter. Neither the complex issue of the public role of religion nor the prospect for cooperation, bridge-building and dialogue among the three "Religions of the Book" that claim to be the Children of Abraham found place and discussion in the EU's Strategy.[33] The future of religious relations in the Mediterranean and the Broader Middle East will become a strategic political issue, notwithstanding the EU's failure to address the matter. The dispute about Danish caricatures in early 2006 demonstrates ample proof of this inescapable tendency.

31 See Cuschieri, Marvin Andrew, *Europe's Migration Policy Towards the Mediterranean: The Need of Reconstruction of Policy-Making*, ZEI Discussion Paper C 168, Bonn: Center for European Integration Studies, 2007.

32 European Union, European Commission, *Green Paper "Confronting demographic change: a new solidarity between the generations"*, March 16, 2005, http://eur-lex.europa.eu/LexUriServ/LexUriServ.do?uri=COM:2005:0094:FIN:EN:PDF

33 See Feiler, Bruce, *Abraham: A Journey into the Heart of Three Faiths*, New York: HarperCollins, 2002.

It was considered a positive tendency of transatlantic reconciliation that the EU and the US Administration of President George W. Bush were ready to frame a new rhetorical compromise on their policies toward the Broader Middle East after two years of the worst transatlantic crisis since World War II.[34] In a Joint Declaration at the annual EU-US Summit on June 26, 2004, at Dromoland Castle in Ireland, both sides agreed to support all forces in the Broader Middle East that are ready to take up the challenge of modernization and democratization. Building human rights and democracy, the rule of law, and sustainable market economies had become a rather vague addition to the phraseology of the war on terrorism. The US and the EU, as well as NATO as the most important military and political link across the Atlantic Ocean, will continue in their gradual and emerging involvement in the world "East of Jordan," as it is now designed.A new US President as of 2009 would not alter this global commitment of the US, challenging the EU to participate in a leadership role. During the peak of British imperialism, the notion "East of Eden" had signified the readiness to go global – and it was a term with immediate significance. In the twenty-first century, new arbitrary efforts to redesign the map could hardly be more successful than old imperial concepts. As for the EU, its proliferation of "policy strategies" and the permanent announcement of "strategic partnerships" are hollow. It sounds imposing and yet it is often lacking the foundation it requires to turn a strategy into reality. As for both transatlantic partners, no reconciliatory communiqué could cover the continuity of grave differences: The Iraq debate was hardly buried when the issue of how to deal with Iran's nuclear ambition was beginning to simmer as the possible next transatlantic dispute.[35] The rise of Iran as a new regional power and its ambition to gain nuclear arms has not found an effective Western answer. To apply the traditional logic of deterrence would require mutual recognition. For Iran this would mean to be recognized by the US as an equal partner, while in the US (and in Israel) Iran is simply considered a growing threat of ultimate danger. It is a sign of improvement in transatlantic relations that the EU and the US coordinated their policies on Iran much better than a few years earlier on Iraq. The EU claimed credit for taming the US and preventing a belligerent escalation while the US administration (and Israel) maintained the right of last resort in case Iran's nuclear build-up becomes too grave a threat to its security or that of Israel.

The military action of the US in 2003 against the regime of Saddam Hussein had provoked unprecedented anti-Americanism across the world. President Bush was singled out to be blamed for a wrong policy choice. Europe was anxiously waiting for a new US President to be installed in January 2009. It could however not be excluded that

34 See Gordon, Philip H., and Jeremy Shapiro, *Allies at War: America, Europe, and the Crisis over Iraq*, New York: McGraw-Hill, 2004; Crowe, Brian, "A Common European Foreign Policy After Iraq?," *International Affairs*, 79.3 (2003): 533-546; Zaborowski, Macin (ed.), *Friends Again?: EU-US Relations After the Crisis*, Paris: European Union Institute for Security Studies, 2006.

35 See Meiers, Franz-Josef, *Transatlantic Relations after the U.S. Elections: From Rift to Harmony?*, ZEI Discussion Paper C 140, Bonn: Center for European Integration Studies, 2004:23-30.

in the absence of an alternative to stabilize and finally democratize Iraq President Bush might eventually be rehabilitated by history. Historians might conclude that the war against Iraq was similar to the way Columbus discovered America - a fatal error that led him to a great success. Thus, Columbus became more famous than Prince Henry the Navigator with all his cautiousness and meticulous sense of detail and complexity. In the end, both the EU and the US under a new President would have to engage together and with all societies and countries in the Broader Middle East if they wanted to succeed in transforming the region that had emerged as the pivotal threat to the West in the early twenty-first century. The countries and societies in the Middle East are too proud and self-assertive to accept the status of objects of a benevolent West forcing them into reforms. The EU and the US will have to recognize their neighbors in the Arab world as subjects of self-determined change toward open and dynamic societies, ready to live in partnership and cooperation among them and with the West. Otherwise, the threat and fear emanating from an unruly Broader Middle East will not wither away for the West. Whenever asked to define its values, the West proudly recalls its Judeo-Christian heritage. The Islamic faith and world will have to be reconciled with this self-assessment if the West wants to have a peaceful future throughout the uncertain course of the twenty-first century.

All in all, the evolution of European Foreign and Security Policy is confronted with one fundamental theoretical challenge. In the past, European integration advanced through negative projects, tearing down borders was the *leitmotiv* of economic integration from the Treaties of Rome to the introduction of a common currency. As for European Foreign and Security Policy, it seems to work, at least so far, only as a positive project, a project that moves forward only if it does not encounter obstacles that could question the anticipated additional gains for all EU member states and institutions. This approach, however, could only generate creeping, piece-meal achievements, insufficient to convince the public at large about the meaningfulness of the overall operation. In matters of foreign and security policy, so it seems, the negative component that was used in economic integration as a driving force, could only come from the outside, pressure on Europe not to tear borders down, but to rather build them up in order to protect Europe against new enemies. This logic, however, was and is as uncomfortable for many as it is unpleasantly realistic. If we were to look for driving forces that can help to create more coherence and a stronger overall EU policy performance in foreign and security matters, it remained uncomfortable to say that the search for an enemy has obviously not lost its age-old function. For the European Union still oscillating between the comfort of portraying itself as a soft power and the rough winds of a world in which hard power prevails, balancing comfort and expectation is equivalent to balancing interests and values, that is to say a precise definition of threats for Europe and a realistic configuration of values relevant to the projection of Europe.

2. Assessing European Interests and Understanding Strategy

Defining interests and formulating a global strategy has never been easy for the European Union. Connecting Europe's past with Europe's global future has been as difficult as the effort to pool the interests of all EU member states and institutional actors under the umbrella of one coherent and common European interest. And yet, gradually, the European Union is becoming a global actor, being forced to answer questions about its interests and underlying strategies.

"Interest" as a political term is a dynamic concept. It cannot be framed in a static way based on experiences and parameters of an ever-valid past. It cannot deny changing circumstances and variable priorities. Yet it remains linked to the root of all politics, geography and history, resources and ambitions. Interests are an expression of the motivation of an actor, be it an individual or a political unit such as the European Union. The most classical study on interests – Albert Hirschman's book "The Passions and the Interests" – has analyzed the considerable changes in the way interests are conceptualized in relation to other sources of human and collective political motivation.[36] Interests relate to actions as they give reasons for an actor's behavior. Interests also reflect the result of a process of assessment that leads to a certain conclusion defined as "interest." In fact, interests are both the product of an assessment and the basis for reasonable or at least comprehensible behavior. As for the European Union, its dynamic and procedural character explains the difficulties in defining intuitive-like interests. Neither the depth of assessment nor the scope of possible action can relate to established patterns of political behavior and tradition. The development of consensual European interests that both grasp the intention of the process of integration and initiate comprehensive actions in pursuing it has grown into a dynamic and ever stronger trajectory. The evolution of common European interests in foreign and security policy will remain subject to a continuous process of "challenge and response." The formation and formulation of common European interests will remain a contingent "product" of the evolving reaction of European Union actors to new challenges and opportunities that are a function of the self-proclaimed global profile and ambition of the European Union. The more the European Union sees itself as global actor, the more it has to recognize the need for a reasonably cohesive Common Foreign and Security Policy with global outreach. As the EU can no longer deny the impact of external developments for the well-being and scope of action of Europe, it has to formulate its Common Foreign and Security Policy as its first priority in the age of globalization.

36 Hirschman, Albert, *The Passions and the Interests: Political Arguments for Capitalism before its Triumph*, Princeton: Princeton University Press, 1977; see also Hindess, Barry, *Political Choice and Social Structure: An Analysis of Actors, Interests and Rationality*, Aldershot: Edwar Elgar, 1989; Bicknell Truman, David, *The Government Process: Political Interests and Public Opinion*, Berkeley: Institute of Governmental Studies, 1993.

The definition of common European interests was reasonably easy as far as the evolution of a common external trade policy was concerned. But once the sphere of hard politics was reached, new and deep gulfs of interests, commitments, resources and ambitions became visible. The classical yet often futile debate about the relationship between interests and values is constantly present. In their classical study about "realism and complex interdependence," Robert O. Keohane and Joseph S. Nye have outlined the characteristics and effects of world politics as seen through the lenses of realist assumptions defining the character of politics as a struggle for power. The dominant character of the nation state, they suggested, cannot deny the existence of multiple channels that connect societies and affect the formulation of policy choices. The agenda of interstate relationships, they argued, "consists of multiple issues that are not arranged in a clear or consistent hierarchy."[37] One of the consequences of this insight is the fact that military security does not consistently dominate and define the agenda. Yet it is part of the agenda of complex interdependence, a truth the European Union had to learn gradually and painfully.

The Wars of Yugoslavian Succession during the 1990's marked a turning point in the European integration history as far as the willingness to resort to pro-active foreign, security and ultimately even defense policies were concerned. Until the outbreak of four consecutive Wars in former Yugoslavia, the idea of a Common Foreign and Security Policy had been a taboo for many. European integration was largely understood as a civilian project and the European Union as a civilian power.[38] As much as this was the correct antithesis to the European history of tragic warfare, it could not provide an adequate answer of an affluent and peaceful continent to the outbreak of violence in its immediate neighborhood. European citizens – confronted with the media coverage of warfare and expulsions in former Yugoslavia – demanded action from their politicians. Confronted with this challenge, integrated Europe had to respond. No matter how slow the response was, no matter how bureaucratic its method of institution-building looked and no matter how much the EU had to recognize American leadership in stopping the murderous atrocities in former Yugoslavia – the EU's Common Foreign and Security Policy began to take shape faster than most others projects of European integration that one could identify in fifty years of history.

The reluctance of the EU to resort to military force as an instrument of projecting its power found an explanation in Keohane's and Nye's assessment of complex interdependences. Military force, they had argued, is hardly used by governments in response to other governments within a region "when complex interdependence

37 Keohane, Robert O., and Joseph S. Nye, *Power and Interdependence: World Politics in Transition*, Glenview: HarperCollins College Publishers, 1989:25.

38 See Schlotter, Peter (ed.), *Europa – Macht – Frieden? Zur Politik der „Zivilmacht Europa"*, Baden-Baden: Nomos, 2003.

prevails."[39] There could have been no doubt about the complex interdependence between integrated Europe and the dissolving Yugoslavia. Keohane and Nye also gave a hint on how to understand the readiness of integrated Europe to change its attitude, no matter how reluctant and belated it might have been. Under conditions of lacking hierarchies among multiple issues, they had argued, "politics of agenda formation and control will become more important."[40] If the EU wanted to maintain and even increase its international scope of action and autonomy, it had to grow out of the self-limiting concept of a "civilian power." It had to develop a European Security and Defense Policy. Its structures did not automatically respond to a common European interest. But the need to contribute to the agenda setting in all matters relevant for any Foreign and Security Policy grew steadily. As the instruments of EU's Foreign, Security and Defense Policy were designed and gradually turned into practice, the goals of EU policies had to be defined as well. The need increased for the formulation of a comprehensive security strategy.

It was questionable whether or not the first EU Security Strategy actually was a strategy. Strategy has been defined as "the bridge that relates military power to political purpose."[41] In the case of the European Union, so it seemed, the opposite was tried, namely to relate an inevitable political purpose to the unavoidable exercise of power. The literature is dominated by academic studies with a clear bias toward the military dimension of strategy. Often, Carl von Clausewitz's famous words are invoked that in strategy, "everything is very simple, but that does not mean that everything is very easy"[42]. If strategy is understood, in a broader sense, as the ability to apply political means to fulfill clearly defined political ends, it is indeed "ultimately about effectively exercising power."[43] As long as the European Union only wanted to be perceived as a benevolent power, it was limiting itself in the projection of a coherent claim to power status.

Strategy requires a clear understanding of one's interest, a realistic notion of one's abilities and a precise concept of one's goals. Modern military strategy reminds us of the fact that "how common it is for imaginative, energetic and determined strategic thinkers and defense planners to forget that the enemy too has preferences and choices."[44] As for the European Union's Security Strategy, the absence of a discussion of the goals of the "others" is significant. This is all the more astonishing as other

39 Keohane, Robert O., and Joseph S. Nye, *Power and Interdependence: World Politics in Transition*, op.cit.: 25.
40 Ibid.: 58.
41 Gray, Colin S., *Modern Strategy*, Oxford: Oxford University Press, 1999:17; see also Elting, John R., *The Super-Strategists: Great Captains, Theorists, and Fighting Men who Have Shaped the History of Warfare*, New York: Charles Scribner's Sons, 1985; Momah, Sam, *Global Strategy: From its Genesis to the Post-Cold War Era*, Lagos: Vista Books, 1994.
42 von Clausewitz, Carl, *On War*, Princeton: Princeton University Press, 1976: 178.
43 Gray, Colin S., *Modern Strategy*, op.cit.: 20.
44 Ibid.

regions in the world are increasingly beginning to reflect on the meaning of European integration for them.[45]

Strategy – from the Greek word "strategos" (general) – is intended to use one's own force and resources to the end that one's "interests will be effectively promoted or secured against enemies, actual, potential, or merely presumed."[46] Historian Paul Kennedy has pleaded for a broader definition of strategy, going beyond the military and encompassing the use of all possible resources of a nation into an integrated approach to pursue one's specific and yet multidimensional interests. Balancing ends and means is a perennial challenge for those who formulate policies intended to implement a strategic calculus. Kennedy underlined the need "to understand that wisdom and judgment are not created in isolation; they are formed, and refined, by experience – including the study of historical experiences".[47] Kennedy summarized his historical findings with the understanding that all great powers were confronted with tests and problems inherently affecting their search for security both in wartime and in peacetime. The essential political character of a grand strategy reminded Kennedy of the American promise: The nature of strategy, he wrote, "is about the implementation of policies which would secure (in the Founding Fathers' words) 'life, liberty, and the pursuit of happiness' for the polity in question, however restricted that policy might be."[48] In doing so, the United States has grown into a strategic superpower, Kennedy argued, by learning from European experience of centuries of balancing power, overcoming warfare and stabilizing peace. It is ironic that in the early twenty-first century, the European Union was forced into its first comprehensive strategy statement by the American dominance in the definition of goals and means in the war against terrorism that had escalated since the terrorist attacks on the United States on September 11, 2001.

As much as military strategy in times of asymmetric warfare must deal with rather chaotic circumstances, the political effort to define a foreign and security strategy has to deal with the enhanced unpredictability of the international order. Chaos theories have entered the sphere of military and political strategy formulation.[49] What has been labeled "the butterfly effect" by chaos theory has to be translated into political categories. The main intellectual challenge is to find an underlying order in a highly

45 See Ortega, Martin (ed.), *Global Views on the European Union*, Chaillot Paper No. 72, Paris: European Union Institute for Security Studies, 2004.

46 Lexicon of Military Terms, 1960, cited in Luttwak, Edward N., *Strategy: The Logic of War and Peace*, Cambridge, Mass.: The Belknap Press, 1987: 240.

47 Kennedy, Paul, "Grand Strategy in War and Peace: Toward a Broader Definition," in: Kennedy, Paul (ed.), *Grand Strategies in War and Peace*, New Haven/London: Yale University Press, 1991: 6.

48 Kennedy, Paul, "American Grand Strategy, Today and Tomorrow: Learning from the European Experience," in: Kennedy, Paul (ed.), *Grand Strategies in War and Peace*, op.cit.: 169.

49 See Gray, Colin S., *Strategy for Chaos: Revolutions in Military Affairs and the Evidence of History*, London/Portland: Frank Cass, 2002; on the theoretical dimension of rational strategy formation see also the relevant mathematical and economic literature such as Koons, Robert C., *Paradoxes of Belief and Strategic Rationality*, Cambridge/New York: Cambridge University Press, 1991; Reinhard Selten, *Models of Strategic Rationality*, Dordrecht/Boston: Kluwer, 1988.

complex behavior of apparently chaotic or unpredictable systems that constitute the contemporary world order: From cyber warfare to climate change, from upheavals in financial markets to terrorism – chaos seems to dominate the agenda of politics, which still claims to be both in control and legitimate to define the monopoly of violence and the regulatory mechanisms of public life. Whether or not under such circumstances any strategy cannot be more than a chaotic and insufficient effort is a serious question. The rather friendly and diplomatic notion of "strategic adjustment" defines the new mood in the strategic community.[50]

This coincides with the rehabilitation of ideas that impact strategic choice. Four dimensions have been identified in recent literature by which ideas impact strategy: they "yield programmatic changes in state behavior in the absence of external change;" they are a source of cognitive change and impact processes "by which ideas gain currency;" they contribute to an "active dynamic between ideas and institutions" and underline the "real, but bounded capacity of government organizations actively to seek out, or to create, new ideas and to institutionalize them;" finally ideas "serve as focal points in elite bargaining, but also play a similar critical role in domestic politics, helping to determine what domestic political coalitions will or will not form."[51] Strategists emphasize "choice" and reflect on "agents of strategy-making."[52] Thus they legitimize its right and they justify the ambition of the European Union to embark on the formulation of a Foreign and Security Strategy that definitely transcends the self-imposed boundaries of a Single Market and the qualities of a "civilian power."

For the EU this does not only require to outline strategic goals, to define interests and to conclude policy choices beyond a gentle diplomatic language; it also requires the continuous assessment of the EU's power to logically project its interests into the realm of global Realpolitik. Since the EU never understood itself as an actor in the international system being able or even willing to enhance its own security by making "all other actors accept an insecure existence"[53] it had to reverse the classical security dilemma. Instead of solely focusing on the notion of self-help in the absence of predictable and norm-abiding behavior by other actors in the global arena, the EU has to conceptualize a security strategy that will make the world safer for all and not only for

50 Trubowitz, Peter, et al. (eds.), *The Politics of Strategic Adjustment: Ideas, Institutions, and Interests*, New York: Columbia University Press, 1998.

51 Trubowitz, Peter, and Edward Rhodes, "Explaining American Strategic Adjustment," in: Trubowitz, Peter (ed.), *The Politics of Strategic Adjustment*, op.cit.: 18.

52 Goldman, Emily O., and John Arquilla, "Structure, Agency, and Choice: Toward a Theory and Practice of Grand Strategy," in: Trubowitz, Peter (ed.), *The Politics of Strategic Adjustment*, op.cit.: 311; on the theoretical role of ideas in the process of institutionalizing European integration see also Parsons, Craig, *A Certain Idea of Europe*, Ithaca/London: Cornell University Press, 2003: 1-33.

53 Rothgeb Jr., John M., *Defining Power: Influence and Force in the Contemporary International System*, New York: St. Martin's Press, 1992: 55; on the economic dimension see Goddard, C. Roe, et al. (eds.), *International Political Economy: State-Market Relations in a Changing Global Order*, Basingstoke: Palgrave Macmillan, 2003; Oatley, Thomas, *International Political Economy: Interests and Institutions in the Global Economy*, New York: Longman, 2004.

itself. In doing so, it was inevitable that the EU would – at least partially – be perceived as antagonistic to some vested interests of the United States.[54] But as much as it would have been illusionary for the EU to define itself as a counter-power to the US, it is unfair to consistently insinuate that the EU is trying to do exactly that. It is more correct to describe the effort of the EU as one of complementing the US by more precisely defining its own interests and strategic goals than ever before.

The formulation of a Security Strategy for the European Union was but one element in "organizing Europe's place in world affairs."[55] Although the European Union still lacks what one analyst has coined "fungibility" – that is to say "the ability to fully transform, and to utilize, the capabilities of the Member States and thereby to put them fully at the disposal of the Union without any loss of efficacy"[56] – its international significance has grown immensely. Its population has outgrown the US, its GDP is almost equal to that of the United States and although its per capita income remains almost 30 percent below that in the US (largely due to the membership of post-communist economies with lower productivity rates), the EU and its leading member states are in a key position as far as the definition of global economic issues is concerned. The EU's account of world trade is higher than the equivalent rate of the US, although it has shrunk in absolute terms due to the rise of other trading regions in the world. The euro has developed into a stable international currency, being recognized as reserve currency across the world. Two third of the membership of the OECD are EU member states and the European Commission itself is an "active participant" under Article 13 of the OECD Convention.

In the United Nations, the then EEC was invited already on October 11, 1974, to participate in the sessions and work of the General Assembly as an observer. The contribution of EU member states to the budget of the United Nations is higher than the US contribution, let alone that of Japan, Russia or China. Only recently, the issue of EU performance in the United Nations has found scholarly attention. The result is telling: The then EC member states reached consensus on 60 percent of all recorded votes in the UN General Assembly in 1979. By 2002 and with the EU in place, this figure had increased to 75.5 percent of the recorded votes in the UN General Assembly. As far as the effect of EU enlargement to post-communist countries of Central Europe was concerned, the trend toward consensual voting behavior already increased before they

54 For a contextualization of this claim see Colson, Bruno, *Europe: Repenser les Alliances*, Paris: Institut de Stratégie Comparée/Economia, 1995.

55 See Kasekamp, Andres (ed.), *Organizing Europe's Place in World Affairs: The European Union's Common Foreign and Security Policy*, Tartu: Department of Political Science, 2001.

56 Whitman, Richard G., *From Civilian Power to Superpower?: The International Identity of the European Union*, Houndmills: Macmillan Press 1998:108; see also Lenzi, Guido, *Paradoxes of European Foreign Policy: Defining the European Security Policy*, Fiesole: European University Institute, 1997; Wessels, Ramses A., *The European Union's Foreign and Security Policy: A Legal Institutional Perspective*, The Hague/Boston: Kluwer, 1999; Mahncke, Dieter, et.al. (eds.), European Foreign Policy: From Rhetoric to Reality ?, Brussels: Peter Lang, 2004.

became formal EU member states in 2004. In 1995, the fifteen "old" EU member states voted identically in 70 percent of the recorded votes, while the twenty-five showed a consensual vote in only 40 percent of the votes. By 2002, the difference had almost vanished: While the "old" fifteen EU member states voted identically in 75.5 percent of the registered votes, the twenty-five states showed a consensus in 62.3 percent of the registered votes.[57]

As far as the details of the EU voting behavior are concerned, the EU Institute for Security Studies concluded that out of 80 recorded votes during the 57th UN General Assembly in 2002, in 33 cases the EU consensus was identical with the votes of the United States. In 47 cases, the EU consensus differed from the votes of the United States, primarily on matters of the Middle East and the quest for a more coercive international regime to implement international criminal law standards. The 26 cases of voting in which the EU member states could not find consensus among themselves were largely related to matters of nuclear disarmament, significant for the special position of the two European nuclear powers France and Great Britain.[58]

In December 2009, immediately following the implementation of the Treaty of Lisbon, for the first time ever a representative of the European Union – the EU's envoy at the United Nations – took the floor and addressed the UN Security Council. The European Union is operating more than 120 delegations in third countries and another five delegations at the seat of international institutions. Beside their deiplomatic work, they fullfil consular duties which are especially beneficial for the many EU member states that are not maintaining national embassies in each country of the world. In the forthcoming years, the delegations of the European Union will become an increasingly strong instrument for the global projection of the role of the EU. Along with the emerging European External Action Service, the EU is in the process of significantly enhancing global visibility. The combined defense spending of all EU member states is not more than 40 percent of the defense spending of the United States. On the other hand, the EU is the leading donor of development aid worldwide. Yet, its global political and strategic profile is suboptimal, to say the least. Although the external profile and influence of the European Union is obvious, its reputation and impact coul be raised. For the time being, it does not seem likely that the European Union will gain a permanent seat in the UN Security Council. Yet, in the end that perspective must be the logical consequence of a coherent global profil of the European Union.

The High Representative of the Union for Foreign Affairs and Security Policy will have to work over a longer period of time in order to gain a similar international

57 See Paul Luif, *EU Cohesion in the UN General Assembly*, Occasional Paper No. 49, Paris: EU Institute for Security Studies, 2003: 29.

58 Ibid.: 57-75, gives all relevant details; see also Johansson-Nogués, Elisabeth, "The Fifteen and the Accession States in the UN General Assembly: What Future for European Foreign Policy in the Coming Together of the 'Old' and 'New' Europe?," *European Foreign Affairs Review*, 9.1 (2004): 67-92; Ortega, Martin (ed.), *The European Union and the United Nations: Partner in Effective Multilateralism*, Chaillot Paper No. 78, Paris: European Union Institute for Security Studies, 2005.

reputation, profile and power usually attributed to the Secretary of State of the United States. Yet, who would have assumed in 2000 that the European Union might at all present a single spokesperson on foreign and security matters to the world, backed by a developing European External Action Service and carried by a growing number of policy strategies and instruments? As usual in politics, the assessment of the global role of the EU is a matter of perspective and proportion: Compared with traditional superpowers, the EU is still "a fleet in being." Compared with its own performance only a decade ago, the European Union has achieved a lot in enhancing its integration in matters of foreign, security and defense policy.

By looking through the various activities and actions of the European Union since the beginning of its foreign affairs posture, the following "stages of institutionalization" of EU's Foreign and Security Policy can been identified:[59] The original agreement among EU member states to cooperate in the field of foreign policy, "and even to establish norms," constituted "the policy domain as an intergovernmental forum." This step was intergovernmental and yet accompanied by thorough skepticism about its rationale and perspective. Information-sharing, as practiced during the phase of European Political Cooperation (EPC), established trust among the institutional actors, permanency in the mechanism of cooperation and growing awareness within the political elite of the EU member states that it would be in their joint interest to strengthen their joint international role by enhancing the level of cooperation, no longer considering a cautious trend toward integration a serious possibility. Organizational steps were taken to underpin this experience, finally establishing governance structures, instruments and mechanisms duly recognized by EU consent and poised to advance into the sphere of solid supranationality.

On a theoretical level, the debate continued between conflicting normative concepts, primarily identified as intergovernmental versus supranational. In reality, a complex web of multilevel and often idiosyncratic overlaps between the two contrasting normative claims evolved. It was unlikely that Europe's Common Foreign and Security Policy would achieve a quantum leap into a Single Foreign and Security Policy during a short period of time. In light of the enormous speed with which Foreign, Security and Defense Policy has taken center-stage as the most important project for the integration process in the first years of the twenty-first century, it was however not unrealistic to assume further and rapid progress in that policy field in which the classical notion of the primacy of national sovereignty is more deeply rooted than anywhere else.

It was largely an academic dispute whether or not intergovernmental cooperation in foreign and security matters could indeed "spill-over" into supranational structures, mechanisms and instruments. The gap between global challenges and Europe's

59 According to Smith, Michael E., *Europe's Foreign and Security Policy: The Institutionalization of Cooperation*, Cambridge: Cambridge University Press, 2004: 32-36; for a more theoretical approach see Krahmann, Elke, *Multilevel Networks in European Foreign Policy*, Aldershot: Ashgate, 2003.

performance remained a permanent issue for media and political actors alike. And yet, multilevel governance has definitively begun to take control of foreign and security matters in a way unforeseeable in the early days of European Political Cooperation in the 1970's.

Declarations and demarches were used as the first instrument of European Political Cooperation in 1970. In 1971 coordination at the UN-level began. In 1973, formal consultations with the US started. 1974 saw the beginning of institutionalized regional political dialogues, beginning with the Euro-Arab dialogue. In 1975, the European Community began to coordinate its positions at the Conference on Security and Cooperation in Europe and started to use economic tools for European Political Cooperation. In 1977, a Code of Conduct for the behavior of EC firms operating in South Africa under apartheid was agreed upon. In 1981, the EC developed peace plans for the Middle East and endorsed military operations by some EC member states as part of the Sinai Force. In 1982, an EC regulation for actions of European Political Cooperation – sanctions against the Soviet Union – was activated. In 1984, the European Community declared a weapons embargo against Iraq and Iran. In 1993, the Treaty of Maastricht enshrined the evolution of a Common Foreign and Security Policy as the consensual goal of all EU member states. By then, the EU agreed on common positions, joint actions and actions taken in conjuncture with the Western European Union ("Petersberg Tasks") on matter of peacekeeping. Since 1998, the EU has presented its first common strategies on matters related to its policies vis-à-vis Russia, the Baltic States and the Ukraine. The publication of the EU Security Strategy in 2003 was the logical continuation and consequence of this sequence of an enlarged commitment to foreign, security and defense matters. The empowerment of the EU's High Representative and the strengthening of human resources and capacities in Brussels was the inevitable next step. In the second decade of the twenty-first century, a new office holder and a revised strategy have to come together to overcome existing policy deficits.[60]

It remains imperative for the European Union to develop more coherence in its foreign, security and defense posture. This can only be done would the EU be ready and capable to precisely define its global ambitions. Institutionalizing coherence cannot be possible without recognizing the primacy of supranational solutions. The EU's High Representative and his staff, but also the relevant Committee for Foreign Affairs of the

60 For an intergovernmental assessment of the actors in Europe's foreign policy see Hill, Christopher (ed.), *The Actors in Europe's Foreign Policy*, London/New York: Routledge, 1996. This volume gives an overview of national political preferences in foreign policy matters, leaving completely out the European Commission and the European Parliament. In his concluding essay, David Allen paraphrases Alan Milward's famous title: "The European Rescue of National Foreign Policy" (288-305); see also Tiersky, Ronald (ed.), *Europe Today: National Politics, European Integration, and European Security*, Lanham: Rowman & Littlefield, 1999; for a broader perspective see Winn, Neil, and Christopher Lord, *EU Foreign Policy Beyond the Nation-State: Joint Actions and Institutional Analysis of the Common Foreign and Security Policy*, Houndmills: Basingstoke, 2001.

European Parliament, should make it one of their priorities to initiate a Europe-wide discourse about the global ambitions and political strategies of the European Union. Should European patriotism grow, it would be imperative to broaden the public debate about European foreign and security matters beyond the core group of institutional actors.

The budgetary perspective of EU's Foreign, Security and Defense Policy must be another matter of grave concern in the process of streamlining decision-making processes. No matter how strong the personal profile of any EU's High Rperesentative may be, no sustainable policy can be implemented without the necessary resources in the institutional structures he or she is leading. In the decades ahead, the European Union will probably face tough battles between fiscal intergovernmentalists, welfare state oriented advocates of the primacy of social and economic redistribution policies inside the EU, and proponents of a coherent and multidimensional global posture of the European Union. In the end, this might turn out to be another inevitable (and therefore welcome) political battle signifying the ever increasing role of the European level in dealing with questions of public concern all across the EU.[61]

3. *"Baptism by Fire:" The Emerging Policy Priorities of the EU*

In a fine study about the impact of EU's Foreign and Security Policy during the 1990's, Roy H. Ginsberg chose a significant subtitle: "Baptism by Fire."[62] Ginsberg was not only studying the institutional provisions of Europe's Foreign and Security Policy, he was also analyzing its feedback and effect, including the external perceptions of this

61 Contributions to this necessary debate also dealt with the practical logistical, organizational and technological dimensions of a Single European Defense, see: European Union Institute for Security Studies (ed.), *European Defense: A Proposal for a White Paper. Report of an Independent Task Force*, Paris: EU Institute for Security Studies, 2004; on the evolving debate about European security see Sauder, Axel, *Souveränität und Integration: Französische und deutsche Konzeptionen europäischer Sicherheit nach dem Ende des Kalten Krieges (1990-1993)*, Baden-Baden: Nomos, 1995; Gasteyger, Curt (ed.), *An Ambiguous Power: The European Union in a Changing World*, Gütersloh: Bertelsmann Foundation Publishers, 1996; Lotter, Christoph, and Susanne Peters (eds.), *The Changing European Security Environment*, Weimar/Cologne/Vienna: Böhler, 1996; von Bredow, Wilfried, et al. (eds.), *European Security*, Houndmills: Macmillan Press, 1997; Holland, Martin (ed.), *Common Foreign and Security Policy: The Record and Reforms*, London/Washington D.C.: Pinter, 1997; Whitman, Richard, *From Civilian Power to Superpower?: The International Identity of the European Union*, Houndmills: Macmillan Press, 1998; Missiroli, Antonio, *CFSP, Defense and Flexibility*, Paris: Institute for Security Studies 2000; Vilanova, Pere, and Nuria Fernandez, *Europa: El Debate sobre Defensa y Seguridad*, Barcelona: Universidad de Barcelona, 2001; Jain, Rajendra K. (ed.), *The European Union in a Changing World*, New Delhi: Radiant Publishers, 2002; Koechlin, Jérome, *L'Europe a-t-elle une adresse?*, Geneva: Edition Georg, 2003.

62 Ginsberg, Roy H., *The European Union in International Politics: Baptism by Fire*, Lanham/Boulder/New York/Oxford: Rowman & Littlefield, 2001; see also Musu, Costanza, "European Foreign Policy: A Collective Policy or a Policy of 'Converging Parallel'?," *European Foreign Affairs Review*, 8 (2003): 35-49; Duke, Simon, "Preparing for European Diplomacy?," *Journal of Common Market Studies*, 40.5 (2002): 849-870.

outcome. Borrowing from economic theory, Ginsberg described the EU's effort of formulating and implementing a Common Foreign and Security Policy as "politics of scale."[63] For the 1990's, Ginsburg concluded that on 72 foreign policy issues, the EU tried to exert an impact on the United States. In 30 cases, or 42 percent, the EU had a significant impact; in 25 cases, or 35 percent, the impact was considerable, in 10 cases, or 14 percent it was marginal, and only in 7 cases, or 10 percent, it was nil.[64]

Only if collective EU action is more than the sum of its constituent parts will costs and risks of foreign and security policy be reduced by pooled sovereignty and resources. Moreover, only then can the potential link between effect and impact be raised. Common action has strengthened the international position of the European Union in areas as distant and unrelated as in the realm of multilateral negotiations on greenhouse gas emissions (Kyoto Protocol of the UN and its follow-up instrument), on issues of human rights (in the setting of the United Nations) and regarding the evolution of security mechanisms since the end of the Cold War (particularly in the context of the Conference on Security and Cooperation in Europe).

Skeptics remain hesitant to recognize the ability of the EU to define common European interests and to exert the necessary political will to pursue them. Yet, special partnerships with other regional integration schemes, pursuit of human rights as precondition for association and cooperation agreements with the EU and conditionality for development aid programs defined by the goal to support rule of law, democracy and civil society have become viable foreign policy instruments that clearly express EU interests. Efforts of a gradual harmonization of norms and laws have become an integral part of the EU's neighborhood policy and will increase the projection of EU interests, both economic and political, in those partner countries.

Foreign and security policies of the European Union are defined and largely determined by an interplay between national and Union actors, international events and the whole range of collective Western actors – notably the United States and NATO – that are intrinsically interwoven into the internal psychology and range of interests determining EU policies. The multilevel system of governance, usually applied in internal EU policies, is more complex in foreign and security matters. The EU's interplay with international institutions and procedures has to be added to the matrix of multilevel governance. EU positions on United Nations matters, EU reactions to US policies, EU governance processes, both ad-hoc and more permanent, and communiqués on events all over the world add to the evolution of European Union policies and interests, the application of its instruments and the contribution of its specific means. Only in rare cases can the EU enjoy the privilege of developing a policy strategy – a grand design – by its own will and choice. This is not a phenomenon the EU is experiencing specifically. Foreign policy strategies are by definition reactive to external

63 Ginsberg, Roy H., *The European Union in International Politics: Baptism by Fire*, op.cit.: 27.
64 Ibid.: 267.

factors and events. The EU can only be measured according to this highly unpredictable and volatile basis of all international relations.

Likewise, the EU has to be measured by the degree of its inactions in foreign policy: From the 1968 uprising in then communist Czechoslovakia (Prague Spring) to the 1986 Libya crisis, from the Greek-Turkish dispute over some Aegean islands in 1996 to the breakdown of law and order in Albania in 1997, the European Union preferred not to act as a broker. In some cases, individual EU member states blocked the EU to operate as an entity: Greece prevented the EU's recognition of Macedonia between 1992 and 1995 and in 1997 France blocked an EU initiative in favor of human rights in China. Most prominent was the failure of the European Union to prevent the outbreak of four Wars of Yugoslavian Succession between 1991 and 1999. And the transatlantic dispute over the need to go to war with Iraq in 2002/2003 ended as the biggest ever dispute inside the European Union, not only preventing a common position to evolve, but also undermining a lot of trust capital the EU had accrued among its member states, and between them and the candidate countries of Central Europe. However, more than any other single external event or internal initiative these two external events – the Wars of Yugoslavian Succession and the Iraq crisis – raised awareness that the European Union needed to be "more active, more coherent and more capable" as the Security Strategy finally admitted in December 2003.[65] By the summer of 2004, the European Union was almost forced to contribute support to the first democratic election in Iraq. An EU participation in a UN led Protection Force in Iraq, as suggested by the Secretary General of the United Nations, did not work out. On June 22, 2005, an EU-US sponsored conference on the future of Iraq held in Brussels signaled a formal end to the policy rift between the EU and the US. Although this conference took place in the EU's own capital, the EU had traveled a long way to reach the new, US-made Iraq. The US and the EU had entered Iraq separately. They would have to stay in together and they would have to leave jointly – and hopefully only with success. For the time being, none of them had a convincing answer of how to turn the violent transformation of Iraq into a stable, democratic and prosperous model for the modernization of any other Arab country. By 2007, a gradual improvement of public security in Iraq became undeniable and yet, a strong foreign presence seemed to remain necessary in order to stabilize the new political and social sytem in Iraq.

Gradually, the European Union had been recognized as a global player.[66] A global player is not a global power yet. This difference marks the structural limitations of the EU's global role. Telling, for instance, is the absence of the European Union in US-led efforts to institutionalize a multilateral scheme for security and stability in North East

65 European Union, *A Secure Europe in a Better World: European Security Strategy*, op.cit.: 17.

66 On the EU's perception in Asia-Pacific see the very comprehensive study by Holland, Martin, and Natalia Chaban (eds.), *The European Union and the Asia-Pacific: Media, Public and Elite Perceptions of the EU*, Abingdon: Routledge, 2007.

Asia, another trouble-spot of world politics.[67] Although the EU had tried to engage in nuclear diplomacy regarding the North Korean ambition to produce an atomic bomb, it could not sustain a cohesive effort of involvement in the resolution of this urgent matter. It simply was not perceived as an "Asian power," no matter its regular cooperation with ASEAN. Whether or not this might remain a temporary or a structural limitation of the projection of EU power will be decided by history. The question must surface in light of the enormous economic stakes of the European Union in the development of Northeast Asia. In China, South Korea, and Japan, the EU had become a leading foreign investor, even surpassing the US at times who has since long established itself as the leading trading partner of the regions economic giants. In 1980, China ranked 25th as a destination for exports from Europe. As consequence of the fundamental changes under way in China since the late 1970's, the EU increased its economic interests, reinforced by diplomatic relations between the EU and China that were established already in 1975. In 2004, China had become the third export market for the EU, surpassed only by the United States and Switzerland. As for investments, the European Union is among the biggest investors in China. In 2000, for the first time the EU ranked as the top investor in China. It does not look as if the EU will do much worse in the years to come. Roughly 80 percent of all European investments in China go to the manufacturing sector. In the long run, however, this can have ambivalent effects on Europe's own manufacturing sector. The competitiveness of China for jobs will constantly grow, along with increased productivity and quality. While the Arab world is threatening Europe with its failure, China seems to increasingly threaten Europe's affluence with its success, given the implication of a projection of China's enormous growth rates of roughly 8 percent on annual average during the past two decades. While economic interests of the EU in North East Asia are beyond doubt – although not thoroughly coordinated on the EU level and often subject to competition among EU member states, notably Germany and France – the absence of concise political and strategic interests of the EU in North East Asia is, at least, surprising. It simply demonstrates the continuous limits of a global role of Europe.

Moreover, the EU remains torn between conflicting aims and diverging national interests. Nowhere is this more evident than in the relationship between its emphasis on human rights and the pursuit of national economic interests among leading EU member states. In spite of the arms ban imposed upon China after the Tienamen Square massacre in June 1989, EU member states, and among them mainly France, sold military equipment in the amount of 281 million US dollars in 2002 alone. When some EU member states contemplated to lift the EU's arms ban on China, they finally had to accept the wish of the Bush Administration in March 2005 not to go ahead with such plans. Europe's North East Asia policy, if there is any, still sails in the shadow of the US. When China used military force in Tibet in spring 2008, the EU was again torn

67 See Fukuyama, Francis, "Re-Envisioning Asia," *Foreign Affairs*, 84.1 (2005): 75-87.

between the goal to defend human rights, economic interests and the possible ramifications of boycotting the Olympic Summer Games 2008 in Beijing.

As the EU's Security Strategy suggested, the European Union needs to conduct foreign and security policies throughout the world defined by the changes in threat assessment and by unfolding globalization opportunities. The global performance of the European Union as multilateral trade negotiator has been recognized since the first decade of the existence of the European Economic Community. Its participation in the Dillon Round of the early 1960's was the first performance of a European external policy. From GATT's Uruguay Round in the 1980's to the WTO Doha Round of the early twenty-first century, the European Union has been recognized as a global economic player. International environmental diplomacy has seen a gradual and firm evolution of the role of the European Union.[68] In political and strategic terms, a breakthrough of a robust and determined single European voice is yet to happen.

The European Union and its member states have acquired a respectable name in international development cooperation, accounting for more than 60 percent of all global development aid. The evolution of an explicit development policy of the European Union has contributed to more visibility and efficiency of the EU's development aid. At the core of the EU's strategy and policy toward the developing world is the mechanism by which the European Union is organizing and executing its relations with the poorest countries in Africa, the Pacific and the Caribbean. Beginning with the first Yaoundé Convention in 1964, linking the then six members of the European Economic Community with 18 associated African states and Madagascar, the EU focused its development policy with the first Lomé Convention in 1975, followed by three subsequent Lomé Conventions and finally leading to the Cotonou Agreement of 2000. The development of these association schemes with most African, Pacific and Caribbean countries mirrored the overall evolution of North-South relations, of experiences and learning processes in development philosophy and the increasing focus of Europe to define priorities in its relationship with a group of countries that mostly had colonial relationships with Europe during the nineteenth and twentieth century. The mechanism of the Lomé Conventions and the Cotonou Agreement increased the export share of many developing countries to Europe. The biggest effect however was the transformation of former colonial "patron/client"-relations into viable and respected relations among partners.

The growing insistence of the European Union to add dimensions of a political dialogue and the threat of conditionality to its instruments of development policy demonstrated another transformation in the relationship with its former colonies. The growing role of the European Community Humanitarian Office (ECHO), established in

68 See Bretherton, Charlotte, and John Vogler, *The European Union as a Global Actor*, London/New York: Routledge, 1999: 80-109.

1992, proves the seriousness of the humanitarian orientation of the EU's relationship with the developing world, most notably in Africa.

The development of almost five decades of European relations with the developing world reflects a fundamental transformation in Europe's relationship with its former colonies. Besides a strong European priority on structured and contractual relations with former colonies in Africa, the Pacific and the Caribbean, the EU increasingly sharpened its policies and instruments in support of the evolution of regional cooperation and integration schemes across the world. This added to the intention of the European Union – as scholars saw it – to strive for "a post-Hobbesian order" in international relations, based on pooled sovereignty and increasingly complex interdependence.[69]

Yet the gap between the world of affluence and the world of poverty remains the biggest concern for long-term stability and moral credibility in the world. While in 2003, the year of the Iraq crisis, the annual US defense expenditure was around 430 billion US dollars and the annual commitment to the occupation in Afghanistan and Iraq was more than 165 billion US dollars per year, official US development assistance was a little over 13 billion US dollars in 2002 and meant to rise to 15 billion US dollars in 2006. The aid record of Europeans is not any better. In 2003, the agricultural subsidies of the EU were seven times higher than the EU's contribution to development aid. Adding direct national development aid contributions does not really improve the EU's record in light of the fact that while the EU as a whole is subsidizing a European cow with 913 US dollars per year, the EU gave eight US dollars per head to the population of sub-Saharan Africa. "European agricultural exports, subsidized by the EUs Common Agricultural Policy (CAP), drive farmers in poor countries out of business – and into destitution," Timothy Garton Ash rightly criticized this horrendous EU policy. In despair he added: "Where are the crowds on the streets of European capitals protesting against the CAP?"[70]

In spite of all idiosyncrasies, flaws and obstacles to implement Europeanized interests, EU foreign policy priorities have become increasingly visible. More often, the European Union tries to project topical powers instead of spatial powers. Not being the center of instability itself any more, Europe tries to project stability, human rights, good governance and market economy worldwide. As long as it remains an incoherent actor, it will often be perceived with skepticism. Spectacular events will always receive more attention than long-term planning and operations by the EU. Capacity-building and a deficit in capacities, will power and instruments, may continue to accompany the strategic discourse about Europe's global role. Complete consistency between strategies and goals, instruments and means may never be achieved in foreign policy. Textbook wisdom and blueprints can hardly be guiding lines for the execution of the global role of

69 See Wind, Marlene, *Sovereignty and European Integration: Towards a Post-Hobbesian Order*, Houndmills: Palgrave, 2001.

70 Garton Ash, Timothy, *Free World: Why a Crisis of the West Reveals the Opportunity of Our Time*, London: Allen Lane, 2004: 170.

Europe. Europe's global role will remain as much actor driven as subject to events, based on common interests and on the specific heritage of some EU member states or interest groups in the European Parliament or the European Commission. There simply is no blueprint for the design of the foreign and security policy of a global actor. But the key ingredients of the EU's foreign policy concept can be identified, both in terms of geographical and in terms of normative priorities. In the pursuit of its external actions, the European Union intends to balance interests and values, genuine experiences of individual member states and an emerging Union interest.

(a) The main decision-making elements in EU foreign and security matters include:

- Common strategies to be agreed upon by the Council: They are defining the objectives of the EU, the scope and duration as well as the means available in order to carry out the strategy.
- Joint actions and common positions to be agreed by the General Affairs Council: These decisions are meant to implement common strategies. Normally, the Council is including the perspective of the European Parliament into its decision-making process.

(b) The most important positive EU foreign policy instruments include:

- Negotiation of trade agreements.
- Negotiation of cooperation and development cooperation agreements.
- Negotiation of association agreements.

The EU is practising several negative instruments as means of political punishment. These foreign policy instruments include:

- Embargo (ban on exports).
- Boycott (ban on imports).
- Delaying the conclusion of agreements.
- Tariff increase, quota decrease or reduction and suspension of aid.
- Delay in granting successive loans.

Since the end of the Cold War, the European Union is increasingly confronted with the evolution of an appropriate system of military-civilian cooperation. During the Cold War, this notion was limited to cooperation between the military and civilian forces in cases of domestic catastrophes and crises inside Europe. In light of the new structure of challenges and confrontations outside Europe, the EU has rather speedily developed new and appropriate mechanisms of "civil-military cooperation" (CIMIC). The EU's police missions in Macedonia and the work of the Provincial Reconstruction Teams of various EU member states in post-Taliban Afghanistan have enabled the European Union to reassess capacities and operational structures of civil-military cooperation and coordination.[71] This important interplay between hard power and soft power will be applied more constantly in future operations. Election observer missions such as in Venezuela, Nigeria or Kenya have added to the global projection of EU interests and values.

Beside its operational outlets, the European Union is engaged in regular political dialogues with all key countries of the world, namely the United States, Russia, China, Canada, Japan, Ukraine, and India through Summits between the respective Head of State and the EU leadership. On a ministerial level, the EU conducts bilateral political dialogues with countries as diverse as New Zealand, Mexico and Armenia, Uzbekistan, Chile and Korea, but also with practically all relevant regional cooperation and integration schemes in the world, notably with ASEAN, MERCOSUR, the Andean Community of Nations (CAN), the Gulf Cooperation Council, ECOWAS, SAARC, the San José Group, but likewise with the non-aligned movement, with the countries of the European Economic Area and with the partner countries of the Euro-Mediterranean Partnership. On the expert level, the European Union conducts regular meetings on all relevant international questions from human rights to drug trafficking, from non-proliferation to consular affairs, from terrorism to all issues relevant in the context of the United Nations. The EU has used the instrument of appointing a special representative contributing to peace-making in the Middle East, Africa, Southeast Europe and Afghanistan.

(c) As far as thematic priorities are concerned, the EU is increasingly developing issue cohesion and global interests in the following policy areas:

- Support of regional cooperation and integration: Support for the development of regional groupings throughout the world reflects the normative consensus in the European Union concerning the value of a multilateral and multidimensional world-order, based on the recognition of regional advantages and forms of cooperative interdependence. From the formulation of the Yaoundé Convention in 1964 to the Euro-Mediterranean Partnership since 1995, the special preference shown for the development of ASEAN, the negotiation of an association agreement with MERCOSUR and with SICA and the negotiation of Economic Partnership Agreements with Caribbean, African and Pacific partner groupings, the European integration process has been linked to the global trend of regional cooperation. The EU's policy objectives are pursued in various ways. The spectrum reaches from rhetorical encouragement to institutional support and a pro-active enhancement of preferential regional schemes of cooperation. Most delicate and complex are the developments in those relationships that obviously

71 See Wenig, Daniel, *Zivil-militärische Zusammenarbeit in der Europäischen Union*, Berlin: Stiftung Wissenschaft und Politik, 2004; Duke, Simon (ed.), *The EU and Crisis Management: Development and Prospects*, Maastricht: European Institute for Public Administration, 2002.

matter most for the EU's own well-being, namely in the complex sphere of EU Neighborhood policies, including the Euro-Mediterranean Partnership ("Barcelona Process") and the new Union for the Mediterranean. Given the proximity of the partner countries and the volatility of the region bordering the Southern shores of the Mediterranean, the EU initiated a highly complex process. So far, however, this process was not able to transform the asymmetric character of the partnership between the EU and the littoral states of the Southern Mediterranean.[72] In spite of all divergence, the EU remains convinced that regional cooperation is the path to enhanced well-being and political stability in any region of the world and thus a contribution to a more balanced and peaceful world-order. Through economic assistance, cooperation agreements and political dialogue the EU is pursuing this policy goal in a very pro-active manner.[73]

- As much as "conditionality" has become a political mantra for the EU since the early twenty-first century in pursuing its foreign policy, including its support for regional cooperation, the struggle for human rights has always been a leitmotif guiding the European Union's relations with other parts of the world. The promotion of human rights – considered to be the cornerstone of a stable political order that is based on democratic values and the rule of law – is much more complex than the promotion of regional integration. However, regional integration can only succeed beyond a certain limit if it is rooted in similar political structures among the participating countries. Moreover, the EU believes, it must be rooted in respect for universally recognized human rights, democratic procedures and rule of law that facilitates the advancement of a pluralistic and lively civil society.
- Starting with the European experience in the struggle against communist dictatorships during the Cold War, the EU's policy of promoting human rights has been included in all international activities of the European Union, most notably in its development policies. The European Union pursues the promotion of human rights with a set of instruments, "but clearly prefers positive to negative measures" as empirical evidence shows[74]. Since 1986, the European Union has provided small amounts of financial support for the promotion of human rights and human rights related institutions in various countries. The various EU funds were finally consolidated in 1994 under one budgetary heading – the European Initiative for Democracy and Human Rights – as requested by the European Parliament. Since then, the budget line has been constantly increased although it is only a small fraction of the overall budget for

72 See Calleya, Stephen, *Evaluating Euro-Mediterranean Relations*, London: Routledge, 2005.
73 See Smith, Karen E., *European Union Foreign Policy in a Changing World*, Oxford: Polity, 2003: 72-85.
74 Ibid.: 110.

the EU's external relations, which itself is a budget of only about seven percent of the whole EU budget.

- Since the 1990's, the European Union has broadened its objective of promoting human rights by suggesting that democracy and good governance are fundamental preconditions for a lasting and solid protection of human rights. Promoting human rights has become a continuous objective of the EU's external relations. The breakdown of communist regimes in Central and Eastern Europe has contributed to a new ideological consensus in Europe – also within the "old" European Union – about the importance of rule of law, democratic procedures and good governance. Good governance became a new catch-word in dealing with the manifold problems of political development and transformation, both inside and outside Europe. The Copenhagen Criteria defining the conditions for EU membership since the early 1990's include the notions of rule of law, democracy and good governance. In negotiating the Cotonou Agreement – the framework for EU's relations with most developing countries – the quest for democratic rule and good governance was likewise ranking prominently for the EU. In the absence of an international codification of the notion of good governance and even of the concepts of rule of law and of democracy, the European Union is obliged to specify its claims and goals unilaterally: Imposing conditionality on development aid, granting aid for programs of democratization, human rights and good governance, observation of and assistance for fair and democratic elections and the use of various diplomatic means have become the main instruments through which the EU tries to support good governance, democracy and rule of law. Almost inevitably, the European Union was confronted with inconsistencies in pursuing different policies vis-à-vis different countries, regimes and regions while at the same time struggling to formulate consensus among its member states, which were pursuing specific interests not always in line with the proclaimed normative goals of the EU. While the EU imposed diplomatic sanctions, for example, on Burma in 1990, on Nigeria in 1995, on Pakistan in 1999 and on Zimbabwe in 2002, France did not shy away from inviting Zimbabwean President Robert Mugabe to attend a Franco-African Summit in 2003. In 2004, the EU threatened Sudan with sanctions without truly manifesting the seriousness of its threat to the regime in Khartoum.[75] The biggest limit of EU policy projections became evident when

75 For an overview of cases of aid suspended and sanctions imposed by the European Union for violations of human rights and democratic principles in third countries between 1988 and 2002 see Smith, Karen E., *European Union Foreign Policy in a Changing World*, op.cit: 205-208. On the EU's diplomatic involvement in Sudan during the Darfur crisis see Bacia, Horst, "Zwischen Einflussnahme und Drohungen: Das Dilemma der EU in der Darfur-Krise," *Frankfurter Allgemeine Zeitung*, September 4, 2004. On the general EU's crisis management in sub-Saharan Africa, with special emphasis on the military operation "Artemis" in Bunia in 2003 see Faria, Fernanda, *Crisis*

the EU tried to prevent the nuclear program of Iran by way of negotiations. These negotiations were able to prolong the illusion that Iran would accept stopping its nuclear ambitions. But eventually, the EU negotiators failed to achieve their original intention. Iran pursued its dangerous path that was aimed from the beginning at strengthening the country's role as the new center of power in the Broader Middle East, no matter global the repercussions.

- Conflict prevention and post-conflict peace-building have become permanent issues of concern for the European Union since its failure to stop the outbreak of the Wars of Yugoslavian Succession during the 1990's. Beginning with the EU Summit in Cologne in 1999, the European Union has developed a broad array of instruments in support of its goal to prevent conflicts from escalating into violence. Preparing the post-conflict conditions for lasting peace is a long-term task. It requires the EU to cope with the complex root causes of conflicts. While the EU failed to resolve the Cyprus question through the EU membership of Cyprus in 2004, it was proud to halt the escalation of political conflicts in Macedonia in 2002. Following the formal, yet internationally controlled independence of Kosovo on February 17, 2008, the EU was ready to supervise the civilian observation mission in Kosovo while at the same time it was obliged to enhance its effort to bring Serbia closer to European Union membership. In the Middle East, the European Union is increasingly getting involved as a peace-keeping force that can succeed only on the basis of a robust mandate.

  Long-term peace building requires new threat assessments, applied instruments and an innovative set of strategies. The European Union is in the process of developing interlocking instruments of soft and hard power. The nature of conflicts unfolding in the twenty-first century forces the EU to constantly broaden its horizon beyond the traditional definition of its role as a soft-power.

- The fight against organized international crime has become another priority in the global projection of EU interests. Although the fight against drugs already has a long history reaching back into the 1970's, only with the end of the Cold War did organized crime become an element of asymmetric and non-governmental "relations" in an increasingly open and disordered world. Trafficking of women and organized prostitution, drug trade, smuggling of goods and even of illegal migrants became notorious concerns for the security systems across Europe – and not only in Europe. More than half a million illegal immigrants arrive in the European Union annually. Although not all of them are criminals, their migration into Europe is a criminal act nurturing fear and prejudice against migrants across the EU.

Management in Sub-Saharan Africa: The Role of the European Union, Occasional Paper No.51, Paris: European Union Institute for Security Studies, 2004.

The European debate about a coherent policy defining the EU as a space of freedom, justice and law became more focused in the aftermath of the horrific terrorist attacks in the US on September 11, 2001. The EU immediately agreed on the terms of a European arrest warrant, including a common definition of terrorism. Europol and the relevant American security institutions maintained very professional and successful means of cooperation that were unaffected by the political crisis between the US and some European governments on the Iraq issue in 2002/2003. The EU has become aware that Europe had been used as a safe haven for terrorists while at the same time Europe could not prevent also becoming a target of terrorism as the Madrid train bombing on March 11, 2004, and the London subway bombings on July 7, 2005, bitterly showed. Nevertheless, instead of reducing the fight against terrorism to a "global war," the European Union tries to tackle the root causes of terrorism and it perceives the preventive fight against terrorism as a policing task across the EU.

4. Europe: Projecting a New Vision of Itself

(1) Hesitantly Returning to a Global Role

The enlargement of the role of the European Union as an international actor is beyond any doubt. Yet, the question of how Europe would ultimately want to position itself in this world remains to be answered. The debate about a European seat on the Security Council of the United Nations is but one rather formal dimension of this evolving issue. The EU claims to represent a modern organization of politics. On the global level, this claim needs to find an echo in a single UN Security Council seat for the EU, representing all its states and citizens. There can be no illusion that France and Great Britain will insist on their global privileges by continuing their membership on the Security Council. Should the issue ever become a matter of real consideration and negotiation, a technical solution would have to be found for recognizing the traditional claim of France and Great Britain. But far from this question, the European Union does not look as if it would approach the issue at all in the foreseeable future. Instead, a useless and time-consuming detour is simmering on the back burner of European Union debates. Germany (and sometimes Italy) has not renounced its ambition to become a permanent member of the UN Security Council. Instead of favoring further national seats on the Security Council of the UN – be it for Germany or for Italy – the European Union could only strengthen its genuine global role if it were able to consensually advocate a common European seat. A European seat on the UN Security Council could be matched by other regional seats for Latin America, Africa, South Asia and the Arab world. These regional seats could be organized in a rotating manner, not unlike the old system of rotating EU presidencies. It would nevertheless create a new dimension for a regionalizing world order.

In order to gain a stronger global presence, the European Union needs more than a political profile in the United Nations. As long as Europe's global identity does not become evident through a cohesive, continuous and consistent global commitment on all possible matters of relevance to mankind, the European Union will not be taken sufficiently seriously as a genuine global player. The first wave of globalization in fifteenth and sixteenth century was driven by European internal dynamics, adventurous European seafarers and explorers, creative merchants and faithful missionaries. It ended as a quest for global dominance and colonial control, followed by a worldwide shrinking of Europe's presence and influence. The new wave of globalization in the twenty-first century is largely defined by American technology and material power. It nevertheless is a wave of globalization that includes the European Union. With the European Union's expanding global role, Europe is returning to the world stage after a century of imperial overstretch, domestic self-destruction and internal rehabilitation. It is a Europe with a completely new global image and reputation. The European Union offers a new contract of partnership to the world.

This ambitious new projection of Europe's interests, claims and goals is linked to the fundamental transformation of European security identity. From the sixteenth century onward, Europeans tended to define security toward each other. From the theological disputes in the Age of Reformation to the military battles of the Thirty Years War, from the conflicts in the age of enlightenment to those in the age of nationalism, Europe was struggling with itself. In doing so, it also had to inevitably struggle with the "rest of the world." Colonial expansion was also a function of internal European conflicts. Imperial overstretch followed colonial expansion and self-destruction followed the imperial overstretch. The cataclysmic escalation of a century long struggle for Europe's identity turned toward a new prospect with the emerging European integration process. European integration has generated a new understanding of Europe's security identity, including in its global dimension. Cooperative patterns of internal European behavior, based on the reciprocal use of resources of the continent, have also begun to define and advance a common approach of the EU to the world at large. The European Union likes to be perceived as an EU that offers partnership to the world and integration or deepened association with its immediate neighborhood.[76] It is in line with this self-perception that the European Union offers to be a partner for intercultural and inter-religious dialogue.

The European Union would also have to position itself in the emerging power quarrels of an increasingly uncertain world order. This includes the relationship of the

76 See Tunander, Ola, et al. (eds.), *Geopolitics in Post-Wall Europe: Security, Territory and Identity*, Oslo: PRIO, 1997; Aggestam, Lisbeth, and Adrian Hyde-Price (eds.), *Security and Identity in Europe: Exploring the New Agenda*, Houndmills: Macmillan Press, 2000.

European Union with the United States of America on the one hand, and with Russia on the other hand. In general terms, the European Union projected its interest to be a friendly and constructive partner with both. But looking at the relationship in more detail, the ambivalence of EU approaches became evident. Regarding the US, the EU had no alternative but to reinvigorate transatlantic relations as the central key for the management of world affairs. Yet, a certain European trend to define Europe against the US and to pretend the possibility of a transatlantic divorce did not stop. Regarding Russia, the EU was aware of the growing authoritarianism in Russia and the potential of threat by Russia because of Europe's energy dependency. Yet, a certain European inclination to pretend a partnership based on equal values and interests with an increasingly unpredictable Russia prevailed. Since the early years of the twenty-first century, the EU relation with Russia was developing into a particular problem for a coherent relationship between the EU's enlargement policies, its neighborhood strategy and the EU's overall global ambition.

- The EU was somewhat ambivalent in its support for the second wave of post-communist democratization revolutions that were unfolding since 2003 in Georgia and in the Ukraine, sweeping into Central Asia by 2005. While the EU took "a clear and even bold initiative"[77] as a resolute mediator in the Ukraine after the election fraud of November 2004, it only reluctantly responded to the long-term ambition of the new president of the Ukraine to join the EU after Victor Yushchenko finally got elected in late December 2004 and was peacefully installed on January 23, 2005, as the country's President. It remained undecided whether or not the EU may finally accept a "European perspective" for the Ukraine. In light of internal uncertainties about the course of the Ukraine, as became manifest in the 2010 Presidential election, the prospect for EU membership seemed to vanish. On the other hand, some observers were beginning to argue that EU membership for Ukraine could be more realistic than EU membership for Turkey. The enlargement debate would eventually also touch the interest Georgia has expressed in joining the European Union, especially after the Russia-Georgian war on South Ossetia in August 2008. Together with Georgia, Armenia and Azerbaijan are member states of the Council of Europe. The Southern Caucasus has become a region of strategic interest for the US and hence for NATO. The European Union would not be able to shy away for all too long from defining its interest in the Southern Caucasus.
- A pro-active enlargement prospect for the Euro-Atlantic institutions toward the Ukraine and the countries of the Southern Caucasus will intensify the growing dilemma of EU policies vis-à-vis Russia. For the time being, the obvious return to authoritarian rule in Russia since 2003 (first under President Putin, then under

77 Bernstein, Richard, "EU diplomacy, the way it's supposed to happen," *International Herald Tribune*, November 26, 2004.

Prime Minister Putin) does not correspond with a coherent and resolute recalibration of EU strategies toward Russia. Not only the European Parliament has become a critical voice as far as Russia's policies in Chechnya, but also the rupture of democratization and the destabilization of the rule of law and the market economy in the Russian Federation, are concerned. On the other hand, the governments of leading EU member states – France and Germany in particular, in 2005 astonishingly joined by Spain – were promoting a policy of engagement and quiet diplomacy vis-à-vis Russia. They were cautious because of European energy dependencies and the long-standing fear "to provoke" Russia. Other EU member states such as Poland with 100 percent dependency on Russian oil imports and 99 percent dependency on Russian natural gas, Slovakia with 100 percent dependency on Russian oil imports and 100 percent dependency on Russian natural gas imports, or Hungary with 100 percent dependency on Russian oil imports and 81 percent dependency on Russian natural gas imports, were much less enthusiastic about hugging the Russian bear.

In November 2003, the EU and Russia had identified four "common spaces" for their future cooperation: A common economic space, a common space of internal security, a common space of external security, and a common space for research, education and culture. In spite of mutual frustrations both on the side of the EU and of Russia, France and Germany were continuing a special relationship with Vladimir Putin's Russia that was irritating[78] other EU partners and the US as well. Most EU citizens and political leaders were categorically rejecting the idea of a possible Russian membership in the EU, even over the long-term. Some analysts, however, expected that in the mid-term an EU-Russia-Treaty could become the framework for a lasting partnership, replacing the existing Partnership and Cooperation Agreement of 1997. The internal EU debate about strategies and policies toward Russia was a constant reflection about the uncertainty that is prevailing in Russia. While some EU member states are inclined to built bridges toward Russia and enhance the degree of engagement, others remain skeptical and worried about Russia's long-term future. They prefer clear borders and the recognition of limits to the EU-Russia partnership. In fact it is astonishing that while the EU and Russia are discussing the deepening of bilateral relations through a long-term treaty, a corresponding "EU-US-Treaty" was obviously not planned for with the same European drive. During the 2007 German EU Presidency, new negotiations on an EU-Russia Partnership Agreement did not begin. Hence the original 1997 agreement was automatically prolongued without any impulse for a new strategic orientation. Polish resistance against too close EU relations to Russia turned EU priorities

78 See Meier, Christian, *Nach dem Gipfel von Den Haag. Russland und das neue Modell der Partnerschaft mit der EU*, Berlin: Stiftung Wissenschaft und Politik, 2004.

toward energy solidarity with Poland and laid to rest German plans for a new "Ostpolitik." For once, intra-EU solidarity was seen as prime interest, not the least in order to facilitate the negotiations that led to the Reform Treaty of December 2007. In order not to provoke Russia too much at the same time the EU did not succeed in formulating a coherent policy toward the Ukraine and the Caucasus as initially expected by the German EU Presidency in early 2007. In June 2007, the European Council only decided on a Central Asia Strategy Paper, not without meeting criticism for its primarily rhetorical nature. In the meantime the EU has produced more strategy papers than strategies and more visions than concrete implementations of foreign policy. It probably should get the benefit of the doubt as a common foreign and security policy has only been emerging for less than two decades. But the gap between EU reluctance and global expectations is clearly rising. The European Union needs to shape its coherent and pro-active global positioning in all aspects of international relations beyond its internal idiosyncratic institutional reform aspirations. The world expects more from Europe and Europe should develop more ambitions and tools to apply them.[79]

(2) The Old World in a New World Order

Multiple political identities and stable internal peace frame the current European encounter of the world. The biggest obstacle to a convincing profile of Europe's latest global projection was inherent in the European approach to global challenges and opportunities: While the political culture in the United States is intuitively universalistic, the European approach favors procedures, incremental approximations to new realities and cautious differentiation. The European Union was hesitant to project its role beyond the next cycle of mandates or fiscal plans. This was not just a matter of projecting visions and futuristic scenarios. The European Union preferred to operate on a pragmatic day-to-day basis. To introduce long-term political planning was inherently alien to the EU. It would require a change in the political culture of the EU and more courage on the side of key EU actors to advance the idea of a more coherent and future-oriented approach to politics. Such a turn in EU behavioral patterns would not require a radical transformation of the political scene in Europe. Relative simple reforms could really make a difference: The European Parliament could introduce the European equivalent of the State of the Union Address regularly delivered by the American President. A regular State of the European Union Address, delivered by the President of

79 See Ferrero-Waldner, Benita, *The EU in the World*, Speech, Brussels, February 2, 2006. http://europa.eu/rapid/pressReleasesAction.do?reference=SPEECH/06/59&format=HTML&aged=0 &language=EN&guiLanguage=en; Lieb, Julia, and Andreas Maurer, *Europas Rolle in der Welt stärken: Optionen für ein kohärentes Aussenhandeln der Europäischen Union*, SWP-Studie S 15, Berlin: Stiftung Wissenschaft und Politik, 2007.

the European Commission, the President of the European Parliament and the President of the European Council would be a refreshing innovation in Europe's political culture.

For two centuries, wars in Europe were part of a sad normalcy. It was a permanent burden to deal with the question of German power inside Europe. It was a permanent problem to externalize intra-European power conflicts through the medium of global imperialism and colonialism. In the end, the internal European conflicts and their global externalization came to an end. Europe's supremacy in the world faded. In 1914, four-fifths of the world's land surface outside Antarctica was under either a European flag or the flag of a nation of European descent.[80] In 1900, 25 percent of world population was European. In 2010, roughly 7 percent of the global population was European. Now, the EU does not consist of more than one percent of the surface of the earth. Colonial dominance over practically all territories outside Europe has come to an end, with the tragic exception of the fringes of Europe where Russia was still involved in a struggle of secession and decolonization with the Muslim people of Northern Caucasus. Whether or not during the twenty-first century Europe would become a museum to the world, a home for the aging, a target of tourism and the leisure playground for its citizens and visitors, or Europe would become the model of a peaceful transformation of conflicts, the laudable expression of unity in plurality, and a dynamic and innovative technological and economic zone in connection with a stable and supreme social model, remains the pivotal question for the European Union to answer. Whether or not by 2019, Europe will once and for all have overcome the unhappy peace order of 1919 and will have positioned itself as a model of regionalization, integration and social inclusion remains to be seen. No path into the future is predestined. Everything depends upon European decisions – and upon European visions about the future of the old continent in a new world order.

The goal of an integrated, truly Common Foreign, Security and Defense Policy of the EU will never be a purpose in itself. It would be the logical precondition for a cohesive global role of the European Union. Much depends on spending, and especially on the readiness of Europe to enhance its common defense spending. The fact that the United Kingdom spent 33.5 billion dollars on defense in 2002 against 26 billion dollars for France and 24.5 billion dollars for Germany, 13 billion dollars for Italy and 7.5 billion dollars for Spain alone does not mean too much. Even the fact that military spending had dropped in France, the United Kingdom and Germany by 13 percent during the 1990's cannot be taken as the sole parameter in comparing US defense spending with European defense spending. A better focus than the simple reference to the share of GDP for defense (down during the 1990's from 3.27 to 2.26 percent in the United Kingdom, from 2.41 to 1.72 percent in France and from 1.55 to 1.16 percent in Germany) would be a comparison between the overall EU defense spending and that of

80 See Roberts, J. M., *The Penguin History of the Twentieth Century: The History of the World 1901 to the Present*, London: Penguin Books, 1999: 89.

the United States. Over the first years of the twenty-first century, defense spending dropped from 60 percent to less than 50 percent of the US budget while the spending for defense equipment had gone down from 40 to 25 percent of the overall budget. However, defense, security and stability in the world of new conflicts, asymmetric warfare and unstable state structures cannot be defined by the degree of military spending and the focus on technology and equipment only. The EU had to admit that its biggest gap vis-à-vis the US is in technology: While the Pentagon is spending about 28,000 US dollars per soldier per year on research and development, the EU member states together are spending four or five times less.[81] While the combined EU defense spending is less than 50 percent of US defense spending, it is substantially higher than the defense budget of Russia, China or Japan. In terms of manpower, the combined EU forces of 1.8 million soldiers are stronger than the 1.5 million US armed forces, twice as many as Russia's military personnel and almost as many as China's. It should also be noted that EU participation in UN Peace Keeping Missions is seven times higher than US participation.[82]

All in all, the defense capabilities of the European Union and its member states are not so irrelevant or small. Yet, the overall efficiency and, even more importantly, the political will to project European interests on a global scale is limited and decisively below the global presence and performance of the United States. As long as security and defense spending will not be pooled on the level of the European Union, the EU will lag behind. It should become imperative for the European Union to assess the cost of non-integration of defense budgets, schemes and instruments.[83] The EU is increasingly confronted with the need to redefine European public goods in fiscal terms, including a European public good in defense and military matters. For the fiscal period 2000 to 2006, the budget of the European Union had amounted to approximately 100 billion euros per annum. While around 51 percent was spent on the Common Agricultural Policy – no matter how many reforms have taken place to reduce this amount of subsidies to a group of approximately 4 percent of the overall EU population – and 28 percent on structural actions – notably for Regional Funds and for Cohesion Funds – only 7 percent of the budget was allocated for expenditures related to external actions, including pre-accession funds. 8 percent of the remaining budget was spent on internal policies and 5 percent on administrative expenditures. For the fiscal period 2007-2013

81 Reid, T. R., *The United States of Europe: The New Superpower and the End of American Supremacy*, New York: Penguin Press, 2004: 180.

82 See Ferguson, Niall, *Colossus: The Price of America's Empire*, New York: Penguin Press, 2004: 238.

83 Instead, academics preferred to stereotypically repeat the theoretical arguments why a Common Foreign and Security Policy could not work – although it was beginning to be proved to the contrary, see Wagner, Wolfgang, "Why the EU's Common Foreign and Security Policy Will Remain Intergovernmental: a Rationalist Institutional Choice Analysis of European Crisis Management Policy," *Journal of European Public Policy*, 10.4 (2003): 576-595.

the EU budget for external actions increased only gradually and was to reach 9.9 percent in 2013 (a total of 50 billion euros for the whole period 2007-2013).

It is, to say the least, unwise for the European Union not to make better use of its defense expenditures and to better pool resources in all relevant fields of external relations. In light of the demographic trend in Europe, it is illusionary to assume that Europe or any of its main countries would substantially increase defense spending in the foreseeable future. But in order to limit the technology and capability gap with the US, it is imperative for Europe to make better use of the existing resources available for security related expenditures. The EU has to develop a solid, albeit limited military capability in order to allow the EU to implement its Security Strategy and to strengthen Europe's influence on EU decision-making. Multiple means have to be utilized, an improved division of labor among EU member states as far as expenditure for defense capabilities is concerned, a better use of the public-private partnership, and the optimal use of the newly established European Defense Agency as far as common procurement policies and production of military equipment is concerned. In this context, the absence of a European tax becomes relevant. The 2007 Reform Treaty (as well as the ill-fated European Constitution of 2004) avoided an answer on the matter of a solid EU revenue allocation. Academic studies continue to raise the matter and link it to the need of defining European public goods, most notably in the sphere of external actions of the EU. It is indispensable for the EU to redefine not only the nature of its fiscal instruments, but also the character of public allowances in support of EU policies. The existing modalities for allocating the EU budget have grown over time and as such they remain highly idiosyncratic as the EU reflects on its position of playing a stronger global role.

The most traditional resources of the EU are linked to community policies already developed during the 1960's and 1970's: Around 12 percent of the union budget originates in taxes on agricultural imports, sugar in particular, and other levies on imports into the European Union. In 1979, the then European Community introduced a quota system by which a certain share of each national value-added tax was to be redirected into the EU budget. This sum amounted to not more than 15 percent of the EU budget during the fiscal period 2000 to 2006 and is not different for the period 2007 to 2013. The biggest share of the EU budget – approximately 70 percent – stems from a quota system based on the Gross Domestic Product of each EU member state.

In February 2004, the European Commission outlined its financial perspectives for the fiscal period 2007 to 2013. The Commission proposed an EU budget of 1.15 percent of the combined Gross Domestic Product of all EU member states. This proposal was strongly refused by the leading net contributors to the EU budget, namely Germany, France, the Netherlands, Sweden, Denmark and Finland. In June 2005, the European Council failed to reach a compromise on the budget perspective for 2007-2013 based on a Luxembourg compromise proposal trying to limit the expenditure ceiling to 1.06

percent of the EU GDP. After a long and daunting period of controversy, the European Council in December 2005 successfully framed the budget perspective for 2007-2013. The basic decision was by definition limiting the future EU scope of action. The EU budget for the period 2007-2013 would not exceed 1.045 percent of the EU's GDP. The EU net budget of 862.3 billion euros was slightly upgraded after the European Parliament refused to agree to the decisions taken by the European Council in December 2005. A new inter-institutional deal was found in early 2006. The budget line for the EU's Foreign and Security Policy was not substantially increased (50 billion euros for the period 2007-2013). It was evident that global expectations and EU resources would not be consistent. As long as the EU was not willing to introduce a European financial constitution, the national net contributing system would genetically limit the scope of action of the European Union.[84]

The lack of a sufficiently communitarized budget for foreign actions of the European Union is also limiting the credibility and coherence of EU development policies. The European Union claims to be the biggest development aid donor worldwide. The EU can say so only by adding the national expenditures. The degree of a genuine EU value added to development policy remains controversial. Development aid is a key policy area for bridging interests and values. In reality, the EU is not yet an autonomous actor. The EU is missing a common and communitarized development aid budget worth the name. Development financing remains a national prerogative. The consequence is permanent confusion about competences and about accountability in development policy matters. Also conceptually, the EU's approach to international development issues could be much more streamlined and stronger.[85] The more the European Union wants to be taken seriously as a global player that acts coherently in all relevant matters of international order-building, the more the EU simply needs a communitarized budget for foreign actions in all relevant fields. And it needs clarity about communitarized competences that go beyond the coordination of 27 or so national preferences and policies, interests and values.

The fundamental question remains unresolved: How to define a European public good and how to organize the appropriate budget to implement it with a certain cohesion and consistency? One way would be to continue along the path of developing further fiscal schemes relative to European challenges, such as an energy tax, an environmental tax, a security tax or to establish a certain quota of nationally existing tax mechanisms, such as corporate tax, explicitly to European tasks. More important, however, than incremental enlargements of European tax instruments would be a coherent European debate – and finally solid political decisions – on the principles

84 For the background of the negotiations in 2004/2005 see Becker, Peter, *Der Finanzrahmen 2007-2013: Auf dem Weg zu einer europäischen Finanzverfassung oder Fortsetzung der nationalen Nettosaldopolitik?*, SWP-Studie S 36, Berlin: Stiftung Wissenschaft und Politik, 2005.

85 See Carbone, Maurizio, *The European Union and International Development: The Politics of Foreign Aid*, Abingdon: Routledge, 2007.

guiding European public goods. According to academic research, two principles may guide the evolution of a European tax system appropriate to bridge the gap between the growing tasks bestowed upon the EU and the current under-funding of the European Union:[86]

- Coupling European tax levies to specific European functions: As seen in the field of external trade, European interests have evolved and will further evolve around specific functions transferred to the European Union. As they have to be financed, the principles of transparency and accountability require a clear coupling of new European tax levies to specific functions granted to the European Union – and the other way around if the functions are to be properly implemented. External affairs have certainly gained consensus in the European Union as an expression of a common interest and thus this policy field should generate a specifically communitarized budget.
- Coupling European tax levies to a specific European objective: A European tax can also evolve – even in an indirect way – around specific objectives, which the EU intends to achieve. As in the case of environmental protection or the regulation of the common market, the EU has demonstrated the ability to define objectives that require public spending by the member states. The evolution of a common market for defense tools can serve the purpose of enhancing European Union fiscal involvement based on increased defense spending among member states; those who do not increase their share might be "punished" via the mechanism of redefining their GDP contribution to the EU budget.

In both cases, the EU must avoid double spending and fiscal competition between the EU level and that of its member states. Should the EU follow the first principle, it will inevitably lead to the creation of a Union budgetary fund for defense spending, the logical consequence of a Common Foreign and Security Policy. Should the EU follow the second principle, it can mean a value added in security and defense policy, but the financial basis would continuously be based on national expenditures in defense and security matters. The application of the first principle would initiate a communitarized budget of the EU. The application of the second principle would prolong the intergovernmental character of European defense and its current nature as the net sum of individual national contributions.

The example demonstrates that the future evolution of Europe's Foreign and Security Policy is not only a matter of grand strategy and global political implication. It is inherently linked to the evolution of Europe's internal structures, to the widely debated "deepening" of European integration. For non-Europeans, the first aspect will be the most important one, for EU member states and taxpayers the second issue is the

86 For the following see Brehon, Nicolas-Jean, "L'impôt européen," in: Lefebvre, Maxime (ed.), *Quel Budget Européen à l'horizon 2013?: Moyens et politiques d'une Union elargie*, Paris: Institut Français des Relations Internationales, 2004: 161-180.

more contested one. If the EU wants to achieve a truly relevant and coherent global role through a cohesive web of external relations, strategies, policies and programs, it will have to organize an adequate European tax mechanism. As this will either curtail spending for domestic programs or require an increase in the overall EU budget, the debates on this matter will be long and daunting. In the first case, the issue of internal solidarity and Union cohesion will be articulated; in the second case, the global responsibility and international expectation toward the European Union will be brought forward as the defining argument. In the end, the relevant decisions will indicate the nature and quality of political leadership in Europe.

(3) Toward European Public Goods in Foreign and Security Policies

A coherent global role of the European Union needs to be recognized as an EU-wide European public good. Only then will the fiscal architecture of the European Union be changed. Setting up a budget line for defense matters in the EU will be as relevant as further progress toward the harmonization of European defense spending through the work of the European Defense Agency. Already during the 1970's, the McDougall Report suggested the need for a parallel development of political and fiscal integration with an emphasis on bringing the function of defense spending to the European level. The report estimated that the EU defense budget would have to be in the order of 2 percent of the overall Gross Domestic Product of the then European Economic Community. Until a "pre-federal" stage would be reached, the European defense budget would have to grow to a ratio of 5 to 7 percent of the overall Gross Domestic Product of the Community. Nothing has substantially changed since the 1970's. It is high time for the EU to move forward on this matter.

Unfortunately, the EU budget structure has not yet overcome its inertia. The risk has even increased that the Union budget will remain too small to meet the tasks already bestowed upon the Union. As a consequence of this fiscal inertia, a re-nationalization of policies could result. This would hardly enhance the efficiency and outcome of policies both in quality and quantity. It would only undermine the need to increase the European added value to make specific policies both more targeted and effective. As far as possible EU defense spending is concerned, the nexus between internal cohesion, the evolution of budgetary federalism and the global projection of Europe as well as its perception worldwide is evident. The creation of a viable defense budget for the European Union would not only strengthen the integration process in the field of defense, it would also enhance the legitimacy of the integration through the creation of visible European public goods. Finally, it would increase the security function of the EU in the field of conflict resolution, crisis management and post-crisis stabilization around the world.

The process of pooling resources in the field of security and defense ranges from joint capabilities – particularly jointly procured and operated equipment – to complementary advantages such as interoperability, lower overhead costs and more effective common doctrines, strategies and missions. It also includes the early realization of such initiatives as the creation of a European Security and Defense College, a European Police Academy and a European Training Institute. Of particular relevance are the efforts to forge a European Defense Industry and to strengthen armaments cooperation through the European Defense Agency.[87] Ultimately, the most sensitive question cannot disappear from the public debate in Europe: Why does the EU still need twenty-seven national armies with their respective infrastructures and personnel? Eurocorps – the first multinational European force formed in 1992 – and the European Battlegroups – operational since 2007 – have shown that these are not theoretical matters. The ultimate key to success or failure of a Common Foreign, Security and Defense Policy of the European Union will be the EU's ability to move from intergovernmental to supranational structures and mechanisms. Only by properly pooling resources and bringing them under one united EU command can the EU become a coherent and capable global actor who makes the best possible use of limited resources.

Europe's standing in the world was defined for most of the twentieth century by the events of 1914 and 1919: 1914 was the beginning of the first European civil war that ended in 1919 with the de-empowerment of Europe at the tables of the Versailles Peace Conference. Between 1914 and 1919, a world broke into pieces that had largely been shaped and defined by Europe.[88] Whether or not the European Union might accomplish its form and function, both in size and depth, remains to be seen. Elections to the European Parliament will take place in 2014 and again in 2019, followed by the appointment of a new European Commission. The fiscal cycle of the EU is currently set for 2007 to 2013 and the next one is due for the period 2014 to 2020. The pending cycle of enlargements may come to a close around 2020.[89] But even beyond 2020, the European Union will continue to evolve, with all the idiosyncratic modes experienced throughout the second half of the twentieth century and during most of the first decade of the twenty-first century. The process of deepening will continue for many more years

87 See Schmitt, Burkhard, *From Cooperation to Integration: Defense and Aerospace Industries in Europe*, Paris: Institute for Security Studies, 2001; James, Andrew D., "European Armaments Cooperation: Lessons for a Future European Armaments Agency," *The International Spectator*, 38:4 (2003): 59-74; Keohane, Daniel, *Europe's New Defense Agency*, London: Centre for European Reform, 2004; Macrae, Duncan, "Defense – European Arms Agency–One Step Forward," *Interavia: Business and Technology*, 59 (2004): 41-42. The European Defense Agency has four mandates: defense capability development, research, acquisition, armaments.

88 See Stefan Zweigs intriguing novel *The World of Yesterday* (paperback reprint by Barnes and Noble, New York, 1990), capturing the spirit of this unique moment better than most historical work.

89 See Rehn, Olli, *Europe's Next Frontiers*, Nomos: Baden-Baden 2007.

and most likely for decades. Its ultimate form and function cannot be projected. It will evolve in reaction, and sometimes in anticipation, of the main global trends.

Whatever the results eventually will be – and transient they will remain as all works of politics are –, the European Union has already left a visible and impressive imprint on the map of world history and geopolitics. Notions of political philosophy have been affected by its existence, also patterns of global trade and economic development, trajectories of geopolitics and power equations, and finally even the global perception of Europe.

"A Secure Europe in a Better World" – the title of the first EU Security Strategy of December 2003 was more than a promise to the world. First and foremost, it was the definition of a challenge to Europe itself. Threats and opportunities for a community of 491 million people and a quarter of the world's GDP will closely coexist in the world of the twenty-first century. They leave the EU with no other choice but to fully become a global actor if it wants to shape its own destiny. In order to do so, the EU has to match aspirations and capabilities, rhetorical goals and politically consensual interests. The EU has to take up responsibility for global security and stability in all its aspects. Only theoretically, the European Union is facing the choice of either being a huge neutral (and hence self-neutralized) zone with an attitude of self-complacent aloofness, or an exemplary, multilateral oriented and pro-active region in strong partnership with the United States. In reality, the choice it faces is either to stay a benevolent yet increasingly marginalized regional power or to become a comprehensive global power with full commitment to the management of world affairs. While the European Union has underperformed in matters of foreign, security and defense policy so far, its very existence and evolution has been more than fifty years evidence of a steep historical learning curve for Europe as a whole. One can expect these European learning processes to continue. Part of the ongoing European learning process remains the steady reinvigoration of transatlantic relations. As the EU's Security Strategy rightly stated, only by "acting together, the European Union and the United States can be a formidable force for good in the world."[90]

The Security Strategy of the EU has recognized the United States as the dominant military actor in today's world. It also reaffirmed the EU's interest in "an effective and balanced partnership with the USA."[91] The EU can be certain that the new US President, following George Bush in January 2009, will take the EU by its word. The United Nations has been considered to be the ultimate and central organ for peace in the world. The Security Strategy of the European Union – an answer, not a counter-proposal to the 2002 National Security Strategy of the US – was a European proposal for a renewed, trusted and lasting partnership with shared responsibilities in a globalized world. In the years ahead, it is dependent on the European Union – be it through

90 European Union, *A Secure Europe in a better World: European Security Strategy*, op.cit.: 13.
91 Ibid.

intergovernmental or supranational mechanisms – to prove the claim of its "2010 Headline Goals" that "the European Union is a global actor, ready to share in the responsibility for global security."[92] On the other hand, it is dependent on the US to take the EU seriously as a partner in global strategic leadership. Also in the future, conflicting interests can hardly be avoided on individual issues. Yet, the political will to work together needs to be the defining element of transatlantic relations again. Should this be the case – and there is no law of nature indicating that it could not happen – the heirs of Christopher Columbus and of Henry the Navigator can ultimately find a common frame of mind again, coupled with the necessary political will (and a solid financial basis) to jointly manage the future of world affairs.

92 Cited in Lindstrom, Gustav, *Enter the EU Battlegroups*, op.cit.: 80.

Conclusion

I.

The twenty-first century is the century of a worldwide region-building and of a multipolar global order. It also is the century of globalization and therefore, as many analysts see it, of Americanization. It is the century of a return of cultural and religious identity into the sphere of public life and politics. Notwithstanding different definitions of region-building and regionalism, disparate degrees of regional integration and unequal approaches to supranationalism: The concept of the autarkic nation state, the Westphalian order of sovereignty and the age of unrelated political and societal processes in different parts of the world has come to an end.[1] Across the world, the states of the twenty-first century are experiencing the limits of their sovereignty and the gains of cooperative behavior. The main challenges of this age are beyond the ability of single states. To realize and exercise autarkic solutions does not work any more. Managing globalization, coping with the challenges of migration, of climate change or of the trends in world financial markets – these prime issues of our time require common approaches and actions of more than one state government. Managing the welfare state and coping with the social agenda of any country, generating sufficient resources to improve the life chances of all citizens, improving education systems and supporting the stability of families and the values they hand to the next generation, persecuting organized crime and dealing with the potential of aggression and violence in modern society – no national effort to cope with these matters can succeed without comparing one's own performance with that of others, without learning from others and without relying on mutual trust in managing the concrete issues stemming from each country's specific constellation together. Wherever trust and the will to cooperate are absent, it is rare that autarkic, seemingly sovereign decisions can work. The costs of cooperative actions may be high. The risks of non-cooperation can be even higher. Often, the gains of cooperation – or of region-building and the pooling of sovereignty – are not properly communicated to the citizenry. This mistake is not a unique European privilege. Suspicion and mistrust in the mechanism of regional interactions can be detected everywhere. Yet, this skepticism cannot deny the facts: Regional cooperation and integration have become global trends because the gains of region-building outweigh the costs of autonomous state sovereignty. The global trend reflects European

1 See Close, Paul, and Emiko Ohki-Close, *Supranationalism in the New World Order: Global Processes Reviewed*, Houndmills: Macmillan 1999.

regional integration. More often, European regional integration is echoed in region-building efforts elsewhere across the globe.[2]

No matter the exceptional role of the United States of America, its shining model of freedom for much of the world, its ever reinvigorating economic dynamic and welcoming community spirit, its cultural attraction and military power: The world order of the twenty-first century may be built around a certain American primacy, yet more than ever it is a world order of regions experiencing power shifts of unpredictable results. Some of the regions of the world are economically stronger than others. Political power and the ability to manage one's own or regional affairs are distributed asymmetrically.

The age of globalization, especially the worldwide presence of new and instant means of communication, has made the concept of center and periphery rather porous. The age of globalization has also brought about the quest for cultural identity and recognition. Migration (and travels of all sorts) accelerates the encounter of cultures and religions, of traditions and values. Sometimes, this happens in confrontational ways. Often, it helps to enrich peoples' lives. The dialogue of cultures and civilizations is one of the most important, promising, yet difficult opportunities of the twenty-first century. The world-order of the twenty-first century combines intra-national and intra-societal, international and transnational realities. How to measure power and power shifts remains a constant challenge. The monopoly of power is no longer defined purely by state actors, as the rise of modern terrorism – mainly in the name of a radical interpretation of political Islam – demonstrates. Yet, the nation states remain central actors in the management of world-order. The supportive role of the United Nations and other global institutions will grow. So does their potential in generating elements of global governance. The UN needs the support of national governments and remains limited by their vetoing capacity. The world-order of the twenty-first century includes elements of cooperation and competition, and it will see stability and conflict. Achievement and stagnation will occur beside hope and fear. It will not end with the creation of a new man. No matter whether human beings visit Mars one day, or not, the world's destiny remains earth-bound as ever it has been.

The political order of the nineteenth century was defined by the European state system and it was dominated by Europe's conflicts and imperial competitions. In the nineteenth century, the United States had hardly been present in the considerations of European powers and it was linked to Europe mostly through the melancholic sentiments of European migrants who had fled hardship, poverty and conflicts in the Old World. At that time though, in Asia the United States behaved not very differently from the European powers, that is to say with military excursions in order to open ports and whole countries, project interests, punish local authorities or engage in outright

2 See Koesler, Ariane, and Martin Zimmek (eds.), *Global Voices on Regional Integration*, ZEI Discussion Paper C 176, Bonn: Center for European Integration Studies, 2007.

colonial rule. Balance of power was hardly kept in more than loose balance. It failed to tame the radicalization of internal pressures and external dynamics that could no longer be controlled by mechanisms of rationality and the experience of conflict. By the mid-twentieth century, totalitarian rule and a thirty years civil war ended in Europe's self-destruction. This was the end of Europe's status as the world's dominant continent.

World War II was a watershed. It forced Europe into a new beginning. The democratic countries of Western Europe began to recalibrate their internal resources and their inter-state relations. The founding of the European Economic Community was unprecedented. The division of Europe into democracies and communist dictatorships, dominated by an expansionist Soviet Union, convinced the United States to stay a European power. The US was ready to help Europe rehabilitate and then reconstruct democratic peace under America's security umbrella. Soviet totalitarianism held millions of Europeans hostage for decades and the Russians as well, bereaving them of almost a whole century. Ironically, the Soviet Union served as the external threat that helped to facilitate reconciliation among Western Europeans, to build a strong Atlantic civilization and to plant the seeds for the struggle for freedom among its own satellites. What had begun with the independence of Latin American republics in the nineteenth century escalated in the mid-twentieth century: Decolonization brought national sovereignty to more than half of the world's population, soon to be labeled the Third World. Following the imperial age, this first wave of globalization, and the global wars of the twentieth century, more than one hundred new countries in Asia, Africa, Latin America, the Caribbean and the Pacific changed the world map. Later, globalization changed the world economy. World War II came to its final end only in 1989, when the Berlin Wall fell, symbolizing freedom as the fall of the Bastille had done during the French Revolution in 1789.

European integration began in 1957 with the goal to promote reconciliation in Europe. Five decades later, it was going through the period of its Second Founding: Internal reconciliation, by and large, had been achieved. The European Union was reframing its constitution in order to reconnect its citizens with the institutions that had developed. The EU did so in order to prepare for a more comprehensive global role. At the end of the first decade of the twenty-first century, the European Union was established as a federation and a polity with increasing global contributions to free trade, stability projection and peace enforcement. European Union has been achieved, including a reasonable balance between its political institutions. But Europeans are still a rare species and ought to be "developed" in the decades ahead: This can only succeed through a better sense of ownership and a shared understanding of European citizenship as a civil duty exerting loyalty and commitment to the European Union.

These questions affect the internal legitimacy of European integration. But the answers given in this process of Europe's Second Founding are essential for the perception and reputation of the EU's global role. It is academic to discuss whether or not the European Union had developed into a regional power and should ever stay as such, or was to become a global power. The European Union is the indispensable partner of the United States in the management of global affairs. It is highly abstract to debate whether or not the European Union should or should not become a super-power. Whether its leaders and citizens like it or not, the EU is increasingly challenged by global developments to take up worldwide responsibility. These processes generate, shape and reinforce the evolution of common European interests. The European Union likes to be portrayed as the world's benevolent power, but hard power will increasingly test the benevolence and competence of the EU. The projection of the EU's interests is a matter of internal coherence and competence, external effectiveness and the ability to influence norm-giving elsewhere. No matter whether or not the EU would wish to be only defined as a consequence of its actions (and non-actions), this self-centeredness is increasingly permeated by global realities: The EU has already been forced substantially to broaden its horizon and activities by an agenda (welcomed or not) that the future has brought (and will continue to bring) to its doorsteps. Important is the fact that the revamped European Union of the twenty-first century encounters the world as a new Europe: No longer a colonizing and imperial Europe, and no longer a divided Europe that exports its own conflicts elsewhere. Instead, it has become a Europe of partnership in pursuit of the promotion of stability, freedom, security and prosperity across the globe. At the same time, however, Europe's former civilization mission has been shaken by internal moral relativism and yet, the European Union likes to be perceived as a community of values. In abstract terms, this claim reflects the political aspiration of the EU. The notion of being a community of values does, however, not coincide with a consensual interpretation of the prime values and their meaning, the religious heritage of Europe and the role of religion in today's Europe.

It is indicative for the new global role of Europe: Europe's internal process of regional integration is finding sympathy and interest in many parts of the world that have been European colonies only one or two generations ago. Other regions strive to emulate European integration, and they do so in their own unique way. They cannot follow European experiences in a static way. Also for Europeans themselves, integration never followed a blueprint. Its first half century of development has been a period of trial and error, with detours, failures and success stories alike. Yet, European integration has become the only innovative contribution to political theory and practical order-building since World War II.

No matter Europe's norms, interests and goals, the European Union is explicitly promoting regional cooperation and regional integration across the world. This policy is an obvious discrepancy with most policy strategies of the United States: Although the US has promoted European integration and cooperation after World War II and although it has supported the creation of the Association of Southeast Asian Nations (ASEAN) in 1967 as a mechanism of defense against communism in Asia, usually the

US is not pro-actively supporting region-building. American concepts of regionalism tend to differ from the European approach: while the US favor free trade, the EU favors institution-building. These objectives are not mutually exclusive. But they can lead to conflicting interests and policy strategies. None of these strategies, of course, can be criticized as neo-colonialism. But it is simply a matter of fact that the EU and the US are pursuing legitimate yet different economic, political and strategic interests in several third regions across the globe. But together, the EU and the US are the main actors in the management of world affairs.

II.

All trends indicate that the world-order of the twenty-first century will be shaped and defined by several contingent factors while power shifts remain difficult to measure. The outcome of the main factors is unpredictable for all those who believe in the open character of history and man. New and so far unexpected realities may completely reshape the global-order over the course of the next decades. For the time being, the following trends can be identified with reasonable certainty as being decisive for the evolution and outcome of the twenty-first century:

(1) Questions of cultural identity, recognition and faith have been moved to the center of the global intellectual debate and political arena. A resurgence of religion can be experienced around the world. It would be superficial to primarily understand this trend as represented by the threatening growth of Islamic fundamentalism. It is certainly the experience with radical and aggressive expressions of religiosity that they can easily transgress the sphere of violence and thus generate terror against innocent people. But it is insufficient to understand the culture of religion primarily through the lens of its excesses. The quest for identity, roots and recognition transcends human and societal interactions. This quest can lead with reason to religious interpretations of human life and society. It cannot be denied that religion has a public meaning. Religion cannot be eliminated from the public sphere without demonstrating authoritarian agnosticism and without provoking religious counter-reactions. The debate about the identity of Europe in the context of the constitution-building of the European Union centered on the meaning of Christianity for the traditions of Europe and, moreover, for the understanding and shaping of today's European Union. While the secularist notion of a clear division between the spheres of religion and politics dominated the debate, the claim for a public role of religion had never been heard that loud in Europe for decades. The insistence of the Christian churches to recognize the Christian view of man as the core of Europe's cultural identity does not contradict the largely secularized reality of many European societies. Religious creed and practized faith are not only a matter of personal belief and certainly not a challenge for inter-religious peace. Religion – in

Christian, Muslim and Jewish connotations alike – is also a challenge to the widely spread libertarian cultural liberalism in the West. Cultural relativism tends to undermine authentic religiosity as a source of free societies. The quest for a new balance between liberalism and religion implies recalibrated reflections about the meaning of authority and freedom, progress and destiny. It is widely recognized that religious concepts of man introduce a dimension of humility and modesty into the sphere of politics. Defining the limits of politics can serve as a shield against authoritarian or even totalitarian aspirations.

Christianity has reconciled with Western democracy. This has been the result of centuries of accommodation and struggle. In the end, both Christianity and the modern concept of democracy have benefited. Anti-Semitism and Islamophobia are condemned by the authorities of all Christian churches in Europe. In the course of the second half of the twentieth century, following the Holocaust and the path of migration into Europe, Islam has become the biggest minority religion next to the dominant Christian faith. The debate about the possible development of a "Euro-Islam" has implications worldwide for the relationship between Islam and democracy, and also for the future relationship between Christians, Muslims and Jews across the Middle East. It remains central that the dialogue among religions and religious cultures around the globe will be based on respect and reciprocity. In many ways, this dialogue is the most important test case for global peace and human equilibrium. The resolution of the Middle East conflict remains at the center of all efforts to translate the inter-religious dialogue into a political reality.

(2) Demographic trends and migration patterns have gained prominence in the public debate in Europe. Both, of course, are world-wide phenomena with repercussions in Europe and elsewhere. Europe's share of world population has shrunk from 20 to 7 percent in the course of one century. Moreover: The aging of the European population does not correspond to trends in most other parts of the world. In light of reduced birth rates, the population in several European countries has begun to shrink (Germany, Poland, Hungary, Estonia, Latvia, Lithuania), while only Cyprus and Ireland can claim net growth rates of their population. The population of most of the non-European regions in the world is still growing, and it is increasingly younger than in Europe. This holds also true for the United States. Europe's population is likely to fall by almost a fifth until 2050 while at the same time the number of people in retirement compared with those in jobs will double from 24 percent (2008) to almost 50 percent. The effect of this dependency ratio – with fewer people in work supporting more people out of work – has economic and cultural implications that are of a reverse nature in practically all other regions in the world.

Europe has changed from being a continent of emigration into a continent of immigration. On a global scale, immigration and emigration coexist with different implications for sender and recipient countries. Migration pattern of a new nature have become a worldwide phenomenon. Two characteristics feature prominently: a)

Migration driven by social and political pressure originates most notably from Russia, Africa and Latin America; more migration due to climate change and the search for a new habitat is already evident in several parts of the world; b) Migration of young and creative people drawn by the attraction of North America or Europe exists across the globe. Migration has human, social, cultural, economic and political implications.

The immediate effects of both types of migration require a wide range of "integration" responses, including the promotion of language skills, the acceptance of cultural and legal patterns, and a host of religious connotations. The management of migration must take into consideration the needs of the countries of origin. It is not rare that the most qualified migrants are much needed in their home country. Yet, they look for better options elsewhere. Especially poor countries can suffer heavy losses from this brain-drain. A balance has to be found between the life chances of the individual and the social needs of each home society. A competent and flexible management of migration must be found that can generate win-win-situations for all.

(3) Globalization has become *the* buzz-word of our age. Time and space have not changed but the human understanding of time and space has changed. Instant communication, many forms of global economic interdependence, activities in world financial markets and the effects of technological discoveries on many spheres of life, including health care and medicine, have brought the globe closer together. It is telling that as a consequence of the de-freezing of the Artic circle and thus the possible free passage through the Bering Sea, the North Pole and access to its natural resources has been included on the agenda of globalization. Globalization has accelerated the speed of human interactions. But this trend has also created a huge gap between those who partake in globalization processes and those who do not or cannot participate. The term "internet-divide" has significance. In the meantime, the opportunities and implications of globalization are present in all regions and continents of the world. They help to cope with problems of "periphery" (such as weather forecasts and hurricane warnings in remote ocean areas). They enhance the dependency of life chances and, partially, of job opportunities. Both in the European Union and in the US, the implications of globalization are experienced as opportunity and as problem. Whenever the European Union contemplates a "European Social Model," the EU cannot deny vast differences between several social models that exist in Europe. Beside, different EU member states have different perceptions of globalization and the opportunities for them. While the EU is confronted with growing challenges of demography and competitiveness, both the EU and the US are the global leaders in generating technological innovation and social dynamics in order to enter new spheres of globalization. Among the Atlantic partners, this will happen as a continuous interplay of competition and cooperation. Both will activate the most creative potential in their societies without a dangerous backlash as long as the results of their developments will help the neglected regions of the world to also actively get involved in the global market economy and in the age of globalization.

As for the social implications of globalization, it is not enough for Europe to take refuge in abstract contemplations about the superiority of a "European Social Model" that hardly exists. The EU and the US need to guide the global quest for an ethical underpinning of successful globalization, including the revitalization of family values and structures. Family values and family structures are of central importance in order to provide children with the necessary moral compass and spine to cope with the challenges of individualism and the permanent discovery of new frontiers that are inherent in the age of globalization. Being rooted in a strong personality is the human precondition to come to terms with ever changing and globalized environments.

(4) The European Union and the United States are increasingly challenged by new rising powers, especially China and India. Between 1500 and 1800, China and India represented 50 percent of world trade. In the age of colonialism and due to the internal struggles in China, their share went down significantly, representing less than 8 percent combined by mid-twentieth century. In the meantime, China and India have regained a share in the world economy of around 20 percent. They will not rest until their vast populations can fully participate in the benefits of the globalized world and its possible levels of affluence and security. For the European Union, the rise of new superpowers poses as many challenges and opportunities as for the US. Global power shifts are, more than a bilateral question. They affect the geopolitical reconfiguration of regional and world affairs.

Although the US and the EU are pursuing a steady policy of engagement vis-à-vis China, in many details they follow different strategies and certainly different tactics. This does not only relate to their cooperation with China, but also to their dealings with the overall geopolitical region of the rising China, including the unresolved partition of the Korean peninsula, the fragility of the balance of power system in Northeast Asia and the absence of regional cooperation, let alone integration in that region. The US favors a system a functioning balance of power in East Asia while the EU promotes multilateralism and regional cooperation. This can lead to new rivalry between the US and the EU, but it can also destabilize the smooth evolution of a genuine Northeast Asian order. It is unclear, how far China would be willing to recognize both the US and the EU as "East Asian powers." It is also unclear, whether or not the US would appreciate the EU as an "Asian power." Moreover, it is unclear, whether or not the EU will want to become an "Asian power," an ultimate precondition if it truly wants to acquire world power status.

As for India, the EU and the US are only in the early stages to recognize and respect the true potential and rising relevance of this great nation. Its diversity equals that of the EU, its democratic traditions are impressive, all the more so in light of the enormous social and cultural pressures inside India. The emergence of a second Asian power has ramifications beyond the region. The power ambitions of Iran, for instance, are, at least indirectly, protected by China and India through their engagement in Iran. Energy supply and access to other natural resources is of essential importance for the rising Asian powers. More than anything else, these preconditions for the rise to global primacy define China's and India's geopolitical interests. The implications for their internal social and political cohesion are not less relevant than their regional posture and global pursuit of interests. The rise of China and India is a clear indication of the reality of a multipolar world. Matters of global relevance, most notably climate change, human rights, global trade issues or the fight against cyber-crime have become much more difficult to be handled for the West on its own terms. New tensions and potential realignments between states, regions and groupings of states are likely.

(5) The challenge of failed or failing states and new forms of threats are also posing a set of concerns that cannot be resolved by simply resorting to the traditional stereotypes of state sovereignty. Terrorism has introduced the phenomenon of asymmetric warfare. Cyber-crime is increasingly understood as a new form of aggression, potentially with as many casualties as the detonation of a huge bomb in a city center. Since the end of the Cold War, the management of failed and failing states has become a continuous concern for the global community. Paradoxically, the Cold War divisions entailed stability and predictability. These are no longer inherent in the nature and performance of states with weak governments that have given up on the imposition of a monopoly of power. Pakistan has turned into a special country of concern, while Iraq and Afghanistan have been at the center of global attention for most of the first decade of the twenty-first century.

The world is torn in its perception of Russia. The peaceful and stable management of the decline of Russia from a threatening super-power with an aggressive ideology to a matter of concern because of Russia's poverty and fragile political culture has been replaced by a new authoritarianism in Russian politics, coupled with a rising self-assertiveness of the country's elite. Whether these are indications of a failed state or in turn indications of a renewed neo-authoritarian claim to world power status is debatable. Yet, Russia holds substantial amounts of natural resources, especially energy resources.

Finally, the EU and the US cannot escape the fact that incomplete globalization does "strike back" and forces the leading economies in the world to better support the majority of the world in its quest for inclusion in the promises of modern affluence and life's opportunities. In particular, the EU and the US will have to "rediscover" the African continent and its development potential as test-case of their moral credibility and political long-term wisdom. The migration pressure Africa is beginning to exert on Europe is an indication of trends to come. In combination with the weakness of many Arab states - who at the same time are controlling energy resources that are essential for Europe - the issue has socio-economic and geopolitical implications that go beyond the traditional agenda of development and culture. The growing presence of China in Africa demonstrates the emergence of new constellations and possibly alliances that presage a new world-order no longer monopolized by the West.

III.

The first wave of globalization in modern history had been initiated by an imperial Europe, followed by an imperial United States. The globalization of the twenty-first century has been initiated by a technologically creative and economically dynamic US, followed by a transformed Europe. Both the US and the EU are bound to manage globalization and to order a world that is enormously asymmetric as far as resources and affluence, freedom and stability, governance and interests are concerned. They can succeed only jointly in pursuing policies of cooperation and gradual inclusion. They continuously need to project their will to stop any force that threatens to undermine the stable evolution of globalization.

Globalization cannot remain an American and European privilege, at best shared with the dynamic societies of Northeast Asia. In its origin, globalization is culturally neutral and primarily a set of technological achievements that redefines our perception of space and time by linking the world as never before. But globalization has obvious effects beyond its original scheme or purpose. It therefore requires stable family structures and other sociological layers everywhere in the world in order to balance the technological dynamics in a way palatable to the human psyche. It requires a form of governance that provides the freedom and breathing space for cultural and religious plurality, technological innovation, economic dynamics and social upward mobility. Global governance has to focus on education and it has to assure the demographic future of each society that projects its purpose beyond the consumption desires of the living. It must respect cultural diversity. Modes of life and work have to be developed that protect the cultural traditions, identities and loyalties of those who are afraid of losing them to a homogenized global culture of entertainment and lifestyle. Technological and economic globalization also calls for a political framework that outlines the norms of conduct for financial, economic and regulatory norms of all sorts. In the end, globalization cannot be complete without global governance. Global governance cannot become sustainable ever if it will not include all societies, countries and regions of the world. To this end, globalization will have to promote a sincere global dialogue among cultures and religions that moves beyond the rhetorical commitment to tolerance. The architects and managers of globalization need to promote a better understanding of the inherent values, practices and rites of cultures and the spiritual creed of religions, including their differences and how to cope with them.

Against this background, European integration appears to be nothing less than anticipated globalization in one region. It provides stability to the world and no longer fear or threat. In its Second Founding, the European Union is reconnecting its original idea with its own citizens and its growing potential with the world at large. Together, the European Union and the United States form the Western circle of stability, in which the highest degree of interactions among two regions in the world takes place. It must be in their interest to project the stability and dynamics of the Atlantic Community beyond their own shores. The EU and the US must favor and actively promote the creation of further circles of freedom, stability and global management. This is the intrinsic implication of the logic of globalization if it is to generate globally with sustainable success. The concentric circles of global governance consist of transnational, intergovernmental, and transgovernmental elements. They also consist of bilateral, multilateral, regional and interregional constellations. The goal of a transformed world is not global harmonization, and certainly not a global government. But surely it must promote global management. Geographical and topical aspects define the multiple layers of global governance in a world of regions and even of continental sub-regions. All indicators in the early twenty-first century point to a continuation of this trend. The United Nations and the World Trade Organization are its most visible expressions. The important work of UNESCO, FAO or WHO, of UNHCR, UNDP and other agencies of the global community should not be underestimated. Non-governmental organizations also contribute to the emergence of a "global consciousness." They all strive for a world in which the successful transformation that has occurred in Europe during the past fifty years can be emulated and multiplied in appropriate ways and through indigenous means.

The European Union contributes to the theoretical and practical redefinition of sovereignty. It has transformed the monopoly of state sovereignty, and it is involved in Europeanizing the notion of popular sovereignty. Along with its global partners and supported by region-building trends in other parts of the world, the European Union is contributing to global governance. As the twenty-first century is unfolding, sustainable human development across the globe is the ultimate test case by which to measure the success of European integration. European integration has started to give the concept of human dignity back to Europe. In the further course of the twenty-first century, European integration must be in the service of human dignity worldwide. Contributing to a world with a more human face, in which the dignity of each human being is valued and cherished, protected and supported, signifies nothing less than the final act of the transformation of Europe from a continent of aggression and division to a world partner in the service of humankind. Unity in diversity could become the motto for such a world in which the European Union is appreciated as an indispensable and reliable partner in global leadership.

Bibliography

Introduction

Armitage, David (ed.), *Theories of Empire, 1450-1800*, Aldershot: Ashgate, 1998.

Chakrabarty, Dipesh, *Provincializing Europe: Postcolonial Thought and Historical Difference*, Princeton: Princeton University Press, 2000.

Chamberlain, Muriel Evelyn, *The Longman Companion to European Decolonization in the Twentieth Century*, London/New York: Longman, 1998.

Deutsch, Karl W., et al., *Political Community and the North Atlantic Area: International Organization in the Light of Historical Experience*, Princeton, N.J.: Princeton University Press, 1957.

European Union, European Commission, *The EU's Relations with the United States of America-Overview*, November 2004, https://europa.eu.int/comm/external_relations/us/intro/index.htm.

Evtuhov, Catherine, and Stephen Kotkin (eds.), *The Cultural Gradient: The Transmission of Ideas in Europe, 1789-1991*, Lanham: Rowman&Littlefield, 2003.

Ferguson, Niall, *Colossus: The Price of America's Empire*, New York: Penguin Press, 2004.

Garton Ash, Timothy, *Free World: Why a Crisis of the West Reveals the Opportunity of our Time*, London: Allen Lane, 2004.

Gerrits, André, and Dirk Jan Wolffram (eds.), *Political Democracy and Ethnic Diversity in Modern European History*, Stanford: Stanford University Press, 2005.

Hosking, Geoffrey, and George Schöpflin (eds.), *Myths and Nationhood*, London: Hurst, 1997.

Huntington, Samuel R., *Who are We? The Challenges to America's National Identity*, New York: Simon&Schuster, 2004.

Kühnhardt, Ludger, *Constituting Europe: Identity, Institution-Building and the Search for a Global Role*, Baden-Baden: Nomos, 2003.

Majone, Giandomenico, *Dilemmas of European Integration: The Ambiguities and Pitfalls of Integration by Stealth*, Oxford: Oxford University Press, 2005.

Raudzens, George, *Empires: Europe and Globalization*, 1492-1788, Stroud: Sutton, 1999.

Rien, Serges T., *Cultural Constructions of Europe: European Identity in the twenty-first Century*, Frankfurt/New York: Peter Lang, 2004.

Scales, Len, and Liver Zimmer (eds.), *Power and the Nation in European History*, New York: Cambridge University Press, 2005.

Schlesinger Jr., Arthur M., *The Disuniting of America: Reflections on a Multicultural Society*, New York: W.W. Norton&Co., 1998.

Springhall, John, *Decolonization since 1945: The Collapse of European Overseas Empires*, New York: Palgrave, 2001.
Waites, Bernard, *Europe and the Third World: From Colonization to Decolonization, 1500-1998*, New York: St.Martin's Press, 1999.
Young, George, "Europeanization," *Encyclopedia of the Social Sciences* Vol. 5, New York: Macmillan, 1937: 623-635.
Van de Kaa, Dirk, et al. (eds.), *European Populations: Unity in Diversity*, Dordrecht/Boston: Kluwer Academic Publishers, 1999.

Chapter I

Af Malmborg, Mikael, and Bo Strath (eds.), *The Meaning of Europe: Variety and Contention Within and Among Nations*, Oxford/New York: Berg, 2002.
Al Sayyad, Nezar, and Manuel Castells (eds.), *Muslim Europe or Euro-Islam: Politics, Culture and Citizenship in the Age of Globalization*, Lanham: Lexington Books, 2002.
Alexander, Larry, *Constitutionalism: Philosophical Foundations*, Cambridge: Cambridge University Press, 1999.
Alting von Gesau, Frans A M. (ed.), *European Unification in the Twentieth Century: A Treasury of Readings*, Nijmegen: Vidya Publishers, 1998.
Bagehot, Walter, *The English Constitution*, Boston: Little Brown, 1873.
Baier-Allen, Susanne, and Ljubomir Cucic (eds.), *The Challenges of Pluriculturality*, Baden-Baden: Nomos, 2000.
Banchoff, Thomas, and Mitchell P. Smith (eds.), *Legitimacy and the European Union: The Contested Polity*, London/New York: Routledge, 1999.
Baneth, Jean, *"Fortress Europe" and Other Myths About Trade*, Washington D.C.: World Bank, 1993.
Bellamy, Richard (ed.), *Constitutionalism, Democracy and Sovereignty: American and European Perspectives*, Aldershot: Avebury, 1996.
Berggren, Niclas, and Nils Karlson, "Constitutionalism, Division of Power and Transaction Costs," *Public Choice*, 117.1/2 (2003): 99-124.
Bonnefous, Edouard, *La construction de l'Europe par l'un de ses initiateurs*, Paris: Presse Universitaire Française, 2002.
Booker, Christopher, and Richard North, *The Great Deception: Can the European Union Survive?*, London: Continuum, 2003.
Bracher, Karl Dietrich, *The Age of Ideologies: A History of Political Thought in the Twentieth Century*, London: Palgrave Macmillan, 1984.
Brague, Remi, and Peter Koslowski, *Vaterland Europa: Europäische und nationale Identität im Konflikt*, Vienna: Passagen Verlag, 1997.

Brand, Michiel, *Affirming and Refining European Constitutionalism: Towards the Establishment of the First Constitution for the European Union*, Florence: European University Institute, 2004.

Brzezinski, Mark, *The Struggle for Constitutionalism in Poland*, Basingstoke: Macmillan, 2000.

Burgess, Michael, *Federalism and European Union: The Building of Europe 1950-2000*, London: Routledge, 2000.

Cederman, Lars-Erik, *Nationalism and Bounded Integration: What it Would Take to Construct a European Demos*, Fiesole: European University Institute, 2000.

Celac, Sergiu, et al., *A Stability Pact for the Caucasus*, Brussels: Centre for European Policy Studies, 2000.

Council of Europe (ed.), *The European Identity: Colloquy in Three Parts Organized by the Secretary General of the Council of Europe*, Strasbourg: Council of Europe, 2001-2003.

Craig, Paul, and Grainne de Burca (eds.), *The Evolution of EU Law*, Oxford: Oxford University Press, 1999.

Craig, Paul, "Constitutions, Constitutionalism and the European Union," *European Law Journal* 7.2 (2001): 125-150.

Davies, Norman, *Europe: A History*, Oxford: Oxford University Press, 1996.

Dedman, Martin, "European Integration: Origins and Motives," *Modern History Review* 9.2 (1997): 30-33.

Dedman, Martin, *The Origins and Development of the European Union 1945-1995*, London: Routledge, 1996.

Delwaide, Jacobus, et al. (eds.), *Die Rheingesellschaft: Mentalitäten, Kulturen und Traditionen im Herzen Europas*, Baden-Baden: Nomos, 2003.

Diez Mendrano, Juan, *Framing Europe: Attitudes to European Integration in Germany, Spain and the United Kingdom*, Princeton: Princeton University Press, 2003.

Dinan, Desmond, *Europe Recast: A History of European Union*, Boulder: Lynn Rieffer, 2004.

Dinan, Desmond (ed.), *Origins and Evolution of the European Union*, Oxford: Oxford University Press, 2006.

Dippel, Horst (ed.), Executive *and Legislative Powers in the Constitutions of 1848-49*, Berlin: Duncker&Humblot, 1999.

Dippel, Horst (ed.), *Die Anfänge des Konstitutionalismus in Deutschland: Texte deutscher Verfassungsentwürfe am Ende des 18. Jahrhunderts*, Frankfurt/Main: Keip, 1991.

Dunkerley, David, et al. (eds.), *Changing Europe: Identities, Nations and Citizens*, London/New York: Routledge, 2002.

Dyson, Kenneth (ed.), *European States and the EURO: Europeanization, Variation, and Convergence*, New York: Oxford University Press, 2002.

Ellis, Joseph J., *Founding Brothers: The Revolutionary Generation*, New York: Knopf, 2000.

Erdödy, Gabor (ed.), *Mitteleuropa: Politische Kultur und europäische Einigung*, Baden-Baden: Nomos, 2003.

Erdödy, Gabor (ed.), *Transformationserfahrungen: Zur Entwicklung der politischen Kultur in den EU-Kandidatenländern*, Baden-Baden: Nomos, 2003.

Eschke, Nina, and Thomas Malick (eds.), *The European Constitution and its Ratification Crisis: Constitutional Debates in the EU Member States*, ZEI Discussion Paper C156, Bonn: Center for European Integration Studies, 2006.

European Union, *Treaty Establishing a Constitution for Europe*, Luxembourg: Office for Official Publications of the European Communities, 2005.

European Union, *Declaration on the Occasion of the Fiftieth Anniversary of the Signature of the Treaties of Rome*, Berlin, March 25, 2007, http://eu2007.de/de/News/download_docs/Maerz/0324-RAA/English.pdf.

European Union, *Treaty of Lisbon Amending the Treaty on European Union and the Treaty Establishing the European Community*, Official Journal of the European Union, C 306/Vol.50, Luxembourg: Office for Official Publications of the European Communities, 2007, https://eur-lex.europa.eu/JOHtml.do?uri=OJ:C:2007:306:SOM:EN:HTML.

European Union, European Commission, *Flash Eurobarometer: Iraq and Peace in the World*, November 2003, http://ec.europa.eu/public_opinion/flash/fl151_iraq_full_report.pdf.

European Union, European Commission, *Flash Eurobarometer: The Future European Constitution*, February 2004, http://ec.europa.eu/public_opinion/flash/fl159_fut_const.pdf.

European Union, European Commission, *Eurobarometer 66: Public Opinion in the European Union*, December 2006, http://ec.europa.eu/public_opinion/archives/eb/eb66/eb66_highlights_en.pdf.

European Union, European Commission, *Eurobarometer 67: Public Opinion in the European Union*, June 2007, http://ec.europa.eu/public_opinion/archives/eb/eb67/eb_67_first_en.pdf.

Ferguson, Niall, *Colossus: The Price of America's Empire*, New York: Penguin Press, 2004.

Frankenberg, Günter, "The Return of the Contract: Problems and Pitfalls of European Constitutionalism," *European Law Journal* 6.3 (2000): 257-276.

Fransen, Frederic J., *Supranational Politics of Jean Monnet: Ideas and Origins of the European Community*, Westport: Greenwood, 2001.

Garton Ash, Timothy, *History of the Present: Sketches and Dispatches from Europe in the 1990*, London: Allen Lane, 1999.

Geddes, Andrew, *Immigration and European Integration: Towards Fortress Europe?*, Manchester: Manchester University Press, 2000.

Gerstenberg, Oliver, "Expanding the Constitution Beyond the Court: The Case of Euro-Constitutionalism," *European Law Journal* 8.1 (2002): 172-194.

Gillingham, John, *European Integration, 1950-2003: Superstate or New Market Economy?*, Cambridge: Cambridge University Press, 2003.

Goenenc, Levent, *Prospects for Constitutionalism in Post-Communist Countries*, The Hague: Nijhoff, 2002.

Goldmann, Kjell, *Transforming the European Nation-State*, London: SAGE, 2001.

Gordon, Phillip H., and Jeremy Shapiro, *Allies at War: America, Europe and the Crisis over Iraq*, New York: MacGraw-Hill, 2004.

Gordon, Scott, *Controlling the State: Constitutionalism from Ancient Athens to Today*, Cambridge, Mass.: Harvard University Press, 2002.

Grant, Charles, *Transatlantic Rifts: How to Bring the Two Sides Together*, London: Centre for European Reform, 2003.

Green Cowles, Maria et al. (eds.), *Transforming Europe: Europeanization and Domestic Change*, Ithaca/London: Cornell University Press, 2001.

Gubbins, Paul, and Mike Holt (eds.), *Beyond Boundaries: Language and Identity in Contemporary Europe*, Clevedon: Multilingual Matters, 2002.

Guehenno, Jean-Marie, *The Typology of Sovereignty*, Washington D.C.: US Institute for Peace, 2000.

Haas, Ernst, *The Uniting of Europe - Political, Social, and Economic Forces 1950-1957*, Stanford: Stanford University Press, 1958.

Harmsen, Robert, and Menno Spiering (eds.), *Euroscepticism: Party Politics, National Identity and European Integration*, Amsterdam: Rodopi, 2004.

Havel, Václav, *Living in Truth*, London: Faber, 1989.

Hewitt, Paul S., "Die Geopolitik der globalen Alterungsprozesse," *Frankfurter Allgemeine Zeitung*, March 23, (2004): 39.

Hewitt, Paul S., "Depopulation and the Aging in Europe and Japan: The Hazardous Transition to a Labor Shortage Economy," *International Politics and Society* 1 (2002), http://fes.de/ipg/ipg1_2002/ARTHEWITT.htm.

Höreth, Marcus, *The Trilemma of Legitimacy: Multilevel Governance in the European Union and the Problem of Democracy*, ZEI Discussion Paper C11, Bonn: Center for European Integration Studies, 1998.

Hye, Hans Peter, *Das politische System in der Habsburgermonarchie: Konstitutionalismus, Parlamentarismus und politische Partizipation*, Prague: Karolinum, 1998.

Janes, Jackson, et al. (eds.), *Ukraine, Europe and the United States: Towards a New Euro-Atlantic Security Architecture*, Baden-Baden: Nomos, 2000.

Jervis, Paul (ed.), *Resolving the European Crisis: Perspectives on the Future of the European Union*, Middlesex: Middlesex University Press, 2005.

Khan, H.A. (ed.), *The Birth of the European Identity: The Euro-Asia Contrast in Greek Thought - 490-322 B.C.*, Nottingham: University of Nottingham, 1994.

Kielmannsegg, Peter Graf, "Integration und Demokratie," in: Jachtenfuchs, Markus, and Beate Kohler-Koch (eds.) *Europäische Integration*, Opladen: Westdeutscher Verlag, 1996: 47-71.

King, Russell, et al. (eds.), *Eldorado or Fortress? Migration in Southern Europe*, Houndsmills: Macmillan, 2000.

Kirsch, Martin, and Pierangelo Schiera, *Denken und Umsetzung des Konstitutionalismus in Deutschland und anderen europäischen Ländern in der ersten Hälfte des 19. Jahrhunderts*, Berlin: Duncker&Humblot, 1999.

Kirsch, Martin, et al. (eds.), *Der Verfassungsstaat vor der Herausforderung der Massengesellschaft: Konstitutionalismus um 1900 im europäischen Vergleich*, Berlin: Duncker&Humblot, 2002.

Kirsch, Martin, *Monarch und Parlament im 19. Jahrhundert - Der monarchische Konstitutionalismus als europäischer Verfassungstyp: Frankreich im Vergleich*, Göttingen: Vandenhoeck&Ruprecht, 1999.

Kirt, Romain (ed.), *Die Europäische Union und ihre Krisen*, Baden-Baden: Nomos, 2001.

Knipping, Franz, Rom *25. März 1957: Die Einigung Europas*, Munich: Deutscher Taschenbuch Verlag, 2004.

Krenzler, Horst Günter (ed.), *Preparing for the Acquis Communautaire: Report on the Working Group on the Eastern Enlargement of the EU*, Florence: European University Institute, 1998.

Kumm, Matthias, *Who is the Final Arbiter of the Constitutionality in Europe?*, Cambridge, Mass.: Harvard Law School, 1998.

Kühnhardt, Ludger, "German-American Relations: What Else Can Go Wrong?," in: *Power and Principle: Prospects for Transatlantic Cooperation*, (ed.) American Institute for Contemporary German Studies, German-American Issues 02, Washington D.C.: AICGS, 2004.

Kühnhardt, Ludger, *Revolutionszeiten: Das Umbruchjahr 1989 im geschichtlichen Zusammenhang*, Munich: Olzog, 1994.

Kühnhardt, Ludger, *Europa neu begründen*, ZEI Discussion Paper C167, Bonn: Center for European Integration Studies, 2007.

Leonhard, Mark, *Why Europe will Run the twenty-first century*, London: Fourth Estate, 2005.

Lipgens, Walter (ed.), *Documents on the History of European Integration Vol. 1: Continental Plans for European Union 1939-1945*, Berlin/New York: de Gruyter, 1985.

Lipgens, Walter (ed.), *Documents on the History of European Integration Vol. 2: Plans for European Union in Great Britain and in Exile 1939-1945*, Berlin/New York: de Gruyter, 1986.
Loth, Wilfried, *Der Weg nach Europa: Geschichte der europäischen Integration 1939–1957*, Göttingen: Vandenhoeck&Ruprecht, 1990.
Mancini, Giuseppe Federico, *Democracy and Constitutionalism in the European Union*, Oxford: Hart Publishing, 2000.
Martinot, Bertrand, *L'EURO: une monnaie sans politique?*, Paris: Hamattan, 2003.
Milward, Alan, *The European Rescue of the Nation State*, London: Routledge, 1992.
Mitrany, David, *A Working Peace System: An Argument for the Functional Development of International Organization*, London: Royal Institute of International Relations, 1943.
Moravscik, Andrew, *The Choice for Europe: Social Purpose and State Power from Messina to Maastricht*, Ithaca: Cornell University Press, 1998.
Murphy, Walter F., "Constitutions, Constitutionalism, and Democracy," in: Greenberg, Douglas, et al. (eds.), *Constitutionalism and Democracy: Transitions in the Contemporary World*, New York/Oxford: Oxford University Press, 1993: 3-25.
Neumann, Iver B., *Uses of the Other: "the East" in European Identity Formation*, Manchester: Manchester University Press, 1999.
Pernice, Ingolf, "Multi-Level Constitutionalism in the European Union," *European Law Review* 27.1/6 (2002): 511-529.
Reinhardt, Wolfgang, *Geschichte der Staatsgewalt: Eine vergleichende Verfassungsgeschichte Europas von den Anfängen bis zur Gegenwart*, Munich: C.H. Beck, 1999.
Renan, Ernest, *Qu'est ce-qu' une nation?*, Toronto: Tapir Press, 1996.
Rifkin, Jeremy, *The European Dream: How Europe's Vision of the Future is Quietly Eclipsing the American Dream*, Cambridge: Polity Press, 2004.
Roussel, Eric, *Jean Monnet 1888-1979*, Paris: Fayard, 1996.
Rubio Lorente, Francisco, *Constitutionalism in the "Integrated" States of Europe*, Cambridge,Mass.: Harvard Law School, 1998.
Sajo, Andras, and Stephen Holmes, *Limiting Government: An Introduction to Constitutionalism*, Budapest: Central European University Press, 1999.
Sampford, Charles, *Beyond the Republic: Meeting the Global Challenges to Constitutionalism*, Sydney: Federation Press, 2001.
Scharpf, Fritz W., *Community and Autonomy Multilevel Policy-Making in the European Union*, Florence: European University Institute, 1994.
Schlesinger Jr., Arthur M., *The Cycles of American History*, Boston: Houghton Mifflin, 1986.
Schulze, Reiner (ed.), *Europäische Rechts- und Verfassungsgeschichte: Ergebnisse und Perspektiven der Forschung*, Berlin: Duncker&Humblot, 1991.

Sim, Stuart, *The Discourse of Sovereignty: Hobbes to Fielding: The State of Nature and the Nature of the State*, Aldershot: Ashgate, 2003.

Tempini, Nadia, *Fortress Europe? EC External Trade Relations and New Protectionism*, London: PNL Press, 1989.

The Economist, Europe's Mid-Life Crisis: A Special Report, March 17-23, (2007).

Tiersky, Ronald (ed.), *Europe Today: National Politics, European Integration and European Security*, Lanham: Rowman&Littlefield, 1999.

Toynbee, Arnold Joseph, *Studies of History: Abridgement of Volumes I-VI*, New York/London: Oxford University Press, 1947.

Tsoukalis, Loukas, *What Kind of Europe?*, Oxford: Oxford University Press, 2005 (rev. ed.).

Van Caenegem, R. C., *A Historical Introduction to Western Constitutional Law*, New York/Cambridge: Cambridge University Press, 1999.

Van Oudenaren, John, *Uniting Europe: An Introduction to the European Union*, Lanham: Rowman&Littlefield, 2005.

Verhofstadt, Guy, *The United States of Europe*, London: Federal Trust, 2006.

Vinen, Richard, *A History in Fragments: Europe in the Twentieth Century*, London: Abacus, 2000.

Von der Groeben, Hans, *Europäische Integration aus historischer Erfahrung: Ein Zeitzeugengespräch mit Michael Gehler*, ZEI Discussion Paper C108, Bonn: Center for European Integration Studies, 2002.

Ward, Ian, "Beyond Constitutionalism: The Search for a European Political Imagination," *European Law Journal* 7.4 (2001): 24-40.

Weiler, Joseph H.H. and Marlene Wind (eds.), *European Constitutionalism Beyond the State*, Cambridge: Cambridge University Press, 2003.

Weiler, Joseph H.H., *Ein christliches Europa*, Salzburg: Pustet, 2004.

Wiener, Antje, "Evolving Norms of Constitutionalism," *European Law Journal* 9.1 (2003): 1-13.

Wirtschaftskammern Österreich, *Bevölkerungsentwicklung*, http://wko.at/statistik/eu europa-bevoelkerungsentwicklung.pdf.

Chapter II

Asmus, Ronald D., and Kenneth M. Pollack, "The New Transatlantic Project," *Policy Review*, 115 (2002): 3-18.

Brimmer, Esther (ed.), *The European Union Constitutional Treaty: A Guide for Americans*, Washington D.C.: Center for Transatlantic Relations, 2004.

Church, Clive H., and David Phinnemore, *Understanding the European Constitution: An Introduction to the EU Constitutional Treaty*, London: Routledge, 2006.

Diedrich, Udo, and Wolfgang Wessels, "Die Europäische Union in der Verfassungsfalle? Analysen, Entwicklungen und Optionen," *Integration* 28.4 (2005): 287-306.

Duff, Andrew, *The Struggle for Europe's Constitution*, London: Federal Trust, 2005.

The Economist, "Europe's Mid-Life Crisis – A Special Report," March 17-23, (2007): 1-20.

Eschke, Nina, and Malick, Thomas (eds.), *The European Constitution and its Ratification Crisis: Constitutional Debates in the EU Member States*, ZEI Discussion Paper C156, Bonn: Center for European Integration Studies, 2006.

Esposito, Frédéric, "The European Referendum: A Tool to Legitimate the European Integration Process?" in: Nagel, Stuart (ed.), *Policymaking and Democracy: A Multinational Anthology*, Lanham: Lexington Books, 2003: 15-37.

Eriksen, Erik Odvar, et al. (eds.), *Developing a Constitution for Europe*, New York/London: Routledge, 2004.

European Union, *Treaty of Nice Amending the Treaty of European Union, the Treaties Establishing the European Communities and Certain Related Acts*, Luxembourg: Office for Official Publications of the European Communities, 2001.

European Union, *The European Convention*, http://european-convention.eu.int.

European Union, *Draft Treaty Establishing a Constitution for Europe: adopted by consensus by the European Convention on 13 June and 10 July 2003: submitted to the President of the European Council in Rome, July 18, 2003*, Luxembourg: Office for Official Publications of the European Communities, 2003.

European Union, *Treaty Establishing a Constitution for Europe*, Luxembourg: Office for Official Publications of the European Communities, 2005.

European Union, *Declaration on the Occasion of the Fiftieth Anniversary of the Signature of the Treaties of Rome*, Berlin, March 25, 2007, http://eu2007.de/de/News/download_docs/Maerz/0324-RAA/English.pdf.

European Union, "Treaty of Lisbon Amending the Treaty on European Union and the Treaty Establishing the European Community," *Official Journal of the European Union*, C 306/Vol.50, Luxembourg: Office for Official Publications of the European Communities, 2007, http://eur-lex.europa.eu/JOHtml.do?uri=OJ:C:2007:306:SOM:EN:HTML.

European Union, European Commission, *The Accession Process*, https://europa.eu.int/comm/enlargement/negotiations/accession_process.htm.

European Union, European Commission, *Flash Eurobarometer 142*, November 10, 2003, http://ec.europa.eu/public_opinion/flash/fl142_convention.pdf.

European Union, European Commission, *Flash Eurobarometer 159*, February 17, 2004, http://ec.europa.eu/public_opinion/flash/fl159_fut_const.pdf.

European Union, European Commission, *Eurobarometer 63: Public Opinion in the European Union*, July 2005, http://ec.europa.eu/public_opinion/archives/eb/eb63/eb63.4_en_first.pdf.

European Union, European Commission, *Eurobarometer 64: Public Opinion in the European Union*, December 2005, http://ec.europa.eu/public_opinion/archives/eb/eb64/eb64_first_en.pdf.

European Union, European Commission, *Eurobarometer 66: Public Opinion in the European Union*, December 2006, http://ec.europa.eu/public_opinion/archives/eb/eb66/eb66_highlights_en.pdf.

European Union, European Commission, *Eurobarometer 67: Public Opinion in the European Union*, June 2007, http://ec.europa.eu/public_opinion/archives/eb/eb67/eb_67_first_en.pdf.

European Union, European Council, *The Laeken Declaration on the Future of the European Union*, December 15, 2001, http://ec.europa.eu/justice_home/unit/charte/en/declarations-laeken.html.

Eriksen Oddvar, Erik et al. (eds.), *Developing a Constitution for Europe*, London: Routledge, 2004.

Höreth, Marcus, Cordula Janowski and Ludger Kühnhardt (eds.), *Die Europäische Verfassung: Analyse und Bewertung ihrer Strukturentscheidungen*, Baden-Baden: Nomos, 2005.

Hug, Simon, *Voices of Europe: Citizens, Referendums and European Integration*, Lanham: Rowman&Littlefield, 2002.

Jopp, Mathias, and Saskia Matl (eds.), *Der Vertrag über eine Verfassung für Europa*, Baden-Baden: Nomos, 2005.

Kühnhardt, Ludger, *Europäische Union und föderale Idee: Europapolitik in der Umbruchzeit*, Munich: Beck, 1993.

Kühnhardt, Ludger, *Erweiterung und Vertiefung: Die Europäische Union im Neubeginn*, Baden-Baden: Nomos, 2005.

Kühnhardt, Ludger, *Europa neu begründen*, ZEI Discussion Paper C167, Bonn: Center for European Integration Studies, 2007.

Loth, Wilfried, *Der Weg nach Europa: Geschichte der europäischen Integration 1939-1957*, Göttingen: Vandenhoeck&Ruprecht, 1990.

Marchetti, Andreas, and Claire Demesmay (eds.), *Der Vertrag von Lissabon: Analyse und Bewertung,* Baden-Baden: Nomos 2010.

McGiffen, Steven P., *The European Union: A Critical Guide*, London: Pluto Press, 2005 (second ed.).

Meny, Yves, "Making Sense of the EU: The Achievements of the Convention," *Journal of Democracy*, 14 (2003): 57-70.

Michalski, Anna, and Matthias Heise (eds.), *European Convention on the Future of Europe: An Analysis of the Official Positions of EU Member States, Future Member States, Applicant and Candidate Countries*, The Hague: Netherlands Institute of International Relations, 2003.

Moravscik, Andrew, *The Choice for Europe: Social Purpose and State Power from Messina to Maastricht*, Ithaca: Cornell University Press, 1998.

Moravcsik, Andrew, "Chastened Leaders need Concrete Policy Successes," *Financial Times*, January 27, 2006, https://news.ft.com/cms/s/27d57ce2-8e93-11da-ae63-0000779e2340,dwp_uuid=39ebf10c- 868e-11da-8521-0000779e2340,s01=1.htm.

Niedermayer, Oskar, "Die öffentliche Meinung zum Europäischen Verfassungsvertrag," in: Jopp, Matthias, and Saskia Matl (eds.), *Der Vertrag über eine Verfassung für Europa*, Baden-Baden: Nomos, 2005: 435-449.

Peers, Steve, and Angela Ward, *The EU Charter of Fundamental Rights: Politics, Law and Policy*, Oxford: Hart Publishing, 2004.

The Rome, Maastricht and Amsterdam Treaties, The Treaty on European Union (Treaty of Maastricht) and the Treaty Establishing the European Communities (Treaty of Rome) Amended by the Treaty of Amsterdam: Comparative Texts, Genval, Euroconfidentiel, 1999.

Schild, Joachim, "Ein Sieg der Angst – das gescheiterte französische Verfassungsreferendum," *Integration* 28.3 (2005): 187-200.

Shaw, Jo, *The Convention on the Future of Europe: Working Towards An EU Constitution*, London: Federal Trust for Education and Research, 2003.

Theiler, Tobias, Political Symbolism and European Integration, Manchester: Manchester University Press, 2005.

Weale, Albert, Democratic Citizenship and the European Union, Manchester: Manchester University Press, 2005.

Wessels, Wolfgang, "The Constitutional Treaty – Three Readings from a Fusion Perspective," *Journal of Common Market Studies* 43 (2005): 11-36.

Chapter III

Ackrill, Robert, *The Common Agricultural Community*, Sheffield: Sheffield Academic Press, 2000.

Barre, Raymond, "Perspectives de la Communauté Économique Européenne après La Haye," *Bulletin de la Communauté Èconomique Européenne* 2 (1970): 9-14.

Burgess, Michael, *Federalism and European Union: The Building of Europe 1950-2000*, London: Routledge, 2000.

Castelain, M.F. (ed.), *The Benelux Economic Union: A Pioneer in European Integration*, Brussels: E.D.J. Kruijtbosch, 1987.

Church, Clive H., and David Phinnemore, *The Penguin Guide to the European Treaties*, London: Penguin, 2002.

Cini, Michelle, *The European Commission: Leadership, Organization, and Culture in the EU Administration*, New York: St. Martin's Press, 1996.

Corbett, Richard, *The European Parliament's Role in a Closer EU Integration*, Basingstoke: Macmillan, 1998.

Davenport, Michael, *Europe's Preferred Partners?: The Lomé Countries in World Trade*, London: Overseas Development Institute, 1995.

Dell, Edmund, *The Schuman Plan and the British Abdication of Leadership in Europe*, Oxford: Oxford University Press, 1995.

Dwan, Renata, *An Uncommon Community: France and the European Defense Community 1950-1954*, Oxford: Oxford University Press, 1996.

Dedman, Martin, *The Origins and Development of the European Union 1945-1995*, London: Routledge, 1996.

Dinan, Desmond, *Europe Recast: A History of the European Union*, Boulder: Lynn Rieffer, 2004.

EFTA (ed.), *EFTA – Past and Future: A Discussion Paper on Achievements in Free Trade and Future Possibilities*, Geneva: EFTA Secretariat, 1980.

Elsig, Manfred, *The EU's Common Commercial Policy: Institutions, Interests and Ideas*, Aldershot: Ashgate, 2002.

European Commission (ed.), *40 Years of the Treaties of Rome: Or the Capacity of the Treaties to Advance the European Integration Process*, Brussels: Bruylant, 1999.

Featherstone, Kevin, *Socialist parties and European Integration: A Comparative History*, Manchester: Manchester University Press, 1988.

Fontaine, Pascal, *A New Idea for Europe: The Schuman Declaration, 1950-2000*, Luxembourg: Office for Official Publications of the European Communities, 2000.

Frey-Wouters, Ellen, *The European Community and the Third World: The Lomé Convention and its Impact*, New York: Praeger, 1980.

Fursdon, Edward, *The European Defense Community: A History*, New York: St. Martin's Press, 1980.

Gehler, Michael, and Wolfram Kaiser (eds.), *Christian Democracy in Europe since 1945*, London/New York: Routledge, 2004.

George, Stephen, and Ian Bache, *Politics in the European Union*, Oxford: Oxford University Press, 2001.

Gillingham, John, *Coal, Steel and the Rebirth of Europe: The Germans and French from Ruhr Conflict to Economic Community*, Cambridge: Cambridge University Press, 1991.

Gillingham, John, *European Integration 1950-2002: Superstate or New Market Economy?*, Cambridge: Cambridge University Press, 2003.

Goldstein, Judith, and Robert O. Keohane (eds.), *Ideas and Foreign Policy – Beliefs, Institutions and Political Change*, Ithaca/London: Cornell University Press, 1993.

Government of Australia (ed.), *Customs Union established by European Economic Community: A Review of Major EEC Activities leading to the Establishment of the Customs Union and some Problems this has created for Australia*, Canberra: Department of Trade and Industry, 1968.

Granvik, Lena, *The Principles of Direct Effect and Direct Applicability in European Community Law*, Abo: Abo Akademi, 1996.

Hallstein, Walter, *United Europe: Challenge and Opportunity*, Cambridge,Mass.: Harvard University Press, 1962.

Hallstein, Walter, *Der unvollendete Bundesstaat - Europäische Erfahrungen und Erkenntnisse*, Düsseldorf: ECON, 1969.

Hayes-Renshaw, Fiona, *The Council of Ministers*, New York: St. Martin's Press, 1997.

Hoscheit, Marc, and Wolfgang Wessels, *The European Council 1974-1986: Evaluations and Prospects*, Maastricht: European Institute of Public Administration, 1988.

Howlett, Darryl A., *Euratom and Nuclear Safeguards*, London: Macmillan, 1990.

Jansen, Thomas, *The European People's Party: Origins and Development*, Basingstoke: Macmillan, 1998.

Judge, David, *The European Parliament*, Basingstoke: Palgrave Macmillan, 2003.

Kanthoor, Willem Frans Victor, *A Chronological History of the European Union 1946-2001*, Cheltenham: Edward Elgar, 2002.

Knipping, Franz, *Rom 25. März 1957: Die Einigung Europas*, Munich: Deutscher Taschenbuch Verlag, 2004.

Krause, Lawrence B., *Sequel to Bretton Woods: A Proposal to Reform the World Monetary System*, Washington D.C.: Brookings Institution, 1971.

Küsters, Hanns Jürgen, *Die Gründung der Europäischen Wirtschaftsgemeinschaft*, Baden-Baden: Nomos, 1982.

Landau, Alice, and Richard G. Whitman, *Rethinking the European Union: Institutions, Interests, and Identities*, Basingstoke: Macmillan, 1997.

Laurent, Pierre-Henri, and Marc Maresceau, *Deepening and Widening*, Boulder: Rienner Publishers, 1998.

Lipgens, Walter (ed.), *Sources for the History of European Integration (1945-1955): A Guide to the Archives in the Countries of the Communities*, Leyden: Sijthoff, 1980.

Lister, Majorie, *The European Community and the Developing World: The Role of the Lomé Convention*, Aldershot: Avebury, 1988.

Magnunssen, Lars, and Bo Strath, *From the Werner Plan to the EMU: In Search of a Political Economy of Europe*, Brussels: Peter Lang, 2001.

Maurer, Andreas, *Die Macht des Europäischen Parlaments: Eine prospektive Analyse im Hinblick auf die kommende Wahlperiode 2004-2009*, Berlin: Stiftung Wissenschaft und Politik, 2004.

Niemann, Anna, Sonja Ana Luisa Schröder, and Meredith Catherine Tunick (eds.), *Recovering from the Constitutional Failure: An Analysis of the EU Reflection Period,* ZEI Discussion Paper C 182, Bonn: Center for European Integration Studies, 2008.

Noack, Paul, *Das Scheitern der Europäischen Verteidigungsgemeinschaft: Entscheidungsprozesse vor und nach dem 30. August 1954*, Düsseldorf: Droste Verlag, 1977.

Nugent, Neill, *The Deepening and Widening of the European Community*, Manchester: Victoria University, 1991.

Odul, Véronique (ed.), *Décision et Indécision dans la Querelle de la Communauté Européenne de Defense, 1950-1954*, Paris: Centre d'Histoire de l'Europe du Vingtième Siècle, 2004.

Oritz Blanco, Luis, *European Community Competition Procedure*, Oxford: Carlendon Press, 1996.

Papaconstantinou, Helen, *Free Trade and Competition in the EEC: Law, Policy, and Practice*, London: Routledge, 1988.

Perron, Régine (ed.), *The Stability of Europe, The Common Market: Towards European Integration of Industrial and Financial Markets 1958-1968*, Paris: Presses de l'Université de Paris-Sorbonne, 2004.

Piattoni, Simona, *Clientelism, Interests, and Democratic Representation: The European Experience in Historical and Comparative Perspective*, Cambridge: Cambridge University Press, 2001.

Riescher, Gisela, *Zeit und Politik - Zur institutionellen Bedeutung von Zeitstrukturen in parlamentarischen und präsidentiellen Regierungssystemen*, Baden-Baden: Nomos, 1994.

Rittberger, Berthold, *Building Europe's Parliament: Democratic Representation beyond the Nation-State*, Oxford: Oxford University Press, 2005.

The Rome, Maastricht and Amsterdam Treaties, The Treaty on European Union (Treaty of Maastricht) and the Treaty Establishing the European Communities (Treaty of Rome) Amended by the Treaty of Amsterdam: Comparative Texts, Genval: Euroconfidentiel, 1999.

The Rome, Maastricht, Amsterdam and Nice Treaties, Comparative Texts, London/New York: Europa Publications, 2003.

Ruane, Kevin, *The Rise and Fall of the European Defense Community: Anglo-American Relations and the Crisis of European Defense 1950-1955*, Basingstoke: Macmillan, 2000.

Scheiman, Lawrence, *Euratom: Nuclear Integration in Europe*, New York: Carnegie Endowment for International Peace, 1967.

Sherrington, Philippa, *The Council of Ministers: Political Authority in the European Union*, London: Pinter, 2000.

Smith, Andy, *Politics and the European Commission: Actors, Interdependence, Legitimacy*, London: Routledge, 2004.

Spierenburg, Dirk, *The History of the High Authority of the European Coal and Steel Community: Supranationality in Operation*, London: Weidenfeld and Nicolson, 1994.

Steinherr, Alfred, *30 Years of European Monetary Integration: From the Werner Plan to EMU*, London: Longman, 1994.

Strasser, Daniel, *Les Finances de l'Europe: Le Droit Budgetaire et Financier des Communautés Européennes*, Paris: Librairie Générale de Droit et de Jurisprudence, 1990.

Swann, Dennis, *Competition and Industrial Policy in the EEC*, London: Methuen, 1983.

Trausch, Gilbert (ed.), *The European Integration from the Schuman-Plan to the Treaties of Rome: Projects and Initiatives, Disappointments and Failures*, Baden-Baden: Nomos, 1993.

Tindemans, Leo, "Report to the European Council," *Bulletin of the European Communities*, Supplement 1 (1976).

Urwin, Derek W., *The Community of Europe: A History of European Integration since 1945*, London/New York: Longman, 1995.

Vaulont, Nicolaus, *The Customs Union of the European Economic Community*, Washington D. C.: European Community Information Center, 1981.

Von der Groeben, Hans, *Aufbaujahre der Europäischen Gemeinschaft: Das Ringen um den Gemeinsamen Markt und die Politische Union (1958-1966)*, Baden-Baden: Nomos, 1982.

Wallace, Helen, *Widening and Deepening: The European Community and the New European Agenda*, London: Royal Institute of International Affairs, 1989.

Wilkens, Andreas (ed.), *Interessen verbinden: Jean Monnet und die europäische Integration der Bundesrepublik Deutschland*, Bonn: Bouvier, 1999.

Wilson, Jêrome, "Négocier de la Relance Européenne: Les Belges et le Sommet de La Haye," *Journal of European Integration History*, 9.2 (2003): 41-62.

Chapter IV

Albert, Michel, and Robert James Ball, *Toward European Economic Recovery in the 1980s: Report to the European Parliament*, New York: Praeger, 1984.

Aldcroft, Derek H., and Michael J. Oliver, *Exchange Rate Regimes in the Twentieth Century*, Cheltenham: Edward Elgar, 1998.

Antohi, Sorin, and Vladimir Tismaneanu (eds.), *Between Past and Future: The Revolutions of 1989 and their Aftermath*, Budapest: Central European University Press, 2000.

Arnold, Anthony, Afghanistan: *The Soviet Invasion in Perspective*, Stanford: Hoover Institution Press, 1981.

Bachtler, John, and Ivan Turok (eds.), *The Coherence of EU Regional Policy: Contrasting Perspectives on the Structural Funds*, London: Kingsley Publishers, 1997.

Ballmann, Alexander, et al., "Delegation, Comitology, and the Separation of Powers in the European Union," *International Organization* 56.3 (2002): 551-574.

Bergström, Carl Fredrik, *Comitology: Delegation of Powers in the European Union and the Committee System*, Oxford: Oxford University Press, 2005.

Beugelsdijk, Maaike, and Sylvester C. W. Eijffinger, "The Effectiveness of Structural Policy in the European Union: An Empirical Analysis for the EU-15 in 1995-2001," *Journal of Common Market Studies* 43.1 (2005): 37-51.

Beverungen, Johannes, *Elite Planning Organizations: Traditionen, Charakteristika, Implikationen der "Trilateral Commission,"* Baden-Baden: Nomos, 2005.

Bruter, Michael, *Citizens of Europe? - The Emergence of a Mass European Identity*, Houndmills: Palgrave Macmillan, 2005.

Buti, Marco, et al. (eds.), *EMU and Economic Policy in Europe: The Challenge of the Early Years*, Cheltenham: Edward Elgar, 2002.

Button, Kenneth, et al., "1992 and the Creation of a Single European Market," *The Antitrust Bulletin* 37.2 (1992): 281-335.

Calleo, David P., and Eric R. Staal (eds.), *Europe's Franco-German Engine*, Washington D.C.: Brookings Institution Press, 1998.

Christiansen, Thomas, and Emil J. Kirchner (eds.), *Committee Governance in the European Union*, Manchester: Manchester University Press, 2000.

Colard, Daniel, "Le Couple Franco-Allemand et la Construction de l'Europe," *Questions Internationales* 11 (2005): 120-123.

Cole, Alistair, *François Mitterrand: A Study in Political Leadership*, London: Routledge, 1994.

Crouch, Colin, and David Marquand (eds.), *The Politics of 1992: Beyond the Single European Market*, Oxford: Blackwell, 1990.

Crozier, Michael, Samuel P. Huntington and Joji Watanuki, *The Crisis of Democracy: Report on the Governability of Democracies to the Trilateral Commission*, New York: New York University Press, 1975.

Dinan, Desmond, *Europe Recast: A History of European Union*, Boulder: Lynn Rieffer, 2004.

Dedman, Martin, *The Origins and Development of the European Union 1945-1995*, London: Routledge, 1996.

De Grauwe, Paul, and Theo Peters (eds.), *The ECU and European Monetary Integration*, Houndmills: Macmillan Press, 1989.

Delors, Jacques, *Mémoires*, Paris: Editions Plons, 2003.

Den Boer, Monica (ed.), *Schengen, Judicial Cooperation ad Policy Coordination*, Maastricht: European Institute of Public Administration, 1997.

Denton, Geoffrey, "Re-Structuring the EC Budget: Implications of the Fontainebleau Agreements," *Journal of Common Market Studies* 2 (1984): 117-140.

El-Agraa, Ali M. (ed.), *The European Union: Economics and Politics*, New Jersey: Prentice Hall, 2001.

Endo, Ken, *The Presidency of the European Commission under Jacques Delors. The Politics of Shared Leadership*, New York: St.Martin's Press, 1999.

Engel, Christian, and Wolfgang Wessels (eds.), *From Luxembourg to Maastricht: Institutional Change in the European Community after the Single European Act*, Bonn: Europa Union Verlag, 1992.

European Communities, European Commission, *Completing the Internal Market: White Paper from the Commission to the European Council (Milan, 28-29 June 1985)*, Brussels: European Communities, 1985.

European Union, European Commission, *The Schengen Acquis: Integrated into the European Union*, Luxembourg: Office for Official Publications of the European Communities, 2001.

Evans, Andrew, *The EU Structural Funds*, Oxford: Oxford University Press, 1999.

Farrell, Henry, and Gregory Flynn, "Piecing Together the Democratic Peace: The CSCE, Norms, and the 'Construction' of Security in Post-Cold War Europe," *International Organization* 53.3 (1999): 505-535.

Ferguson, Niall, *Colossus: The Price of America's Empire*, New York: Penguin Press, 2004.

FitzGerald, Garret, *All in a Life: An Autobiography*, Dublin: Gill and Macmillan, 1991.

Fielder, Nicola, *Western European Integration in the 1980s: The Origins of the Single Market*, Bern/New York: Peter Lang, 1997.

Flandreau, Marc (ed.), *International Financial History in the Twentieth Century: System and Anarchy*, Cambridge: Cambridge University Press, 2003.

Garrett, Geoffrey, "The European Community's Internal Market," *International Organization* 46.2 (1992): 533-560.

Garton Ash, Timothy, *The Uses of Adversity: Essays on the Fate of Central Europe*, London: Penguin, 1989.

George, Stephen, *An Awkward Partner: Britain in the European Community*, Oxford: Oxford University Press, 1998.

Gibson, Heather D. (ed.), *Economic Transformation, Democratization and Integration into the European Union: Southern Europe in Comparative Perspective*, Basingstoke: Palgrave, 2001.

Goodby, James E., *CSCE: The Diplomacy of Europe Whole and Free*, Washington D.C.: Atlantic Council of the United States, 1990.

Gowland, David, and Arthur Turner, *Britain and European Integration 1945 – 1998: A Documentary History*, London/New York: Routledge, 2000.

Hallaba, Saadallah A.S., *Euro-Arab Dialogue*, Brattleboro, Vt.: Amana Books, 1984.

Heller, Mark, *The Soviet Invasion in Afghanistan: Motivations and Implications*, Tel Aviv: Center for Strategic Studies, 1980.

Hendriks, Gisela, and Annette Morgan, *The Franco-German Axis in European Integration*, Cheltenham: Edward Elgar, 2001.

Howarth, David J., *The French Road to European Monetary Union*, Houndmills: Palgrave, 2001.

Joubert, Chantal, and Hans Bevers, *Schengen Investigated: A Comparative Interpretation of the Schengen Provisions on International Police Cooperation in the Light of the European Convention on Human Rights*, The Hague/Boston: Kluwer, 1996.

Kaiser, Wolfram, and Jürgen Elvert (eds.), *European Union Enlargement: A Comparative History*, London/New York: Routledge, 2004.

Kissinger, Henry A., *American Foreign Poliy*, New York: W.W. Norton & Company, 1974.

Kirchner, Emil J., *The European Parliament: Performance and Prospects*, Aldershot: Gower, 1984.

Knipping, Franz, *Rom 25. März 1957: Die Einigung Europas*, Munich: Deutscher Taschenbuch Verlag, 2004.

Kühnhardt, Ludger, *Revolutionszeiten – Das Umbruchjahr 1989 im geschichtlichen Zusammenhang*, Munich: Olzog, 1994.

Kumar, Krishan, *1989: Revolutionary Ideas and Ideals*, Minneapolis: University of Minneapolis Press, 2001.

Lewis, Paul, and Paul Webb (eds.), *Pan-European Perspectives on Party Politics*, Leiden/Boston: Brill, 2003.

Lucarelli, Bill, *The Origins and Evolution of the Single Market in Europe*, Aldershot: Ashgate, 1999.

Magiera, Siegfried, *The Emergence of a "Europe of Citizens" in a Community without Frontiers*, Speyer: Forschungsinstitut für Öffentliche Verwaltung, 1989.

Maitland-Walker, Julian, "The Societas Europae: Useful Corporate Vehicle or Political Stalking Horse?," *European Competition Law Review* 12.3 (1991): 97-100.

Mayes, David G. (ed.), *The Evolution of the Single European Market*, Cheltenham: Edward Elgar, 1997.

McKenzie, George, and Anthony J. Venables (eds.), *The Economis of the Single European Act*, London: University of Southhampton, 1991.

Morgan, Roger, and Clare Tame (eds.), *Parliaments and Parties: The European Parliament in the Political Life of Europe*, New York: St. Martin's Press, 1996.

Padoa-Schioppa, Tomasso, et al., *Efficiency, Stability and Equity: A Strategy for the Evolution of the Economic System of the European Community*, Oxford: Oxford University Press, 1987.

Pedersen, Thomas, "Political Change in the European Community: The Single European Act as a Case of System Transformation," *Cooperation and Conflict* 27.1 (1992): 7-44.

Reif, Karlheinz (ed.), *European Elections 1979/81 and 1984: Conclusions and Perspectives from Empirical Research*, Berlin: Quorum, 1984.

Riboud, Jacques, *The Case for a New EU: Towards another Monetary System*, New York: St. Martin's Press, 1989.

Rodokanakis, Stavros, "Fifteen Years (1988-2002) of Structural Funds' Intervention: Critical Evaluation and Impacton conomic and Social Disparities among EU Countries and Regions," *The European Union Review* 8.1-2 (2003): 65-105.

Ross, George, *Jacques Delors and European Integration*, New York: Oxford University Press, 1995.

Seers Dudley, and Constantine Vaitsos (eds.), *The Second Enlargement of the EEC: The Integration of Unequal Partners*, New York: St. Martin's Press, 1982.

Swann, Dennis (ed.), *The Single European Market and Beyond: A Study of the Wider Implications of the Single European Act*, London: Routledge, 1992.

Sweeney, Jane P., *The First European Elections: Neo-Functionalism and the European Parliament*, Boulder: Westview Press, 1984.

Taylor, Alan R., *The Euro-Arab Dialogue*, Washington D.C.: Middle East Institute, 1978.

Thatcher, Margaret, *Downing Street Years*, New York: HarperCollins, 1993.

Tsoukalis, Loukas, *The Politics and Economics of European Monetary Integration*, London: Allen and Unwin, 1977.

Ungerer, Horst, *A Concise History of European Monetary Integration: From EPU to EMU*, Westport/London: Quorum Books, 1997.

Urwin, Derek W., *The Community of Europe: A History of European Integration since 1945*, London/New York: Longman, 1995.

Völker, Edmond (ed.), *Euro-Arab Cooperation*, Leyden: Sijthoff, 1976.

Webber, Douglas (ed.), *The Franco-German Relationship in the European Union*, London: Routledge, 1999.

Weigel, George, *Witness to Hope: The Biography of Pope John Paul II.*, New York: HarperCollins, 1999.

Wessels, Wolfgang, "Comitology: Fusion in Action. Politico-Administrative Trends in the EU System," *Journal of European Public Policy* 5.2 (1998): 209-234.
Ye'or, Bat, *Eurabia: The Euro-Arab Axis*, Madison, NJ: Fairleigh Dickinson University Press, 2005.
Young, John W., *Britain and European Unity: 1945-1992*, Basingstoke: Macmillan, 1993.

Chapter V

Barrass, Robert, and Bernard Steunenberg (eds.), *Widening the European Union: The Politics of Institutional Change and Reform*, London: Routledge, 2002.
Becker, Peter, *Der EU-Finanzrahmen 2007-2013: Auf dem Weg zu einer europäischen Finanzverfassung oder Fortsetzung der nationalen Netosaldopolitik?*, SWP-Studie S36, Berlin: Stiftung Wissenschaft und Politik, 2005.
Biermann, Rafael, "Robert Schuman's Perspective of Peace and Stability through Reconciliation: A Legacy of Continuing Actuality Also for the Balkans?," *Ankara Review of European Studies*, 1 (Autumn 2001): 45-60.
Bischof, Günter, et al. (eds.), *Austria in the European Union*, New York: Transaction Publishers, 2002.
Bofinger, Peter and Eric Mayer, *The Stability and Growth Pact - Time to Rebuild!*, Würzburg: University of Würzburg, 2004.
Bowley, Graham, "EU Gets Failing Grade on Competitiveness," *International Herald Tribune*, November 5, 2004.
Brimmer, Esther, and Stefan Fröhlich (eds.), *The Strategic Implications of European Union Enlargement*, Washington D. C.: Center for Transatlantic Relations, 2005.
Brok, Elmar, "Der Nutzen wird verschwiegen," *Frankfurter Allgemeine Zeitung*, March 1, (2004).
Brusis, Martin, and Janis A. Emmanouilidis (eds.), *Thinking Enlarged: The Accession Countries and the Future of the European Union*, Bonn: Europa Union Verlag, 2002.
Calleya, Stephen, *Is the Barcelona-Process Working?*, ZEI Discussion Paper C75, Bonn: Center for European Integration Studies, 2000.
Calleya, Stephen, *Evaluating Euro-Mediterranean Relations*, London: Routledge, 2005.
Cameron, Fraser (ed.), *The Future of Europe: Integration and Enlargement*, London: Routledge, 2005.
Corbett, Richard, *European Parliament's Role in Closer EU Integration*, Basingstoke: Palgrave, 2001.
Craig, Paul and Gráinne de Burca (eds.), *The Evolution of EU Law*, Oxford/New York: Oxford University Press, 1999.

Dimitrakopoulos, Dionysssis G., *The Changing European Commission*, Manchester: Manchester University Press, 2004.

Dimitrova, Antoaneta C. (ed.), *Driven to Change: The European Union's Enlargement Viewed from the East*, Manchester: Manchester University Press, 2004.

Dyson, Kenneth, and Kevin Featherstone, *The Road to Maastricht: Negotiating Economic and Monetary Union*, Oxford: Oxford University Press, 1999.

Eiff, Hansjörg, *Zum Problem des Kosovo-Status*, ZEI Discussion Paper C144, Bonn: Center for European Integration Studies, 2005.

European Parliament, *Composition of the European Parliament: Historial Data,* http://europarl.europa.eu/parliament/archive/elections2009/hist_composition_en_txt.html.

European Union, "Treaty of Lisbon Amending the Treaty on European Union and the Treaty Establishing the European Community," *Official Journal of the European Union*, C 306/Vol.50, Luxembourg: Office for Official Publications of the European Communities, 2007,
https:// eur-lex.europa.eu/JOHtml.do?uri=OJ:C: 2007:306:SOM:EN:HTML.

European Union, European Commission, *The Treaty of Nice: A Comprehensive Guide*, http://europa.eu/scadplus/nice_treaty/bodies_en.htm#PARLIAMENT.

European Union, European Commission, *The Treaty of Nice: A Comprehensive Guide*, http://europa.eu/scadplus/nice_treaty/council_en.htm#VOTES.

European Union, European Commission, *Europe In Figures. Eurostat Yearbook 2006-07*, Luxembourg: Office for Official Publications of the European Communities 2007, http://epp.eurostat.ec.europa.eu/cache/ITY_OFFPUB/KS-CD-06-001/DE/KS-CD-06-001-DE.PDF.

European Union, European Commission, *Eurobarometer 67: Public Opinion in the European Union*, June 2007,
http://ec.europa.eu/public_opinion/archives/eb/eb67/eb_67_first_en.pdf.

Featherstone, Kevin, and Claudio M. Radaelli (eds.), *The Politics of Europeanization*, Oxford: Oxford University Press, 2003.

Ferguson, Niall, *Colossus: The Price of America's Empire*, New York: Penguin Press, 2004.

Frankfurter Allgemeine Zeitung, "Der Hochtechnologiestandort Europa ist bedroht," November 17, (2005): 13.

Fuller, Thomas, "EU Get's a 'Bargain' in Expanding East," *International Herald Tribune*, December 17, 2002.

Gehler, Michael, "Präventivschlag als Fehlschlag: Intentionen und Konsequenzen der EU14-Sanktionsmassnahmen gegen Österreich im Jahre 2000," in: Loth, Wilfried (ed.), *Das europäische Projekt zu Beginn des 21.Jahrhunderts*, Leverkusen: Leske&Budrich: 352-382.

George, Stephen and Ian Bache (eds.), *Politics in the European Union*, Oxford, Oxford: University Press, 2001.

Grabbe, Heather, *The Constellations of Europe: How Enlargement Will Transform the EU*, London: Centre for European Reform, 2004.

Grabbe, Heather, *The EU's Transformative Power: Europeanization through Conditionality in Central and Eastern Europe*, Houndmills: Palgrave Macmillan, 2005.

Grin, Gilles, *The Battle of the Single European Market: Achievements and Economic Thought, 1945-2000*, New York: Columbia University Press, 2003.

Hall, Ronald, et al. (eds.), *Competitiveness and Cohesion in EU Policies*, Oxford: Oxford University Press, 2001.

Heipertz, Martin, and Amy Verdun, "The Do that Would Never Bite," *Journal of European Public Policy* 11 (October 2004): 765-780.

Hosli, Madeleine O., *The Euro: A Concise Introduction to European Monetary Integration*, Boulder: Lynne Rienner, 2005.

Iral, Hubert, *Between Forces of Inertia and Progress: Co-Decision in EU Legislation*, ZEI Discussion Paper C114, Bonn: Center for European Integration Studies, 2003.

Jacobs, Andreas (ed.), *Euro-Mediterranean Cooperation: Enlarging and Widening the Perspective*, ZEI Discussion Paper C131, Bonn: Center for European Integration Studies, 2004.

Knipping, Franz, *Rom 25. März 1957: Die Einigung Europas*, Munich: Deutscher Taschenbuch Verlag, 2004.

Kohl, Helmut, *Ich wollte Deutschlands Einheit*, Berlin: Propyläen Verlag, 1996.

Korkman, Sixten, *Economic Policy in the European Union*, London: Palgrave Macmillan, 2005.

Kreppel, Amie, "Moving Beyond Procedure: An Empirical Analysis of European Parliament Legislative Influence," *Comparative Political Studies*, 35.7 (2002): 784-813.

Kühnhardt, Ludger, "Europa als Wertegemeinschaft – Verlierer der Österreich-Krise 2000?," *Wiener Zeitschrift zur Geschichte der Neuzeit* 1 (2001): 73-80.

Kühnhardt, Ludger, *Die Europäische Union – Fragen zur Erweiterung*, Berlin: Auswärtiges Amt/Europäische Kommission (3rd ed.), 2003.

Kühnhardt, Ludger, *Erweiterung und Vertiefung: Die Europäische Union im Neubeginn*, Baden-Baden:Nomos, 2005.

Liddle, Roger, and Frédéric Lerais, *Europe's Social Reality: A Consultation Paper from the Bureau of European Policy Advisers*, 2007, http://ec.europa.eu/citizens_agenda/social_reality_stocktaking/docs/background_document_en.pdf.

Lodge, Juliet (ed.), *The 2004 Elections to the European Parliament*, Basingstoke:, Palgrave Macmillan, 2005.

Maier, Felix (ed.), *Managing Asymmetric Interdependencies within the Euro-Mediterranean Partnership*, ZEI Discussion Paper C101, Bonn: Center for European Integration Studies, 2002.

Marchetti, Andreas (ed.), *Ten Years Euro-Mediterranean Partnership: Defining European Interests for the Decade Ahead*, ZEI Discussion Paper C154, Bonn: Center for European Integration Studies, 2005.

Marchetti, Andreas, and Martin Zimmek (eds.), *Annäherungen an Europa: Beiträge zur deutschen EU-Ratspräsidentschaft 2007*, ZEI Discussion Paper C 175, Bonn: Center for European Integration Studies, 2007.

Maurer, Andreas, *Die Macht des Europäischen Parlaments: Eine prospektive Analyse im Hinblick auf die kommende Wahlperiode 2004-2009*, Berlin: Stiftung Wissenschaft und Politik, 2004.

Mazzucelli, Colette, *France and Germany at Maastricht: Politics and Negotiations to Create the European Union*, New York: Garland, 1997.

Milos, Ivan, "Das beste Steuersystem der EU," *Frankfurter Allgemeine Zeitung*, September 3, (2005): 13.

Moyer, Wayne, and Timothy Edward Josling, *Agriculture Policy Reform: Politics and Process in the EU and US*, Aldershot: Ashgate, 2002.

Norris, Floyd, "Tough EU Rules?," *International Herald Tribune*, March 22, 2005.

Occhipinti, John D., *The Politics of EU Police Cooperation: Toward a European FBI?*, Boulder: Lynne Rienner, 2003.

Pius XI., *Encyclical Letter Quadragesimo Anno*, London: Catholic Truth Society, 1946.

Pöttering, Hans-Gert, *Von der Vision zur Wirklichkeit: Auf dem Weg zur Einigung Europas*, Bonn: Bouvier, 2004.

Pöttering, Hans-Gert, *Defending Europe's Values – For a Citizens' Europe*, Program Speech to the European Parliament, Strassbourg, February 13, 2007, https://europarl.europa.eu/president/ defaulten.htm?home.

Puetter, Uwe, *The Eurogroup: How a Secretive Circle of Finance Ministers Shape European Economic Governance*, Manchester: Manchester University Press, 2006.

Quinlan, Michael, *European Defense Cooperation: Asset or Threat to NATO*, Washington D.C.: Woodrow Wilson Center Press, 2001.

Rahimi, Ashkaan, *The Evolution of EU Asylum Policy*, ZEI Discussion Paper C142, Bonn: Center for European Integration Studies, 2005.

Schimmelfennig, Frank, and Ulrich Sedelmaier (eds.), *The Politics of European Enlargement: Theoretical Approaches*, New York: Routledge, 2005.

Schimmelfennig, Frank, and Ulrich Sedelmeier (eds.), *The Europeanization of Central and Eastern Europe*, Ithaca: Cornell University Press, 2005.

Schwarz, Hans-Peter, *Die Zentralmacht Europas: Deutschlands Rückkehr auf die Weltbühne*, Berlin: Siedler, 1994.

Schwarz, Karl-Peter, "Mehr Unternehmen, weniger Arbeitslose, gleiche Staatseinnahmen," *Frankfurter Allgemeine Zeitung*, August 26, (2005): 13.

Szabo, Stephen, *The Diplomacy of German Unification*, New York: St.Martin's Press, 1992.

Wittschorek, Peter (ed.), *AGENDA 2000: Herausforderungen an die Europäische Union und an Deutschland*, Baden-Baden: Nomos, 1999.

Zelikow, Philip, and Condoleezza Rice, *Germany United and Europe Transformed: A Study in Statecraft*, Cambridge, Mass.: Harvard University Press, 1995.

Zielonka, Jan (ed.), *Europe Unbound: Enlarging and Reshaping the Boundaries of the European Union*, Abingdon: Routledge, 2002.

Zielonka, Jan, *Europe as Empire: The Nature of the Enlarged European Union*, Oxford: Oxford University Press, 2006.

Chapter VI

Ahrens, Geert-Hinrich, *Diplomacy on the Edge: Containment of Ethnic Conflict and the Minorities Working Group of the Conferences on Yugoslavia*, Washington D. C.: Woodrow Wilson University Press, 2007.

Altmann, Rüdiger and Eugene Whitlock (eds.), *European and US Policies in the Balkans: Different Views and Perceptions, Common Interests and Platforms*, Berlin: Stiftung Wissenschaft und Politik, 2004.

Arendt, Hannah, *Essays in Understanding, 1930-1954*, New York: Harcourt Brace & Company, 1994.

Asmus, Ronald D., *Opening NATO's Door: How the Alliance Remade Itself for a New Era*, New York: Columbia University Press, 2002.

Asmus, Ronald D., "Europe's Eastern Promise: Rethinking NATO and EU Enlargement," *Foreign Affairs*, Vol. 87.1(2008): 95-106.

Baldwin, Matthew, et al., "Trade and Economic Relations," in: John Peterson/Mark A. Pollack (eds.), *Europe, America, Bush: Transatlantic Relations in the Twenty-First Century*, London/New York: Routledge, 2003: 29-46.

Bannermann, Edward, et al. (eds.), *Europe after September 11th*, London: Centre for European Reform, 2001.

Bark, Dennis L., *Americans and Europeans Dancing in the Dark, Or Our Differences and Affinities, Our Interests, and Our Habits of Life*, Stanford: Hoover Institution Press 2007.

Barroso, José Manuel, "Hands Across the Ocean," *International Herald Tribune*, April 27, 2007: 6.

Bermann, George A., et al. (eds.), *Transatlantic Regulatory Cooperation: Legal problems and Political Prospects*, Oxford/New York: Oxford University Press, 2001.

Bertram, Christoph, "Europe's Best Interest: Staying Close to Number One," *Internationale Politik und Gesellschaft* 1 (2003): 61-70.

Biermann, Rafael, *Schattenjahre: Das Scheitern der internationalen Konflikteinwirkung im Kosovo vor Kriegsbeginn*, Paderborn: Schöningh, 2005.

Brandon, Henry (ed.), *In Search of a New World Order: The Future of US-European Relations*, Washington D.C.: Brookings Institution, 1992.

Bronstone, Adam, *European Union – United States Security Relations: Transatlantic Tensions and the Theory of International Relations*, New York: St. Martin's Press, 1997.

Busch, Marc L., *Transatlantic Trade Conflicts and GATT/WTO Dispute Settlement*, Fiesole: European University Institute, 2002.

CIA, *World Factbook 2007*, https://cia.gov/library/publications/download/download-2007/index.html

Council of the European Union, *Presidency Conclusions of the Brussels European Council*, 21/22 June 2007, http://consilium.europa.eu/ueDocs/cms_Data/docs/pressData/ en/ec/94932.pdf.

Croci, Osvaldo, and Amy Verdun (eds.), *The Transatlantic Divide: Foreign and Security Policies in the Atlantic Alliance from Kosovo to Iraq*, Manchester: Manchester University Press, 2006.

Dedman, Martin, *The Origins and Development of the European Union, 1945-95*, London/New York: Routledge, 1996.

Dembinski, Matthias, and Kinka Gerke (eds.), *Cooperation or Conflict? Transatlantic Relation in Transition*, Frankfurt/New York: Campus, 1998.

De Vasconcelos, Alvaro, and Marcin Zaborowski, *The Obama Momentum: European and American Perspectives,* Paris: The European Union Institute for Security Studies, 2009.

Derrida, Jacques, and Jürgen Habermas, "Nach dem Krieg: Die Wiedergeburt Europas," *Frankfurter Allgemeine Zeitung*, March 31, 2003: 33;

Derrida, Jacques, and Jürgen Habermas, "Europe: plaidoyer pour une politique extérieure commune," *Libération*, June 2, 2003.

Dinan, Desmond, *Europe Recast: A History of the European Union*, Boulder: Lynne Rienner, 2004.

Drozdiak, William, "Betting on the EU," *Newsweek*, May 10, 2004: 28-29.

Duchêne, François, *Jean Monnet: The First Statesman of Interdependence*, New York/London: W.W. Norton & Co., 1994.

Egan, Michelle (ed.), *Creating a Transatlantic Marketplace: Government Policies and Business Strategies*, Manchester: Manchester University Press, 2005.

Frankfurter Allgemeine Zeitung, “Europäer wollen Weltmacht sein,” September 7, 2005: 6.

European Union, European Commission, Directorate-General for External Relations, (ed.), *European Union Relations with the United States*, Luxembourg: Office for Official Publications of the European Communities, 2002.

Ferguson, Niall, *Colossus: The Price of America's Empire*, New York: Penguin Press, 2004.

Galantière, Lewis (ed.), *America and the Mind of Europe*, London: H. Hamilton 1951.

Gardner, Anthony L., *A New Era in US-EU Relations? The Clinton Administration and the New Transatlantic Agenda*, Aldershot: Ashgate, 1997.

Garton Ash, Timothy, *Free World: Why a Crisis of the West Reveals the Opportunity of Our Time*, London: Allen Lane, 2004.

German Marshall Fund of the United States, and Compagnia di San Paolo(eds.), *Transatlantic Trends 2004*, https://transatlantictrends.com.

Gompert, David, and R. Stephen Larrabee (eds.), *America and Europe: A Partnership for a New Era*, Cambridge: Cambridge University Press, 1998.

Grant, Charles, *Transatlantic Rift: How to Bring the Two Sides Together*, London: Centre for European Reform, 2003.

Hackett, Clifford P. (ed.), *Monnet and the Americans: The Father of a United Europe and his U. S. Supporters*, Washington D.C.: Jean Monnet Council, 1995.

Hamilton, Daniel S., and Joseph P. Quinlan, “We Can't Afford this trans-Atlantic Squabble,” *International Herald Tribune*, November 5, 2004.

Hamilton, Keith, and Patrick Salmon (eds.), *The Year of Europe: America, Europe and the Energy Crisis, 1972-74*, Abingdon: Routledge, 2006.

Hearden, Patrick J., *Architects of Globalism: Building a New World Order During World War II*, Fayetteville: University of Arkansas Press, 2002.

Hensel, Howard M. (ed.), *The United States and Europe: Policy Imperatives in a Globalizing World*, Aldershot: Ashgate, 2002.

Heuser, Beatrice, *Transatlantic Relations: Sharing Ideals and Costs*, London: Royal Institute of International Affairs, 1996.

Hitchcock, William I., *The Struggle for Europe: The Turbulent History of a Divided Continent - 1945 to the Present*, New York: Anchor Book, 2004.

Isaacson, Walter, and Evan Thomas, *The Wise Man: Six Friends and the World They Made*, New York: Simon and Schuster, 1986.

Jabko, Nicolas, and Craig Parsons (eds.), *The State of the European Union: Vol. 7 - With US or Against US? European Trends in American Perspective*, Oxford: Oxford University Press, 2005.

Kagan, Robert, *Of Paradise and Power: America and Europe in the New World Order*, New York: Knopf, 2003.

Kennedy, John F., *Address at Independence Hall*, Philadelphia, July 4, 1962, http://jfklibrary.org/Historical+Resources/Archives/Reference+Desk/Speeches/JFK/003POF03IndependenceHall07041962.htm.

Kupchan, Charles A., *Power in Transition: The Peaceful Change of International Order*, New York: United Nations University Press, 2002.

Kühnhardt, Ludger, *Contrasting Transatlantic Interpretations: The EU and the US Toward a Common Global Role*, Stockholm: Swedish Institute for European Policy Studies, 2003.

Kühnhardt, Ludger, *Stufen der Souveränität: Staatsverständnis und Selbstbestimmung in der Dritten Welt*, Bonn: Bouvier, 1992.

Kühnhardt, Ludger, *System-opening and Cooperative Transformation of the Broader Middle East: A New Trans-Atlantic Project and a Joint Euro-Atlantic-Arab Task*, EUROMESCO Papers 26, Lisbon: Euro-Mediterranean Study Commission, 2003.

Kühnhardt, Ludger, and Hans-Gert Pöttering, "EU-USA – Plädoyer für einen Atlantischen Vertrag," *Integration*, 26.3 (2003): 244-250.

Kurki, Christian et.al.(eds.), *The Great Regression?: Financial Crisis in an Age of Global Interdependence,* Helsinki: The Finnish Institute of International Affairs, 2009.

Leech, John (ed.), *Whole and Free: NATO, EU Enlargement and Transatlantic Relations*, London: Federal Trust for Education&Research, 2002.

Lindley-French, Julian, *Terms of Engagement: The Paradox of American Power and the Transatlantic Dilemma post-11 September*, Paris: European Union Institute for Security Studies, 2002.

Lugar, Richard, *The Future of Transatlantic Relations: Euro-Atlantic Community and the Continuing US Role in Europe*, London: HMSO, 1993.

Lundestad, Geir, *"Empire" by Integration: The United States and European Integration*, Oxford: Oxford University Press, 1998.

Lundestad, Geir (ed.), *No End to Alliance: The United States and Western Europe: Past, Present and Future*, Houndmills: Macmillan, 1998.

Mahncke, Dieter, et al. (eds.), *Redefining Transatlantic Security Relations: The Challenge of Change*, Manchester: Manchester University Press, 2004.

Maier, Charles S. (ed.), *The Cold War in Europe: Era of a divided continent*, Princeton: Markus Wiener, 1996 (3rd ed.)

Marchetti, Andreas (ed.), *The CSCE as a Model to Transform Western Relations with the Broader Middle East*, ZEI Discussion Paper C137, Bonn: Center for European Integration Studies, 2004.

Melandri, Pierre, *Les Etats-Unis face à l'unification de l'Europe – 1945-1954*, Paris: Pédone et Publications de Sorbonne, 1980.

Monar, Jörg (ed.), *The New Transatlantic Agenda and the Future of EU-US Relations*, London/ Boston: Kluwer Law International, 1998.

Monnet, Jean, *Mémoires*, Paris: Fayard, 1976.
Neuss, Beate, *Geburtshelfer Europas? Die Rolle der Vereinigten Staaten im europäischen Integrationsprozess 1945-1958*, Baden-Baden: Nomos, 2000.
Nye, Joseph, *The Paradox of American Power: Why the World's Only Superpower Can't Go it Alone*, Oxford/New York: Oxford University Press, 2002.
Peterson, John, and Mark A. Pollack (eds.), *Europe, America, Bush: Transatlantic Relations in the Twenty-First Century*, London/New York: Routledge, 2003.
Pollack, Mark A., and Gregory C. Shaffer (eds.), *Transatlantic Governance in the Global Economy*, Lanham: Rowman & Littlefield, 2001.
Pollack, Mark A. (ed.), *The New Transatlantic Agenda at Five: a Critical Assessment*, Fiesole: European University Institute, 2002.
Reinicke, Wolfgang H., *Deepening the Atlantic: Toward a New Transatlantic Marketplace?*, Gütersloh: Bertelsmann Foundation Publishers, 1996.
Schnabel, Rockwell, *The Next Superpower: The Rise of Europe and its Challenge to the US*, Lanham: Rowman&Littlefield, 2005.
Schönwald, Matthias, "'The same – should I say – antenna'. Gemeinsamkeiten und Unterschiede im europapolitischen Denken von Jean Monnet und Walter Hallstein (1958-1963)," in: Wilkens, Andreas (ed.), *Interessen verbinden: Jean Monnet und die europäische Integration der Bundesrepublik Deutschland*, Bonn: Bouvier, 1999: 289-297.
Schwabe, Klaus, "The United States and European Integration - 1947-1957," in: Wurm, Clemens (ed.), *Western Europe and Germany: The Beginnings of European Integration, 1945-1960*, Oxford/New York: Berg Publishers, 1995: 115-135.
Schwabe, Klaus, "Jean Monnet, die Vereinigten Staaten und die Rolle Europas in der Atlantischen Völkergemeinschaft," in: Wilkens, Andreas (ed.), *Interessen verbinden: Jean Monnet und die europäische Integration der Bundesrepublik Deutschland*: xxx-xxx.
Silva, Michael, and Bertil Sjogren, *Europe 1992 and the New World Power Game*, New York: Wiley, 1990.
Sloan, Stanley, and Peter van Ham, *What Future for NATO?*, London: Centre for European Reform, 2002.
Sloan, Stanley, *NATO and Transatlantic Relations in the twenty-first century: Crisis, Continuity or Change?*, New York: Foreign Policy Association, 2002.
Sloan, Stanley, *NATO, the European Union and the Atlantic Community: The Transatlantic Bargain Reconsidered*, Lanham: Rowman&Littlefield, 2002.
Stemplowski, Ryszard, and Laurence A. Whitehead (eds.), *After the Attack: "Several Europe's" and Transatlantic Relations*, Warsaw: Polish Institute of International Affairs, 2002.
Suri, Jeremi, *Power and Protest: Global Revolution and the Rise of Détente*, Cambridge, Mass.: Harvard University Press, 2003

Thiele, Ralph D., "Projecting European Power: A European View," in: Brimmer, Esther (ed.), *The EU's Search for a Strategic Role: ESDP and its Implications for Transatlantic Relations*, Washington D. C.: Center for Transatlantic Relations, 2002: 67-82.

United States Congress, House, Committee on International Relations, Subcommittee on Europe, *Renewing the Transatlantic Partnership: A View from the United States*, Hearing Before the Subcommittee, June 11, 2003, Washington D.C.: US G. P. O. Congressional Sales Office, 2003.

United States Congress, House, Committee on International Relations, Subcommittee on Europe, *The Future of Transatlantic Relations: A View from Europe*, Hearing before the Subcommittee, Washington, June 17, 2003, Washington D.C.: US G. P. O. Congressional Sales Office, 2003.

Urwin, Derek, *The Community of Europe: A History of European Integration since 1945*, London/New York: Longman, 1995

Van Oudenaren, John, "E Pluribus Confusio: Living with the EU's Strctural Incoherence," *The National Interest*, Fall (2001): 23-37.

Van den Broek, Hans, et al., *Transatlantic Relations in the 1990s: The Emergence of New Security Architecture*, Washington D.C.: Brassey's, 1992.

Wells, Sam, and Ludger Kühnhardt (eds.), *The Crisis in Transatlantic Relations*, ZEI Discussion Paper C143, Bonn: Center for European Integration Studies, 2005.

Wilkens, Andreas (ed.), *Interessen verbinden: Jean Monnet und die europäische Integration der Bundesrepublik Deutschland*, Bonn: Bouvier, 1999.

Wikipedia, http://en.wikipedia.org/wiki/EU.

Winand, Pascaline, *Eisenhower, Kennedy, and the United States of Europe*, Houndmills: Basingstoke, 1997.

Zaborowski, Marcin, and David H. Dunn (eds.), *Poland: A New Power in Transatlantic Security*, London/Portland: Frank Cass, 2003.

Zaborowski, Macin (ed.), *Friends Again?: EU-US Relations After the Crisis*, Paris: European Union Institute for Security Studies, 2006.

Zelikow, Philipp, and Condoleezza Rice, *Germany Unified and Europe Transformed: A Study in Statecraft*, Cambridge, Mass.: Harvard University Press, 1995.

Chapter VII

Albrow, Martin, *The Global Age: State and Society beyond Modernity*, Stanford: Stanford University Press, 1997.

Albrow, Martin, and Darren O'Byrne, "Rethinking State and Citizenship under Globalized Conditions," in: Henri Goverde (ed.), *Global and European Polity? Organizations, Policies, Contexts*, Aldershot: Ashgate, 2000: 65-82.

Al Sayyad, Nezar, and Castells, Manuel (eds.), *Muslim Europe or Euro-Islam: Politics, Culture, and Citizenship in the Age of Globalization*, Lanham: Lexington Books, 2002.

Amin, Ash, and Nigel Thrift (eds.), *Globalization, Institutions, and Regional Development in Europe*, Oxford: Oxford University Press, 1994.

Andersen, Svein S., and Kjell A. Eliasen (eds.), *The European Union: How Democratic is it?*, London: Sage, 1995.

Archibugi, Daniele, David Held, and Martin Koehler (eds.), *Re-Imagining Political Community:Studies in Cosmopolitan Democracy*, Cambridge: Polity Press, 1998.

Ariès, Paul, et al. (eds.), *L'Europe Globalisée: la fin des illusions*, Paris: Hamattan, 2002.

Arnull, Anthony, *The European Union and its Court of Justice*, Oxford: Oxford University Press, 2003.

Axtmann, Roland (ed.), *Globalization and Europe: Theoretical and Empirical Investigations*, London/Washington D.C.: Pinter, 1998.

Barber, Benjamin, *Jihad vs. McWorld*, New York: Times Books, 1995.

Barry, John, et al. (eds.), *Europe, Globalization and Sustainable Development*, London/New York: Routledge, 2004.

Beck, Ulrich, *Was ist Globalisierung?*, Frankfurt: Suhrkamp, 1997.

Bieler, Andreas, and Adam David Morton (eds.), *Social Forces in the Making of the New Europe: The Restructuring of European Social Relations in the Global Political Economy*, Houndmills: Palgrave, 2001.

Bodin, Jean, *Les six livres de la République*, Paris: Fayard, 1986.

Boyer, Robert, and Pierre-Francois Souyri, *Mondialisation et régulations: Europe et Japon face à la singularité américaine*, Paris: Découverte, 2001.

Brewer, Thomas L. (ed.), *Globalizing Europe: Deepening Integration, Alliance Capitalism, and Structural Statecraft*, Northampton: Edward Elgar, 2002.

Cavanna, Henry (ed.), *Governance, Globalization and the European Union: Which Europe for Tomorrow?*, Dublin: Fourt Courts, 2002.

Cooper, Robert, *Breaking of Nations: Order and Chaos in the Twenty-First Century*, London: Atlantic Books, 2003.

Cuyvers, Ludo (ed.), *Globalisation and Social Development: European and Southeast Asian Evidence*, Northhampton: Edward Elgar Publishers, 2001.

De Tocqueville, Alexis, *De la démocratie en Amérique*, Paris: J. Vrin, 1990.

Dinopoulos, Elias, et al. (eds.), *Globalization: Prospects and Problems*, Abingdon: Routledge, 2007.

Ducatel, Ken, Juliet Webster, and Werner Herrmann (eds.), *The Information Society in Europe: Work and Life in the Age of Globalization*, Lanham/Boulder: Rowman&Littlefield, 2000.

Duignan, Peter, and L.H. Gann, *The United States and the New Europe*, Oxford: Oxford University Press, 1994.

European Union, European Commission, *Flash-Eurobarometer 151b*, November 2003, http://ec.europa.eu/public_opinion/flash/FL151bGlobalisationREPORT.pdf.

Fernandez Jilberto, Alex E., and Andre Mommen (eds.), *Regionalization and Globalization in the Modern World Economy: Perspectives on the Third World and Transitional Economies*, London/New York: Routledge, 1998.

Friedman, Thomas, *The Lexus and the Olive Tree*, New York: Farrar, Straus, Giroux, 2000 (rev. ed.).

Fürtig, Henner (ed.), *Abgrenzung und Aneignung in der Globalisierung: Asien, Afrika und Europa seit dem 18. Jahrhundert*, Berlin: Das Arabische Buch, 2001.

Garton Ash, Timothy, *Free World: Why a Crisis of the West Reveals the Opportunity of Our Time*, London: Allen Lane, 2004.

Goddard, C.Roe, et al. (eds.), *International Political Economy: State-Market Relations in a Changing Global Order*, Basingstoke: Palgrave Macmillan, 2003.

Goldmann, Kjell, *Transforming the European Nation-State: Dynamics of Internationalization*, London: Sage Publishers, 2001.

Gruber, Lloyd, *Globalization and Political Conflict: The Long-Term Prognosis,* American Institute for Contemporary German Studies, Seminar Papers 15, Washington D.C.: AICGS, 2001.

Hambleton, Robert, H.V. Savitch, and Muray Stewart (eds.), *Globalism and Local Democracy: Challenge and Change in Europe and North America*, New York: Palgrave, 2002.

Hirschhausen, Christian von, and Jürgen Bitzer (eds.), *The Globalization of Industry and Innovation in Eastern Europe: From Post-Socialist Restructuring to International Competitiveness*, Cheltenham: Edward Elgar, 2000.

Hirst, Paul, "The Myth of Globalization," in: Vellinga, Menno (ed.), *The Dialectics of Globalization: Regional Responses to World Economic Processes, Asia, Europe, and Latin America in Comparative Perspective*, Boulder: Westview, 2000.

Höreth, Marcus, *Stille Revolution im Namen des Rechts?*, ZEI-Discussion Paper C78, Bonn: Center for European Integration Studies, 2000.

Horman, Denis, *Mondialisation excluante, nouvelles solidarités: Soumettre ou démettre l'OMC*, Paris: Harmattan, 2001.

Hudson, Wayne, and Steven Slaughter (eds.), *Globalisation and Citizenship: The Transnational Challenge*, Abingdon: Routledge, 2007.

Huntington, Samuel P., *The Clash of Civilizations and the Remaking of World Order*, New York: Simon&Schuster, 1996.

Johansson, Karl Magnus, and Peter Zervakis (eds.), *European Political Parties Between Cooperation and Integration*, Baden-Baden: Nomos, 2001.

Kampny, Marian, and Aldona Jawlowska (eds.), *Identity in Transformation: Postmodernity, Postcommunism, and Globalization*, Westport: Praeger, 2002.
Keohane, Robert O., "Hobbes's Dilemma and Institutional Change in World Politics: Sovereignty in International Society," in: Holm, Hans-Henrik, and Georg Sorensen (eds.), *Whose World Order?: Uneven Globalization and the End of the Cold War*, Boulder: Westview, 1995: 165-187.
Kierzkowski, Henryk (ed.), *Europe and Globalization*, New York: Palgrave, 2002.
Kindley, Randall W., and David F. Good (eds.), *The Challenge of Globalization and Institution Building: Lessons from Small European States*, Boulder: Westview, 1997.
Kokkinos, Theodore, *Economic Structure-Functionalism in European Unification and Globalization of the Economies*, Frankfurt/New York: Peter Lang, 2000.
Kühnhardt, Ludger, *Die Universalität der Menschenrechte: Studie zur ideengeschichtlichen Bestimmung eines politischen Schlüsselbegriffs*, Munich: Olzog, 1987.
Kühnhardt, Ludger, *Stufen der Souveränität: Staatsverständnis und Selbstbestimmung in der Dritten Welt*, Bonn/Berlin: Bouvier, 1992.
Kühnhardt, Ludger, *Von der ewigen Suche nach Frieden: Immanuel Kants Vision und Europas Wirklichkeit*, Bonn: Bouvier, 1996.
Kurki, Kristian et.al.(eds.), *The Great Regression?: Financial Crisis in an Age of Global Interdependence,* Helsinki: The Finnish Institute of International Affairs, 2009.
Lafougère, Michel, *L'Europe Face au Défi de la Mondialisation: les consequences socials de la reconstruction des économies en Europe*, Strasbourg: Editions du Conseil de l'Europe, 1998.
Loch, Dietmar, and Wilhelm Heitmeier (eds.), *Schattenseiten der Globalisierung*, Frankfurt: Suhrkamp, 2001.
Locke, John, *Two Treatises on Government*, London: Cambridge University Press, 1967.
Loth, Wilfried, and Wolfgang Wessels (eds.), *Theorien europäischer Integration*, Opladen: Leske&Budrich, 2001.
Maier, Hans, *Die ältere deutsche Staats- und Verwaltungslehre*, Munich: C.H. Beck, 1980 (rev. ed.).
Marsilius of Padua, *Defensor Pacis*, New York: Arno Press, 1979.
Maurer, Andreas, and Wolfgang Wessels (eds.), *National Parliaments on their Ways to Europe: Losers or Latecomers?*, Baden-Baden: Nomos, 2002.
Meehan, Elizabeth, *Citizenship and the European Community*, London: Sage, 1993.
Meier Dallach, Hans-Peter, and Jakob Juchler (eds.), *Postsocialist Transformations and Civil Society in a Globalizing World*, Huntington: Nova Science Publishers, 2001.

Milward, Alan S., *The European Rescue of the Nation-State*, London/New York: Routledge, 2000.

Montesquieu, Charles de Secondat, Baron de, *De l'esprit des lois*, Paris: Garnier, 1977.

Moravcsik, Andrew, *Choice for Europe, Social Purpose and State Power from Messina to Maastricht*, Ithaca: Cornell University Press, 1998.

Mueller-Graff, Peter-Christian (ed.), *Die Europäische Gemeinschaft in der Welthandelsorganisation, Globalisierung und Weltmarktrecht als Herausforderung für Europa*, Baden-Baden: Nomos, 1999.

Nederveen Pieterse, Jan, and Bikhu Parekh (eds.), *The Decolonization of Imagination: Culture, Knowledge and Power*, London/New Jersey: Zed Books, 1995.

Niedermayer, Oskar, and Richard Sinnott (eds.), *Public Opinion and Internationalized Governance*, Oxford: Oxford University Press, 1995.

Pollack, Mark A., and Gregory C. Shaffer (eds.), *Transatlantic Governance in the Global Economy*, Lanham: Rowman&Littlefield, 2001.

Prodi, Romano, *"The European Dimension" - Progressive Governance for the XXI Century*, Conference Proceedings, Florence, November 20 and 21, 1999, European University Institute/New York University School of Law, 2000: 8-17.

Reding, Viviane, *Die Rolle der EG bei der Entwicklung Europas von der Industriegesellschaft zur Wissens- und Informationsgesellschaft*, ZEI-Discussion Paper C84, Bonn: Center for European Integration Studies, 2001.

Rodemer, Horst, and Hartmut Dicke (eds.), *Globalisierung, Europäische Integration und internationaler Standortwettbewerb*, Baden-Baden: Nomos, 2000.

Roloff, Ralf, *Europa, Amerika und Asien zwischen Globalisierung und Regionalisierung: Das interregionale Konzert und die ökonomische Dimension internationaler Politik*, Paderborn: Schöningh, 2001.

Ronge, Frank, *Legitimität durch Subsidiarität: Der Beitrag des Subsidiaritätsprinzips zur Legitimität einer überstaatlichen politischen Ordnung in Europa*, Baden-Baden: Nomos, 1998.

Sassen, Saskia, and Kwame Anthony Appiah (eds.), Globalization and its Discontents, New York: New Press, 1998.

Schirm, Stefan A., *Globalization and the New Regionalism: Global Markets, Domestic Politics and Regional Co-Operation*, Cambridge: Polity Press, 2002.

Segbers, Klaus, and Kerstin Imbusch (eds.), *The Globalization of Eastern Europe*, Münster: Lit Verlag, 2000.

Siedentop, Larry, *Democracy in Europe*, London: Allen Lane, 2000.

Strange, Susan, "Europe's Future in the Global Political Economy," in: Row, Thomas (ed.), *Reflections on the Identity of Europe: Global and Transatlantic Perspectives*, Bologna: Baiesi, 1996: 27-33.

Sykes, Robert, Bruno Palier, and Pauline Prior (eds.), *Globalization and European Welfare States: Challenges and Chances*, Houndmills: Palgrave, 2000.

Sweeney, Simon, *Europe, the State, and Globalisation*, Harlow: Pearsons, 2005.

The Rome, Maastricht and Amsterdam Treaties, The Treaty of the European Union (Treaty of Maastricht) and the Treaty Establishing the European Communities (Treaty of Rome) Amended by the Treaty of Amsterdam, Comparative Texts, Genval: Euroconfidentiel, 1999.

Tilly, Charles (ed.), *The Formation of National States in Western Europe*, Princeton: Princeton University Press, 1975.

Van Ham, Peter, *European Integration and the Postmodern Condition, Governance, Democracy, Identity*, London/New York: Routledge, 2001.

Van Houtum, Henk, Martin van der Velde, and Frans Boekema, "Borders and Interaction," in: Goverde, Henri (ed.), *Global and European Polity?:Organizations, Policies, Contexts*, Aldershot: Ashgate, 2000: 269-282.

Van Oudenaren, John, "E Pluribus Confusio: Living with the EU's Structural Incoherence," *The National Interest*, Fall (2001): 23-37.

Verdun, Amy, *European Responses to Globalization and Financial Market Integration*, Houndmills: Macmillan, 2000.

Vibert, Frank, *Europe Simple, Europe Strong*, Cambridge: Polity Press, 2002.

von der Gablentz, Otto, et al. (eds.), *Europe 2020: Adapting to a Changing World*, Baden-Baden: Nomos, 2000.

Weber, Steven (ed.), *Globalization and the European Political Economy*, New York: Columbia University Press, 2001.

Weiler, Joseph H.H., "Community, Member States and European Integration: Is the Law relevant?," *Journal of Common Market Studies*, 21.1/2 (1982): 39-56.

Wiarda, Howard J., *European Politics in the Age of Globalization*, Fort Worth: Harcourt Publishers, 2001.

Zielonka, Jan, *Europe as Empire, The Nature of the Enlarged European Union*, Oxford: Oxford University Press, 2006.

Zloch-Christy, Illiana, *Eastern Europe and the World Economy. Challenges of Transition and Globalization*, Cheltenham: Edward Elgar, 1998.

Chapter VIII

Abadie Aicardi, Oscar, *Fundamentos Historicos y Politicos del Mercosur*, Montevideo: Melibea Edicciones, 1999.

Acharya, Amitav, *The Quest for Identity, International Relations of South East Asia*, Oxford: Oxford University Press, 2000.

Ajulu, Rock, "Thabo Mbeki's African Renaissance in a Globalising World Economy: The Struggle for the Soul of the Continent," *Review of African Political Economy*, 28.37 (2001): 27-42.

Al-Alkim, Hassan, *The GCC States in an Unstable World, Foreign Policy Dilemmas of Small States*, London: Saqi Books, 1994.

Algorta Pla, Juan, *O Mercosul e a Communidade Europeia: Uma Abordagem Comparativa*, Porto Alegre: Editorial de Universidade, 1994.

Arnold, Christian, *La experiencia de la Union Europea y sus anecdotas para la Communidad Andina de Naciones (CAN)*, ZEI Discussion Paper C145, Bonn: Center for European Integration Studies, 2005.

Asmus, Ronald D., and Kenneth M. Pollack, "The New Transatlantic Project," *Policy Review*, 115 (2002): 3-18.

Aggarwal, Vinod K., and Edward A. Fogarty (eds.), *EU Trade Strategies: Between Regionalism and Globalism*, Houndmills, Palgrave Macmillan, 2004.

Bhargava, Kant K., *EU-SAARC: Comparisons and Prospects for Cooperation*, ZEI Discussion Paper C15, Bonn: Center for European Integration Studies, 1998.

Barrios, Raul (ed.), *Communidad Andina de Naciones, Desafios Politicos y Percepciones de la Sociedad*, La Paz: Friedrich Ebert Stiftung, 1999.

Becak, Peggy, *Mercosul, Uma Experiencia de Integracao Regional*, Sao Paulo: Editora Contexto, 2000.

Braun, Ursula, *Der Kooperationsrat am Golf: Eine neue Kraft?: Regionale Integration als Stabilitätsfaktor*, Baden-Baden: Nomos, 1986.

Bridges, Brian, *Europe and the Challenge of the Asia-Pacific*, Cheltenham: Edward Elgar, 1999.

Caetano, Gerardo, and Ruben M. Perina (eds.), *La Encrucijada Politica del Mercosur: Parlamentos y Nueva Institutionalidad*, Montevideo: Impresora Editorial, 2003.

Camara de Comercio de la Republica de Cuba (ed.), *Cuba, el Caricom y sus Paises Miembros*, Havanna: Camara de Comercio, 2001.

Casas Gragea, Angel Maria, *El Modelo Regional Andino: Enfoque de Economia Politica Internacional*, Quito: Universidad Andina Simon Bolivar, 2003.

Cheru, Fantu, *African Renaissance: Roadmaps to the Challenge of Globalization*, London/ New York: Zed Books, 2002.

Chirathivat, Suthipand, et al. (eds.), *Asia-Europe on the Eve of the twenty-first century*, Bangkok: Saksopha Press, 2001.

Christie, John, "History and Development of the Gulf Cooperation Council: A Brief Overview," in: Sandwick, John A. (ed.), *The Gulf Cooperation Council: Moderation and Stability in an Interdependent World*, Boulder: Westview Press, 1987: 7-20.

Clapham, Christopher, et al. (eds.), *Regional Integration in Southern Africa: Comparative International Perspectives*, Johannesburg: The South African Institute of International Affairs, 2001.

David, Harald, *Die ASEAN zwischen Konflikt, Kooperation und Integration*, Hamburg: Institut für Asienkunde, 2003.

de la Ossa, Alvaro, "Der zentralamerikanische Integrationsprozess: Ende einer Entwicklungsalternative," *IBERO-Analysen* 6 (December 2000).

Dearden, Stephen J. H. (ed.), *The European Union and the Caribbean*, Aldershot: Ashgate, 2002.

Dent, Christopher M., and David W.F. Huang (eds.), *Northeast Asian Regionalism: Learning from the European Experience*, London: Routledge, 2002.

Diamint, Rut (ed.), *La OTAN y los Desafios en el MERCOSUR: Comunidad de Seguridad y Estabilidad Democratica*, Buenos Aires: Nuevohacer, 2001.

Diedrichs, Udo, *Die Politik der Europäischen Union gegenüber dem Mercosur: Die EU als internationaler Akteur*, Opladen: Leske&Budrich, 2003.

The Economist, "South American Summitry - Fraternity at 3,300 Metres," December 11, 2004: 47.

Fairlie Reinoso, Alan, *Las relaciones Communidad andina – Union Europea y la Zona de Libre Comercio del Sur*, Lima: Centro de Investigaciones Sociales, Economicas y Politicas, 2000.

Farrell, Maryl, et al. (eds.), *Global Politics of Regionalism: Theory and Practice*, London: Pluto Press, 2005.

Fasano, Ugo (ed.), *Monetary Union Among Member Countries of the Gulf Cooperation Council*, Washington D.C.: International Monetary Fund, 2003.

Fawcett, Louise, and Andrew Hurrell (eds.), *Regionalism in World Politics, Regional Organization and International Order*, New York: Oxford University Press, 1995.

Gates, Carolyn L., and Mya Than (eds.), *ASEAN Enlargement: Impacts and Implications*, Singapore: Institute of Southeast Asian Studies, 2001.

Genge, Manelisi, et al., *African Union and a Panafrican Parliament*, Pretoria: Africa Institute of South Africa, 2000.

Giacalone, Rita (ed.), *CAN-Mercosur a la Sombra del ALCA*, Merida: Editorial Venezolano, 2003.

Gonzalez Nunez, Gerardo, and Emilio Pantojas Garcia, *El Caribe en la Era de la Globalization*, Puerto Rico: Publicaciones Puertorriquenas, 2002.

Haines Ferrari, Marta (ed.), *The Mercosur Codes*, London: BIICL, 2000.

Hänggi, Heiner, et al. (eds.), *Interregionalism and International Relations*, Abingdon/New York: Routledge, 2005.

Hentz, James J. and Morten Boas (eds.) *New and Critical Security and Regionalism: Beyond the Nation-States*, Aldershot: Ashgate, 2003.

Hettne, Björn, and Fredrik Söderbaum, "Civilian Power or Soft Imperialism? The European Union as a Global Actor and the Role of Interregionalism," *European Foreign Policy Affairs Review* 10.4 (2005): 535-552.

Hoa, Tran Van, and Charles Harvie (eds.), *New Asian Regionalism: Responses to Globalisation and Crises*, Basingstoke: Macmillan, 2003.

Holland, Martin, *The European Union and the Third World*, Houndmills: Palgrave, 2002.

Inter-American Development Bank (ed.), *Beyond Borders: The New Regionalism in Latin America*, Washington D.C.: Inter-American Development Bank, 2002.

Jaguaribe, Helio, and Alvaro de Vasconcelos (eds.), *The European Union, Mercosul and the New World Order*, London/Portland: Frank Cass, 2003.

Jonson, Lena, and Clive Archer (eds.), *Peacekeeping and the Role of Russia in Eurasia*, Boulder: Westview, 1996.

Kalam, Abul, *Subregionalism in Asia: ASEAN and SAARC Experiences*, New Delhi: UBS Publishers, 2001.

Kelsey, Jane, *A People's Guide to PACER: The Implications for the Pacific Islands of the Pacific Agreement on Closer Economic Relations (PACER)*, Suva: Pacific Network on Globalisation, 2004.

Kim, Samuel S. (ed.), *The International Relations of Northeast Asia*, Lanham: Rowman&Littlefield, 2004.

Kösler, Ariane, *The Southern African Development Community and its Relations to the European Union: Deepening Integration in Southern Africa?*, ZEI Discussion Paper C169, Bonn: Center for European Integration Studies, 2007.

Kösler, Ariane, and Martin Zimmek (eds.), *Global Voices on Regional Integration*, ZEI Discussion Paper C 176, Bonn: Center for European Integration Studies, 2007.

Krasner, Stephen D., *Sovereignty: Organized Hypocrisy*, Princeton: Princeton University Press, 1999.

Kühnhardt, Ludger, *Constituting Europe: Identity, Institution-Building and the Search for a Global Role*, Baden-Baden: Nomos, 2003.

Kühnhardt, Ludger, *System-Opening and Cooperative Transformation of the Broader Middle East: A New Transatlantic Project and a Joint Euro-Atlantic-Arab Task*, EUROMESCO Papers 26, Lisbon: Euro-Mediterranean Study Commission, 2003.

Kühnhardt, Ludger, *Northeast Asia: Obstacles to Regional Integration. The Interests of the European Union*, ZEI Discussion Paper C 152, Bonn: Center for European Integration Studies, 2005.

Kühnhardt, Ludger, *African Regional Integration and the Role of the European Union,* ZEI Discussion Paper C 184, Bonn: Center for European Integration Studies, 2008.

Lauer, Rene, *Las Politicas Sociales en la Integracion Regional: Estudio Comparativo de la Union Europea y la Comunidad Andina de Naciones*, Quito: Universidad Andino Simon Bolivar, 2001.

Lavergne, Real (ed.), *Regional Integration and Cooperation in West Africa: A Multidimensional Perspective*, Trenton/Asmara: Africa World Press, 1997.

Le Gras, Gilbert, *The New New World: The Re-Emerging Markets of Latin America*, London: Reuters, 2002.

Leonhardt, Wolfgang, *Spiel mit dem Feuer: Russlands schmerzhafter Weg zur Demokratie*, Bergisch-Gladbach: Lübbe, 1996.

Luciani, Giacomo, and Felix Neugart (eds.), *The EU and the GCC: A New Partnership*, Munich: Bertelsmann Stiftung, 2005.

Magen, Amichai, and Shlomo Shpiro, *Towards a Comprehensive Security Approach in the Middle East: Lessons from the European Experience in Justice and Home Affairs Cooperation*, Tel Aviv: The Tami Steinmetz Center for Peace Research, 2003.

Marchetti, Andreas (ed.), *The CSCE as a Model to Transform Western Relations with the Broader Middle East*, ZEI Discussion Paper C137, Bonn: Center for European Integration Studies, 2004.

Martin, Guy, *Africa in World Politics: A Pan-African Perspective*, Trenton/Asmara: Africa World Press, 2002.

Mattli, Werner, *The Logic of Integration: Europe and Beyond*, Cambridge/New York: Cambridge University Press, 1999.

Max Planck Institut für Ausländisches und Internationales Privatrecht (ed.), *Rechtsquellen des Mercosur*, Baden-Baden: Nomos, 2000.

Mbeki, Thabo, *The African Renaissance, South Africa and the World*, https://unu.edu/unupress/mbeki.html.

Meeting of the Leaders of CIS Member States, October 6./7. 2002, https://cis.minsk.by/english/meet_cis.htm.

Melber, Henning, The New African Initiative and the African Union - A Preliminary Assessment and Documentation, Uppsala: Nordiska Afrikainstitutet, 2001.

Minkner-Bünjer, Mechthild, "Zentralamerika zwischen regionaler Integration und Eingliederung in die Weltwirtschaft im "Schlepptau" der USA," *Brennpunkt Lateinamerika*, 13 (July 2002): 129-142.

Montoya, Carlos Alberto, *Teoria de la Integracion, Los Procesos de Integracion Economica en America Latina*, Medellin: Eafit Fondo Editorial Universidad, 2000.

Moon, Woosik, and Bernadette Andreosso-O'Callaghan (eds.), *Regional Integration - Europe and Asia Compared*, Aldershot: Ashgate, 2005.

Murray, Philomena, "Towards a Research Agenda on the European Union as a Model of Regional Integration," *Asia-Pacific Journal of EU Studies* 2.1 (2004): 33-51.

Nabers, Dirk, "Das ASEAN Regional Forum (ARF)," in: Maull, Hanns W., and Dirk Nabers (eds.), *Multilateralismus in Ostasien-Pazifik: Probleme und Perspektiven im neuen Jahrhundert*, Hamburg: Institut für Asienkunde, 2001: 89-117.

Nakhleh, Emile A., *The Gulf Cooperation Council: Policies, Problems and Prospects*, Westport/London: Praeger, 1986.

Nathan, K.S., *The European Union, United States and ASEAN - Challenges and Prospects for Cooperative Engagement in the twenty-first century*, London: ASEAN Academic Press, 2002.

Nazarkin, Yuri K., *Peace-Keeping Operation in the CIS*, https://ieis.lu/books/future_role_of_russia/nazarkin.pdf.

Nerys Fernandez, Wilson, *MERCOSUR, Estados Unidos, ALCA: Globalizacion y Regionalizacion en el Cambio del Siglo*, Montevideo: Fundacion de Cultura Universitaria, 2000.

Neue Zürcher Zeitung, "Eine 'pazifische Union' am Horizont?," August 9, 2004.

Orijako, Desmond T., "Road to the African Union (AU): Opportunities and Challenges," in: African Union (ed.), *The African Union Directory 2002, 1st Heads of State Summit*, Mauritius: Millenium African Communications, 2002.

Ortiz Mena, Antonio, *Regional Integration in the Americas and the Pacific Rim*, La Jolla: California Center for Iberian and Latin American Studies, 1997.

Pacific Islands Forum, *The Pacific Plan*, https://forumsec.org.fj/docs/PPlan/Final%20Draft%20%Pacific%20Plan%20'sept%202005.pdf.

Payne, Anthony, and Paul Sutton, *Charting Caribbean Developments*, Gainesville: University Press of Florida, 2001.

Peterson, Erik R., *The Gulf Cooperation Council: Search for Unity in a Dynamic Region*, Boulder: Westview, 1988.

Plummer, Michael G., "The EU and ASEAN: Real Integration and Lessons in Financial Cooperation," *The World Economy*, 25 (2002): 1469-1500.

Pollard, Duke (ed.), *The Caricom System: Basic Instruments*, Kingston: The Caribbean Law Publishing House Company, 2003.

Potholm, Christian P., and Richard A. Fredland (eds.), *Integration and Disintegration in East Africa*, Lanham: University Press of America, 1980.

Ramazani, R. K., *The Gulf Cooperation Council: Record and Analysis*, Charlottesville: University Press of Virginia, 1988.

Sader, Emir (ed.), *ALCA: Integracao Soberana ou Subordinada?*, Sao Paulo: Expressao Popular, 2001.

Scheffler, Thomas, "'Fertile Crescent,' 'Orient,' 'Middle East:' The Changing Mental Maps of Southwest Asia," *European Review of History*, 10.2 (2003): 253-272.

Shibuya, Eric, "The Problems and Potential of the Pacific Islands Forum," in: Rolfe, Jim (ed.), *The Asia-Pacific: A Region in Transition*, Honolulu: Asia-Pacific Center for Security Studies, 2004: 102-115.

Smith, Malinda S. (ed.), *Globalizing Africa*, Trenton/Asmara: Africa World Press, 2003.

Strezhneva, Marina, *Social Culture and Regional Governance: Comparison of the European Union and post-Soviet Experiences*, Commack: Nova Scotia Publishers, 1999.

Telò, Mario, Europe: *A Civilian Power? - European Union, Global Governance, World Order*, Houndmills: Palgrave Macmillan, 2006.

Trenin, Dmitri, *The End of Eurasia: Russia on the Border between Geopolitics and Globalization*, Moscow: Carnegie Endowment for International Peace, 2001.

Ulrich, Stephan, *Die zentralamerikanische Integration: Stand und Entwicklungsperspektiven*, Berlin: Deutsches Institut für Entwicklungspolitik, 2000.
Van Hoa, Tran, and Charles Harvie (eds.), *New Asian Regionalism: Responses to Globalisation and Crises*, Basingstoke: Macmillan, 2003.
Vera-Fluixa, Ramiro, *Regionalbildungsansätze in Lateinamerika und ihr Vergleich mit der Europäischen Union*, ZEI Discussion Paper C73, Bonn: Center for European Integration Studies, 2000.
Vigevani, Tullo, and Marcelo Passini Mariano (eds.), *ALCA: O Gigante e os Anoes*, Sao Paulo: Editora Senac, 2001.
Wichmann, Peter, *Die politischen Perspektiven der ASEAN: Subregionale Integration oder supranationale Kooperation*, Hamburg: Institut für Asienkunde, 1996.
Yeung, May T., et al. (eds.), *Regional Trading Blocs in the Global Economy: The EU and ASEAN*, Cheltenham: Edward Elgar, 1999.
Zippel, Wulfdieter (ed.), *Die Beziehungen zwischen der EU und den Mercosur-Staaten: Stand und Perspektiven*, Baden-Baden: Nomos, 2002.
Zimmek, Martin, *Integrationsprozesse in Lateinamerika: Aktuelle Herausforderungen in Mittelamerika und der Andenregion*, ZEI Discussion Paper C153, Bonn: Center for European Integration Studies, 2005.

Chapter IX

Althusius, Johannes, *Politica Methodice, with an introduction by Carl Joachim Friedrich*, New York: Arno Press, 1979.
Arts, Will, et al., *The Cultural Diversity of European Unity: Findings, Explanations and Reflections from the European Value Study*, Leiden/Boston: Brill, 2003.
Aston, Nigel, *The French Revolution, 1789-1804: Authority, Liberty and the Search for Stability*, Houndmills: Palgrave Macmillan, 2004.
Baker, Keith Michael, *The French Revolution and the Creation of Modern Political Culture*, Oxford: Pergamon Press, 1987.
Barraclough, Geoffrey, *European Unity in Thought and Action*, Oxford: Blackwell, 1963.
Becher, Mathias, *Charlemagne*, New Haven: Yale University Press, 2003.
Berlin, Isaiah, *The Age of Enlightenment*, Boston: Houghton Mifflin, 1956.
Boemecke, Manfred, et al. (eds.), *The Treaty of Versailles: A Reassessment After 75 Years*, Cambridge: Cambridge University Press, 1998.
Boussière, Eric, et al. (eds.), *Europe: The European Idea and Identity, from Ancient Greece to the twenty-first century*, Antwerp: Mercatorfunds, 2001.
Burckhardt, Jacob, *Weltgeschichtliche Betrachtungen*, Stuttgart: Kroener, 1978 (12th ed.).

Campbell, Peter R., *The Origins of the French Revolution*, New York: Palgrave Macmillan, 2005.
Carr, Craig L., *The Political Writings of Samuel Pufendorf*, New York: Oxford University Press, 1994.
Convention to Amend the Revised Convention for Rhine Navigation, signed at Mannheim on 17 October 1868, Strassbourg 20. November 1963, London: H.M. Stationary Office, 1967.
Coudenhove-Kalergi, Richard von, *Paneuropa*, Vienna: Paneuropa-Verlag, 1923.
Coudenhove-Kalergi, Richard von, *Crusade for Pan-Europe: Autobiography of a Man and a Movement*, New York: G.P. Putnam's Sons, 1943.
Craxton, Derek, and Anuschka Tischer, *The Peace of Westphalia: A Historical Dictionary*, Westport: Greenwood, 2002.
Danylyszyn, Daniel William, *"Prisoner's of Peace:" British Policy Towards Displaced Persons and Political Refugees within Occupied Germany 1945-1951*, London: University of London, 2001.
De Ménil, Lois Pattison, *Who Speaks for Europe?: The Vision of Charles de Gaulle*, New York: St.Martin's Press, 1978.
Dedman, Martin, *The Origins and Development of the European Union, 1945-95*, London/New York: Routledge, 1996.
De Rougement, Denis, *The Idea of Europe*, New York: Macmillan, 1966.
Dunn, Richard, and Mary Maples Dunn, *The World of William Penn*, Philadelphia: University of Philadelphia Press, 1986.
Dushnyck, Walter, *Refugees are People: The Plight of Europe's Displaced Persons*, New York: America Press, 1947.
Ferrell, Robert H., *Peace in Their Time: The Origins of the Kellog-Briand Pact*, New York: W.W. Norton, 1969.
Foley, Bernhard J. (ed.), *European Economies Since the Second World War*, Basingstoke: Macmillan, 1998.
Gaedicke, Herbert, and Gert von Eynern, *Die produktionswirtschaftliche Integration Europas: Eine Untersuchung über die Aussenhandelsverflechtuntg der europäischen Länder*, Berlin: Junker und Dünnhaupt, 1933.
Gallagher, Clarence, *Church Law and Church Order in Rome and Byzantium: A Comparative Study*, Aldershot: Ashgate, 2002.
Gilbert, Martin, *The Origins of the "Iron Curtain" Speech*, Fulton, Missouri: Winston Churchill Memorial/Westminster College, 1981.
Griffiths, Richard, *Explorations in OEEC History*, Paris: Organization for Economic Cooperation and Development, 1997.
Groenendijk, Kees, *In Search of Europe's Borders*, The Hague: Kluwer, 2003.

Gruner, Erich, "Die Schweizerische Eidgenossenschaft von der Französischen Revolution bis zur Reform der Verfassung," in: Schieder, Theodor (ed.), *Handbuch der Europäischen Geschichte*, Vol. 5., Stuttgart: Klett-Cotta, 1981: 968-986.

Haas, Mark L., *The Ideological Origins of Great Power Politics, 1789-1989*, Ithaca: Cornell University Press, 2005.

Hamilton, Richard F., and Holger H. Herwig, *The Origins of World War I*, Cambridge: Cambridge University Press, 2003.

Harbutt, Fraser J., *The Iron Curtain: Churchill, America and the Origins of the Cold War*, New York: Oxford University Press, 1986.

Heath, John Everett, *Place Names of the World: Europe - Historical Context, Meaning and Changes*, Basingstoke: Macmillan, 2000.

Herriot, Édouard, *The United States of Europe*, London: George Harrap, 1930.

Hitchcock, William I., *France Restored: Cold War Diplomacy and the Quest for Leadership in Europe, 1944-1954*, Chapel Hill: University of North Carolina Press, 1998.

Hitchcock, William I., *The Struggle for Europe: The Turbulent History of a Divided Continent, 1945 to the Present*, New York: Anchor Book, 2004.

Hueglin, Thomas, *Early Modern Concepts for a Late Modern World: Althusius on Community and Federalism*, Waterworld, Ont.: Wilfrid Laurier University Press, 1999.

Hoerder, Dirk, et al. (eds.), *People on the Move: Migration, Acculturation, and Ethnic Interaction in Europe and North America*, Providence: Berg, 1993.

Holtz, Uwe (ed.), *50 Jahre Europarat*, Baden-Baden: Nomos, 2000.

Hugo, Victor, *The United States of Europe*, Boston: World Peace Foundation, 1914.

Huizinga, Johan M., *Mr. Europe: A political Biography of Paul Henri Spaak*, London: Weidenfeld&Nicholson, 1961.

Jackson, Julian, *Charles de Gaulle*, London: Haus, 2003.

Jellinek, Georg, *The Rights of Minorities*, London: P.S. King&Son, 1912.

Jessop, T.E., *The Treaty of Versailles: Was it Just?*, London: Thomas Nelson, 1942.

Joll, James, *The Origins of the First World War*, London: Longman, 1984.

Jukes, Geoffrey, *The First World War*, New York: Routledge, 2003.

Kant, Immanuel, *Perpetual Peace*, translated by Benjamin F. Trueblood, Washington D.C.: American Peace Society, 1897.

Kanthoor, Willem Frans Victor, *A Chronological History of the European Union, 1946-2002*, Cheltenham: Edward Elgar, 2002.

Kelley, Judith, *Ethnic Politics in Europe: The Power of Norms and Incentives*, Princeton: Princeton University Press, 2004.

Knipping, Franz, *Der 25. März 1957: Die Einigung Europas*, Munich: Deutscher Taschenbuch Verlag, 2004.

Krebs, Gerhard, and Dieter Oberländer, *1945 in Europe and in Asia: Reconsidering the End of World War II and the Change of the World Order*, Munich: Iudicium, 1997.

Kühnhardt, Ludger, *Von der ewigen Suche nach Frieden: Immanuel Kants Vision und Europas Wirklichkeit*, Bonn: Bouvier, 1996.

Larres, Klaus, *Churchill's Cold War: The Politics of Personal Diplomacy*, New Heaven: Yale University Press, 2002.

Leboutte, René (ed.), *Migrations et Migrants dans une Perspective Historique: Permanences et Innovations*, Brussels/New York: Peter Lang, 2000.

Liddle, Peter, et al., *The Great War, 1914-1945*, London: HarperCollins, 2001.

Lipgens, Walter, *A History of European Integration*, Oxford: Clarendon Press, 1982.

Lipgens, Walter (ed.), *Documents on the History of European Integration, Vol.1.: Continental Plans for European Union, 1939-1945*, Berlin/New York: Walter de Gruyter, 1986.

Lipgens, Walter (ed.), *Documents on the History of European Integration, Vol.2: Plans for European Union in Great Britain and in Exile, 1939-1945*, Berlin/New York: Walter de Gruyter, 1986.

Lipgens, Walter (ed.), *Documents on the History of European Integration, Vol.3: The Struggle for European Union by Political Parties and Pressure Groups in Western European Countries 1945-1950*, Berlin/New York: Walter de Gruyter, 1988.

Macmillan, Margaret, *Peacemakers: Six Months that Changed the World*, London: John Murray, 2001.

May, Alex, *Europe at the Crossroads: The European Union of Federalists and the Process of European Integration, 1946-54*, London: South Bank European Papers, 1997.

Marjolin, Robert, *Architect of European Unity: Memoirs 1911-1986*, London: Weidenfeld&Nicholson, 1989.

Marwick, Arthur, et al., *Total War and Historical Change: Europe, 1914-1955*, Buckingham, PA: Open University Press, 2001.

Morrissey, Robert, *Charlemagne and France: A Thousand Years of Mythology*, Notre Dame: Notre Dame University Press, 2003.

Murray, Philomena B., and Leslie Holmes (eds.), *Europe - Rethinking the Boundaries*, Ashgate: Aldershot, 1998.

Murray, Philomena B., and Paul B. Rich (eds.), *Visions of European Unity*, Boulder: Westview Press, 1996.

Naimark, Norman, *Fires of Hatred: Ethnic Cleansing in Twentieth-Century Europe*, Cambridge, Mass.: Harvard University Press, 2001.

Naimark, Norman, *The Russians in Germany: The History of the Soviet Zone of Occupation 1945-1949*, Cambridge, Mass.: Harvard University Press, 1995.

Neiberg, Michael S., *Fighting the Great War: A Global History*, Cambridge, Mass.: Harvard University Press, 2005.

Ouin, Marc, *The OEEC and the Common Market: Why Europe needs an Economic Union of Seventeen Countries*, Paris: Organization for European Economic Cooperation, 1958.

Pagden, Anthony (ed.), *The Idea of Europe: from Antiquity to European Union*, Washington D.C.: Woodrow Wilson Center Press, 2002.

Page Moch, Leslie, *Moving Europeans: Migration in Western Europe since 1650*, Bloomington: Indiana University Press, 2003.

Sarolea, Charles, *The Policy of Sanctions and the Failure of the League of Nations*, London: International Publishing Company, 1936.

Schwimmer, Walter, *Der Traum Europa: Europa vom 19. Jahrhundert in das dritte Jahrtausend*, Berlin/Heidelberg/New York: Springer, 2004.

Shackleton, Robert, *Montesquieu: A Critical Biography*, London: Oxford University Press, 1961.

Sheehan, Michael, *The Balance of Power: History and Theory*, New York: Routledge, 1996.

Smith, M. L., and Peter M. R. Stirk (eds.), *Making the new Europe: European Unity and the Second World War*, London/New York: Pinter, 1990.

Spiering, Menno, and Michael Wintle (eds.), *Ideas of Europe since 1914: The Legacy of the First World War*, Basingstoke: Palgrave Macmillan, 2002.

Stirk, Peter M. R. (ed.), *European Unity in Context: The Interwar Period*, London/New York: Pinter, 1989.

Stirk, Peter M. R., *A History of European Integration since 1914*, London/New York: Pinter, 1996.

Stirk, Peter M. R., and David Weigall (eds.), *The Origins and Development of European Integration: A Reader and Commentary*, London/New York: Pinter, 1999.

Stirk, Peter M. R., and David Willis (eds.), *Shaping Postwar Europe: European Unity and Disunity - 1945-1957*, New York: St. Martin's Press, 1991.

Story, Joanna, *Charlemagne: Empire and Society*, Manchester: Manchester University Press, 2005.

Sworakowski, Witold S., *Bibliography of Books, Pamphlets, and Articles in Periodicals, Dealing with Federation Plans for Central and Eastern Europe, Developed during the Second World War*, Stanford: Stanford University Press, 1964.

Taylor, Alan J.P., *The Struggle for Mastery in Europe - 1848-1918*, Oxford: Clarendon Press, 1954.

Thio, Li-Ann, "Battling Balkanization: Regional Approaches Toward Minority Protection Beyond Europe," *Harvard International Law Journal*, 43.2 (2002): 409-468.

Van der Dussen, Jan, and Kevin Wilson (eds.), *The History of the Idea of Europe*, New York: Routledge, 1993.

Wentholt, Wyger, *A Study of Monetary and Economic Situations in International Relationship: Freedom of Navigation on the Rhine is a Western European Interest*, Amsterdam: W. Wentholt&Co., 1957.

Wilson, Woodrow, *8 January 1918: President Woodrow Wilson's Fourteen Points*, http://wwi.lib.byu.edu/index.php/President_Wilson%27s_Fourteen_Points.

Zurcher, Arnold J., *The Struggle to Unite Europe, 1940-1958: An Historical Account of the Development of the Contemporary European Movement from its Origin in the Pan-European Union to the Drafting of the Treaties for Euratom and the European Common Market*, Westport: Greenwood, 1975.

Zwerin, Michael, *A Case for the Balkanization of Practically Everyone: The New Nationalism*, London: Widerworld House, 1976.

Chapter X

Adshead, Maura, *Developing European Regions?: Comparative Governance Policy Networks and European Integration*, Aldershot: Ashgate, 2002.

Al Sayyad, Nezar, and Martin Castells, (eds.), *Muslim Europe or Euro-Islam: Politics, Culture, and Citizenship in the Age of Globalization*, Lanham: Lexington Books, 2002.

Annett, Anthony, et al. (eds.), *Reforming the Stability and Growth Pact*, Washington D.C.: International Monetary Fund, 2005.

Bache, Ian, and Matthew Flinders (eds.), *Multi-Level Governance*, Oxford: Oxford University Press, 2004.

Bankowski, Zenon, and Andrew Scott, *The European Union and its Order: The Legal Theory of European Integration*, Oxford: Blackwell, 2000.

Baus, Ralf Thomas, *Rechtspopulistische Parteien*, Sankt Augustin: Konrad Adenauer Stiftung, 2005.

Bellamy, Richard, and Alex Warleigh, *Citizenship and Governance in the European Union*, London: Continuum, 2001.

Bellamy, Richard, et al. (eds.), *Lineages of European Citizenship: Rights, Belongings and Participation in Eleven Nation-States*, Houndmills: Palgrave, 2004.

Bogdanor, Vernon, "A Constitution for a House Without Windows," *EU Constitution Project Newsletter*, July 2004, www.fedtrust.co.uk.

Bomberg, Elizabeth, and Alexander Stubb (eds.), *The European Union: How does it Work?*, Oxford: Oxford University Press, 2003.

Bonoli, Giuliano, et al. (eds.), *European Welfare Futures: Towards a Theory of Retrenchment*, Cambridge: Polity Press, 2000.

Bowley, Graham, "EU Bends Fiscal Rules with Treaty in Trouble," *International Herald Tribune*, March 23, 2005.

Brunila, Anne, et al. (eds.), *The Stability and Growth Pact: The Architecture of Fiscal Policy in EMU*, Houndmills: Palgrave, 2001.

Buigues, Pierre A., and Patrick Rey (eds.), *The Economics of Antitrust and Regulation in the Telecommunication Sector*, Cheltenham: Edward Elgar, 2004.

Capotorti, Francesco, *The European Union Treaty: Commentary on the Draft Adopted by the European Parliament on 14 February 1984*, Oxford: Clarendon Press, 1986.

Cafruni, Alan, and Patrick Peters (eds.), *The Union and the World: The Political Economy of a Common European Foreign Policy*, The Hague: Kluwer, 1998.

Church, Clive H., and David Phinnemore, *Understanding the European Constitution: An Intoduction to the EU Constitutional Treaty*, New York: Routledge, 2006.

Cini, Michelle, *European Union Politics*, Oxford: Oxford University Press, 2003.

Corbett, Richard, et al., "The European Parliament at Fifty: A View from the Inside," *Journal of Common Market Studies*, 41 (2003): 353-373.

Cuschieri, Marvin Andrew, *Europe's Migration Policy Towards the Mediterranean: The Need of Reconstruction of Policy-Making*, ZEI Discussion Paper C168, Bonn: Center for European Integration Studies, 2007.

De Búrca, Gráinne, *EU Law and the Welfare State: In Search of Solidarity*, Oxford: Oxford University Press, 2005.

Dinan, Desmond, *An Ever Closer Union: An Introduction in the European Integration*, Houndmills: Palgrave Macmillan, 2005 (3rd ed.).

Dobson, Lynn, and Andreas Follesdal (eds.), *Political Theory and the European Constitution*, London: Routledge, 2004.

Donnelly, Brendan, "After the European Council, a Referendum to Win," *EU Constitution Project Newsletter*, July 2004, https://fedtrust.co.uk.

Drake, Helen, *Jacques Delors: A Political Biography*, New York: Routledge, 2000.

Eliasen, Kjell A., and Marit Sjovaag (eds.), *European Telecommunication Liberalisation*, London: Routledge, 1999.

European Union, European Commission, *Trans-European Network: Implementation of the Guidelines 1998-2001*, Luxembourg: Office for Official Publications of the European Communities, 2004.

European Union, European Commission, *The Trans-European Transport Network: Revised Proposals on Guidelines and Financial Rules 2004*, Luxembourg: Office for Official Publications of the European Communities, 2004.

European Union, European Commission, *Building our Common Future: Policy Challenges and Budgetary Means of the Enlarged Union*, https://europa.eu.int/eu-lex/LexUriServ/site/eu/comm/2004/com2004_0101en02.pdf.

European Union, European Commission, *A New Start for the Lisbon Strategy*, http://ec.europa.eu/growthandjobs/pdf/COM2005_024_en.pdf.

European Union, European Commission, *Statistical Annex to European Economy*, March 16, 2005, http://ec.europa.eu/economy_finance/publications/publication477_en.pdf.

European Union, European Commission, *Eurobarometer 225: Social Values, Science and Technology*, June 2005, http://ec.europa.eu/public_opinion/archives/ebs/ebs_225_report_en.pdf.

Eurostat, *European Demography in 2003*, August 31, 2004, http://epp.eurostat.ec.europa.eu/cache/ITY_PUBLIC/3-31082004-BP/EN/3-31082004-BP-EN.PDF.

Feldstein, Martin J., *The Euro and the Stability Pact*, Cambridge, Mass.: National Bureau of Economic Research, 2005.

Fishkin, James, and Peter Laslett (eds.), *Debating Deliberative Democracy*, Malden, Mass.: Blackwell, 2003.

Frankfurter Allgemeine Zeitung, "Einstieg in die Steuerharmonisierung;" September 13, 2004: 19.

Furlong, Paul, and Andrew Cox, *European Union at the Crossroads: Problems of Implementing the Single Market Project*, Wyberton: Earlsgate Press, 1995.

Garton Ash, Timothy, *Free World: Why a Crisis of the West Reveals the Opportunity of Our Time*, London: Allen Lane, 2004.

Geddes, Andrew, *The Politics of Migration and Immigration in Europe*, London: Sage, 2003.

Green Cowles, Marie, and Desmond Dinan (eds.), *Developments in the European Union*, Houndmills: Palgrave Macmillan, 2004.

Greenwood, Justin, *Interest Representation in the European Union*, Houndmills: Palgrave Macmillan, 2003.

Hammond, Andrew, *The Balkans and the West: Constructing the European Other - 1945-2003*, Aldershot: Ashgate, 2004.

Hardy, Sally, *An Enlarged Europe: Regions in Competition?*, London: Regional Studies Association, 1995.

Hennis, Marjoleine, *Globalization and European Integration: The Changing Role of Farmers in the Common Agricultural Policy*, Lanham: Rowman&Littlefield, 2005.

Hix, Simon, *The Political System of the European Union*, London: Palgrave Macmillan, 2005 (2nd rev.ed.).

Hommers, Ina, *Die Migrationspolitik der EU,* ZEI Discussion Paper C 196, Bonn: Center for European Integration Studies, 2009.

Hooghe, Liesbet, and Gary Marks, *Multi-Level Governance and European Integration*, Lanham: Rowman&Littlefield, 2001.

Jaspers, Karl, *The European Spirit*, London: SCM Press, 1948.

Johnson, Debra, and Colin Turner (eds.), *Trans-European Networks: The Political Economy of Integrating Europe's Infrastructure*, Houndmills: Palgrave Macmillan, 1996.

Koenig, Christian, et al. (eds.), *EC Competition and Telecommunications Law*, The Hague: Kluwer, 2002.

Kok, Wim, *Facing the Challenge: The Lisbon Strategy for Growth and Employment*, Luxembourg: Office for Official Publications of the European Communities, 2004.

Kreppel, Amie, *The European Parliament and Supranational Party System: A Study in Institutional Development*, Cambridge/New York: Cambridge University Press, 2002.

Kroes, Rob, *Them and Us: Questions of Citizenship in a Globalizing World*, Urbana: University of Illinois Press, 2000.

Kupchan, Charles A. (ed.), *Nationalism and Nationalities in the New Europe*, Ithaca: Cornell University Press, 1995.

Leggewie, Claus, *The Emergence of Euro-Islam?: Mosques and Muslims in the Federal Republic of Germany*, Bad Homburg: Herbert Quandt Stiftung, 2002.

Lodge, Juliet (ed.), *The 2004 Elections to the European Parliament*, Basingstoke: Palgrave Macmillan, 2005.

Mahncke, Dieter, et al. (eds.), *European Foreign Policy: From Rhetoric to Reality?*, Brussels/New York: Peter Lang, 2004.

Marginson, Paul, and Keith Sisson (eds.), *European Integration and Industrial Relations: Multi-Level Governance in the Making*, New York: Palgrave Macmillan, 2004.

McCormick, John, *Understanding the European Union: A Concise Introduction*, Houndmills: Palgrave Macmillan, 2005 (3rd ed.).

Nugent, Neil, *The European Commission*, Houndmills: Palgrave Macmillan, 2001.

Nugent, Neil, *The Government and Politics of the European Union*, Houndmills: Palgrave Macmillan, 2003 (5th ed.).

Paton, Nic, "Europe's Crisis: It's Not Just the Politics, It's the Leadership;" *Management Issues, News and Research*, June 24 (2005), https://management-issues.com/display_page.asp?section=research&id=2273.

Pescatore, Pierre, *The Law of Integration: Emergence of a New Phenomenon in International Relations, based on the Experience of the European Communities*, Leiden: Sijthoff, 1974.

Peterson, John, and Elizabeth Bomberg, *Decision-Making in the European Union*, London: Palgrave, 1999.

Pollack, Mark A., "Delegation, Agency, and Agenda Setting in the European Community," *International Organization*, 51.1 (1997): 99-134.

Rato, Helena, *Europeanization Impact on Multi-Level Governance in Portugal: Patterns of Adaptation and Learning, 1988-1999*, Oeiras: Instituto Nacional de Administraçao, 2004.

Reid, T.R., *The United States of Europe: The New Superpower and the End of American Supremacy*, New York: Penguin Press, 2004.

Reiffenberg, Benno, *Does the European Spirit Still Live?*, Hinsdale, Ill.: H. Regnery Co., 1948.

Richardson, Jeremy, *European Union: Power and Policy-Making*, New York: Routledge, 2006 (3rd ed.).

Riketta, Michael, and Roland Wakenhut (eds.), *Europabild und Europabewusstsein: Bestandsaufnahme der europäischen Forschung und sozialpsychologische Forschungsperspektiven*, Frankfurt/London: IKO Publishers, 2002.

Sandholtz, Wayne, and Alec Stone Stewart, *European Integration and Supranational Governance*, Oxford: Oxford University Press, 1998.

Scott, Joanne, *Development Dilemmas in the European Community: Rethinking Regional Development Policy*, Buckingham: Open University Press, 1995.

Siedentop, Larry, *Democracy in Europe*, London: Penguin Press, 2000.

Snyder, Francis, *The Europeanization of Law: The Legal Effects of European Integration*, Oxford: Hart Publisher, 2000.

Steunenberg, Bernard, and Jacques Thomassen (eds.), *The European Parliament: Moving Toward Democracy in the EU*, Lanham: Rowman&Littlefield, 2002.

Tallberg, Jonas, *European Governance and Supranational Institutions: Making States Comply*, London: Routledge, 2003.

Terluin, Ida J., *Rural Regions in the EU: Exploring Differences in Economic Development*, Utrecht: Koninklijk Nederlands Aardrijkslundig Genootshap, 2001.

Tonra, Ben, and Thomas Christiansen (eds.), *Rethinking European Foreign Policy*, Manchester: Manchester University Press, 2004.

Turro, Mateu, *Going Trans-European: Planning and Financing Transport Networks for Europe*, Amsterdam: Pergamon, 1999.

Van Aaken, Anne, et al. (eds.), *Deliberation and Decision: Economics, Constitutional Theory and Deliberative Democracy*, Aldershot: Ashgate, 2004.

Van Grinsven, Peter, *The European Council under Construction: EU Top Level Decision-making at the Beginning of the New Century*, The Hague: Netherlands Institute of International Relations, 2003.

Van Schendelen, Rinus, *Machiavelli in Brussels: The Art of Lobbying in the EU*, Amsterdam: Amsterdam University Press, 2005 (2nd ed.).

Wajahat, Ali, "Europe's Leadership Crisis," *Daily Times*, August 24 (2005), https://dailytimes.com.pk/default.asp?page=story_29-6-2005_pg3_5.

Ward, David, *The European Union Democratic Deficit and the Public Sphere: An Evaluation of EU Media Policy*, Amsterdam: IOS Press, 2002.

White, Brian, *Understanding European Foreign Policy*, Houndmills: Palgrave, 2001.
Zentrum für Türkeistudien (ed.), Euro-Islam: Eine Religion etabliert sich in Europa, ZfT Aktuell, 102 (2004).
Zielonka, Jan, *Paradoxes of European Foreign Policy*, The Hague: Kluwer, 1998.

Chapter XI

Almond, Gabriel, and Sidney Verba, *The Civic Culture: Political Attitudes and Democracy in Five Nations*, Princeton: Princeton University Press, 1963.
Baimbridge, Mark, and Philip Wyman, *Fiscal Federalism and European Economic Integration*, New York: Routledge, 2003.
Beach, Derek, *The Dynamics of European Integration: Why and When EU Institutions Matter*, Houndmills: Palgrave Macmillan, 2005.
Boucher, Stephen, et al., "Europe and its Think-tanks: A Promise to be Fulfilled," *Notre Europe*, October 15, 2004, www.NotreEurope.asso.fr.
Born, Hans (ed.), *The 'Double Democratic Deficit': Parliamentary Accountability and the Use of Force under International Auspices*, Aldershot: Ashgate, 2004.
Brenner, Michael J., *Technocratic Politics and the Functionalist Theory of European Integration*, Ithaca, N.Y.: Center for International Studies Cornell University, 1969.
Cappelletti, Mauro, et al. (eds.), *Integration Through Law: Europe and the American Federal Experience*, Berlin/New York: W. de Gruyter, 1995.
Checkel, Jeffrey T., "Social Construction and European Integration," in: Christiansen, Thomas, et al. (eds.), *The Social Construction of Europe*, London: Sage Publications, 2001: 50-64.
Cini, Michelle, and Angela K. Bowne (eds.), *European Union Studies*, Houndmills: Palgrave Macmillan, 2006.
Cooper, Robert, "The Post-Modern State," in: Mark Leonard (ed.), *Re-Ordering the World: The Long-Term Implications of September 11*, London: The Foreign Policy Centre, 2002: 11-20.
Delanty, Gerard, and Chris Rumford, *Rethinking Europe: Social Theory and the Implications of Europeanization*, Abingdon: Routledge, 2005.
Deutsch, Karl W., et al., *Political Community and the North American Area: International Organization in the Light of the Historical Experience*, Princeton: Princeton University Press, 1957.
Deutsch, Karl W., *The Analysis of International Relations*, Englewood Cliffs N.J.: Prentice Hall, 1968.
Dinan, Desmond, *Encyclopedia of the European Union*, Houndmills: Palgrave Macmillan, 2005 (2nd rev.ed.).

El-Agraa, Ali M. (ed.), *The European Union: Economics and Policies*, London/New York: Prentice Hall, 2001.

Fabbrini, Sergio, "Transatlantic Constitutionalism: Comparing the United States and the European Union," *European Journal of Political Research*, 43 (2004): 547-569.

Ferguson, Niall, *Colossus: The Price of America's Empire*, New York: Penguin Press, 2004.

Follesdal, Andreas, Federalism, Stanford Encyclopedia of Philosophy, http://plato.stanford.edu/entries/federalism.

Forsyth, Murray, "The Political Theory of Federalism: The Relevance of Classical Approaches," in: Joachim Jens Hesse and Vincent Wright (eds.), *Federalizing Europe?: The Costs, Benefits, and Preconditions of Federal Political Systems*, Oxford. Oxford University Press, 1996: 25-45.

Frankfurter Allgemeine Zeitung, "Stadt der Lobbyisten," February 1, (2005): 17.

Frey, Bruno S., and Reiner Eichenberger, *The New Democratic Federalism for Europe: Functional, Overlapping, and Competing Jurisdictions*, Cheltenham: Edward Elgar, 1999.

Friedrich, Carl Joachim, and Robert R. Bowie (eds.), *Studies in Federalism*, Boston: Little, Brown, and Co., 1954.

Friedrich, Carl Joachim, *Trends in Federalism in Theory and Practice*, New York: Praeger, 1968.

Gehler, Michael et al. (eds.), *Towards a European Constitution: A Historical and Political Comparison with the United States*, Vienna: Böhlau, 2005.

Haas, Ernst B., *Beyond the Nation State: Functionalism and International Organization*, Stanford: Stanford University Press, 1964.

Haas, Ernst B., "The Study of Regional Integration: Reflections on the Joy and Anguish of Pretheorizing," in: Leon N. Lindberg and Stuart A. Scheingold (eds.), *European Integration: Theory and Research*, Cambridge, Mass.: Harvard University Press, 1971: 3-42.

Haas, Ernst B., *The Obsolescence of Regional Integration Theory*, Berkeley, Institute of International Studies Working Paper, 1975.

Hermann, Peter (ed.), *European Integration Between Institution Building and Social Process: Contributions to a Theory of Modernization and NGOs in the Context of the Development of the EU*, Commack, N.Y.: Nova Science Publishers, 1999.

Hoffmann, Stanley, "Obstinate or Obsolete? The Fate of the Nation-state and the Case of Western Europe," *Daedalus, Journal of the American Academy of Arts and Sciences*, 95 (1966): 862-915.

Hooghe, Liesbet, and Gary Marks, *Multi-Level Governance and European Integration*, Lanham: Rowman&Littlefield, 2001.

Howell, Kerry E., *Discovering the Limits of European Integration: Applying Grounded Theory*, Huntington, N.Y.: Nova Science Publishers, 2000.

Jachtenfuchs, Markus, "The Governance Approach to European Integration," *Journal of Common Market Studies*, 39.2 (2001): 245-264

Kelemen, Daniel R., *The Rules of Federalism: Institutions and Regulatory Politics in the EU and Beyond*, Cambridge, Mass.: Harvard University Press, 2004.

Kuhn, Thomas, *The Structure of Scientific Revolutions*, Chicago: University of Chicago Press, 1962.

Kühnhardt, Ludger, *Europäische Union und föderale Idee: Europapolitik in der Umbruchzeit*, Munich: C.H. Beck, 1992.

Lenaerts, Koen, et al. (eds.), *Two Hundred Years of U.S. Constitution and Thirty Years of EEC Treaty: Outlook for Comparisons*, Brussels: Story-Scientia, 1988.

Leonard, Dick, and Mark Leonard (eds.), *The Pro-European Reader*, Houndmills: Palgrave Macmillan, 2002.

Lindberg, Leon N., and Stuart A. Scheingold, *Europe's Would-Be Polity: Patterns of Change in the European Community*, Englewood Cliffs, N.J.: Prentice Hall, 1970.

Lindberg, Leon N., *The Political Dynamics of European Economic Integration*, Stanford: Stanford University Press, 1963.

Loewenstein, Karl, *Political Power and the Government Process*, Chicago: The University of Chicago Press, 1965 (2nd ed.).

Macmahon, A.W., *Federalism: Mature and Emergent*, New York: Doubleday, 1955.

Majone, Giandomenico, "The Rise of the Regulatory State in Europe," *West European Politics*, 17.3 (1994): 77-101.

Maurer, Andreas, *Die Macht des Europäischen Parlaments: Eine prospektive Analyse im Hinblick auf die kommende Wahlperiode 2004-2009*, Berlin: Stiftung Wissenschaft und Politik, 2004.

Milward, Alan, *The European Rescue of the Nation State*, London: Routledge, 1992.

Mitrany, David, *The Progress of International Government*, New Haven: Yale University Press, 1933.

Mitrany, David, *The Functional Theory of Politics*, London: Martin Robertson&Company, 1975.

Molle, Willem, *The Economics of European Integration: Theory, Practice, Policy*, Aldershot: Ashgate, 2001.

Moravcsik, Andrew, *Negotiating the Single Act: National Interests and Conventional Statecraft in the European Community*, Cambridge, Mass.: Minda de Gunzburg Center for European Studies, Harvard University, 1989.

Moravcsik, Andrew, *Why the European Community Strengthens the State: Domestic Politics and International Cooperation*, Cambridge, Mass.: Minda de Gunzburg Center for European Studies, Harvard University, 1994.

Moravcsik, Andrew, *De Gaulle and Europe: Historical Revision and Science Theory*, Cambridge, Mass.: Minda de Gunzburg Center for European Studies, Harvard University, 1998.

Moravscik, Andrew, *The Choice for Europe: Social Purpose and State Power from Messina to Maastricht*, Ithaca, N.Y.: Cornell University Press, 1998.
Morgan, Glyn, *The Idea of the European Superstate: Public Justification and European Integration*, Princeton: Princeton University Press, 2005.
Murray, Philomena, "Towards a Research Agenda on the European Union as a Model of Regional Integration," *Asia-Pacific Journal of EU Studies*, 2.1 (2004): 33-51.
Nelsen, Brent F., and Alexander Stubb (eds.), *The European Union: Readings on the Theory and Practice of European Integration*, Houndmills: Palgrave, 2003.
Nicolaidis, Kalypso, and Robert Howse (eds.), *The Federal Vision: Legitimacy and Levels of Governance in the United States and the European Union*, New York: Oxford University Press, 2001.
Peterson, John, "Decision-making in the European Union: Towards a Framework for Analysis," *Journal of European Public Policy*, 2.1 (1995): 69-94.
Peterson, John, and Elizabeth Bomberg, *Decision-Making in the European Union*, London: Palgrave, 1999.
Pollack, Mark, "Delegation, Agency, and Agenda Setting in the European Community," *International Organization*, 51.1 (1997): 99-134.
Pollack, Mark A., and Gregory Schaffer (eds.), *Transatlantic Governance in the Global Economy*, Lanham: Rowman&Littlefield, 2000.
Pollack, Mark A., *International Relations Theory and European Integration*, Fiesole: European University Institute, 2000.
Pollack, Marc, *The Engines of European Integration: Delegation, Agency and Agenda Setting in the European Union*, Oxford: Oxford University Press, 2003.
Richardson, Jeremy J. (ed.), *European Union: Power and Policy-making*, London/New York: Routledge, 1996.
Risse-Kappen, Thomas, "Exploring the Nature of the Beast: International Relations Theory and Comparative Policy Analysis Meet the European Union," *Journal of Common Market Studies*, 34.1 (1996): 53-80.
Rosamond, Ben, *Theories of European Integration*, Houndmills: Palgrave, 2000.
Sandholtz, Wayne, and Alec Stone Sweet (eds.), *European Integration and Supranational Governance*, Oxford: Oxford University Press, 1998.
Sbragia, Alberta (ed.), *Euro-Politics*, Washington D.C.: Brookings Institution, 1992.
Scharpf, Fritz W., "The Joint-Decision Trap: Lessons from German Federalism and European Integration," *Public Administration*, 66 (1988): 239-278.
Schmitter, Philippe, "A Revised Theory of European Integration," in: Lindberg, Leon N., and Stuart A. Scheingold (eds.), *European Integration: Theory and Research*, Cambridge, Mass.: Harvard University Press, 1971: 232-264.
Stehn, Jürgen, *Towards a European Constitution: Fiscal Federalism and the Allocation of Economic Competencies*, Kiel: Institute of World Economies, 2002.

Verdun, Amy, *The Euro: European Integration Theory and Economic and Monetary Union*, Lanham: Rowman&Littlefield, 2002.

Wakonen, Jouko, *Implications of Federalism and the Principle of Subsidiarity in the Case of Science and Technology Development in Europe*, Turku: Turun yliopisto, 1995.

Waltz, Kenneth, *Theory of International Politics*, New York: McGraw Hill, 1979.

Wallace, William (ed.), *The Dynamics of European Integration*, London: Pinter, 1990.

Wessels, Wolfgang, "An Ever Closer Fusion: A Macropolitical View on Integration Processes," *Journal of Common Market Studies*, 35.2 (1997): 267-301.

Wiener, Antje, and Thomas Diez, *European Integration Theory*, Oxford: Oxford University Press, 2004.

Wind, Marlene, *Europe Towards a Post-Hobbesian Order?: A Constructivist Theory of European Integration, or How to Explain European Integration as an Unintended Consequence of Rational State-Action*, Fiesole: European University Institute, 1996.

Chapter XII

Abernethy, David B., *The Dynamics of Global Dominance: European Overseas Empires, 1415-1980*, New Haven: Yale University Press, 2000.

Ahrens, Geert-Hinrich, *Diplomacy on the Edge: Containment of Ethnic Conflicts and the Minorities Working Group of the Conferences on Yugoslavia*, Washington D.C.: Woodrow Wilson Center Press, 2007.

Anderson, Benedict R., *Imagined Communities: Reflections on the Origin and Spread of Nationalism*, London/New York: Verso, 1991.

Arendt, Hannah, "On the Nature of Totalitarianism: An Essay in Understanding," in: Arendt, Hannah, *Essays in Understanding 1930-1954*, New York: Harcourt, Brace and Company, 1994: 328-360.

Bairner, Alan, *Sport, Nationalism, and Globalization: European and North American Perspectives*, Albany: State University of New York Press, 2001.

Behning, Ute, *Trends of Europeanization in Social Welfare Politics*, Wien: Institut für Höhere Studien, 2002.

Bellamy, Richard, and Alex Warleigh, *Citizenship and Governance in the European Union*, London/New York: Continuum, 2005.

Benhabib, Seyla, "On European Citizenship," *Dissent*, 45.4 (1998): 107-109.

Betten, Lammy, "The EU Charter on Fundamental Rights: A Trojan Horse or a Mouse?," *International Journal of Comparative Labour Law and Industrial Relations*, 17.2 (2001): 151-164.

Biermann, Rafael, *Schattenjahre: Das Scheitern der internationalen Konflikteinwirkung im Kosovo vor Kriegsbeginn*, Paderborn: Schöningh, 2005.

Booth, W. James, "Communities of Memory: On Identity, Memory, and Debt," *The American Political Science Review*, 93.2 (1999): 249-263.

Börzel, Tanja A., and Thomas Risse, *When Europe Hits Home: Europeanization and Domestic Change*, Fiesole: European University Institute, 2000.

Bracher, Karl Dietrich, *The Age of Ideologies: A History of Political Thought in the Twentieth Century*, London: Palgrave Macmillan, 1984.

Bracher, Karl Dietrich, *Europa in der Krise: Innengeschichte und Weltpolitik seit 1917*, Frankfurt/Berlin/Vienna: Propyläen, 1979.

Calleo, David P., *Rethinking Europe's Future*, Princeton/Oxford: Princeton University Press, 2001.

Delouche, Frédéric (ed.), *Illustrated History of Europe: A Unique Portrait of Europe's Common History*, London: Cassell, 2001.

Dunkerley, David, et al. (eds.), *Changing Europe: Identities, Nations and Citizens*, London/New York, Routledge, 2002.

Emanuel, Susan, "A Community of Culture? The European Television Channel," *History of European Ideas*, 21.2 (1995): 169-176.

European Union, "Treaty of Lisbon Amending the Treaty on European Union and the Treaty Establishing the European Community," *Official Journal of the European Union*, C 306/Vol.50, Luxembourg: Office for Official Publications of the European Communities, 2007, http://eur-lex.europa.eu/JOHtml.do?uri=OJ:C:2007:306:SOM:EN:HTML.

European Union, European Commission, *Eurobarometer 1*, July 1974, http://ec.europa.eu/public_opinion/archives/eb/eb1/eb1_en.pdf.

European Union, European Commission, *Euro-Barometer: European Election Special*, May 21, 1984, http://ec.europa.eu/public_opinion/archives/eb/eb21/eb21_en.pdf.

European Union, European Commission, *Eurobarometer 41*, July 1994, http://ec.europa.eu/public_opinion/archives/eb/eb41/eb41_en.pdf.

European Union, European Commission, *Eurobarometer Spring 2004: Public Opinion in the European Union*, July 2004, http://ec.europa.eu/public_opinion/archives/eb/eb61/eb61_en.pdf.

European Union, European Commission, *Eurobarometer 68: Public Opinion in the European Union*, December 2007, http://ec.europa.eu/public_opinion/archives/eb/eb68/eb68_first_en.pdf.

European Union. European Commission, *Eurobarometer 71: Public Opinion in the European Union,* September 2009, https://ec.europa.eu/public_opinion/archives/eb/eb71_std_part1.pdf.

European Union. European Commission, *Eurobarometer 72: Public Opinion in the European Union,* November 2009, https:// ec.europa.eu/public_opinion/archives/eb/eb72/eb72_first_en.pdf.

Featherstone, Kevin, and Claudio M. Radaelli (eds.), *The Politics of Europeanization*, Oxford/New York: Oxford University Press, 2003.

Fichte, Johann Gottlieb, *Der geschlossene Handelsstaat (1800)*, Hamburg: Meiner, 1979.

Fossum, John Eric, and Philip R. Schlesinger (eds.), *The European Union and the Public Sphere: A Communicative Space in the Making*, Abingdon: Routledge, 2007.

Garcia, Soledad, *European Identity and the Search for Legitimacy*, London: Continuum International Publishing, 1993.

Gehler, Michael, *Zeitgeschichte im dynamischen Mehrebenensystem: zwischen Regionalisierung, Nationalstaat, Europäisierung, internationaler Arena und Globalisierung*, Bochum: Dieter Winkler, 2001.

Gellner, Ernest, *Culture, Identity, and Politics*, Cambridge: Cambridge University Press, 1987.

Gleason, Abbott, *Totalitarianism: The Inner History of the Cold War*, New York: Oxford University Press, 1995.

Green Cowles, Maria, et al. (eds.), *Transforming Europe: Europeanization and Domestic Change*, Ithaca: Cornell University Press, 2001.

Haltern, Ulrich, "Pathos and Patina: The Failure and Promise of Constitutionalism in the European Imagination," *European Law Journal*, 9 (2003): 14-44.

Harmsen, Robert, and Thomas M. Wilson, *Europeanization: Institution, Identities and Citizenship*, Amsterdam: Rodopi, 2000.

Herder, Johann Gottfried, *Philosophical Writings*, Trans. Michael N. Forster, Cambridge/New York: Cambridge University Press, 2002.

Herf, Jeffrey, *Divided Memory: The Nazi Past in the two Germanys*, Cambridge, Mass.: Harvard University Press, 1997.

Herrmann, Richard K. et al. (eds.), *Transnational Identities: Becoming European in the EU*, Lanham: Rowman&Littlefield, 2005.

Hodess, Robin B., "The Role of News Media in European Integration: A Framework of Analysis for Political Science," *Res Publica*, 39.2 (1997): 215-227.

Holmes, Leslie (ed.), *Citizenship and Identity in Europe*, Ashgate: Aldershot, 1999.

Howe, Paul, "A Community of Europeans: The Requisite Underpinnings," *Journal of Common Market Studies*, 33.1 (1995): 27-46.

Hroch, Miroslav, *Das Europa der Nationen: Die moderne Nationsbildung im europäischen Vergleich*, Göttingen: Vandenhoeck&Ruprecht, 2005.

Huntington, Samuel P., *American Politics: The Promise of Disharmony*, Cambridge, Mass.: Belknap Press, 1981.

Jensen, Ole B., and Tim Richardson, *Making European Space: Mobility, Power and Territorial Identity*, London: Routledge, 2004.

Jones, Alun, and Julian Clark, *Europe and Europeanization: An Empirical Exploration*, Abingdon: Routledge, 2007.

Jordan, Andrew, *The Europeanization of British Environmental Policy: A Departmental Perspective*, Basingstoke: Palgrave Macmillan, 2002.

Kaelble, Hartmut, "The Historical Rise of a European Public Sphere," *Journal of European Integration*, 8.2 (2002): 9-22.

Kostakopoulou, Theodora, Citizenship, Identity, and Immigration in the European Union: Between Past and Future, Manchester/New York: Manchester University Press, 2001.

Kostakopoulou, Theodora, "Why a 'Community of Europeans' could be a Community of Exclusion," *Journal of Common Market Studies*, 35.2 (1997): 301-309.

Kühnhardt, Ludger, "An EU Constitutional Twist: No Representation Without Taxation," *European Affairs* 4.2 (2003): 76-81.

Kühnhardt, Ludger, et al., *Das Weimarer Dreieck*, ZEI Discussion Paper C72, Bonn: Center for European Integration Studies, 2000.

Kühnhardt, Ludger, *Constituting Europe: Identity, Institution-Building and the Search for a Global Role*, Baden-Baden: Nomos, 2003.

Kühnhardt, Ludger, *Erweiterung und Vertiefung: Die Europäische Union im Neubeginn*, Baden-Baden: Nomos, 2005.

McLaren, Lauren M., *Identity, Interests and Attitudes to European Integration*, Houndmills: Palgrave Macmillan, 2006.

Meehan, Elisabeth, *Citizenship and the European Union*, ZEI Discussion Paper C63, Bonn: Center for European Integration Studies, 2000.

Mill, John Stuart, *Considerations on Representative Government*, South Bend: Gateway, 1962.

Milward, Alan, *The European Rescue of the Nation-State*, London/New York: Routledge, 1992.

Naimark, Norman, *Fires of Hatred: Ethnic Cleansing in Twentieth-Century Europe*, Cambridge, Mass: Harvard University Press, 2001.

Nessler, Volker, *Europäische Willensbildung: Die Fraktionen im Europaparlament zwischen nationalen Interessen, Parteipolitik und Europäischer Integration*, Schwalbach: Wochenschau Verlag, 1997.

Odermatt, Peter, "The Use of Symbols in the Drive for European Integration," in: Leersen, Joseph Th., and Menno Spiering (eds.), *National Identity: Symbol and Representation*, Amsterdam: Rodopi, 1999: 217-240.

Pagden, Anthony (ed.), *The Idea of Europe: From Antiquity to the European Union*, Washington D.C.: Woodrow Wilson Center Press, 2002.

Pommerin, Reiner, "Die europäische Hauptstadt," in: Salewski, Michael (ed.), *Nationale Identität und Europäische Einigung*, Göttingen: Muster-Schmidt-Verlag, 1991: 18-31.

Popp, Susanne, "Auf dem Weg zu einem europäischen 'Geschichtsbild': Anmerkungen zur Entstehung eines gesamteuropäischen Bilderkanons," *Aus Politik und Zeitgeschichte*, 7.8 (2004): 23-32.

Pöttering, Hans-Gert, *Defending Europe's Values – For a Citizens' Europe*, Program Speech to the European Parliament, Strassbourg, February 13, 2007, https://europarl.europa.eu/president/defaulten.htm?home.

Ratzinger, Joseph Cardinal (Pope Benedict XVI), Homily "Pro Eligiendo Romano Pontifice," Vatican, April 18, 2005, https://vatican.va/gpll/documents/homily-pro-eligiendo-pontifice_200.

Reid, T.R., *The United States of Europe: The New Superpower and the End of American Supremacy*, New York: Penguin Press, 2004.

Ross, George, and Andrew Martin, *European integration and the Europeanization of Labor*, Madrid: Centro de Estudios Avanzados en Ciencias Sociales, 1998.

Semetko, Holli A., et al., "Europeanised Politics, Europeanised Media? European Integration and Political Communication," *West European Politics*, 23.4 (2000): 121-141.

Schild, Joachim, "Europäisierung nationaler politischer Identitäten in Deutschland und Frankreich," *Aus Politik und Zeitgeschichte*, 3.4 (2003): 31-40.

Schout, Adriaan, *Internal Management of External Relations: The Europeanization of an Economic Affairs Ministry*, Maastricht: European Institute for Public Administration, 1999.

Scully, Roger, *Becoming Europeans? Attitudes, Behaviour and Socialization in the European Parliament*, Oxford: Oxford University Press, 2005.

Shaw, Josephine, *Citizenship of the Union: Towards Post-National Membership?*, Jean Monnet Working Paper Series 6, Cambridge, Mass.: Harvard Law School, 1997.

Smith, Mitchell P., *Who are the Agents of Europeanization? EC Competition Policy and Germany's Public Law Banks*, Fiesole, European University Institute, 2001.

Sternberger, Dolf, *Verfassungspatriotismus*, Frankfurt/Main: Insel Verlag, 1990.

Steunenberg, Bernard, and Jacques Thomassen (eds.), *The European Parliament: Moving Toward Democracy in the EU*, Lanham: Rowman&Littlefield, 2002.

Taylor, Paul, *The End of European Integration: Anti-Europeanism Examined*, Abingdon: Routledge, 2007.

De Tocqueville, Alexis, *Democracy in America*, Trans. Harvey C. Mansfield and Delba Winthrop, Chicago: University of Chicago Press, 2000.

Vibert, Frank, *Europe Simple Europe Strong: The Future of European Governance*, Cambridge: Polity Press, 2001.

Weiler, Joseph H. H., and Marlene Wind (eds.), *European Constitutionalism Beyond the State*, Cambridge: Cambridge University Press, 2003.

Wilson, Kevin, and Jan van der Dussen (eds.), *What is Europe? The History of the Idea of Europe*, London/New York: Routledge, 1995.

Chapter XIII

Asmus, Ronald D., and Kenneth M. Pollack, "The New Transatlantic Project," *Policy Review*, 115 (2002): 3-18.

Aggestam, Lisbeth, and Adrian Hyde-Price (eds.), *Security and Identity in Europe: Exploring the New Agenda*, Houndmills: Macmillan Press, 2000.

Aydin, Mustafa, *Europe's Next Shore: the Black Sea Region after EU Enlargement*, Occasional Paper 53, Paris: European Union Institute for Security Studies, 2004.

Bacia, Horst, "Zwischen Einflussnahme und Drohungen: Das Dilemma der EU in der Darfur-Krise," *Frankfurter Allgemeine Zeitung*, September 4, 2004.

Batt, Judy, et al., *Partners and Neighbours: A CFSP for a Wider Europe*, Chaillot Papers 64, Paris, European Union Institute for Security Studies, 2003.

Becker, Peter, *Der EU-Finanzrahmen 2007-2013: Auf dem Weg zu einer europäischen Finanzverfassung oder Fortsetzung der nationalen Nettosaldopolitik?*, SWP-Studie 36, Berlin: Stiftung Wissenschaft und Politik, 2005.

Bernstein, Richard, "EU Diplomacy, the Way it's Supposed to Happen," *International Herald Tribune*, November 26, 2004.

Biscop, Sven, and Jan Joel Andersson (eds.), *The EU and the European Security Strategy*, Abingdon: Routledge, 2007.

Bredow, Wilfried von, et al. (eds.), *European Security*, Houndmills: Macmillan Press, 1997.

Brehon, Nicolas-Jean, "L'impôt européen," in: Lefebvre, Maxime (ed.), *Quel Budget Européen à l'horizon 2013? Moyens et politiques d'une Union elargie*, Paris: Institut Français des Relations Internationales, 2004: 161-180.

Bretherton, Charlotte, and John Vogler, *The European Union as a Global Actor*, London/New York: Routledge, 1999.

Brimmer, Esther (ed.), *The EU's Search for a Strategic Role: ESDP and its Implications for Transatlantic Relations*, Washington, D.C.: Center for Transatlantic Relations, 2002.

Calleya, Stephen, *Evaluating Euro-Mediterranean Relations*, London: Routledge, 2005.

Carbone, Maurizio, *The European Union and International Development: The Politics of Foreign Aid*, Abingdon: Routledge, 2007.

Carlsnaes, Walter et al. (eds.), *Contemporary European Foreign Policy*, London: Sage, 2004.

Colson, Bruno, *Europe: Repenser les Alliances*, Paris: Institut de Stratégie Comparée/Economia, 1995.

Crowe, Brian, "A Common European Foreign Policy After Iraq?," *International Affairs*, 793 (2003): 533-546.

Cuschieri, Marvin Andrew, *Europe's Migration Policy Towards the Mediterranean: The Need of Reconstruction of Policy-Making*, ZEI Discussion Paper C168, Bonn: Center for European Integration Studies, 2007.

Dannreuther, Roland (ed.), *European Union Foreign and Security Policy: Towards a Neighbourhood Strategy*, London: Routledge, 2004.

Duke, Simon (ed.), *The EU and Crisis Management: Development and Prospects*, Maastricht: European Institute for Public Administration, 2002.

Duke, Simon, "Preparing for European Diplomacy?," *Journal of Common Market Studies*, 40.5 (2002): 849-870.

Dwan, Renata (ed.), *Building Security in Europe's New Borderlands: Subregional Cooperation in the Wider Europe*, Armonk, New York/London: EastWest Institute, 1999.

Elting, John R., *The Super-Strategists: Great Captains, Theorists, and Fighting Men who Have Shaped the History of Warfare*, New York: Charles Scribner's Sons, 1985.

Frankfurter Allgemeine Zeitung, "Entwicklungsfinanzierung bleibt nationale Aufgabe," September 9, 2005.

Frankfurter Allgemeine Zeitung, "Europäer wollen Weltmacht sein," September 7, 2005.

European Union, *A Secure Europe in a Better World: European Security Strategy*, Paris: EU Institute for Security Studies, 2003.

European Union, "Treaty of Lisbon Amending the Treaty on European Union and the Treaty Establishing the European Community," *Official Journal of the European Union*, C 306/Vol.50, Luxembourg: Office for Official Publications of the European Communities, 2007,
https://eur-lex.europa.eu/JOHtml.do?uri=OJ:C: 2007:306:SOM:EN:HTML.

European Union, European Commission, *European Neighbourhood Policy: Strategy Paper*, May 12, 2004,
http://ec.europa.eu/world/enp/pdf/strategy/strategy_paper_en.pdf.

European Union, European Commission, *EU Strategic Partnership with the Mediterranean and the Middle East: Final Report*, June 23, 2004,
http://ec.europa.eu/external_relations/euromed/publication/2004/euromed_report_78_en.pdf.

European Union, European Commission, *A World Player: The European Union's External Relations*, July 2004,
http://ec.europa.eu/publications/booklets/move/47/en.pdf.

European Union, European Commission, *Green Paper "Confronting demographic change: a new solidarity between the generations"*, March 16, 2005,
http://eur-lex.europa.eu/LexUriServ/LexUriServ.do?uri=COM:2005:0094:FIN:EN:PDF.

European Union Institute for Security Studies (ed.), *European Defense: A Proposal for a White Paper, Report of an Independent Task Force*, Paris: EU Institute for Security Studies, 2004.

Eurostat, *European Demography in 2003*, August 31, 2004, https://epp.eurostat.cec.eu.int/cache/ITY-PUBLIC/3/31082004-BP/EN/3-31082004-BP-EN.PDF.

Everts, Steven, "Two Cheers for the EU's New Security Strategy," *International Herald Tribune*, December 9, 2003.

Faria, Fernanda, *Crisis Management in Sub-Saharan Africa: The Role of the European Union*, Occasional Paper 51, Paris, EU Institute for Security Studies, 2004.

Feiler, Bruce, Abraham: *A Journey into the Heart of Three Faiths*, New York: HarperCollins, 2002.

Ferguson, Niall, *Colossus: The Price of America's Empire*, New York: Penguin Press, 2004.

Ferrero-Waldner, Benita, *The EU in the World*, Speech, Brussels, February 2, 2006, http://europa.eu/rapid/pressReleasesAction.do?reference=SPEECH/06/59&format=HTML&aged=0&language=EN&guiLanguage=en.

Foster, Georg D., "Research, Writing, and the Mind of the Strategist," *Joint Force Quarterly*, 14.7 (1996): 111.

Fukuyama, Francis, "Re-Envisioning Asia," *Foreign Affairs*, 84.1 (2005): 75-87.

Garton Ash, Timothy, *Free World: Why a Crisis in the West Reveals the Opportunity of Our Time*, London: Allen Lane, 2004.

Gasteyger, Curt (ed.), *An Ambiguous Power: The European Union in a Changing World*, Gütersloh: Bertelsmann Foundation Publishers, 1996.

Geographica Slovenica (ed.), *Political Geography in the twenty-first century: Understanding the Place, Looking Ahead*, Ljubljana: Institute of Geography, 2001.

Gillespie, Richard and Richard Youngs (eds.), *The European Union and Democracy Promotion: The Case of North Africa*, London: Frank Cass, 2002.

Ginsberg, Roy H., *The European Union in International Politics: Baptism by Fire*, Lanham/Boulder/New York/Oxford: Rowman&Littlefield, 2001.

Goddard, C. Roe, et al. (eds.), *International Political Economy: State-Market Relations in a Changing Global Order*, Basingstoke: Palgrave Macmillan, 2003.

Gordon, Philipp H., and Jeremy Shapiro, *Allies at War: America, Europe and the Crisis over Iraq*, New York: MacGraw-Hill, 2004.

Gray, Colin S., *Modern Strategy*, Oxford: Oxford University Press, 1999.

Gray, Colin S., *Strategy for Chaos: Revolutions in Military Affairs and the Evidence of History*, London/Portland: Frank Cass, 2002.

Grevi, Giovanni et.al (eds.), *European Security and Defense Policy: The first 10 years (1999-2008),* Paris: The European Union Institute for Security Studies, 2009.

Hill, Christopher, *The Actors in Europe's Foreign Policy*, London/New York: Routledge, 1996.

Hindess, Barry, *Political Choice and Social Structure: An Analysis of Actors, Interests and Rationality*, Aldershot: Edwar Elgar, 1989.

Hirschman, Albert, *The Passions and the Interests: Political Arguments for Capitalism before its Triumph*, Princeton: Princeton University Press, 1977.

Holland, Martin (ed.), *Common Foreign and Security Policy: The Record and Reforms*, London/Washington D.C.:Pinter, 1997.

Holland, Martin, and Natalia Chaban (eds.), *The European Union and the Asia-Pacific*, Abingdon: Routledge, 2007.

Jain, Rajendra K. (ed.), *The European Union in a Changing World*, New Delhi: Radiant Publishers, 2002.

James, Andrew D., "European Armaments Cooperation: Lessons for a Future European Armaments Agency," *The International Spectator*, 38.4 (2003): 59-74.

Johansson-Nogués, Elisabeth, "The Fifteen and the Accession States in the UN General Assembly: what Future for European Foreign Policy in the Coming Together of the 'Old' and 'New' Europe?," *European Foreign Affairs Review*, 9.1 (2004): 67- 92.

Kasekamp, Andres (ed.), *Organizing Europe's Place in World Affairs: The European Union's Common Foreign and Security Policy*, Tartu: Department of Political Science, 2001.

Kennedy, Paul, *Grand Strategies in War and Peace*, New Haven/London: Yale University Press, 1991.

Keohane, Daniel, *Europe's New Defense Agency*, London: Centre for European Reform, 2004.

Keohane, Robert O., and Joseph S. Nye, *Power and Interdependence: World Politics in Transition*, Glenview: HarperCollins College Publishers, 1989.

Koechlin, Jérome, *L'Europe a-t-elle une adresse?*, Geneva: Edition Georg, 2003.

Koons, Robert C., *Paradoxes of Belief and Strategic Rationality*, Cambridge/New York: Cambridge University Press, 1991.

Krahmann, Elke, *Multilevel Networks in European Foreign Policy*, Aldershot: Ashgate, 2003.

Kühnhardt, Ludger, *The Lakes of Europe*, ZEI Discussion Paper C104, Bonn: Center for European Integration Studies, 2002.

Kühnhardt, Ludger, *System-Opening and Cooperative Transformation of the Greater Middle East: A New Trans-Atlantic Project and a Joint Euro-Atlantic-Arab Task*, EUROMESCO Papers 26, Lisbon: Euro-Mediterranean Study Commision, 2003.

Lenzi, Guido, *Paradoxes of European Foreign Policy: Defining the European Security Policy*, Fiesole: European University Institute, 1997.

Lieb, Julia, and Andreas Maurer, *Europas Rolle in der Welt stärken: Optionen für ein kohärenteres Aussenhandeln der Europäischen Union*, SWP-Studie S15, Berlin: Stiftung Wissenschaft und Politik, 2007.

Lindstrom, Gustav, *Enter the EU Battlegroups*, Chaillot Paper 97, Paris: European Union Institute for Security Studies, 2007.

Lotter, Christoph, and Susanne Peters (eds.), *The Changing European Security Environment*, Weimar/Cologne/Vienna: Böhler, 1996.

Luif, Paul, *EU Cohesion in the UN General Assembly*, Occasional Paper 49, Paris: European Union Institute for Security Studies, 2003.

Luttwak, Edward N., *Strategy: The Logic of War and Peace*, Cambridge, Mass.: The Belknap Press, 1987.

Macrae, Duncan, "Defense-European Arms Agency – One Step Forward," *Interavia, Business and Technology*, 59 (2004): 41-42.

Mahncke, Dieter, et al. (eds.), *European Foreign Policy: From Rhetoric to Reality?*, Brussels: Peter Lang, 2004.

Marchetti, Andreas (ed.), *Ten Years Euro-Mediterranean Partnership: Defining European Interests for the Next Decade*, ZEI Discussion Paper C154, Bonn: Center for European Integration Studies, 2005.

Marchetti, Andreas, *The European Neighbourhood Policy: Foreign Policy at the EU's Periphery*, ZEI Discussion Paper C158, Bonn: Center for European Integration Studies, 2006.

Marsh, Steve, and Hans Mackenstein (eds.), *The International Relations of the European Union*, Edinburgh: Pearsons, 2005.

Frankfurter Allgemeine Zeitung, "Mehr Geld für Europas Nachbarn," December 5, 2006.

Meier, Christian, *Nach dem Gipfel von Den Haag: Russland und das neue Modell der Partnerschaft mit der EU*, Berlin: Stiftung Wissenschaft und Politik, 2004.

Meiers, Franz-Josef, *Transatlantic Relations after the U.S. Elections: From Rift to Harmony?*, ZEI Discussion Paper C140, Bonn: Center for European Integration Studies, 2004.

Missiroli, Antonio, *CFSP, Defense and Flexibility*, Paris: Institute for Security Studies, 2000.

Momah, Sam, *Global Strategy: From its Genesis to the Post-Cold War Era*, Lagos: Vista Books, 1994.

Musu, Constanza, "European Foreign Policy: A Collective Policy or a Policy of 'Converging Parallels'?," *European Foreign Affairs Review*, 8 (2003): 35-49.

Oatley, Thomas, *International Political Economy: Interests and Institutions in the Global Economy*, New York: Longman, 2004.

O'Brennan, John, *The EU and the Western Balkans*, Abingdon: Routledge, 2007.

Ortega, Martin (ed.), *Global Views on the European Union*, Chaillot Paper 72, Paris: European Union Institute for Security Studies, 2004.

Ortega, Martin (ed.), *The European Union and the United Nations: Partners in Effective Multilateralism*, Chaillot Paper 78, Paris: European Union Institute for Security Studies, 2005.

Ortega, Martin (ed.), *Building the Future: The EU's Contribution to Global Governance*, Chaillot Paper 100, Paris: European Union Institute for Security Studies, 2007.

Parsons, Craig, *A Certain Idea of Europe*, Ithaca/London: Cornell University Press, 2003.

Pflüger, Friedbert, *Ein neuer Weltkrieg? Die islamistische Herausforderung des Westens*, Munich: Deutsche Verlags-Anstalt, 2004.

Rehn, Olli, *Europe's Next Frontiers*, Baden-Baden: Nomos, 2007.

Reid, T.R., *The United States of Europe: The New Superpower and the End of American Supremacy*, New York: Penguin Press, 2004.

Reiter, Erich, "Die Sicherheitsstrategie der EU," *Aus Politik und Zeitgeschichte*, B 3.4 (2004): 26-31.

Roberts, J. M., *The Penguin History of the Twentieth Century: The History of the World 1901 to the Present*, London: Penguin Books, 1999.

Rothgeb Jr., John M., *Defining Power: Influence and Force in the Contemporary International System*, New York: St. Martin's Press, 1992.

Rühl, Lothar, *ESDP and Intervention Strategies in Reaction to US and NATO*, ZEI Discussion Paper C137, Bonn: Center for European Integration Studies, 2004.

Sauder, Axel, *Souveränität und Integration: Französische und deutsche Konzeptionen europäischer Sicherheit nach dem Ende des Kalten Krieges (1990-1993)*, Baden-Baden: Nomos, 1995.

Schlotter, Peter (ed.), *Europa – Macht – Frieden? Zur Politik der "Zivilmacht Europa"*, Baden-Baden: Nomos, 2003.

Selten, Reinhard, *Models of Strategic Rationality*, Dordrecht/Boston: Kluwer, 1988.

Smith, Karen E., *European Union Foreign Policy in a Changing World*, Oxford: Polity, 2003.

Smith, Michael E., *Europe's Foreign and Security Policy: The Institutionalization of Cooperation*, Cambridge: Cambridge University Press, 2004.

Telò, Mario, Europe: *A Civilian Power? European Union, Global Governance, World Order*, Houndmills: Palgrave Macmillan, 2006.

Tiersky, Ronald (ed.), *Europe today: National politics, European integration, and European Security*, Lanham: Rowman&Littlefield, 1999.

Tocci, Nathalie, *The EU and Conflict Resolution: Promoting Peace in the Backyard*, Abingdon: Routledge, 2007.

Trubowitz, Peter, et al. (eds.), *The Politics of Strategic Adjustment - Ideas, Institutions, and Interests*, New York: Columbia University Press, 1998.

Truman, David Bicknell, *The Government Process: Political Interests and Public Opinion*, Berkeley: Institute of Governmental Studies, 1993.

Tunander, Ola, et al. (ed.), *Geopolitics in Post-Wall Europe: Security, Territory and Identity*, Oslo: PRIO, 1997.

U.S. National Security Strategy, *A Balance of Power that Favors Freedom*, December 2002, http://usinfo.state.gov/journals/itps/1202/ijpe/pj7-4rice.htm.

Vilanova, Pere, and Nuria Fernandez, *Europa: El debate sobre defensa y seguridad*, Barcelona: Universidad de Barcelona, 2001.

Von Clausewitz, Carl, *On War*, Princeton: Princeton University Press, 1976.

Wagner, Wolfgang, "Why the EU's Common Foreign and Security Policy will Remain Intergovernmental: a Rationalist Institutional Choice Analysis of European Crisis Management Policy," *Journal of European Public Policy*, 10.4 (2003): 576-595.

Weng, Daniel, *Zivil-militärische Zusammenarbeit in der Europäischen Union*, Berlin: Stiftung Wissenschaft und Politik, 2004.

Wessels, Ramses A., *The European Union's Foreign and Security Policy: A Legal Institutional Perspective*, The Hague/Boston: Kluwer, 1999.

Whitman, Richard G., *From Civilian Power to Superpower? The International Identity of the European Union*, Houndmills: Macmillan Press, 1998.

Wind, Marlene, *Sovereignty and European Integration: Towards a Post-Hobbesian Order*, Houndmills: Palgrave, 2001.

Winn, Neil, and Christopher Lord, *EU Foreign Policy Beyond the Nation-State: Joint Actions and Institutional Analysis of the Common Foreign and Security Policy*, Houndmills: Basingstoke, 2001.

Zaborowski, Macin (ed.), *Friends Again?: EU-US Relations After the Crisis*, Paris: European Union Institute for Security Studies, 2006.

Zweig, Stefan, *The World of Yesterday*, New York: Barnes and Noble, 1990.

Conclusion

Close, Paul, and Emiko Ohki-Close, *Supranationalism in the New World Order: Global Processes Reviewed*, Houndmills: Macmillan, 1999.

Koesler, Ariane, and Martin Zimmek (eds.), *Global Voices of Regional Integration*, ZEI Discussion Paper C 176, Bonn: Center for European Integration Studies, 2007.

Index

The author

Ludger Kühnhardt, born 1958, has been Director at the Center for European Integration Studies (ZEI) of Bonn University since 1997. Prior to this, he was Professor of Political Science at Freiburg University, where he also served as Dean of his faculty. He has been a Visiting Professor at Stanford University, Dartmouth College, Seoul National University, St.Antony's College Oxford, College of Europe (Bruges), Cape Town University and Jena University. He regularly lectures at the Catholic University Milan (ASERI), the Diplomatic Academy Vienna and the Mediterranean Academy of Diplomatic Studies Malta. Prof. Kühnhardt was a Public Policy Scholar at the Woodrow Wilson International Center for Scholars in Washington D.C. and has served as speechwriter for former German President Richard von Weizsäcker. Author of more than thirty books, he has been advisor to the Secretary General of the Council of Europe and to the President of the European Parliament. In 2004, he received the European Science Award of the European Foundation for Culture.